SCIENCE OF RELIGION: STUDIES IN METHODOLOGY

Religion and Reason 13

Method and Theory
in the Study and Interpretation of Religion

MOUTON PUBLISHERS · THE HAGUE · PARIS · NEW YORK

Science of Religion
Studies in Methodology

*Proceedings
of the Study Conference of the
International Association for the History
of Religions, held in Turku, Finland
August 27-31, 1973*

Edited by
LAURI HONKO
*University of Turku
Finland*

MOUTON PUBLISHERS · THE HAGUE · PARIS · NEW YORK

The photographs in this book were printed
with the financial support of UNESCO

ISBN: 90-279-7782-8
Jacket design: Jurriaan Schrofer
© 1979, Mouton Publishers, The Hague, The Netherlands
Printed in Great Britain

Preface

This volume contains the proceedings of the study conference of the International Association for the History of Religions on 'Methodology of the Science of Religion' held in Turku, Finland, August 27-31, 1973. The Finnish Society for the Study of Comparative Religion, a member society in the I.A.H.R., was responsible for the organization of the conference. I would like to express my thanks to the Committee of the Society for their interest and support. My special thanks are due to my colleagues on the Organizing Committee of the Conference, Haralds Biezais (vice-chairman, Turku), Åke Hultkrantz (Stockholm), Juha Pentikäinen (Helsinki), Helmer Ringgren (Uppsala) and Eric J. Sharpe (Lancaster), whose expertise was of great assistance. The practical arrangements for the conference were taken care of by an efficient team of junior staff, mainly drawn from the Department of Comparative Religion and Folklore at the University of Turku. The able secretary of the conference, Aili Nenola-Kallio, devoted a great deal of time to the correspondence and preparations necessary. I would like to express my warm thanks to all of these staff.

It was my task to edit the proceedings of the conference into some kind of documentation of those methodological questions which dominated the conference and have been to the forefront in comparative religion in general. The papers of the eighteen main speakers and thirtyone commentators, together with the summaries of the subsequent discussions, printed in this book should achieve this purpose, and also represent the results of highly successful cooperation. A complete list of all the participants can be found in the report on the technical arrangements for the conference in *Temenos* 9, Turku 1974, pp. 15-24. The good atmosphere which prevailed during the conference was the result of the contributions of all the participants.

The editing of this book, and in particular of the taped discussions, would not have been possible without grants from the Finnish Ministry of Education, the University of Turku Foundation, and the Donner Institute for Research in Religious and Cultural History. Unesco had made a grant towards the costs of the conference. My sincere thanks are also due to Gun Herranen, who gave unstinting assistance in the various stages of the preparation of the manuscript, Keith Battarbee, who prepared the summaries of the discussions and carried out the translations necessary, and my wife Märta Honko, who helped me with the name-index.

Finally I should like to thank Jacques Waardenburg, Editor of the Religion and Reason series, who invested much time in compiling the subject index, and the representative of the publisher, A.J. van Vliet, for encouragement and cooperation.

Turku, November 1978   LAURI HONKO

Contents

List of Participants

Speakers

J. van Baal, Professor of Cultural Anthropology at the University of Utrecht. Sitiopark 8, P. O. Box 57, Doorn, NL.

James Barr, Professor of Semitic Languages and Literatures at the University of Manchester. University of Manchester, Dept. of Near Eastern Studies, Manchester M13 9PL, GB.

Ugo Bianchi, Professor of History of Religions at the University of Bologna. Via Principe Amedeo, 75, I-00185 Rome, Italy.

Haralds Biezais, Professor of History of Religions at Åbo Akademi. Köpmansgatan 15 D, SF-20100 Åbo 10, Finland.

Svein Bjerke, Dr. Phil., Lecturer in Comparative Religion at the University of Oslo. Apalveien 51, Oslo 3, Norway.

Carsten Colpe, Professor of Iranian Studies and History of Religions at the University of Berlin. Schützallee 112, D-1 Berlin 37, BRD.

Kurt Goldammer, Professor of History of Religions at the University of Marburg. 3571 Amöneburg-Bmf, Krs. Marburg/Lahn, An der Winneburg 1, BRD.

M. Heerma van Voss, Professor of History of Ancient Religions at the University of Amsterdam. Koningin Emmalaan 12, Voorschoten, NL.

Lauri Honko, Professor of Folkloristics and Comparative Religion at the University of Turku. Satakielenkatu 8, SF-20600 Turku 60, Finland.

Åke Hultkrantz, Professor of History of Religions at the University of Stockholm. Seglarvägen 7, S-181 62 Lidingö, Sweden.

Joseph Kitagawa, Professor of History of Religions at the University of Chicago. Divinity School, Univ. of Chicago, Chicago, Ill. 60637, U.S.A.

James L. Peacock, Professor of Anthropology at the University of North Carolina at Chapel Hill. Dept. of Anthropology, Chapel Hill, North Carolina 27514, U.S.A.

Juha Pentikäinen, Professor of Comparative Religion at the University of Helsinki. Käpyläntie 29, SF-00600 Helsinki 60, Finland.

Helmer Ringgren, Professor of Old Testament Exegetics at the University of Uppsala. St. Johannesgatan 21 A, S-752 21 Uppsala, Sweden.

Anna-Birgitta Rooth, Professor of Ethnology at the University of Uppsala. Ovre Slottsgatan 14 C, S-752 35 Uppsala, Sweden.

Kurt Rudolph, Professor of History of Religions at the Karl Marx University in Leipzig. Karl-Marx-Platz 9, DDR-701 Leipzig.

Melford E. Spiro, Professor of Anthropology at the University of California at San Diego. Dept. of Anthropology, La Jolla, Calif. 92037, U.S.A.

Jacques Waardenburg, Dr. Theol., Reader in Islamics and Phenomenology of Religion at the University of Utrecht. 375 Utrechtse Weg, Amersfoort, NL.

Commentators

Prof. Dr. Th. P. van Baaren, Instituut voor godsdiensthistorische beelddokumentatie der Rijksuniversiteit te Groningen, Nieuwe Kijk in 't Jatstraat 104, Groningen, NL.

Prof. Dr. Jan Bergman, Box 511, S-751 20 Uppsala, Sweden.

Prof. Dr. C. J. Bleeker, Churchill-laan 290, Amsterdam, NL.

Dr. Gerben J. F. Bouritius, Postelse Hoeflaan 99a, Tilburg, NL.

Prof. Dr. Manfred Büttner, Kiefernweg 40, D-463 Bochum, BRD.

Liz. Horst Cain, 365 Marburg/Lahn, Am Schützenplatz 12, BRD.

Prof. Dr. Walter H. Capps, University of California, Institute of Religious Studies, Santa Barbara, Calif. 93106, U.S.A.

Prof. Dr. Ileana Chirassi-Colombo, Via delle Aiuole 4, I-34141 Trieste, Italy.

Lic. Ulf Drobin, Religionshistoriska institutionen vid Stockholms universitet, Fack, S-104 05 Stockholm, Sweden.

Prof. Dr. Carl Martin Edsman, Vasagatan 5 C, S-752 24 Uppsala, Sweden.

Prof. Dr. Mircea Eliade, Swift Hall 403, University of Chicago, Chicago, Ill. 60637, U.S.A.

Dr. Asok K. Ghosh, Dept. of Anthropology, University of Calcutta, 35, Ballygunge Circular Road, Calcutta 700019, India (absent).

Dr. Anthony Jackson, Dept. of Social Anthropology, University of Edinburgh, Edinburgh E118 9LL, GB (absent).

Prof. Dr. J. H. Kamstra, Peppinghof 37, Abcoude U, NL (absent).

Prof. Dr. William Klassen, University of Manitoba, Dept. of Religion, Winnipeg 19, Manitoba, Canada R3T 2N2.

Prof. Dr. Hans-J. Klimkeit, Religionswissenschaftliches Seminar der Universität Bonn, 53 Bonn, Seminargebäude, Am Hof 34, BRD.

Mrs. Aili Nenola-Kallio, Västäräkinkatu 1 B 56, SF-20600 Turku 60, Finland.

Dr. G. C. Oosthuizen, Dept. of Science of Religion, University of Durban-Westville, Durban, Natal, South Africa.

Prof. Dr. Hans H. Penner, Darmouth College, Dept. of Religion, Hanover, New Hampshire 03755, U.S.A.

Prof. Dr. Edmund F. Perry, Northwestern University, Dept. of Religions, 2006 Sheridan Rd., Evanston, Ill. 60201, U.S.A.

Dr. Leander Petzoldt, D-7987 Weingarten, Pädagogische Hochschule, Kirchplatz 2, BRD (absent).

Dr. habil. Zygmunt Poniatowski, 00-95 Warszawa, os. Przyjaźń, domek 169, Poland.

Prof. Dr. Reinhard Pummer, University of Ottawa, Faculty of Arts, Religious Studies, Ottawa, Ontario K1N 6N5, Canada.

Mr. Michael Pye, Department of Theology and Religious Studies, University of Leeds, Leeds LS2 9JT, GB.

Prof. Dr. Eric Segelberg, Svartbäcksgatan 26, S-753 32 Uppsala, Sweden.

Prof. Dr. Eric J. Sharpe, Dept. of Religious Studies, University of Sydney, Sydney, N.S. Wales, Australia 2006.

Prof. Dr. Ninian Smart, University of Lancaster, Dept. of Religious Studies, Cartmel College, Bailrigg, Lancaster, GB.

Prof. Dr. Robert F. Spencer, University of Minnesota, Dept. of Anthropology, 210 Ford Hall, Minneapolis, Minnesota 55455, U.S.A.

Prof. Dr. Annemarie de Waal Malefijt, 552 Riverside Drive, 6C New York, N.Y. 10027, U.S.A.

Prof. Dr. R. J. Zwi Werblowsky, The Hebrew University of Jerusalem, Faculty of Humanities, Jerusalem, Israel.

Liz. Hans Wissman, 6900 Heidelberg, Werderstr. 20, BRD.

Introduction

by
LAURI HONKO

THE ORIGINS OF THE CONFERENCE

Every five years the world's historians of religion meet for the General Congress of the International Association for the History of Religions (I.A.H.R.). These are stimulating occasions, but what happens is what always happens on congresses with several hundred participants and a dozen sections meeting simultaneously: you end up in the cafeteria, simply talking to someone you've always wanted to meet. It is no accident that people so often refer to 'informal contacts' in their reports from large-scale conferences. It is also symptomatic that this kind of comment does not occur in reports from workshops with 10-20 participants, despite the fact that these are as a rule organized in a more informal way: workshop reports always speak of 'efficient and intensive work'.

When in Stockholm in August 1970 the I.A.H.R. Executive Board entrusted the Finnish Society for the Study of Comparative Religion, and the University of Turku, with the organization of a study conference in 1973, we immediately recognized that the size of the conference and the choice of theme would be decisive factors for the conference's success. We decided to try to achieve an ideal size and mode of work by limiting the number of active participants to 50 and by maximizing the proportion of discussion, thus aiming at something both of the representativeness of the large-scale congress and of the inventiveness of the small workshop. The idea of parallel sections was rejected; and all the participants should be able to follow everything that might be said in the papers, commentaries, and subsequent discussion. Since the programme was to consist of three subtopics, each comprising three sessions, it seemed feasible to offer each active participant one formal contribution, by inviting two participants per session to present a paper (18 in all) and inviting the remaining two thirds of the participants to act as commentators. It seemed important to ensure that none of the sessions should include only one formal paper, and that the formal commentaries should act as stimuli for discussion. With the time for each session restricted to two hours, and in view of the importance attached to discussion, it was clear that the formal contributions must be distributed to the participants in advance. Despite the time of the year (the conference was held in Turku from 27 to 31 August 1973) the participants cooperated splendidly and the conference secretariat was able to duplicate and send out by post approximately 50,000 pages of material in advance.[1] In the sessions themselves there was a careful balance in the use of time between main speakers and commentators: the main speakers were only allowed briefly to summarize their major points, while the commentators were permitted a few minutes more. The general principle was that at least 45 minutes must be left for open discussion in each session. These arrangements worked rather well, not least due to effective chairmanship, and instead of more or less passive listening to papers being read, the conference was dominated by energetic discussion. What in fact resulted was a five-day continuous methodological debate, in which the different research traditions and theoretical approaches were in constant confrontation.

In choosing 'Methodology of the Science of Religion' as the theme of the conference we were conscious of the fact that research into religions has undergone marked division into diverging schools, partly on the basis of methodology, and partly by language and culture area. In practice it is extremely rare for these schools to encounter each other face to face. The absence of a common body of theory has allowed students of religion to pursue their research under a variety of orientations, e.g. historical, phenomenological, philological, psychological, sociological, anthropological, and ethnological, without any very concrete need to maintain contact or to cooperate with each other. The fact that comparative religion is variously located within faculties of humanities, theology, or social sciences, on the one hand, and the continuity of national or culture-area schools of research, on the other, have both con-

---

1. See the conference secretary's report on the technical administration of the conference: Aili Nenola-Kallio, 'Report on the Study Conference of the I.A.H.R. on "Methodology of the Science of Religion", held in Turku, Finland, August 27-31, 1973', *Temenos* 9 (1974), pp. 15-24.

tributed to the emergence of widely contrasting research environments. In these environments the nature and development of comparative religion has been far more powerfully influenced by locally defined objectives for teaching and research than has generally been openly admitted.

It would hardly have been necessary to arrange a conference, however, merely to establish the fact that the situation in comparative religion is characterized by a kind of disparate poly-methodology. There were, however, other factors. At the turn of the 1970s it was becoming clear that Western science, not least in the humanities and social sciences, was undergoing a profound process of self-examination, which seemed to be leading to the breakdown of certain older paradigms and even, possibly, to the emergence of new ones. This process was part of a wider social and cultural development which no community exposed to the influence of the Western industrialized world could completely escape. For science this breakdown shattered the belief in the necessity of a cumulative acquisition of knowledge, undermined naive optimism about research, aroused greater willingness to take part in interdisciplinary cooperation, and gave rise to totally new fields such as 'science of science'. Self-sufficient and insular sciences emerged as open-minded interested partners in the exchange of experiences and opinions with their neighboring sciences and in the search for new possibilities for integration and a new identity. In other words, the splendid isolation of the academic world was coming to an end, and the demand for socially relevant research was penetrating deep into both internal discussion within the sciences and the choice of topics for research by individual scholars. In the background there was the profile of the Third World and the problems of global development, which were leading to the on-going revision of the Eurocentric world picture.

With this background in mind it seemed interesting to direct the conference's work towards defining the methodological status of and potential new lines of development in the scientific study of religion. There were a host of questions to which we could not know the answers in advance. What are the dominant metatheoretical trends in comparative religion at the moment? What traces of personal theory would come to the surface in methodological discussion among a representative gathering of historians of religion? Which specific theories — old or new — would attract most attention? What is the position of the well-established methodological schools, and what new approaches are arising?

What are the current burning questions in history of religions, i.e. questions to which people would constantly recur even in the space of a short conference? How would the different schools of research regard each other, at a time when it was particularly difficult to point to any one dominant paradigm?

These were the questions to which we expected to obtain answers; but in order for the answers to have significance, it was necessary to select a representative sample of scholars from the field and a set of relevant themes. The Organizing Committee set about solving these problems collectively. Most of the Committee's members were from Finland and Sweden. The institutionalized study of history of religions has long been established in Sweden, while in Finland it is not yet two decades old as a university subject. Turku is in an interesting position in this regard, with its two universities — one Finnish-language and one Swedish-language — each with its chair in history of religions (both of which are attached to the humanities faculties). Åbo Academy, the Swedish-language university, does have a Faculty of Theology, to which the Professor of History of Religions from the Faculty of Humanities belongs as an 'adjunct member', whereas there is no theological faculty in the Finnish-language University of Turku, though teaching in theology is provided on a limited scale within the Faculties of Humanities and Education. The University of Turku's chair has been heavily oriented in the direction of empirical cultural research, fieldwork, and a folkloristic-anthropological approach to methodology. In conjunction with the chair at the Åbo Academy there is also an important special library, the Steiner Library at the Donner Institute for Research in Religious and Cultural History, which has made it possible to provide both teaching and research over a very wide range of the various fields within history of religions. An extremely important link between students of religions throughout Finland has been the Finnish Society for the Study of Comparative Religion, which has from the beginning been multidisciplinary in nature and enjoys good overseas relations, especially with the Scandinavian countries. The Society publishes the joint Nordic yearbook, *Temenos*.[2] It therefore should be said here that the choice of Turku as the venue for the conference represented both challenge and recognition for the youngest of

2. Lauri Honko, 'The Finnish Society for the Study of Comparative Religion in 1963-1973', *Temenos* 9 (1974), pp. 5-14.

the comparative religion schools in the Nordic countries. It is also significant that while the majority of chairs in history of religions within Europe are located in faculties of theology, the members of the Organizing Committee represented the research environment of the humanities.

The Organizing Committee picked three themes around which the study conference was to be built. 'Oral and written documentation of the religious tradition' was a topic that had stimulated workers over a wide range of research fields, e.g. exegetes of the Bible and Koran, archeologists and historians of religions investigating the remains of prehistoric cultures, philologists working in text and source criticism, anthropologists using techniques of interview and observation, and folklore scholars interested in genres and contexts of tradition. 'The future of the phenomenology of religion' implies a question both about the past and the future: what is the value of the phenomenological research traditions which have dominated comparative religion for so many decades? Are they still usable, and if so, in what form? Have there arisen new approaches to research which might be attracting increasing attention? Two possible examples of relatively new approaches which were mentioned were ecology of religion and anthropology of religion. 'Religion as expressive culture' concentrated attention on those theories and approaches applicable in the analysis of the widest and most varied topic of investigation, i.e. the cultural forms and meanings of religious expression. Ritual behavior, the language of religion, and the depth structures of religious expression were selected as areas within which to examine the validity of theories and their need for development in the attempt to explain largely unique cultural realities by means of more general scientific categories.

It should be pointed out that the organizers selected the themes for each session but that the speakers were free within the context of each theme to choose the title of their paper themselves. They were thus able to define the theme more closely in accordance with their own areas of interest. The commentators had to be invited, however, at a stage when the themes for the sessions, and the names of the main speakers, were known, but not the final titles of the papers. In addition to commentary, the commentators were encouraged to put forward other points of view on the theme of the session. This arrangement was intended to ensure a comprehensive treatment of the various themes, but it also helps to account for the fact that many of the commentaries read more like independent papers. Since the themes for the sessions had been left relatively broad, matters were also raised in discussion which had not been the subject of detailed treatment in the papers or commentaries. Consequently the discussions (which have been summarized below on the basis of taped recordings) should reflect the main points of current interest among historians of religions extremely well.

The main language of the conference was English, though both German and French were also used. In editing this volume all the contributions have been put into English. It was tempting during editing to cut certain of the rather lengthier contributions which had had little influence on the subsequent discussion, but the editor has opted instead for documentation; accordingly, this volume depicts the conference as it actually took place. All the contributors have had the opportunity to examine their texts, but only on two cases did this lead to significant changes (Bianchi shortened his paper and Spiro partly rewrote his). Four of the commentators (Ghosh, Jackson, Kamstra, and Petzoldt) were unable to be present in person at the conference, but their commentaries were distributed in the appropriate sessions. The documentation of the discussions took far more time than one would have expected, and the transcriptions of the tapes and summarizing of the discussion necessitated the assistance of two qualified staff members.

THE RESULTS OF THE CONFERENCE

If one assumes that teaching, fieldwork (or equivalent study of primary material), the writing of books, and participation in conferences constitute the cornerstones of academic work, then it is clear that conferences are of importance both for the individual academic and for the research community which any particular branch of science constitutes. The research community, especially, takes shape most clearly on conferences, which represent the social manifestation of scholarly work. Apart from some possible decisive, and usually inchoate, youthful experiences, conferences are not to any great extent events of socialization. The majority of speakers arrive on a conference with their opinions already formed, and few people can resist the temptation to expound (possibly at length) their pet ideas, which have usually already been published elsewhere in one form or another. Despite all this, a conference is more than people talking past one another, or the mere repetition of what has been said before. For a few transient days the research community becomes a reality. Processes of adaptation are set in motion. The participants begin to react to the situation, to a topic, or to each other, in a manner that can only be described as creative, critical, and unique. They are prepared to communicate with each other, but unprepared to surrender much of their scholarly identity, with the consequence that a conference's basic mode of action is polite confrontation. Even if the debate rarely leads to unanimity, it does provide a cross-section revealing the status and strength of differing schools of research. And often – as on the Turku conference – there arises a feeling of unity and a liberal atmosphere which makes possible open and constructive criticism, and interaction between different schools. Something at least of what one has learnt is taken home afterwards.

What then did we learn from this conference? I do not wish to go into the special points raised by each session or paper; the reader can trace these for himself with the aid of the Table of Contents and the Index, and by reading the book itself. Nevertheless it may be appropriate to present some general findings about the methodological profile of comparative religion on the basis of the evidence provided by this conference.

Part of any methodology remains unformulated, and implicit. Every discipline, indeed every scholar, holds certain fundamental assumptions which have not been expressed explicitly but which profoundly influence the strategy of research and its scientific conclusions. If only scholars were capable of recognizing and making explicit these fundamental assumptions, there would be no need to speak of metatheory or personal theories. As it is, however, these terms are necessary both on the individual level ('personal theory') and on that of the discipline ('metatheory') in order to distinguish those unstated but influential fundamental assumptions from explicit claims and assumptions relating to recognized theory and special theory, e.g. functionalism, Van der Leeuw's phenomenology of religion, Bellah's theory of religious evolution, or Steward's cultural ecology. Often scientific debate is concerned with special theories, but it can be very valuable to compare the same speaker's opinions on a variety of topics. A certain consistency can then be traced, which does not originate in the research problems under investigation but in the scholar himself. What is involved here is as it were a

methodological 'stance' or personal bias, which can often be better labelled by reference to some key expressions or favorite concept than by
the stricter and more demanding term 'theory'. The key expression for
one person may be 'historical investigation', for a second 'tradition', for
a third 'empiricism', for a fourth 'context', and so on. Personal theory
usually includes a number of favorite concepts, which can partly be read
between the lines. Bias may occur either in a general theoretical starting
point or in the choice of research techniques (interview or observation?
a qualitative or quantitative approach?), and it can be equally dominant
in the presentation of one's own hypothesis or in the critique of someone else's theses.

A further methodological critique is implied in the terms 'general
theory', 'middle-range theory', 'low-order proposition', 'modes of observation', and 'the real world of things and events' ('raw data'). These
constitute the steps on a ladder of transformation by means of which an
investigator can move either upwards, inductively, towards higher abstractions, or downwards, deductively. This zigzag movement has its
own rules; information cannot be transformed arbitrarily. What was
noticeable on this conference was the lack of a general theory, and the
poor success of methodological imperialism. There is a view that history
of religions is not really a branch of science at all, but a collection of
scholars who happen to be working on religion. Many participants expressed the wish to achieve clarification of the recurrent basic assumptions on the basis of which religions are studied: in other words people
were wanting metatheory, in the hope that it would provide elements to
unite historians of religions. For at the moment comparative religion has
the appearance more of a multi-disciplinary and poly-methodic field,
in which a number of middle-range theories can be found, though not
even these are commensurable or compatible with each other. Methodological problems emerge already at the grass-roots level, where the raw
data of a religion are subjected to classification. Modes of observation
and the arrangement of data were seen as especially problematic. Consequently comparative religion can be seen as being more closely related
to cultural research in the humanities than to sociology or psychology,
even in the case of empirical research. The zigzag movement of induction
and deduction is located on a lower rung of the data-transformation
ladder in history of religions than in sociology or psychology. Whereas
the sociologist makes a single, planned grass-roots expedition to gather

data and then returns to the plane of middle-range theories to relate his data to the existing corpus of knowledge, the historian of religion is as it were at the mercy of his raw data, and constantly has to return to this, ready to revise his hypotheses if new material gives cause to do so. From some points of view this may appear a weakly formalized research procedure, but in fact it need not represent weakness at all: on the contrary, it is precisely in this way that the historian of religions is able to elicit information about a phenomenon which the sociologist or psychologist, trapped in his own frame of reference, would probably not even recognize.

I referred to methodological imperialism. Father Wilhelm Schmidt, Rudolf Otto, Gerardus van der Leeuw and Mircea Eliade no longer rule (if they ever did). There is no theory or method in existence which can predominate over the others, within comparative religion at any rate. The most convincing demonstration of this fact on the conference was Ugo Bianchi's heroic attempt to integrate anthropology of religion, for instance, into his own research approach, which is that of historical investigation. The attempt was tolerated, but failed to win support.

There were three disciplinary 'clusters' — history of religions, phenomenology of religion, and anthropology of religion—which formed a triangle within which the major methodological discussions were carried on. Naturally the internal contradictions of these disciplines also cropped up, but these were of secondary importance or belonged to the sphere of personal theory. Both psychology of religion and sociology of religion in the strict sense of these terms were absent, though concepts from these fields were employed by the anthropologists of religion. A theological element occurred in various contexts but never at any stage succeeded in gaining control of the discussion. The research into folklore and oral tradition, on the other hand, did occasionally come to the fore, especially due to Swedish and Finnish contributors.

The debate between the phenomenology and the history of religions has been part of the programme of symposia in comparative religion for decades; and the conclusion that both phenomenology and history are essential and that they complement each other is also familiar. On this conference, history had the more effective protagonists of the two. The phenomenological front was scattered: there were a few unconditional supporters of the old phenomenology à la Van der Leeuw, but in general this approach was labelled as intuitive, metaphysical, or non-

empirical, and it found little support. It is significant that none of the
newer hermeneutic modes of investigation has, as yet, found acceptance
in phenomenology of religion either. It became clear, however, that some
people wanted to save phenomenology by creating a balance between
positivism and hermeneutics, or rather between an empirical approach
to research and an interpretative understanding. It was especially interesting that the reformers and supporters of phenomenology viewed the
possibility of an alliance with anthropology of religion favorably, while
the strongest defenders of a historical approach went into the attack
against anthropology.

Cultural anthropology still enjoys a strong position within the scientific study of religion, not least due to its fieldwork techniques and
methodology of cultural comparison. A kind of bifurcation appears for
instance in the significance which anthropologists investigating religion
accord to the relation 'man—the "otherworldly" (god, etc.)' in comparison with the relation 'man—society'. It is the latter relation which has
always been central both for cultural and social anthropology. Religion
has often been seen as a tool by means of which people and communities
can be subjected to real influence in a practical and functional manner.
Discussion arose at the conference as to whether religious symbols are
manipulative in nature or not; and the dominant trend appeared to support the opinion that the existence of a symbol cannot be explained
anything like exhaustively in terms of economic, social, or similar causes.
If symbols are tools, they are so only in a very general sense – i.e. tools
of language, thought, and living. The man—'otherworldly' relation continues to hold an important position in the metatheory of religious studies, despite the fact that some anthropologists do not consider it capable
of operationalization (cf. the discussion of the term *numen*), while for
some historians of religions this appeared to be a question to which different religions would in an inductive approach provide different answers. On the whole it seems that it was precisely the anthropologists
and folklorists who most often came in for criticism, sometimes on the
grounds that their methods of investigation were those of the natural
sciences, sometimes because of their objective typologies, which were
even seen as a threat to humanist scholarship. On the other hand it was
a known anthropologist, De Waal Malefijt, who returned the humanist
ball with the observation that the word 'man' had been rare on the
conference (not to mention 'woman' or 'student'). The conference, a

gathering of people considering abstract problems, very much reminded her of Harris or Lévi-Strauss, who leave man out of the picture. She left it to her audience whether this was a compliment or not.

If ecological thinking and linguistic structuralism are currently the central movements in cultural research, a word or two about these will not be out of place. Structuralism came up rather less than had been expected. It would appear that traditional philologists are closer to the majority of historians of religions than are the supporters of general linguistics. There were not very many people interested in the applications of Lévi-Strauss' structuralism, nor even in the latest communication theories. It was indicative that the term 'depth structure' (which had been adopted as the title for one of the sessions mainly from syntactical theory) turned out to be unproductive when applied to the study of religion. The discussion of the language of religion was perhaps most worthwhile on the subject of the problems of translation; neither of the papers on this topic took up the link with general linguistics.

Ecology was more strongly represented, though it was not accepted uncritically. There are no doubt various reasons for this caution towards the possible applications of cultural ecology in comparative religion. One was probably the fact that those who most profoundly supported Bleeker's appeal 'Retournons à la philologie et à l'histoire' are equally cautious towards ecology of religion as they are towards sociology, psychology, or anthropology of religion. A second cause for caution lies in the fact that Steward's ecology of religion can be seen as an anthropological variant of historical materialism. There was however more constructive criticism: the hope was expressed that ecology of religion would come down from the generalizing heights of the macro-level to actual villages and towns in order to carry out empirical, holistic investigation of the role of religion in various environments. A limitation in this respect to natural economies, e.g. hunting and fishing cultures, would be too narrow. (Geography of religion does not limit its investigation of the relation between religion and the environment in this way.) It was somewhat paradoxical that the critics of ecological determinism fell in a sense into the same determinism when they put the question how social organization and religion can be the same in differing natural environments, or how communities living in the same natural environments can have differing religions. Anyway, it appears that if a static functionalism and to some extent also structuralism are on the way out, then the ecological approach and the related set of problems concerning social development and cultural change are on the way in. Problems relating to evolution and to the process of development came up in the sessions on both ecology of religion and ritual processes. It is conceivable that the processual approach characteristic of anthropology may come to form a valuable counterbalance to the purely behavioral or purely historical approaches.

It is perhaps scarcely surprising that problems of comparative work emerged as one of the most important themes of the conference. Comparative religion has repeatedly been driven to consider the validity of its comparisons and their methodological basis; but this time there was the same profound polarization in evidence which characterizes all cultural research. Many other fields, and especially cultural anthropology, present researchers with paired concepts such as emic and etic, intra- and inter-cultural, particular and universal, idiographic and nomothetic, real and nominal, etc. These oppositions have in fact been sharpened in proportion as the weakness of the categories and classes of traditional phenomenology is recognized. A class such as 'sacred stone', for instance, may be dismissed as empty, since the examples, collected from around the world, are incompatible. The fact that one is unquestionably dealing with a 'stone' and with 'something sacred' does not offer any guarantee that one can make an intelligent comparison; on the contrary, the speculative generalizations built up on material gathered in this way can sometimes appear metaphysical, and sometimes quite simply wrong. In these comparisons the context of the phenomenon has often unavoidably or deliberately been ignored; if it had not been, then many of the classes would have disintegrated. It is no coincidence that students of religion nowadays lay such stress on the importance of context, irrespective of whether they are philologists practicing textual analysis, historians investigating various kinds of documents, philosophically oriented phenomenologists, psychologists and sociologists investigating the relation between the individual and the community, or anthropologists, folklorists and ethnologists, constantly refining their fieldwork techniques. Once it was the functionalists who stressed the importance of context; but it is worth noting that although functionalism has lost support, the significance attached to context is not diminishing in the slightest.

The frustrations occasioned by phenomenological comparisons are not enough in themselves to explain the orientation towards particularism and intra-culturalism. A highly decisive role has been played by the development of techniques, especially in fieldwork, to the point where they far more effectively register the informant's own sense of reality and the way in which the community under investigation perceives the world. The development of interview and observation techniques, especially of certain participant techniques, has turned the investigator into a marginal being in a new sense, operating in the (often temporary) field of interaction between two cultures. It easily happens that empirical cultural research leads one into conflict with the conventions of the academic community. The human knowledge and experience which are jointly created in personal contact with the representatives of another culture are no longer as closely bound to the predetermined categories as they used to be. There is, naturally, more to this than the mere development of research techniques. Countless cultures have been transformed from being passive objects into being the active determinants of their own universe, and in interactive research the investigator is as much the object of investigation as his informant. Nor is the audience for research limited to the European academic community. In cultural research, as it frees itself from Eurocentrism and asymmetry, the comparison of cultures and of religious phenomena occurring in them is all the more essential as an encounter between new spiritual fields where, previously, passive primitives underwent discovery.

This trend became apparent at many points on the conference, although one might also have expected to encounter outspoken opponents of it. For example, the question was raised as to where the concepts needed in cultural research could be obtained from; and there was anxiety that the concepts used in research do not do justice to the reality of the culture being investigated. Some supporters of traditional phenomenology went so far as to consider recognizability to be an essential test, i.e. that the representatives of a religion should not be alienated by the picture of their religion which science draws.

This does not mean, of course, that comparative religion should give up being comparative. There were also those on the conference — perhaps the majority — for whom it would be quite unimaginable to present the data at the core of religious studies other than comparatively. Accordingly, the discussions on taxonomy, classification, and definition were lively, with the focus on, for instance, the typology of religion, the classification of rites, and the comparison of various higher religions. An examination of the criticism put forward against generalizations reveals three main types; (1) some participants did not believe in religious universals, but emphasized uniqueness; (2) there were those who wished to refute some generalization based on comparison, by reference to empirical material — usually to one or two counter-examples; (3) there were those who preferred to avoid committing themselves to definitive conventions and generalizing hypotheses at the outset of an investigation, and to preserve most of the object of investigation as *terra incognita* to be cautiously explored by means of induction, e.g. historical methodology. It is probably significant that there was no demand for the quantitative verification of generalization; this probably indicates that comparative religion is still dominated by the older qualitative phenomenological approach to comparison rather than the methodology of modern cross-cultural research. Nevertheless, neither historical nor hermeneutic particularism is adequate for the study of religions; besides these we shall continue to need flexible universal categories (though not such as to exclude exceptions or borderline cases) in order to make the transfer of results from one investigation to another possible. Research into development, ecology of religion, and structuralism all presuppose generalization, reduction, and comparison. Nor are the drafting of cognitive maps or the investigation of symbols and meanings likely to prove very fruitful without an empirical and comparative approach to the investigation. In general any investigation of 'rules' or 'systems' presupposes a comparative approach, whether one is dealing with micro- or macrosystems, or with intra- or inter-systemic comparisons.

If various methodologies are considered along the 'hard'–'soft' dimension, on which a 'hard' methodology is characterized by its reliance on quantitative methods where applicable and by the strict operationalization of the basic terms of the investigation, while a 'soft' methodology is recognized by the absence of these features, then it would seem that the Turku conference was open towards 'soft' methodologies but that a need was felt to close ranks around a more strictly defined terminology, which ought to be specific to comparative religion and not merely a collection of more or less ill-assorted concepts from different disciplines. The conference was unable to meet this need, nor will other conferences in the near future be able to do so. The situation can be seen as in some ways typical of a science which depends for its existence on an interdisciplinary spirit and poly-methodological liberalism. Although this situation undoubtedly has its good sides (intellectual flexibility, interaction between different schools of research, freedom from methodological imperialism), it does seem — on conferences at least — inevitably to lead to a sort of 'defensive' methodology. Since the scholars present have little in common except the fact that they are investigating religion, concentration on religion comes to the fore. But at what cost? Astonishingly enough, at the cost of concentration on man, or on society, and even on culture as a whole. Consequently we are left with the question whether the science of religion could in future afford to progressively redefine its boundaries so as to include not only religious systems, and their internal, central, i.e. 'religious' phenomena, but also the relations of religious systems to other social, cultural and economic systems. This is a crucial question; for there are many uses for religious traditions, every individual belongs to other systems as well as religious ones, and every religious community is involved in a wider process of social development. The history of the academic study of religions to date has shown that this form of scholarship in itself cannot provide information about the 'otherworldly' — god, etc. — except in an indirect manner. It is the empirical investigation of religious traditions, of man and his community, which alone can open the road, not to the 'otherworldly', but to those realities of which the concept of the 'otherworldly' is an inherent part. It is the task of the academic study of religions to describe, understand, and explain that part: not in isolation or independence, however, but in its context, against the background of cultural symbol systems and socio-economic structures.

Helmer Ringgren

M. Heerma van Voss

Juha Pentikäinen

Anna-Birgitta Rooth

Joseph Kitagawa

Kurt Rudolph

Haralds Biezais

Carsten Colpe

Åke Hultkrantz

Svein Bjerke

Ugo Bianchi

Melford E. Spiro

Lauri Honko

James Peacock

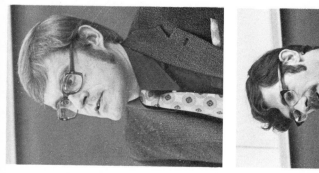

James Barr

Jacques Waardenburg

J. van Baal

Kurt Goldammer

PART ONE

Oral and Written Documentation
of Religious Tradition

Preliterate Stages and Formation of the Canon in Book Religions

HELMER RINGGREN   *Problems of the Formation and Function of a Canon*

The principle of canonical scripture is well expressed in the Biblical book of Deuteronomy (4:1f.), where it says: 'And now, O Israel, give heed to the statutes and the ordinances which I teach you, and do them... *You shall not add to the word which I command you, nor take from it*'. This passage refers to the Law, given by Yahweh through Moses. Other Biblical passages refer to the words of prophets or to the word of God in general. Jeremiah receives the injunction: 'Speak to all the cities of Judah ... all the words that I command you to speak to them; *do not hold back a word*' (26:2). In the Book of Proverbs (30:5f.) we read: 'Every word of God proves true... *Do not add to his words...*'. This latter passage may be late, but the idea that all three passages express is the same: there is a divinely revealed word, to which nothing should be added and from which nothing should be taken. In other words: the divine word is normative and should not be changed, either by addition, or by subtraction.

The existence of canonical writings in many religions involves two main problems of methodological interest, namely: (1) the origin of the canon, and (2) the function of the canon in the life and belief of the religion in question.

As for the origin of the canon, the problem is really a double one. Two questions should be asked: (1) What is the generally accepted theory of its origin? and (2) What can be ascertained with the aid of historical criticism? The first question is closely tied up with the problem of function, and the second one is of considerable interest for the historian of religion.

I shall illustrate my point by referring to the Biblical material, primarily the Old Testament, and then proceed to some comparative viewpoints.

The accepted theory concerning the Old Testament canon receives
its earliest known expression in Flavius Josephus' book *Against Apion*
(ca. 95 AD) (I, 8). Here the writer discusses the trustworthiness of historical writings and states that the Greek writers often contradict one
another. Then he goes on to say: 'We have not an innumerable multitude
of books among us disagreeing from, and contradicting one another,
but only twenty-two books, which contain the records of all the past
times; which are justly believed to be divine; and of them five belong
to Moses, which contain his laws and the traditions of the origin of
mankind till his death. As to the time from the death of Moses till the
reign of Artaxerxes, king of Persia, the prophets, who were after Moses,
wrote down what was done in their times in thirteen books. The remaining four books contain hymns to God, and precepts for the conduct
of human life.

Josephus adds that history has also been written after the time of
Artaxerxes, but these works do not have the same authority attributed
to them, 'since there has not been an exact succession of prophets since
that time' and he further comments that 'no one has been so bold as
either to add anything to (these books), to take anything from them,
or to make any change in them'.

A somewhat different account of the origin of the sacred books of
Judaism is given in the 14th chapter of the Ezra Apocalypse (also called
2 Esdras or 4 Ezra). Here we find Ezra lamenting the disappearance of
the holy books: 'Thy law has been burned, and so no one knows the
things that have been done or will be done by thee'. Thereupon he
receives the instruction to prepare writing tablets and take with him
five men, well versed in the art of writing, and withdraw with them to
a certain place. This done, he receives from God a cup to drink, and
his heart is filled with understanding and wisdom, and he is able to
dictate the contents of the sacred books to his secretaries. So, within
forty days, 94 books were written, and Ezra was told to make public
24 books, while the remaining 70 should be kept secret 'for the wise
among your people'. These 24 books obviously correspond to the 22
books of Josephus and constitute the existing canon.

The essential thing in these two accounts seems to be that the books
of the canon are inspired by God and therefore reliable, maybe even

infallible. Divergent as they are, they cannot also represent the historical truth, and as a matter of fact, none of them does. The historical truth, as far as it can be ascertained, is considerably more complicated.

The various writings of the Old Testament do not seem to have been written with the intention of producing a canon. The Law (i. e. the Pentateuch) is the result of a long process of growth. The historical books were obviously written for no other purpose than to relate historical events. It is interesting to observe that the author(s) of the Books of Chronicles feel(s) free to make changes in their sources, to correct them by adding material or by omitting certain passages. The books of the prophets, of course, had the authority of the prophetical word: it was the word of God through the mouth of the prophet. But prophetical words could be enlarged or applied to new situations by means of slight changes.

The first part of the canon to obtain such status was obviously the Pentateuch; the earliest documentation is our quotation above from Deuteronomy, the final collection of the whole Pentateuch is somewhat later. The 'praise of famous men' in Eccls. (Ben Sira) 44-49 also presupposes the collection of 'the former and the later prophets', including the twelve minor prophets, as one book (49:10). The introduction to the Greek translation of this book refers to 'the law and the prophets and the others that followed them', which seems to allude to the three parts of the present Hebrew canon. The literature of Qumran seems to have contained the same collection of canonical writings. The same is true of the New Testament. There is however, evidence that the Book of Psalms in certain manuscripts from the beginning of our era contained a number of psalms which are not found in the canonical book and some of the canonical psalms in a different order. A final decision on the contents of the canon was reached at a meeting in Jabne about 100 AD.

The canon thus fixed was normative for all aspects of Jewish religion. Its divine origin gave it authority. Questions of belief and practice were discussed and solved according to Scripture. The Mishna treatise Sanhedrin states (10,1) that 'he has no part in the world to come who says: There is no resurrection of the dead (in the Torah), and: The Torah is not from God (literally: Heaven)'. The second statement emphasizes the divine origin of Scripture; the first statement, according to the variant reading of some manuscripts, reminds us of Jesus' argument with the Sadducees, Mt 22:22-33, in which he shows by a reference to Ex 3:6 that the resurrection of the dead can be deduced from the Torah.

The method used in the quotation of support from Scripture is especially interesting, in so far as little attention is paid to the context in which a scriptural passage appears. Very brief passages are separated from their context and made to carry the burden of proof by themselves. Examples abound in the rabbinical literature. One example might suffice to illustrate the point. Mishna Sanhedrin 10,3 says: 'The people of the flood has no part in the world to come and they will not arise (*qūm*) in the judgment (*dīn*), for it says (Gen 6,6): "My spirit shall not 'judge' (*jādōn*) man forever". (The verbal form *jādōn* has probably nothing to do with *dīn* 'to judge'; more probably it means 'reign' or 'remain in', but the similarity in sound suggests the idea of 'judgment' (*dīn*)). The people of Sodom have no part in the world to come; but they will arise in the judgment. R. Nehemiah said: Neither the first, nor the latter will arise in the judgment, for it says (Ps 1:5): "Therefore the wicked will not stand (or: arise) in the judgment, nor the sinners in the community of the righteous". 'Therefore, the wicked will not stand in the judgment', that is the people of the flood; 'nor the sinners in the community of the righteous', that is the people of Sodom. Then they said to him: 'They will not arise (stand) in the community of the righteous, but they will arise in the community of the wicked.' (The text of Ps 1:5 has no specific reference to the people of the flood, not to the people of Sodom; but the use of the verb *qūm* 'to stand', 'to arise' suggests some connection with resurrection, and the word *mišpāṭ* suggests the idea of judgment.)

This, and numerous other examples, show that the authority of canonical Scripture is such as to permit far-reaching conclusions on the basis of the mere association of ideas.

On the other hand, this very method implies considerable freedom in the application of a scriptural passage. The Habakkuk commentary from Qumran quotes Hab. 2:16 'You are sated with ignominy instead of glory. Drink, you yourself and stagger (*har^cel*)!' The last word of this text appears in the Massoretic text as *hē^cārel* 'show your foreskin', but the Qumran text prefers another variant reading, changing the order of two consonants. It goes on to say: 'This means the priest, whose ignominy was greater than his glory, because he did not circumcise the foreskin of his heart, but walked in the ways of drunkenness'. In other words, the commentary applies both the variant readings: *hēᶜārel* suggests that the heart of the priest was uncircumcised, *harᶜel* suggests his drunkenness.

The use of the Old Testament canon in the New Testament follows the same rules. Mt 2:15 quotes Hos 11:1 'Out of Egypt I called my son' in order to prove that the flight into Egypt was predicted in the Old Testament. But the context in Hosea proves beyond doubt that the words refer to the deliverance of the people of Israel from Egypt. Variant readings are often used in order to make the scriptural proof clearer as is discussed at length by K. Stendahl in his dissertation *The School of St. Matthew.*

In some cases two Old Testament passages are combined, e. g. Mt. 21:5 'Say to the Daughter of Zion: Lo, your king comes, humble and riding on a donkey and on the colt of an ass'. This is an obvious combination of Is. 62:11 'Say to the daughter of Zion: Lo, your salvation (LXX your saviour) comes...', and Zech. 9:9 'Rejoice much, o daughter of Zion; exult, o daughter of Jerusalem; lo, your king comes to you, righteous and victorious, he is humble and riding on a donkey, and on the colt of an ass'. Both texts are canonical and can be combined without difficulty. On the other hand, the quotation from Is. 62 is not literal, and the quotation from Zech. 9 is considerably abridged. That is, the text is normative as a proof text, but there is a certain freedom in its use as far as the exact wording is concerned. But the gospel makes Zech. 8 refer to two animals, because it sticks strictly to the wording of the Hebrew text, against the real meaning of the text (the words used in parallellism refer to one and the same animal which is also the usual rabbinic interpretation).

Another interesting example is Paul's argument in Gal. 3:16f., where he says that the promises were given to 'Abraham and his seed', not to those who come from this seed; consequently the promises refer to one single person, that is, to Jesus Christ. The main point is that the Hebrew singular *zaera*ᶜ 'seed' must refer to one person since it is singular. This argument runs counter to Hebrew grammar, since *zaera*ᶜ is a collective noun and practically never refers to one person. Nevertheless, Paul's use of this argument shows that even grammatical details of the canonical text are considered as important for the correct use of the text.

The obvious conclusion to be drawn from these examples is that there was no formulated principle for the use of the canonical text. It was taken for granted that the text was sacred and normative and reliable, but in spite of this the exact wording of the text was not always observed. We might ask if this could possibly be due to the fact that the authors of the New Testament quoted from memory, but it is doubtful whether this explains all cases. The main point is, however, that whatever the methods of exegesis applied are, both Jews and Christians regarded the canonical text as normative and as the true basis for the discussion of questions of belief and religious practice.

What, then, was the function of the Jewish canon in Judaism and in early Christianity? It was used, first of all, to establish correct religious practice. This is in accordance with the fact that religious practice was extremely important in Judaism. But, as we have seen, it was also used to deduce the correct doctrine of Judaism. Questions of belief (e. g. the belief in resurrection) were solved on the basis of Scripture. This use of the canon becomes natural as soon as doctrinal questions come to be regarded as important. Thirdly, Scripture was applied to present events as prediction. This is true in the community of Qumran, where events in the life of its founder, the Teacher of Righteousness, and other events in the life of the sect, were interpreted with the aid of Scriptural passages. It is also true of early Christianity in so far as Jesus Christ was regarded as the fulfilment of prophecy and scriptural passages were adduced to prove the Messianic claims of Jesus.

Christianity thus accepted the Jewish canon, but in addition it gradually developed a canon of its own, i. e. the New Testament. Jesus accepted the Scriptures but claimed an authority of his own for their interpretation ('But I say unto you...'). Gradually, the letters of Paul and the Gospels came to be regarded as fundamental to the Christian faith. But as late as ca. 150 AD Justin the Martyr denotes the Gospels not as sacred Scripture, but as the 'remembrances' of the apostles. In the Christian church the authority was first of all Christ himself, then the apostles as eyewitnesses of his work, but also the witness of the Holy Spirit.

In the second half of the 2nd century AD, the conflicts with Gnosticism and with Marcion necessitated the establishment of a normative collection of documents of the Christian faith. And so gradually, in the course of the 3rd century, a specifically Christian canon was developed.

The criteria, e. g. as set forth by St. Augustine, were three: (1) the book should derive from an apostle, (2) it should be in general use in the church, and (3) its doctrine should be in accordance with the apostolic teaching. There were discussions as to whether certain books should be regarded as canonical or not, but in the main the New Testament as we have it was established as normative for the Christian church.

It is interesting that the main interest seems to be the establishment of Christian doctrine as against other doctrines that were rejected as heretical. This ties in with the general interest in doctrine in the early Christian church and is certainly due to the philosophical interest current in the environment in which the church grew up.

This doctrinal interest has remained in the Christian church. Though no theory of the canon and its inspiration seems to have existed from the beginning, various such theories were developed in the course of time. The most elaborate of these is perhaps that developed by protestant orthodoxy in the 17th century, which can be characterized as that of verbal inspiration. A text that is verbally given by God can be used as the infallible basis for the formulation of the Christian faith. Any article of faith must be proved by a reference to one or more scriptural passages (*loca probantia*).

However, the last centuries have brought about a considerable change in the attitude towards the canon in many Christian quarters. It was the acceptance of historical criticism of the Biblical documents that brought about this change. The Biblical books were not regarded as dictated by God word by word but as human documents containing the witness of human beings to the acts of God. These documents should be interpreted in the same way as other historical documents, using historical criticism, and taking into account the general cultural background of their times. The consequence was that the canon had only a relative value as the basis of Christian faith. Isolated passages could not be used as *loca probantia*, and a historical development was traced within the Bible. As a result of this, the situation with regard to the authority of the canon is rather confused. While the churches officially recognize the Bible as canonical, theologians feel that they have considerable freedom in using it for the establishing of what is Christian faith. For these theologians it is rather the spirit and general tendency of the Bible that are normative than separate passages. In a way this situation is rather unique. No other religion possessing canonical scriptures has developed such a freedom in its attitude to its normative documents. It should, however, be emphasized again that this attitude is not accepted by all the Christian churches. Nevertheless, it constitutes a special problem when the function of the canon is concerned.

The situation in Islam is altogether different. From the very beginning it was the ambition of the Prophet Muhammad to give his people a sacred Scripture corresponding to the holy books of the other book religions. Even if the Qurᵓan was colllected and given its first shape only after Muhammad's death, this fact must be taken into account. There was also a theory of inspiration from the beginning. Muhammad refers to a Heavenly book and to revelation sent down from Heaven. Thus every word revealed to Muhammad was literally the word of God.

Thus the authority of the Qurᵓan was established beyond any doubt, and any controversy, be it in matters of religious practice or of doctrine, could and should be settled on the basis of a passage from the Qurᵓan. In cases of doubt, recourse was had to the Prophet's *sunna*, i. e. traditions relating what he had done or said in various situations. Collections of traditions were made and gradually assumed a kind of half-canonical significance. It is interesting to note that these collections contain material regarding both religious practice and questions of doctrine. Probably the latter became more significant as the interest in theoretical or theological questions grew in Islam.

The use of the Qurᵓan reminds us to some extent of the use of Scripture in Judaism. Even very brief isolated passages can be used as proof-texts, and they can also be applied to things that are completely alien to their original context. This method of quotation reaches its climax in the exegesis of Islamic modernism, where brief sentences from the Qurᵓan are applied to modern conditions that are completely alien to their meaning in the original context. This seems to be done on the tacit assumption that the word of God is infallibly correct however brief the quotation may be and whatever the context in which it is used.

There are scattered instances of a reaction against this way of using the Qurᵓan. One is Daᵓud Rahbar's book *God of Justice*, in which the author tries to harmonize the contradictory passages concerning free will and predestination by placing them into the context of Qurᵓanic teaching as a whole. A few attempts have been made to interpret the Qurᵓan against its historical background. But from this to the attitude of historical criticism in Christianity there is a long step. The verbal inspiration and infallibility of the Qurᵓan remain undisputed.

The formation of a canon is a historical problem. Whether it is a gradual process, as in Judaism and Christianity, or a conscious creation, as in Islam, it seems to be a function of what people expect from their religion, what kind of questions it is supposed to settle. Or rather, there is a kind of reciprocal influence: the formation of a canon is religion's answer to the questions people ask, but at the same time the canon influences the questions and contributes to the formation of a special type of religion. In a way the problem of the function of the canon is bound up with that of its formation. On the other hand, the use of the canon may change in the course of time: when the canon of Judaism was developed, its use as prediction was probably not foreseen; and the modern Christian interpretation of the Bible was certainly not in the mind of those who established the canon. The function of sacred scripture in different environments is a topic well worth phenomenological study.

M. HEERMA van VOSS   *Methodology and the Egyptian* Book of the Dead

The importance of the New Kingdom *Book of the Dead* (*BD*) as a primary source for the knowledge of ancient Egyptian religion is generally recognised. On the methods of exploring it, however, comparatively little[1] has been said.

My paper is meant to contribute to a discussion on this topic. In presenting it I would like to stress three points arising from my experience:
1. sources other than papyri are regularly neglected, to our disadvantage;
2. pictures ('vignettes' and others) should be examined for their own sake: they often lead to a better or a fuller understanding of the corresponding spell;

---

1. E.g. by de Buck: *Jaarbericht ... Ex Oriente Lux* III/9 (1944), pp. 9-10; *Bibliotheca Orientalis* 2 (1945), esp. p. 44; *The Journal of Egyptian Archaeology* 35 (1949), pp. 87-8.

3. hieroglyphic mss. of the creative XXIth Dynasty lie under an un-
deserved doom due in the first place to Naville.[2] One may compare
my observations on the Leiden Papyrus T3.[3]
These three remarks could be well illustrated in the case of spell 161,
which is offered here as a model.

Naville[4] knew only the version in his Pb, my Document No.1. The
same applies to the most recent authors.[5] In fact, quite a number of
New Kingdom sources can be quoted. The following list is meant to
give characteristic examples, not to be exhaustive.

A. Papyri
Doc. 1.   Owner: Neferwebenef.
          Paris, Louvre, Pap. III 93 (Inv. No. 3092; Naville's Pb).
          Edition: S. Ratié, *Le papyrus de Neferoubenef (Louvre III 93)*,
          Le Caire, Institut français d'Archéologie orientale, 1968, pl. XIV.
          Period: Dyn. XIX.
Doc. 2.   Owner: Hori.
          Cleveland, Ohio, Cleveland Museum of Art, 21. 1032.
          Two details: J. D. Cooney, *The Bulletin of The Cleveland Muse-
          um of Art* 55 (1968), p. 266, Fig. 9.
          Period: Dyn. XXI.

B. Coffins and sarcophagi
Doc. 3.   Owner: Meh(u).
          Moscow, Pushkin Museum II a 5249.
          Edition: I. A. Lapis, *Vestnik drevnej istorii* 4/56 (1956), pp. 157-
          160, pl. 2 and 3, 2 pp. hand-copy.
          Mummiform; wood.
          Period: Dyn. XVIII.

---

2. E. g.: *Das aegyptische Todtenbuch der XVIII. bis XX. Dynastie*. Einleitung,
Berlin, 1886, p. 35.

3. Cf. 'Preliminary report' in: D. Sinor, *Proceedings of the Twenty-Seventh International Congress of Orientalists, Ann Arbor, Michigan, 13th-19th August 1967*,
Wiesbaden, Harrassowitz, 1971, p. 48; *Zwischen Grab und Paradies*, Basel, Morf,
1971; *De spreuk om de kisten te kennen*, Leiden, Brill, 1971.

4. Publication of note 2, p. 184.

5. E. g. S. Ratié (see Doc. 1), p. 47.

Doc. 4. Owner: Thothhotep.
Paris, Louvre D 3.
Photograph: Breasted und Ranke, *Geschichte Aegyptens*, Wien, Phaidon (1936), T. 8.
Mummiform; granite.
Period: Dyn. XIX.

Doc. 5. Owner: N. N.
London, British Museum 66654.
Edition: Bimson and Shore, *The British Museum Quarterly* 30 (1965/6), pp. 105-8, pl. XXI.
Mummiform model; glass.
Period: Dyn. XVIII (?).

Doc. 6. Owner: Yuya.
Cairo 3668 (No. of 'Brief Descr.').
Edition: Davis, Maspero, Newberry, and Carter, *The Tomb of Jouiya and Touiyou*, London (1907), pl. VI.
Rectangular; wood.
Period: Dyn. XVIII.

Doc. 7. Owner: Wabset.
Khartum 14408.
Edition: J. Leclant, *Kush* 11 (1963), pp. 141-158, pl. XXXVI; cf. *Soleb II. Les nécropoles*, Firenze, Sansoni (1971), pp. 125-132 (T 5 c 2).
Rectangular; sandstone.
Period: Dyn. XVIII.

C. Shrines

Doc. 8. Owner: Tutankhamon.
Cairo 239 (Carter's No.).
Edition: Piankoff and Rambova, *The Shrines of Tut-Ankh-Amon*, New York, Pantheon Books (1955), pl. 19-22, Fig. 20/5; shrine IV.
Wood with gold foil.
Period: Dyn. XVIII.

D. Tomb walls

Doc. 9. Owner: Nefertari.
In situ, Valley of the Queens, Tomb 66, West Side Room (= IV).

Edition: Thausing und Goedicke, *Nofretari*, Graz, Akademi-sche Druck- und Verlagsanstalt (1971), Fig. 114/6.
Period: Dyn. XIX.

It is clear that *BD* 161 refers to the physical intactness of the deceased. The text of Pb (Doc. 1), however, is difficult to translate.[6] One of the crucial passages is the final phrase. A papyrus from Dynasty XXI (Doc.2) now corroborates an emendation in the orthography. The corrected reading says that the mummy-bandages have been unrolled (thus allow-ing free movement in the hereafter).

The mention of Kebehsenuf, one of the four sons of Horus, is natural because of their indispensable function in the preservation of the body. He does not occur in the vignettes; they show no god except Thoth, the principal character. According to the title and the late rubric, Thoth is engaged on breaking open heaven in order that each of the four winds may enter the deceased's nose. The latter is to be seen in Doc. 2, mummified and facing the former. Curiously enough, Categories B-D usually depict not merely Thoth, but the four brothers and Anubis, the chief divine embalmer, as well. Why are these always absent from the papyri?

Once again, Doc. 2 throws light on a problem. Our spell figures there[7] point to one absent in Doc. 3-9, viz. *BD* 151 A dealing with the sarco-phagus-room in the tomb and portraying all five gods full-sized. Appar-ently, there was no need to repeat them for a designer who had to cope anyway with four big figures of Thoth opening the sky (and of the deceased) as against only a few lines of text. This must also apply to Doc. 1, where the vignette of 161 adjoins one serving as a combined (albeit abridged[8]) illustration for *BD* 151 A, 155 and 156.

This explanation presents itself again in the case of Isis and Nephthys. That they (well known for their funeral cares and mentioned in the

6. Cf. P. Barguet, *Le Livre des Morts des anciens Égyptiens*, Paris, Les Éditions du Cerf (1967), p. 227. The rubric is found in late papyri only, but makes a reli-able impression: see below.

7. Unpublished. My colleagues in the Department very kindly provided me with photographs (these were shown at the Turku conference).

8. The complete picture of 151 A ranks with those of the burial (*BD* 1) and the opening of the mouth (*BD* 23) in Pb; they precede all other spells of the ms.: Ratié, *op. cit.*, pl. I-III.

rubric) accompany the gods is certain in Doc. 9, and may be so in many other instances.[9] These goddesses, too, occur in the picture of *BD* 151 A (Doc. 2). The same could be said concerning the udjat-eye(s).

To sum up: without Doc. 2 (text and vignettes) and categories B-D, many details, indeed the very import and impact of *BD* 161, would have escaped us.

Commentary   by Jan Bergman

To start with I would like to give some general remarks on the main theme, 'Oral and written documentation of religious tradition'.

A concentration on 'Pre-literate stages and formation of the canon in book religions' covers some moments of the complicated interaction between oral and written tradition, which can coexist for long periods of time, some traditions being transmitted orally, others by scriptures (e. g. in Rabbinic Judaism[10] and in Iran[11]). But even when the written canon has been established, some processes of the oral transmission are of great importance, viz. listening to the read tradition and memorizing by heart. (It is a matter worth considering, that the two most consistent book religions (the Jewish religion and Islam) are the most eager ones to stress the importance of learning the holy tradition by heart!). Thus these later stages of the typical book religions are also of methodological interest even for those working only with oral traditions.

Within these religions, however, one may find an obvious ideological trend towards stressing the original book-form of the canon, to the disregard of any oral tradition (e. g. the conception of the Torah as pre-existent before the creation; that of the Koran as a heavenly book in the care of Allah; cf. also the statement of Dēnkart, that Zoroaster himself had written the 1,200 chapters of the original Avesta).

Many typical features of oral tradition can exist in written tradition

9. E. g. on head and foot in Category B.
10. See the brief outline: B. Gerhardsson, *Memory and Manuscript*, Uppsala, 1961, Chapter I.
11. Summary: G. Widengren, 'Holy Book and Holy Traditions in Iran', in: *Holy Book and Tradition*, ed. by F. F. Bruce and E. G. Rupp, Manchester, 1968, pp. 36ff.

without justifying the conclusion that the text contains an actual oral tradition, for diverse reasons, of which I will mention two: (a) the copy may have been written from dictation, which causes mishearings etc.;[12] (b) the text can have been originally intended for reciting and thus appeal more to the ear than to the eye.

When thinking of formation of canon, the particular case of the Veda's — not only compared with the Torah, the Bible etc. but also with the Tipitaka — must be kept in mind: No historical revealer, no 'concilia' etc. — but mythical statements about their divine ever-existing character — guarantee their canonical status.

In many religious cultures the fixation of the traditions, let us call it 'canonization', is not attained by means of scriptures but by drawings etc. (That is why it would be better to speak of 'drawing cultures' etc., instead of the negative expression 'illiterate cultures'.) Here the interaction between oral tradition and drawings etc. needs to be studied.

In the ancient Egyptian civilization the representations of statues and reliefs are more 'canonic' than are the reproductions of the texts (cf. below on the vignettes of the *Book of the Dead*).

SOME COMMENTS ON THE PAPER OF PROF. HELMER RINGGREN

First of all I would like to agree with H. Ringgren that the questions about the function(s) of the canon — original or intended function, changes of function, actual function(s) etc. — are of great importance and cannot be separated from the questions under discussion.

It is an interesting fact that the O. T. formulae quoted on p. 3 as excellent expressions of the principle of canon seem to have originated in a quite 'uncanonical' context, viz. Egyptian wisdom literature[13] without any claim to divine origin or inspiration. Thus, the formulae *in se* are not witnesses of canonicity.

12. Cf. for the Egyptian wisdom literature A. Volten, *Studien zum Weisheitsbuch des Anii*, Copenhagen, 1937-38, pp. 8ff.

13. For the often supposed Egyptian background see Z. Žába, *Les Maximes de Ptahhotep*, Prague, 1956, pp. 169f. (vv. 608-609) and S. Morenz, *Gott und Mensch im Alten Ägypten*, Heidelberg, 1965, pp. 26f. (M., commenting upon the new interpretation, wants to retain the usual translation, at least for a passage in *The Teaching of Cheti*, 10:3.)

As an example of the principle of 'sticking strictly to the wording of the Hebrew text' H. Ringgren cites Mt. 21:5. Another well known instance of this is Jn 19:23-24 (referring to Ps. 22:18). In the first case, however, I think we can add a special reason why Mt. makes Zech. 8 refer to two animals; I see here an application of Hab. 3:2 (according to LXX): ἐν μέσῳ δύο ζῴων γνωσθήσῃ 'You will be recognized between two animals'. (Its application to the Bethlehem event is well attested, and its application to other 'epiphanies' seems very plausible.) This suggestion is made not principally to throw some light on the passage in question but to illustrate a very important principle in interpreting canonical texts: *Scriptura per Scripturam explicatur.*[14]

The example from the Habakkuk commentary from Qumran is illustrative of the appreciation of the Divine Word. According to my view, both the variant readings are kept not for fear of making a bad choice but in the conviction of the inexhaustible richness of the Divine Word, which cannot be exhausted by one single word or one single interpretation (cf. also the *quadriga* interpretation of the Scripture, ascribing four different senses to the biblical wordings).

The special liturgical use of only parts of the canon in fact evidently limits the text mass of the canon (cf. the fixed text series in some churches *contra* a *lectio continua* of the whole Torah in the synagogues). When parallel traditions exist, the liturgical preference of one of these tends to make the other(s) obsolete: How many Christians consider the Lord's Prayer according to Luke 11 as canonical?

So the liturgical texts can, in fact, function as a sort of canon for the canon. In the formation of the N. T. canon a *regula fidei* or *regula veritatis* had the function of deciding whether scriptures were to be considered as canonical or not. Further, the N. T. functions as a canon for the (understanding of the) O. T. and Christ for the whole Bible (cf. 'was Christum treibt' of Luther). In studying and interpreting Holy Scriptures an acquaintance with such regulative 'canons' is necessary, if one wants to have a relevant idea of this or that book religion.

As a concluding remark I want to point out some canonic materials which could be dangerous for the persistence and the definitiveness of the canon in question. In the Koran we have the problematical abroga-

---

14. Cf. the well known saying of Hillel (or of a pupil) about the Torah in Ab. V, 22: 'Turn it this way and turn it that way, for all is therein'.

tion formulae: S.2:106 'If we abrogate an *āya* or consign it to oblivion, we offer something better than it or something of equal value'; S.16: 101 'If we put an *āya* in the place of another — and Allah surely knows best what he sends down...'; cf. further S.13:39 'Allah blots out, and he establishes whatsoever he will, and with him is the Original Book (*umm al-kitāb*)'. These formulae are evidently in conflict with the canonical formulae discussed above. Dissenssion about what is *nāsikh* (the abrogating) and what is *mansukh* (the abrogated) and disagreement regarding the number of verses to which the rule must be applied (the extremes are: more than 250 verses — 5 verses) are bound to cause exegetical problems.[15] Also S.3:7 is worth mentioning in this connection: 'He it is who has sent down to you the Book, of which there are some verses that are of themselves perspicuous (*muḥkamāt*) — they are the Original Book (*umm al-kitāb*) — and others are ambiguous (*mutashābihāt*).'[16]

Another type of canonical saying, which threatens to surpass the limits of the canon in question, is that represented by the Messianic prophecies in the O.T. and the promises concerning the Paraclete in John. These passages naturally play a most important role when the religion in question encounters new prophetic religions (e. g. Dt.18:18, adopted by Christians — and after many others by the Aḥmadiyya; and Jn 16:13, applied by Mani to himself and later on by a series of other prophets).

A SHORT REMARK ON PRE-LITERATE STAGES AND ORAL TRADITION IN ANCIENT EGYPT

Old Egyptian religion is certainly no book religion in the strict sense of the word, but a religion with many books and an appreciation of writing and of scribes which is quite outstanding.[17] The general background

---

15. For the abrogation see *Shorter Encyclopedia of Islam*, p. 275 (F. Buhl) with further references; J. M. S. Baljon, *Modern Muslim Koran Interpretation*, Leiden, 1968, pp. 48ff.; R. Wielandt, *Offenbarung und Geschichte im Denken moderner Muslime*, Wiesbaden, 1971, pp. 38f.

16. See Baljon, *op. cit.*, pp. 51ff.

17. See S. Morenz, *op. cit.*, pp. 19ff.; C. J. Bleeker, *Religious Traditions and Sacred Books in Ancient Egypt* (in the collection above, note 11) pp. 20ff.; J. Leipoldt und S. Morenz, *Heilige Schriften*, Leipzig, 1953, passim.

for a 'book religion' was, in this respect, a most advantageous one. And I am convinced, that, if Echnaton had succeeded in bringing his personal mission through, his written 'teaching (*sb3*)', mentioned in some contemporary texts, would have been established as canon in the strict sense of the word. The conspicuous dominance of writing, inaugurated according to the Egyptians by the god Thoth himself,[18] puts the oral tradition totally into the shade. The unexpected appearance of the imposing text mass in the Pyramid of Unas, which in later periods was considered as the standard text, presupposes a long and complicated period of transmission, in which oral tradition must have played a considerable role. Unfortunately, we are not able to give any details concerning the procedure of this transmission.[19] References to records in some chapters of the Book of the Dead – and in some medical papyri – which tell us about the finding of the text in question in the times of Usaphais (1st dyn.) or of Mycerinus (4th dyn.) are of little value as they are, probably, fictions.[20] As regards the rich Egyptian wisdom literature, learning by heart is well attested, but the role of writings is always stressed, so that conclusive proofs of oral tradition are lacking even for this genre. No Egyptian record is known to me where one finds a strict order not to commit this or that to writing (as is often the case in the Indoeuropean civilizations).

SOME COMMENTS ON THE PAPER OF PROF. M. HEERMA VAN VOSS

Prof. M. Heerma van Voss' paper is evidence of the sort of painstaking studies which are very necessary in order to get a better understanding of the utterly confused and complicated traditions that form the Egyptian book of the Dead. In discussing methodological matters one always

18. Some instances: D. Müller, *Ägypten und die griechischen Isis-Aretalogien*, Berlin, 1961, pp. 22f. (Thoth, however, is also the lord of the spoken words.)
19. Cf. the cautious remarks by H. Brunner, *Grundzüge einer Geschichte der altägyptischen Literatur*, Darmstadt, 1966, pp. 11f. The hypotheses of Sethe need to be revised on the basis of the results of the researches of S. Schott and others (see J. Spiegel, 'Die religionsgeschichtliche Stellung der Pyramiden-texte', in *Orientalia* 22, 1953, pp. 129ff.).
20. See D. Wildung, 'Die Rolle ägyptischer Könige im Bewusstsein ihrer Nachwelt I', *MÄS* 17, Berlin, 1969, pp. 21ff., 217ff.

runs the risk of forgetting the fact that our progress basically depends on such research.

As an Egyptologist I can not refrain from giving some detailed remarks, from which, however, methodological points can be drawn.

The vignette adjoining that of 161 in Doc. 1 is interpreted as 'a combined (albeit abridged) illustration for BD 151A, 155, and 156'. The abridgement, however, only concerns chapter 151 (NB: the accompanying text is that of 151B), not 156 and 155 (this is the order of texts and vignettes in Doc. 1). In his note 8 the author refers to 'the complete picture of 151A' in the beginning of the papyrus (Ratié, *op. cit.*, pl. I-III). In this picture, however, we find only two of the four figures of the 'summary' in the illustration discussed (the Djed and the jackal/Anubis). For a complete picture we have to look at PapBM 10010 (= Naville, *op. cit.*, T. CLXXIII): here we recognize all the four protecting symbols of the sides of the sarcophagus, which have entered Doc. 1 as a sort of 'summary' of the comprehensive scene of the sarcophagus-room in the tomb. The selection of one of the many protecting quartets is well understandable as a counterpart to the adjacent Thoth-quartet illustrating chapter 161 (which is also one of many possible quartets). The number four symbolizes the cosmic totality, which — according to the macrocosmos-microcosmos ideology — is represented by the four walls of the sarcophagus-room and reflected on the four walls of the sarcophagus itself. Especially categories B and C in the author's inventory, being three-dimensional, help us to read the two-dimensional vignettes of the papyri. Thus, the shrine of Tutanchamon (Doc. 8) provides a good illustration of the important fact that even the comprehensive picture to 151A in PapBM 10010 (referred to above) is not complete: Isis and Nephthys are both connected as well with the east as with the west; together with the four Horus children appears another divine quartet, and so on.

The important lesson to learn from this observation is the following: Even if the vignettes of the papyri are, at least sometimes, more reliable than the accompanying texts, they only give a limited approach to the actual ceremony. What is 'canonic' are the basic funerary ceremonies, in the view of the ancient Egyptian; the texts and the vignettes in the Books of the Dead give merely selections of important moments. In the current state of research we know very little about the principles for these more or less different selections. Careful collection and detailed registration of the immense materials concerned could give us some clues to understanding these principles.

One detail ought to be underlined. The mention of Kebehsenuf in 161 is, as far as I know, the only instance in the Book of the Dead where he appears alone (elsewhere — one can find 10 cases[21] — he is always accompanying the other three Horus children). In 151A, however, his importance according to the text seems to surpass that of his brothers. His connection with the West, the most important cardinal point in the funerary context, and his special care of the mummy ($s3\underline{h}$), mentioned in 161, could help us to explain why he — and not one of the others — appears alone here. As the concluding member of the quartet he can, however, also stand for the whole quartet.

Commentary   by Carl-Martin Edsman

'In India, from the oldest times, up till the present day, the spoken word, and not writing, has been the basis of the whole of the literary and scientific activity', M. Winternitz emphasizes in his classical *History of Indian Literature* (Engl. transl. 1927-33, I, 33). Mainly with the help of this solid scholar I should like to draw the attention of this Study Conference to some other book religions than those treated in the two opening lectures and, with reference to the subject of the 1st session, concentrate on the pre-literate stages. As further both folklorists and anthropologists are well represented among the hosts and the members of the Conference they may perhaps also be interested in the interrelation between their methods and those of biblical scholarship, not always known among non-exegetes. I leave phenomenological-comparative and terminological questions aside as well as the history of the formation of any single canon. The last restriction also excludes a description I had originally intended to give of how a canon is established in our own days, namely the three sacred books of one of the older Japanese 'New Religions', Tenrikyo.

The oral teaching of the *guru*, the spiritual leader, is not the source

21. See P. Barguet, *op. cit.*, the index p. 290 (s. v. Qebehsenouf).

of all learning, in ancient and modern India alone. This method has to a certain extent survived also in the university teaching of Western Europe. A Swedish undergraduate in Berlin and Paris just before the Second World War made the following remark, when he observed how his foreign fellow-students spent their days listening to the lectures of their professors and were busy in the evenings rewriting and copying their notes: 'In our country we have discovered the existence of the art of printing and read books instead of hearing lectures, and so we save a lot of time.' The latest, supposedly progressive, university reforms in Sweden have in fact reintroduced the pre-Gutenberg times and made such a statement impossible.

There are at least two answers to the question why ancient India did not make use of the art of writing, already well known at that time. Certainly the priests were interested in the very profitable privilege of teaching the higher castes: 'If a Shudra hears the Veda, his ears shall be stopped with molten tin or lac, if he repeats the sacred texts, his tongue shall be cut out, if he stores them in his memory, his body shall be struck in two', it says in an old law-book (I, 35f.). But conservatism in religious matters has also contributed to the preservation of the old method of oral transmission of the texts, well established before the Indians learnt the new art of writing. So the unique prestige of the teacher is very understandable: he is equal to or superior to the physical father of the pupil, he is regarded as an image of the god Brahman, whose heaven is open to the faithful disciple. This high position of the guru finally depends on his transmission of a holy tradition. The sacred texts required, moreover, quite a different method of learning from the secular ones. 'Word for word, with careful avoidance of every error in pronunciation, in accent, in the manners of recitation, the pupil had to repeat them after the teacher and impress them on his memory' (I, 37). The result of this accuracy was that the correctness of the texts was better guaranteed by oral transmission than by written manuscripts, which, incidentally, only date from later times, most of them from the last few centuries (I, 38 ff.).

The Veda ('knowledge') is, in contradistinction to a single work such as the Muslim Koran or a definitive collection of books such as the Christian Bible and the Buddhist Tipitaka, a whole literature. It consists of hymns, prayers, incantations, benedictions, sacrificial formulas and litanies, commentaries on sacrifice and philosophical meditations on

God and man. It has been from the oldest times considered as divine revelation and designated as *shruti* ('hearing'), 'breathed out' by the God Brahman, and 'visioned' only by the ancient seers. Nor do the opponents of Brahmanic religion, the Buddhists, deny the divine origin of the Veda. But they accuse the Brahmans of falsifying the texts, which therefore in their present form are full of errors (I, 52 ff.).

The oral transmission of the texts explains two opposing impressions gained by the Western reader from the later written and printed manuscripts: some commentaries contain indeed many repetitions, but at the same time the sentences may be so short and aphoristic, that they now need completions to be understandable (I, 270 f.; cf. 203). Perhaps one might compare the last characteristic with the peculiarity of university lecture-notes in our days: only the writer himself can comprehend them, as long as the oral presentation remains in his memory; when it is lost, they are incomprehensible to him too. As a matter of fact, Vedic texts were also written down when they were no longer understood (I, 302).

With Buddhist sacred writings we are on firmer historical ground than in the case of the almost prehistoric Vedic literature. The preaching of the Buddha falls into the decades before and after 500 B.C. His speeches and sayings have been faithfully preserved in the oral tradition of his disciples, since Gotama himself did not write down his words. What the Pāli canon of the Buddhists puts into the mouth of Buddha might in some famous cases really be original utterances, especially the metrical verse aphorisms (*gāthā*) with their stable form (II, 1 ff.; cf. II, 117).

According to Buddhist tradition a canon was established by three councils, the first immediately after the death of the Buddha, the second a hundred years afterwards and the third at the time of the famous king Ashoka about 250 B.C. The learned monk Tissa Moggaliputta, who organized the last one, which is historically the best testified and most important, sent his pupil Mahinda, the younger brother or son of Ashoka, as a missionary to Ceylon. He brought with him the Buddhist texts, which, according to the Ceylon chroniclers were first transmitted orally and two hundred years later written down (II, 4-8).

It is significant that no manuscripts of sacred books are mentioned in the Buddhist canon, although the art of writing was well-known at that time and regarded as a distinguished branch of learning. If we nowadays call a person well-read, the corresponding attribute of the Buddhist brethren was 'rich in hearing'. The memory of the monks played the same role in the first four hundred years of Buddhist history as later — as also in the history of Christianity — the monastic libraries. Still living oral tradition could also be incorporated into already existing scriptures (II, 185), and, like written texts, it could inspire artists (II, 254).

The coexistence of oral and written tradition is confirmed by the Chinese pilgrim Fa-hien, who travelled in North India at the beginning of the 5th century A.D. He found the first 'basket of the discipline of the order' (Vinayapitaka) of the Buddhist canon only in oral transmission, without any manuscripts, until he came to Pātaliputra, where a Mahāyāna monastery possessed a copy of the Vinaya (II, 8). To warrant the continuation of the doctrine and the rules of the order the monks constantly had to memorize, recite and expound the different texts. They got special epithets according to their concentration on different parts of the canon and on different practical duties (II, 11, 17). One of the dangers which threaten the existence of Buddhism in the future, says a recurring prophecy, is that the monks will not any longer be interested in hearing and learning (*not*: reading!) the texts (II, 76 f.). There are also instructions to prevent such a development. If, for instance, the important confession formula, which must be regularly recited in the assembly, is in danger of being forgotten, the ancient rule prescribes: 'From amongst those monks one monk shall without delay be sent off to the neighbouring community. To him shall be said: Go brother, and when you have memorized the confession formula, the full one or the abridged one, then return to us.'

A peculiarity belonging to Buddhist scriptures, namely the many repetitions, is also explained by their oral origin. If a Westerner hears that the New Testament parable of the Prodigal Son has got a striking parallel in Buddhism, he is disappointed when he goes to the Buddhist version, which is very prolix. But in this and other cases the intention of the Eastern storyteller was a double one: firstly to help the memory of the listener, and secondly to obtain a rhetorical effect. The late Danish indologist P. Tuxen has compared the impression which the recitation of the repetitions brings about on the ears of a Buddhist audience with the delight which the recurring motifs in the musical compositions of Bach or Wagner gives to a Western concert hall public (II, 68).

Every folklorist reader of H. Gunkel's famous commentary on Genesis, published in 1901, must say to himself: This sounds quite modern. The different types of oral tradition (*Gattungen*) correspond to, for instance, the *Einfache Formen* by Jolles. The emphasis on the 'situation in life' (*Sitz im Leben*), to which the special kind of story belongs, can be compared with the importance laid on the function of myth by Malinowsky. Where did Gunkel get his points of view from, so revolutionary in Old Testament scholarship? One of his pupils, W. Baumgartner, has given the answer in his foreword to a facsimile edition of Gunkel's Genesis commentary published in 1964 and 1966. There he clearly traces the germanistic (E. Schmidt), ethnological (W. Wundt) and folkloristic (A. Wuttke, K. Bücher, O. Böckel) inspiration of his master.

The Uppsala Orientalist H. S. Nyberg also underlined the significance of oral transmission in his *Studien zum Hoseabuche* (1935) and initiated a lively discussion on this subject among Nordic scholars. One of them, the late Norwegian O. T. nestor S. Mowinckel, who himself was a pupil of Gunkel's at Giessen, has given a balanced synthesis of the whole question in *The Interpreter's Dictionary of the Bible* (s. v. 'Tradition, Oral', 1962). As evidence of the reliability of oral tradition compared with written documents, he points to old Norwegian family traditions. The bibliography includes, among other works, A. Olrik, 'Epische Gesetze der Volksdichtung' (*Zeitschrift für deutsches Altertum* 51, 1909); H. Ellekilde (ed.), *Nogle grundsaetninger for sagnforskning* (1921); K. Liestøl, *Norske aettesogor* (1922); Idem, *The Origin of the Icelandic Family Sagas* (1930); K. Krohn, *Die folkloristische Arbeitsmethode* (1926).

One of the last contributions to the combination of exegetical and folkloristic methods comes from a countryman of Mowinckel's, Th. Boman, *Die Jesusüberlieferung im Licht der neueren Volkskunde* (1967). The last paper I have seen on the same subject is written by P. Gaechter, 'Die urchristliche Überlieferung verglichen mit der irischen Gedächtniskultur' (*Zeitschrift für katholische Theologie* 95, 1973). Cf. also A. Schoors, *I am God Your Savior. A Form-Critical Study of the Main Genres in Is. XL-LV* (Supplement to *Vetus Testamentum*, 24), Leiden 1973. In his monograph *Oral Tradition: A Study in Historical Methodology*, transl. by H. M. Wright (1965, 1969), J. Vansina takes up the relation of oral tradition to written history, and makes the following remark: 'Few historians have gone into the methodological problems raised by oral tradition'. This statement does not apply so much to Biblical scholars; and among others their work on this field seems to be a good legitimation of the subject of this session.

Discussion   Chairman: Th. P. van Baaren

The first session was opened by the chairman of the conference as a whole, Lauri Honko, who extended a welcome on behalf of the Organizing Committee to all of the participants. Replying, the chairman of the first session, Th. P. van Baaren, thanked the Organizing Committee for their work in arranging the conference, and then invited the first speaker, Helmer Ringgren, to present his paper.

Ringgren began by identifying two problems, namely the formation, and function, of a religious canon. He drew a distinction between canons which had emerged gradually, such as the Jewish and Christian, and those written with the express purpose of creating a canon, such as the Qurʾan or the Book of Mormon. In addition, he pointed to the existence of a third type, not dealt with in his paper, such as the Sumerian religious literature or the Egyptian Book of the Dead, where a selection, maybe involving redaction and even recomposition, is carried out (e. g. at the time when the language in question ceases to be spoken) in order to establish a normative text. Turning to the question of function, he suggested that a canon could be defined as having religious authority, and also as being a definitive text, which nothing may be added to or taken away from. It might have several uses: as the correct ritual text in liturgical use; as containing rules for the correct behaviour of the believers; or as the basis for the establishment of true doctrine. The last two functions often occurred together. Finally, he read the closing paragraph of his paper, in which he emphasized the possibility of change in the use of a canon, and urged the desirability of the phenomenological study of these uses.

The second speaker was M. Heerma van Voss, who wished first to explain how it came about that his paper mentioned neither 'canon' nor 'book religion', the two topics of the first session: the paper had originally been written with session 1c, Literary Source Criticism, in mind, and had subsequently been transferred to 1A. Hence he would like to add a commentary to the paper, with reference to the question of canons and book religions.

It was difficult to speak of a canon in the case of ancient Egypt: the Pyramid Texts, the Coffin Texts, and finally in chronological order the Book of the Dead, showed a progressive selection and fixing of texts; yet even in Ptolemaic times, c. 300 B.C., it was only possible to state that the texts in the Book of the Dead were more or less fixed; the Book of the Dead was still perhaps in the stage preceding a canon proper. Nevertheless, he thought it possible to speak (as Helmer Ringgren had done) of Egyptian religion as a book religion, even if not in the usual sense of the term. Turning then to his paper, he said that too often in scholarly literature the Book of the Dead was identified with the papyri alone, to the exclusion of other texts and of the important 'vignettes', i. e. pictures; whereas in fact both the vignettes and the wall pictures from the tombs could make an important contribution to the understanding of the text. His paper was intended to illustrate this point, taking spell 161 from the Book of the Dead as a model, and he supplemented this by showing and commenting in detail on some slides of Document 2, the Cleveland papyrus, especially since it was not reproduced in the available literature. What emerged from a study of the non-papyrus material was that false conclusions could easily be drawn on the basis of the papyri in isolation: e. g. that in this spell 161, the only gods who were important were Thoth and one of the sons of Horus, whereas the other materials clearly indicated that all of Horus' children were involved. It was therefore highly misleading to limit the sources studied to the papyri.

The first commentator to speak about the two papers was Jan Bergman. Picking out some points from his commentary for special emphasis, he said that one should not confine the consideration of oral tradition to preliterate phases, since it was quite possible for written and oral traditions to coexist, with some material being transmitted orally and some by scriptures. He then went on to add an extra point about the formation of a canon, with special reference to the Vedas: i. e. that they had not been defined as canonical by any special councils, etc., as was the case in some other religions; nor could this be seen as a difference between East and West, since in the case of Buddhism 'canonization' had in fact taken place. This distinction in canon formation should also be borne in mind when considering the question of function.

Reading for the most part from his prepared text, Bergman also however added an extra point about the distinction frequently made between 'book religions' and 'cult religions', arguing that in most cases 'book religions' were 'cult religions' as well, involving the liturgical use of their books within their cults. The final point in his paper, he said, was intended for M. Heerma van Voss, as from one Egyptologist to another: he agreed entirely on the inadequacy of restricting consideration to the written papyri, but would like to widen the perspective even further, so as also to include some of the three-dimensional pictures on the coffins.

The second commentator to speak was Carl-Martin Edsman, who remarked on the applicability of the considerations about written and oral transmission to the delivery of conference papers. His own contribution, he said, was more of a supplement than a commentary, and relied on Winternitz' work to emphasize the coexistence of oral and written traditions, e. g. in Hinduism and Buddhism. His second point was to emphasize the importance of an interdisciplinary understanding of comparative religion, especially in the cooperation between the humanities and theology. This could be illustrated by the important work being done on Old Testament and New Testament studies by means of the methodology and terminology of folklore studies. In addition to Gunkel and Mowinckel, who were mentioned among others in his paper, he would also like to refer to the Norwegian scholar Thorlief Boman's monograph, *Die Jesusüberlieferung im Licht der neueren Volkskunde* (1967).

He went on to present an illustration which reasons of space had excluded from his paper, about one of the older new Japanese religions, Tenrikyo, where it was possible to study the actual process of formation of a canon in progress. Tenrikyo had originated in 1837, when an itinerary priest had come to carry out a ritual to cure a woman, Miki Nakayama, her husband Zembei, and their son Shuji, of sudden attacks of pain. During the ritual, Miki, who had been acting as the medium, suddenly went into a trance, in which she spoke as follows: 'I am the True and Original God. I have been predestined to reside here. I have descended from Heaven to save all human beings, and I want to take Miki as the Shrine of God, and the mediatrix between God and men'

(H. Thomsen, *The New Religions of Japan*, 1963, p. 34). According to the historians of Tenrikyo, Miki had 'endeavoured to teach them by Her words, by Her writings, and by Her life, always putting Herself in the place of others, and performed wonders before their eyes, so that She might convince them of the authenticity of Her being His Temple' (*A Short History of Tenrikyo*, 1958, p. 3); but she had then also written down the revelations she had received in a book called *Ofudesaki*, i. e. 'The tip of the writing brush' (C. B. Offner and H. van Straelen, *Modern Japanese Religions*, 1963, p. 58). This book was deliberately written in poetry, partly in order to assist memorization, and using the relatively simple 99-character phonetic Japanese alphabet (supplemented by a few Chinese signs); but it also used many metaphors, which the Tenrikyo authorities stress are not always easily explained. In Miki's original manuscript (preserved at Tenji), the legitimation of the book is as follows: 'What I have spoken hitherto was forgotten by you, so I have decided to commit it to writing by the tip of Her pen' (*A Short History*, pp. 53ff., 5).

The chairman then invited the speakers to reply to the commentators, adding what he called the 'ritual request' to keep the answers short. Ringgren declined; Heerma van Voss wished only to say, in reply to Bergman, that while he agreed on the importance of the Egyptian tomb figures, in the case of spell 161 they had not been of assistance; and that in some cases (e. g. Tutenkhamun's tomb) the sculptors had taken artistic licence to include the figures of gods who definitely did not belong there. Otherwise he was in agreement with the points raised in the commentary.

Before opening the discussion to the floor, the chairman interpolated the observation (which he thought had largely been overlooked) that it was possible to study the contemporary process of canon formation in the many small religions continually springing up all over the world. The first speaker from the floor was Zwi Werblowsky, who stressed the distinction between the emergence of sacred scripture or literature, and the conscious or semi-conscious process of canonization. The texts in question might have been in existence for a long time before the latter process took place: it was a response to a new historical situation, and it necessitated the formulation of criteria for the selection of the canon, which in turn modified the notion of holy scripture. Many canonical texts clearly were definitely literary compositions − e. g. the

Qurʾan, the Book of Mormon, and many late Mahāyāna Buddhist Sutras — in contrast to the crystallization of oral traditions, e. g. of what the Founder had said. He suggested that one should also distinguish between the concepts of sacred scriptures, on the one hand, and canonical scriptures on the other (a point reverted to later by Ninian Smart). It would have been valuable to look at the 'sacred' (in quotation marks) books of the Chinese tradition: Confucius, etc.; authoritative works, whose 'sacredness' or 'canonicity' were very different from those of the traditions discussed. He recalled that Max Weber had specifically used the term 'book religion' of the Chinese tradition. Similarly, picking up van Baaren's remark, he suggested (not facetiously) that comparative religion also ought to look at the current process of formation of secular canons, e. g. the works of Chairman Mao. Finally, he turned to the question of the use of canonical scriptures as a locus on which to anchor authority. From a sociological point of view, the question how authority was legitimated was a very important one, and he suggested that this use of the sacred literature (which often resembled an inkblot test, in that anything could be projected onto it) was a far more significant question than that of the liturgical use of canonical literature in rituals, for instance.

G. C. Oosthuizen reported the phenomenon of religious movements in Africa in which tremendous authority was attributed to the canonical literature, which was however kept locked up by the prophets, so that the people in the movement had never read it.

Hans-J. Klimkeit questioned the definition of the word 'canonized'. Two of the criteria which had been mentioned were divine authority, and being a criterion for religious doctrine or behaviour; but it seemed to him that these could not be applied to all religions, e. g. Mahāyāna Buddhism, where it was in any case difficult to say which texts were canonical and which were apocryphal. He suggested that comparative religion still needed to arrive at a definition of the canonical which would be applicable to all religions. Replying, Carl-Martin Edsman said that for southern Buddhism, this question had been solved: the Council of 54-56 had recited, and thus definitively laid down, the canon. Klimkeit said that the problem arose more in the case of Mahāyāna Buddhism, especially in Tibet. Despite the real differences between the Tandjur/Bstan-hgyur and the Kandjur/Bkah-hgyur, the Tibetan canon was vast, and included virtually everything written which could have significance for Mahāyāna Buddhism. Ringgren suggested that the concept of 'authoritative literature' varied between religions, and that phenomenology should take this into account.

The next contribution was by Carsten Colpe, who said that the descriptions and investigations of the formation and functions of canons presented so far had been good, but he suggested that at a conference devoted to problems of methodology this was not adequate. Methodology would require the setting up of some general rules, the *logos* of the method; and it should also be applicable to other things besides the canon. He turned for an analogy to classical scholarship, which illustrated the secular yearning for an authoritative text; there might be 20 or 30 editions of a particular author, each one changing a word here and there, although this might not add anything to our understanding of the author beyond what had been known 100 years ago. Maybe this secular analogy suggested a psychological connection between the aim of an authoritative text, as something that could be leant on, in a secular context and in religion.

Ringgren disagreed. He did not think that the student of a classical text such as Plato or Aristotle or Livy would use this text in order to establish a doctrine or correct behaviour. Such a text ought to be 'authoritative', but would not be used in the same way as that of a religious canon. He also argued that the study of religious canons did not require a specific methodology, but used the methods of history, literary history, literary criticism, sociology (as Werblowsky had suggested), and so forth. Bergman countered, however, by pointing out that the role of authors such as Homer was sometimes very like that of a religious canon: the Gnostics, for example, while they did not quote from Aeschylus, did treat quotations from Homer, Hesiod, etc., in very much the same way as they treated quotations from the Old and New Testament prophets.

Colpe agreed that there was an important difference between the authority an editor was looking for and the authority a believer was looking for. The first point he was thinking of, however, was that the editor of a text could become so personally committed to 'his' text, and to its authoritativeness, that it could serve as a locus for rules of personal behaviour and for a *Weltanschauung*; and secondly, a good philologist who had edited a text would insist on rejecting interpretations or readings based on words or motifs not strongly stressed in the text (sometimes to the embarrassment of historians of religion). In this way, it seemed to him, the 'authority' of secular and of religious texts was partly analogous, e. g. in its function of guaranteeing a security of conscience (religious or non-religious).

Ninian Smart reverted to Werblowsky's distinction between sacred and canonistic authoritativeness, which he thought had been implicit in the papers, but had been brought out much more clearly by Werblowsky. The distinction would have methodological implications; and it raised the question whether sacredness or canonicity could exist without each other. He thought it could. There was no doubt about the possibility of non-canonical sacred texts, which might be quite non-authoritative, with reference to both belief and practice. It was on the other hand difficult to see how a canonical text could avoid being authoritative: authoritativeness and canonicity were closely related concepts. He compared this to the concept of the guru. In the pure form of the 'guru syndrome', the guru's authority was total: he must be believed, no matter what he said. From a theological point of view, therefore, the question of canonicity was one of authoritativeness in religion: and it posed the question why a written source of authority might be preferred to other forms of authority, institutionalized or non-institutionalized.

The chairman offered a summary of the main points which had been put so far. It was clear, firstly, that texts should be differentiated from each other, e. g. as (1) canonical, (2) authoritative, and (3) other sacred texts, or rather, with decreasing authoritative value (reading for edification, etc.); and secondly, the important question was why in some religions a written text should be used, and in others an oral transmission or some other form.

The concept of 'canonicity' was questioned at a fundamental level by Michael Pye; he stressed that it was a term which had originated in one specific culture, and which comparative religionists were now attempting to apply more generally, although it carried overtones quite inapplicable in other cultures. He referred to the terms used in Buddhism, and in China and Japan (*sutra, ching*, and *kyō*), which denoted both the extended 'canon' of Mahāyāna, and also the Confucian 'canon'; and he wondered how the concept would have developed if comparative religionists had started from 'ching' instead of from 'canon'. The methodological problem involved was: how could a concept be developed for use in comparative studies which would be free from the initial definitions implicit in one culture?

Van Baaren suggested that since it was necessary to make use of words, it was better to start from those one was familiar with, than to borrow those from another culture (which one usually misunderstood). This point was followed up by Werblowsky, who compared the situation where one takes a familiar word from one's own culture and gradually 'polishes it up', with that where one might borrow a loanword and only discover after thirty years of hard scientific work how wrong one's understanding of it had been. As long as people did not speak an ad hoc special scientific metalanguage, they must start from the cultural limitations of their existing languages. He suggested that doing comparative religion was (to quote Mussolini) 'vivere pericolosamente', and that one constantly had to stick one's neck out. While it might be misleading to try to apply the Christian term 'canon' to Mahayana Buddhism, this was probably preferable to the way in which terms such as 'mana' and 'tabu' had been appropriated and misused. There were methodological dangers, however one acquired one's terminology, but they seemed to be less by lopping off the misleading associations from a term from one's own tradition than by starting with a completely unknown term from another tradition.

Ugo Bianchi agreed with Pye. What was important, he believed, was to be conscious. Comparative religionists did not have the right to start from definitions (not even comparative definitions), nor to proceed by deductive procedures. In the question of religious terminology, he felt that it was justified to proceed dialectically between what was known (i. e. scientifically experienced), and that which needed to be clarified by means of philologically- and historically-minded research.

The concept of 'inspiration' was then questioned by William Klassen. He suggested that one perhaps ought to draw a distinction between inspiration where the deity was deemed to have dictated the text directly, and where it was written by a human instrument. Christianity and Judaism differed on this point. He also questioned what the term 'canon' had really meant historically in Christianity. In the 16th or 17th centuries, it had referred to authoritativeness; but he suggested that in the 2nd century it had meant simply the 'rule of truth'. In the light of recent Gnostic findings, it seemed likely that the canonical collection had in any case been in existence earlier than had been thought; but what that meant was that Christianity's concern for the truth had been in existence before the question was raised as to which books belonged to the canon and which did not.

The fact that the concept of 'inspiration' varied was supported briefly by Ringgren, e. g. between the time of the formation of the Jewish and Christian canons, and its later interpretation in the western Christian church, and in the case of the Qurʾan, which was obviously based on the concept of inspiration as it had developed in the book religions in Mohammed's time.

The chairman brought the session to a close by referring to Werblowsky's quotation about 'living dangerously', which he thought was the right slogan for the conference: he looked forward to the time when all the participants could sit by the fire telling their children and grandchildren about the week when they had lived so dangerously in Turku.

Taxonomy and Source Criticism of Oral Tradition

JUHA PENTIKÄINEN *Taxonomy and Source Criticism of Oral Tradition*

ORAL TRADITION AND THE STUDY OF RELIGION

In trying to assess objects for research in the study of religion from a present-day perspective, it is in my opinion quite clear that more attention needs to be paid to oral tradition than has been the case in the past. It seems that here is a question of an area within comparative religion which has been largely neglected and whose share of the volume of research in the discipline has hitherto been very small. In fact, many scholars seem, consciously or unconsciously, to have excluded orally transmitted information concerning religious traditions from their field of research.

It is a mistake to look upon the study of religion as a purely historical field of study.[1] Rather, we should be prepared to accept the fact that the study of religion covers a multiplicity of research objects and methods and to regard 'history of religion' as but one field for research within the study of religion along with the phenomenology, sociology, psychology and anthropology of religion. In each of these segments of the study of religion it would be interesting to study not only the written relics of past religions and cultures but also the considerable religious information which is transmitted orally both in literate and non-literate cultures. It is clear that the proportion of this type of information is greatest in the case of totally non-literate cultures. Today more and more of the

---

1. From this point of view the international name of this association I.A.H.R. is too limited.

cultures of the third world are crossing the threshold from the non-literate to the literate. Consequently, oral tradition material should be considered an area of great importance nowadays and one where the need for research is very pressing.

Specialists within each of the different segments of the study of religion should attempt to chart the special problems encountered in studying oral tradition and individuals and communities whose religious beliefs are transmitted, either in part or totally, orally: in the absence of ancient written sources historical deductions, too, must be made on the basis of oral tradition. Even when dealing with the historical religions of literate cultures it is well to bear in mind that most of them too have had a pre-literate or pre-historical stage which cannot be charted without the aid of the methods placed at our disposal, e. g. by archeology, folkloristics and ethnological text analysis. In general the importance of archeological methods is from the viewpoint of history of religion the greater the older the cultures and religions in question. Although linguistics and archeology are important ancillary sciences when studying the history of religion, their significance should none-theless not be over-estimated. Experience has shown that archeologists have made considerable blunders in stating that some object or find has had a ritual or mythical function when they have been uncertain as to whether it might have served some other purpose. Scholars of religion with a leaning towards linguistics have at times put too much trust in doubtful etymologies as religious historical evidence. What is needed is discussion and cooperation between different disciplines, since the worst blunders seem to have been made when embarking alone upon investigations of the 'no man's land' situated on the edges of different disciplines' traditional fields of study or lying between them. This seems to have been the case as far as orally transmitted information about religious traditions is concerned.

There is reason to ask why scholars of religion, whose task it is to identify their areas for research and to be fully conversant with what religion is, have not been more resolute in using all possible materials of religious information. The sociology and psychology of religion, for example, have long thrived among western peoples and in Christian societies. As a result there is a large volume of literature dealing with the personalities of mystics, with Christian attitudes and secularisation and with the typologies of Western Christian sects and denominations, while corresponding studies of other, principally unwritten, religions are almost entirely lacking. Is it that the sociology and psychology of religion lack the methods whereby the peoples and communities of non-literate cultures could be interviewed and studied? In defence of religious phenomenologists it may be said that they have made sincere attempts to find examples among the religions of non-literate cultures. However, it is possible to criticize the ways in which the question of how representative the material is and how valuable it is as source material have frequently been overlooked. Consequently, single, even unique, notes have at times mistakenly been used to characterize the culture or religion of a particular area. Religious anthropologists cannot be accused of lack of interest in non-literate religions. On the other hand, it may be said that they have often neglected the taxonomy of their materials and been satisfied to study tradition as if it were a homogeneous mass of knowledge acquired by rote.

The Swedish folklorist, C. W. von Sydow, sharply criticized scholars of 'primitive religion' in the 1940's, accusing them in particular of neglecting source criticism. A result of this has been that conclusions have been drawn about religion on the basis of such traditional genres as folktales and ficts which have no value as religious evidence. 'The school of Comparative Religion is thus incapable of seeing independently which categories of tradition are of importance for the study of religion and which have nothing to do with religion at all; they have contented themselves in good faith, with the material prepared by former scholarship, and have now and then added some detail which might seem relevant. Reliable scientific work in the field of primitive religion presupposes broadly based studies of popular tradition and a thorough knowledge of all its several categories'.[2] In reviewing this criticism in the light of the 1960's perspective, Lauri Honko pointed out: 'Slightly modified, this still holds true'.[3] Future historians of comparative religion will, I think, come to look upon the end of the 1960's and the beginning of the 1970's as the turning point when the position of oral tradition

2. C. W. von Sydow, *Selected Papers on Folklore Published on the Occasion of his 70th Birthday*. Sel. and ed. by Laurits Bødker, Copenhagen, 1948, pp. 166-188, esp. 168-170.

3. Lauri Honko, 'Memorates and the Study of Folk Beliefs', *Indiana State Univ. Folklore Institute Journal* 1 (1964), pp. 5-19, esp. p. 7.

began to grow stronger as an object of study in comparative religion. This conference alone is testimony to such a development.

ORAL TRADITION AND LITERARY TRADITION

Tradition is a key concept in the study of cultures and also of religions. A minimum definition can be given, according to which tradition includes 'culture elements handed down from one generation to another'.[4] We are thus concerned with information that continues uninterruptedly over at least one generation. At the root of the word tradition lies the Latin verb *tradere*, which contains the aspect of continuity. Another important aspect of tradition is its social character. For this reason, tradition and 'individual knowledge' are concepts which should not be regarded as identical. The choice made by society, in other words social control, is of crucial importance in the gradual formation of traditions. If an individual's information lacks continuity, if it is not handed down, if the information is not accepted by the whole society or one of its groups or sub-cultures, then we are not dealing with a tradition. Since the presentation of a tradition is controlled behaviour, the information takes on a fixed form, and becomes stereotyped. The principal channels by which a tradition is transmitted are education and upbringing. In studying these processes anthropologists distinguish between enculturation (internalization of culture) and socialization (integration into society and its norms).[5]

Whether we are dealing with oral or literary tradition depends on the way in which it is communicated. Oral tradition is communicated by means of speech, from speaker(s) to listener(s). This communication must be considered social behaviour which requires reciprocity between at least two individuals. For reciprocity to occur there must exist a certain fund of common knowledge and certain common expectations, i. e. 'common culture'. Individuals cannot, for example, communicate religious messages to each other unless they understand each other's language and share to some extent a common linguistic or paralinguistic

4. See Åke Hultkrantz, *General Ethnological Concepts, International Dictionary of Regional European Ethnology and Folklore* 1(1960), Copenhagen, pp. 229-231.
5. For details see my article 'Depth Research', *Acta Ethnographica Academiae Scientiarum Hungaricae* 21 (1972), Budapest, pp. 127-151.

code.[6] We may represent the communication of oral tradition in the following way:[7]

Social Context

Message

Speaker . . . . Listener

Contact

Common Code

When a speaker sends a message to his listener, the prerequisites of mutual communication are always contact, interaction between the individuals in question, and the code or context that they have in common at, say, the level of language. In a social situation this makes the message sensible and endows it with meaning.

Literate tradition is transmitted with the aid of the printed word and, in modern times, also via mass media (mass lore).[8] Often, in education and upbringing, literate societies make use of the methods of both oral and written communication in transmitting knowledge from generation to generation. An important problem in our present-day cultures is interference between the different modes of transmission. When dealing with book religions, for example, many interesting questions arise concerning the pre-literate stage of a tradition and its eventual evolution into a written form.[9]

The following diagram illustrates the course of a religious tradition transmitted orally. The starting point is an event or experience felt to be religious or given a religious interpretation, and the end occurs when it is recorded for the first time. In favorable circumstances the birth

6. Dell Hymes has written on the problems of the 'Ethnography of Speaking' in several of his articles, e.g. 'The Ethnography of Speaking', *Anthropology and Human Behavior*, ed. by Thomas Gladwin and William S. Sturtevant, Washington, 1962, and Introduction: 'Toward Ethnographies of Communication', *American Anthropologist* 66 (1964), e.g. pp. 2-13.

7. Cf. Roman Jakobson, 'Closing Statement: Linguistics and Poetics', *Style in Language*, ed. by Thomas A. Sebeok, New York, 1960, p. 353.

8. On communication in narrative situations see Robert A. Georges, 'Towards an Understanding of Storytelling Events', *Journal of American Folklore* 82 (1970), pp. 316ff.

9. Cf. Jan Vansina, *Oral Tradition. A Study in Historical Methodology*. London, 1965, p. 21.

and canonization of a new religion may also follow the same pattern as that shown here:

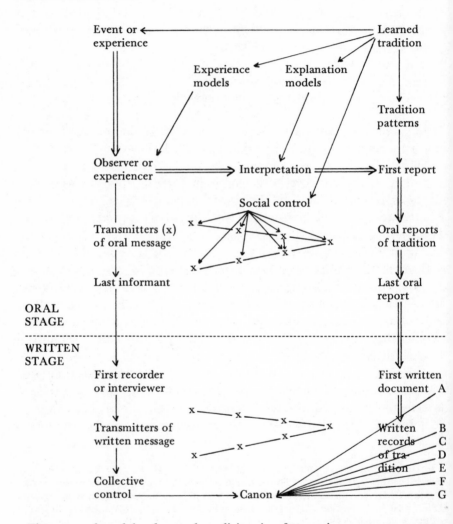

The part played by learned tradition is of great importance at every stage of the transmission of a religious message. Nobody can experience or interpret an event as religious if he is not already acquainted with religious experience and explanation models of the tradition.[10] A religious

10. Cf. L. Honko, *op. cit.*, pp. 16-17.

experience is always a question of the actualization of a belief within some supranormal frame of reference. The patterns of content, style, structure and language,[11] already familiar from learned tradition, regulate each oral communication in the chain of transmission. It is through the agency of these patterns, too, that the tradition is preserved and gradually takes on a stereotyped form. In studying religious events, there occurs the important problem of the processes of interpretation; these may be individual or social events which are controlled or regulated by individuals who exercise some kind of authoritative power in their social groups. In this way a uniquely experienced event is partly absorbed into the traditions of a society. The study of the pre-literate stage of religious tradition presupposes that the chain by which the experience or event is communicated is examined in detail. Each informant in the chain plays an important part, but of particular significance are the experiencer of the event, i. e. the eyewitness, and the last informant, the person who actually relates the oral message or commits it to writing. It is at this point that the oral stage in the transmission of the tradition comes to an end and the written stage begins. The analysis of the written stage is just as interesting a task as the study of the oral process of transmission. In general it is a condition for the formation of a religious canon that there exists collective control of tradition materials. There should also be a collective interpretation process in which account may be taken of background factors from the culture which have undergone some temporal or spatial transition. The entire store of religious tradition does not usually become absorbed into the canon of a religion, but part of it is excluded and remains in the category of tradition.

The pre-literate and literate communication of religious tradition has been characterized above as a process, underlying which is the idea that the scholar of religion should not be content simply to study texts but should also try to determine the functional context of the written texts. Furthermore, holistic analysis of the communication of religious tradition is a part of source criticism, which is an extremely complex question. Since 'literary source criticism' is the subject of a separate

11. For details see my paper 'Oral Transmission of Knowledge', prepared for the IXth International Congress of Anthropological and Ethnological Sciences, Chicago, August 28–September 8, 1973, published in *The Anthropological Study of Education*, edited by C. J. Calhoun and F. A. J. Ianni, pp. 11-28, Mouton, 1976 (Series World Anthropology).

session of this conference, I shall here concentrate on problems concerning the taxonomy of oral tradition, measurement of religiosity and
the demands of source criticism as far as fieldwork on oral tradition is
concerned.

THE PRINCIPLES OF THE TAXONOMY OF ORAL TRADITION

The question of classification of material is one that enters into every
research situation. In order to carry out his analysis properly, the scholar
must approach his material systematically and decide upon a terminology which will enable him to make known his results and to present the
empirical material of the research on which his conclusions are based.
In actual fact the results will be better understood and the information
value of his concepts will be much greater if the scholar uses a generally
accepted terminology.

In classifying and analyzing tradition the scholar needs genre concepts.
which can form the basis of a taxonomy of oral tradition. However,
the use of genre concepts is not without its problems for the simple
reason that the same concept has been used by different scholars to
mean several different things. It is for this reason that the terminological
analysis of tradition genres advanced by Lauri Honko[12] should be followed. An attempt should be made to determine the criteria (content,
form, style, structure, function, frequency, distribution, origin, age,
context, etc.) on which concepts of genre can be based or on which
they should be based in the normative sense. In doing so, account
should be taken of the fact that some concepts can be determined on
the basis of a single criterion (e. g. migratory legend on the criterion of
distribution) while for others it will be necessary to have a number of
criteria (e. g. myth). The second task of such a terminological analysis
should be to indicate the relationship between different genres: are the
concepts synonymous, hyponymous, overlapping, oppositional or do
they operate on totally different levels? There is no need, in comparative
religion, for the whole battery of terms used in folkloristics: a considerably more limited selection of concepts will suffice for practical

12. Lauri Honko, 'Genre Analysis in Folkloristics and Comparative Religion',
Temenos 3 (1968), Helsinki, pp. 62-64.

purposes. However, religious genres require particular attention: these are the concepts which are of importance for evaluating religiosity.[13] In fact, the scholar may set up as his goal the formulation of the minimum terminology for both himself and his reader that he needs in any single situation where research is involved. If, in this connection, he decides to use a term in a way which deviates from that in which it is usually used, then it is his duty to explain to his audience the principles on which he has based his taxonomy.

In one of my articles ('Grenzprobleme zwischen Memorat und Sage')[14] I have dealt, in detail, with the kind of hotchpotch of terms and meanings that can arise if scholars do not recognize the difference of principle involved between real and nominal terminologies. It was C. W. von Sydow's ambitious aim to develop for folkloristics the kind of genre terminology which Linnaeus applied to botany. His underlying thought was that tradition genres existed in the mouths of the people like flowers in a field and that it was the folklorist's duty to pluck and name them in the order prescribed by Nature. Instead of popular names von Sydow gave the concepts scientific definitions (Memorat, Fabulat, Dit, etc.) and tried to prove that the distinctions between the concepts were of general and international validity.[15] What was involved was a real organization of tradition genres. Many anthropologists have pursued a similar approach but have been rather more modest insofar as they have used popular names without usually claiming that their terminology could be applied cross-culturally. An exception to this, however, is William Bascom. In his article 'The Forms of Folklore: Prose Narratives'[16] he tries to show that the trichotomy of myth—legend—folktale is valid in all cultures. He starts with an operational definition and ends, after having presented real genre systems in various cultures, by putting forward his conclusion that the system is cross-culturally applicable. The article is an interesting one even if Bascom's definitions and claims need further study.[17]

13. I have dealt with this problem more thoroughly in my article 'Quellenanalytische Probleme der religiösen Überlieferung', *Temenos* 6 (1970), Turku, pp. 110-118.
14. *Temenos* 3 (1968), Helsinki, pp. 136-164.
15. E. g. C. W. von Sydow, 'Kategorien der Prosa-Volksdichtung', and 'Popular Dite Tradition; A Terminological Outline', in *Selected Papers on Folklore* (see note 2), pp. 60-88 and 106-126.
16. *Journal of American Folklore* 78 (1965), Philadelphia, pp. 6-15.
17. Cf. the criticism by L. Honko in his article 'Der Mythos in der Religionswissenschaft', *Temenos* 6 (1970), Turku, pp. 52-55.

In a nominal system the terms are regarded rather as having been created by the scholar for reasons of expediency than as real, existing units. The use of some concept of genre is consequently based on an agreement reached between scholars. The purpose of such an agreement is to bring about a more effective interaction between the empirical material and the terminology with the aid of a system of ideal types.[18] If the term used for the ideal type does not reflect reality, it can be re-defined or replaced by a better ideal type. C. Scott Littleton's article 'A Two-Dimensional Scheme for the Classification of Narratives'[19] is an example of the kind of distinction based on the use of polar ideal types.

Acknowledging the existence of real and nominal genre systems would, in my opinion, also mitigate the inconsistency that exists between genre systems used in archives and operational genre systems that can be used in research. From time to time archivists, in their efforts to set up cataloguing systems, have called for the international recognition of their distinctions in terminology on the part of scholars as well.[20] They have justified this demand by pointing out that their terminology is based on an extremely wide body of materials. In doing so, however, they have lost sight of the fact that the aims of the archivist are quite different to those of the scholar who has to grapple with a special type of material. An archive system must be practicable and handy to use: it need not necessarily have a scientific foundation. The most important thing is that the system should facilitate the finding of material and the characterization of the total mass of material. Consequently, it has usually been necessary to resort to compromise solutions in systematizing the materials to be classified and their cultural background. These systems cannot, as they stand, be applied to individual research situations. By this I do not imply any criticism of the attempts that have been made to achieve conformity in the principles underlying international archiving systems.[21] However, it is my view that a solution to questions of ter-

18. Max Weber, *The Methodology of Social Sciences*, Glencoe, 1949, p. 89. L. Honko, 'Genre Analysis', pp. 61-64.

19. *Journal of American Folklore* 78 (1965), Philadelphia, pp. 24-26.

20. Cf. my article 'Grenzprobleme zwischen Memorat und Sage', pp. 156-158.

21. Cf. papers published in *Die Tagungen der Sagekommission der 'International Society for Folk-Narrative Research'*, Antwerp 1963, Budapest 1964, etc. Cf. Wayland D. Hand, 'Status of European and American Legend Study', *Current Anthropology* 6:4 (1965), Chicago.

minology is more likely to be reached by scholars, at the round table of a symposium, for example, than among the shelves of archives.

GENRE ANALYSIS IN THE STUDY OF RELIGION

For a scholar of religion genre analysis is of interest principally as a source critical method. The main question is similar to that which plagues the historian; namely, how well does tradition material reflect reality? The question put by the scholar of religion is what source value oral tradition has for measuring religiosity. Basically the problem is one of function analysis. The main question which arises is what meaning and source value different tradition materials have in the study of religious phenomena. The study of religion requires fewer terms than folklore because many tradition genres fall outside its sphere of interest. Among the valid criteria for recognizing tradition genres, one problem in particular — that of truth value, which must be included in the field of function — arises more often than others: 'Is the tradition believed in or not?' and 'In what way is it believed?' For the scholar of religion it is useful to have a system which accords different source values to different genres according to how they communicate elements belonging to the supranormal sphere.

Before using the term 'religious', we must be sure that the information being studied has some religious use, meaning or function. Use and meaning are, then, regarded as two aspects of context.[22] By 'use' is meant the situation in which the tradition is used, presented and actualized. 'Meaning' denotes the other aspect of context: the ideas, attitudes and evaluations which the bearer of the tradition gives to his material. From our experience of studying religion in the field we know that use can be observed; but in order to elicit the meaning of a tradition, we must interview the bearer of the tradition. It has been observed that even in small communities and cultures the meanings of the same phenomenon may vary considerably from person to person. It is therefore necessary for the scholar to interview several informants before drawing conclusions about the meanings of a tradition if unnecessary

---

22. E. g. Alan Dundes, 'Metafolklore and Oral Literary Criticism', *The Monist* 1966:4, La Salle, Illinois, p. 506.

and erroneous generalizations are to be avoided.[23] The analysis of religious tradition is always function analysis.[24] In order to study religion, religiosity, or religious behavior, the scholar needs a definition or clearly delimited view of what religion is. It has been emphasized that religion is an institution belonging to the universal aspects of culture. It is Spiro's view[25] that ideas about the meaning of religion coincide to a great extent. But conflicting ideas have been advanced in answer to the question: 'What phenomena go to make up religion?' and 'What are the invariables of religion?'[26] Of the many definitions of religion some have been real — aiming to be empirical and of general validity — while others have been only nominal — religion has been explained using terms of which the meaning is already known. It is my view that scholars of religion should no longer content themselves with conclusions that culminate in assumptions as to the religiosity or non-religiosity of a certain phenomenon, custom or tradition. Instead there is every reason to give belief, religion and religiosity dimensions which would differentiate the concept of the different invariables and functions of religion at the individual, social and cultural level. In this way it would be possible to make distinctions between cognitive, affective, conative, social and cultural levels of religion:

1. the cognitive dimension comprises the conscious, intellectual factors such as an individual's or society's awareness of their religion, their *Weltanschauung*, their view of the universe, of the supernatural figures that dominate their beliefs, etc. Religion is usually characterized by the fact that people are convinced of the existence of one or more supernatural powers who watch over their fate, their needs and their values;

---

23. Pentikäinen, 'Depth Research', pp. 140-144.
24. E. g. R. K. Merton, *Social Theory and Social Structure*, Glencoe, 1949, pp. 50-53, 61-81. L. Honko, 'Funktioanalyyttisesta tutkimustavasta' (On the Function Analytic Method), *Sananjalka* 3 (1961), Turku, pp. 152-165. J. Pentikäinen, *The Nordic Dead-Child Tradition* (Folklore Fellows Communications 202), Helsinki, 1968, pp. 113-118.
25. Melford E. Spiro, 'Religion: Problems of Definition and Explanation', in *Anthropological Approaches to the Study of Religion*, ed. by M. Banton, (A.S.A. Monographs 3), Crawley, Sussex, 1968, pp. 85-124.
26. Th. P. van Baaren, 'Systematische Religionswissenschaft', *Nederlands theologisch tijdschrift* 24:2, pp. 81-88. Cf. Åke Hultkrantz, 'Anthropological Approaches to the Study of Religion', *History of Religions* 9:4 (1970), pp. 337-352.

2. the affection level refers to the problems surrounding religious feelings, attitudes and experiences. Man feels that he is dependent on something supernatural and at the same time feels some kind of link with it. A religious experience is a state of interaction between the natural and the supernatural, a state in which a religious person or, rather, tradition acting through him, actualizes a meeting with one of the figures that dominate his beliefs;
3. the conative aspect of religion is religion seen as a form of behavior. Included here are rites, social conventions, such as sacrifices, prayers and spells with the aid of which the individual or society can achieve by traditional methods some kind of union with religious figures. Besides ritual, religions usually presuppose certain ethical behavior, the observation of certain norms, in order that the rewards promised by the religion may be obtained and the punishments avoided;
4. the social factor forms a fundamental part of every religion. Religion presupposes existence of a group whose duty it is to watch over views and to carry out certain tasks. The members of this group work together in order to achieve the goals imposed on them by the religion;
5. the cultural level of religion concerns the dependence of religion, both in time and place, on the ecological, social and cultural environment in which the religion is practiced.

It is important that we adopt a holistic approach when exploring a religious tradition. This means a study of the religion both vertically and horizontally in its cultural and social context. We must take stock, for example, of the natural and other ecological environment, the way in which these are reflected in social and economic life and, further, the different reciprocal effects they have on religious needs.

Recognition of religious genres is not the only problem confronting the scholar of religious tradition. He must also determine which dimensions of religion and religiosity different tradition genres refer to. The question 'Is the tradition believed in or not?' is not as important as the following problems: 'In what way is the tradition believed in? How does belief regulate individual and social behavior? How widespread within a certain society is a belief? Who preserve the tradition and who change it? What manifest or latent functions do different religious genres have in the life of individuals or the society?'

DEMANDS MADE BY SOURCE CRITICISM ON FIELDWORK IN THE STUDY OF
RELIGION

When studying oral tradition, source criticism must be extended beyond
text analysis to those situations in field studies where a religious narrative
is committed to writing or a religious event, for example the enactment
of a rite, is verbally described. Anna Birgitta Rooth terms the source
analysis of the collecting of tradition materials 'ethnographical source
criticism'. 'Philological and ethnological criticism of the sources are
both practiced at the writing desk. Such criticism only begins after the
text is written down, whereas ethnographical criticism must be practiced
before and during the collection of the material.'[27] This means that the
method of collection, interviewing technique, observation, the parts
played by the interviewer and observer and the choice of roles and informants as well as other details of fieldwork must be clearly reported or
described. It is important that the scholar should subject the reliability
and validity of his material to source criticism. He should subject himself to questioning, too, if he has collected the material himself. As far as
source criticism of fieldwork is concerned, it has proved useful to have
matrices which the fieldworker can use when recording details worthy of
note in an interview or observation situation.[28] The actual circumstance
in which a tradition is recorded is, from the point of view of source
criticism, a key situation, since any mistakes or oversights made at this
stage are apt to be multiplied in any further study of the material.

I hope that there will be a lively discussion of the source criticism
and taxonomy of religion seen from the viewpoint of comparative
religion. I conclude by presenting a few details from my own research,
which is religio-anthropological in its methods. Since the object of
study is non-literate, the main problems here concern the taxonomy
and source criticism of an oral tradition.

My study *Individual, Tradition Repertoire and World-View*, on Marina
Takalo (1890-1970), a Karelian bearer of tradition, is a religio-anthropological study which deviates from most earlier studies of individual
tradition bearers in that it concerns the whole tradition repertoire of
one individual. Mrs. Takalo was illiterate, which means that oral com-

---

27. Anna Birgitta Rooth, *The Complexity of Source Criticism*, pp. 1-7.
28. Pertti J. Pelto, *Anthropological Research*, New York, 1970, pp. 67 ff.

munication was the sole process by which information was formed and transmitted. The first phase of the study was free interview (1960-1965): at this stage the interviewer's only active role was to propose new subjects of conversation. During this type of interview, Mrs. Takalo communicated a collection of tradition, which later was revealed to be the tradition repertoire of Mrs. Takalo (by repertoire we understand the actively selected tradition material which is at the complete command of the tradition bearer). She knew the content, style, texture and structure of this material so well that she enjoyed reciting it. She communicated this material quite spontaneously and immediately as a new subject turned up. Thirty per cent of the tradition material known to Mrs. Takalo was included in the repertoire. We may speak about the threshold of repertoire which was crossed by a tradition at the reproduction phase, when it changed from latent into active. After free interviews we began directive ones, where attention was paid to source-critical and contextual questions. A special questionnaire was used for this type of interview. The following information was solicited: (1) the source of information ('From whom did you hear the tale?'), (2) the age of the information ('How old were you then?'), (3) the use ('What was going on when you were told this story?'), (4) the context of the learning situation ('How was the story told? Who were present? What did the listeners do? Who interpreted the story?'), (5) the function ('Why did he tell this to you? What did the hearers think about the story?'), (6) the meaning ('What do you think about the story? Do you believe in it? Do you like it? Did other people believe it?'), (7) the classification of genres by the tradition bearer ('What did you call this story?'), (8) the observations of the bearer of tradition concerning the frequency, distribution, etc., of an item ('Have other people told you this? When? In what way was the story different?'), and (9) the process of transmission ('When did you yourself first tell this? In what situation? When did you last tell this?'). Mrs. Takalo's memory was very accurate: she was able to remember the source and the learning situation in 92 per cent of the cases. The reliability of source-critical and contextual information was checked by repeated interviews.

In considering the religion of Marina Takalo, it has been interesting to observe the information she supplied on the following topics: (1) the individual religious view of life and the world and its formation, (2) the personal religious frame of reference, its actualization in a supranormal experience, and the interpretation of the experience, (3) ritual behavior (in rites of passage, rites of crisis, and calendrical rites), (4) the religious groups Mrs. Takalo was a member of, (5) religious education (in these groups), (6) the religious roles played by Marina Takalo, (7) the relation of Mrs. Takalo's individual world view to the collective tradition, in her native parish of Oulanka (in the part of Karelia bordering on the White Sea), (8) the dependence of religious views on the ecological environment and changes in it, (9) the changes in religious ideas during a lifetime, (10) the influence of religion on personality.

When we analyze oral tradition, the first questions should concern source criticism and function analysis. Before one can even call a tradition religious, it is necessary to determine the function of the material studied. We have to find out the different genres of religious tradition and to explain what is measured by each of them. As far as religious prose tradition is concerned, Mrs. Takalo has told saint's legends, myths, legends of origin, memorates, legends and folk beliefs.

A folk belief is not a narrative genre: it expresses a supranormal assertion in a generalizing statement, for example 'there is a spirit in the forest'. A memorate is an experiential narrative — a description of a supranormal experience undergone by the narrator or somebody close to him, and it is the most reliable source for the scholar of religion. It represents an empirical tradition; the surest way of recognizing a memorate is by its authenticity from the standpoint of perception psychology. By taking into account the perception-psychological and social-psychological factors we may decide how authentically the memorate being studied describes the supranormal experience. Compared to a memorate, a legend is a secondary source for the scholar. The most important distinguishing features of a legend are to be found in the content. It is typical of a legend that the contents are stereotyped and follow a certain plot-formula. We may show, by means of comparison, that this formula is repeated in variants of the same legend and often in variants of a legend belonging to the same group. A considerable number of legends are intricately constructed around a certain formula-like dialogue pattern. Lucidity of plot and a certain impersonality is typical of the legend. Details, which are typical of the memorate, unnecessary for the plot, but necessary for the description of the experience, are not found in legends, which survive on the basis of narrative interest.

A folk belief is a statement, a memorate, a detailed report of a supra-

normal experience, while a legend is a lucid, stereotyped narrative totality, with a clear plot. A folk belief is always a generalization – a religious
saying – and therefore its reliability must be proved by careful frequency analysis. The same is also true of legend analysis, which also
includes comparison and the study of form, style, structure and content
in order to separate the stereotyped material from the unique experiential information. Memorates are the most reliable source for the
student of religious tradition, because they reveal the situations in which
the religious tradition was actualized and began to influence behavior.
From memorates we may also learn about the social contexts of beliefs,
about religious experiences, their experiences and interpreters, and
about the society which preserves the tradition.

Myths deal with cosmogonic events and the community regards them
as holy and true. Usually myths are told orally but they can also be
acted out in their own ritual contexts. Myths crop out at all levels of
religiosity. They provide answers to man's cognitive questions about
the why and wherefore of things. They foster attitudes and religious
feelings, offer models for cognitive behavior, create and establish religious groups and explain such things as the genesis of different cultural
elements. Myths are found not only in oral and written tradition but
also in prehistoric material and in religious art.

Marina Takalo categorizes narrative genres using her own 'natural'
terminology and seems to be quite aware of when she is relating a folktale ('tale', 'story that has no truth in it', 'amusing account'), when she
is telling a legend ('story of holy men'), a tale ('story', 'hearsay', 'event')
or memorate ('experienced event', 'nearby event'). She also has a feeling for the meaning, function and use of different stories, and in the
course of telling them, she selects the code appropriate to the genre
from among the possible alternatives. In each case this means a choice
between different norms governing content, form, style, texture and
structure.

The memorates told by Marina Takalo are interesting from this point
of view because it can be shown in every case how many links there
are in the chain from the experiencer down to Marina Takalo. There
are 58 memorates founded on her personal experiences, that is to say
45 per cent of the whole memorate material. There are 59 second-hand
memorates in which Takalo is the third narrator, that is to say 46 per
cent. And there are 8 third-hand memorates, that is only 7 per cent.

The number of 4th-hand memorates is only 3, i. e. 2 per cent. We may conclude that memorate tradition must be continually renewed. In actual folk belief there are always new experiences which for their part strengthen the belief tradition. In the Takalo tradition, as well as in other depth research material, I have observed that in memorates there are regularly two links at the most in the chain between the person who experiences the supernatural being and the narrator (that is to say, where the experiencer is the 1st narrator and Takalo is the 4th). In the identification of a memorate, the explanation of the context of the narrative situation thus provides a reliable criterion. It is also interesting to observe that in memorates, details describing the experience, but unnecessary from the point of view of plot, are the more sparse the more links there are in the chain and the further one gets from the moment of experience. We may therefore say that identification of memorates requires analysis of both the narration and the experience situation.

It is worth noting that different genres seem to transmit information about the various aspects of a religion in different ways. Thus, myths, folk beliefs and legends deal chiefly with the cognitive aspects of religion, and memorates with their affective elements. At the same time the conative level manifests itself above all in rites and in ritualistic descriptions of such behavior as sacrifice, prayer or charms. In Russian Karelia, where Takalo lived the first part of her life, there was a caste-like system of sects of Old Believers within the Orthodox Church; Takalo's knowledge about these sects, their norms and rituals, memberships, etc., is unique and detailed.[29]

29. For more detailed information see J. Pentikäinen, 'Depth Research', pp. 138-140. The writer's study in Finnish of Marina Takalo's religion, *Marina Takalon uskonto* (Forssa, 1971) is a religio-anthropological study of a single individual's religious repertoire.

ANNA-BIRGITTA ROOTH   *On the Difficulty of Transcribing Synchronic Perception into Diachronic Verbalization*

In this paper I would like to draw attention to (1) the necessity of transferring socio-cultural behavior (as well as psychological and physiological processes) from the dimension of human/organic life into the oral/verbal dimension (i. e. texts and symbols) for taxonomic studies; (2) the consequences that this transfer from one dimension into another has for the material described; (3) what oral/verbal tradition is, what the important factors are as to the validity of the testimony, and how the fieldworker can contribute to a correct presentation of the oral/verbal records.

MATERIAL AND IMMATERIAL CULTURE IN TAXONOMIC STUDY

When one is dealing with material culture, its elements, like houses, furniture, agricultural or handicraft tools etc., can easily be studied as regards their forms. The important thing is that the forms of the material elements of culture do not change as long as the material exists. The form is not changed during the lifetime of the implement or the article. The material articles or artefacts, can, if we are lucky, be preserved for many thousands years and become excellent objects of study for archeologists and ethnologists.

The elements of immaterial culture, like folk-tales, legends, beliefs, behavior — the whole verbal and oral traditions — do not allow direct research until they have been transferred into a new medium, namely into writing (or into photography or film in the case of movements: the technique of working, dance-steps, or the way to hold a violin, etc.). A. Olrik and M. Moe have pointed out some characteristics of the folk-tale, and thus also the externally observable forms of the folktale, the instruments of taxonomy.[30]

However, even the fact that scholars have been able to identify recurrent characteristics and elements of form, which in their turn are the

30. For the discussion of processes and products see A.-B. Rooth, *Folklig Diktning, Form och teknik*, Uppsala 1965, pp. 139ff.

basis for a division into genres, shows that the immaterial culture also has forms which can be studied. Those who have worked with concrete objects — whose form can be visually described and which remain unchanged as long as they are untouched by the ravages of time — can easily be tempted to believe that the immaterial and the visually undescribable material is as fugitive as an impulse, a caprice or an idea, so that an attempt to find a taxonomy is futile.

It is to the credit of earlier scholars that we can talk about genres or categories today in terms of the observed and described characteristics which make the elements of form or style, which are the criteria of genres. It is also quite clear that a folktale, a legend, or a proverb can be misinterpreted or distorted — or even improved. Scholars have been able to identify the reasons for change. There are also border areas between genres, which has sometimes been used as an argument for the futility of talking about genres at all.

The taxonomy and the criterion of form are a scientific way of classifying material, but are maybe also among man's oldest ways of expression. To arrange the pearls in a necklace according to their size, or to arrange pearls or teeth or bones according to a certain harmonic repetition, are among man's first documented attempts at systematic order — though here for aesthetic reasons.

In the development of a scientific idea, classification takes place in a similar way and according to similar principles, i. e. on the basis of external, recurrent, more or less identical forms. It seems to be in the nature of science that there is basic research, which must be founded on the special characteristics or forms of the objects of study, and which can then form the basis for further systematization. Classification according to forms and similarities operates, in fact, mathematically, just like the study of quantities. Relation and comparison are necessary in order to bring out similarities and dissimilarities in quantity, size, form, function and so on. The use of this mathematical principle in research is just as necessary for the study of elements — not only of material products (articles, implements, etc.) but also for the study of immaterial products (folktales, legends, riddles, etc.).

The observable elements of form were used by Linnaeus as a basis for the classification of flowers. Darwin used the same principle for the classification of species. The humanists have in turn borrowed the term taxonomy from the natural sciences.

Classification according to form — the form criterion, as ethnologists call it — is a necessary basis. Only when the basic facts are known can one proceed to analysis, systematization, and eventually arrive at a synthesis.

THE DIMENSION OF SOCIO-CULTURAL LIFE. TRANSFER FROM THE MEDIUM OF SPEECH INTO WRITING.

Morphological study, or the study of forms, is natural in the study of materia, of a 'body' (an object or artefact) which has observable external forms. In a transferred sense we can also talk about 'forms' and 'characteristics' when studying 'immaterial material' (a contradiction in terms). This has no 'body' or materia, that is to say somatic basis — but through the description of observed immaterial phenomena we can study it morphologically, which provides the basis for the taxonomic classification of the 'material'.

We are using a symbolic language, which continually creates semantic problems because the 'material' has no body or materia. This immaterial material (a tale, legend, dite, fict, memorate, thoughts, ideas, etc.) is verbally realized in speech but it is in fact only as a text that it becomes concrete, scientifically analyzable material.

I am well aware of the fact that it is possible to describe speech as sound-waves, which can be transferred onto phonograms and oscillograms and analyzed.[31] Through the curves of the oscillograms we discover the morphological forms, which also here can be of help in taxonomic study (cf. below).

Even Gunkel saw the two different dimensions — writing and life. He uses the term 'der Sitz im Leben' and in this way tries to see the Old Testament text as if lifted out of — or set into — its context in real life.

It is not my intention to try to establish if Gunkel was the first, the greatest or the only thinker with this idea. He pointed it out in a brilliant way. In the exegetics of the Old Testament the pastoral life and agricultural customs of the Jews, their beliefs and cult-life, have perpetually been regarded as a mirror when interpreting the Old Testament.

31. A.-B. Rooth, 'Storytelling among the Athabascan Indians of Northern Alaska' (stencil), Lund, 1970, Appendix 1. Oscillogram.

It is as a rule very difficult to transpose a part of real life into a text. It is easier for the writer, with a clear aim, and a circle of readers to turn to. — The intention of the author is ultimately to determine for himself and communicate to his readers his own observations.[32] This could apply to Turgenyev's sensitive descriptions of scenery, or the horrifying descriptions of the inner life by Dostoyevskiy, or Moa Martinsson's precise descriptions of the life of industrial workers or farm laborers. What all these authors have in common is that they use observations from real life and transfer them into prose, and they all have a compulsion to do this with aesthetic finesse.

A new, and still unusual form of expression is to be found in P. O. Sundman's literary work: the attempt to transfer everyday life into everyday prose. For those who listen carefully to everyday language it brings the joy of recognition. This is the way in which common people talk, who have not been trained to polish their language. The code or message is more important than the verbal form.

O. Lewis works in the same way — to get as close as possible to everyday events and let the individual tell them in his own language with his own evaluations. This is the method of the literary, 'anthropological' novel, which is very close to the memorate. It uses an autobiographical way of describing things. Both the autobiography and the memorate are important forms of documentation for ethnologists.

We have little comparative material, and that is why I have turned to authors' ways and methods of describing observations from real life. The fieldworker is in a situation similar to that of the author when transferring observations into written statements. It is difficult for the fieldworker to transmit mental processes such as thoughts, ideas and beliefs held by the informant and verbalized by the informant into a statement that the recorder has to tape and to write down.

In interviewing and in participant observation the fieldworker has to transfer elements of belief that are perhaps usually not verbalized — or at least seldom in the form acquired in this process of transferring the material from one dimension to another. Or the fieldworker has to describe a rite or custom that has been experienced by the informant but never verbalized until the informant or recorder put it into words.

---

32. Cf. G. W. Allport, 'The Use of Personal Documents in Psychological Science', *Social Science Research Council Bulletin* 49, New York, 1942, pp. 67 ff.

Thus the written record may give us a belief, that may never have been more than an idea or the result of a mental process in the informant's mind, and never before verbalized until the moment of recording when it was put into words and written down. In this process — transfer via oral/verbal media to the written document — a verbal form is given to the element (the rite, the idea, etc.) which is of importance later for the study of taxonomy.

In *Folklig diktning* I had reason to comment upon this artificial form given to customs and beliefs and originally quite alien to them.[33] There is a belief that it is unlucky to kill a spider. But how is this belief presented in real life and how is it presented in the verbalized form of the written documents filed in our archives? And how is that belief passed on in the process of transmission?

In the folklore archives we may have a written document stating 'It is unlucky to kill a spider', or 'To kill a spider brings bad luck'. But the belief is not transmitted in these forms in real life. Most likely in a certain situation a mother stops her child from killing a spider, saying at the same time something like: 'Don't do that! Don't you know it's unlucky to kill a spider!' Or two girls are together in a room and one points to a spider and says: 'There's a spider! That means good luck!' In the verbal formalization the written document will probably say 'To see a spider means good luck'.

These 'beliefs' as well as the rules and taboos connected with them are very interesting, although we usually get them in a very distorted form, even if their contents are correct. Åke Hultkrantz has also pointed out that these types of information tend to be gathered at the end of anthropological/ethnological books or papers presenting material collected in the field.[34]

It is true that we often find a list of taboos or beliefs presented as odds and ends after the presentation of the corpus of the text. This awkward presentation is mostly due to the fact that it is extremely difficult to describe this type of material. Whereas real life is 'holistic', diachronic, multidimensional and possible to grasp with more than one of our senses, this is impossible as soon as it is verbalized. Then it

33. A.-B. Rooth, *Folklig Diktning, Form och teknik*, Uppsala, 1965, pp. 94ff.
34. A.-B. Rooth, *Folkdikt och folktro*. Handböcker i etnologi utgivna av N.-A. Bringéus och Mats Rehnberg, Stockholm, 1971, p. 17.

can only be either heard or read. When situations in life, behavior, mental processes, etc. are transferred from one dimension to another — where only one sense or one physiological instrument, the ear, can be used — the verbalization brings about of necessity a splitting up in parts which can only be presented in chronological order. Just like Alice in Wonderland we have 'to start from the beginning' and go on to the end.

When customs and social events are described in interviews, they pass over into verbal communication and are recorded as such as a kind of oral tradition now fixed in a written document in our folklore archives. These types of oral/verbal tradition ought really to be identified as a kind of socio-cultural text describing rites, ceremonies, customs, etc. The customs and events were never intended for verbal or oral transmission. There were to be lived, and experienced as part of man's behavior and socio-cultural life. But in answer to the ethnologist's questions, verbal statements were given, and when passing through the oral/verbal media these statements were (like other oral traditions) subjected to changes and subjective alterations. Although all the texts in our archives have passed through oral/verbal media, it is necessary to remember the basical differences these texts had in their 'Sitz im Leben' according to their meaning, purpose and function. Even if we have a whole stock of written verbal/oral documents in our archives, it is only part of them that were originally intended to be oral/verbal testimonies. The study of these categories of oral tradition has for a long time been of interest to scholars.[35] When studying the material elements or the products of culture it is precisely the character of the material — the materia — which is important. As pointed out above, it is visually perceptible and describable. Research-workers can work on the nature of

35. Jan Vansina in his *Oral Tradition* lays out a scheme of different types of oral traditions. He states that no typology of oral tradition has ever been made. Now this is an understatement. To mention only Scandinavia, scholars such as A. Olrik, Moltke Moe, Kaarle Krohn, Antti Aarne, C. W. von Sydow devoted part of their scholarly work directly or indirectly to describing the morphology of different kinds of oral tradition, thus laying out the foundation for the different genres or categories such as tale, legend, fict, memorate, etc. It is of interest to compare Vansina's terms with those that von Sydow outlined 25 years before Vansina and to see how fairly close Vansina's terms come to von Sydow's, although independently of him. It is also of interest to note that Pentikäinen in his paper on depth study has been able to demonstrate the accuracy of some of von Sydow's categories.

the material (wood, fibre, metal, etc.), its surface, which is measurable, etc. With help of the object, of pictures or photographs, one can give the reader or the listener a possibility to perceive quickly all its forms and characteristics.

With immaterial products it is quite a different situation — with the tale, the folksong, the riddle, etc. Their medium is the word — the verbal form of expression, which thus becomes part of the communication.

In so-called high cultures, i. e. cultures with writing, this originally verbal and oral material can be transferred from speech into a new medium, the written form, the physiological receiver of which is the eye, not the ear. But this oral material was originally intended for the ear.

These are obvious points, but scholars have often neglected what happens when oral and verbal material like everyday speech, rhetoric, tales, legends, etc. are transferred for reception by another physiological instrument. Here, once again, we have the dilemma of the fieldworker — when his task is to transfer from one medium, the spoken word, into another, the written word.

Within ethnology it has therefore, as a rule, been easier to work with the material products of culture, which are immediately visible and perceptibly observable. Through seeing we get an immediate holistic impression, which is important for fast perception. With speaking and hearing as the media we have to wait for the chronological listing of the words which are intended to form the meaning and the code. (In this connection, one imperative is a convenient form of code, so that perception is immediate for the receiver.) A long message does not give a holistic impression until all the more important words have been registered. I shall not here touch upon fields which belong to linguistics. I only want to point out the differences between media and thus on their importance for morphological study and hence for source criticism.

Some ethnologists have in recent years to a certain extent begun to realize that the process of transfer concerns not only the spreading of an article where it gives impulses — but the spreading of an idea. This insight is, of course, something that ethnologists or researchers into religion, who have worked with immaterial culture all the time, have been forced to use as a starting point in their work. Their material does not become concrete and scientifically analyzable until it can be transferred from the dimension of socio-cultural life into, if you like, the dimension of materia. Through writing it is materialized in symbols on paper from the dimension of the process of thinking via the medium of sound (speech), to the medium of writing on paper.

This transfer from one dimension to another, via one medium into another, has another parallel in modern scientific research. Many different physiological processes defy proper analysis until they are transferred by means of various recording apparatus (for instance gaschromatographs and electrocardiographs) into written messages in the form of gaschromatograms or cardiograms etc.

These technical possibilities do not exist for ethnologists. Man (the research-worker, the fieldworker), not the machine, has to transfer his observations and reactions into writing to be able to analyze and classify them. Thus there are also new opportunities of changes, additions or eliminations, which means that the fieldworker may influence the material.

IMPORTANT FACTORS FOR SOURCE CRITICISM

How can we practice source criticism? What are the pertinent questions as to the validity and stability of oral traditional elements (such as tales, legends, epical songs, dites, ficts, riddles, communicative elements such as greetings, nicknames, symbols and similes, sayings and proverbs, formulas etc.)? Even this list of the many different kinds of oral elements is evidence of the complexity and differences inherent in each kind of oral element.

The difference from material elements, with their stability of form – because of their solid materia – has been pointed out above. But the eerie stuff of oral elements has also been shown to have 'forms' and to be a possible object for morphological studies, i.e. a basis for taxonomy.

Now, what is important to the fieldworker collecting oral traditions – what is to be noted in order to present important clues as to the validity of the reported element? (If these clues are not given, other scholars at their desks are left in the dark as to the validity of the oral testimony and cannot evaluate the texts.) I have already in another paper drawn attention to some factors as well as to the complexity of source criticism based on my experience in working on mythology

among the Athabascan Indians of Northern Alaska.[36] Here I would like
to draw attention to some observations of other important factors.

1. *The validity of time and space mentioned e. g. in memorates of self-
experienced customs/behavior or supranormal experience.* The space
factor (i. e. topography, locale or place) tends to be more accurate than
the time factor in the memories of the individuals used as informants.
Where a custom or rite was performed (e. g. the act of churching at the
threshold in the church) is easier to remember than at what time it was
performed, i. e. how much time had elapsed between the birth and the
reunion with the congregation.[37] Still more difficult is to ascertain —
perhaps decades later — why a certain custom like this was performed.
The reason offered may be the result of subsequent, retrospective interpretation.

2. *The importance of the custom or memorate per se.* The validity of a
testimony may be due to the importance attached to the custom or
memorate
a. by the group — for the effect that it is supposed to have (e. g. myths
   and rites in connection with world renewal)
b. by an individual for emotional/psychological reason (e. g. a girl for
   wearing her first long dress, or a special love affair or a song composed
   in praise of a dead husband)
c. by the social status or special importance of the performers of the
   ceremony, rite or recital (be it a king, a high priest or witch-doctor
   who is performing)
d. by the social status of the individual who is the object of the rite,
   ceremony, recital or list (e. g. the funeral or wedding of an important
   member of the society endowed with land and titles).

3. *Intensity.* The intensity with which an individual takes part in a custom or with which he listens to a story is of further importance. How
intensely he has enjoyed the telling of a tale or the singing of a song

36. A.-B. Rooth, 'The Complexity of Source Criticism', *Verhandlungen des
XXXVIII. Internationalen Amerikanistenkongresses.* Stuttgart-München 12. bis 18,
August 1968, Band III, München 1971, pp. 395 ff.
37. A. Gustafsson, *Kyrktagningsseden i Sverige.* (Skrifter fran Folklivsarkivet i
Lund nr. 13), Lund, 1972, p. 169.

depends on his personal interest at the time — whether he listened to the stories willingly or unwillingly. (Some informants may state that as children they were more interested in playing outside than in sitting in the house listening to the stories.) Another important point here is the role which the individual is performing. Is he passive or active? If he is active is it in an important or in a minor part in the performance? (e. g. an Indian's role in the ceremony of the 'pow-wow' changes according to his gradual acquisition of ceremonial knowledge and mastership.)

4. *Frequency.* Another factor of importance for the validity of a testimony is the frequency with which a custom is repeated or how often and how long a person has been exposed to a custom (partaking in it passively or actively) or a tale etc., having the opportunity to listen to it repeatedly, and thus facilitating the learning process. Repetition is learning, as the proverb has it. Thus the frequency with which a custom or oral element is repeated is of special importance among the factors of validity. This is an excuse for dwelling a little longer on the frequency of repetition.

I once drew the attention to the frequency factor, pointing out that despite a very long interval, special knowledge (how to make a hat of rushes) could be actualized in a given situation.[38] Thus a technique could be remembered for decades (in this case over 40 years) although not practiced until the right material (rushes), the right situation (resting at the side of a trout stream), the right set of persons (an older man wishing to make a young boy happy by making a hat of rushes for him) presented itself and actualized a special technical knowledge, that of making a hat of rushes, thus suddenly reviving a very old, special, if not prehistoric technique: that of plaiting rushes.

The frequency with which a custom or an oral element occurs is also of importance for practical fieldwork. Customs, behavior or oral traditions belonging to or related to daily life, everyday material, is more prone to be observed by and described by the fieldworker, whereas customs and oral traditions more seldom repeated may easily be overlooked. Hence the method of participant observation must necessarily be complemented by interviews in order to record the more unusual

---

38. A.-B. Rooth, 'The Offering of the First Shed Tooth and the Tooth-Formula. A Study in a "Physiological" Custom' (stencil), Lund, 1970, pp. 4 ff.

or more seldom repeated customs and oral traditions. As behavior and verbal/oral expressions often go together (e. g. rite and magic formula) it is important to have both vouched for, as they complete and elucidate each other.

When speaking of oral tradition we are perhaps first of all thinking of traditional forms such as tales, legends, myths, epical songs, dites, ficts, riddles, proverbs and formulas. But we also have other categories, such as memorates describing personal experiences, at first or second hand. There are also popular pedagogical traditions that, consciously or not, transmit the knowledge of technical methods (often a motoric technique), the right time for sowing and harvesting, the use of the plants, magic or rational cures, etc. The training of the muscles and the motoric nerves are often completed with oral instructions.

Beside these traditions of knowledge we have the many beliefs and views concerning space and time, creation and eschatology, concepts of the world and nature, omens and divination, magic and religious concepts. In recording all these types of material it is vital to the scholars that the fieldworker should try to get not only the contents but also the informant's personal attitude to the material, the intensity with which he may believe in some of the traditions or his indifference to other material. Does he believe·or not? How deeply or intensely does he believe? These are important questions.

It is not necessarily true, however, that the statement, the actual text, will reveal anything about these problems. It may perhaps be evident only from the way that the informant speaks and looks. Thus his voice, his mimicry, and his gestures may elucidate what he believes in and how intensely.

The material presented from the Athabascan Indians is of importance for the understanding of the 'myths' as narratives and for the value they have in everyday life and for the proper understanding of 'rites' as actions. Both these categories were part of the informants' earlier everyday life and part of their practical knowledge, or at least considered by them as practical knowledge. For the modern discussions of terminology and categories such as myths, memorates, rites, etc., we need this type of material from a civilization where the myths and stories have until recently been part of what is considered the real world. Much more so since modern terminology is mostly based on material that was collected in Europe, where the function had perhaps been reduced to one of mere entertainment, and collected in a period when the field-worker picked and chose material as to whether it seemed interesting or uninteresting to him, and when he accepted the convention that the material should be properly rewritten for editing or archiving. Material from civilizations like those of the Indians and Eskimos of northern Alaska is necessary for the whole discussion of 'myths' and 'legends' and the classification of these categories of oral tradition.

Today it is very difficult to get material representative of the myths and 'religion' of semi-nomadic hunting and fishing civilizations. And yet this type of material is necessary if we want our terms to be applicable also to non-European material.

When we want to define and use a term such as myth we must also consider cultures outside our own Western culture area. Then this type of material is necessary as a basis for terminological definitions. To be able to make these definitions we must know the forms in which the different informations have been given, as well as the attitude of the informant to the myths or stories related.

As the belief in the myth or the legend has been considered important for the definitions by many scholars, it must be pointed out that the stories that the Indians believed in could not be characterized as 'legend', which is a term based on the Eurasiatic genre.

The stories, which I would like to call 'myths' because of their relations to the beliefs and philosophy of the Indians, have the same time-perspective as that in the chimerates of the Eurasiatic tradition. It happened once, long ago, 'in the old time', 'when men were animals or animals were men'. (This corresponds to the phrase in European tradition 'in that time when the animals could talk'. It is mostly just a phrase in our European animal tales and fables, but in the Indians stories it refers to something that is considered to be the truth.) Although the myth has the time-perspective of the chimerate it does not use the phantasy world of the chimerate. Instead it uses a local setting, as does the legend, and is partly realistic like the legend. The myths take place in the same localities that the Indians live in. It is in the neighborhood of the villages, where their people live, fish and hunt.[39] Where the

39. Because these myths had the time-perspective of the chimerates and space-perspective of the legends I had one of my students to work on these factors in a

legends and fabulates speak of things that have happened to near relatives or neighbors, e. g. meeting with supernatural beings, the characters
in the myths are now animal, now man, and we hear practically nothing
of the supernatural beings which the Eurasiatic tradition abounds in.
It is usually a man, an Indian (who in the old time also was an animal)
who once experienced something for the first time. In that respect the
myths are close to the explanatory legends or aetia of the Eurasiatic
tradition, and also close to the animal tales of Eurasia. But where the
animal tales, at least in Europe, very often are mostly considered to be
humorous or entertaining, these animal tales, or myths as I would like
to call them, are very often stated as being part of the Indians' beliefs
or philosophy.

We know little and we need to know more about the stories and the
beliefs in the stories. I have tried in another paper to draw attention to
the functions of the stories in order to show the deeper meaning of
many of them.[40] That does not mean that we do not have also joculates,
which were perhaps told only for the sake of the joke and not in order
to be believed or to prove anything.

It is necessary to mention where in the story the storyteller and his
audience find cause for laughter. Many of the points may not be as easily appreciated by a western listener as by the Indians, whose interest
has been centered around wild animals. In an economic system based
on hunting and fishing the knowledge about wild animals adds to the
interest and appreciations of a good imitation of different animals or of
jokes about animals. Thus the Indians will be able, probably more than
is possible for a member of a western urban civilization, to enjoy the
good performance or the impersonations of for example the gestures
and movements of an animal or its plaintive voice of animal, the culture
hero or trickster in a dilemma.

An analysis of the traditions about Crow, or Raven (or Choolian as
the Eskimos call him) will show that he is a popular buffoon in many
stories. He is strangled in the cache when he tries to steal from the
cached meat; he loses his beak when he is stealing the bait off the hook

---

paper for the Alaska Seminar, Kerstin Erikson, 'Stildrag i athapaskiska myter. A
cross-cultural study', Lund, 1971.

40. A.-B. Rooth, 'Storytelling among the Athabascan Indians of Northern Alaska'
(stencil), Lund, 1970, pp. 1 ff., 12 ff., 16 ff.

of the fisherman. Or he eats the oil from the gut in a slough when the animals are busy trying to fill it. He pretends to be sick so he can sneak back, steal and eat the food that is left in the village when he has lured the others to move to another camp. We can see from the stories and motifs that Raven or Crow as a buffoon is especially popular. But it is also noticeable that Raven or Crow in some of the stories acts as a kind of creator or instigator. Charlotte Titus tells the story where Raven or Crow has deceived the people to run away (so that he can have the whale to himself), by telling them that pestilence will follow if they eat a whale that died in that special way. Then he realizes that he is alone with the whale meat and therefore he creates all the moieties that are the social basis for the 'potlatch-economy' system.

In the story of 'Crow marries a goose', Crow is not able to follow the summer birds although they try to carry him when he is too tired. Finally he is dropped in the ocean whereupon his magic power is shown in that he wishes a pole to come up on which he can rest. And from this resting place he starts to collect drift wood with his hook or send helpers to collect sand from the bottom of the sea and in this way he creates Alaska.

In another story he is fighting with the bear. Both are acting as a kind of fighting culture hero, from whose gigantic paddle strokes islands emerge. There is in these myths the power and ability of a godlike being although in a zoomorphic form.

Still more important is the information accompanying the narration of the myths and additionally supplied by the informants. What the Crow wishes will come true. If you say anything to the crow beware that you do not say anything stupid or wish anything stupid because the Crow can grant you your wishes. The child who had been teasing the crow, 'Come and eat my eyes! Come and eat my eyes!' is found dead in the evening by the unhappy parents. This story made Bessie Charlie turn to her grand-daughter and say: 'Maxine, do not say anything stupid to the crow! Say something nice! — No, you had better not say anything at all.' Bessie meant that Maxine might say something stupid and if she did, that could come true. Better safe than sorry. In this educational warning to the grand-daughter, Bessie's belief in the power of the crow is shown and hence the necessity to be careful. Here we have explicitly expressed Bessie Charlie's absolute belief in the crow and its supernatural power. But these examples of actual belief are much more difficult to record than the stories which have a traditional verbal form made for telling and retelling. For the beliefs there are no such forms ready to hand for verbal transmission. The informant has to formulate the verbal expression in such a connection or in such a situation as Bessie Charlie did.

Often Crow's or Raven's importance as a culture hero or trickster has only been described implicitly through the stories and myths. It is very rare to have the informations about rites and customs giving the explicit belief in the importance and omnipotence of the crows or ravens as real birds or animals. The sacrifice is made to the birds, the crows or ravens. Still it seems that there is a personification and deification of the birds, Crow and Raven, into an anthropomorphic being. In the stories Crow or Raven is consistantly changing; now he is an animal, now an anthropomorphic being.

A fieldworker taking part in a hunt might see the hunters, when flaying the killed animal, throw or place a piece of meat on a sandbar or bank. It cannot be recognized what reason this is done for only by participant observation. The recorder must also ask the hunter why it is done. In this case the custom was revealed because Moses Charlie was telling in his myth about the crow who got caught in a trap and how the man excused himself saying: 'I did not set this trap for you!' He releases the crow and ever since, he has caught lots of animals in his traps. Here again is evidence for the importance of the crow in giving good luck in hunting. It was also stated by Moses Charlie in connection with the myth that you must offer a piece of meat to the crow in order to get good luck in hunting.[41]

In this case I may point out that it was through the grandchild of Moses and Bessie Charlie that I first learnt that she (Bessie) used to ask the crow for fish and to give or offer the crow a piece of meat or a piece of cloth for its nest. Through all these different pieces of material about the crow — humorous stories as well as myths — where Crow is acting like a culture hero or in the customs connected with hunting or in asking the crow for what you wish, one gets a picture of Crow not only as a buffoon and trickster but also as a culture hero and an animal with godlike powers.

41. A.-B. Rooth, *The Alaska Expedition* (Acta Universitatis Lundensis 1972), Lund, 1972, see alphabetical index to Crow, Raven and Choolian.

How the crow has come to get his supposed power is beyond the scope of this paper. Here I wanted to draw attention to the complexity of Crow's nature (the trickster and the animal) in connection with rites, beliefs and myths. It is then extremely important that the recorder presents the informant's statement in the right context.

In the paper mentioned[42] I have commented upon the differences of oral technique and behavior observable in the act of story-telling among the informants and in their comments on the material delivered. There are often both jokes and humorous points in the myths mixed with actual explicit belief showing the informants' own attitude to Crow, Raven or Choolian. It is then very important that the fieldworker reports not only the contents of the myths but when and where the informant laughs and when he is very insistent or in some way or other states his own belief in what has been told, whether it is in mimicry, gestures or in the pitch of his voice.

It is very much indeed to be hoped that oral traditions will be more extensively analyzed by fieldworkers. The oral traditions of semi-nomadic hunters and fishers are rapidly disappearing, and with them our only source of information. In North America I would say that we have at the best five to ten years left to secure material that will be invaluable for the answers to the problems presented here. It is to be hoped that the present group of scholars may work as a pressure group to get scientific institutions to harvest these types of information before it is permanently too late.

---

42. A.-B. Rooth, 'Storytelling among the Athabascan Indians in Northern Alaska' (stencil), Lund, 1970, pp. 61 ff.

*Excerpts from the oscillogram made after the story-telling
of Catherine Trefont*

Upper diagram: frequences (pitch) measured in Hz along the vertical axis
Lower diagram: loudness measured in dB along the vertical axis

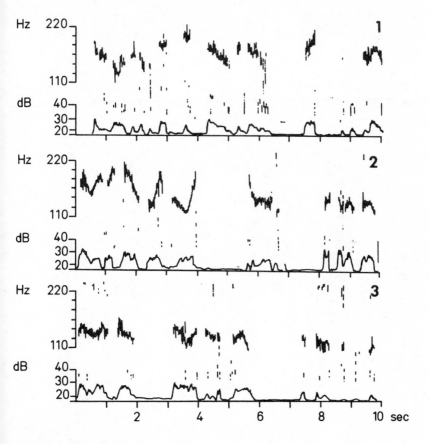

1. From the story
2. From a discussion between the informant and the recorder
3. From the story after the short discussion

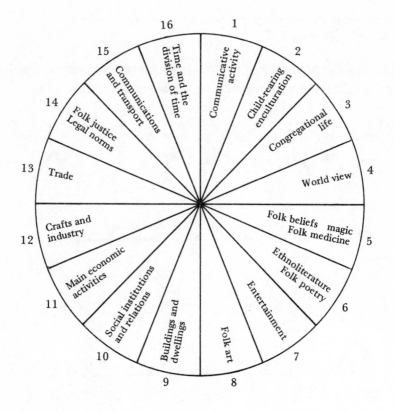

Commentary   by Leander Petzoldt

APPROACHES TO RESEARCH INTO ORAL TRADITION

The field of oral tradition certainly does not constitute folklore studies' own domain, since there are widely varying disciplines, such as literary criticism, ethnology, and cultural anthropology, which work on the same material and analyze it in accordance with the aims of their subjects. In view of this fact, it becomes clear that there will *a priori* be several possible ways of dealing with it. For literary criticism, for example, there will be the allocation to a particular genre, and the investigation of the history of the material or the motifs; for ethnology, an approach oriented towards the elaboration of elements specific to the culture; and for cultural anthropology, finally, an approach with comparative cultural aims, investigating the genesis, development, and function of the cultural heritage, conceptions of faith, and behavior. But, not least, oral tradition offers to comparative religion vital, and sometimes its only, source material.

If we put the oral tradition with its narrative texts at the centre of our studies, the variation in the relevance of the different approaches becomes immediately clear, since the methods mentioned here, whose questions are oriented towards traditional disciplines, are far from producing a total picture of the phenomenon known as oral narrative tradition. Essentially, they refer to content and material, and in the individual texts, all they see is a vehicle for the transmission of specific conceptions, while the specific structure and form of the individual narrative genres is ignored. One of the most important advances in scientific development in our time, it seems to me, is the abandonment of the traditional division between the natural sciences and the humanities. By this I do not intend to support the external or inappropriate transfer of natural-scientific methods and concepts to the humanities, but merely emphasize the fact that empirically motivated theories contribute to the unification of science. A model of a 'theoretically sound empirical science' has been put forward on the basis of structuralism,[43]

43. Manfred Bierwisch, *Modern Linguistics: Its developments, methods, and*

which formulates general laws, and attempts to 'account for the phenomena in terms of their underlying patterns'.

The structuralist method was introduced by Ferdinand de Saussure at the beginning of the century into linguistics (which had until then been oriented towards history and genesis, in the hands of the Neo-grammarians), and was then adopted in ethnology, sociology, psychology, mathematics, formal logic, and poetics, and has finally, in modern linguistics, returned to its source. Wladimir Propp's *Morphologie des Märchens* appeared in German translation almost 45 years late, in 1972; it is an important work, and not only for narrative research. Here he attempts a 'Beschreibung der Märchen auf der Grundlage ihrer Bestandteile sowie deren Beziehungen untereinander und zum Ganzen'.[44] What makes Propp's investigation particularly important for folklore studies is its method, which can be applied, with modifications, to the most widely varying genres of profane or religious text. Propp, for the first time, investigated a genre of oral tradition from new aspects, especially that of function. Propp's working method makes it possible for higher laws to be identified much more precisely than with traditional methods; e. g., for sagas: construction, figures, schemes of events, and problems of communication and of tradition. Propp's morphological method reveals itself to be based on genuine structuralist approaches, which have been developed above all by Lévi-Strauss in myth research.

It must be admitted that structuralism now means different things to different people; but what all these conceptions have in common is the fact that by establishing the formal relations between the elements that constitute a phenomenon, what this system of relations constitutes, in the realization of the specific possible combinations of these elements, is precisely the structure. Phenomena and ways of behavior of all kinds are thus no longer regarded in isolation, but investigated against the background of their systematic relations. 'In fact when examined from this point of view, surprisingly many phenomena, from folklore to religious concepts and complex aesthetic problems, become approachable in a rational way, and begin to lend themselves to precise description.'[45]

---

problems (Janua Linguarum, series minor 110, The Hague/Paris, 1971, p. 10. Translated from 'Strukturalismus und Linguistik', *Kursbuch* 5 (1966), pp. 77-152.

44. W. Propp, *Morphologie des Märchens*, tr. K. Eimermacher, München, 1972.

45. Bierwisch, *op. cit.*, p. 10.

FEATURES OF SPOKEN LANGUAGE AND OF WRITTEN TEXTS

What seems to be essential in this method, however, is its value as exact statement, which, if we apply structural analysis to 'folklore', makes it possible to proceed inductively to a presentation of the laws, basic categories, conceptual schemes, models, and structures, which underlie the popular oral tradition. One can see this best by looking at the range of concepts in structural linguistics. In the following, however, when I speak of popular texts with reference to popular tradition, I am merely acknowledging the fact that the whole of our historical research material (which we mainly owe to the activities of 19th-century collectors) is fixed in written form.

In narrative research, we simply term all texts 'oral tradition' which have been recorded from the mouth of an informant, irrespective of whether they have been recorded directly on tape or taken down in shorthand or longhand. For the purposes of research on motifs or on content in general, these documents can be treated in exactly the same way. If these documents are made the basis for further research, however, e. g. if they are studied with reference to their social background or to the intentions of the speaker or narrator, then we have to reduce the material critically to its genuinely documentary content, and crucial differences emerge between these texts in their relevance for research. It must be critically queried whether they really reproduce oral texts, with all the features of 'spoken language', or whether they have been shortened or subjected to literary or stylistic revision. It was only with the invention of the electromagnetic recording device (1934) that it became possible to gain access at will to the simultaneity of the process of formulation and of articulate utterances, which is the characteristic of spoken language. This also becomes 'accessible' in the sense that both the temporal and spatial simultaneity of the speaker's and hearer's situation can be recorded. In order to make the difference between oral tradition and literary tradition vividly clear, it is not enough to emphasize the linguistic, temporal, and spatial simultaneity. The differences between an orally recorded saga and one that has been worked over as literature, to take a concrete example, correspond (apart from their divergent structure) to the differences between spoken and written language. The spoken language, which traditionally includes everyday speech and dialects, is characterized by spontaneity of expression, which is motivated by the structure of communication, and not given formal or stylistic shape. I am of course referring by 'spoken texts' to those where the speaker has no written text to read from or to memorize: in other words to an oral tradition to which the concept of a 'memory culture' ('Gedächtniskultur') could also be applied.[46] In contrast to the reading out of a literary text, in which a public factor operates which diverges from the everyday situation of colloquial language, spoken texts are less strictly formed either by the linguistic standard or by grammatical coding: sentence contamination (i. e. badly planned sentences), interjections (the irruption of an emotional element), and anacolutha (i. e. broken sentence constructions and parentheses as isolated sequences outside the syntactical continuum), are all signs of a high degree of spontaneity, and of the character of spoken language as a dialogue involving the hearer's reactions.[47] A visual representation of the forms of linguistic communication in oral and literary transmission respectively, using the signs used in linguistics, produces the following differentiated model:

speaker . . . . (spontaneous). . . . . . $\overset{dialogue}{\ldots \ldots}$ . . .hearer

S . . . .(M) . . . . A

writer . . . .(edited). . . . . . $\overset{monologue}{\ldots \ldots}$ . . . .reader

The sender S (i.e. speaker or writer) adresses himself via a medium M (soundwaves or graphic transcription) to an addressee A (i.e. hearer or reader). The fundamental differences between spontaneous and edited expression, and between dialogue and monologue structures, must be recognized in working on written texts in the oral tradition; for the ideal case, in which records of popular tradition reveal the characteristics of spoken language, is relatively rare. The majority of the German tale and saga texts are admittedly recorded in dialect, as a result of the social origins of the narrators, but they have been transposed by the recorders (as a result of their social origins and for editorial consider-

46. Cf. P. Gaechter, *Die Gedächtniskultur in Irland*, Innsbruck, 1970.
47. I am grateful to my colleague R. Müller, Kassel, for his comments on the question of 'spoken language'.

ations) into the standard or written language, which necessarily means the loss of crucial linguistic features. Yet it is precisely those features which are needed to make it possible to interpret popular texts not merely formally and in terms of content, but with reference to their function, their genesis, their value in a communication network, and their basic spiritual position. I would like to illustrate this by referring to an oral-tradition sentence taken from a tape recording made in the Black Forest in 1972.[48] The narrator is describing the moment in the Genevieve legend when the disloyal Golo is attracted to Genevieve, who is completely at his mercy. The following sentence contamination is typical: 'Un der hett also immer uf die Genofeva, die hett ihm sehr gefalle, un da hett er denkt, wart nur dich, hiirat ich dich'. Paraphrased in the written language, this takes up several sentences: 'Und der hatte also immer auf die Genofeva (ein Auge geworfen). Die hat ihm sehr gefallen, deshalb dachte er: Warte nur, dich heirate ich (will ich heiraten)'.

In addition to the features of spoken language already mentioned (sentence contamination, parenthesis, anacoluthon), another striking feature is the way in which the sentences are strung together paratactically; but it is mainly the many sentence contaminations that one notices here. According to traditional grammar, these phenomena are deficient; but our grammar is oriented towards a standard high form of the language, and it is only modern linguistics which has attempted to find a function instead of a defect in these phenomena, which are normal, i. e. characteristic, of oral narrative texts.

The linguistic picture given in the dialect version is not the same as that in the written-language paraphrase. The oral example gives expression to an essentially more intense modality. The explanation about being attracted to Genevieve is so strongly stressed that in the first half of the sentence, part of the statement is actually omitted, and in the second half, following a parenthesis and the interjection 'Wart nur', the idea of being able to marry her leads into the statement of the intention to marry her. In the written-language paraphrase, this is not nearly so strongly expressed. Linguistically, the motivation for this behavior is economy in the formulation in the text, aiming, with the hearer in

48. From a tape recording by J. Künzig and W. Werner, Institute for Eastern German Ethnology, University of Freiburg. The texts are to be published soon on records under the title *Volkslesestoffe aus mündlicher Überlieferung*.

mind, above all at the progress of the content: i. e. maximum content in minimum time.[49] This is also a distinguishing feature of the code used. The concept of linguistic codes was introduced into linguistics by Basil Bernstein in 1966.[50] He makes a distinction between 'restricted codes' and 'elaborated codes'. In 'restricted codes', which are what primarily interest us here, both sentence structure and in extreme cases vocabulary are completely predictable, both for the speaker and the hearer. This means that the speaker has a relatively limited range of lexical and syntactical choice. The speaker (and the hearer) are in possession of a 'common, extensive set of closely-shared identifications and expectations consciously held'.[51] Incompleteness of expression is replaced by the presence of a shared symbolism or collective mythology. The restricted code indicates that 'the social relationship will be one of an inclusive kind'. 'The meanings are likely to be concrete, descriptive or narrative rather than analytical or abstract' (as they are in elaborated codes). The high degree of predictability implies that 'some meanings are likely to be dislocated, condensed and local', which is particularly true on the level of the dialect speaker. This does not, however, necessarily mean that dialect speakers use a restricted code, although dialect naturally constitutes a class-specific social symbol, while every code symbolizes a specific social identity. Nevertheless, it must be emphasized that 'restricted codes are not necessarily linked to social class'.[52] Specific examples of restricted codes include 'ritualistic modes of communication', in which 'all the words, and hence the organizing structure irrespective of its degree of complexity, are wholly predictable for speakers and listeners'.[53] Forms of this kind are to be found in 'relationships regulated by protocol, types of religious services, cocktail-party routines, and (particularly important in this context) 'some story-telling situations'.

In specific areas of the oral tradition, as the sentence from the Genevieve legend showed, the meanings are sharply condensed. This is par-

---

49. This does not imply anything about the quality of the information, as becomes clear from the example of redundance.

50. Basil Bernstein, *Class, Codes and Control*, vol. I, London, Routledge & Kegan Paul, 1971; republished, St Albans, Paladin Books, 1973; see esp. chaps. 6 & 7.

51. Bernstein (Paladin ed.), p. 149.

52. Bernstein, *ibid.*

53. Bernstein, pp. 147-148.

ticularly clear when proverbs or proverbial manners of speaking are being used, which are also recognized in the standard language as a sign of 'popular' ways of speech. In proverbs and proverbial language, kinds of behavior, intentions, and opinions are made paradigmatically concrete and raised to the level of the collective experience of life. This concretization in formulaic language betrays the speaker's limited desire, or perhaps ability, for abstraction. In this way a whole genre of popular short prose becomes the indicator of a restricted code; for the users of such a code tend to make use of proverbial and formulaic language, without being aware of its regressive tendency, equipped as such a form of language is with predetermined formulas. This further reveals an essential element of restricted codes: their predictability, which is determined both lexically, through a limited vocabulary, and through the availability of a collective symbolism. The application of these linguistic categories to popular oral text material offers an exact tool for source criticism of the oral tradition. This tool also makes it possible to deal with extra-linguistic features of spoken language.

EXTRA-VERBAL COMPONENTS OF ORAL TRADITION

Oral communication consists of verbal and extra-verbal, or paralinguistic, components. The verbal component refers to the selection, combination, and organization of the words. In the context of the narrative texts which interest us here, and their oral transmission, which are, as we saw, determined a restricted code, the paralinguistic components take on increased importance. A speaker who uses a restricted code develops a high degree of sensitivity to extra-verbal signals, which 'become a major channel for transmitting individual qualifications'.[54] Restricted codes have no room to express individual differences verbally; in a restricted code, these can only be transmitted through extra-linguistic or extra-verbal signals, such as rhythm, intonation, mimicry, and gesture: in other words, the expressive phenomena that accompany an utterance. It was not sociolinguistics, however, which first pointed out the extra-verbal phenomena that accompany spoken language or narrative. In an essay on the language of gesture of tale-narrators, Haiding writes:

54. Bernstein, p. 149.

'Einzelne Erzähler ringen zuweilen mühsam um den sprachlichen Ausdruck und suchen das Geschehen besonders durch Gebärden zu verdeutlichen'.[55] The Irish folklorist Delargy describes very vividly the mimicry and gestures of an Irish tale and saga narrator: 'Sein durchdringender Blick ruht auf meinem Angesicht, seine Glieder zittern, wie er, ganz versenkt in seine Geschichte, und alles andere vergessend, seine ganze Seele ins Erzählen legt. Offensichtlich sehr ergriffen von der Erzählung, macht er viele Gesten und versucht, durch die Bewegungen des Körpers, der Hände, des Kopfes Hass und Ärger, Furcht und Humor auszudrücken wie ein Schauspieler in einem Theaterstück. Bei gewissen Stellen verstärkt sich seine Stimme, dann wird sie wieder beinah ein Wispern. Er spricht ziemlich schnell, aber seine Aussprache ist immer deutlich'.[56]

As has been said, however, it was not linguistics that first pointed out the presence of extra-verbal components in the oral tradition. In the early 1950's, a folklorist had already studied the popular basis of the language of gesture, and concluded: 'Über den enggezogenen Kreis der sprachlichen Verständigung wirkt die gleiche Haltung verbindend, und Mimik und Gestik, also Gesichtsausdruck und Gebärde der einzelnen Körperteile werden noch verstanden, wenn die Sprache im engeren Sinn bereits ihren Verständigungswert verloren hat'.[57] This remark points to exactly what is meant here. With the methods of linguistics, however, these observations can be placed in context, and functionally interpreted within the framework of a theory of language.

REDUNDANCE AND AUTHENTICITY OF WRITTEN TEXTS

A further distinguishing feature of the oral tradition, especially of narrative texts, is redundance. This is a feature of a spoken language under which is understood the frequent repetition of information in sequences which add only little to what has already been said.[58] This does not conflict with the example quoted from the Genevieve legend, which

55. Karl Haiding, *Von der Gebärdensprache der Märchenerzähler*, Helsinki, 1955, p. 14 (FFC No. 155).
56. Gaechter, *op. cit.*, p. 50.
57. L. Schmidt, in *Festschrift f. A. Spamer*, Berlin, 1953, p. 234.
58. Cf. Bernstein, *op. cit.*

offers maximum content in minimum time, as I put it, but does not in this way raise the information value. The capacity of the code, in other words, is not fully exploited for information; and this is a phenomenon that is probably connected with the limitations of human reception capacity.[59] No studies on redundance in popular narrative texts have so far been published, but it is certainly more than 50 percent. This brings me to one of the essential problems of narrative research. What we find nowadays in 19th-century German and central European collections of legends and tales are mainly texts which were taken over from anthologies, topographical and statistical publications, or the literature of curiosities and prodigies, if not in fact from the literary, i. e. chronicle, tradition. They are characterized by being stylistically smoothed off, culturally formed, and put by the recorder into acceptable grammatical form. Naturally this means that repetitions and tautologies in particular, which are the special forms of redundance, are deleted. After all, the major example are the Brothers Grimm. It would be a mistake to think that the pieces reprinted in the legends of the Brothers Grimm are living popular tradition or material from the oral narrative tradition. Orally recorded sagas in this collection form only 54 items, which, in a total of 585 items, makes just 9 percent. Even these legends have been worked on and altered stylistically, which is not criticism of the philological precision of the editors, for both in the time of the Brothers Grimm and later, mythological research was mainly material-oriented; it is only nowadays that the questions of form, narrative position, style, intention, social determination, and in general everything that could be termed the 'biology' of the legend or tale, has been seen as problematical. The results of a method of legend and tale collection which is, in our sense, uncritical and unphilological, are pieces which do not correspond to the oral narrative tradition quantitatively, not to mention any other criteria. It can be demonstrated that this is not a technical problem, but one of the collector's attitude towards his material, by reference to the plentiful transcriptions of legends and tales from the Irish tradition. 'So brauchte Sean Delargy (the founder of the Dublin Folklore Archive) zur Niederschrift *einer* Geschichte die Stunden von Mittag bis zum Ein-

---

59. Precise statistical measurements have been published, especially in the literature in English. The redundance in the literature in Modern English is round about 50 percent. Cf. H. Vermeer, *Einführung in die linguistische Terminologie*, Darmstadt, 1971, p. 40.

bruch der Nacht. Im Archiv der Folklore Commission in Dublin liegen Niederschriften von Geschichten, welche einzeln 24 000, ja 36 000 Wörter enthalten.'[60]

But we do not need to go so far afield to find examples. One of the few collectors to collect tales and other narratives during the last few years, in quite epic proportions, comments on this problem: '... ein Zehn-Minuten-Märchen vom Durchschnittstyp ist entweder nur eine Inhaltsangabe des eiligen Erzählers für eilige Sammler, bzw. der Sammler hat in seiner Aufnahme psychisch-methodisch oder technisch versagt. Das gut erzählte Märchen will seine Leute wie ein guter Film möglichst mehr als eine Stunde unterhalten'.[61]

This is confirmed by other collectors and researchers into narrative, such as Walter Anderson, Georgios Megas, Will-Erich Peuckert, and Reidar Th. Christiansen, to mention only a few. These observations point towards an important function of the oral tradition: redundance cannot, therefore, simply be defined as the linguistic incompetence of the speaker, but represents, together with the features of spoken language that have been mentioned, an important criterion for the oral tradition.

Discussion   Chairman: Åke Hultkrantz

The first speaker at the second session was Juha Pentikäinen, who proposed to summarize the main points in his paper and to read short extracts from it. He said it fell into five sections, dealing respectively with (1) oral tradition and the study of religion, (2) the relationship between oral and literary traditions, (3) the principles of the taxonomy of oral tradition, (4) genre analysis and the study of religion, and (5) the demands placed on fieldwork in the study of religion by source criticism. This last section was largely based on his own fieldwork experience. One observation, in the light of the discussion at the first session (on canons), was that we should pay more attention to the formation and function of canons as a process, and that in order to do so it was ex-

---

60. Cf. Gaechter, *op. cit.*, p. 51.
61. A. Cammann, *Westpreussische Märchen*, Berlin, 1961, p. 13.

tremely useful to be able to study oral material, using observation, interviews, etc., so as to get at the tradition behind the text.

In presenting his paper, Pentikäinen was able to illustrate the last section (about the Karelian tradition-bearer, Marina Takalo) with a number of slides, including photographs of her (one of which showed her reading a charm in a sauna: she had had some shamanistic features in her personality, and one of the interesting questions was the relationship for her between the old ethnic religion and the Old Believer sect of Orthodoxy to which she belonged).

The second speaker, Anna Birgitta Rooth, also presented a summary of and read extracts from the main points of her paper, which was concerned with various aspects and consequences of the act of transferring socio-cultural behavior and similar 'non-material materials' into the oral/verbal medium involved in ethnological research. In addition to the discussion reprinted above in her paper, she also showed an oscillogram recording of the special technique used by an Athabascan Indian woman in telling a story: she had talked very monotonously and slowly, which had given a certain mysterious quality to the story (a myth important for the hunting traditions); Rooth wanted to be able to record this special quality of speech with an oscillograph, thereby describing the speech into a different medium – drawn into curves – which can be analyzed by the eye. This exemplified the process she was talking about: i.e. that when situations in life, behavior, mental processes, etc., are transferred from one dimension into another, in which only one physiological instrument (e.g. the ear) can be used, then this verbalization of necessity brings about a splitting up of the holistic and multi-dimensional nature of real life, into parts which can only be presented in chronological order.

Following the presentation of the two papers, the chairman, Åke Hultkrantz, commented that both of the speakers were both versed in history and science of religion, and also folklorists. He also pointed out that Turku was an international centre for taxonomy and genre analysis. In the absence of the commentator, Leander Petzoldt, Hultkrantz then presented a summary of the main points from the written commentary.

Replying to Petzoldt's commentary, Pentikäinen said that many of the points were valuable, but probably applied to early German folklore archives much more than to collections based on modern fieldwork.

Rooth then asked if she might offer a commentary on her own paper. She wished to draw attention to a diagram published by Cornelius Oswood, in *Ingalic Mental Culture* (Yale University Publications in Anthropology 56, p. 16), which was an attempt to show the complexity and difficulty of an anthropologist making a recording from an informant — a situation in which the minds, and universes, of the informant and the anthropologist impinged on each other in many ways. She found the diagram, like Oswood's work in general, very illuminating. Secondly, she wished to distribute a diagram which showed how ethnology was nowadays constituted in Sweden. It divided the subject into 16 sections, eight of them representing verbal and mental culture, and eight representing material culture.

Speaking from the floor, Lauri Honko questioned the use of the term 'memorate' in the two main papers. He thought that the term itself might be unfamiliar to many, and asked Anna Birgitta Rooth whether she would accept a definition of memorate as 'a detailed report of a supernatural experience'. Rooth replied that while one could decide to limit the term to supernatural experience, what von Sydow had had in mind when he coined the term did not need to be anything supernatural; it could, for instance, be something from one's childhood; what it referred to was the first telling of something the person had experienced, and the term had been created with the definite purpose of explaining how, from this first-hand telling of experience, legends or *Sagen* gradually developed.

L. Honko commented that he understood the Sydowian concept, but that it needed modification. It was probably not correct always to assimilate memorates to legend, as German scholarship tended to do. One could therefore draw a distinction between different types of report: memorates (oriented towards the supernatural), chronicates (towards the historical), joculates (towards the humorous), etc. While terminology did not of itself create results, it did enable one to be more exact in one's analysis. He went on to comment on the diagram in Pentikäinen's paper, which had been creatively crossbred from a number of sources, including Jan Vansina's *Oral Tradition* and a flowchart in one of Honko's articles (cf. note 3 to Pentikäinen's paper). However, he was unsure about the function of the canon in the diagram in its present form, which he thought needed further comment.

Robert Spencer wanted to raise a number of questions about Petzoldt's commentary, especially the question of the relationship between folklore and literature. Spencer recognized a kind of 'rivalry' between the Finnish and German approaches to folklore; yet both of them seemed to lead towards an objective, typological orientation, which tended to exclude or reduce the effectiveness of the humanistic element. He suggested that literary criticism, with its humanistic orientation, could contribute a lot here, where much of the sense of the life in the folklore would otherwise be lost.

Rooth was also interested in the analogy drawn with literature, and extended it by commenting on some writers, such as the anthropological novels of Oscar Lewis — who represented a kind of material very close to memorate, if the connection with the supernatural was not insisted on — or the Swedish novelist P. O. Sundman, who wrote in everyday language, with all its incoherences and incorrect language, etc. This represented something quite new, in trying to capture not only the way ordinary people live but also the way in which they use language to talk about it.

Hans Penner suggested that at the core of both of the main papers was the issue of belief. He discussed the difficulty, in fieldwork, of analyzing from a belief statement to what the belief actually was, and of proceeding from a belief statement to either semantics or structural systems analysis. Accordingly, he asked the two speakers to clarify what they understood by 'belief'. Pentikäinen pointed out that this actually involved definitions for folklore, belief, and folk belief. In his paper he had offered a definition of folk belief, as a 'supranormal assertion in a generalizing statement'. As to belief, the question to be answered first was whether it should be defined on the basis of meaning or on the basis of use, function, etc., or on the basis of all these. Fieldwork experience indicated wide variation in the meaning of belief even within the same community, which would make it necessary to investigate the frequency of belief. He emphasized a multi-dimensional, functional approach in defining the concept of belief and its relationship to the community and cultural environment.

The chairman, Hultkrantz, interposed to draw attention to a number of articles about belief and belief systems in recent issues of *Temenos* and in the latest issue of *Current Anthropology*.

In Th. P. van Baaren's opinion, a very formal definition of belief was necessary in science of religion, and he offered the following as an (admittedly rather clumsy) working hypothesis: that belief consisted of those statements, etc., etc., which were accepted by a community or an individual but which could not be checked (or which the believer believed could not be checked) empirically.

The title of this session, 'Taxonomy and Source Criticism of Oral Tradition', implied, said Honko, a lot of thinking when confronted with different kinds of oral tradition – thinking which led both to optimism and to frustration. Without genre taxonomy, one was likely to put gods, etc., which only appeared in fact in certain kinds of prayers, for instance, on the same level as those which appeared in prose narrative, and mix them together in a kind of methodological porridge. The optimism arose because taxonomy provided a spoon with which one could dip into that porridge; but the frustration arose because it was difficult to achieve agreement on the definitions and categories required. Probably it was very idealistic to imagine that one day one would achieve a general taxonomy of oral tradition, but he continued to be optimistic.

The question of folk belief, and especially the problems associated with anthropological research in modern societies, were taken up again by J. van Baal. He supported the definition of folk belief put forward by van Baaren, i.e. on the basis of the unverifiability of the belief. Modern folk belief was extremely vague; the believers were increasingly unwilling to talk about it, and its lack of form made research into it very difficult. Participant observation had been a good method in societies where life was carried on publicly, but it was of little use against the privacy of modern society. Studying modern religion was an important task, but one which was methodologically increasingly difficult.

The whole idea of taxonomy, however, was then questioned by Anne-Marie de Waal Malefijt. American anthropology, she said, was dominated by a wish to understand; classification might be important or not. Listening to the discussion about 'belief', she had been struck by the recurrence of words such as 'frustration', 'vagueness', 'unverifiability', and even 'porridge': definition and content did not seem to be in close relationship to each other. She therefore questioned whether it was at all necessary to find a definition for 'belief', since it appeared to be an ineffable and indefinable concept. Surely what was important was not whether people believed or not in a certain way, but how they acted communally. On the other hand, when Hultkrantz suggested that this was to reduce the discussion to one on the value in general of taxonomy in religion, de Waal Malefijt said that that was not what she had intended, although Hultkrantz repeated that that would in his opinion be the consequence of what she had said. G. C. Oosthuizen was afraid of a confusion between 'belief' and 'conviction', if 'belief' was not adequately defined; but van Baaren countered by suggesting that the difference between these terms was that 'belief' was 'conviction in a religious context'.

Rooth argued strongly in favor of flexibility in the use of the term. Ethnology included a section concerned with 'folk belief', but there could be varying meanings of 'folk', of 'belief', and — if the latter were defined by reference to the religious — of 'religious'. Moreover it was particularly difficult in oral tradition, because, for example, narratives might make use of fixed formulas or pedagogical rhetorical traditions in order to transmit knowledge: e. g. should the statement 'I believe this is the right time for sowing', whose function was to transmit technical knowledge, be interpreted as 'belief'? In addition to traditional knowledge, there were also many beliefs in use concerning space and time, creation, eschatology, concepts of the world of nature, omens, divinations, magic and religious concepts: here 'concepts' overlapped with 'beliefs'.

In bringing the session to a close, the chairman welcomed the way in which the discussion had showed that the members of the conference belonged to differing traditions and schools of thought. He hoped that similar clashes would continue to take place, since they would make the discussion on the conference more interesting and more valuable.

Literary Source Criticism

JOSEPH M. KITAGAWA   *Early Shinto: A Case Study*

It is not an easy task to discuss the role of literary source criticism within the context of 'Oral and Written Documentation of Religious Tradition'. The notion of literary source criticism, as usually adopted by Biblical scholars in contradistinction to form criticism, tradition history criticism and redaction criticism, assumes for the most part the existence of sacred writings which have some kind of canonical authority. This implies that the religious documents in question are integrally related to the doctrines or dogmas which have been determined and preserved by the religious community, whereby there is a normative perspective from which one can engage in critical study of the religious documents. Such an understanding of literary source criticism is relevant in dealing with the sacred books of Judaism, Christianity, Islam, and to a certain extent those of Hinduism and Theravada Buddhism. But in dealing with religious traditions which do not recognize canonical or sacred scriptures as such, the historian of religions is compelled both to examine religious and non-religious documents through literary source criticism as well as other types of form criticism, and also to explore the meaning and structure of myths, legends, folklore, rituals, symbols and the religious community itself. Indeed, even when the historian of religions is primarily concerned with the literary source criticism of certain religious documents – in every case but more so in the case of religious traditions which do not recognize canonical scriptures – he must study 'religious data in their historical connections not only with other religious data but also with those which are not religious, whether literary, artistic, social or what not'.[1] As a case in

1. Raphael Pettazzoni, *Essays on the History of Religions*, trans. by H. J. Rose

point, I now turn to the nature of the task required in literary source criticism of early religious documents in the native Shinto tradition of Japan.

RELIGIOUS DOCUMENTS

At the outset, it must be explicitly stated that Shinto tradition has never officially acknowledged any document as canonical literature, although the following classics have acquired semi-canonical status. They are:

Kojiki (The Records of Ancient Matters), compiled in 712 A. D.[2]

Nihongi or *Nihon-shoki (The Chronicles of Japan)*, compiled in 720 A. D.[3]

Norito (Ritual Prayers), Book VIII of *Engi-shiki (The Procedures of the Engi Era)*, compiled in 927 A. D.[4]

Also, the following documents are regarded as 'Classics' (*koten*):

Semmyō (The Imperial Proclamations), taken from *Shoku-Nihongi (The Chronicles of Japan, continued)*, compiled in 797 A. D.[5]

Kogoshūi (Gleanings from Ancient Stories), compiled in 807 A. D.[6]

Ryō no Gige (Commentary on the Legal Code), especially the section on 'Jingi-kan' (Department of Kami-affairs), compiled in 833 A. D.[7]

(Leiden: E. J. Brill, 1954), p. 216.

2. See Basil Hall Chamberlain (tr.), *Ko-ji-ki: 'Records of Ancient Matters'*, supplement to *TASJ (Transactions of Asiatic Society of Japan)*, Vol. X (1882); and Donald L. Philippi (tr. with an Introd. and Notes), *Kojiki*, Princeton University Press and University of Tokyo Press, 1969.

3. See William George Aston (tr.), *Nihongi: Chronicles of Japan from the Earliest Times to A. D. 697*. 2 vols., London, 1896; 2 vols. in 1, London, 1956.

4. See E. M. Satow, 'Ancient Japanese Rituals', *TASJ*, VII, Part 1 (1879), 97-132; IX (1881), 182-211; Karl Florenz, 'Ancient Japanese Rituals', *TASJ*, XXVII, Part 1 (1899), 1-112; Donald L. Philippi (tr.), *Norito (A New Translation of the Ancient Japanese Ritual Prayers)*, Tokyo, 1959; and Felicia Gressitt Bock (tr. with Introd. and Notes), *Engi-Shiki (Procedures of the Engi Era)* Books VI-X, Tokyo, Sophia University, 1972, pp. 57-105.

5. See Zachert Herbert, *Semmyo, die Kaiserlichen Erlasse des Shoku-Nihongi*, Berlin, 1950.

6. See Genchi Kato and Hikoshirō Hoshino (tr. and annot.), *The Kogoshūi: Gleanings from Ancient Stories*, Tokyo, 1926.

7. See George B. Sansom, 'Early Japanese Law and Administration', Part I, *TASJ* (2), IX (1932), 67-109; Part II, XI (1934), 117-49.

Engi-shiki (Procedures of the Engi Era), Books I-X, compiled in
927 A. D.[8]
Shinsen-shojiroku (The New Compilation of the Register of Families),
compiled in 815 A. D.[9]
Fudoki (Topographical Records) of the Provinces of Hitachi, Harima,
Izumo, Hizen and Bungo, etc., commenced in 713 A. D.[10]
Manyoshu (Collection of Myriad Leaves), compiled around 766 A. D.[11]

ORAL TRANSMISSION AND WRITTEN RECORDS

While this is not the occasion to trace the prehistory of Japan or the
development of the Japanese language, it is safe to assume that the
inhabitants of the Japanese islands who introduced rice cultivation
somewhere between the first century B. C. and the first century A. D.,
spoke Proto-Japanese, from which the modern Japanese dialects developed.[12] Scholars point out that the phonology of Proto-Japanese
was somewhat different from that of modern Japanese, and that the
vocabulary of Proto-Japanese, which was quite limited, was destined
to be greatly enriched under the impact of the Sino-Korean civilization
starting from the 5th or 6th century A. D. Nevertheless, the structure of
the Japanese language has remained remarkably unchanged throughout
the ages. Its syllabic structure is very simple, while it is abundant in
homonyms (words with the same pronunciation but different meanings).
And, as the ancient Japanese did not develop a written script, their
myths, legends, lore, songs, beliefs and rites were committed to memory
and transmitted from mouth to mouth for generations.

Meanwhile, the gradual stratification of Japanese society during the
3rd, 4th and 5th centuries resulted in the development of the Yamato

8. Felicia Gressitt Bock (tr. with Introd. and Notes), *Engi-Shiki (Procedures of the Engi Era)*, Books I-V, Tokyo, Sophia University, 1970; Books VI-X, 1972.
9. See Ryusaku Tsunoda, *et al.*, (compls.) *Sources of Japanese Tradition*, New York, Columbia University Press, 1958, pp. 87-90.
10. See Michiko Yamaguchi Aoki (tr. with an Introd.), *Izumo Fudoki*, Tokyo, Sophia University, 1971.
11. See The Nippon Gakujutsu Shinkokai (tr.), *The Manyoshu*, Tokyo, Iwanami Shoten, 1940; New York, Columbia University Press, 1965.
12. For the identity of Proto-Japanese, see my 'Prehistoric Background of Japanese Religion', *History of Religions*, Vol. 2, No. 2 (Winter, 1963), 313-16.

Kingdom. The Yamato Kingdom, a confederation of semi-autonomous powerful clans brought together under the leadership of the Imperial Clan, imposed its authority over others by means of military power as much as by the claim of its solar ancestry. It even established a military base at Mimana, in the southern tip of the Korean peninsula. During the 5th and 6th centuries, some of the Japanese monarchs dispatched official envoys to the Sung Court in China, too. It was through these contacts that the Sino-Korean civilization and Buddhism penetrated Japan. One of the most important by-products of the Sino-Korean civilization was the introduction of the Chinese script, which was appropriated by the Japanese as their own written script.

According to the official chronicle, it was during the reign of the 15th legendary emperor, Ōjin, around the turn of the 5th century A. D., that the two Confucian scholars, Achiki and Wani, came from Paekche, Korea, to the Japanese court. Along with them the Confucian Analects and the 'Thousand-Character Classics'[13] were introduced to Japan.

In the course of time, some of the Japanese intelligentsia learned the use of literary Chinese (called *kambun* in Japanese), which was used for writing historical and official records for many centuries. For example, most portions of the *Nihongi (Chroniques of Japan)* and the *Shoku-Nihongi (Chroniques of Japan, Continued)* were written in literary Chinese. Another system used Chinese characters (*kanji* in Japanese) in a hybrid *kambun* style in which the characters were read in Japanese. Still another system utilized Chinese characters only for their sound value, disregarding their lexical meaning, in order to express Japanese sounds. This system was called the *Manyō-gana* (a form of syllabary used in the *Manyōshū* or the *Collection of Myriad Leaves*), which became the forerunner of the *hiragana* and *katakana* syllabaries. At any rate, with the adoption of the Chinese script as their own, the Japanese were able to put in writing the ancient traditions which had been heretofore transmitted orally.

The impact of the Sino-Korean civilization not only gave new impetus to the development of the Japanese language, but also provided the opportunity or a medium for Japanese poets and writers to express

13. Philippi, *Kojiki*, p. 285, note 7, points out: 'The Thousand-Character Classics as we know it today became current at a later period; probably some other compilation was known by that name, or the later work was assigned an erroneously early provenance.'

themselves in Chinese (*kambun*) as a viable option. For example, Professor Keene cites the conspicuous example of Prince Ōtsu (662-87), who wrote two poems — one in Japanese verse and the other in Chinese — shortly before his execution. According to Keene, the first one, which is included in the *Manyōshū*, is 'purely Japanese in feeling', while the second 'not only used Chinese language and allusions but attempts to give philosophical overtones lacking in the simple Japanese verse'.[14] No doubt, the practice of expressing oneself both in Japanese and Chinese writing or verse has greatly enriched cultural life in Japan. On the other hand, it presents a series of complex hermeneutical problems for our attempts to analyze literary characteristics or to determine the literary units of both the religious and non-religious documents of early Japan.

EQUATION OF NATIONAL COMMUNITY AND RELIGIOUS COMMUNITY

The most salient feature of Japanese religion is that throughout its history there was no religious community as such apart from the national community. Accordingly, there were no religious documents as such outside of the ancient memories and traditions, history myths, lore, legends, rituals and laws of the national community. Underlying the notion of the religio-national community was the seamlessness of the early Japanese world of meaning. That is to say, to the early Japanese the 'world', comprised as it was of various facets, divisions and realms, was nevertheless a one-dimensional monistic universe. It had a unitary meaning-structure, based on the *kami* (sacred) nature which pervaded

14. Donald Keene (compl. & ed.), *Anthology of Japanese Literature — from the earliest era to the mid-nineteenth century* (New York: Grove Press, 1955), p. 21. The two poems are translated as follows:

> Today, taking my last sight of the mallards
>   Crying on the pond of Iware,
>   Must I vanish into the clouds!
>   (from the *Manyōshū*)

> The golden crow lights on the western huts;
>   Evening drums beat out the shortness of life.
>   There are no inns on the road to the grave —
>   Whose is the house I go tonight?
>   (from the *Kaifūsō*)

the entire universe, which was essentially a 'sacred community of living beings' endowed with spirits or souls.

The penetration of Sino-Korean civilization and Buddhism during the 5th and 6th centuries brought about not only a series of social, cultural and political changes in Japan, but also a variety of new ways of ordering the meaning of the world. Inevitably, the simple structure of the ancient religio-national community took on a multi-dimensional character. For example, in the earlier days the Yamato Kingdom was ruled by monarchs, who were no more than tribal chieftains, and whose actions were dictated by the precarious will of the *kami*, transmitted to them through dreams and divination. But, with the penetration of Sino-Korean civilization and Buddhism, the religio-national community of Japan could no longer depend solely on integrating principles based on communal rules and paternalistic authority as in the old days.

It was Prince Shōtoku (573-621), who ruled as the regent around the turn of the 7th century, who was quick to recognize the emerging pattern of the religio-national community by upholding the centrality of the particular experience of the Japanese as expressed in the native Shinto tradition, while at the same time promoting Confucianism and Buddhism. Indeed, the central motif running through the so-called 'Seventeen-Article Constitution' of Shōtoku is the harmony of the religio-national community, based on the exalted image of the sovereign, this image now attaining cosmological significance.[15]

Following Shōtoku's death, the Japanese nation became highly centralized along the Sui and T'ang Chinese imperial model, and the affairs of the nation were administered by bureaucrats trained in Confucian learning. Yet the Confucian principle of Tao was homologized with, and was made subordinate to, the authority of the emperor, who by virtue of his descent from the Sun Goddess Amaterasu, the mythological ancestress of the imperial clan, was destined to reign over the nation. Moreover, the Sovereign came to be regarded as the 'manifest kami' (*akitsu-kami*), whose divine will is communicated by a series of 'imperial rescripts'. The religio-political structure, thus developed in the 7th cen-

15. In the third article of Shotoku's Constitution we read: 'The lord is Heaven, the vassal is Earth. Heaven overspreads, and Earth upbears... Therefore is it that when the lord speaks, the vassal listens... Consequently when you receive the imperial commands, fail not to carry them out scrupulously.' Cited in Tsunoda, *et al.*, *Sources...* (cf. above note 9), p. 50.

tury, is referred to as the 'Ritsuryō (imperial rescript) State'. It was in effect a form of 'immanental theocracy'. It was the religio-national community, under the inspiration of the immanental theocratic principle, which produced the semi-canonical documents, such as the *Kojiki (The Records of Ancient Matters)*, *Nihongi (Chronicles of Japan)*, *Norito (Shinto Ritual Prayers)*, and *Semmyō (The Imperial Proclamations)*.

LITERARY CHARACTERISTICS OF EARLY SHINTO DOCUMENTS

It is well nigh impossible to make generalizations concerning the literary characteristics of the semi-canonical documents and classics of the early Shinto tradition. In this connection, it might be interesting to note that the compilation of the *Kojiki* and *Nihongi* was ordered by Emperor Temmu in 673 A. D., in order to justify his accession to the throne after he usurped it from the Emperor Kōbun. Yet, these two documents are very different in literary form and style as well as in scope.

The *Kojiki* is divided into three scrolls (*maki*). The First Scroll deals with six main themes of heavenly myths, i. e. (1) cosmogonic myths, (2) myths concerning the two kami — Izanagi ('He Who Invites') and Izanami ('She Who is Invited'), (3) myths concerning the Plain of High Heaven in which Amaterasu (the Sun Goddess) is the central figure, (4) myths of the Izumo region, (5) myths regarding the offering of the Izumo region of Japan to the heavenly kami, and (6) myths concerning the descent of Ninigi, the grandson, of Amaterasu, from heaven with the divine mission to rule Japan. The Second Scroll deals with earthly myths, probably better characterized as the Yamato myths, consisting of accounts of the first 15 legendary emperors, beginning with Jimmu, who is portrayed as the great-grandson of Ninigi. The Third Scroll gives genealogical and anecdotal accounts of the Yamato monarchs from the 16th Emperor, Nintoku, to Empress Suiko (reigned 592-628 A. D.), the 33rd sovereign. According to the Preface of the *Kojiki*, a court attendant called Hiyeda no Are was commanded by Emperor Temmu (in 673 A. D.) to learn the contents of 'genealogical accounts of the imperial family'[16] and the 'myths and legends of the imperial clan'.[17]

16. *Sumera mikoto no hitsugi.*
17. *Saki-no-yo no furu-goto.*

The task of compilation of the *Kojiki*, however, was completed in 712 A. D. by Ō no Yasumaro.

The *Nihongi*, which is divided into 30 scrolls provides — apart from the first two dealing with the heavenly myths — chronological accounts of the Yamato monarchs from the first legendary emperor Jimmu to Empress Jitō (697 A. D.). The chronology of the *Nihongi* is based on the Chinese calendar system called *kanshi*.[18] While the *Nihongi* consciously used many available documents and traditions — indeed alternative interpretations of the same events are carefully recorded throughout the book — its format is clearly modelled after the Chinese dynastic histories. Unlike the *Kojiki*, which utilizes the Chinese scripts to express Japanese language and ideas, the *Nihongi* is written in literary Chinese.

Obviously, the compilers of the *Kojiki* and *Nihongi* had access to a vast amount of materials — myths, legends, folklore, court documents, etc. Being men of letters of the 7th and 8th centuries in Japan, they were also very well acquainted with the literary, legal, and philosophical traditions of China. But they made every effort to make full use of the Japanese materials, especially the heavenly myths handed down in the imperial clan tradition. Moreover, the chroniclers 'historicized' the earthly or 'Yamato' myths. Chief among these is the account of the legendary first emperor, Jimmu, who presumably led his followers from Kyushu — where his great-grandfather Ninigi had descended from heaven — via the Inland Sea and the mountain roads of the present Wakayama prefecture up to Yamato, the central region of Japan, where he established the Yamato Kingdom, and was enthroned as the first emperor. In this connection, while we readily acknowledge the structural similarities between the mythical accounts of Jimmu's military

---

18. J. H. Kamstra, *Encounter or Syncretism: The Initial Growth of Japanese Buddhism*, Leiden, E. J. Brill, 1967, pp. 59-65. Kamstra states: 'Its nature can be discovered in the word *kanshi* itself. *Kan* in an indication of the Five Elements, after these had been divided by *yin* and *yang* into two groups of five, the older named *e* and the younger 'brother' named *to*. Thus there were in total ten "*kan*", or rather, five pairs of older and younger brothers. *Shi* has two meanings, namely "nucleus" and "something which is divided within itself". This original meaning was later extended to that of the two verbs for division and addition. Therefore *shi* is a means by which the above-mentioned ten *kan* may be subdivided further. Of these *shi* there were twelve altogether: the twelve signs of the zodiac... In this system the years are indicated by combining one of the ten *kan* with one of the twelve *shi*. Thus 120 combinations can be brought about...'

campaign from Kyushu to Yamato and the proceedings of the enthrone-
ment ceremonies prescribed in the *Engi-shiki*, we have little basis to
determine which came first — the rituals or the myths.

Norito is a general term, referring to a series of stylized prayers addressed to various *kami*. The *Engi-shiki*, compiled in 927, preserves 27
representative forms of *Norito*. As Mrs. Bock rightly points out, 'the
language of the *norito* differs from the Chinese style (*kambun*) of the
other books of the Engi-shiki, showing that *norito* had entirely different
sources — some of which are earlier than the time of the Taika Reforms
(mid-7th century) and some of which are later'.[19] Usually the *Norito*
begins with words praising *kami*, followed by lists of offerings and the
identity of the petitioner and the reciter, closing with the subject of
the prayer. In earlier days, before the *Norito* became stylized, there
must have been simpler forms of petitions and supplications. Implicit
in the *Norito* is the ancient Japanese notion of *koto-dama* (the spiritual
power residing in words), according to which beautiful words, correctly
pronounced, were believed to bring about good whereas ugly words or
beautiful words incorrectly pronounced were believed to cause evil.
There is good reason to assume that the ritualized format of the *Norito*,
as contained in the *Engi-shiki*, must have been influenced by Buddhist
sutra reciting, which became popular from the 6th century A. D. onward.[20]

The *Semmyō (Imperial Proclamations)* were recited on special occasions, such as the accession of the new emperor, abdication of the
throne, dispatching ambassadors to China, death of important ministers,
etc. Unlike the *shō-choku (Imperial Rescripts)* which are written in
literary Chinese, the *Semmyō* are written in the so-called *Semmyō-gaki*
style, combining large characters and small-size characters used as
Manyō-gana, both following Japanese reading. It is to be noted that
the *Norito*, which addressed to the Heavenly and Earthly *kami*, and
the *Semmyō*, which expresses the decrees (*ō-mikoto*) of the Sovereign
as the 'manifest Kami', were written in the same *Semmyō-gaki* style. A
little over sixty *Semmyō* are cited in the *Shoku-Nihongi (Chronicles of
Japan, Continued)*, which is the official chronicle covering the years
700-790.

19. Bock, *Engi-Shiki, Books VI-X* (cf. above note 8), p. 57.
20. Enchō Tamura, *Fujiwara Kamatari*, Tokyo, Hanawa-shobo, 1966, p. 21.

A few words might be added to describe the other Shinto classics. The *Kogoshūi (Gleanings from Ancient Stories)*, compiled in 807 A. D., presents the traditions of early Shinto as transmitted in the Imbe priestly family.

The section on 'Jingi-kan' ('Department of Kami-Affairs') of the *Ryō no Gige (Commentary on the Legal Code)*, compiled in 833 A. D., embodies the contents of various legal codes, the earliest being that of 662, and their revisions. The 'Jingi-kan' section provides regulations regarding the status, number and duties of Shinto priests and officials, important festivals of the religio-national community, as well as fixed scales of offerings and taxes for Kami-affairs.

The first ten books of the *Engi-shiki (Procedures of the Engi Era)*, compiled in 927 A. D., are by far the most complete documents regarding the institutionalized form of Shinto as developed within the framework of the *'Ritsuryo (Imperial Rescript) State'*. The contents of the first ten books are: 'Festivals of the Four Seasons' (I & II), 'Extraordinary Festivals' (III), 'The Shrine of the Great Kami in Ise' (IV), 'The Institution of the Consecrated Imperial Princess (*Itsuki-no-miya* or *Saigu*)' (V), 'Regulations concerning the Quarters of Consecrated Imperial Princess' (VI), 'Accession Ceremonies' (VII), 'The Norito or Ritual Prayers' (VIII), and 'Register of Kami' (IX & X).

The *Shinsen-shōjiroku (The New Compilation of the Register of Families)* was completed in 815 A. D. It divides the aristocracy of 8th century Japan into three arbitrary categories — descendants of heavenly and earthly kami, descendants of imperial and other royal families, and descendants of naturalized Chinese and Koreans. The Preface frankly admits the impossibility of such a task, and yet the compilers of the record 'mythologized' historic facts regarding genealogies in order to solidify the foundation of the religio-national community.

The Japanese rulers also commenced in 713 A. D. the compilation of the *Fudoki (Topographical Records)* of various provinces. Judging from the material available concerning the Provinces of Hitachi, Harima, Izumo, Hizen and Bungo, one can get valuable insights into local traditions, which had little relation to the Shinto tradition that was handed down through the imperial clan.

The *Manyōshū (Collections of Myriad Leaves)* is a collection of poems. While it was compiled in the 8th century, that is, nearly two centuries after the introduction of Sino-Korean civilization and Buddhism, the *Manyō* poems betray amazingly little effect of the continental influence. And, as was mentioned earlier, the recording of these verses by using the sound value of the Chinese scripts fostered the so-called *Manyō-gana* (a form of syllabary).

LITERARY SOURCE CRITICISM

Even such a superficial account as given above indicates the enormous difficulties involved in attempting literary source criticism of early Shinto documents. In Japan, literary source criticism of the classics was pioneered by Shimokawabe Chōryū (1624-86), Keichū (1640-1701) and Kada Azumamaro (1669-1736). It was Kamo Mabuchi (1697-1769), however, who devoted his life to the study of the *Manyōshū* and established the foundation of National Learning (*Koku-gaku*). In his advice given to the celebrated Shinto scholar, Motoori Norinaga (1730-1801), Mabuchi states: 'I, too, aspired from the outset to unravel the book of kami (that is, the *Kojiki*). But to do this, one must first free oneself from *kara gokoro* (the Chinese spirit) and seek the true spirit of antiquity. To grasp the spirit of antiquity, one must understand ancient words. To understand ancient words, one must clarify the *Man'yoshu*. Therefore, I have devoted myself to studies in the *Man'yoshu'*.[21] Inspired by Mabuchi's advice Norinaga wrote voluminous commentaries on the *Kojiki*, which had long been overshadowed by the *Nihongi*. His work has been regarded as authoritative by the subsequent scholars and the Japanese classics.

In the modern period, Japanese historical scholarship was greatly stimulated by Western historical studies, especially the school of von Ranke. In this situation, able scholars like Kume Kunitake (1839-1931) and Tsuda Sōkichi (1873-1961) engaged in textual criticism of the Japanese classics. In the words of Professor Kamstra, 'Just as the "Formgeschichtliche Schule" in the West resolved (the problem of) Holy Scripture, (Tsuda) analyzed the Japanese sources. In this way, he attempted to penetrate to historical facts which had remained hidden until now'.[22] The study of early Shinto and Japanese classics

---

21. Cited in Shigeru Matsumoto, *Motoori Norinaga 1730-1801*, Cambridge, Mass., Harvard University Press, 1970, p. 69.
22. Kamstra, *op. cit.*, p. 53.

was also aided by the contribution of a number of able Western scholars.

Unfortunately, academic freedom was greatly curtailed during World War II. However, since the end of the war a host of scholars have resumed critical studies of the myths, rituals, beliefs, literature and institutions of early Japan. One of the most interesting lines of inquiry in this respect has been pursued by scholars of early literature, poetry and history. For example, following the publication of Ishimoda Shō's essay on the 'Heroic Age' in early Japan in 1948,[23] a series of controversies have been carried on as to whether or not there was a 'Heroic Age' in Japan, and whether or not some of the legendary heroes mentioned in the *Kojiki* and *Nihongi* could be compared to Homeric heroes, based on the literary analysis of certain songs called 'Kume-uta', etc. The historian of religions who is concerned with early Shinto will benefit much from the literary source criticism of the early Shinto classics, as for example the *Kodai-kayo-ron (Essays on Ancient Songs)* by Tsuchihashi Yutaka.[24] But, how to reconcile literary source criticism and form criticism, and how to relate the study of religious documents to the study of symbols, rituals, institutions, etc., remain serious methodological problems.

KURT RUDOLPH   *The Position of Source Research in*
                    *Religious Studies (*Religionswissenschaft*)*

J. Wach's perspective division of religious studies into history of religions and comparative or systematic religion is derived from the two basic methods applied within what is the special field of religious studies (the religions, their traditions and forms of expression in history and in the present): the philological-historical and the comparative-systematic. In addition, there are sociological, psychological, and ethnological methods, which are often closely associated with the two constitutive methods mentioned. The integrity and relative autonomy of religious

23. Shō Ishimoda, 'Kodai kizoku no eiyū jidai', *Ronshū-shigaku*, Tokyo, Sanseido, 1948.

24. Kyoto, Sanitsu-shobō,1960; especially Chap. 6 'Kumeuta to eiyū monogatari: eiyū-jidai no mondai ni yosete' (I owe this citation to Prof. Manabu Waida).

studies are grounded in the dialectical application of these methods within their specialized field: it is only a balanced relationship between them, i. e. their mutually self-correcting application in the various lines of work and research, which can guarantee and help to substantiate the originality of religious studies (cf. here my comments on 'Das Problem der Autonomie und Integrität der Religionswissenschaft' in *Ned. Theol. Tijdschr.* 27 (1973), pp. 105-131).

For history of religions as a whole, the basic method is the 'philological-historical'. This refers to the working method developed in these fields, and especially in the field of source research, since the origins of scientific philology and historiography in the nineteenth century. The critical spirit of the 19th-century generations of researchers, refusing to accept the tradition without questioning it, is still fundamental today, and is thus closely connected with the successive development of modern religious studies. It is no exaggeration to state that the essential methods of enquiry for work on sources in the widest sense were established and elaborated in this period: the 20th century has brought only extensions or further development, e. g. with reference to typology. The same is true of methodology in sociology, as a glance at Marx, Engels, and Durkheim illustrates, and also in psychology, as is shown, for example, by Dilthey and Wundt. In order to form a picture of the historical method, it is therefore highly fitting to take J. G. Droysen's *Historik* of 1881, or his *Grundriss der Historik* of 1882 (both ed. R. Hübner, 1936, 6th ed. 1971). Bernheim's well-known *Lehrbuch der historischen Methode* (6th ed. 1908), is, though later, less stimulating. Droysen divides historical material into three groups: remains, sources, and monuments, each of which possesses its own original and differentiated character. It is the art of 'heuristics' to open up this material and render it fruitful for historical enquiry, with the aid of the 'ancillary sciences', including in this case philology and archeology, since these provide the basic preconditions for the historical use of the sources. Criticism of the sources proceeds in conjunction with this work, and is one of the most fundamental components of modern historical research; I would almost say the most important, for the results of historical work, as we shall see, fundamentally depend on it. The methods of source criticism are extremely varied, and have nowadays been further refined as a result of new discoveries (e. g. in the field of sociology); mastery of them forms a basic tool in the historian's equipment. 'Das

Ergebnis der Kritik', says Droysen, 'ist nicht die eigentliche historische Tatsache, sondern was von derselben an Resten, Auffassungen, usw. noch vorliegt' (*op. cit.*, p. 148); it makes possible 'eine verhältnismässig sichere und korrekte Auffassung' (*ibid.*, p. 339). What follows is interpretation, the aim of which is 'in den vergangenen Geschehnissen Wirklichkeiten mit der ganzen Fülle von Bedingnissen, die ihre Verwirklichung und Wirklichkeit forderte, zu sehen' (*ibid.*). It is only interpretation that allows the material to 'speak' (cf. *ibid.*, p. 152). There are a large number of forms of interpretation, which could also be categorized under 'hermeneutics'; Droysen mentions 'pragmatic interpretation', 'the interpretation of conditions' (which includes technological and nowadays economic interpretation), 'psychological interpretation', and 'the interpretation of the powers of ideas and morals', which expresses for him the core of his idealistic basic position. All of these exegetical approaches are still in use, reinforced by newer ones, in particular by sociological interpretation and by the critical interpretation of ideology.

This brief characterization of the historical method on the basis of one of its classic exponents is intended to illustrate the basis on which work in history of religions has so far relied, insofar as it applies itself to this method. What must be done now is to show how far modern religious studies (1) must continue to rely on this 'classical model', in order to subsist as a historical science, while on the other hand (2) demonstrating their originality. What is particularly important here is (3) to establish the position of source research in history of religions.

1. Since the religions, in their historical form, with all their historically accessible tradition and forms of expression, are the primary object of religious studies (as a disciplinary description), then insofar as they wish to be taken seriously as scholarship, they must first work with the customary philological and historical methods.

In the case of periods and cultures which made no distinction between a religious and profane sphere in the modern sense (such as all the old traditional religions), the historian of religions has available for his purposes almost the entire surviving material, including religious buildings and monuments; in the case of religions still in existence, he has in addition the present living expressions, such as cults, community life, etc. The most important literature with a specifically religious character or an unambiguously religious function consists of the following: holy scriptures (in various literary genres), rituals, hymns, prayers, homilies, dramas, 'historical' writings (chronicles, hagiographies, and the like), mythologies (collections of myths), and theological writings (including apologetics). The progressive separation of religion, culture, and society (e. g. in the world religions) also leads to the stronger development of an autonomous religious literature.

The majority of these 'sources' are not fundamentally distinct from the other material available to the historian. There is, at first, no need for a special heuristic and hermeneutic method to open up these sources: the texts must be edited and prepared according to philological and critical procedure, including translation, and the first stage of their commentary and exegesis, e. g. with reference to chronology, authorship, structure, etc., follows the usual historical rules.

The type of source analysis and historical evaluation most commonly employed recently in several branches of religious studies is research into tradition and the history of form. This type of research was first tried out and developed in Old Testament scholarship, and later extended to the New Testament and early Christian literature. It has sadly only been applied very timidly so far in the other relevant areas of religious studies. Its aim is the elucidation of specific clusters of traditions, with the aid of stylistic, formal, and genre-historical criteria (which have in some cases first been elaborated in the methods of this research) and of the statements, e. g. teachings, contained in the text. There can be no doubt about the extraordinary fruitfulness of this method, but it cannot continue in the long run without relaying on literary criticism and history, i. e. on the source as actually transmitted.

This literary criticism belongs to the oldest procedures of philological research, dating back to Alexandrian times. Since the appearance of history of tradition and genre, it has frequently retreated in importance, and has in fact often been violently rejected; nevertheless, it continues to be an important tool for the source researcher, in particular because it remains much more closely tied to the actual transmitted text, and remains within the chronological-historical framework. This latter is very frequently not observed in research on history of tradition, which works of necessity on the hypothesis of either oral or written traditions which it is often impossible to define closely, e. g. in Gnostic research. For this reason, closer cooperation between history of tradition and literary criticism and history will be necessary in the future.

A further working method, which has long been well established especially in research on legends, is motif research, which traces the 'migration' and use of specific forms of expression, technical terms, pictorial language or symbols, phrases and phraseology, i. e. of *topoi*, in order to be able to deduce a traditional connection. This method has also repeatedly justified itself, but it embodies serious dangers, whenever it is followed in too much isolation from the literary context and the historical chronology; its results are only convincing and usable in connection with the history of literature and of tradition, and with source criticism in general.

Closely associated with motif and tradition research, and with their sources of error, there is also 'pattern research'. This was stimulated by Anglo-American cultural anthropology, and has been especially pursued in Uppsala; it has proved extremely fruitful for work in history of religions in the last few decades, especially in the Middle East. The 'patterns' which it traces in the historical tradition from their (usually hardly recognizable) beginnings to the decadent final forms, are frequently only recognizable through daring reconstruction and hypotheses. This procedure could be described as 'archeological': for instead of being satisfied with a statement found, in a meaningful form, in a given context, it reflects on the ultimate origins (which are often prehistorical, and ethnologically verified), and attempts to understand the present meaning in terms of its hypothetical beginnings (e. g. Old Testament passages, for instance in the Psalms, in terms of the ancient oriental ideology of sacral kings); in other words, it creates a semantic link which actually only exists for the consciousness of the modern researcher. Pattern research is very close to general history of ideas; one could treat it as a variation of the latter. Like the latter, it pays too little attention to the changes that can take place as a result of the adoption of this kind of set forms of thought ('ideas', 'patterns', or 'topoi') into a different context, and to their historical and social relevance.

The same can be said about structural research as about motif and pattern research. With its aim of fathoming the inner 'tissue' of a historical or philological phenomenon, this kind of research has been practiced for a long time, but under other names (e. g. 'Gestalt' or 'system') and using different working methods. It makes its appearance nowadays, however, with completely new ambitions and methods of enquiry.

Structural research has been fed by French structuralism. It has been particularly prominent in the field of the analysis of myths and rites, and less so in the field of history of religions proper (with the exception of structuralist interpretations of literary texts of religious origin). As a combination of sociology and Indo-Germanic philology or linguistics, the structural research of G. Dumézil opened up new aspects of religious studies, to my knowledge before C. Lévi-Strauss, and initiated a discussion that is still continuing today. It is this branch which is, provisionally, the prime object for criticism, since it has published an elaborated model: the 'tripartite world of thought' of the Indo-Europeans. Its basic assumption of a kind of 'schema' leads it to leap too quickly over source research from a historical-chronological and critical point of view, and to put down roots in places where no soil has been identified to grow in. This kind of structural research is an attempt to carry out a historical enterprise with non-historical means; it ultimately depends on, and takes refuge in, the functioning of an incomprehensible — because unconscious — structure of consciousness. Nevertheless, it has provided many stimuli, and will continue to do so, especially if — as appears to be the case — it more and more firmly reintegrates the historical enterprise in its calculations, i. e. if it understands historical events and structure as a dialectical 'conflict', without which the perception of the object is impossible. 'Die zwiefache Betrachtungsweise des wissenschaftlichen Objekts wird uns nicht mehr wie ein ausschliesslicher, nicht zu beseitigender Gegensatz erscheinen, sondern als wesentliche Bedingung des Fortschritts'.[25]

On another track, on the other hand, there is a more traditional structural research, which sets out to grasp the 'assembly' ('Gefüge': S. Morenz) or the 'disposition' ('Habitus': W. Baetke) of a religion or religious phenomenon, by means of a combination of historical and phenomenological work, as we shall show later (p. 106). This research is concerned with structure as an organic unity.[26]

The newest method to become available to history of religions stems from modern linguistics, which has developed a textual semantics, linguistics, or grammar which analyzes religious texts as 'Objekt im Spiegel

25. G. Granger, in his suggestive article 'Geschehen und Struktur in den Wissenschaften vom Menschen', 1959; German ed. in *Der moderne Strukturbegriff*, ed. by H. Naumann, Darmstadt, 1973 (Wege der Forschung CLV), pp. 207-248; cf. also A. J. Greimas, 'Struktur und Geschichte', *ibid.*, pp. 421-434.
26. Cf. Granger, *op. cit.*, p. 210.

textlinguistischer Kategorien'.[27] To my knowledge, however, such questions have to date only been put with the purposes of linguistics itself and of theology in mind,[28] and they cannot therefore be dealt with at greater length here. This approach will be necessary in future, however, for the working-out of a formal theory of the interpretation of religious texts, and the primary interest will fall on general semantics in religious texts, i. e. the meaning they convey. It should be observed that the 'religious' element in such texts can only be seen, from a linguistic point of view, in terms of function or pragmatics, and has accordingly been termed a 'textpragmatische Kategorie'.[29]

Finally we must point out the possibility of trying out 'multivariate factor analysis' in religious studies, in cases where adequate constituents are available to make this kind of analysis seem worthwhile. Up to now, such procedures have only been used in order to make the contents of religious texts more accessible through the provision of an improved index and glossary (e. g. for the Koran). It would be worth enquiring whether this method, which has been developed in cybernetics and data processing for the analysis and recognition of repeated events and statements, could not also be deployed within comparative religion. An internationally-organized working project of this type could achieve an enormous reduction of labor for several generations to come by mastering the mass of material, and set comparative religion on a genuinely universal basis, not to mention the scientific exactitude and insight into new connections that would be gained (perhaps even a mathematical structure, which would allow thematization on a geometrical model). The major difficulty would be the actual programming itself.

2. The working methods described here which are now being used, or offered for use, in history of religions, confirm the fact that for history of religions to work appropriately, it must rely on historical science and philology. Its originality, which is what we shall now investigate, also depends on three further components:

---

27. Cf. P. Hartmann, in *Sprache und Sprachverständnis in religiöser Rede*, ed. by Th. Michels and A. Paus, Munich, 1973, pp. 109-134.

28. Cf. *ibid.*, pp. 85 ff., 135 ff., 171 ff.

29. Cf. P. Hartmann, *op. cit.*, p. 116.

— the objective: the object, i. e. religions and their phenomena;[30]
— the methodological: the dialectical combination of specialized research and comparison (comparatistics, systematics, phenomenology), i. e. of specialized and general working methods;
— the ideologically critical: the dispute, from the point of view of historically-gained insights, with the religions' own self-understanding, and the decisive demarcation of the differences from individual theologies (dogmatisms) and religious movements.

In this context we can only go into detail about the second component, the methodological one.

The 'hermeneutic circle' often invoked in religious studies, first conjured up by Schleiermacher, and later by Dilthey and now Gadamer, is of limited value as a methodological principle, and has just recently been interpreted as a kind of rationalization of the 'minority complex of the humanities' in relation to the natural sciences.[31] Its affinity to Hegel's idealistic dialectic (especially in the *Phenomenology of Mind*) can easily be demonstrated.[32] The epistemological relativism cultivated out of this 'vicious circle' leads not so much to historical understanding, as to non-perception, i.e. to the denial of objective perception altogether. Observation of the time- and place-bound nature (bias of interests!) which led to this circle and its history of operation (which is its main justification) being transformed all the way into a method, forces one to the conclusion that these limitations need to be adequately reflected on and objectivized in order to achieve objective historical perception.[33]

The equally common invocation of 'feelings' as a means of perception in religious studies must also be ruled out, since such irrationalism makes a mockery of scientific verification, which can only operate in terms of articulated and demonstrable judgments.[34] Subjective, emotional interpretation does not represent a perception of real connections:

30. Cf. my paper 'Das Problem der Autonomie und Integrität der Religionswissenschaft', mentioned p. 99 above, pp. 108 ff.
31. W. Becker, *Hegels Phänomenologie des Geistes*, Stuttgart, 1971, pp. 12-16.
32. *Ibid.*
33. Cf. the critique by Betti in *Die Hermeneutik als allgemeine Methodik der Geisteswissenschaften*, Tübingen, 2nd ed. 1972, pp. 20 ff., 34 f., 40, 51; and H. Albert, 'Theorie, Verstehen und Geschichte', *Zeitschrift für Allgemeine Wissenschaftstheorie*, I (1970), pp. 2-23.
34. Cf. Betti, *op. cit.*, p. 25.

'sie zeugt nur von der psychologischen Genesis einer Hypothese im Geiste des Historikers'.[35]

All textual interpretation also depends on a whole series of previous decisions, which in many cases are based on unobjectivized theoretical assumptions: these include, for example, even the identification of the source as a source, and the determination of its significance.[36] The hermeneutic working methods described above in section 1 illustrate this: their theoretical preconditions determine not only the interpretation of the sources, but their choice as well. They should therefore be applied in as complex a way as possible, in order to ensure some degree of reliable perception.

The interweaving of comparative (general) and specialized working methods, which is characteristic − or ought to be so − of religious studies, also applies to source research in this field, as the following considerations indicate.

The philological-historical method does admittedly represent the essential and main means of work in history of religions, but it is inadequate by itself, and requires supplementation by the comparative-systematic method. For history of religions, interpretations and readings need to be not only philologically and historically plausible, but also 'religionswissenschaftlich', i.e. they must do justice to the results of comparative-systematic religious studies.[37]

The historian of religions needs therefore to complement his philological and historical work with the endeavor to keep as wide a range of analogical or parallel phenomena in mind as possible, so as to be able to approach the investigation of the individual phenomenon in ways that go beyond the limits of simple philology and history and also simultaneously contribute to the finer definition and operationalization of the technical terms of religious studies.

An important tool in this procedure is the 'typological' method, which starts from the historical data, but − for reasons of systematic methodology (generalization) − moves on from them to reach forward to an overall perception. Max Weber attempted this with his idealistic-typical working method, which J. Wach has adopted for the field of

---

35. *Ibid.*
36. Cf. H. Albert, *op. cit.*, p. 18.
37. Cf. for example Baetke, *Kleine Schriften*, Weimar, 1973, p. 213.

religious studies. The dangers of this method are well-known (the bed of Procrustes!), and I myself have pointed them out in various places previously; what we are concerned with here is its usefulness in the task of history of religions.

Several of the methods described above (p. 102-104) rely on the inclusion of comparative-systematic work, i. e. cannot be applied successfully without this. To some extent, then, we obtain for source research in religious studies a specific working method, which one could call complex or combined, a point of intersection, as it were, between the diachronic and the synchronic.

Let us take, as an example, the investigation of magic. Starting from the task of investigating a special area (for instance magic in Greco-Roman culture) on the basis of the available material, the historian of religions (in contrast to the classicist) has the additional task of obtaining aids to interpretation from both related and more distant religious and cultural areas (for instance from the Middle East), in order (a) to achieve a better understanding of the singularity of the specific object of enquiry (i. e. Greco-Roman magic, presuming that this can be proved to exist); and to contribute to (b) the establishment of convergences, parallels and influences, and (c) to the clarification of magic in general. A large number of religious phenomena may be investigated in this manner. I hold the same position here, in relation to comparative studies, as Goethe once formulated: 'Wir sollten, dünkt mich, immer mehr beobachten, worin sich die Dinge, zu deren Erkenntnis wir gelangen mögen, voneinander unterscheiden, als wodurch sie einander gleichen'.[38]

3. As my comments indicate, source research occupies a dominant position in religious studies. It is the 'basis' of their work, on which the 'superstructure' of comparative-systematic religion and of phenomenology of religion depend.[39] Geo Widengren has just recently in an essay illustrated very well the value of source criticism for history of religions, using the example of biographical data about the founders of the great religions.[40]

---

38. 'Die Natur', *Werke* X, p. 369. Cf. also my above mentioned paper 'Das Problem der Autonomie', p. 118 ff.

39. On the relationship of these two concepts, cf. my comments, *op. cit.*, p. 121 ff.

40. *Historia Religionum*, ed. by Bleeker and Widengren, I (1969), pp. 1-22; cf. my review, in *ThLZ* 98 (1973), col. 413 ff.

The priority of source research results from the fact that advances or new discoveries in this field frequently lead to, or should lead to, a change or shift in the field of comparative-systematic religion or in phenomenology of religion. Since this unfortunately does not always happen, comparative religion frequently finds itself being scientifically discredited. I am thinking, for example, of the typological definitions given by G. van der Leeuw for the religions in his *Phänomenologie der Religion*, which rely on a very one-sided, subjective, and preferential selection of secondary literature. Similarly, Heiler's descriptions of the divinities of death and resurrection in his *Wesen und Erscheinungsformen der Religion* cannot stand up to expert examination.[41]

Just how fundamentally source research, and in particular its supreme form, source criticism, enters into religious studies is shown for example by W. Baetke's work in the field of Germanic religious history. His demonstration that the dynastic sagas (*ættsögur*) are legendary and above all poetic in character, and moreover dependent on Christian ecclesiastical and late classical thought (as had previously been demonstrated in the case of the Edda) penetrates directly into the definition of the essence of Germanic religion, and thus indirectly into comparative religion. There are thousands of such examples.

Recently new sides of Christian religious history have been opened up, both through the discovery of new texts from the beginnings (I refer to the Gnostic codices of Nag Hammadi), and for the Middle Ages through a deeper fundamental investigation of the heretical movements, which will have considerable significance for religious studies. The Leipzig medievalist, E. Werner, has applied the approach of history of religions in close combination with sociological (Marxist) analysis, and produced important contributions to a new picture of medieval church history.

The old controversy as to whether the Gnostic world religion of Manicheism originated as a Christian heresy or in Iran has been resolved beyond question by the appearance of a new source (the Cologne Mani Codex) in favor of the former view, as had already been indicated by the Coptic texts from Medinet Madi.[42]

41. Cf. P. Lambrechts, *Med. Kon. Vlaams Acad. Wet. Kl. der Lett.*, XXVI, Nr. 6, Brussels, 1964.
42. Cf. my essay in the *Mélanges d'histoire des religions offerts à H.-Ch. Puech*, Paris, 1974, p. 471-486.

In history of religions, the undeniable fundamental task of source research can however only proceed when the demands of comparative-systematic religion are taken into account as set out above (p. 106-107), unless, that is, religious studies are to 'get stuck' at the level of philological-historical processing. That was why I spoke of a kind of dialectic between history of religions and comparative-systematic religion, which demarcates their working methods: history of religions delimits the generalizations and summaries of comparative-systematic religion (or phenomenology of religion), but the latter extend the work of history of religions in specialized fields into a universal frame of reference, and contribute to the process of discovery: there is both give and take.

In conclusion, I would not like to finish these brief remarks on some of the methodological problems of history of religions without recalling that, as N. Hartmann has so clearly put it, there is 'keine vorgreifende Methodenerkenntnis vor der Sachkenntnis, deren Methode sie zum Gegenstand macht' (*Das Problem des geistigen Seins*, 3rd ed. 1962, p. 30). Every method is 'allemal bedingt durch den Gegenstand einerseits und durch die Struktur des verwickelten Aktes, den wir Erkenntnis nennen, anderseits' (*ibid.*). Both factors are valid, without reservations. Every object requires, then, in the concrete sense, its own method, which science ceaselessly works on: not abstractly, but practically, in its devotion to its object and its proper area of study. 'Die Methode erwächst ihr unter den Händen in der Arbeit an der Sache' (*ibid.*, p. 31). Knowledge of the subject, and awareness of methodology, go hand in hand. Therefore: 'Alles Wissen um die Methode ist sekundär, Sache nachträglicher Reflexion' (*ibid.*). Once it has been raised to reflection, however, it determines further progress in the knowledge of the subject, by which it is in turn, however, controlled. These observations point directly towards problems discussed in other sections of our symposium, however. It would be welcome if a subdiscipline were founded within religious studies for this purpose, primarily dedicated to the questions of 'Theory' and of 'Research on Basic Principles'.

Commentary   by Ileana Chirassi Colombo

1. With reference to Prof. Kitagawa's most interesting paper, I must state in advance that unfortunately my knowledge of the problems relating to early Shinto is too superficial to allow a thorough discussion in this peculiar field. I can however offer evidence that analogous, even if not similar, problems arise when we are dealing with source criticism referring to archaic Greek religion. We can avoid the superficial comparison, which has already been made at the level of common mythical motifs like the Izanagi = Orpheus theme. Like archaic Japan, archaic Greece offers to the historian of religions many sources which cannot be considered canonical or sacred scripture, but which have the greatest interest as they deal with myth. I mean the Homeric Poems (Iliad and Odyssey), the Hesiodic Poems (Works and Days and Theogony), the Hesiodic Corpus including the Catalogues of women and Eoiae, the Poems of the Epic Cycle including various poems relating to the fall of Troy as well as different arguments like the War of the Titans, the Oidipodeia or the Story of Oedipus, the whole Theban Epic and other items which survived only in indirect and late tradition,[43] the so-called Homeric Hymns, a later collection in which the five major hymns can be dated roughly from the 8th to the 7th century B. C. for the Hymn to Dionysos. All this extant production is under the huge shadow of the lost poetry which can be regained only through new discoveries or the possible but difficult new collation of the late quotations as in the case of the 'Orphic Literature'.[44] On the whole all this can be assumed to represent the set of the hexameter poetry, near which lyric poetry holds a position of its own, and appears on the documentary level a little later.[45]

Since the studies of Milman Parry, already old, the discovery of the

43. For a new collection of Greek epic fragments see Huxley, *Greek Epic Poetry*, London, 1969, passim.

44. The unique collection still available is Kern, *Orphicorum Graecorum Fragmenta*, Berlin (1923), 1963 — The problem of Orpheus, Orphism, and the chronology is still an open question (see F. Böhme, *Orpheus*, Bern, 1970, passim).

45. On the possible chronological primacy of lyric poetry rooted in the lost periods of the 'Oral' culture, see C. Gallavotti, *Atti e Memorie del Primo Convegno di Micenologia*, II, p. 853, Roma, 1968.

formulaic structure of the Greek hexameter, the typical meter of the epic poetry, has called the attention of scholars to the oral beginnings of Greek hexameter poetry, that is of the great part of the early Greek mythical tradition. The subsequent decipherment of the Linear B Tablets revealing the existence of a Greek-speaking culture which seems to have used writing only for administrative purposes in the Greek bronze age has given support to Parry's theory, while raising new problems.[46] The existence of the polytheistic pantheon in the Bronze Age where it was possible to find many names of deities familiar to Greek historical religion many centuries later has aroused the well-founded opinion of the presence of a rich mythology which could have survived as oral tradition through the so-called Dark Age after the collapse of Mycenaean power about the 13th century B. C. or a little later.[47]

As it is beyond any doubt that Mycenaean tradition perpetuated itself in linguistic as well as in different cultural aspects of Greek truly historical civilization, we cannot deny the persistence of poetic and in this case mythical traditions handed down to the limit of the X − IX − VIII century B. C. when most probably epic poetry and in a larger sense hexameter poetry became to be patterned approximately in the way we have it in the Homeric and Hesiodic corpus. Since hexameter poetry and especially epic poetry appears as a complex result of manifold linguistic and cultural experiences,[48] we must suppose that many things were modified during the cultural developments so that even

46. See Notopoulos, *Homer, Hesiod and the Achean Heritage of Oral Poetry*, Hesperia, 1960, p. 177 ff.; Kirk, *The Songs of Homer*, Cambridge, 1962; for a presentation and discussion of theories also J. B. Hainsworth *The Flexibility of the Homeric Formula*, Oxford, 1968, passim; M. Durantesulla, *Preistoria della Tradizione Poetica Greca*, Roma, 1971, passim.

47. Even after a severe criticism the presence of the following names on the Linear B tablets can be considered sure: Zeus (diwe), Poseidon (Poseidao), Dionysos (Diwonusajo), Enyalios (Enuwario), Hephaistos (Apaito), Ares (Are), Hera (Era), Diwia (Dia), Erinys (Erinu), Eileithyia (Ereutija). We can add also the similarity in religious terminology revealed by words like: ijereja - ijereu = hiereia - hiereus, priestess and priest, ijero = hieron = temple - sacred place, shrine; the frequent use of potinia, potnia, an epiclasis of goddess like potinija Asiwija = potnia Asia (Athena Asia?). We must add also the presence of the name teo = theos = god and the significative plural *pasiteoi* = to all gods.

48. M. Durante, *op. cit.*, p. 1 'I Poemi Omerici sono il punto di arrivo di una lunga vicenda di esperienze'; the same can be said of all hexameter poetry as well as for the early lyric.

mythology could have been manipulated to meet new formal and historical requirements.

This is of the greatest importance for the historian of religions because hexameter texts dealing with myth are the first available source concerning religious problems in a historical perspective even if, like the early Shinto documents, they are not canonically recognized as such. Prof. Kirk rightly points out in his last book on the analysis of myth that the Iliad, even if it concerns the roughly historical fact of an Achean expedition to Asia Minor, is to be considered on the whole actually mythical. We have to note in fact that the fall of Troy always appears to have been consistently chosen as the dividing-line between a previous mythical time and a subsequent historical one by poets as well as by the first logographoi and historians.[49]

As in the case of the Japanese *Kojiki* and *Nihongi* the matter of Greek hexameter poetry looks more historico-mythical (that is, 'heroic') rather than purely 'religious'. Now the modern analysis of myth as fostered by formalism and structuralism can give a great help for the historical approach to such problems. First of all it must be pointed out that the main problem is to look at the text itself as it appears and try to catch the exact meaning involved. Secondly it is suggested that no distinction should be made between the so-called religious myths (myths of gods) and heroic myths or legends (myths where human beings are involved): gods and human beings are both to be considered as mythical categories acting as such on the mythical level according to mythical 'laws'. Thirdly it is suggested that myth as an independent activity of mind may coincide with religion insofar as a religion system, like a mythological system, tries to give a taxonomic, that is, an ordered interpretation of human reality.

In this sense Herodotus' statement about poets like Homer and Hesiod as religious teachers is of the greatest importance: 'these (Homer and Hesiod) are they who taught the Greeks the descent of the gods and gave to all their several names, and honors, and arts, and declared their outward forms'.[50] This acknowledgment of the religious value of myth

---

49. Kirk, *Myth, its Meaning and Functions*, Cambridge, 1970, p. 33; see also I. Chirassi Colombo 'Morfologia di Zeus' (to be published); idem 'Heros Achilleus/Theos Apollon', paper presented to the Convegno sull'analisi della mitologia classica, Urbino, 7-12 maggio 1973.

50. Herod. II, 53 (transl. A. D. Godley, Loeb ed.).

is quite important to understand the active role of poets, *aoidoi*, which we can easily translate as mythtellers in pre-literate and early literate Greece.[51] The equation myth = religion is not contradicted by the so-called allegorical hermeneusis of Homeric texts as it appears in a fragment of Theagenes of Regium, VI B. C. (in schol. Hom. B ad Il XX, 67; Porph. Quaest. Hom. I, 240,14). This rather testifies the beginning of a split in a myth making society and the existence of an already stratified and multi-levelled cultural reality. In any case allegorical hermeneusis of myth which can follow through the whole antiquity until our days always signifies the religious relevance of myth itself.[52] To come back to what is our main concern, the first problem for the historian of religions is how to make use of the mythical texts for his aims, in this case how to understand religious structure or archaic Greece. For this purpose there may be in a certain sense only minor importance, even if always some importance, in the typical research about the origin of this or that name, or of this or that theme. That is to say for instance that after having established that there is more than one typology in common between Hesiod's *Theogony* and the correspondent mythical traditions in Mesopotamic, Phoenician and Hittite poetry, the historian of religions must be aware that the Hesiodic text has a structure and a meaning of its own, and full autonomy, and that his task is to deal with textual significance in relation to the culture which is being considered. This will prove to be the real historico-religious approach to the text itself.

Notwithstanding the analogies already hinted at, the Japanese early texts like the *Kojiki* and *Nihongi* are in a very different position from the early Greek written sources. We know they were collected and written down by imperial order, that is, we know the function this mythology was supposed to assume in support of an imperial ideology. Many things in the internal disposal of the roles of personages can be explained within this perspective, even if, of course, to gain the pure mythical message, we can omit this secondary function.

There is nothing similar in Greece, where we can have serious doubts about Homer and even Hesiod as fully historical personages, and where

51. *aoidòs* which is the only word used in the significance of poet in Homer is the true oral singer, as it can be considered the *nomen agentis* of *aeido*.
52. Jean Pépin, *Mythe et Allégorie*, Paris, 1958.

we don't find until much later a centralized political power which could express and support anything similar to the religious-national community which developed in Japan from the 4th-5th centuries A.D. downward. It is quite interesting however to ask what role we may ascribe to the wandering poet, the *aoidòs*, in the Greek world during the centuries which followed the Mycenaean collapse. In a certain sense we may assign to the *aoidòs* a great part in the development of a common supertribal poetry acting as a catalyzing unitary force on the linguistic as well as on the ideological level.[53] It is quite interesting in this regard that hexameter couplets appeared frequently among the earliest inscriptions in Greece since the second half of the 8th century.[54] This can be assumed as proof of the existence of a widespread ancient common poetical tradition, to which we must assign the memorization and, from a certain point onward, the transcription of different pieces of mythology at a literary level.[55] What is impossible to define is the reason why at a certain point writing was adopted on a large and regular scale, and not only for administrative reasons as in Mycenaean times. The answer to this question can be given on different levels as we can try to explain on different levels the sudden disappearance of the Mycenaean syllabic writing and the different alphabetic system which came into use four centuries after. What we can maintain is that writing does not necessarily affect the formal narrative structure of myth even if at a certain point writing could have helped to establish a standardized tradition active at the educational and political level.

   Up to a certain point we can even suppose that writing helped to

53. Durante, *op. cit.*, p. 158 ff.; Kirk, 'The Songs', *op. cit.*, p. 58 ff.

54. L. H. Jeffery, *The Local Scripts of Archaic Greece*, Oxford, 1961, p. 68, pl. 1; p. 90, pl. 7; p. 235, pl. 47; p. 245, pl. 45. Of particular interest is the so-called Nestor cup of Ischia bearing an hexameter inscription referring to the well-known passage in the XI book of the Iliad.

55. The link between the poet and Memory was felt as an active one even during the literary period: the poet is always protected by the Muses, the daughters of Mnemosyne. At the same time different facts confirm the persistence of an oral poetical tradition through more recent centuries. Epic poems were sung during the Nemean games by the so-called Homeridai, a *genos* or corporation of *aoidoi* of the Island of Chios, about which we have a lot of interesting but rather confusing data (see Wade-Geri, *The Poet of the Iliad*, Cambridge, 1952. To this we may add the mythical tales in prose which could have been conveyed to the first prosa-writers, the logographoi (see Wardmann, 'Myth in Greek Historiography', *Historia*, 1960, p. 430 ff.).

establish a standard pantheon, the Olympic one, as a common religious feature in archaic and classical Greece. In any case we have to note that Greek tradition does not possess fixed 'liturgical' collections like the Japanese *Norito*. The so-called Homeric Hymns, which are in praise of different gods of the pantheon, cannot be considered in any way prayers, but rather pieces of mythical narrative, the oldest ones at least. This fact may be further proof of the religious significance accorded to myth in the broadest sense of the word. So the first task of the historian of religions dealing with an archaic piece of myth is to use a method of analysis which could give him the meaning of myth, that is the basic meaning of his text.

The philological as well as the purely historical methods have to be accompanied by an analysis which takes into account the narrative structure and the semantic taxonomy involved. We will give a short and incomplete example of the usefulness of an approach of this kind to the text.

If we choose one of the Homeric Hymns, the Hymn to Aphrodite which is numbered fifth in the A.H.S. edition, we can make the following remarks: a purely philological and historical approach will give a lot of contradictory notes, which will not help us to fix the date or the place of the composition except with a certain degree of uncertainty.[56] What is true is that the language makes frequent use of the common formular structure involved in hexameter poetry (we can add oral as well as written poetry) while the content assures us of a widespread cult to the goddess Aphrodite especially centered in the eastern Mediterranean area. But a 'deep' reading could make us aware of the rich 'logical' significance of the Aphrodite sphere in Greek mythical thought.

We will see that we do not need to pay too much attention to the hypothesis that the hymn was composed at the suggestion of a supposed court on the Aegean coast of Asia Minor who could have been interested in renewing an old tradition about the divine birth of the ancestor Aeneas as a peculiar support for claims of supremacy. This hypothesis is

---

56. Allen Halliday, *Sikes*, 1936, 2, Oxford, comment p. 347 ff. We chose this hymn even if it is considered later among the major hymns of the Corpus, because it has been largely discussed from a philologico-historical point of view in recent times and because of certain particular features (see E. Heitsch *Aphroditen Hymnos, Aeneas und Homer*, Göttingen, 1965, passim; A. Hoekstra, *The Sub-Ethic Stage of the Formulaic Tradition*, London, 1969, p. 39 ff.)

obviously based on the prophecy of eternal kingship assured to Anchises'
descent in Hymn v. 196-7, equated to the analogous prophecy in Iliad
Y 307, and it is much more 'mythical' than 'historical'.[57] I will briefly
summarize the content: the poet affirms his wish to sing to golden
Aphrodite, who can subdue all creatures, even the immortal gods. Only
three hearts she cannot bend: Athena, who delights in wars and first
taught craftsmen to make chariots of war and cars and maidens to know
goodly arts in the house; Artemis, the huntress who loves archery and
the slaying of wild beasts and the cities of right men; and Hestia, the
first born and the youngest too of the children of Kronos, who refused
marriage and obtained from Zeus high honor in the midst of the house
instead of marriage. In order to punish Aphrodites' presumption, Zeus
casts upon her the desire for a mortal man so that she should not be
innocent of mortal love. So she fell in love with the handsome Anchises,
who was tending cattle on Mount Ida. To meet him the goddess filled
herself with fragrance and covered herself with gold, and then went to
Mt Ida, followed by wild beasts who mated together in the wilderness.
She appeared to the godlike shepherd disguised as a mortal woman,
claiming to be a Phrygian princess whom Hermes had stolen away to be
Anchises' wife. Anchises is suddenly seized by love and lies with her,
not really knowing what he is doing. The goddess puts soft sleep upon his
eyes, only afterwards revealing her true being. She also announces that
a son will be born who will reign among the Trojans, and his children's
children after him. His race will be the most like to the gods of all mortal
men in beauty and stature. They will be dear to the gods like Ganymede
who was stolen away by Zeus to be the immortal cup-bearer of the
gods; or Tithonus whom Eos carried away giving him the gift of immortality without avoiding the obsessive presence of an eternal old
age. Aphrodite will not give immortality to Anchises and his child will

57. Wade-Gery, *op. cit.*, p. 24, n. 62; Cassola, *La Ionia nel Mondo Miceneo*, Na-
poli, 1957, p. 67, n. e. The references in ancient writers are too slight to give any
real support. Even the famous passage in Strabo (607c) where it is stated that two
families of Skepsis, a town near Mount Ida, claimed descent from Scamandrius the
son of Hektor and Ascanius the son of Aineias to hold certain royal prerogatives
until recent times, must be considered cautiously. The claim may rather be considered as the mythical *ktiseis* assigned to various heroes of the Trojan war on their way
home in late sources. Here we can see myth as a charter to evaluate an established
situation. But against Malinowski, this is only a secondary meaning of myth, even
if an important one!

be reared by the long living nymphs who rank between mortals and immortals. Lastly the goddess forbids the hero to reveal the real birth of Aineias, otherwise Zeus will smite him with a thunderbolt. The tale ends on this frightening tabu which gives room for a further movement of the narrative in the sequence prohibition-infraction.

The piece is built with all the common themes of the Greek mythology: we can see with Kirk the punishment of presumption, the trick of disguise, the love between a mortal and a goddess. We cannot however stop at this 'thematic simplicity'. There is something else in the narrative structure which appears interesting in the context of a wider evaluation of myth with regard to Greek religious features. Applying a kind of Proppian analysis we can follow the procedure of the mythical language as it appears in a large part of Greek mythology. It can be summarized according to Greimas in the sequence A F non c = imposition vs acceptance; reaction vs fullfilment; consequence.[58] The role of actors however is here of primary importance to gain the inner significance that is the structure which takes in charge and distributes the meaning at the semantic level. The first sequence develops a series of semantic oppositions subject-antisubject which defines the Olympic role of Aphrodite. We can read the oppositions in the semiotic carré where we can put

Aphrodite	Athena		$S1$		$S2$
		as			
Artemis	Hestia		$\overline{S2}$		$\overline{S1}$

involving:

free love	maidenhood as state
himeros *peithos* *apate*	technical skill in housekeeping activities and in warrior arts
free wilderness	cultural life

58. Greimas, *Sémantique structurale*, Paris, 1966.

free maidenhood as state	maidenhood as established choice
hunting	antimarriage
song and dancing	special honors
polis	*oikos*
no free wilderness	cultural life
cultural life	

Reciprocal interchanges between these oppositions define the relative evaluation of female status on the ground of the main opposition nature/culture. It oscillates from the super-evaluation of Aphrodite's status which reflects a feminine super-freedom at sexual level beyond the limits of legal *gamos*, that is for Greek thought beyond the limits of cultural life (legal *gamos* is hinted at by Aphrodite only in the fictitious speech to Anchises), to the super-choice of Hestia. On a rapport of contradiction she denies sexuality, exalting the high position of an integral feminine status as a countermark of the unity and fixity of the *oikos*.[59] In this semantic space the value expressed by Artemis and Athena on the level of an antisexual attitude signifies: (1) the display of a 'civic' life in a condition of no-nature where wild beasts can be hunted; (2) the display of technical crafts which matches the report of contrariety with the sphere of *himeros* and *apate* to support the *kosmesis* of Aphrodite.

These oppositions don't exploit the whole range of situations regarding the first cultural problem: marriage/no marriage/anti-marriage. The set should be completed with the examination of the mythical role of Demeter and Hera on this level. This however is out of our present purposes.

Aphrodite acting in connection with *apate*, deception, appears involved in an ambiguous situation on the syntax level: in a double sequence she is the punished and the punisher, appearing as the object given to the hero Anchises by Zeus and as the subject who gives the Aineias object to Anchises as a gift according to a schema: D − O − D2. This structure is quite interesting because involves the whole of heroic Greek mythology where the hero acts at a same time as the winner and the victim.[60]

59. On the value of Hestia in this sense see the interesting article by J. P. Vernant, 'Hestia − Hermes', *Homme*, 1963, p. 12 ff.

60. See on this peculiar aspect of Greek mythology, I. Chirassi Colombo, 'Heros Achilleus − Theos Apollon', *op. cit.*

The double situation of Aphrodite is marked on the semantic level by the value of *apate* detailed as *eoikòs* and *homoios* (Anchises is *démas athanatoisin eoikòs* and Aphrodite appears *parthénō adméte mégethos kai eidós homoíē*).[61] Anchises acts *ou sapha eidos*, his experience appears as an oneiric happening where the power of *erōs* can join the furthest opposition between men and gods. Reality on the contrary is marked by the newly established distance between the two categories: the awakened Anchises is the hero-victim and the receiver of the gift of posterity through a famous genealogy. This position of reciprocity men—gods is better defined by the most important opposition mortal—immortal, which plays a prominent role in the organization of Greek mythology.[62]

Anchises will not receive immortality from Aphrodite, but as he is dear to the gods, he will have posterity. Myth faces the problem of mortality vs immortality on a multiple semantic level which blurs the simple binarism men/gods = mortals/immortals. Aphrodite herself introduces the variants: Ganymede is immortal among immortals through Zeus' choice; Tithon is immortal but deprived of eternal youth; the nymphs are long-living but not immortal.

We can set out the following semantic graduated categories:
  immortality as status of gods
  immortality as exceptional destiny
  long life of nymphs as ambiguous beings
  posterity of heroes like Anchises and Aineias
This could be expressed by the logical hexagon of Blanché:

MI

M _____ I   M = mortality / I = immortality

MI = mortality and immortality together

$\overline{M}$ $\overline{I}$ $\overline{MI}$ = neither mortality nor immortality
  $\overline{MI}$

61. Hom. Hymn. Aphr. v.85-91; see Rivier, 'Sur les fragments 34 et 35 de Xenophane', *Rev. Phil.*, XXX (1956), 51ff. On the problem of ambiguity in Greek archaic thought, M. Detienne, *Les Maîtres de vérité dans la Grèce archaïque*, Paris, 1973, (2), p. 51ff.
62. See on the problem my remarks on the sacrifice of the Divine Being in Greek Polytheism, paper presented to the XII Congress of the I.A.H.R., Stockholm, 1970.

The mythical data correspond exactly:

	Nymphs	
thnetoi		*athanatoi* (Aphrodite)
Ganymede		Anchises—Aineias
	Tithonus	

Myth expresses with logical coherence the main pitfalls in Greek thought: the problem of reality vs irreality equated to the problem of mediation between human/divine = mortals/immortals. Having explored all the logical solutions the answer is that mediation is possible only at the level of *erōs—apate*, that is in the 'mimetic' frame of what is *similar* or analogous (like Aphrodite to a human girl or Anchises to a god), but not in the realm of the *identical*.

The final solution is pointed out in the reality of history in genealogy, that is the solution of the *tempus continuum* which absorbs the mythical value of the prophecy of the *longum regnum* for Anchises' posterity and looks like the superimposed, even if logical, necessity of the human state.

A reading like this does not exhaust all the possibilities of the text. It is however quite profitable for a historian of religions as the hymn is defined a 'brilliant piece' of literature or used as a source for historical speculation but appears on the contrary to be a true document of the logical organization of Greek archaic myth and of its relevance to the religious problems of the time. I think that such a reading could be significant for the early Shinto texts too.

2. First of all, I would like to express my complete agreement with Prof. Rudolph's statement about integrity, that is, complete autonomy of the History of Religions against the manifold attacks from different and even opposite sides.

The task of primary importance is to define what is the object of historico-religious hermeneutics. Just facing this problem we meet the first difficulty, which is the definition itself we choose to label our discipline: history of religion or of religions.

It is of the greatest importance to call attention to the plural. On the one hand it takes into account the 'universal' value of what J. Wach defined as *Vergleichende Religionswissenschaft* in its deep connection with phenomenology; on the other hand it emphasizes primarily the connotation of 'historical'. What does 'historical' mean? In its broader meaning it conveys all the hermeneutical tools, from textual philology to archeology, to sociology, used in order to embrace the whole space of a culture in the dynamic development in which religion takes part.[63] As a consequence of this historical approach we must choose, from the various definitions of religion, that one which can best define religion from a historical point of view.[64] I am perfectly aware that every definition will be an incomplete one. We can give our preference to one which tries to explain religion as the complex behavior of a cultural group toward an extra-human reality which appears shaped in accordance with the inner taxonomic needs of the culture itself.[65]

In this perspective I am perfectly aware that this ignores the problems of the hermeneutics of truth of religion or of the nature of the divine — the *noesis theou* — which ancient scholars defined as the proper field of theologians (Plut. *De def. or.*, 410b).[66] Of much more concern is the sociological approach to religion (see on this point T. Parson's paper on 'Theoretical development of the sociology of religion', 1949) which can go hand in hand with the historical methodology dealing with religion as a cultural product. Psychology of religion with its peculiar field of interest can be for the historian of religions a helpful but only a secondary way of looking at problems. To come back to our main problem, which concerns *Quellenforschung* in a historico-religious analysis I cannot but agree with Prof. Rudolph's repeated issues about the

63. On the meaning of history in relation to historico-religious methodology, see the recent introductory article by A. Brelich, 'Perchè storicismo e quale storicismo (nei nostri studi)' in *Religioni e Civiltà* N. S. I. 1970-72, p. 1 ff. Prof. Brelich points out the necessity to go beyond the limits of a pure philology of history avoiding at the same time the Crocian historicism which deeply affected historical disciplines in Italy.
64. For a very detailed and useful survey of methodological approaches, see R. Pummer, '*Religionswissenschaft* or Religiology?'
65. See Clifford Geertz, 'Religion as a Cultural System', in *Anthropological Approaches to the Study of Religion*, ed. M. Banton, London, 1969, p. 1-46.
66. I refer to problems like those raised at the 11th International Congress of the I.A.H.R. at Claremont as well as to the most recent Gensichen proposals for an integration between *Religionswissenschaft* and Theology, 'Tendenzen der Religionswissenschaft' in H. Simers and H.-R. Reuter, eds., *Theologie als Wissenschaft in der Gesellschaft*, 1970, pp. 28-40.

priority of this in our studies. There are however some points which should be made clear:

1. The mastership of philological-linguistic tools can be complete and refined only in one or perhaps two different cultural domains: hence the necessity for the scholar to have one specialization of his own.[67]

2. At the same time he must avoid isolation, which dooms history of religions to be split into a myriad of ultraspecialized trends within the single specialized field. How can this danger be avoided? First of all, I agree with the necessity of the mastery of one field. However, the philology which a historian of religions needs must not be of the traditional type, which can even be left as an operational activity to the text philologist *stricto sensu*. What the historian of religions needs is the possibility of direct control over the philological and semantic problems of a text. In any case the historian of religions can cooperate with the philologist so that through a joint exploration it should be possible for them to widen their reciprocal experience and have the possibility of a textual approach in a wider sense even in more than one particular field. In any case however it is necessary for the historian of religions to be aware of the prior concern with philological problems when he faces textual problems of any kind of one or more ancient and modern cultures. This awareness should avoid what Prof. Rudolph rightly defines as the use of an 'one-sided secondary literature', which van der Leeuw employs in his (still fascinating) *Phänomenologie der Religion*. Secondly, the historian of religions must work within a comparative, that is, a multicultural and multifunctional frame. As far as this is concerned he needs a typology which only phenomenology of religions can supply, or rather, what would be necessary would be a new comparative methodology developing from pure phenomenology and taking into account the peculiar needs of the historian of religions. What would be of particular interest would be a new morphological analysis of certain religious features which could allow the development of a common religious terminology beyond unicultural limits. This would also provide a specialized semiology, as powerful tool for further analysis in the comparison of religions. I mean that it would be useful in this perspective to re-examine all commonly used terminology — supreme being, spirits, divine beings,

---

67. On the point see A. Brelich, *Situazione attuale degli studi di Storia delle Religioni*, Acta Class. Univ. Debr., 1967, p. 3 ff.

heroes etc... in a wide programme which could use the method of a 'multivariate factor analysis' which Prof. Rudolph rightly indicates as a useful way into text analysis. Another and perhaps the most important problem hinted at is the so-called *Strukturforschung* as applied by Lévi-Straussian structuralism. It deserves here actually more space, for different reasons. First of all structuralism faces the problem of myth as a whole: what myth is; what the concern of myth is with legend, history, literature, folklore tradition; what it means for a culture which lives on myth, as many really do even beside the 'incidental' fact whether myth is believed, is transformed into faith, or not. This is not the place here to enter into details. A survey of such problems, made not by a structuralist but by a classical scholar of excellent philological background, can be found in a useful recent volume by Kirk, *Myth, its Meaning and Functions* (Cambridge, 1970). Some points can however be considered here. Structuralism is not the unique way to look at myth, but certainly the first approach to a mythical text after it has been previously collected (in the case of oral tradition) or philologically established in the case of written tradition. At this point the structural suggestion to look at the 'text' itself — a suggestion derived from the experience of Russian formalism — may prove to be of great usefulness.

The discovering of the formal-structural law of mythical thought as reflected in mythical language, that is in mythical texts, may help us to understand the positions and actions of personages, the relation between historical facts and their narrative formalization, and may even help in the case of ancient tradition which comes to us in different split contexts, to overcome the diachrony of sources.[68]

At the same time this procedure can help one to enter the deep meaning of the text, not only of a purely 'mythological' one but also of one which could appear quite well established from a canonical point of

---

68. As an attempt in this direction see my own paper presented to the Convegno sull'analisi della mitologia classica, Urbino 7-12.5.1973, 'Heros Achilleus/Theos Apollon'. A previous attempt appears also in my book I. Chirassi, *Elementi di Culture Precereali nei Miti e Riti Greci*, Roma, 1968, where the horticultural complex in Greek mythology is explored in its historico-genetical as well as in its semantic and mythical implications. A very interesting review of theories of myth and of the usefulness of new methods can be read in P. S. Cohen, 'Theories of Myth', *Man*, 1969, p. 337ff.

view, because it is primary involved in the semantic investment of problems which — we may agree — express the meaning at a 'deep' level.[69]

This could help to establish mythical structural patterns in different cultural contexts beyond the limits of the old comparativism. I wish now to refer here to a recent book. It can be considered one of the best examples of Lévi-Strauss methodology, applied within the framework of a rigorous philological correctness: *Les jardins d'Adonis* by Marcel Detienne (Paris, 1973). The author reveals the structure which ties together in an organized system the different and perhaps opposed and apparently trivial elements of Greek myth and ritual which come to us in a fragmentary textual tradition embracing epic and lyric poetry, theatrical pieces, botanical treatises, glossaries etc. The opposition between Demeter—Persephone/Myrrha—Mintha translates and is translated as the opposition between cereals and aromatic plants, including, on different semantic levels, the logical contrast between sexuality/chastity; incest/marriage; disorder/order; dampness/dryness etc. These dyads of oppositions interrelate reciprocally to define a taxonomy of different fields such as agriculture, social position of women, family rights, calendar time reckoning, etc. All these items are related to 'religion' as they concern the divine personalities of a polytheistic pantheon, religious rites and festivals like the Thesmophoria and the Adonia which have actual reality in the Greek world.

The methodology involved opens new prospects as it tries to reach the deep structure and consequently the deep meaning of all the data involved, including the apparent historical one. The acknowledgment of the Semitic origin of Adonis can be for instance reckoned as a historical turning-point, but it is a matter of greater importance to discover the the role this Oriental origin plays in the organization of Greek myth, that is 'religious' thought, as reflected in our texts.[70]

So I completely agree with Prof. Rudolph when he requires a thorough acquaintance with the primary sources of information and their

69. A questionable but interesting analysis of this kind applied to a canonical religious text is E. Leach, *Genesis as Myth, Discovery XXIII, 1962. Genesis as Myth and other essays*, London, 1969. On the problem of 'deep structure' in text analysis see A. Greimas, *Du sens*, Paris, 1970.

70. See on the point M. Detienne, *op. cit.*, p. 273. For similar remarks on the role of Thrace in Greek thought in the religious perspective see I. Chirassi Colombo, *The Role of Thrace in Greek Religion*, Sofia, 1972.

critical establishment; but I must also draw attention to the necessity of making use of all the devices which help to clarify the meaning of the text, or the established oral tradition, once it has reached the optimum available standard of correctness. I also think that the meaning of the text can be completed only with reference to its cultural environment and this is the primary purpose for a historian, even if the philological hermeneutics must come first chronologically. In any case a formal interpretation of texts can even give a contribution to the solution of philological difficulties at the level of a correct edition of the text itself as well as possibly opening new perspectives in dealing with historical problems of antiquity.[71] I also agree on the importance of every new document as a source of information which can confirm or definitively put aside a hypothesis, as in the case of the new Mani-Codex. I may only quote the incidence of the decipherment of Linear B tablets for new perspectives in problems of archaic Greek religion.

On the other hand I cannot be sure about the usefulness of a new subdiscipline which should be developed inside *Religionswissenschaft*, equated with phenomenology.[72] The theoretical approach to a history of religions can only arise in the context of a historical methodology open to all new techniques, structuralism included.

Commentary   by William Klassen

This response is written from the perspective of Biblical scholarship, the area of my work as a teacher and researcher. Primary attention will therefore be paid to issues which intersect with this area of work in the field of religious studies.

71. As an example of formal semiology applied to philological problems, see the microanalysis of a passage in Euripides' Medea as proposed by B. Gentili, 'Il "letto insaziato" di Medea', S.C.O.,1972, p. 60ff. For a formal analysis of myth concerning historical problems see also the long essay by D. Sabbatucci, 'Mito e demitizzazione nell'antica Roma' in *Rel. e Civ.*, N.S.I., 1970-72; and R. Buchler-H. A. Selby, *A Formal Study of Myth*, Austin,1968 (rev. G. Kutkdjian, 'Etude formelle du mythe', *L'Homme*, 1963 (3), p. 5ff.

72. On this point see Rudolph, 'Die Problematik der Religionswissenschaft als akademisches Lehrfach', *Kairos*, 1967, p. 22-42.

In passing, a comment may be allowed which deals with a point made by Prof. Kitagawa and which has emerged at various points in our discussions: the effect of canonical status upon the work of the student of the text. It would appear to me that much has changed in this regard. In an analysis of e. g. Rudolf Bultmann's *Theology of the New Testament* and the works of Cullmann and E. Stauffer it becomes clear that on many occasions noncanonical sources are used for an understanding of the situation of the Early Church and at no point is the reader told that such a distinction is important. Indeed in the work of Bultmann one has the distinct impression that on certain points the Apostolic Fathers are more enlightening than are the deutero-pauline writings. Furthermore it has been vigorously debated whether the Gnostic finds in Egypt may not in fact provide us with sayings of Jesus which antedate the canonical gospels. It could be argued that in effect, the canonical question is being opened up by such developments.

Prof. Rudolph has, in my judgment, observed what the critical issues are in our dealing with the sources: Is there a distinctly 'religious' approach to the texts or does it follow the classical model? Does a proper approach to the text in any way move beyond the purely rational? Does in fact the concern with method sometimes take the place of a concern with the discovery of the contents in our analysis of the sources?

Above all he has called attention to the fact that whatever other sources may be available to us in our understanding of a given religion, when we are dealing with a text it has a kind of sovereignty which cannot be ignored. It is almost a tyrannical authority for whatever other evidence indicates; in source criticism the scholar must ask about the integrity and genuineness of the text, he must inquire what it is saying. This involves him in a detailed study of the meaning of the words being used and their relation to each other in the sentences as well as the larger literary type or genre in which they appear. When analyzing the Gospels in the New Testament he cannot ignore the novelty of this literary type, when looking at the Apocalypse of the New Testament he must note not only its similarities with that type of literature in Judaism but also its striking differences.

Let me illustrate with a concrete example. According to Luke's Gospel Jesus said to his disciples: 'Love your enemies'. A critical analysis of this saying would need to ask whether it is a saying which can logically be traced back to Jesus or whether the Early Church had reasons for imputing such a teaching to their Master. If such a teaching had been attributed to the great Jewish teachers and to Hellenistic ethical teachers and perhaps even attributed to Socrates then it might be understandable to believe that the Early Church placed this saying upon the lips of Jesus. None of this seems to be the case and there are strong reasons to believe that this saying goes back to Jesus himself; so much so that Bultmann has said that if Jesus taught anything at all he taught this. Suppose, however, that we discover a text from the Old Testament or the Jewish wisdom literature of pre-Christian times which contains these words verbatim – if so then the critic will certainly be inclined to believe that the teaching is not original with Jesus. In fact it has often been asserted that Jesus was the first to teach this course of action but when we look at some of the Stoic teachers (Epictetus, Musonius Rufus) then we must at least say that ideas similar to that were being promoted by the Stoics. Did not Socrates come very near to it in his attitude towards those who sought his death? The point is that a critical analysis of the text demands a look at the *Umwelt* in which it was written. When other texts exist which antedate the text we are studying with similar or identical ideas then our work as source critics demands that we consider the possibility of dependency etc. Certain objective standards can then guide us. We can date certain texts and although analogy does not always indicate genealogy, where the possibility of dependence of one author upon another appears it must be taken seriously by the critic.

The value of a religious teaching is not called into question merely because it has been discovered elsewhere. In so-called historical religions especially it is considered part of its development that it shows its historical reality by accepting influences from other religions of its culture.

The contributions of Dilthey and Schleiermacher to modern hermeneutics is recognized by Prof. Rudolph. While the basic importance of *Einfühlung* (empathy) for accurate interpretation is today widely recognized, it is my impression that Biblical scholars are so wrapped up with method (form criticism, redaction criticism, structural analysis etc.) that little time is left over for *Sachkritik* or an analysis of content. Goethe once commented about certain literary critics of his day that they were so skilled at dissecting the literary classics that nothing was left of value when they were done and few people were able to see the contents of the documents. While this is not yet true in Biblical studies two trends, one good, the other not so good seem to be present which need watching.

First the bad one. There is a heightened subjectivity which does not pay enough attention to what the text itself says. Examples could be cited here from many sources. I give only two.

In Bultmann's commentary on I John all cultic materials are consigned to a redactor and the only reason given is that John himself has no interest in cultic materials. Such a highly subjective judgment is hardly acceptable. Likewise Ernst Fuchs is inclined to see in the parables of Luke 15 the most critical part of the gospel story. In making that judgment no regard is paid to the fact that the parable of the prodigal son appears in only one source and that not even in our oldest Gospel!

What Fuchs does, however, is something which is now often recognized: that the Biblical narrative is primarily interested in telling a story and that the source critic must treat these sources as a story — not a rational treatise trying to defend an orthodox position. The sources came into being within the life of a community and whatever may be the exact credit we bestow upon the original writer(s), upon the redactors or upon the community in which they were formed, we know that these sources must be looked upon in the context of that community.

It is the conviction of an increasing number of scholars who work with the Biblical text that careful source criticism can only benefit from other disciplines, provided of course that it does not lose sight of its primary mandate: to understand that text within the context of the society and culture in which it was born.While certain presuppositions will haunt each one who seeks that understanding he is not condemned to a hermeneutical circle if he works consciously with those presuppositions and is rigorously honest in working with the sources he has at his disposal.

Commentary   by Eric Segelberg

Dr. Rudolph's paper, 'The Position of Source Research in Religious Studies', is certainly an extremely enlightening and systematically presented work, based on an interpretation of religion and the science of religion which is generally accepted among scholars, a strictly historical approach which consequently has use for strictly historical methods, the philological-historical and the comparative-systematical methods used dialectically. He develops his review of the traditionally accepted methods including what has recently been added to the methodological arsenal mainly by refining the one or the other method and occasionally by adopting more contemporary views, thereby approaching religion from a slightly different angle than before.

Dr. Kitagawa on the other hand presents a case study which enables the reader to follow the way of tackling the Early Shinto religion as known from its literary sources.

To be the third commentator upon these two papers which are so different in their approach, is a rather difficult task and it seems to me that the best way is to comment upon a few points of Dr. Rudolph's, later adding a few special remarks.

The philological critical approach as well as the comparative systematical has been used in Biblical Exegesis by several generations of scholars; the various types of research recorded under those headings are generally accepted, their strength as well as their weakness is acknowledged and appreciated.

Such methods which attempt to reach behind the written or orally carefully handed over sources are especially interesting and at the same time more open to criticism, the causes for misinterpretation being more numerous. Two methods which — to use Rudolph's term — are both to some extent archaelogical, are *Patternforschung* (pattern research) and the structuralism of Dumézil.

It seems obvious that the study of patterns has brought forth a good deal of fresh understanding of the ancient religions in the Near East. Its basic hypothesis seems to be that people in the Near East at the beginning of historical times were able to grasp a kind of general understanding of their entire life and life situation, an interpretation which is religious. This may be wrong, but it seems likely that leading personalities, chief ideologists, were able to present a kind of general theory. This basic understanding pervades the entire life of people and society, its focus being the cult where the king plays the central and decisive role. In the process of disintegration, which is certainly a slow process, slower in some areas than in others, it seems sometimes hard to decide whether the pattern is also actually related to a cultic system or not. Here is a point where the limits of the method become apparent. The sources may be scanty, and their interpretation is always tricky when it comes to the question of cultic facts. Here we are not obliged to illustrate our point by resorting merely to Akkadian or Sumerian or other early sources. The Gnostic texts themselves, written during a historical period when sources are not scarce, are rich in evidence that we do not really know whether we have just a pattern of thought or a cultic, liturgical reality behind a pattern of thought which once must have been related to a kind of cultic-mythic system.

The criticism of Rudolph seems, however, correct in principle. There is a danger that we take too little into account the changes which occur when ideas or patterns or parts of patterns are accepted in other more or less related cultures or religions or which occur in one and the same culture during the course of history. There should, however, be means whereby one could make this kind of method more precise, e. g. by studying more carefully the rules of religious encounters or rather religions in encounter, such as the ways in which a younger, and growing, intellectually and perhaps also politically stronger religion relates to religions of opposite qualities.

The other archaeological method is that of Dumézil. Rudolph describes the method as follows: 'Its basic assumption of a kind of 'schema' leads it to leap too quickly over source research from a historical-chronological and critical point of view, and to put down roots in places where no soil has been identified to grow in. This kind of structural research is an attempt to carry out a historical enterprise with non-historical means; it ultimately depends on, and takes refuge in, the functioning of an incomprehensible — because unconscious — structure of consciousness.'

The criticism of this method may be worth some discussion, especially since it seems likely that uncertainty about its validity is one reason why the theories and as it seems the results of Dumézil's research have not been widely known or accepted in the English-speaking world. In his preface to the English edition of the *Archaic Roman Religion*, Mircea Eliade points out that this is the first work of Dumézil's ever to be translated into English, critical comments no doubt having been published previously.

As to the non-historical method, one has to agree that material from different epochs and different cultures has been used. The evaluation of the material is certainly often quite difficult. But would not the historian working in the time between history and pre-history run into similar problems? The combination of various methods, e.g. philological method, analysis of myths, comparative study of myths etc., seems to give a great amount of plausibility to the results of research following the method or methods here discussed.

Rudolph characterizes the method as carrying out historical enterprise with a-historical means. Would it not be possible to say instead that the method reminds us of the reconstruction of Minoan frescoes of Thera, where the remaining fragments set off the original structure of the masterpiece? A further discussion, however, might be justified.

Rudolph refers to the most recent trends in modern linguistics, 'textual semantics, linguistics, or grammar'. He indicates that these methods have so far not been adopted in the science of religion. It would probably be valuable to examine these methods more closely in order to explore in detail what we can gain by turning to such methods, and we should be grateful to Dr. Rudolph if he would kindly further elaborate this modern method to find its advantages.

What has been said about multivariate factor analysis as applied to the history of religion and run as international team work is something worthwhile discussing here and the I.A.H.R. is the obvious body to start acting along such lines in the case of approval.

We might further ask: to what extent could such an enterprise be of any value in solving the problems of early Shinto, the very methodological problems of research being largely unsolved, as Prof. Kitagawa has shown in his paper.

Or, to turn to another field which has also been studied for centuries, and which has a great deal to contribute both to New Testament studies and the studies of the Early Church as well as late Judaism, namely Mandaeism: in spite of all the excellent work by a great number of scholars, literary source criticism has not been able to tell us the dates of the major works or parts thereof. The nature of the Mandaean—Manichaean relation has not been solved; the relationship between Mandaeism and the Western Gnosis is not known in its entirety. Dr. Widengren's study of Parthian loanwords in Mandaic has contributed to fixing the time of the decisive Mandaean—Parthian encounter, stating a period *ante quam non*; Schou-Pedersen discussed some of the crucial texts especially such referring to Christian influence on the Mandaeans; Rudolph has analyzed the doctrinal contents in the central areas of anthropology, soteriology etc. and he has tried to draw a general picture of the religious world in which Mandaeism forms an important part. In spite of all those and other studies there are a great number of problems to be solved. The lack of success is partly due to the lack of scholars in the field but partly it may also be due to our inability to solve some literary source problems by means of the methods available. Therefore, in spite of all the progress that has been made, we must ask with Kitagawa if we have the right tools necessary for this work. Let us hope that the following discussion will help to solve some of the problems.

Discussion   Chairman: James Barr

The first speaker to present his paper was Joseph Kitagawa. He took a number of points from his paper for special emphasis, especially the difficulty of discussing source criticism in the context of 'Oral and Written Documentation of Religious Tradition'. Literary source criticism had originally been a variant of textual studies, concentrating on the literary pattern and characteristics of sources, but then proceeding from that to questions about the settings and motivations which had originally prompted the scriptures, thus ending up as an attempt to delineate the process of scripture formation as a history of writing and editing. This presupposed, however, that one was dealing with a fixed canon of scriptures; it was therefore applicable to Judaism, Christianity, Islam, and perhaps Theravada Buddhism; but in dealing with religious traditions which do not recognize a canon as such, the historian of religions must examine all the available documents, both religious and non-religious (e. g. political, sociological and legal). As a case in point, he wished to talk about the problems relating to early documents in the Japanese Shinto tradition.

One difficulty resulted from the interaction of early oral and subsequent written transmission, since early Shinto had been entirely oral in transmission, and Proto-Japanese had had a very simple structure, and was rich in homonyms: since the ancient Japanese had had no written script, their myths, legends, lore, songs, beliefs, and rites were all committed to memory. Writing had been made possible by the introduction of Chinese characters, and with them, the philosophical, religious, and literary influence of the early Sino-Korean civilization, which raised a number of serious hermeneutical problems. In the case of the documents written to preserve a oral tradition, however, it was the oral tradition, and not the documents, which had possessed sacred character. On the other hand, the codification of Shinto had been carried out within a unified religio-national community which he characterized as a kind of 'immanental theocracy', and they represented a double process of the historicization of myth and the mythologization of history. Source criticism and other forms of research had been going on into early Shinto since the 17th century, and especially since the Second World War, but the absence of any canon, or of a valid distinction between religious and secular texts, meant that it was always the total culture which had to be examined, and that there could never be certainty as to the appropriate methodology.

Kitagawa was followed by the second speaker, Kurt Rudolph. He said that his paper was in part based on discussions in a working group which he belonged to in Leipzig, which also included philologists and orientalists. Their experience of working together had been extremely positive, and it had also pointed towards the value of interaction between different methodologies. He did not want to take up time by presenting his paper in detail, but described its main parts as: (1) a discussion of J. G. Droysen's fundamental ground-lying work; (2) a survey of new methods; (3) a characterization of the unique features of *Religionswissenschaft*, within an interdisciplinary context; and finally (4) he drew attention to his closing remarks about the discussion of methodology: he was sceptical about the value of a general discussion on this – each specialist must choose the methodology appropriate to his specialty – but he did reiterate his suggestion of a subdiscipline of methodological discussion within *Religionswissenschaft*, and thought that despite the doubts expressed by Ileana Chirassi Colombo in her commentary it might find support among others.

The three commentators, Ileana Chirassi Colombo, William Klassen, and Eric Segelberg, then presented their prepared comments, mainly in the form printed in this volume. Kurt Rudolph replied directly to a couple of points raised by Chirassi Colombo: he emphatically agreed on the need to develop a common agreed terminology; certain words, such as 'symbol', 'magic', or 'mysticism', for example, had acquired such a wide usage that it was almost impossible to be sure what was being meant. He suggested that it might be useful to hold a future study-conference on just one of these controversial terms, so as to work towards an agreed usage. On methodology, he wished to refer to the work of a Czech orientalist, B. Hruška, especially to his article 'Zur Geschichte Sumerischer Religion' (*Archiv Orientalni*, 1971, p. 190ff.), in which the final section traced the history of the methodology of *Religionswissenschaft* from positivism to logistics.

In presenting the second commentary, William Klassen said that he was speaking from the perspective of New Testament scholarship, and in addition to his written commentary he added some remarks on the impact of new sources on NT work. The discovery and study of the Dead Sea scrolls, for instance, meant that scholars such as Rudolph Bultmann or C. H. Dodd could no longer be treated as authoritative interpreters. Similarly, while the late Prof. Brandon had regarded the non-mentioning of the Zealots in the New Testament as highly significant, what was one to do when the Essenes were not mentioned either? — or for that matter, St Paul's mother (an omission alleged to be very important psychoanalytically)? He felt, in fact, that extreme caution was called for in dealing with the science of sources.

Following Klassen's commentary, he and Rudolph discussed the meaning of the term *Sachkritik*, which Klassen had used. Rudolph asked whether it meant that source criticism should always be preceded by close attention to the text itself. Klassen replied that he meant both simultaneously, and Rudolph agreed with this, though he argued that source criticism could not be deferred; and he went on to remark that in his paper he had criticized the tradition-historical method particularly sharply because, having so totally dismissed the older literary scholarship, he felt it was a house built on sand; literary scholarship had the advantage of being built on rock.

The point about *Sachkritik* was subsequently taken up by Carsten Colpe, who said that in New Testament scholarship, particularly, despite source criticism, literary criticism, and the history of redaction, what was missing was any criterion for the establishment of brute historical facts. For instance, Ernst Lohmeier had discussed in *Galiläa und Jerusalem* the so-called Galilean and Jerusalem traditions in early Christianity, yet no one had yet established whether there really had been one, and only one, community in each place. Part of the difficulty, he suggested, lay in the untranslatable German concept of *Geschichtlichkeit*, which meant not only the historicity of a particular fact but also the historically relative character of the tradition. Historians of religion were happy when talking about tradition, and on safe ground, since the existence of the (written) tradition was indisputable; things became difficult when one asked about the brute facts, and this, following on from *Quellenkritik*, it was the task of *Sachkritik* to overcome.

Th. P. van Baaren wished to make two brief remarks on Rudolph's emphasis on the historical study of religion: firstly, that while most of the material studied in history of religion so far had been gathered by anthropologists, the major task of theory formation would in future have to be dependent on our own religious environment; and secondly, that all the material which could not, in any sense, be considered text, and which had so far largely been ignored, was also of crucial value.

Another point from Rudolph's paper was taken up by Helmer Ringgren, namely the role of 'feelings' (*'Gefühle'*). Ringgren argued that although the subjective element should be avoided as much as possible, 'empathy' (*'Einfühlung'*) was very important. Absolute objectivity was, by its nature, impossible: every scholar was dependent on a frame of reference, e.g. in his selection of a topic for research, and in his selection and interpretation of facts; what mattered was to be aware of this. Ringgren also picked up one point from the disagreement the previous day between Bleeker and van Baaren over the former's rule about producing descriptions of religions which the believers would recognize. He suggested that Bleeker's rule was a good control, but there was a dilemma, since a scholarly analysis would inevitably lead to results not immediately recognizable by the believer. Van Baaren agreed; and the chairman brought the discussion back to the topic of the day, 'Oral and Written Documentation', where Ringgren continued by challenging what Rudolph had said about the Icelandic sagas. If Dumézil was right in looking not for historical details but for structures, he suggested that the sagas could be useful sources through having preserved certain structures common to other Indo-European religions. It all depended what questions one asked the sources.

Before asking for further comments from the floor, the chairman said that two themes had emerged so far: the specific question of source criticism, which was the official topic, and also the question of objectivity. He requested speakers to give preference to the former. Nevertheless, the next speaker, R. J. Zwi Werblowsky, announced that he did intend to say something about objectivity since he believed it to be impossible. His first point, however, concerned Dumézil: he questioned whether, even if Dumézil's analysis of structures (tripartite or not) in Indo-European material was correct, this could justify any conclusions about Indo-European society. One must distinguish between the question of the correct analysis of the literary sources, and that of the jump to an alleged underlying social reality. Turning to Kitagawa's paper, he welcomed the inclusion of the *Norito* and the *Semmyo*. The former represented traditional prayer formulas, *hieroi logoi* which were not sources in the sense of being mythological accounts but did have semi-canonical authority; the latter made him also think of the Imperial Rescripts in Japan in the 19th and 20th centuries, especially those on education, which had contributed to the modernization of Japan: a supreme example, he suggested, of a canonical document, which should perhaps be compared with a papal encyclical in relation to the question of canonicity and sacred authority.

A major problem facing the historian of religion, he went on, was the tendentiousness of the texts, which gave, not the whole picture, but the ideology of the group who wrote or produced them. What Colpe had called the brute facts were missing: at the end of the 1st century A. D., for instance, Judaism might have consisted to half a per cent of Qumran covenanters and 80 per cent of Pharisees, but there was no Pharisaic documentation extant (irrespective of what Josephus had written). Reverting to the question of objectivity and selectivity, he said that among scholars the problem was less acute, since each of them had his own bias but through confrontation at conferences and in journals they cancelled each other out. What was more worrying, then, was the selectivity in the sources themselves. They happened to be able to study the literary or archeological remains of certain groups, such as the tiny little unimportant backwater sect of Qumran (laughter!), yet the real picture might be quite falsified.

Yet another reply to Rudolph's paper came from Carl Martin Edsman, as a correction to what had been written about the 'Uppsala school' — to which he himself did not belong. This had not studied 'culture pattern', but 'cult pattern', e.g. the cult pattern of the New Year festival, and had in fact been criticized by the 'culture pattern' school; its inspiration, moreover, had come from earlier Nordic scholars, such as

Grönbech, Pedersen, and Mowinckel. Edsman went on to correct what he suspected was a false current impression of theology. Modern theological scholarship on the New Testament, for example, had derived its methods from classical and oriental philology, and if it found itself moving in a circle — the criteria for judging the text having to be derived from the text itself — this was a problem shared, for example, by the indologist studying the *Mahābhārata*. Indeed the language of living religion could provide assistance in discussing another question which had come up, of the difference between faith and belief; cf. 'Faith gives sustenance, assurance to our hopes, and makes us certain of realities (or perhaps 'things') we don't see' (Hebrews 11: 1): the two English words 'faith' and 'belief' corresponded to the distinction between how you believe and what you believe. He finished with a quotation from Wilfred C. Smith's *Islam in Modern History*: 'The work will fail if it does not enable non-Muslims to understand better the behavior of the Muslims they observe, books by Muslim authors that they read, and Muslims that they meet. It will fail also if intelligent and honest Muslims are not able to recognize its observations as accurate, its interpretations and analyses as meaningful and enlightening. For both groups it will fail if it does not serve in some small way to further a mutual comprehensibility. In such a study there are tests of validity.'

Ulf Drobin took issue with another point from Rudolph's paper, where he drew consequences from the proof of the post-Christianized character of the dynastic Icelandic sagas for the determination of Germanic religion and for comparative religion in general. This was however not source criticism: it was extrinsic interpretation by Baetke.

Jan Bergman reverted to the value of Dumézil's work, and immediately conceded that even if one made use of his tripartite functionalism, differentiated research had to be carried out for each culture. Nevertheless, the fact, for example, that the war-and-reconciliation pattern between the first two functions and the third one in Dumézil's system generally and in some details appears in the Indian, the Roman, the Nordic/German (etc.) mythologies could, at least, help us not to jump to historical conclusions concerning any local confrontation in India, in Scandinavia etc.

At this point the discussion returned to the theme of objectivity. Haralds Biezais expressed serious disquiet at what Ringgren had said about the impossibility of the latter: this would mean the denial of science, scientific nihilism. When Ringgren apologized, and said he had omitted the initial statement, that objectivity must always remain the primary ideal, Biezais contended that that was precisely the point: if objectivity was no more than an (unattainable) ideal, science was done for. On the other hand he found Werblowsky's formulation — that the biases of individual scholars cancelled each other out — a methodologically acceptable statement. As for Dumézil, he went on to say, there was nothing wrong with his research, and he had been perfectly justified in putting forward hypotheses and theories: what was dangerous was when hypotheses became dogmas. The tripartite theory did not in fact fit the historical relations among many Indo-European peoples; what this showed was the necessity of the constant checking of theories against empirical facts.

The next question concerned Kitagawa's paper: Walter Capps was interested in the parallels which had been stated between myth and ritual, and in the implications of the demand that the scope of research should be widened to include form criticism of myth, legends, folklore, rituals, symbols, and the religious community itself: did this mean that similar structural parallels would occur there as well? Replying, Kitagawa said that this would not necessarily be the case: it happened to be so with this material. Possibly the precise parallels between the myth and the ritual of the emperor's coronation was coincidence, but it was a very fishy one. He wished however to repeat the importance of studying the nature of the religious community, which after all represented the context within which the questions of canonicity and sacrality had to be evaluated. He was very uneasy about the idea of sole dependence on literary source criticism.

Summing up, Rudolph picked out two points for especial mention: the question of Baetke's reading of the Icelandic sagas, and the question of objectivity. He had not meant to imply that Dumézil's methodology was totally unacceptable, nor to say that the Icelandic sagas were of no value at all: merely that there was little in them, beyond possibly a number of formulas, which could be shown to date back to the pre-Christian era, and that both Baetke, and the Icelandic scholars themselves (who were far more critical about the transmission of the sagas than the Swedish scholars) considered their value as evidence to relate not to Germanic religion, but to the Christianization of the North. Dumézil was an impressive and fascinating writer, but he did tend to skate over the problems raised by source research rather too easily. He went on to say that he shared Biezais' disquiet at the cultivation of a-historicism. Even if absolute objectivity was unattainable, science and scholarship must aim at least at relative objectivity. The over-emphasis on subjectivity was a plague on their discipline, as for instance in Gadammer's recent book. In oriental studies, for example, and Qur'an research, there were facts that had been established a hundred years earlier, which still held good and were being confirmed today: and that was what scientific objectivity referred to.

PART TWO

The Future of the Phenomenology of Religion

Evaluation of Previous Methods

HARALDS BIEZAIS   *Typology of Religion and*
                    the Phenomenological Method

1. The typology of religion is a familiar concept in research in history of religions,[1] and has become of particular relevance recently in connection with the difficulties associated with the current crisis in phenomenology of religion.[2] I wish to comment here on a few recently published opinions. For instance Lanczkowski, acknowledging these difficulties, has sought a way around them precisely in the typology of religion, or typology of religious history (*religionsgeschichtliche Typik*) as he calls it: 'Vor die Aufgabe gestellt, Pluralismus und Wandel der Religionen

1. Special reference may be made to sources such as H. Frick, *Vergleichende Religionswissenschaft* (Sammlung Göschen 208), Berlin, 1928, pp. 13 ff., and G. Mensching, *Vergleichende Religionswissenschaft*, Heidelberg, 1949, pp. 33 ff.
2. Th. P. van Baaren, 'Systematische Religionswissenschaft', *Nederlands Theologisch Tijdschrift* 24 (1970), p. 81: 'Nach dem Sturm und Drang des 19ten Jahrhunderts und dem Heldenzeitalter der ersten Hälfte dieses Jahrhunderts ist es ziemlich still geworden um die Vergleichende Religionswissenschaft (Phänomenologie der Religion). Es scheint mir am besten, diesen zweiten Namen so schnell wie möglich zu vergessen (...) weil, wie immer deutlicher wird, die ältere 'Phänomenologie' sehr einseitig und fehlerhaft ist.' Cf. also the sharp criticism by J. van Baal, *Symbols for communication* (Studies of developing countries 11), Assen, 1971, pp. 90 ff., and K. Rudolph, 'Religionsgeschichte und "Religionsphänomenologie" ', *Theologisch Literaturzeitung* 96 (1971), pp. 241 f. Even the phenomenologists themselves are divided and sceptical: M. Eliade, *The quest*, Chicago, 1969, p. 8: 'Actually, the divergences between these two approaches (phenomenology and history) are more marked. In addition there are a certain number of differences – sometimes quite perceptible – within the groups that, for the sake of simplification, we have termed "phenomenologists" and "historians".' (Cf. *ibid.*, p. 36). Cf also C. Bleeker, 'The contribution of the phenomenology of religion to the study of the history of religions', in *Problems and methods of the history of religions* (Studies in the history of religions 19), Leiden, 1972, p. 41.

wissenschaftlich zu erfassen, bietet sich der Religionsforschung eine Methode dar, die als religionsgeschichtliche Typik bezeichnet werden kann. Indem sie sich als sachgemässe Art der Erfassung von Pluralismus und Wandel der Religionen anbietet, kann sie zu ihrem Teil dazu beitragen, das Spannungsverhältnis, das zwischen zwei Forschungsrichtungen der Religionswissenschaft, der historischen und der phänomenologischen, häufig deutlich wird, fruchtbar zu nutzen und damit zu enschärfen. Hierbei geht es allerdings nicht allein um die Verwirklichung der in allen Auseinandersetzungen über die Beziehungen zwischen Religionsgeschichte und Religionsphänomenologie im Prinzip anerkannten Forderung, die phänomenologische Erarbeitung von Typen und Strukturen müsse genauestens auf historischen Tatbeständen basieren und sich von deren fortschreitender Erkenntnis ständig überprüfen lassen. Es handelt sich vielmehr um eine noch engere geistige Verflechtung beider Forschungsweisen. Denn einer religionsgeschichtlichen Typik ist es aufgegeben, in einer der traditionellen Religionsphänomenologie entsprechenden Weise typische Erscheinungsformen herauszustellen, die historische Vorgänge zum Inhalt haben. Die reine Religionsgeschichte genügt der gegebenen Aufgabe nicht, weil sie der Sicht des Wesentlichen sowohl mit einer Überfülle von Material als auch mit der Darstellung des geschichtlichen Weges jeweils einer Religionswelt im Wege steht und damit nicht gerecht wird der hier gebotenen systematischen Zueinanderordnung analoger Erscheinungen des Wandels in verschiedenen Religionen und des Pluralismus zu verschiedenen Zeiten.'[3]

We may summarize this statement under the following points: firstly, that Lanczkowski refers to a method of religious research which he calls the 'typology of religious history'. Secondly, he justifies the necessity of this method on the grounds that religious research has the task of investigating 'religious pluralism and change', which is not possible in any other way. He also mentions as a subsidiary motive the fact that one would be able to 'make good use of, and thus ease, the tension which is becoming constantly more apparent between two tendencies in history of religions, i. e. the historical and the phenomenological'. This would lead to 'a much closer intellectual interweaving of both kinds of research'. A further task is 'to present typical hypostases ... in

3. G. Lanczkowski, *Begegnung und Wandel der Religionen*, Düsseldorf, 1971, pp. 29f.

a manner conforming to traditional phenomenology of religion'. The historical method is incapable of this, for two reasons. First of all, there is the vast quantity of material; secondly, its reproduction of the complicated historical process itself. Neither of these facts, however, prevents the perception of a 'systematic correlation of analogous phenomena'. Despite the fact that the typology of religious history which has been suggested must proceed cautiously and 'in a manner conforming to traditional phenomenology of religion', it can be stated that it had itself expressed the desire to achieve a shift of emphasis.

It remains questionable whether Lanczkowski has really noticed or adequately emphasized all the weaknesses of the historical and phenomenological methods which he mentions, but he has undoubtedly seen the difficulties into which the phenomenological method, formerly so highly respected, has run during the last ten years.

Even such a loyal champion of Van der Leeuw's phenomenological method as Bleeker has been compelled to concede considerable weaknesses even in his master, and to attack them,[4] or, as he puts it, to define his position with respect to the criticisms of the phenomenological method: 'In my opinion the task of the phenomenology of religion is threefold, in the sense that this science discovers three dimensions in the religious phenomena, which are correlated though they should be clearly distinguished. The phenomenology of religion has to make inquiries into: (1) the theoria of the phenomena, (2) the logos of the phenomena, (3) the entelecheia of the phenomena. The theoria of the phenomena discloses the essence and the significance of the facts, for instance the religious meaning of sacrifice, of magic, of anthropology. The logos of the phenomena penetrates into the structure of different forms of religious life. Religion is never an arbitrary conglomerate of conceptions and rites, but always possesses a certain structure with an inner logic. The entelecheia of the phenomena reveals itself in the dynamics, the development which is visible in the religious life of mankind.'[5]

4. Bleeker, *op. cit.*, p. 41: 'In my opinion a vulnerable side of Van der Leeuw's phenomenology is that too many elements of the philosophical phenomenology have been incorporated into it, in the form of speculations about the deeper meaning of the concept: phenomenon. Thereby the phenomenology of religion transgresses the boundary of its competence.' Cf. *ibid.*, p. 39, and also 'Wie steht es um die Religionsphänomenologie?' *Bibliotheca orientalis* 28 (1971), p. 307.
5. *Op. cit.* (n. 2), p. 42. The same thing is shown in his review of G. Widengren, *Religionsphänomenologie (op. cit.* in n. 4, pp. 306f.).

Bleeker's statement thus not only makes his own position unambiguously clear, but also the philosophical basis of this entire school. The
philosophical concepts mentioned here may be able to help in the systematization of perceptions, but — understandably — they can tell us
nothing about historical reality itself.

It was precisely this attempt by Bleeker to define his phenomenological method more precisely which provoked Bianchi to the justifiable
question whether it is possible to reconcile the historical and phenomenological methods. Their exchange of views goes briefly as follows:
'Does Prof. Bleeker think it possible to somehow unify historical and
phenomenological research by that concept of "historical typology"
I tried to elaborate in my paper, i.e., the possibility of analogous,
comparable, parallel historical formations in different cultures? Could
one imagine of a comparison which could be at the same time and in
the same context historical and phenomenological, constructing its
concepts not only by means of phenomenological generalization but also
by means of concrete individualization of historical processes, i.e. of
religious "worlds", engaged, as they are, in phenomena of diffusion, convergence, innovation, divergence, parallel development, and so on, and
thus resulting to the concept of a (more or less) "analogical" (i.e. not
"univocal" nor "equivocal") meaning of words as "religion", "prayer",
"sacrifice" etc.? This would be useful also in order to escape the *impasse*
caused by the necessity of having a previous idea (if not a precise definition) of the object of the research and the impossibility of getting
such an idea or definition before having carefully studied that very
object.

Bleeker.— This last question is not easy to answer to; it raises many
problems and we have little time to talk it over very quietly. But I can
give a provisional answer. In my opinion there is and there will remain a
difference of procedure between history of religion and phenomenology
of religion. As to typology of religion, it is more or less included, in
my opinion, in the phenomenology of religion. There are types of
phenomenology of religion that you could classify as typology.

Bianchi.— What about a 'historical typology of religions'?

Bleeker.— Yes, historical typology. I am not so in favor of using that
notion. I don't exactly understand what is the import of that word.
History is evolution, it is a process. Can you really in this process distinguish different types?

Bianchi.— An analogy between historical processes, between historical developments; "parallel" evolution within separate cultures...

Bleeker.— Yes, but that is another matter. You mean a comparison between different processes, of typological structure. That could be done, but then the question arises: where are you to locate this study? There is, as we know, a general history of religion, next to the particular history of religions; perhaps this would be the best place to locate this kind of research.'[6]

One can only conclude, from this discussion, that there is no unanimity between these two loyal representatives of the phenomenological school about typology of religion. There is the same confusion in their use of the terms 'typology', 'structure', 'parallels', 'general history of religion', and 'particular history of religions'. Bleeker does not believe in Bianchi's 'historical typology of religion', while Bianchi is dissatisfied with the existing phenomenology of religion.[7] The question that he is concerned with is whether it is possible to unite the historical and phenomenological methods, or whether it would not be better to speak of a typological or morphological method. This problem points to the need for a clear definition of religion, in order then to be able to discuss appropriate methods of research.[8]

What result does Bianchi reach, and how does he justify his position? He wishes to introduce a new method, 'historical typology of religions'. In contrast to the phenomenological method, this would be capable of leading to insights 'not only by means of phenomenological generalization but also by means of concrete individualization of historical processes, i. e. of religious "worlds", engaged as they are'. The differences

6. Bleeker, *op. cit.* in n. 2, p. 52 ff.

7. In point of fact Bianchi set out already in 1958 to demonstrate his typology in practical form, and this becomes even clearer in the expanded Swedish edition of his polemic against Mensching (*Religionshistoriska problem*, Halmstad, 1968, p. 120), as Hultkrantz (in 'The phenomenology of religion: aims and methods', *Temenos* 6 (1970), p. 79) has quite rightly realized.

8. Bianchi, 'The definition of religion. On the methodology of historical-comparative research' in *Problems and methods...* (*op. cit.* in n. 2), pp. 20 f.: 'Thus, this relation between the definition or concrete, progressive (in the real meaning of the word) research of the definition, and the progress (or, the "methodos", which means etymologically the same) of the research, is essential. And this suggests the question of what this method must be: should it be a "phenomenological" method, or rather a typological or morphological one, or should it be a historical method, or some combination of both?'

and similarities between religions are given, historical facts; they should therefore be investigated using historical methods. The phenomenological method has so far failed to achieve this. Bianchi believes that he has found a solution, according to which the difficulties which arise from the demonstration of parallels between different religions, i. e. 'least common denominators' or a 'nucleus', can be overcome by restricting oneself strictly to the historical basis. When the religious content in question is checked from the point of view of 'historical continuity and discontinuity', it is revealed as belonging to different types. So far, it is clear that Bianchi has recognized the weakness of the phenomenological method and — if nothing more — has once again stressed the necessity of the historical context. On the other hand, his statements on the concept of types, or, to be more accurate, of historical types, are unclear, as Bolgiani has already correctly observed: 'I have the impression if it is not mistaken, that Bianchi used such expressions as 'typology' and 'phenomenology' rather indiscriminately, when it seems to me that in the current state of "religious sciences" we cannot purely and simply equate them. To set the bounds of the problem correctly it strikes me that we ought to distinguish between "typology", "morphology" and even "phenomenology" of religions. To reduce religious phenomenology simply to a "typology" of religions does not seem to me to be entirely right: indeed I feel that it entails the risk of confusion and misunderstanding.'[9]

From these comments, the following points emerge: (1) the recognition that the phenomenological method is one-sided and, as a result of its philosophical orientation, leads to abstract generalization; it is not capable of grasping and explaining the historically given religious reality; (2) the methods recommended are 'historical typology' and 'historical

---

9. *Problems and methods...* (*op. cit.* in n. 2), p. 26. Bianchi has excused himself on the grounds of the loose use of the term typology in Italy: 'When we talk of typology here in Italy we think of certain obsolete polemics with historicism, that was ignoring "History of Religions" for the reasons given above. When we mention phenomenology we especially think of scholars such as Wach, Van der Leeuw and Bleeker; when we mention morphology then our mind goes especially to Eliade.'
Nevertheless, he is ultimately forced to admit that he himself uses the term typology imprecisely: 'Now since, in my opinion, phenomenology, as we understand it here, is often hinting too empirically or too intuitively at "meaning", "structure", "system" or "whole", I prefer to speak of typology. But I do admit that there is a certain tendency to mix the terms, and use them indifferently.'

typology of religions', with a special emphasis on the desirability of sticking to the historical facts in using them. The comments fail to get beyond 'desirability', however, for no convincing justification is put forward for this necessity or possibility; (3) the comments on the relation of the phenomenological method to the typological method contain serious confusions. This discussion is fruitless in its present stage, for two reasons. Attention is paid neither to the fact that the question of typology has been exhaustively discussed for several decades, and that this concept is employed in history of religions and in theology, nor to the results which this had led to. The current discussion would achieve greater significance if these results were noted and made use of. It will therefore now be necessary to spend some time on the perceptions so far achieved by typology, in order to then approach an assessment of the phenomenological method.

2. Goppelt, for example, published his dissertation *Typos. Eine typologische Deutung des Alten Testaments im Neuen* as early as 1939, in which he offers an extensive survey of the definition and usage of typology in the interpretation and hermeneutics of the scriptures of the Christian church, and writes: 'Begriff und Methode der *Typologie* sind, offensichtlich unter dem Einfluss des NT, von den ersten Anfängen an *in der kirchlichen Exegese und Hermeneutik* heimisch (...). Soweit wir sehen können, hat Paulus den Gebrauch des griechischen Wortes τύπος (Adj. τυπικός) als Ausdruck für die Vorausdarstellung des Kommenden in einer vorlaufenden Geschichte angebahnt.'[10] We may ignore the author's theological intentions, which are revealed in the last words; it remains nevertheless true that this word has established itself in the tradition of the Christian church and of European culture.[11] When we take into consideration that Goppelt wishes to make use of a strictly typological method in his work, we can see that he is compelled to define it more precisely, and to demonstrate its distinction from other methods. 'Gegenstand typologischer Deutung können nur ge-

10. L. Goppelt, *Typos. Die typologische Deutung des Alten Testaments im Neuen*, (Beiträge zur Förderung christlicher Theologie 2. 43), Gütersloh, 1939, pp. 4f.
11. The Greek word τύπος in its original meaning would best be translated as 'mould' or 'impression', and is connected with various other words with related semantic meanings. This is more fully surveyed and analyzed by A. Blumenthal, 'τύπος und παράδειγμα', *Hermes* 63 (1928), pp. 391ff.

schichtliche Fakta, d. h. Personen, Handlungen, Ereignisse und Einrich-
tungen, sein, Worte und Darstellungen nur insofern, als sie von solchen
handeln. Eine typologische Deutung dieser Objekte liegt vor, wenn sie
als von Gott gesetzte, vorbildliche Darstellungen, d. h. 'Typen' kom-
mender, und zwar vollkommenerer und grösserer Fakta aufgefasst
werden.'[12]

Nevertheless, it is clear even here — if we ignore the author's specific
theological interests — that we can only speak of typological interpretation when 'set, ideal images, i. e. types' are previously available and
properly followed; when there is no intensity between the historically
given reality, i.e. the facts, and the types, then this constitutes merely
a repetition of the facts, not in any way their typological exegesis. A
typological interpretation or method presupposes a type (a theological
type — set by God) within the researcher's own consciousness. Goppelt
subsequently distinguishes his view, which is basically correct, from
various of its parallels, especially from the allegorical interpretation of
facts: 'Gegenstand der allegorischen Auslegung sind nicht die Fakta oder
auch der Wortsinn einer Darstellung als ganzer, sondern ihre Begriffe
und Wendungen. Sie sucht in ihnen, sie als Metaphern auffassend,
"neben dem buchstäblichen Sinn des Textes oder bisweilen auch unter
völligem Ausschluss desselben eine andere, hiervon verschiedene und
vermeintlich tiefere Bedeutung".[13] Die Geschichtlichkeit des Berichte-
ten und damit der Wortsinn des Textes ist für die Allegorie gleichgültig,
für die Typologie (und wenigstens letzterer auch für die symbolische
Deutung) Grundlage. Wohl aber sieht der Allegorist diese Doppelsinnig-
keit nicht als eingetragen, sondern als vom Text gewollt und gegeben
an.'[14]

He thus rejects the search for 'a suspected deeper meaning' in the
religious text. This applies to a large extent both to the older and to
modern religious phenomenology.[15] Two points worthy of attention
emerge from this statement. Firstly, typology can only deal with facts
given in space and time, i. e. with historical reality. Secondly, typology
is concerned with the interpretation of these facts, and uses for this

12. Goppelt, *op. cit.*, pp. 18f.
13. F. Torm, *Hermeneutic des NT*, Göttingen, 1930, p. 213.
14. Goppelt, *op. cit.*, p. 19.
15. F. Heiler, *Erscheinungsformen und Wesen der Religion* (Die Religionen der
Menschheit 1), Stuttgart, 1961, pp. 4f., 565.

purpose a 'set type'. We shall return to this expression later. It seems that the group of historians of religion that grew up around Otto, and who carried out serious and comprehensive work on the problem of religious typology, has nowadays been forgotten. Mensching, for example, published his first work in this field as long ago as 1931,[16] in which he firmly distinguished general history of religion, and phenomenology, from typology: 'Die moderne Religionswissenschaft sieht sich heute vor die Aufgabe gestellt, einen neuen Zweig am Baume ihrer Erkenntnis zu fördern. Es handelt sich um das, was man mit dem Terminus 'Typologie' am treffendsten bezeichnet. Worauf kommt es dabei an? Die Religionstypologie setzt die Arbeit der allgemeinen Religionsgeschichte mit ihrer Feststellung dessen, was in concreto da ist und was gemeint wird, voraus. Sie richtet sich mit ihrer Arbeit nicht auf die phänomenale Wirklichkeit der Religion, sondern auf ihr abstraktes Wesen. Diese Fragestellung schliesst die Vermutung ein, dass innerhalb der bunten Welt religionsgeschichtlicher Phänomene Gesetze walten und typische Entwicklungen nach konstatierbaren Notwendigkeiten sich vollziehen. Die Tatsache der Parallelen wird erst von dieser Betrachtungsweise aus in ihrer letzten Tiefe und zugleich in ihrer absoluten Notwendigkeit begriffen werden können. Die heute je und dann bereits erfasste Aufgabe (vgl. besonders Heinrich Frick, *Vergleichende Religionswissenschaft,* 1928) wird also vorwiegend darin bestehen, typische Gemeinsamkeiten der religiösen Entwicklung, typische Ähnlichkeiten und Unterschiede in der religiösen Ideenbildung usw. zu erkennen.'[17]

In complete contrast to Goppelt, Mensching concedes that the attention of typology is directed to the 'abstract essence' of religion, whereas the history of religion is only concerned with concrete data. He also distinguishes phenomenology from typology by showing that

16. He published his dissertation *Typologie ausserchristlicher Religion,* for example, as early as 1931 — in *Zeitschrift für Missionskunde und Religionswissenschaft* 46, now in *Topos und Typos.* Motive und Strukturen religiösen Lebens (Untersuchungen zur allgemeinen Religionsgeschichte N. F. 8), Bonn, 1971, pp. 157 ff. — and in 1938 his *Vergleichende Religionswissenschaft* (2nd ed. 1949), which is actually the first full-scale work in which a comprehensive typology of religion is presented. He deals systematically with the same theme in *Die Religion,* Stuttgart, 1959. In fact Mensching has been dealing with typology ever since 1929, when the author of these lines heard him lecture on this topic at the Latvian University in Riga.

17. Mensching, *Topos und Typos...,* p. 157. Mensching also examines here Hegel's approaches to the non-Christian religions, which, in his opinion, fulfil in principle the requirements of typology.

the former is concerned with isolated facts, events, and concepts. He has made his point of view even clearer in his book published in 1959: 'Die Phänomenologie der Religion stellt solche Parallelen fest, nicht aber das, was wir als Typologie bezeichnen wollen. Worin besteht der Unterschied? Der Phänomenologie hat es mit Einzelmomenten im Erscheinungsbild der Religion zu tun. Sie stellt z. B. fest, dass quer durch die Religionen das 'heilige Wort' eine numinose Grösse ist, die in mancherlei verschiedenen, aber jeweils in verschiedenen Religionen bezeugten Abwandlungen und Anwendungsformen auftritt. Zum Aufgaben- und Problembereich der Phänomenologie gehört die Erforschung und Darstellung der Erscheinungswelt der Gottesverehrung, der Gottesvorstellung usw. Davon unterscheiden wir das Problemgebiet der *Typologie*. In ihr handelt es sich darum, die Religionen als *Ganzheiten*, als Organismen zum Gegenstand der Betrachtung zu machen, und zwar nach beiden Seiten hin: nach der Seite *typischer Gemeinsamkeiten in der Ganzheit* und *typischer Einmaligkeit in der Ganzheit*.'[18] These words give us an accurate characterization of phenomenology: it is concerned with 'individual features in the total phenomenon of religion' (Einzelmomente im Erscheinungsbild der Religion). What does this mean? Firstly, in a positive sense: if phenomenology wishes to remain in the field of the empirical sciences, then it can only deal with the given, concrete, total phenomenon, or, as we would say, with the facts of religious history. The majority of phenomenologists of religion commit themselves to this position, with their repeated statement that they wish to respect the facts of religious history.[19] Secondly, in a negative sense: this dis-

---

18. Mensching, *Die Religion*, p. 78.

19. In this context one could point to extreme opinions, such as that that the history of religion can only possibly be successfully studied if the phenomenological method is employed: 'In my opinion you can only study history of religion fruitfully if you apply this method of the phenomenology of religions, that means that you try to find the religious value, the structure, the essence of the phenomena' (Bleeker, *op. cit.* in n. 2, p. 52). Cf. also Eliade, *The quest*, p. 8. The extremism of this attitude was already recognized earlier by Bianchi, despite the fact that he himself for the most part belongs to the phenomenological tendency, and he attacked it with justification: 'Tuttavia bisogna dire che equivoci e ingenuità comparatiste alla maniera del vecchio comparatismo, voglio dire) non mancano presso gli odierni fenomenologi della religione. Né mancano arbitrarietà e soggettivismi. In realtà, la loro scienza, se scienza autonoma la fenomenologia della religione si può chiamare, non può fare a meno della storia: pena la trasformazione dei materiali di studio in pezzi senza vita, o ai quali si attribuisce un'altra vita, o pena la minore o addirittura

tinction between phenomenology and typology gives expression to the significant recognition that the concern with 'individual features in the total phenomenon' makes it impossible for phenomenology to speak about what it regards as its main task, i. e. about the essence of particular phenomena or of religion. This impossibility can be illustrated by the phenomenologists' comments on the discovery of the axis or centre of the world. This is seen either in a tree growing on the summit of a holy mountain, or in the site of an altar, in the central row of pillars in a temple, in an arrow driven into the ground, or in the intersection of the decumanum and the cordo, etc.[20] It is obvious that these individual features have no meaning when isolated from their historical context. These individual features do not disclose the meaning of the phenomenon of the 'axis of the world' or the 'centre of the world': that is to say, they do not offer a religious phenomenology of these phenomena. This statement illustrates the fact that it is impossible for the phenomenological method to carry out the task it has set itself, i. e. to disclose the essence of religious phenomena. It is unable to do this in consequence of its atomizing character, and this is one of the causes which has provoked hostile criticism against it. This one-sidedness, with which phenomenology deals with individual features, is on the other hand counterbalanced by the demand to respect the totality within which the individual features are embedded; yet before we can more closely examine this demand, for respect above all for the totality, we must return to the way in which the concept of types has up to now been used.

Mensching's use of the idea of types is influenced by Frick. The latter has pointed out that the term 'type' is used in two senses: *'Die Worte Typus und typisch* haben verschiedene Bedeutung je nach der Blick-

---

dubbia fondatezza scientifica delle conclusioni. Sembra quindi che la fenomenologia della religione, nonché porsi in contrasto o in posizione di indipendenza rispetto alla storia, non possa neppure fare a meno del continuo controllo da parte di questa (il che del resto è riconosciuto — almeno in teoria — dai fenomenologi)' (*Problemi di storia delle religioni*. Universale studium 56, Roma, 1958, p. 19).

20. Other phenomenologists would probably find it difficult to surpass the wealth of fantasy and unjustified claims found in the words of F. Kuiper, a loyal disciple of the phenomenology of Eliade, on this same subject: 'It may therefore be sugsted, as a mere working hypothesis, that the pre-natal correlate of the tree rising from the primordial hill is to be found in this developing spinal marrow' ('Cosmogony and conception: a query', *History of religions* 10 (1970), p. 125).

richtung des Vergleichs. "Typisch" ist einmal Gegensatz zu "singulär" (...) zu einmaligen, individuellen Erscheinungen'.[21] The second meaning emerges when one considers that: 'in jedem Glied (...) sich der Charakter des Ganzen (offenbart), im demselben Stück also liegen ineinander das mit anderen Gemeinsame und das Besondere. Das Besondere ist hier so viel wie das Typische eines organischen Gebildes. Damit haben wir einen zweiten Sinn für das Wort Typus gefunden'.[22] 'Der Begriff des Typus ist doppeldeutig: einerseits bezeichnet er ein *Gemeinsames* innerhalb verschiedener Religionsorganismen, andererseits aber auch das "typisch" Einmalige und Eigenartige jeder Religion.'[23]

The introduction of the concept of types arises, as we saw before, from the need to systematize.[24] Pointing out the double function or varied usage of the concept tells us little, however, about its content. Nor does the restriction of its use to the metaphor 'centre of life' give us any better an understanding: 'Die nächste Aufgabe ist daher, die Fülle der religionsgeschichtlichen Gestalten auf ihre jeweilige *Lebensmitte* hin zu untersuchen. Es entsteht auf diese Weise eine *Typologie der Religionen*. Wir verzichten dabei auf die in der "Allgemeinen Religionsgeschichte" gegebenen Einzelheiten und richten den Blick auf die innere

---

21. Cf. Frick, *op. cit.*, pp. 13 f., also 86. Both Mensching, *Vergleichende Religionswissenschaft*, p. 33, and indirectly W. Baetke ('Aufgabe und Struktur der Religionswissenschaft', *Grundriss des Theologiestudiums* 3 (1952), Gütersloh) refer to this.
22. *Ibid.*, p. 14.
23. Mensching, *Die Religion*, p. 33.
24. This highly-motivated necessity of typology has also met with disagreement. Baetke, *op. cit.*, pp. 216 ff., is extremely sceptical about it. He justifies his negative opinion on purely practical grounds, i. e. 'dass ein solches Unternehmen heute verfrüht ist, da eine zureichende Charakteristik auch nur der wichtigsten Religionen noch nicht vorliegt' (p. 217). However, he was also compelled to introduce a principle of systematization, though without calling it that, and only mentioning it in the results: 'Für eine Systematik der religiösen Phänomene empfiehlt sich folgende Einteilung: a) Das religiöse Subjekt; b) Das religiöse Objekt; c) Die Beziehung beider zueinander; d) Die Auswertung der Religion auf das Gemeinschaftsleben' (p. 219). Rudolph also invokes his master Baetke in adopting an attitude of rejection towards typology, but also, significantly, for practical reasons: because it is still in its infancy — '(da diese) noch sehr in den Kinderschuhen steckt' ('Die Problematik der Religionswissenschaft als akademisches Lehrfach', *Kairos* 9 (1967), p. 30). It is however difficult to see why the principle which he recommends, of economic stages ('Wirtschaftsstufen'), and of a consequent division of religions into religions of gatherers and hunters, of planters and cultivators, and of cattle-farmers (*ibid.*), should be any better. One can just as well describe these religions as typical forms in the history of religions.

Lebenseinheit, die doch in jeder Religion, die eine organische Ganzheit bildet, gegeben sein muss.

'Der Typologie der Religionen tritt dann die Typologie *der* Religion zur Seite, in der die andere Sinnmöglichkeit des Begriffs Typus (Typus als das Gemeinsame) zu Grunde gelegt wird, und zwar in verschiedener Hinsicht: wir werden eine Typologie der Erscheinungsformen, eine Typologie der Strukturen, der Entwicklung und der religiösen Erlebnisse zu unterscheiden haben.'[25]

If we replace the concept 'religion' by the term 'totality' here, then we can say that in the one case it is the typical common features in the totality, and in the other the typical unique features in the totality, that are being recognized.[26] On the basis of this kind of theoretically-grounded typology, it is possible to systematize the facts of religious history. It is quite another question, however, whether the defenders of this theory are able to do this in practice; but that is a question to be approached in another context.[27] What is important here is to reaffirm the fact that the historians of religion were forced by the same difficulties, i. e. the mass of factual material, to look for their principle of systematization in types, in contrast to the phenomenologists, as long ago as the 1920s. It is particularly important to stress the fact that the chosen normative principle of systematization is abstract in nature.

25. Mensching, *Vergleichende Religionswissenschaft*, p. 33. Cf. criticism on this point in Baetke, *op. cit.*, pp. 217f.

26. This is similar to the distinction in a different terminology between 'history of religion' and 'history of religions' (cf. Bleeker, *op. cit.* in n. 2, p. 43).

27. It would be appropriate here to remind him to his own comment on the previous typological attempts: 'Solche Versuche, eine Typologie der Religion zu gewinnen, liegen bereits in grösserer Zahl vor. G. van der Leeuw hat darüber ausführlich in seiner *Phänomenologie der Religion* berichtet. Es handelt sich um Typologien, die man auch als Einteilungen der Religionen bezeichnen könnte, d. h. man versucht, die ganze Religionswelt nach *einem* Einteilungsprinzip aufzugliedern. So teilte z. B. N. Söderblom die Religionswelt ein in animistische, dynamistische und Urheber-Religionen, F. Heiler in mystische und prophetische Religion, H. Frick in Religionen der Werke und Religionen der Gnade usw. Gemeinsam ist diesen Versuchen zweierlei: einerseits fassen sie den Begriff Typus auf als Zusammenfassung notwendiger Wesensgemeinsamkeiten, andererseits aber – und hier trennen wir uns von ihnen – glaubt man, mit *einem* Einteilungsprinzip auszukommen. Typologie in unserem Sinne soll mehr leisten als nur eine Einteilung der Religionen zu bieten unter zwei oder drei Kategorien' (Mensching, *Die Religion*, pp. 78f.). Heiler also makes his own division, which in his own opinion, however, forms a subdivision within phenomenology (cf. Heiler, *op. cit.*, pp. 18f.).

3. In this context, Van der Leeuw completely supports the position of Otto, Frick, and Mensching as to the abstract nature of types, and emphasizes it even more strongly: 'Der Typus hat keine Realität. Auch ist er nicht eine Photographie der Wirklichkeit. Er ist, wie die Struktur, zeitlos und braucht in der geschichtlichen Wirklichkeit nicht vorzukommen. (...) Er hat aber Leben, eigenen Sinn, eigenes Gesetz.'[28]

What is of interest to us, however, are his comments, as a classic authority in phenomenology, on the introduction of types into history of religions. How does he understand types, and how does he obtain them? He starts from the situation of the historian, which is characterized by the wish to reconstruct. The real question is, therefore: how is reconstruction possible, and how is it carried out? Van der Leeuw is forced, like the other researchers mentioned, to recognize that 'reality is a maze of lines', into which the researcher draws in his own basic lines: Van der Leeuw calls these 'structure'. The concept of structure is of extreme importance for the further development of his thinking. He characterizes it as follows: 'Die Struktur ist ein Zusammenhang, der weder nur erlebt, noch, logisch oder kausal, nur abstrahiert, sondern der *verstanden* wird. Sie ist ein organisches Ganzes, das sich nicht in seine Teile zerlegen, sondern aus seinen Teilen verstehen lässt, ein Gewebe von Einzelheiten, das sich nicht durch Addierung derselben oder Deduzierung der einen aus den andern zusammensetzen, sondern nur als Ganzes wiederum *verstehen* lässt'.[29]

A number of different descriptions are used here, such as: structure, context (Zusammenhang), organic totality (organisches Ganzes), network of details (Gewebe von Einzelheiten), and meaningfully-organized reality (sinnvoll gegliederte Wirklichkeit). These are synonyms, which are used to clarify the concept of structure. The structure is supposed

---

28. Van der Leeuw, *Phänomenologie der Religion*, Tübingen, 1956, pp. 771 f. He expresses his approach extremely unfortunately, however, as follows: 'Die "Seele" kommt als solche nie und nirgends vor. Es wird immer nur eine bestimmte Art der Seele geglaubt die, in dieser ihrer Bestimmtheit, einzig ist. Ich kann sogar sagen, dass die Seelenvorstellungen zweier Menschen, sogar im selben Kultur- und Religionskreis, nie ganz und gar dieselben sind. Es gibt aber einen *Typus* der Seele, einen verständlichen Zusammenhang verschiedener Seelenstrukturen. Dieser Typus ist zeitlos. Er ist nicht wirklich. Aber er ist lebendig und zeigt sich uns. Was aber tun wir, damit wir ihn auch wirklich schauen?' In this text 'soul' ('Seele') is actually meant as 'concept', not as a 'type'.

29. *Ibid.*, p. 770.

to disclose the meaning of the reality. Inasmuch as these synonyms are used only for clarification, we do not need to enquire into them in more detail. Van der Leeuw's hope is to be able to use this understanding of the concept of structure to reveal, and to comprehend, the deeper meaning in history, in the empirically given facts, and in their context. It is from this basic orientation that he approaches the concept of types. A structure is experienced instantaneously, without its meaning being recognized; but this does not reveal the total truth, for the understanding is never restricted to the instantaneous experience.

'Das verstandene Erlebnis wird in und vom Verstehen einem grösseren objektiven Zusammenhang eingeordnet. *Jedes Einzelerlebnis ist schon Zusammenhang*, jeder Zusammenhang ist noch immer Erlebnis. Das meinen wir, wenn wir neben Strukturen von *Typen* reden.'[30]

In other words, Van der Leeuw employs the concept of types alongside the concept of structure in order to represent the relationships which emerge once the meaning has been recognized. An experiential situation is created, in which understanding, or the recognition of the context in the meaningful, takes place: that is to say, relationships are established between what is understood and the person who understands it. He describes this situation quite explicitly, and correctly, on the basis of Husserl's philosophy of phenomenology,[31] as a situation of observation: 'Diese Verhältnisse sind aber immer *erschaubare* Verhältnisse, *"verständliche Beziehungen"*. Sie sind nie faktische Verhältnisse, kausale Beziehungen. Selbstverständlich schliessen sie die letzteren nicht aus, aber sie sagen nichts über sie aus. Sie gelten nur im verständlichen Zusammenhang. Einen solchen Zusammenhang, gleichgültig, ob er einer Person, einer geschichtlichen Situation, einer Religion gilt, nennen wir: *Typus* oder *Idealtypus*'.[32]

It is particularly important here to notice the expression 'erschaubare

30. *Ibid.*, p. 771. Cf. on this point K. Goldammer, *Die Formenwelt des Religiösen* (Kröners Taschenausgabe 264), Stuttgart, 1960, p. XVII.
31. Van der Leeuw, 'Confession scientifique', *Numen* 1 (1954), p. 12: 'Mon but était de pénétrer jusqu'à l'essence des phénomènes religieux'. Cf. Bleeker, 'The phenomenological method', *Numen* 6 (1959), p. 99: 'Nobody can fully understand the trend of a phenomenology of religion, as e. g. that of Van der Leeuw, if he does not realize how strongly the Husserlian principles have influenced this scholar'. Meanwhile Bleeker has begun to doubt this (cf. *op. cit.* in n. 2, p. 41), apparently under the influence of Eliade (cf. also Hultkrantz, *op. cit.*, p. 72).
32. Van der Leeuw, *Phänomenologie...*, p. 771.

Verhältnisse', observable relationships, which Van der Leeuw associates completely with phenomenological philosophy. 'Das sich Zeigende zeigt sich im Bilde'[33] : that which reveals itself, reveals itself pictorially, and can only be grasped through 'observable relationships'. In other words, this is an act of recognition. The picture is the form in which the phenomenon appears, with the aid of which the recognizer enters within the act of recognition into 'observable relationships'. In this way the contextual meaning, i. e. the type or ideal type, as it is expressed in the quotation, is revealed within the empirical reality (in this case, within religious history). The type, understood in this way, becomes an integrating constituent part of the process of recognition. Or, to express this in Van der Leeuw's terminology: the type has no reality, but it gives the contextual meaning of man's observable relationships with the divine. Not only Van der Leeuw, but the whole phenomenological school (Otto, Söderblom, Heiler, Wach, Eliade, *et al.*) are led by the desire to achieve the recognition, or rather the vision, of the essence of religion. This represents the attempt to establish direct contact, with the aid of the phenomenological method, with the holy, the divine, and the irrational.[34] It is hardly surprising that several writers have

---

33. *Ibid.*, p. 771.

34. Rudolph (*op. cit.* in n. 24, pp. 34ff.) offers a deeper examination and an evaluation of the research of this group of phenomenologists. He also demonstrates their deeper theological motives: 'Ausgangspunkt der verhängnisvollen Entwicklung der deutschen Religionswissenschaft — im Unterschied zur vorausgehenden guten historisch-philologischen Tradition — ist der bekannte Marburger Theologe Rudolf Otto (1869-1937). In seinen zahlreichen, weitverbreiteten Veröffentlichungen vertrat er die Auffassung, dass die Religionswissenschaft dazu dienen solle, das 'Numinose', das heisst die göttliche Wirklichkeit, mit Hilfe einer Analyse des religiösen Gefühls zu erfassen. Der scheinbar äusserliche wissenschaftliche Rahmen der Untersuchungen Ottos, besonders in seinem bekannten Buch *Das Heilige* (...) kann darüber nicht hinwegtäuschen, dass er der Religionswissenschaft die Aufgabe einer *Theologia naturalis* zuweist, so wie es vor ihm schon N. Söderblom beabsichtigt hatte. Der Begriff 'numinos' dient R. Otto und seiner Schule als eine Art ontologischer Gottesbeweis auf psychologischer Grundlage. Wir greifen hier ganz deutlich die Wirkung von Schleiermachers Religionsphilosophie (bzw. -psychologie). Verantwortlich für Ottos Konzeption ist (abgesehen vom Einfluss des Neofesianismus) auch seine starke Hinneigung zur Mystik; sie bestimmte sein Denken wesentlich. Auf diese Weise hat Otto den wissenschaftlich-historischen Charakter der Religionswissenschaft untergraben und sie in eine Pseudo-Theologie und Religionspsychologie verwandelt.' It is worth remarking that he only mentions in his text this group of German researchers; without doubt, one of the most flagrant representatives of this tendency should also be included here — Eliade, who has provoked criticism even among his

recently very sharply attacked the phenomenological method as a method of scholarly research. The claim that 'the phenomenology of religion never pretended to be science of the essence of religion'[35] is – as the foregoing commentary has shown – unjustified.[36] No doubt there do exist various tendencies and groupings among the phenomenologists.[37]

To sum up: the approaches to the typological method discussed here

---

fellow-phenomenologists on account of his prophetic mission (cf. Bleeker, *op. cit.* in n. 4, p. 306). A much more far-reaching criticism of Eliade's methods, and of phenomenology in general, can be found in Baird, *Category formation and the history of religions* (Religion and Reason 1), The Hague, 1971.

35. Bleeker, *op. cit.* in n. 31, p. 104.

36. Bleeker himself exemplifies this quite explicitly: 'The student of the history of religions and of the phenomenology of religion starts his study with an intuitive, hardly formulated, axiomatic notion of what religion is. His ultimate aim is an inclusive formulation of the essence of religion'. This has been quite correctly seen by the critics of the phenomenological method, e. g. Baird, *op. cit.*, p. 4: 'While there are significant differences between Mircea Eliade and C. J. Bleeker, they are united in proceeding with the essential-intuitional method. They are finally after the 'essence' of religion.' J. Waardenburg, in 'Religion between reality and idea', *Numen* 19 (1972), p. 187, argues similarly, and also in the same place characterizes Bleeker's position in general (pp. 183 ff.). This can be confirmed from the work of other phenomenologists' as the following examples illustrate: e. g. R. Pettazoni, 'Aperçu introductif', *Numen* 1 (1954), p. 4: 'La phénoménologie religieuse ignore le développement historique de la religion ("von einer historischen 'Entwicklung' der Religion weiss die Phänomenologie nichts": Van der Leeuw). Elle s'attache surtout à découper dans la multiplicité des phénomènes religieux les diverses structures. C'est la structure qui seule peut nous aider à déceler le sens des phénomènes religieux indépendamment de leur situation dans le temps et l'espace et de leur appartenance à un milieu culturel donné. Par là la phénoménologie religieuse atteint une universalité qui nécessairement échappe à une histoire des religions adonnée à l'étude des religions particulières et qui, de ce fait, est exposée au fractionnement inévitable de la spécialisation. La phénoménologie n'hésite pas à se poser en science *sui generis* essentiellement différente de l'histoire des religions ("die Religionsphänomenologie ist nicht Religionsgeschichte": Van der Leeuw).' Heiler, *op. cit.*, p. 16, is even clearer: 'Die fünfte methodische Forderung ist die phänomenologische Methode: vom φαινόμενον gilt es zum εἶδος, zum Wesen vorzustossen. Die Erscheinungen sind nur zu untersuchen um des Wesens willen, das ihnen zugrunde liegt, und im Blick auf dieses. Man darf nie an der äusseren Schale hängen bleiben, sondern muss überall hindurchbohren zum Kern der religiösen Erfahrung; von den feststehenden Formen (Kultformen und Dogmen) müssen wir zum unmittelbaren religiösen Leben vordringen.' Cf. also Eliade, *op. cit.*, p. 9, and 'Methodological remarks on the study of religious symbolism' in *The history of religions*, ed. by M. Eliade and J. Kitagawa, Chicago, 1970, p. 88; Van der Leeuw, *op. cit.* in n. 31, p. 12.

37. There is a good summary in Waardenburg, *op. cit.*, pp. 199 ff.

show that they are based on the concept of 'types', which is understood in a number of ways:

1. The facts given in religious history have to be sorted into groups, on the basis of characteristics which can be established empirically. The resulting groups may be regarded as empirically-based types, and history of religions may concern itself with their representation.

2. Types may be understood as an abstract, normative principle of systematization, which can help one to find one's way among the empirical phenomena of the religious life. The systematization is carried out in this case on the basis of the similarity or divergence of the characteristics of the phenomena in question. Types operate here as a category of scientific theory.

3. By means of phenomenology, types can establish direct relationships between the object to be understood and the person understanding it, between the spheres of the empirical and the transcendental, and thus they can reveal contextual meaning. In this case, the typological method becomes a special epistemological method of speculative comparative religion.

After this discussion, we can turn again to the crisis of phenomenology mentioned at the beginning, and to the demand for a typological method. The relationship of this method to the phenomenological method must be defined in terms of the three alternative interpretations mentioned here of the concept of types. The first and second alternatives allow the typological method to be employed within the limits of empirical history of religions; they also make it radically different from the intuitive phenomenological method.[38] It also fulfils the requirements set by the empirical nature of history of religions.[39] In the case

38. Baird, *op. cit.*, pp. 2 ff., 74 ff., also, with justification, describes the phenomenological method as intuitive, mainly on the basis of his analysis of Eliade's and Bleeker's work.

39. Van Baaren, *op. cit.*, p. 83: 'M. E. sollen theologische Aussagen über die Wahrheit und Unwahrheit der Religion nicht zeitweilig eingeklammert werden, sondern endgültig gestrichen werden aus dem Sprachgebrauch all jener Wissenschaften, zu denen auch die Religionswissenschaft gehört (...). Der Sprachgebrauch der Religionswissenschaft lässt keine Aussagen zu, die wissenschaftlich weder verifiziert noch falsifiziert werden können.' Cf. Goldammer: 'Religionswissenschaft ist eine empirische Wissenschaft, auch als Systematik (...). Das Transzendieren in die hinter ihnen stehende Wirklichkeit und Existenzerfahrung muss einem jeden einzelnen überlassen bleiben, der sich damit beschäftigt.' Cf. also Rudolph, *op. cit.* in n. 24, pp. 38 ff., and 'Der Beitrag der Religionswissenschaft zum Problem der sogenannten

of the third alternative, the typological and phenomenological methods become identical (Van der Leeuw), and must be regarded as a specific path of recognition within history of religions which has passed beyond the boundaries of empirical research.

CARSTEN COLPE   *Symbol Theory and Copy Theory as Basic Epistemological and Conceptual Alternatives in Religious Studies*

1. The disciplines 'history of religions' and 'historical theology' deal, among other things, with problems which are methodologically on two different levels. An especial difficulty consists of the fact that these problems have to be overcome in the execution of one and the same scientific task. Moreover this difficulty is overshadowed by the epistemological reservation (*aporia*) that the results of historical and critical work in theology and history of religions are dependent not only on the criterion whether the hermeneutic principles immanent in this work have been correctly applied, but also on prior decisions which are often binding on the exegete or historian even when they have been taken without him, or when he is unconscious of them. This can be demonstrated not only in direct, detailed exegetical or historical work, but in fact better in the examination of particular tendencies in biblical and historical scholarship; not only textual work, therefore, but a critical overview of the research also takes on its own internal importance. This could be termed either 'methodology', or '(contributions to) the logic of research (in OT or NT studies, religious scholarship, or church history)'.[40]

In the history of research, both of these levels can be recognized,

---

Entmythologisierung', *Kairos* 12 (1970), p. 184; R. Pummer, '*Religionswissenschaft* or religiology?', *Numen* 19 (1972), p. 21.

40. This further concept, which goes beyond that of both dialectical and of formal logic, is not only the basis of various modern forms of scientific logic, but was used as early as 1922 by Ernst Troeltsch in giving his book *Der Historismus und seine Probleme*, Tübingen, 1922, the subtitle: 'The logical problem of the philosophy of history'.

even when the researchers themselves fail to distinguish clearly between them. First of all, what is involved is the level of historical and critical research in general. The growth and the fields of application of this research are familiar. The identification of 'religion' as a field of application is, on this level, usually simply presupposed. Yet in fact it is not self-evident on this level, but must take place on another level. Once the identification has been made — we may ignore here the question as to what theological or philosophical premisses it has been made on — then a causal-genetic explanation for the growth of religion is required, which is different from the historical-genetic explanation,[41] and yet must be acknowledged as a part of the history of research in which we are interested here. For epistemological and conceptual theory in religious studies, then, it is not only the theoreticians and actual practitioners of the historical-genetic explanation, i. e. the representatives of philosophy of history, methodology, and historiography, who are of interest, but also those thinkers who have concerned themselves with the relationship of 'spiritual' to material 'being', or of the 'superstructure' to the 'basis': from Aristotle via the scholastic ontologists to Leibniz and Hegel, from there to Saint-Simon, Comte, and Marx, and finally to N. Hartmann, Lenski, Parsons, and the neo-Marxists.

It is the last-mentioned, moreover, who have most clearly recognized the epistemological *aporia* mentioned at the beginning. They are in the habit of criticizing forms of science which fail to recognize this *aporia* as 'ideology'. This usage can be adopted, and this problem cannot be ignored, if the real task is to be achieved: the theoretical illumination of the basic structures of historical and causal explanation in carrying out research in religious studies.

2. The necessary preliminary neutralization of the ideological factor is important, not only for religious studies, but also for theology; in fact there are certain further implications here which make the problem for religious studies appear simpler. Therefore we shall concentrate for

41. What is meant here is mainly the 'Hempel-Oppenheimer model', which has not even been properly applied in epistemology in history of religions; cf. C. G. Hempel, 'The function of general laws in history', in H. Feigl and W. R. Sellars, *Readings in Philosophical Analysis*, New York, 1949, pp. 459-471; Hempel, *Aspects of Scientific Explanation*, New York/London, 1965; W. Dray, *Laws and Explanations in History*, Oxford, 1957, 1970.

the time being on theology, which may however stand for religious studies as well.

The theological legitimacy of the attempt at ideological criticism cannot be demonstrated by the fact that the logic of science — in this case, of theology and religious studies — is founded solely within these sciences themselves and can be demanded only by them. For the logic of other disciplines, e.g. philosophy or the social sciences, is not introduced from outside either, for instance as an axiomatic system or dialectical principle: it rather constitutes an *organon* produced, or at least initiated, by these sciences' internal *aporiae* with the aim of pursuing them more adequately.

Criteria may however be expected, as possible results of theological self-reflection,[42] which admit of the re-examination of claims more qualified than those merely concerned with the verification or falsification of scientific propositions — i.e. precisely the claims which theology, as theology, must make. For these claims to be met, theology must above all avoid the false step that could transform its utterances (which in the first instance can be recognized positively as having been gained through historical and critical method) into an utterance system, no longer verifiable by reference to the experience of Christian belief, let alone other forms of reality. Once such a transformation has taken place it is hardly surprising that theology is seen as ideology,[43] i.e. in the currently dominant pejorative sense of the word.

Nowadays this no longer refers to the kind of false science which theology still put up against the truths of secular, empirical natural science in the 19th century: nowadays it refers to the fixation of social and intellectual issues which can easily be imputed to theology as being alien or even hostile to reality, and to this extent as ideological. Some examples of such issues are: the 'electness' of some men before others, which then hardens into a 'natural condition' (e.g. non-Semites before 'Semites', whites before blacks, property-owners before the poor); the

---

42. The fact that logic of science is nowadays no longer based on for instance the premises of Kant's critique of reason, but simply on the self-reflection of nomological and hermeneutic science, is demonstrated by J. Habermas, *Zur Logik der Sozialwissenschaften*, Frankfurt a.M., 1970, pp. 77-91.

43. On the ideologization of science — not of theology — cf. also J. Habermas, 'Technik und Wissenschaft als "Ideologie" ', in the book of the same title, Frankfurt a.M., 1968, pp. 48-103.

hypostatization of words by ignoring their pragmatic reference (e. g. the word of God without having regard to the motivation of the biblical speaker, or ecclesiastical confessions of faith without reference to the alternatives possible on the road towards consensus or compromise); the justification of the status quo, even including obvious inhumanities, by appealing to the order of creation, instead of questioning this status quo through consideration of our ignorance of God's future. Another example is the transformation of historicism, one of the greatest mental revolutions which the western mind has experienced,[44] into a reactionary attitude of mind which limited itself, in tracing new tendencies, to those tendencies in the past which were capable of establishing just connections with succeeding and contrasted periods. This is represented, for example, by those upholders of historical theology who loved to shock the parishes and impress the students as paragons of a critical stance towards tradition right up to the 1960s, but swung over to the conservative or even reactionary camp in proportion to the parishes' and students' loss of respect for individualism and relativism.

These fixations of social and intellectual issues, and others like them, have only too often been accompanied by the occurrence of a fundamental danger to Christian belief itself, namely, even here, by ideologization.[45] This ideologization could not have manifested itself so fundamentally as has sometimes happened and still happens, however, if it had not been borne by theology. The quality of theology as theology must therefore prove itself by showing how far it is capable of annulling its own ideologization in those cases where this has taken place. Theoretically speaking, the ideological criticism of theology would also be conceivable in the interests of a class, i. e. one which sees itself as being free of religion and thus as altogether free, and which is in conflict with another class that uses religion for its own ends and develops theology for this purpose — that is to say, most plausibly, with that class which also supported historicism, i. e. the bourgeoisie. If one looks for constructive results from this kind of criticism of theology, however, then the object suspected of ideology is simply exchanged: it now becomes the class which is free of religion and critical of theology

---

44. Cf. F. Meinecke, *Die Entstehung des Historizismus*, Munich, 1959, p. 1.
45. Cf. H.-G. Drescher, 'Ideologie und christlicher Glaube', *Das Gespräch* 40, Wuppertal, 1962, p. 16.

which itself cannot demonstrate that it is not ideologized, since it already bears some of the essential features of ideology: the claim to be non-ideological; the unity of its vision of the world; the claim to the monopoly of truth; the rejection of examination whether their theory accords with reality, by reference to the possibility of establishing this accordance at any time through praxis.

Ideological criticism is most likely to achieve its aim, therefore, if it comes to pass as a self-critique by theology itself. This expectation predicates the conviction that it is a constitutive feature of the essence of theology that it alone, as the 'nomothetic' science (in the sense here of *theologia thetica*) is capable of developing the possibility (as *theologia critica*) of surveying both its own substance and also its tools for the inquiry into this substance. This can take place through the constant joint application of these same theories, which should assist both historical perception and the explanation of the growth of religion.

3. The tendency of the methodological reflection which is now at stake must be different from that pursued so far, if only because in the history of ideas and in scientific policy this other has been relegated to a distressingly inferior position. This started with Plato's hatred of Democritus, and continued when the Christian church permitted only one part of the monumental work of Thrasyllus, who edited both Plato and Democritus, to stand, i.e. the Corpus Platonicum. One could call the tendency which needs to be restored to authority 'materialistic'. If this is followed, then the substance lifted from history for theology must of necessity display an aspect in contrast to the usual one. The relationship between the new tools established by methodological criticism and this substance, however, is by no means equally contrasted. It is far rather an exact analogy to that relationship which we should grasp between the historicity of faith and of theology and that dimension of history, which was opened up above all through the biblical belief in God.[46] The

46. It is impossible to go here into all the variations that have been undergone in protestant theology on the theme of 'faith and history' since for instance Reinhold Niebuhr's book of that title (New York, 1949). The evaluations of historicity in Gadamer, Bultmann, Gogarten, and Kamlah, with special reference to its emergence in Christian thinking, are described by G. Bauer in *'Geschichtlichkeit'. Wege und Irrwege eines Begriffs*, Berlin, 1963, pp. 154-166. One could also refer to the corresponding qualification of theology by representatives of dialectical theology.

relationship which we have to establish is, indeed, analogous to that just described, but the poles between which it exists are different: this is the reciprocal relation between the materialist character of ideological criticism of specific theological positions, and the materialist view of the conditions under which 'religious' documents — including biblical, Christian ecclesiastical, and Jewish — came about. This reciprocal relation has not yet been clarified, not even by a science that (in however varied and partisan a manner) sees itself as 'materialist'. This is a task that needs to be done.

First of all, it must be made clear that materialist interpretation is no less theologically legitimate than any other kind of interpretation: neither in relation to its object, nor in relation to its methodological execution. For there should be no theological position conceivable from which it would be possible to argue that interpretation is to be carried out exclusively on the syntactical level: i.e. that it should consist of the investigation on the one hand of the relations between the utterances and concepts in the texts, and on the other hand between the sum of these and the scholarly conceptual apparatus and theological utterances of the exegete or historian. It can only make theology a more competent science for the pursuit of truth if the pragmatic connection is investigated between, on the one hand, itself and its representatives, and on the other between the utterances and concepts in the source and their speakers and users.

In the context of these two pragmatic connections, 'materialism' means no more than that, with reference to the exegetes or historians, the conditional nature of their results should also be investigated in relation to their own bonds to their social environment, on which they depend for their existence as scholars; and that with reference to the text under exegesis, the co-conditioning of its wording by the social conditions, and especially the working conditions, under which its authors lived, should also be investigated.

It may be objected that in this way the concept of matter has already acquired symbolic character, and should therefore be avoided. Marx's interpretation of history does not offer any statement about the relationship between mind and matter, but sets out to explain the history of ideas, legal relations, and religions through the history of production and the property orders resulting from this, which do not necessarily have to be termed 'material'. Accordingly, even Marxists have recognized that the expressions 'materialist conception of history' and 'historical materialism' (introduced by Engels)[47] are misleading, and have recommended for example the expressions 'realistic' or 'empirical' conception of history instead.

The objections entailed here may be fully conceded, as soon as the introduction has been successfully accomplished of better concepts, which are not simultaneously claimed by too many other schools, as is the case with 'realistic' and 'empirical' conceptions of history. Meanwhile, we must be satisfied with saying that this concept of materialism is different from that according to which mind is the product of matter, matter has temporal precedence over mind, etc. It also follows from this that religious utterances and religion in general will certainly be conceded to be influenced by social circumstances in the widest sense, but not to be produced by them. This is also a different concept of materialism from that which constitutes a vulgar basis-superstructure schema; that is to say, this is not a constitution of causal relations between the sum of material economic conditions (including specific conditions of production and class) and a system of ethical, political, religious, and philosophical positions (including their respective conceptualizations) which varies in relation to these economic conditions. It should be observed that in the *locus classicus* where this problem, and its vulgarization, are presented, consciousness is said to be 'determined',[48] whereas the word ought to be, as it is in the preceding sentence, 'conditioned'.[49] It is a precise grasp of this 'conditional' relation, and also incidentally of the 'correspondential' relation, between the forces and conditions of production on the one hand and the juridical, political,

47. E. g. in his review of Marx's *Critique of Political Economy*, MEW 13, p. 469; and the Introduction to *Anti-Dühring*, MEW 20, p. 25. The critics of these expressions included not only E. Bernstein and K. Vorländer, but above all M. Adler, who nevertheless entitled his fundamental work the *Lehrbuch der materialistischen Geschichtsauffassung*, Berlin, 1930. The immediately following remarks are based on the four chapters in which Adler is particularly concerned with the demarcation between the 'materialist conception of history' and 'philosophical materialism'. These chapters have unfortunately been omitted in the new edition of St. Wirlandner and K. Blecha, *Grundlegung der materialistischen Geschichtsauffassung*, Vienna, 1964; cf. *ibid.*, p. 93, note 62.

48. K. Marx, Preface to the *Critique of Political Economy*, 1859, MEW 13, p. 9.

49. This was pointed out by G. Müller, in a review of F. Tomberg's *Basis und Uberbau*, 1969, in *Zeitschrift für philosophische Forschung*, 1973, p. 325.

and religious superstructure on the other, which guarantees the dialectical character of this relation.

4. The distinction from a non-dialectical concept of materialism raises the question whether, in tracing back from specific concepts and conceptions, the appropriate epistemological theory is available with which one could start work on the conditions for the growth of these concepts and conceptions and also on the conditions for their valid interpretation. While the symbolic character of the concept of matter, mentioned above, might suggest attempting to make use of a developed symbol theory, there are theories on the 'realistic' or 'materialistic' side, ranging from the *adaequationes intellectus et rei* to naive copy theory, which claim to have solved the problems in question already, or deny their existence altogether. It ought to be possible, however, to bring symbol theories and copy theories into alignment at least in a common consciousness of the problem, if one uses both of them primarily as epistemological theories, which is in any case what they both aim to be and what they were originally developed as. This can be done by working from an earlier difference on the conception of nature, a difference that starts out from so precisely the same theoretical point that one could almost imagine that E. Cassirer and V. I. Lenin had met each other in personal debate. Heinrich Hertz is the first modern scientist to have effected a decisive turn from the copy theory of physical knowledge to a purely symbolic theory. The basic concepts of natural science no longer appear as mere copies and reproductions of immediate material data; rather, they are represented as constructive projects of physical thinking – and the only condition of their theoretical validity and significance is that their logical consequences must always accord with the observable data.[50] 'In Wirklichkeit zeigt die philosophische Einleitung H. Hertz' zu seiner 'Mechanik' den üblichen Standpunkt des Naturforschers, der durch das Professorengeheul gegen die 'Metaphysik' des Materialismus eingeschüchtert ist, aber dennoch die naturwüchsige Überzeugung von der Realität der Aussenwelt nicht überwinden kann'.[51] The question is whether a symbol theory (as furthest developed, fol-

50. E. Cassirer, *Philosophy of Symbolic Forms*, transl. by Ralph Manheim, New Haven-London, 1953-1957, III. 20.
51. V. I. Lenin, *Materialism and Empiriocriticism*, German ed. by F. Rubiner, Moscow, 1947, pp. 302f.

lowing H. Hertz and others, by E. Cassirer) would not achieve even more, if the perception — for which is necessary for a symbol to come into being — was carried out 'materialistically', thus altering the character of the symbol; and whether a copy theory (as developed most consistently, in opposition to Hertz, by Lenin and others) would not be more likely to reach its fullest performance capacity, specifically as an epistemological theory, if the isomorphism between the 'subject' and the 'object' of the perception were understood not structurally but functionally, and if symbols with epistemological value were introduced in order to make this functionalism manifest.

5. While these questions are frequently handled in controversy about nature-oriented and matter-oriented conceptualization, this happens astonishingly seldom in connection with the phenomena of the historical world — perhaps because the distinction between nature and history itself is judged to have come about on the basis of false premises. In order to avoid epistemological short circuits, however, it should be at least hypothetically maintained.

If, accordingly, past history is taken as the object not only of historical research, but also of an epistemological attitude which aims at clarifying both the premises on which historical results are achieved and the *a priori*'s of the exegete and historian (the latter not under transcendental but social-psychological criteria), then a paradoxical discovery is made. Those historical theologians and religious scholars whose search for the 'seat' of the objectivations they are investigating in the 'life' of the historical, social, state, or working world remains a mere postulate or pauses at the most simplistic distinctions,[52] and who thus in fact only deal with the syntactics of the superstructure, ought therefore to be grateful if it could be demonstrated that what they have found out is a symbolization (however this has come about) of, and

---

52. Some examples from historical theology: 'festival/working-day'; 'Jesuan/community-formation'; 'pre-Easter/post-Easter'; 'Judaizing/free of the Law'; 'eschatologically oriented/early catholic'; 'heresy/the Great Church'; 'Pentecostal/official'. The distinctions in Christology, which are often only formally precise, but semantically meaningless or at least not yet clarified, and which science has simply adopted from the history of dogma, belong here, too. Some examples from history of religions: 'primitive/high'; 'spirits/gods'; 'animist/animatist'; and a host of other distinctions made in phenomenology of religion.

thus the essential part in, excerpts from real history. Yet it is precisely these who insist that what they have found out is in fact a copy of the real things. Thus things that are capable of combination are made to belong together — many theologies of the evangelists or of the community, and many totemisms and fetishisms, have seen the light of science in this way —; neighboring or temporally-consecutive facts are made into historically-induced or dependent facts — e. g. Jewish apocalyptics became Iranian, the Christian Gnosis was made Jewish, and the idea of world domination Christian —; and that which is conceptual is made concrete.

Social historians, on the other hand, even those who work 'materialistically', would be generally expected to be completely content once they have uncovered the soft pillow of the 'basis'. Yet it is they who are aware of how difficult it is, from the historical material, to confirm their fundamental methodological insistence on demonstrating that being is not 'determined' by consciousness, but consciousness by being. They speak, correctly, of 'mediations' between being and the products of consciousness, and it is only their 'fideism'/'idealism' complex that prevents them from seeing these mediations for what they are, namely transformations, which involve a symbolizing perception and mastery of being, just as symbolically-informed thinking will continue to be necessary for their historical and genetic explanation. This probably even applies to those mediations which occur according to Marx in religion[53] and according to Stalin in language.[54]

6. What has been said here about the tacit or explicit supporters of copy and symbol theories must of necessity form general theses. These now need verification, differentiation, and of course correction. What

---

53. Cf. J. Kadenbach, *Das Religionsverständnis von Karl Marx*, Munich/Paderborn/Vienna, 1970.

54. It is remarkable that about the only insight of Stalin's which it would have been worth maintaining in inner-Marxist discussion, i. e. that language is neither part of the basis nor of the superstructure, but a social phenomenon independent of class (J. V. Stalin, *Der Marxismus und die Fragen der Sprachwissenschaft*, Berlin, 1951) — an insight which has already made it possible for Marxists and non-Marxists to achieve a broad consensus in the application of philological and linguistic methods — has virtually disappeared from that discussion since de-Stalinization. Cf. for example the significant silence in A. Kosing and W. Segeth, s.v. 'Sprache', in: G. Klaus and M. Buhr (eds.), *Philosophisches Wörterbuch*, Berlin, 8th ed. 1971, pp. 1033 ff.

is needed, therefore, is to describe as precisely as possible what a symbol theory and what a copy theory is, in research in historical theology and in history of religions; where and why one or the other occurs; which objects each of them is by preference applied to; and finally, what their respective results are like. The comments that follow are merely intended as stimuli for the discussion at the conference.

On the side of symbol theories, the writings of Ernst Cassirer[55] on the one hand and of A. N. Whitehead[56] on the other, which conjoin in the work of Susanne Langer,[57] are of value, as is some of Paul Tillich, though only in his pre-Platonist period.[58] The range of copy theories stretches from Nicolai Hartmann[59] to Lenin[60] and also embraces the theologians and historians of religions characterized above. The congruity of symbol and copy theories in reality, or at least how they ought to converge in the basic problems of epistemological theory, was what, on a grand scale, 'Austro-Marxism' attempted to show.[61] Yet even such a determined opponent of neo-Kantian tendencies in Marxism as G. V. Plekhanov was willing to concede something to symbol theories from the natural sciences — not that of H. Hertz, but that of H. von

55. From *Substanzbegriff und Funktionsbegriff*, 1910, and *Zur Einsteinschen Relativitätstheorie*, 1921, and the *Philosophy of Symbolic Forms* (German ed. 1923-1929, English ed. 1953-1957), up to *Determinismus und Indeterminismus in der modernen Physik*, 1937, but not any longer in the *Essay on Man*, 1944, where the whole of epistemological theory has slithered into an anthropology of man as 'animal symbolicum'.

56. Since: *Symbolism, its Meaning and Effect*, 1927.

57. *Philosophy in a New Key. A study in the symbolism of reason, rite, and art*, New York, 1942. For a survey of symbol theories, leading to the empirical side, see: Shulamith Kreitler, *Symbolschöpfung und Symbolerfassung. Eine experimentalpsychologische Untersuchung*, Munich/Basle, 1965.

58. Thus, for example, in *Die sozialistische Entscheidung*, 1932 (reprinted, Offenbach, 1948: pirate off-prints of this edition available), pp. 26-28 on the control of space, and pp. 58, 60, and 67 on symbols. For material on Tillich's later Platonism, see Peter Schwanz, 'Plotin und Tillich', *Kairos* 14 (1972), pp. 137-141. This, like Cassirer's *Essay on Man*, certainly justifies the suspicions by materialists of idealism in symbol theories, though the fault here lies not in the theory, but in the inability of its champions to carry it through consistently.

59. *Grundzüge einer Metaphysik der Erkenntnis*, 1921.

60. See note 12 above. Original edition, 1909. In the German Moscow edition, 1947, cf. especially pp. 29-43.

61. Two anthologies: H. J. Sandkühler and R. de la Vega (eds.), *Marxismus und Ethik*, Frankfurt a.M.,1970 ('Theorie' series); *Austromarxismus*, Frankfurt a.M./Vienna, 1970 ('Politische Texte' series). Cf. also note 47 above.

Helmholtz.[62] It looks very much as though Alfred Schmidt[63] and L. Kolakowski[64] are nowadays attempting a materialist epistemological theory which would avoid merging into ideas of 'reflection', and which is not intended to be a neo-Kantian-Marxist synthesis. The objects which symbol theory has been applied to are mainly language, myth, and numbers (Cassirer), the Christian tradition (Tillich), and communication signs and artistic representation (Whitehead and Langer). Copy theories have been applied to the datum of religion (Feuerbach) and of matter (from Engels' *Anti-Dühring*, 1st ed. 1878, up to Lenin).

Finally we must pay attention to the two kinds of mutual confusion that take place: between symbols of the basis and the superstructure, and between both of these together and their scholarly interpretation. The former is the case, for example, where material nature is a constitutive part in mythologies and statements about creation;[65] where one specific concept of space is constitutive for mythical and a different one for non-mythical thinking;[66] where a theological Pythagoreanism is based on numbers;[67] and where the understanding of time as one of either absolute or relative alternatives natures between material and symbolic contents of the future. A confusion between historically-given symbols and symbols which belong to the interpretation directed towards them took place for example in Romantic religious studies (which were, after all, not restricted to the Romantic period) — for instance in their productive explanations of myths, or in their own creation of myths, which the Romantics legitimated by the appeal to history. And in historical theology, as in religious studies, a confusion always takes

62. 'Materialismus oder Kantianismus?' *Neue Zeit* 17 (1898-99), pp. 589-596. 626-632; *Grundprobleme des Marxismus*, Berlin, 1958.

63. *Der Begriff der Natur in der Lehre von Karl Marx*, Frankfurt a.M., 2nd ed., 1971, pp. 107-113, 'Zum Begriff der Erkenntnistheorie bei Marx'; *Emanzipatorische Sinnlichkeit. Ludwig Feuerbachs anthropologischer Materialismus*, Munich, 1973, pp. 81-91, 'Elemente einer materialistischen Erkenntnistheorie'.

64. *Traktat über die Sterblichkeit der Vernunft*, Munich, 1967, pp. 163-168, 'Ist der Verstehende Materialismus möglich?'; *Die Gegenwärtigkeit des Mythos*, Munich, 1973, pp. 50-60, 'Der Mythos in der Logik'.

65. M. Jammer, *Concepts of Mass*, Cambridge, Mass., 1961. The history of alchemy is also relevant here.

66. M. Jammer, *Concepts of Space*, Cambridge, Mass., 1954.

67. Cf. G. Sauter, 'Die Zahl als Schlüssel zur Welt. Johann Albrecht Bengels "prophetische Zeitrechnung" im Zusammenhang seiner Theologie', *Evangelische Theologie* 26 (1966), pp. 1-36.

place between thing and concept when the theologian's or historian's symbols are not maintained as epistemological and critical, but lead to a construct of historical facts which is then taken for the thing itself. Nazi OT scholars, for example, appraised the Jews as a special kind of minority in the population, with consequences for the investigation of the 'remnant' in the OT; and the 'discovery' of eschatology and of the delay in the Parousia had an ideologically political function in the setting-up of theories of history and secularization. Only if religious studies are able to undo these confusions[68] will they be able to make a contribution to the controversies of our time.[69]

Commentary   by C. J. Bleeker

The notion of previous methods which should be evaluated, suggests that there exist novel methods, differing from the old ones and better than those previous methods. I doubt whether the previous methods

68. Perhaps I may allude here to the essays in which I have attempted to exemplify this, though I cannot claim to have mastered the problems of the basis and the superstructure: 'Theoretische Möglichkeiten zur Identifizierung von Heiligtümern und Interpretationen von Opfern in ur- und parahistorischen Epochen', *Abh. Akad. Göttingen* 3/74 (1970), pp. 18-39 (the retracing of psychological *a priori*'s, and their reproduction in imagined facts, to transcendental *a priori*'s); 'Zarathustra und der frühe Zoroastrianismus', in: *Handbuch der Religionsgeschichte*, ed. J. P. Asmussen and J. Laessoe, Göttingen, 1972, II. 319-357 (the difference between social determination and conditioning); 'Zur mythologischen Struktur der Adonis-, Attis- und Osiris-Überlieferungen', in: *Lišan mithurti* (Festschrift W. v. Soden), ed. by W. Röllig, Kevelaer/Neukirchen, 1969, pp. 23-44 (dissolution of the imagined universality of the mythologeme of gods of death and resurrection through a critique of the 'die-and-rise-again' symbol); 'Der Begriff "Menschensohn" und die Methode der Erforschung messianischer Prototypen', *Kairos* 11 (1969), pp. 241-263; 12 (1970), pp. 81-112; 13 (1971), pp. 1-17; 14 (1972), pp. 241-257 (the rejection of the symbol of primordial man, *Urmensch*, as an explanatory category for 'Son-of-Man' Christology); 'Das Phänomen der nachchristlichen Religion in Mythos und Messianismus', *Neue Zeitschrift für systematische Theologie und Religionsphilosophie* 9 (1967, pp. 42-87) (an attempt to develop Cassirer's mythos theory further, without new mythopoia).
69. An improved and expanded version of this paper, based in part on the discussions at the conference, will appear under the title 'Zur Logik religionswissenschaftlicher und historisch-theologischer Erkenntnis', in: *Theologie und Wirklichkeit. Festschrift für Wolfgang Trillhaas*, Göttingen, 1974.

can be taken as an unity, to be opposed to more recent methods. This is the first difficulty which I encounter, when I try to find a starting-point for my remarks on the methodology of the science of religion. My second stumbling-block is that there is no clear *communis opinio* about the nature, the aim and the contents of the science of religion. Apparently it is a complex of different disciplines, each with a different outlook on the subject in question. If philosophy of religion, for example, is reckoned as part of this system, it is evident that the approach of this discipline to religion must differ considerably from the way in which a historian of religion tackles his problems.

In my opinion the first requirement for a scholar is that, like a good cobbler, he sticks to his own last. I shall gladly grant to everybody the liberty of interpreting the meaning of the science of religion in his own way and of studying the part of this discipline which has his predilection and I am quite willing to learn from the results of his investigations, but in regard to my own contribution to this discussion I feel myself only competent to shed light on the methods of the two sciences which I have pursued for half a century, namely the history of religions and the phenomenology of religion.

My first remark is that I doubt whether it is useful to digress on different methods without first asking about their presuppositions. For method is only a practical measure. The scholarly method is always the outcome of the principle and the aim of the discipline in question. Therefore the first step should be to define the principle and the object of the two sciences mentioned.

This is no easy task, because opinions differ. In such a case it is advisable to start by stating what cannot be the aim of the history of religions and of the phenomenology of religion. This procedure has the advantage that I can thereby discard certain conceptions which to my mind are misconceptions of the character of the sciences in question. This judgment applies in the first place to the opinion of the people who think that the history of religions and the phenomenology of religion should mainly serve to foster world-peace and social harmony, by creating mutual understanding among the adherents of the different religions. It is to be hoped that these high benefits for humanity may be additional results of the studies which we have in view. But theoretically these studies are a purely scholarly affair. Secondly it is wrong to assume that these disciplines are meant to create a picture of the religion of the future. The presupposition of this conception seems to be the idea that traditional theology has lost its authority, so that the science of religion has to step into its place. In certain cases and in certain circles science of religion has actually replaced theology. But it would be erroneous to take this as a general rule. In fact, students of the history of religions and of the phenomenology of religion belong to different religious confessions and churches, or profess no religion; what unites them is the unbiased study of religion as a phenomenon of historical and current interest.

The aim of the two disciplines at stake can be no other than the description and the understanding of religion as a human phenomenon with a deeper dimension. By presenting this definition I am fully aware of the fact that I am conjuring up a series of problems, into which I unfortunately for lack of time cannot enter. Let me simply stress that in my opinion a religio-historical explanation should never be a reduction of religion to non-religious factors, either anthropological, or psychological, or sociological. It is certainly not superfluous to emphasize this principle. At this juncture, now that the God-is-dead theology has captured the mind of many people, and the social sciences and cultural anthropology are flourishing, one now and then gets the impression that the right view of the true nature of religion is in danger of being lost. It should therefore be clearly pointed out that religio-historical research is not primarily meant to understand religious man as such, but should have the ambition of clarifying how man finds his attitude towards divine reality. Religion is not in the first place man's attempt to integrate himself into society, but is the effort to maintain his stand over against the overwhelming cosmic forces which influence human life, both individually and collectively.

As concerns the history of religions I have the feeling that the word 'history' can be misleading. It suggests that the task of the historian of religions is the description of the development of the religion in question. In certain cases, for instance Christianity, Judaism, and Islam, this end can be achieved. In other cases the idea is irrelevant to the research. The sources of Mandeism do not provide sufficient points of support for a historical development. In the study of the Ancient Egyptian religion, which maintained its original pattern throughout the ages, it is no use paying much attention to the question whether and how the conceptions and the rites have changed. I am the last to underestimate the importance of all kinds of painstaking philological, archeological or historical inquiries into the nature of different religions. I would even like to stress that we should clearly realize that religio-historical research can be effected at various levels. That means that different methods should be applied. But ultimately the real aim of the history of religions is to get insight into the character, the idea, and the pattern of the religion in question, totally or partly. Apart from the factual knowledge required there is only one reliable method, namely following the principle of Nathan Söderblom, who declared that in order to understand the religion of the African negroes one should learn to think in black.

The phenomenology of religion is today exposed to renewed criticism. I do not have the time to argue that both the name and the discipline in its traditional shape should be maintained. The phenomenology of religion proves its right of existence, because it can clarify the sense and the structure of the constitutive elements of religion, such as sacrifice, prayer and magic. It is evident that the two sciences are closely related and that they should continuously cooperate. That means that the phenomenology of religion is fully dependent on the material which the history of religions provides it with. On the other hand the phenomenology of religion offers the heuristic principles which help historians of religions to find the clue to difficult problems.

As to methodology, there actually exists only one general rule, i. e. that one should study the religious phenomena both critically, unbiasedly, in a scholarly manner, and at the same time with empathy. Furthermore it depends on the approach to a certain side of the religions in question whether one will use sociological, psychological or anthropological standards. This should not alter the general line of conduct.

These considerations lead finally to two remarks on the evaluation of methods. In the first place I am firmly convinced that the average historian of religions should abstain from speculations about matters of method, which can only adequately be solved by students of philosophy and of philosophy of religion. He has not been trained for the solution of these problems, he has no solid knowledge of the subject, it leads him only to dabbling. Moreover he needs all his time and energy to increase his philological and historical capacities. Secondly we should test to a higher degree than has been done up to now, the concepts with which we try to understand a certain religion. For a Festschrift

I wrote an article on 'Some remarks on the religious terminology of the Ancient Egyptians'. Starting out from the observation by S. Morenz that the Egyptian language lacks words for the notions 'religion', 'piety', and 'belief', I consulted the German-Egyptian part of the famous *Wörter-buch der aegyptische Sprache*. This led me to some interesting conclu-sions: on the one hand it appeared that the Ancient Egyptians had not yet reached the level of sophistication on which we are living, thinking and talking about the religions of the world. On the other hand one learns to detect the religious terms in which the typical Egyptian reli-gious consciousness expressed itself. I sometimes wonder whether the adherents of the religions which we are studying would recognize their belief in the picture which we present them. This means that the true evaluation of methods would be to retain only those methods which let religious people themselves testify their faith. In conclusion I offer a variant of the saying by Rousseau, 'retournons à la nature', namely: retournons à la philologie et à l'histoire.

Commentary   by Walter H. Capps

In the 'Epistle to the Reader', in the introductory portion of his *Essay Concerning Human Understanding* (1671-1687), the English philos-opher, John Locke, offered the following commentary on the state of corporate intelligence in his time: 'The commonwealth of learning is not at this time without masterbuilders, whose mighty designs in ad-vancing the sciences will leave lasting monuments to the admiration of posterity; but everyone must not hope to be a Boyle or a Sydenham, and in an age that produces such masters as the great Huygenius and the incomparable Mr. Newton, with some other of that strain, 't is am-bition enough to be employed as an under-labourer in clearing ground a little and removing some of the rubbish that lies in the way to knowl-edge.'

Having introduced my subject with Locke's almost iconoclastic state-ment, I run the risk, I know, of creating the expectation that my con-tention will pertain to the rubbish that has accumulated in the study of religion. But this is neither my suggestion nor my insinuation. Nor do I want to say in straightforward, simple fashion that the pathway to knowledge in *Religionswissenschaft* has been cluttered by the grand, all-encompassing, systematic thought patterns of the prominent master builders. Of course, this is always partially true, whether one is talking about the history of sciences, philosophy, or religion. But there is a significant second side to the issue which should not be overlooked. Though some of the master builders' substantive contentions have become obsolete, and though the systematic configurations of their thought patterns have become unfashionable, the grand theories will always be looked upon as being monumental. Whatever else they did, they helped put a subject in focus. They also gave design, shape, and direction to an emerging field of studies. These large stylistic constructive contributions must always be appreciated even in times when intellectual interests move in other directions. For not until after the visionary stage has been accomplished does it dawn on anyone that something like Locke's critical, reflexive measure is the next necessary step.

Thus, acknowledging the greatness of the master builders, one must contend nevertheless that it is appropriate to be involved in the more menial tasks of 'clearing the ground a little'. Religious studies cannot progress simply by adding theory to theory or by piling one systematic-configurative account upon another. Nor are large advances to be found in restricting oneself to issues and questions internal to the science of religion, or even in negotiating the casual border hostilities between, say, the history, phenomenology, and philosophy of religion. Similarly, it can no longer suffice to take all prime constructive cues from developments within other fields and disciplines. This, as we know, has been a dominant pathway to knowledge in the field. 'Evolutionism', for example, loomed large in other fields and disciplines; gradually 'evolutionism' came to loom large too in the science of religion. Phenomenology came to loom in other fields and disciplines; true to form, phenomenology found its way into the science of religion. 'High gods', 'sky gods', and astral myths gained prominence in certain areas of the study of religion; then, progressively, their influence became pervasive. Recently, structuralism has become a major component of a variety of fields and disciplines; gradually, more and more, and even dramatically, structuralism has become prominent in the science of religion. And this pattern will continue as long as the stimulus-and-response syndrome continues as a chief source of creativity.

No matter how well such enterprises are embarked upon, the fact remains that the science of religion is ripe for ground-clearing, for it is not always clear about its conceptual basis. More specifically, the science of religion is unsure of its second-order tradition. I shall cite some examples: When one studies philosophy, he is introduced not only to long-standing philosophical issues, but to philosophers and to philosophical schools. To study philosophy is to engage in philosophical reflection and to learn to find one's way into the reflections of Plato, Aristotle, Descartes, Russell, Wittgenstein, and the others. The same is true, too, in psychology. In studying psychology, one is introduced to problems and issues that belong to the field, and he is also forced to become acquainted with the history and theory of psychology. And this implies knowing one's way into Freud, Jung, Adler, Rank, Erikson, Sullivan, Maslow, and the others. But it is difficult to do the same in the science of religion. The prime difficulty is due to the fact that the subject-field has no clear, direct, self-sustaining second-order tradition. The scholar within the field comes to sense that the theories of E. B. Tylor, Émile Durkheim, Max Weber, Sir James Frazer, Max Müller, Rudolf Otto, Gerardus van der Leeuw, and the others, have something to do with one another. On closer inspection, they seem to exhibit certain intriguing family likenesses. But one can never be quite sure. For, as is obvious, such personages come from a variety of fields, represent a variety of disciplines, and hardly ever enter the science of religion from the same standpoint or on the same grounds. A good case can be made that the principle contributions and the prime discoveries within the field have ordinarily been made by persons who are self-conscious practitioners of methods and disciplines of other fields: anthropologists, sociologists, philosophers, historians, psychologists, sometimes historians of art. Much of the time the formative contributions have not come from within the field, but from the outside, as it were. Thus, if a sense of a second-order tradition is to be recovered, one cannot expect to look for a chain of communication that bears any resemblance to apostolic succession. Instead, it is disparate, disjointed, flexible, and accumulated or even created rather than discovered. Its sources lie here and there, and its ingredients are always arbitrarily assembled. But no matter how difficult it is to recover, the field cannot get along without a sense of an underlying, second-order tradition. It cannot hope to be instrumentally self-conscious without knowing how to arrange its second-order literature. It cannot pretend to find its way until it can relate to its past in narrative form.

Because there is no clear, conscious second-order tradition in the science of religion, there is profound uncertainty regarding the configuration, boundaries, and self-definition of the field. This fact has been made apparent by the large number of definitional questions that continue to be unresolved. For example, is the science of religion a subject or a field? Is it a discipline or is it multi-disciplinary? Does it have a proper subject, or does the multiplicity of its interests prohibit a common focal point?

Answers to such questions are seldom convincing if only because of the enormous range of subjects which the science of religion claims to comprehend. For, strictly speaking, the science of religion is neither a discipline nor a subject. Rather, it must be designated as a 'subject-field' within which a variety of disciplines are employed and a multiplicity of subjects treated. It is a subject-field before it is anything more discrete than this. And when it becomes more discrete it lends definitional exactness, methodological precision, and specific focus to the objects of its attention.

This is simply another way of saying that what the scholar does within the subject-field depends upon where he is standing. Where he stands influences what he discovers. Furthermore, where he stands and what he discovers are implicit in what he is trying to do. All of these factors, in turn, form his conception of the field and help set the operational definition he gives to religion. Consequently, when one looks within the academy for analogs to the science of religion, he should pay attention to fields which have just recently emerged, for example, 'environmental studies' or even 'ethnic studies'. In all such cases, the name of the enterprise indicates that the subject-field is a collectivity within which a variety of useful endeavors occur which draw upon a large number of disciplines, methodologies, and tutored sensitivities.

In this paper so far, I have attempted to register two contentions. Both belong to the concern for a 'ground-clearing', reflexive action within the science of religion. The first pertains to the need for a clearly articulated second-order tradition within the subject-field. Without the awareness of such a tradition, it is difficult to find orientation and establish identity. The second contention points to the massive disparateness of the subject-field. With regard to this disparateness, I want now to be more specific. When the second-order tradition of the subject-field is conceived, it must possess both sufficient dynamism and flexibility to sustain the following kinds of variability.

VARIETIES OF OPERATIONAL DEFINITIONS

Within the large subject-field, there are several clusters of subjects, topics, and foci which lend a regulative definition to the word 'religion'. Some methodologies treat religion as religions, for example, and spend their energies describing one or more religious tradition. In such approaches, religion is understood to refer to an organism. The organism has component parts, and tends to function well when those parts are in harmony.

But other methodologies are not trained upon religious traditions, just as philosophers do not always think in terms of philosophical schools and ideologies (Platonism, Aristotelianism, existentialism, positivism, and the like). Instead such methods focus upon religious quotients or religious factors. They are sensitive to the religious components of the development of the personality. They identify the religious factors which inform cultures. There treat religious dimensions to social, ethical, and political life.

In addition to the two large postures already cited, there is an orientation to the field which is motivated neither by religion as tradition or organism nor by religious factors and quotients, but, as it is said, by religion itself, or 'the nature or essence of religion' if you will. For this temperament, it is not enough to concentrate on the prominent patterns of religious institutionalization or upon religious qualities that register elsewhere: rather, it is necessary to get to the heart of the matter. Consequently, this approach is preoccupied with questions about what religion is, what its fundamental components are, how it is to be defined. Under the same rubric, one can list the apparently perpetual, ongoing quest to locate the range of human experience to which religion properly refers (feelings, actions, thoughts, imagination, etc.). In all of this, religion is construed as being something other than an adjective modifying a noun or a noun that can become pluralized.

MULTIPLE METHODOLOGICAL INTERESTS AND INTENTIONS

The range of the subject-field is compounded further because the multiple subject is also approached from multiple intentions and vested interests. Some methods, for example, are equipped only to describe religious phenomena, whether such phenomena be organisms, quotients, distinguishing elements, or structures. Others attempt to transcend 'mere description' and engage in exercise in comparison and contrast. Comparison and contrast, in turn, can be of the internal kind (when applied to one and the same organism), or it can be of the cross-cultural or even cross-disciplinary kind. But some methods function not only to compare and contrast, but, more ambitiously, to systematize and synthesize. That is, they have been designed to build systems of unification or patterns of similarity.

This is sufficient multiplicity. But the multiplicity is further compounded when the various methodological intentions are coupled with deepseated convictional goals. Scholars engage in descriptive, comparative, isolative, and synthesizing work, sometimes, in order to defend religion, demonstrate its utility, verify it, explain it away, or, frequently, to give it a theological sanction. Admittedly, these examples of convictional intent hardly ever display themselves in such unambiguous manner; but the point is worth making that elements of evaluation and sanction possess a formative place in methodological dispositions. In various degrees, every scholar in the field does what he does in order to show the significance, relevance, meaningfulness, uniqueness, connection, or utility of religion, in either positive or negative terms.

DISTINCTIONS BETWEEN LARGE CONTROLLING QUESTIONS

In addition to variations of foci and methodological proclivities, the subject-field called the science of religion has also been influenced by a multiplicity of large controlling questions. Here we have reference to the comprehensive philosophical or ideational issues under which the tasks and methods of scholarship were conceived. For example, when one looks back across the past one hundred fifty years, he recognizes that a large portion of the second-order tradition was inspired by the desire to identify religion's *sine qua non*. From Immanuel Kant — perhaps from Descartes — onward, a large host of scholars and methodologists have concentrated attention within the science of religion on the discovery of first principles. Their methods have been tailored to reduce all qualities, characteristics, and aspects of religion to those components that are absolutely basic. The goal is to analyze complex entities so that an unambiguous simple core-element might be identified. Then, this fundamental simple element is understood to be indispensable. Whether it be Kant's moral compulsion, Schleiermacher's 'feeling of absolute dependence', Otto's 'numinous', Freud's 'illusion', Feuerbach's 'projection', Nygren's 'agape', Tillich's 'depth dimension', Goodenough's 'protection against the tremendum', etc., etc., the isolated core-element is regarded as that without which religion would not be what it truly is.

But there are other questions under whose influence the science of religion has taken shape. In addition to the concern for religion's essence, the tradition also reflects a pervasive interest in revocering religion's origin. Here, the attempt to disclose an underlying core-element is merged with the awareness that realities are affected by the passage of time. Thus, the quest for the *sine qua non* becomes transposed into an interest in tracing back to religion's *primordium*. It is here that I would place the work of E. B. Tylor, Andrew Lang, R. R. Marett, Wilhelm Schmidt, Frazer, Müller, perhaps Durkheim, and (as we scholars are wont to say) 'a host of others'.

Furthermore, when the attempt to find the fundamental core-element (whether logical *sine qua non* or chronological *primordium*) is abandoned, there is still much that can be done to lend description to the relationship that exists between the pluralized (rather than singularized) components (or perceptible features) of religion. Methodologically, one can regard the phenomenology of religion as having been formed out of a pluralized, detemporized attempt to put the various elements of religion — the irreducible simples — in meaningful order. Thus, instead of trying to identify the single, definitive core-element, or providing an account of religion's origin and development, scholars in phenomenology have seemed content to give a comprehensive description to the manner and form in which religious phenomena appear in human experience. Rather than searching for underlying causes, essences, or exhaustive explanations, they have focussed on the manifest, descriptive features of phenomena. Their eventual goal is to provide a complete account of a thing's form, structure, and distinguishing lines. All of them have assumed that within the proper manner of viewing — which combines empirical techniques with a kind of intuitive grasping of the subject — such manifestable features 'stand out' for the investigator to perceive.

Our subject can only be treated in sketch here. But even in sketch, the large variety of interests, methods, intentions, materials, subjects, skills, questions, and issues referred to should indicate that the science of religion is a large, dynamic subject-field within which a variety of selected subjects is approached by means of numerous disciplines under the influence of multiple attitudes and methodological sets of interests. This variety should demonstrate that there is no single, common subject which is treated by all, regardless of their backgrounds, who claim association with the science of religion. There is no single subject within the science of religion which is common to all endeavors. Furthermore, the science of religion perhaps owns no agreed-upon center. It possesses no single, identifiable core-element. And the more specific subjects within the field do not share a common likeness. The enterprises sponsored within the subject-field may have direct and indirect associations with each other. They possess family likenesses, to be sure. But such likenesses need not rest on a common property; such associations need not be organic. Rather, the science of religion is a collectivity in which a variety of useful endeavors occur which draw upon a large number of disciplines and involve a multiplicity of subjects.

At the same time, the very disparateness of the subject-field makes consciousness and articulation of a second-order tradition all the more necessary and crucial. For collectivities and traditions function to give formation and to sustain arrangement and direction. The components of collectivities are ingredient in the composition of second-order traditions. Collectivities are composed: they are always at least partially idiosyncratic. They consist of peculiarities, not of logical steps. Their function is rather odd-job, not regular and forensic. They are given to perimeter settings, not necessarily to definitional exactness. And while they carry a formative junction, they are not causal. A tradition, too, is formed, not caused. It is composed, not deduced. It has a certain spontaneity and flexibility; it is never forced. It is like a design applied delicately and lightly rather than a necessary conclusion of a sequential, discursive series.

The science of religion owns such patterns of arrangement, and they have not yet been enunciated. And, as we have suggested, this is a commentary on the sheer diversity and immensity of the subject. Perhaps it testifies too to the embryonic nature of the field. It may well be that the science of religion is just now reaching the stage of its corporate life cycle, where, in the words of Erik Erikson, after knowing that it can make things and make them well it seeks to align its capacities with its sense of endowment, opportunity, and heritage. At earlier moments, it sought place, purpose, and competence. Now, as the cycle indicates, it is also a matter of fidelity.

Until a second-order tradition is found and nurtured, scholars may find themselves engaged in tasks that are obsolete even before they are undertaken, communication from within the subject-field outward will be frustrated by an untranslatable vocabulary, and the familiar stimulus-and-response syndrome will prevail as the chief source of a creativity always at least once-removed. More seriously, until a second-order tradition becomes conscious, all methodological stances seem doomed to maintain a rigid focus on permanence (norms, laws, structures, and recurrent patterns) within the science of religion. At some future point, the turn must be taken away from permanence to processes of change, motion, movement, and spontaneity. Eventually, instead of straining to identify the underlying pattern of stability of religious phenomena, future methodologies must become equipped to come to terms with the change factor: the moving, inconstant, spontaneous, irregular, discontinuous, non-forensic, once-only, explosive, surprise element. Instead of focusing on 'arrested pictures' or moments of stopped action, as all past and/or present methodologies seem to do, future approaches must find access to the dynamics of catalytic and kinetic realities.

But this is to shift our topic to new ground. It is necessary first to clear that ground a little.

Commentary   by Hans-J. Klimkeit

1. H. Biezais' clear presentation actually leads us into two different areas worthy of discussion: (1) the problem explicitly addressed, i.e. typology of religion and its relation to history, phenomenology and morphology,

and (2) the further-reaching question concerning hermeneutics in religious studies. This latter question is always entailed in a reflection on
the premisses of phenomenology.

Let us speak first about the former problem, and begin by commenting on the relationship between typology and history. Two possible
forms of such a relationship are chosen for study here. First of all,
reference is made to the 'typology of religious history', or historical
typology, proposed by Lanczkowski; it is intended to mediate between
history of religions and phenomenology, and to ensure, or at least aim
at, a coordination of both. The danger that facts can be processed (or
even constructed) without being adequately grounded in and checked
against history, is fully recognized, and a corrective function is hence
assigned to the proposed historical typology. Fundamentally, one must
grant this scholarship its right.

One might add that Joachim Wach's approach practically led in the
direction of this kind of historical typology. In his later years, at any
rate, Wach saw the greatest — and ultimate — possibilities for comparative religious studies in type-formation (Wach, *Types of Religious
Experience*, p. 229). But he avoids the danger of a self-satisfied typology,
for he observes, in accordance with Dilthey, that typology should serve
only to look deeper into history.

What seems in fact to be more problematical (as Biezais emphasizes,
in common with Bleeker) is the establishment of an overarching, rather
than mediating, 'historical typology of religions', as proposed by Bianchi. Here, the problem of identifying religion without presuming specific
ideas about it, is not at all escaped, but merely put aside. Furthermore,
there will be understandable objections on the part of the historian,
for such an undertaking would demand the acceptance of concepts,
the nature and implications of which can only be apprehended in phenomenology. It is equally questionable whether phenomenology is
capable of carrying out its task on the concrete level which history
must require.

The fact that there are differences in the level of abstraction when
bruta facta or *phenomena* are described, points to a crucial issue that
has been the subject of increasing attention in German historical research
and methodology: the question whether historiography is possible at
all without preconceived general notions and type concepts, e. g. the
concept of 'a state', 'a nation', 'a prophet', 'a reformer', etc., with all

that implies (see Th. Schieder, F. Wagner, F. G. Maier, R. Wittram, and K.-G. Faber, to mention but a few). This leads us, again, to the advantage of a 'mediating typology' which could become valuable as a corrective to phenomenological as well as historical studies, if it considers the types and crypto-types always necessary in historical description.

The relationship of typology to phenomenology and also to morphology (which systematizes its material according to purely formal principles) is indeed manifold, as is clearly shown in Biezais' paper. But the whole question seems to be rather barren when studied in such a general manner. The systematic allocation of specific concepts of types, which Biezais undertakes at the end of his paper, is therefore all the more welcome.

The first of these possibilities — summarized on p. 160 — practically comes close to Weber's 'ideal type'; at any rate, a clearer definition, and to some extent a legitimation, of such a type concept could be found in Weber. (This cultural or sociological concept of type is naturally distinct from van der Leeuw's hermeneutic concept thereof.)

The second concept of type suggested is an 'abstract ... principle of systematization', and it undoubtedly offers a good working tool, worthy of further elucidation, if it is capable of being modified, corrected, and challenged by the concrete facts themselves, and insofar as its 'normative character' is not based on premises which resist investigation.

The third concept of type, finally, discloses 'contextual meaning' by establishing 'by means of phenomenology ... direct relationships between the object to be understood and the person understanding it'. This notion corresponds closely to the concept of the phenomenon in classical, hermeneutically oriented phenomenology. It is questioned here as a usable means of empirical research. But there seems to me to be a misunderstanding here, deriving from a false interpretation of R. Otto, if this concept of type, or phenomenon, is thought of as supposedly establishing 'direct relationships ... between the spheres of the empirical and the transcendent'. According to Otto, and many other phenomenologists, this can refer at most to the transcendental in the Kantian or neo-Kantian sense as that which is *a priori*, i.e. prior to and independent of all experience. This should not be conceived of metaphysically, however, as an ontological proof of God's existence, in any way. There is no attempt here 'to establish direct contact, with the aid of the phenomenological method, with the holy, the divine, and the irrational', even if Otto did predicate numinous experience as the basis of his method.

No doubt, even with a corrected understanding of Otto – and we refer here to A. Paus' differentiated analysis of his premises – and with a well defined phenomenological method such as that supported by Van der Leeuw, there remains much in this approach which needs critical re-examination on the basis of modern hermeneutics and scientific theory. First and foremost, the concept of 'essence' (*Wesen*) and hence also of '(intuitive) perception of essence' (*Wesensschau*) seem to have become problematic, even in philosophy. (I dare say that the analytical concept of 'structure', which replaces that of 'essence' in some quarters today, is no less problematic because of its formal nature.)

To reject the phenomenological method altogether as unempirical, and therefore unscientific, would mean letting the baby out with the bath-water. The notion of science on which such an attack is based needs to be critically examined itself, for it claims to be the sole legitimate empirical tool with which reality may be grasped. The scientific description of reality which we must strive for, however, is more than a matter of completely objectifiable validity, as in the classical natural sciences. Beyond the historical and typificatory processing of the material, the legitimate ultimate aim will always entail an interpretation of being, i.e. of human existence, itself. If this is not recognized consciously, it will at least determine the presentation of facts unconsciously, which seems all the more problematic.

What E. Staiger has said about the interpretation of literary, poetic material can also be applied to the description and analysis of religious material: 'Es ist seltsam bestellt um die Literaturwissenschaft. Wer sie betreibt, verfehlt entweder die Wissenschaft oder die Literatur. Sind wir aber bereit, an so etwas wie Literaturwissenschaft zu glauben, dann müssen wir uns entschliessen, sie auf einem Grund zu errichten, der dem Wesen des Dichterischen gemäss ist...' (E. Staiger, p. 10).

If the hermeneutics of religious studies were reformulated so as to follow up the working methods of the so-called 'positivist', analytical-empirical branches of research, conceding these orientations their right, but integrating them hermeneutically, it would then be in a position to uphold the legitimate claim of phenomenology, which is precisely that it wishes to grasp the living element in religion. It is necessary to incorporate the empirical and at the same time the nomological-analytical working methods into an ideographical-analytical framework (cf. P. Masson). This is not the place to expand on such a form of hermeneutics. It could be pointed out, however, that there is much that is valuable in this respect in the thought of H.-J. Gadamer and his school, especially in its dispute with the so-called 'Critical Theory'.*

2. The attempt to place methodological enquiry in religious studies into relation with the current discussion in the humanities and social sciences — at least in the German-speaking world — deserves special attention, since the roots of many methods in use today are still partly to be found in philosophical reflections which were carried out several decades ago. It is not simply that the premisses of religious studies need to be brought 'up to date', as it were, or rejuvenated, in the sense of a beautifying 'facelift'; it is also that the work on the religious data is partly conditioned — as Colpe rightly emphasizes — by unconscious premisses that shape the researcher's approach in crucial ways. Work in history of religions, like all historical work, as well as any form of intercultural or comparative study, will therefore always need to be oriented in two directions: towards the matter in hand, i. e. the concrete data of history, and towards the preconditions and premisses that precede one's own work in the field. In neither area of work will the ultimate establishment of truth as objectifiable validity be possible.

* Bibliography:
Faber, K. G., *Theorie der Geschichtswissenschaft*, Munich, 1971.
Masson, P., *Traditionelle soziale Werte der Tukuna und das 'Verstehen'*, Unpub. diss., Bonn, 1973.
Maier, F. G., 'Der Gesetzesbegriff in den historischen Wissenschaften', *Studium Generale* 19 (1966), 657-670.
Paus, A., *Religiöser Erkenntnisgrund: Herkunft und Wesen der Aprioritheorie Rudolf Ottos*, Leiden, 1966.
Schieder, Th., 'Der Typus in der Geschichtswissenschaft', *Studium Generale* 5 (1952), 228-234.
——, *Geschichte als Wissenschaft*, Munich/Vienna, 1965.
Staiger, E., *Die Kunst der Interpretation* (dtv Wissenschaftliche Reihe), Munich, 1971 (first published 1955).
Wach, J., *Types of Religious Experience*, London, 1951.
Wagner, Fr., 'Analogie als Methode geschichtlichen Verstehens', *Studium Generale* 8 (1955), 703-712.
Wittram, R., *Das Interesse an der Geschichte*, Göttingen, 1958.

As far as methodological enquiry is concerned, the maximum aim can only be a higher degree of reflection, never the disclosure of permanently valid methodical principles.

This leads us into the modern problematic of scientific theory. The location of Colpe's paper within the current German discussion on the issue prompts me to state my own position in the light of this discussion itself. Since the complex which we are concerned with has in fact remained largely restricted to the German world, a fuller exposition of this intellectual landscape seems necessary.

The crucial concept, which provides us with access to the heart of the matter, is that of ideological criticism. It implies that all forms of ideology that pretend to give a valid interpretation of man and his existence need to be criticized, since they are determined by a preconceived world view, arrived at independent of a searching analysis of the facts themselves. Naturally, religion, or the religious world view, are also regarded as ideological in this sense. The need of the hour – so say the representatives of 'ideological criticism' – is the elimination of such non-factual elements in the description, or interpretation, of the world, for they conceal the actual relationships determining man's being.

This ideological critique derives its basis from the idea that the interpretative, non-factual elements in a presentation of historical or sociological state of affairs will be directed by specific interests, unconscious as yet (i. e. not as yet made conscious through reflection), and in the final analysis determined by class. Such latent interests are aimed at perpetuation, reinforcement, and fixation (this is a central idea) of given patterns and structures from the past.

In the case of religious studies that aim at an understanding not determined by any reductionism, this means that here, too, structures from the past are illegitimately perpetuated by their very appreciative description. By an appreciative, not critical, 'understanding' of the religiousness of the past beyond a mere reconstruction of historical facts, those past forms of faith are elevated into a sphere where they will be safe from socio-psychological attack; made into absolutes, and accorded the aura of the immutable: exempt from enquiry, irreducible, possessing absolute value, and holy. Faced with this state of affairs, the demand which ideological criticism makes is for self-examination, the disclosure of concealed intentions, and the consequent demolition of ideological embellishment, both on the level of presentation and of methodology.

The application of this claim to theological enquiry undoubtedly carries special implications, but it is also of relevance for religious studies which are not seen as being tied to Theology. For any form of religious studies which aims at more than the mere establishment of historical facts and the illumination of their historical-causal relations, must feel itself addressed by the problems raised in ideological criticism, just as the most rationalistic historical criticism is also challenged, precisely because of its obscured premises. Above all, however, religious studies will have to deal seriously with the problem of ideological criticism, if they aim not only at the description of dogmatic ideas in their origins and structure, but also at rendering piety visible — not only at the explanation of the structures of religious ideas and traditionally-determined institutions, but also at disclosing past forms of belief —, in short, not only at the assembly and reconstruction of museum material, but at adequately grasping and honoring the living element in and within religion.

The notion of ideology which is at the basis of ideological criticism, and which — as we saw — also subsumes religion under its concept, accusing it of masking reality, derives from the idea that in an ideological, or religious, world view, factual reality is concealed by an interpretative addition which thought adds to reality. This kind of addition has no right to exist, however, since it originates neither in reality, nor in thinking that accords with reality, but in other sources, which are not immediately transparent to the perceiver. The picture of reality presented through such additions is a deception, and, as a result of the latent, concealed character of its sources, it is ultimately a self-deception, an unconscious distortion of reality.

The crucial objection made by ideological criticism, therefore, is that the ideological — and thus also religious — view of reality is invaded by elements which are alien to the essence of true perception. These illegitimate elements are defined more closely as elements which serve the practical interest of domination of the world. This secret, voluntative interest, which inserts itself into perception as its guiding principle, determines the ideological, or religious, version of reality, which hence pictures the world of man not as it is, but as it ought to be according to concealed wishes.

This concealed bias in an ideological or religious interpretation of the world, which presents itself in the false guise of an idea ostensibly satisfying the requirements of perception, reveals its true nature in the perpetuation (or 'fixation') of inherited structures by their uncritical description. For the ideological critic, there is no truth that survives all ages, or which could be located spiritually, neither can there be any systems or patterns which remain the same, i. e. 'fixed'. Time itself reveals the false 'fixation' of a version of the world through the progress of development. It becomes apparent that it is no longer appropriate to the age: (social) reality has already become different from what ideology or religion would have us believe. The ideological or religious world view reveals itself as historical, for it has become obsolete. True perception, which is timeless and ahistorical, and based solely on the immutability of logical precepts, is thus opposed to an ideological interpretation of the world.

The conception of ideology on which ideological criticism is based is furthermore determined by its relation to time, inasmuch as ideology — and thus religion — are understood in sociological terms. Ideology and religion — so it is believed — are always crucially co-determined through respective given social factors. This unilateral sociological orientation excludes other dimensions of interpretation. The dimensions of personality, or culture, for instance, are all projected onto the social level, or traced back to social frames of reference.

For the representative of ideological criticism, the ideological or religious image of the world is bound up with a social entanglement. Ideas propounded by religion or ideology must always be traced to the corresponding social interests and conditions whence they derive. Hence they represent a superstructure, dependent upon a certain social basis. The duality of the basis/superstructure pattern as propounded by Marxism remains very much alive here. It is obvious that the relation between the 'basis' and the 'superstructure', i. e. between sociological 'being' and ideological 'consciousness' suspended above it, constitutes a problem of particular urgency in ideological criticism.

Here, now, three basic questions arise:

1. First of all, it must be pointed out that this criticism of ideology is to be seen against the background of German idealism. The conception that it is the mind (*der Geist*) which creates for itself the body, is a basic dogma in German idealist thinking; it has dominated, and continues

to dominate not only philosophy, psychology and anthropology, but also sociology, history and in fact widely differing fields of study. The mental premises and intellectual structures conditioning a given object of investigation are accorded such priority that sight is only too easily lost of the concrete pressures and objective social living conditions which determine the matter in its entirety. These concrete facts are too easily regarded as secondary and derivative over against intellectual preconditions. Now in ideological criticism, that polarity is merely reversed. The duality between social being and mental consciousness is maintained, albeit in sublimated form, but 'material', social objects are accorded the priority of importance, and intellectual factors derived from them. Here the fallacy of idealism is not overcome, but merely turned upside down. It must be asked whether it would not be better to overcome the 'idealism complex' by enriching the dimensions of reference of reality, rather than simply by reversing it into a 'material-ism complex'. Being and consciousness, and also religion, are at least also determined by the dimensions of culture and personality, just as undeniably and unambiguously as being is conditioned by consciousness and consciousness by being, as Max Weber has pointed out. In research into religion, the question therefore arises not only as to its sociological frame of reference, but as to all its conceivable dimensions of reference. It would be ideological to exclude *a priori* any dimension which a pred-icated methodology cannot explore. We shall return to this question under point 3.

2. The image of reality characterized by a polarity between being and consciousness is paralleled within ideological criticism by the latent premise of a dualistic image of man. A conscious, intellectual upper layer, which operates according to constant, logical laws, and is capable of empirical, objectivist perception of reality, is paralleled by an un-conscious depth layer, which entertains concealed intentions that ille-gitimately influence the act of perception and determine it ideologically. In contrast to the eternal constancy of the logical laws in the top layer of man's thinking, these latent and opaque impulses and interests from below are conditioned by time and determined by class. Constant and recurrent archetypes from the lower, unconscious layer only derive from the researcher's class-determined intentions, although they represent themselves as true perception.

Now it should be impossible to point to any scientifically or philo-

194 Evaluation of Previous Methods

sophically compelling position which would make the adoption of this image of man predicated by ideological criticism necessary. Nor should it be possible to point to any scientific or philosophical position which would make the adoption of the Marxist class-struggle model (even in its sublimated neo-Marxist form) necessary. This model is however fundamental to the image of man as an integral part of society which we find in ideological criticism. This position thus in its turn reveals itself as the crypto-ideological result of an ideological escalation. In neo-Marxist discussions, the criterion for historical perception and social action is derived from a chosen, 'historical' class ('history' here includes past, present and future); the question arises whether this class does not thus take over the role of the decisive social reference-group which was once accorded to a chosen race. The justification of this class perspective will certainly be no less ambiguous than that of the racial perspective.

3. Thirdly, the validity of the epistemological theory in ideological criticism needs to be examined. The demand for unrestricted examination of every single attempt to describe or interpret the world must be accepted as basically valid. The postulate that all representations of reality should be critically explored is scientifically legitimate, and moreover necessary in the interests of our freedom. Every idea which claims to interpret reality must submit to probing investigation, and to enquiry as to its real reasons and background. This also applies to every religious idea which belongs to history and which is picked out and interpreted by the researcher. Every value and criterion that is taken for granted, every spiritual and social context, must be constantly probed as to its genetic and causal origins. There is no interpretation or prejudice which may exempt itself a priori from rational examination.

This claim by ideological criticism must be acknowledged; in fact it must be followed through to more radical and consistent conclusions, and applied to ideological criticism itself. But when that is done, the fundamental epistemological premise of ideological criticism is itself revealed as being determined by bias. This consists of the idea that a true view of reality is only possible by means of a specific immanent epistemological tool (which incidentally has only been revealed as universally valid in the present era of ideological criticism). The tool consists of checking thought by applying it to the objects of possible, finite experience. This is the logical principle that must always be observed.

But the extent to which truth and reality can be checked here is limited by the boundaries of that logic. In this way, the boundary of reality becomes identical with that of this form of perception.

The crucial premise here is that every idea claiming to interpret reality (e. g. the idea of God) can be analyzed fully by ideological criticism in terms of historical or socio-psychological categories if only submitted to a searching examination. It is further assumed that its full sense is disclosed if it is analyzed into elements stemming from the conscious, intellectual sphere and elements from the unconscious realm of latent volition. But is it thereby agreed that an idea which cannot be fully reduced to the objective reasons which speak for it and to those which unconsciously stand behind it, is 'illegitimate', or inevitably distorts reality instead of disclosing it?

Certainly we recognize the necessity of disclosing as far as possible the causal and functional referents that serve to explicate a religious idea, or phenomenon. But by only putting it into the straitjacket of causal and genetic explicability, we run the risk of concealing its full significance. Squashing the phenomenon into the Procrustes' bed of a calculative hither-and-thither, forbidding it to express itself fully (that is to say to express itself in categories which cannot be exhaustively grasped by this epistemological theory), and imposing on it a reduction to experience, verifiable by means of its accordance with praxis – all this shortens its phenomenality. The only things which are being illuminated here are the conditions under which it occurred. There cannot exist any legitimate scientific position, however, which would question the openness of allowing the phenomenon to speak beyond the frames of reference that serve to explain it causally and genetically. The living encounter of man with man can already serve as an example. The meaning of such an encounter is not exhausted by an illumination of the historical conditions, social involvements and psychological interactions which determine it. A live encounter does not resolve itself (like a natural phenomenon) into the conditions of its becoming.

Hence the ultimate criterion which must be required here is that of freedom from bias in the face of all experience of reality. This is required not by any metaphysics, but by the dignity of man himself.

The question that arises in the basis of this general background is: what are the positive and negative premises of ideological criticism that have been adopted in Colpe's paper?

The epistemological theory Colpe is aiming at strives to illuminate 'the basic relationship between historical and causal explanation' in religious research. Hence genetic and causal explicability are crucial issues. The problem thus corresponds to that in ideological criticism. The criteria called for in this theory apparently also correspond to those of ideological criticism for here, too, the epistemological tool consists of checking by application to possible present experience. Fortunately, the short-sightedness of the check-proof method required by ideological criticism is abandoned in Colpe's theory, for verification need not be entirely immanent to science, though it is still to be carried out by showing up accordance with experiential praxis. But it is emphasized that Theology has special claims to make in respect to verifiability: claims that go beyond 'those merely concerned with the verification or falsification of scientific propositions'. It is to be appreciated that the 'verification' demanded here involves such a wide concept of reality that it even includes the experience of faith. This goes far beyond the normal epistemological postulate of ideological criticism, and in consequence, both 'verification' and 'praxis' must be understood in a modified sense. The whole problem comes close to the question of hermeneutics, with its well-known circle co-determined by the researcher's experience. The form of hermeneutics aimed at by Colpe is, however, normative (in the sense used by Habermas) rather than historical, as is indicated by the concern to relativize historicity. His hermeneutical circle is determined by 'the reciprocal relation between the materialist character of ideological criticism..., and the materialist view of the relations under which 'religious' documents ... come about'. Here the term 'materialist' refers to the basis/superstructure schema; it implies that concrete, socio-economic circumstances condition – though not crudely or deterministically – both the religious documents and their understanding today. Hence not the documents and their understanding alone are to be related to one another hermeneutically, but also the concrete 'bases' of both. Hereby, the social conditions prevailing today have normative character for the interpretation of the text.

The idea that such an epistemology is adaptable to theological statements that take as their norm the present social scene, seems disputable within theology. But be that as it may – such a socially based and praxis oriented conception is hardly useful in non-normative historical and comparative religious studies.

The implications of this whole epistemology have already been referred to above. The main idea is that the 'fixation' of social and intellectual states of affairs have to be overcome, also in theology, and in all forms of religious study. Let us refer again to the concept of time in ideological criticism. According to it, the progress of development itself determines the nature of the theological 'truth' to be expounded today — insofar as the term 'truth' can be applied in this context at all, for it seems to be replaced by the concept of a (theological) 'substance' revealing different aspects at different times. The interpretation is to take place against the background of a view of history, oriented towards society and praxis, which comprehends past, present and future. History here is clearly, and as usual in Marxism, not merely something to be thought about and contemplated, but also to be done in anticipation of a specific social goal. But here, the very ideological 'fixation' that is to be avoided comes in through the back door. The interpretation is 'fixed' — not historically, but teleologically! The whole epistemology thus reveals itself as crypto-ideological.

Again, it is a theological question whether the praxis of social reform can be a legitimate norm for theological interpretation of historical texts or not. But it is quite clear that no present social reform intentions whatsoever can provide the point of orientation for non-theological religious studies; for these are not nomothetic, and must therefore reject any normative demand made on them, whether it be the conscious 'justification of the status quo' or the demand for reform.

It must be appreciated in Colpe's paper, nevertheless, that the basis-superstructure complex is not thought of deterministically. What is repeatedly stressed is that religious texts are co-conditioned, or conditioned among other things, by social factors. (In the case of the exegete or interpreter, who is supposedly also subject to such dependency, it is not entirely clear to me whether this co-conditioning has not been inconsistently turned into a conditioning, i.e. being conditioned by, social relations and even material interests. This would contradict the broader concept of reality already put forward, however.) At any rate, a deterministic schema is rejected for texts and sources. The question then arises as to what further factors determine and influence the religious phenomenon (i.e. here, the texts for exegesis), and possibly also the interpreter, and how these are taken account of in this epistemology: in other words, how they can be grasped with the aid of this theory.

Maybe this will be clearer when the 'precise grasp of this "conditional" relation, and also incidentally of the "correspondential" relation, between the forces and relations of production on the one hand and the juridical, political, and religious superstructure on the other' is available in a fully formulated version. The type of relation obtaining between basis and superstructure is already suggested, however, by the concepts 'symbol' and 'copy'. The problems connected with both concepts are intended to be related to each other epistemologically. In other words, the religious or intellectual superstructure can either be thought of as a symbol, or as a copy, of the socio-economic base, and both theories should be related to each other in an epistemological consideration. (Their mutual relation in a 'common consciousness of the problem' does however contradict the title, which speaks of 'symbol theory and copy theory as basic ... alternatives'.)

If the relationship between basis and superstructure is viewed in terms of symbol theory, the superstructure is to be seen as being mediated symbolically (i. e. the symbol here mediates between the basis and the superstructure: 'the perception ... which is necessary for the symbol to come into being' must be carried out 'materialistically', i. e. it must be regarded as being 'co-determined' and 'influenced' by social relations in the widest sense).

If this is the case, the symbol does not remain what it is; it is questionable whether there is any congruence with the conventional concept of symbols, though this could not be an objection to the use of the term in the meaning indicated. It should perhaps, however, be pointed out that every symbol in the conventional sense can also be read as a symbol in the new sense, but not vice versa.

It is obvious that special problems will arise in those cases where not only the symbol, but even the perception associated with it, possesses a distinct, non-social, geographical dimension of relevance. The basis-superstructure schema, or the division between social being and consciousness, cannot simply be applied here, since a new dimension — that of the natural preconditions — simultaneously determines both levels. As a result there will be difficulties of interpretation, especially in the allocation to the level of being or of consciousness, for such natural phenomena can certainly have a direct bearing on consciousness, without having to be of social relevance beforehand. Consequently, there will be difficulties also in the abolition being demanded of the confusion between 'symbols of the basis and of the superstructure'.

As far as copy theory is concerned, the superstructure is seen as a 'function' of the base, and such relationships are to be represented by 'symbols with epistemological value'. But what are such symbols like, concretely? Are they also the concepts which the text makes use of? It would appear that 'objectivations' in the widest sense are meant, at any rate those that are unambiguously 'seated in life' and thus represent 'the symbolization of ... excerpts from *real history*' (commentator's emphasis). It must be borne in mind, however, that as a result of the further development of copy theory and its approach towards symbol theory, the symbols (or objectivations with symbolic value) introduced are not 'copies of the real things', but 'transformations', which mediate between 'being and the products of consciousness', and 'which involve a symbolizing preception and mastery of being, just as symbolically-informed thinking will continue to be necessary for their historical and genetic explanation'.

The question of the 'ban' issued here on the mental combination of these conceptual objectivations seems to me a weighty one. Surely all orderly thought consists of association and differentiation. How else can intercultural comparison be possible, and therefore cultural anthropology in general — not to mention comparative religion? There is no doubt that one must be aware of the danger of confusion between concrete historical facts and their 'symbols' on the level of consciousness, and of the even greater danger of idealist-ontological or even historical objectification, i. e. of the 'construction of facts' through mental association. Yet how is reality, including purely real history, to be grasped except by means of mental associations? Relatedness between the thing and the concept is inevitable in thought, and it is in fact far more necessary than the pure social historians would have us believe: for they themselves cannot manage without general concepts, and conceptions of types, gained outside their material, in the representation of the most concrete objects. Even the pure *homo oeconomicus* (or *sociologicus*) who forms the 'basis' can only be grasped as an ideal type (in Weber's sense of emphasizing certain aspects and disregarding others also there): in reality — fortunately — the pure *homo sociologicus* does not exist.

Once we have made it clear that the types, patterns and structures obtained by comparisons are hermeneutic, not historical or ontological, in character (when 'symbols are ... maintained as epistemological and critical', as Colpe says), we can use them freely and thereby hope for a major contribution to the expansion of our image of man.*

Finally, we should look once again at the anthropological problem. An epistemological theory without any conscious anthropological foundation, one which is 'quasi-idealist' (and in terms of the history of philosophy a return to Hegelianism) by maintaining that the principles of true insight alone remain constant, arouses unease. But it is already a philosophical question whether an epistemology, whatever its nature, must not constantly relate to an image of man and ground itself anthropologically. What Colpe's paper undoubtedly achieves is to provide vital stimuli for the illumination of questions in the foreground of this problem, and thus in the real field of the methodology of religious studies.

Commentary   by Reinhard Pummer

In the last analysis, typological schemata are also heuristic principles, as Goldammer has pointed out.[70] It is, therefore, in this context, that a *Religionstypologie* or typology of religion has to be seen. In the light

---

* The observations in this Commentary are partly based on ideas put forward by Prof. Dr. Klaus Hemmerle in his inaugural lecture as Privatdozent at the University of Bonn on 11 June 1969, which has unfortunately not yet been published, but is available in MS. Other sources used were:

Albert, H. and Topitsch, E. (eds.), *Werturteilstreit*, Darmstadt, 1971.

Apel, K.-O. *et al.*, *Hermeneutik und Ideologiekritik*, Frankfurt a.M., 1971.

Faber, K.-F., *Theorie der Geschichtswissenschaft*, Munich, 1971.

Landgrebe, L., *Phänomenologie und Geschichte*, Darmstadt, 1968.

Nipperdey, Th., 'Bemerkungen zum Problem einer historischen Anthropologie', in: *Die Philosophie und die Wissenschaften. Festschrift Simon Moser*, Meisenheim am Glan, 1968, pp. 350-370.

——, 'Kulturgeschichte, Sozialgeschichte, historische Anthropologie', in: *Vierteljahrschrift für Sozial- und Wirtschaftsgeschichte* 55 (1968), pp. 145-164.

Rohrmoser, G., *Das Elend der kritischen Theorie*, Freiburg i.Br. (Rombach Huchschul paperback 13), 1970.

Schneider,Th., 'Der Typus in der Geschichtswissenschaft', *Studium generale* 5 (1952)

——, *Geschichte als Wissenschaft*, Munich/Vienna, 1965.

Theunissen, M., *Gesellschaft und Geschichte. Zur Kritik der kritischen Theorie*, Berlin, 1969.

70. K. Goldammer, *Die Formenwelt des Religiösen*, Stuttgart, 1960, p. 118.

of Prof. Biezais' analysis, the relationship between phenomenology of religion and typology of religion is therefore to be determined in the following way: if 'phenomenology of religion' means the empirical comparative research and not the intuitive search for essences behind the data, typology is one of the tasks of the comparative study of religions and religious elements. If, further, *Religionswissenschaft* comprises two major divisions, i. e. history of individual religious traditions and the systematic study of religious concepts, actions, social associations and states of mind,[71] typology of religion falls under the second aspect. It has to elaborate 'a standardized set of categories, of types of religious items'[72] that make scientific comparisons possible.

Apart from this general consideration, the following aspects may be underlined:

1. In trying to clarify the concept of type for *Religionswissenschaft* it is certainly necessary to analyze the use of 'typos' within this discipline and also within Christian theology, as Prof. Biezais has done. But it is equally necessary to take into account what anthropology and history have to say on the subject. In both fields the concept is in use and theoretical discussions have been and are being carried on.[73] As for other problems too, *Religionswissenschaft* cannot ignore these cognate disciplines.[74] On the contrary, it needs to incorporate the work done by them, otherwise it will perpetuate some of the fruitless and confused discussions of the past and thus isolate itself more and more.

The anthropological use of type has been brought to bear on certain areas of *Religionswissenschaft* by Hultkrantz within the framework of a religio-ecological approach.[75] In his opinion, it is in such a context

71. Cf. M. Pye, *Comparative Religion: An Introduction through Source Material*, Newton, 1972, Introduction.

72. N. Smart, *The Phenomenon of Religion*, London, 1973, p. 41.

73. For anthropology see Ford and Steward, 'On the Concept of Types', *American Anthropologist* 56 (1954), pp. 42-57; for history see R. Wittram, *Das Interesse an der Geschichte*, Göttingen, 1968 (c. 1958), pp. 54-58; Th. Schieder, *Geschichte als Wissenschaft*, 2, überarbeitete Auflage, Munich, 1968, pp. 46-50; K.-G. Faber, *Theorie der Geschichtswissenschaft*, Munich, 1971, pp. 89-103.

74. Cf. Pummer, '*Religionswissenschaft* or Religiology?', *Numen* 19 (1972), pp. 118f., and K. Rudolph, 'Das Problem der Autonomie und Integrität der Religionswissenschaft', *Nederlands Theologisch Tijdschrift* 27 (1972-73), pp. 118.

75. Å. Hultkrantz, 'Type of Religion in Arctic Hunting Cultures: A Religio-Ecological Approach', in: H. Hvarfner, ed., *Hunting and Fishing*, Luleå, 1965, pp. 265 ff.

that typology can be of greater value than in other areas.[76]

A brief consideration of the possible benefits of including the findings of historians regarding type and typology in the work of *Religionswissenschaft* was recently offered by Rudolph.[77] However, future attempts at utilizing typological methods in *Religionswissenschaft* must concern themselves in more detail with anthropological and historical discussions in this regard.

2. To utilize Christian typological explanations in *Religionswissenschaft* does not seem feasible. As Goppelt himself remarks, the word τύπος in the sense of a prefiguration of a future event, person, etc., goes back to the biblical thought world.[78] The theological method of interpretation based on this concept is used in the New Testament and Christian exegesis and hermeneutics. Its two presuppositions are: (1) the type is set or posited (*gesetzt*) by someone, i. e. God, and (2) there is an intensification (*Steigerung*) between type and antitype, i. e. the type prefigures more perfect and greater *Fakta* to come. The latter condition makes it impossible to transfer this understanding of typology to *Religionswissenschaft*. For, even if it is the researcher and not God who posits a norm according to which the data are to be systematized, it is not at all clear why an intensification of qualities should be a precondition for the possibility of speaking of types of religious data.[79]

3. Mensching speaks of two kinds of *Religionstypologien*: one is the typology of religion*s* and the other the typology of *the* religion.[80] The former is based on the meaning of τύπος as the unique or specific characteristics of individual religions.[81] Its task is to determine the respective

76. Å. Hultkrantz, 'The Phenomenology of Religion: Aims and Methods', *Temenos* 6 (1970), pp. 68-88.

77. Rudolph, *op. cit.*, pp. 122-124.

78. L. Goppelt, *Typos. Die typologische Deutung des Alten Testaments im Neuen*, Gütersloh, 1939.

79. Cf. P. Bläser ('Typos in der Schrift', *Lexikon für Theologie und Kirche*, 2nd. ed., 10 (1965), cols. 422f.): 'Voraussetzung für die Existenz eines T.(ypos) ist der Glaube an ein kontinuierliches Heilshandeln Gottes, das im Raum der Verheissung die gleichen Wesenszüge trägt wie bei der Erfüllung', and: 'Da der T. als T. nach Gottes Plan auf die eschatolog. Realität bezogen ist, kann seine Existenz nur vom ntl. Anti-T. her erkannt werden'. Especially the latter fact makes the biblical notion of type unfit for the purpose of *Religionswissenschaft*.

80. G. Mensching, *Die Religion*, Stuttgart, 1959, and *Vergleichende Religionswissenschaft*, Zweite, neubearbeitete Auflage, Heidelberg, 1949.

81. Mensching, *Vergleichende*, p. 33.

Lebensmitte of the various religions.[82] It compares religions as whole organisms (*Ganzheiten*).[83] The typology of *the* religion is based on the meaning of τύπος as that which is common to several entities.[84] It makes cross-religious comparisons in order to determine systematically formal and essential analogies.[85] One arrives thus at a typology of manifestations, of structures, of development, and of religious experiences.[86]

As to Mensching's typology of religion*s*, its usefulness has been questioned repeatedly, as Prof. Biezais mentions.[87] The reason for the limited value of it lies in the procedure of establishing fundamental characteristics of whole religious traditions. These characteristics are short formulas that do not do justice to the variety which exists within each of them. Thus they are of little help in understanding the respective religions.

The typology of *the* religion as developed by Mensching is in principle another name for phenomenology of religion as understood in this paper. It elaborates types of religious items that are apt to shed light on each other. Conceived of in this way, the heuristic value of this kind of typology is obvious.

4. Typological phenomenology concerns itself also with historical processes, as Bianchi has stated.[88] However, difficulties connected with such an undertaking have caused the phenomenology of 'arrested pictures' to be far more developed than the so-called historical phenomenology.[89] Whether it is desirable or not to elaborate the latter will again depend on its heuristic value. It is interesting to note that

---

82. *Vergleichende*, p. 33, and *Die Religion*, p. 20, where Mensching offers a definition of *Lebensmitte*.

83. *Vergleichende*, p. 77; *Die Religion*, p. 78.

84. *Vergleichende*, p. 33.

85. *Vergleichende*, p. 77.

86. *Vergleichende*, p. 33, and the organization of the whole book *Vergleichende*.

87. Cf. above p. 154, n. 24; see now also Rudolph, *op. cit.*, p. 124.

88. U. Bianchi, 'The Definition of Religion. On the Methodology of Historical-Comparative Research' (in: U. Bianchi, C. J. Bleeker and A. Bausani, eds., *Problems and Methods of the History of Religions*, Leiden, 1972, pp. 15-34, and discussion pp. 26-34), pp. 22f., and in C. J. Bleeker, 'The Contribution of the Phenomenology of Religion to the Study of the History of Religions' (*ibid.*, pp. 35-54, and discussion pp. 45-54), pp. 52f.; Biezais, above pp. 146f.

89. M. Pye, 'The Transplantation of Religions', *Numen* 16 (1969), pp. 234f.; 'Syncretism and Ambiguity', *Numen* 18 (1971), p. 85; and *Comparative Religion*, pp. 24f.

history too used typology more for historical phenomena *in Ruhe* than for those in motion.[90]

5. Finally, there is the problem concerning the expression 'phenomenological method' (and, one may add, 'typological method'). As is well known, the question has been raised whether there exists any special method of phenomenology of religion or whether one should rather speak of a phenomenological perspective.[91] Discipline, method, and perspective have all been used in characterizing phenomenology of religion.[92] In the light of what has been said above, it seems preferable to speak of a phenomenological method in *Religionswissenschaft* since it may evoke associations with philosophical phenomenology.

In summary, typologies are useful and instructive as heuristic principles, but it would certainly be wrong to make them an end in themselves.[93]

Commentary   by Eric J. Sharpe

This comment has been prepared only on the basis of Prof. Biezais' paper 'Typology of Religion and the Phenomenological Method'. Prof. Colpe's paper 'Symbol Theory and Copy Theory' deals with questions lying entirely outside the present writer's field of competence, and he therefore offers no direct response to it.

For more than four years now I have been engaged in an attempt to write a book on the history of methodological thought as it affects the 'discipline' of comparative religion (or the history of religions, or *Religionswissenschaft*, or religious studies). The wisdom of anyone's

90. Schieder, *op. cit.*, p. 48.

91. Hultkrantz, *op. cit.* in n. 76, pp. 83f.; N. G. Holm, Review of U. Bianchi, C. J. Bleeker, A. Bausani, eds., *Problems and Methods of the History of Religions* (Leiden, 1972), *Temenos* 8 (1972), pp. 141.

92. C. J. Bleeker, 'The Phenomenological Method', *Numen* 6 (1959), pp. 96-111; 'Wie steht es um die Religionsphänomenologie?', *Bibliotheca Orientalis* 28 (1971), pp. 306f.; and *op. cit.* in n. 88, p. 39.

93. Cf. Goldammer, *op. cit.*, pp. XVII and 117. In history, Schieder has said: 'Typenbildungen sollen das geschichtliche Verstehen erleichtern, vertiefen...' (*op. cit.*, p. 49).

undertaking such a task may of course be questioned; it has been time-consuming and sometimes tedious, but on the other hand it has been extremely instructive. From such a protracted study one learns (among other things) that no method, however novel, is without antecedents, and few altogether without followers — though the followers themselves may be either unconscious of the degree of their indebtedness to earlier traditions of scholarship, or privately convinced of their own extreme originality.

Scholarly fashion is, in fact, a curious thing. In its intricacy and its interplay of presuppositions (acknowledged or unacknowledged), material and applied method, it shows many resemblances to the complex object on which its attentions are focussed. Like religion, too, its traditions are cumulative. No scholar, whatever the nature of the material on which his researches are based, leaves his field exactly as he finds it. Ideally, he will add one more stone to a scholarly cairn — though occasionally the stone he adds to the top of the cairn he may previously have prised out of the foundations. Nevertheless, as a rule it will be the same cairn, standing on the same eminence; seldom will a real attempt be made to begin an altogether new edifice. Even should an attempt be made, it will seldom succeed, unless by a process of elaborate disguise.

This image may already have become too elaborate. It was designed, however, to demonstrate my conviction that in matters such as these, the scholar's scope for methodological novelty, though theoretically unlimited, in practice may be really very limited indeed. It may perhaps be objected that the history of comparative religion (and I shall continue to use this form of words for the sake of convenience) is already of bewildering complexity, and that a subject of such vast human scope ought to be virtually limitless in its possibilities. In some senses this is undoubtedly true. But the history of scholarly inquiry over the past hundred or so years does not in fact speak very strongly for human ingenuity, save in one respect, to which I shall return in a moment.

But before doing so I may perhaps be permitted to record my slight disappointment that little attempt has been made, even in a section of a methodological conference devoted to 'Evaluation of Previous Methods', to state clearly and unambiguously what those methods actually are. The history of ideas, as it affects the phenomenology of religion, is by no means self-evidently well known, and I would suspect that among our delegates there are many views current on the subject of how we have arrived at the methodological position or positions we now occupy, and of course on the even more important subject of what those positions actually are. Some systematic clarification of those particular questions would certainly have been most useful.

The ingenious aspect of modern scholarship to which I referred a moment ago is in the field of terminology. One understands the analytical philosophers' obsession with the values of words, since no small part of the recent history of Western scientific inquiry in the humanities has been a history of conflicts between competing terminologies. Perhaps this is no more true of comparative religion than of others among our sister-subjects; but the phenomenon is certainly to be found in our area, and the confusion which can result when a new terminology (or the reintroduction of an old terminology, perhaps with a new conceptual framework: one might reflect on the history of the words 'animism' and 'fetish' for instance) is assumed to be, and mistaken for, a new method, is something with which I fancy we are all familiar enough.

Prof. Biezais has invited us to reflect on a form of procedure which may be called 'the typology of religion', the stated purpose of which is to overcome the problems created by the presence in the world of vast numbers of in some ways distinctively different, and yet in other ways strikingly similar, religious traditions.

The Lanczkowski quotation with which he begins reminds us at once that this is no new problem. The problem of *Pluralismus und Wandel der Religionen*, we have had with us for a good many years now; and what varies is not the problem as such, but rather the steps which each successive scholarly generation takes to try and overcome it (or at least to understand it). We are also introduced at this early stage to that well-known and, I fear, fundamental tension between two *Forschungsrichtungen*, the historical and what is here called the 'phenomenological' — that is, between the work of those individual scholars who are content to study more or less within the bounds laid down by one religious tradition, and those individual scholars who with an eye to more remote goals attempt to ford streams, cross bridges, and otherwise obtain some total understanding of 'religion-as-such'. *Typik* in the study of religion, it is claimed, can overcome those tensions by concentrating on a systematic *Zueinanderordnung* of analogous manifestations.

To this initial statement one can only comment that the method as such is clearly that of descriptive phenomenology, albeit under another name. Why, one wonders, should the new name be necessary? It certainly would not have been necessary, had the existing terminology been unambiguous. We shall return to this question.

The short dialogue which is next quoted between Professors Bleeker and Bianchi begins to illustrate the existing tension between 'historical' and 'phenomenological' approaches to the study of religion. I say 'begins to', not because of the dimensions of the extract, but rather because of the linguistic framework within which it has had to be placed. English can be a very slippery language indeed, and I am sure that both our distinguished colleagues would have been happier had some other medium for their interchange of ideas been possible. But three main points emerge well enough nevertheless.

The first is, as Prof. Biezais points out, that Prof. Bleeker's concepts reveal the 'philosophical' basis of the whole phenomenological school, serving as they do towards systematization of *Erkentnisse*, but contributing little to the understanding of the historical reality itself. And yet Prof. Bleeker always explicitly repudiates the suggestion that his position is 'philosophically' conditioned at all. I am sure that he would not want to be labelled as a philosopher. Conceivably we have here yet another area in which some semantic tidying up is necessary, in the interests of deciding, for the purposes of intelligent discussion, where 'philosophy' might be regarded as beginning and ending.

The second point is equally serious. When Prof. Bianchi asks Prof. Bleeker whether it is at all possible to bring about a rapprochement between the historical and phenomenological methods, he is asking a question frequently discussed during the past few decades, but never even provisionally resolved. The task is of course one to which very many scholars have applied themselves, at one time or another. But it is evident that if such a rapprochement is possible, it cannot take place purely within the framework of the categories supplied by historical method. As long as the ultimate explanation of the essence of religion was believed to be discoverable within the area of religious genetics, then the historian and the (descriptive) phenomenologist might well unite under a common banner. This seems no longer to be possible. *Wesen* is no longer a matter of genetics. Historical categories have simply not been designed for the refined tasks involved in modern scholarship, and these categories ought not to be forced to serve contingencies for which they were not designed. It would seem to follow that whatever categories may conceivably be used will have to be both broad and flexible (and perhaps even interchangeable, imprecise and impressionistic), and that they are therefore unlikely in principle to be acceptable, or even understandable by the historian as long as he is working as a pure historian. The result, then, will not be history. Whether it will therefore be 'philosophy' again depends on the precise shade of meaning one wishes to give that word.

Thirdly, on the matter of typology, the question is asked: 'Where are you to locate this study?' This assumes that the study of typology is capable of being delineated and separated from other studies; such an assumption may or may not be justified. One suspects, however, that the question of 'location', as posed here, may not be unrelated to the patterns of existing university teaching posts in Europe. My reflection is simply that changing patterns of university teaching, particularly in the English-speaking world, may cause questions of this kind to appear somewhat anachronistic. A multidisciplinary and polymethodic department would have no difficulty in 'locating' a course of religious typology.

Prof. Biezais' own comments on this discussion are somewhat pessimistic in tone. Typology, whether 'historical' or 'phenomenological', as discussed in this context, he sees as being too imprecise a concept to serve any useful purpose in a scientific discussion. This may not necessarily be the case, however. The individual typologist, like the individual phenomenologist, may know well enough where the boundaries of his subject go, where it begins and ends, and what its conditions are. Regrettably, though, there is no external authority capable of ensuring that two typologists (or two phenomenologists, for that matter) are going to define their terms in more than approximately the same way. The difficulty experienced by scholars in such areas as these when they have to try to communicate with one another is already occasionally noticeable.

It is not difficult for Prof. Biezais to demonstrate in continuation that 'typology' is very far indeed from being a new and therefore neutral word. It has been familiar to New Testament scholarship for decades, and has a place in the later history of Christian thought. The Hegelian 'types' about which Mensching was writing in 1931 are also important. The later Hegelian strain, which Mensching to some extent seems to reflect, can also be seen in such a context as this, from Nathan Söderblom's *Naturlig religion och religionshistoria* (1914): 'Christianity is an extremely heterogeneous phenomenon. Is it desirable — even if it were possible — to deprive it of its proper character? *It is the task of scholarship to distinguish, sharply and distinctly, the different types of religion in their essence* (my italics: the Swedish here is '... religionens olika typer i deras väsen'). But in real life they do not appear distinctly: they enter into manifold relationships with one another. This is not due only to inconsistency and indecision, which every conscious human life has the duty of eliminating from itself. Rather it often has to do with the fact that reality demonstrates connections which scholarship, for the sake of clarity, has for the time being to leave aside...' (p. 53). What Söderblom is here saying, it seems to me, is that typology on the Hegelian pattern may be an interesting interim exercise, but that sooner or later its limitations are bound to manifest themselves.

Mensching, on the other hand, says that typology presupposes the work of the historian (a customary sentiment, when expressed in the context of phenomenology), that it determines what is concretely there and what it signifies (*was gemeint wird*). And further, that 'it does not turn in its work to the phenomenal reality of religion, but towards its abstract essence (*Wesen*)'. But in a later context he states that typology has to do with religions as organisms, as totalities — and here the Hegelian reference is somewhat clearer.

It is evident by this stage that 'typology' is liable to be canvassed in what appear to be two divergent senses. A 'horizontal' sense, in which each 'religion' is a 'typical' structure and totality (and in this area, the work of Prof. W. Cantwell Smith, in *The Meaning and End of Religion*, should be borne in mind; abstractions and reifications are of value only as long as their true nature remains recognized; once this sense is lost, they become tyrants); and a 'vertical' sense, corresponding exactly to the concerns of descriptive phenomenology back to Chantepie de la Saussaye. And perhaps the vertical and horizontal lines express the question asked, in such a different frame of reference, at the dawn of the comparative study of religion: 'Are the individual religions species of the genus religion?'

The reference to Mensching prompts a further question. In his view, typology is particularly valuable as a means of penetrating to the abstract essence (*Wesen*) of religion, that is, to the ultimate pattern, or *ratio*, at the heart of the religious phenomena. Some are certainly liable to ask, however, whether this provides for all the contingencies. In short, the question is liable to be asked what might happen if there should prove to be no ultimate *ratio*, no final pattern to be discovered? Or alternatively, what initial methodological procedure would be appropriate for the investigator who is convinced *a priori* that no such final pattern exists?

These questions are not facetious ones. All our existing methods, from unilinear evolutionism to structuralism, have begun with the same assumption of the final rationality of the universe. Could one only find the right key, it is argued (or hoped, or assumed), the lock must burst open. But the analogy may be a false one. The assumption of rationality may be a mirage. Alternatively, the phenomenon of religion may best be compared to a living organism rather than to an enclosed and locked cabinet; in either case it would follow that no one mode of explanation, no one method, can ever expect to provide more than a limited insight into such a complex human totality.

Prof. Biezais further emphasizes his mistrust of existing phenomenological method when he suggests that because of its atomistic character, that is, because of its incurable tendency to separate the *Erscheinungs-formen* of religion from the only total contexts within which they can be understood, '... the phenomenological method cannot fulfil its self-imposed task, of showing the essence of religious manifestations'. This again may not always be true, though the 'world-axis' illustration is well chosen, and certainly demonstrates the point. Some manifestations, however, may be better suited than others to phenomenological analysis. But I would certainly agree in essence with this judgment, and elsewhere I have discussed the concept of 'faith' with this problem in mind (Eric J. Sharpe and W. Cantwell Smith, 'Dialogue and Faith', *Religion*, October 1973).

But to separate any manifestation from its total context may be to separate it from that which alone can make it intelligible, either to the believer himself (who is still, despite Kristensen, far too seldom taken seriously into account), or to the observer. Further — and to take the most pessimistic outlook possible — to proceed from here to place side by side a dozen or so decontextualized phenomena may have a totally undesirable side-effect: a quite independent pattern may be produced which is relevant to, and recognizable in, none of the original contexts at all. This particular result is not unknown in the structural analysis of myth.

Another (albeit 'unscientific') aspect of the question of particularity and context may be considered here. Phenomenologies and phenomenologists, typologies and typologists, do not of course live and work in a religious or cultural vacuum. Present-day climates of opinion, particularly in certain of our universities, are tending away from religions-in-particular, and strongly towards religion-in-general. By this means one escapes the depressing imperfections of existing traditions, by moving out into the indistinct fields of phenomenology; manifestations lead, after all, to essences, do they not? But the possibility should at least be borne in mind that, however vigorously one may apostrophize the historical method, the desire to ignore, bypass or reconstruct history is strongly present. This situation is perhaps not unlike that which accompanies every process of religious disintegration, where the talk is all of 'essences' — the boundaries beyond which a process of secularization must not be permitted to go.

The question, then, is whether typological theories of the kind which Prof. Biezais has described, can serve any useful purpose in elucidating religion as it actually exists. He believes that they can not. Phenomenologies of the descriptive type he will allow; but philosophical or quasi-philosophical constructions he views with the utmost suspicion, mainly because of their apparent or actual lack of respect for the historical contexts from which their material has been drawn. Either one works in full awareness of all the manifold relationships involved in every religious manifestation, or one does not. The choice seems simple.

In the last resort, however, there are boundaries across which limited and fruitful cross-cultural analysis is eminently possible. Surely, too, there must be a degree to which historical context and background may simply be taken for granted (to deny this, and claim that every scholar must always do all the background work afresh on every occasion is of course a comprehensive vote of no confidence in every scholar's work save one's own).

What may not be taken for granted, on the other hand — and this brings us back to our initial point of departure — is that when words, and particularly methodological words, are used freely, they are always being used in the same sense. This need not be the case. Sometimes, as here, it is evidently not the case. It is a matter, then, of examining, not words only, but presuppositions, and particularly the hidden and unacknowledged presuppositions which govern both the choice of the words the phenomenologist (or the typologist) uses, and the way or ways in which he uses them.

It may seem cynical, but I would consider it highly appropriate, to end this brief comment with a quotation. The article from which it is taken was written more than sixty years ago; and while not wishing to suggest that phenomenological method has made no progress since then, it may be salutary to reflect how appropriate these words still in many ways seem. The year, then, is 1909; the writer, Andrew Lang: '... The common mistake is to suppose that there is a 'science' of religion. We have only collections of disputable facts, and a welter of conjectures: not knowledge but opinions. There can be no short and cheap cuts to reasonable familiarity with a subject of this nature. A man must work hard at first hand to know how little can be known' ('Scientific Short Cuts', *The Morning Post*, October 1, 1909).

Discussion   Chairman: R. J. Zwi Werblowsky

The chairman opened by prophesying a worthwhile discussion, since although having to suggest new methods for the future was never popular, nothing was more enjoyable than demonstrating the inadequacy of the methods of the past. The first of the paper speakers, Haralds Biezais, refrained altogether from presenting his paper orally, since it had been available in written form; but Carsten Colpe, the author of the second paper, wished to add some comments to what he had written, especially in view of the discussions that had taken place at the conference. He began by discussing the difficulty of translating some of the terms he had been using from German into English — e. g. 'Abbildtheorie' and 'Erkenntnistheorie' (translated in this volume as 'copy theory' and 'epistemological theory' respectively). His main comments, however, fell under five points: Juha Pentikäinen's discussion of terminology; a comment on Cassirer; a critique of previous treatment of the 'Sitz im Leben' of religious studies; Feuerbach's critique of religion; and an ideological critique of 'Religionswissenschaft'.

In his paper (see session II) Juha Pentikäinen had suggested a differentiation within science of religion, firstly, with reference to the object of study, between the 'cognitive dimension' and 'real terminologies', and secondly, with reference to the subjects, i. e. the scholars, between the 'cognitive dimension' again and 'nominal terminology'. There was an apparent tautology in the recurrence of the term 'cognitive dimension', and this reflected the tendency for what Pentikäinen called 'real terminology' simply to be repeated within science of religion: e. g. the scientific study of myth or mythology being itself called 'mythology'. A critical discrimination was therefore needed between cognition in religion, and the scholars' own cognition; and he suggested this could be achieved through a critical concept of 'symbol', which could be found best in Cassirer's philosophy of symbolic forms, and Colpe accordingly meant something rather different by 'symbol' from what was usually meant by 'religious symbol'. His second point also related to Cassirer, who had shown that many concepts which had formerly referred to substantial things now referred to functions. Examples of this were the way in which 'number', and, within science of religion, 'soul', had developed from being substantial concepts to being functional ones. (The term 'function' here was taken from Cassirer's *Substanzbegriff und Funkstionsbegriff*, and his books on Einstein's theory of relativity, and was therefore quite different from the theory of 'functionalism' in science of religion. Colpe agreed with the point being made by the title of Spiro's conference paper, 'Symbolism and Functionalism', though their usage of 'functionalism' was not the same.) Colpe wanted to draw a distinction between the functions of a symbol and of a belief in a society.

Thirdly, he took up a point made by Anna Birgitta Rooth about the need to identify the 'Sitz im Leben' of folklore, science of religion, etc. This had often been left undone, or done on an abstract level which had nothing to do with sociology. The formal denotations used in historical philology for 'Sitz im Leben' — such as 'vor-österlich', 'nach-österlich', etc. — were quite inadequate, since they said nothing about the actual 'Sitz' in the life of an actual community. This pointed in the direction of a materialistic interpretation of the origin of expressions. He had tried to show how even post-Marxist thinkers such as Adler and Vorländer, who had been able to see Marxist thinking in the tradition of 19th-century critical philosophy, came very close to this critical understanding of symbol and function, or of the symbolic and functionalist use of concepts. Adler (in his *Lehrbuch der materialistischen Geschichtsanschauung*) was dealing with the relation between expressions and material conditions. These relations were not material: Adler called them 'geistig', or 'spiritual', which was precisely the concretion of the symbolical reference between expressions and the material basis, which Cassirer had also been dealing with, and it was for this reason that he had been trying to develop Cassirer's ideas in the direction of post-Marxist thinking.

Colpe's fourth point was the importance of Feuerbach's critique of religion. Not all religion was projection, as Feuerbach had suggested; there remained a small essence which could not be reduced in this way. However, by applying Feuerbach's critique wherever possible, one could reduce religion to its essential minimum, and thus make the concept of 'religion' more exact. Wherever non-religion could be proved, it should be proved, since it was too pretentious to claim the existence of religion as an ontic system in opposition to the secular. His fifth point, accordingly, was an attack on the tendency in science of religion to do the opposite of this, i. e. to expand the concept of 'religion' as widely as possible, in the attempt to legitimate itself as science. In this way 'Religionswissenschaft' became a kind of substitute theology, and what he had tried to do in his paper was to apply the principles of ideological criticism to 'Religionswissenschaft'.

Finally, Colpe wished to reply briefly in advance to two points raised by the commentators in their written papers. He thought that Hans Klimkeit had misunderstood the point when he argued that the 'common consciousness of the problem' which Colpe had attributed to both symbol theory and copy theory was in contradiction to talking about them as 'basic ... alternatives'; they were alternative solutions to a jointly-recognized problem; and taking up C. J. Bleeker's closing remark ('Retournons à la philologie et à l'histoire') he said that he claimed to be in philology and in history, but that what was important was to recognize one's dependence both on the choices which history had made for one, and on one's own presuppositions of thinking; and this was the reason behind the ideological critique which he had been offering here.

Restraining himself from immediately joining in the discussion (good chairmen, like good children, ought to be seen and not heard), Werblowsky invited the commentators to respond to the papers. Both C. J. Bleeker and Walter H. Capps had in fact had to write their papers in advance of receiving Biezais' and Colpe's papers, so that their commentaries referred to the topic in general. Both of them chose simply to present or summarize their papers as written, which centred round the uncertainties of the intellectual traditions in science of religion or history of religions. Hans Klimkeit offered an English summary of his paper (which had been written in German), but also elaborated on some of the points. In his commentary on Biezais, he had concentrated on the author's distinction between three concepts of 'type', and the conclusions that these led to, and in his commentary on Colpe, on criticizing the adequacy of a historico-sociological interpretation of religion. What emerged from both of these commentaries was the question of the 'essence' of religion — what Capps had called the 'dynamic' element, which was always there with and among the other elements — and he agreed that this idea of 'Wesensschau', or perception of essence, was philosophically problematic. Nevertheless, he thought that there were avenues of approach in science of religion which could provide a new hermeneutical basis for the phenomenological method: especially in view of its intention to look at its material not only historically and typologically, but in a manner that would open up an understanding of the existence of man himself. He had tried to suggest a hermeneutic which could give phenomenology such a meta-historical (but anthropologically-, not ontologically-founded) basis. On the other hand he was not happy about Colpe's paper, in which he had rightly rejected the German idealist tradition in philosophy, and had also rejected materialist determinatism, but was nevertheless still arguing in terms of a dualism between two layers: one consisting of the socio-economic factors, and the other of ideas reflecting these. He pleaded in favor of the recognition of a multiplicity of categories that went to the making of symbols, including socio-economic factors, and consciousness, but also others such as nature or culture. Then it would certainly be possible to see symbols as a transformation of these various categories, mediating between them.

The fourth commentator was Reinhard Pummer. Summarizing his paper, he said it fell into two parts, a general discussion, and a specific commentary on Biezais' paper, to which however he would like to add a few further points: firstly, on the need for 'Religionswissenschaft' to take into account not only the achievements of typology and theology, but also history and anthropology; secondly, on Goppelt's term 'typos', which he felt might be usable within Christianity, but was inappropriate in history of religions, since it involved an intensification ('Steigerung') between type and antitype which was not applicable in the latter. He agreed, however, with Biezais' rejection of Mensching's *Religionstypologie*. Finally, he questioned the term 'phenomenology' altogether, and referred back to Walter Capps' point about the phenomenology of arrested pictures versus historical phenomenology (though it seemed to him that historical phenomenologists too had concentrated on phenomena in stasis rather than in motion). The associations of the term 'phenomenological method' with philosophical phenomenology also disturbed him, and he would prefer not to use the term at all.

Eric Sharpe concentrated on presenting a few salient points from his paper. He said that many aspects of the history of ideas were not in fact as familiar as they should be (it was all too easy to indulge in name-dropping of illustrious scholars in remote languages, particularly in the English-speaking world, where the knowledge of other languages was notoriously limited); the problem of knowing how one had arrived at the present methodological position, and of evaluating it, was extremely important. He thought that the two *Forschungsrichtungen* described by Biezais – the historical and the phenomenological – represented a fundamental contrast of approach that was likely to continue for many years to come, and he suggested that a rapprochement between them would not be possible (if at all) within the categories provided by the historical method. As long as the ultimate explanation of the essence of religion had been believed to be discoverable through evolutionism, the historian and the phenomenologist of religion had been able to unite; but this was no longer possible. He went on to say that the problems of methodology were in fact often problems of terminology, and that 'new methods' often turned out to be no more than new terms. Similarly, problems often arose through different scholars using the same term (e.g. 'typology') in different senses, since they were starting out from different presuppositions. It was the presuppositions, then, which needed investigation. Finally, one such basic presupposition in history of religions for the past 100 years had been the quest for an underlying *ratio* of religion; but students and younger researchers were now beginning to question whether such a *ratio* did in fact exist, and even if this appeared to be a naive question, it was one which should be taken seriously.

One point that troubled R. J. Zwi Werblowsky was the polarization implicit in much of what had been said between a historical and a non-historical orientation in history of religions, with the latter being exclusively identified with a certain type of phenomenology. Even if it were conceded (which he questioned) that phenomenology really was non-historical, it would certainly not be the only non-historical methodology: Lévi-Straussian structuralism, for instance, was a total negation of phenomenology, yet it was also completely non-historical.

Th. P. van Baaren disagreed with Bleeker's suggestion that the believers of a religion understood it better than a specially-trained non-believers. This, he thought, was a fundamental methodological error, and was fully understood as such in for example the study of art and literature. He also wished to second the need for what Capps had called a 'second-order tradition', which in turn necessitated a reliable and widely-accepted terminology; and this was something which a conference on methodology, such as this one, should be working towards.

The important question, suggested Juha Pentikäinen, was the future of phenomenology of religion. He considered that the Weberian concept of 'ideal types' was a good starting point, but would also like to mention four ways in which it was possible that phenomenology of religion could be made more empirical (though he did not think it possible to answer the question as to the essence or nature of religion empirically). Religion ought to be studied from a structural point of view, and he asked for other's opinions as to the value of the structuralism of Lévi-Strauss, or of Propp and Dundes, respectively. The second method would be cross-cultural research, which would mean a more statistical approach to comparative religion; the third would be the ecological, i. e. the relationship between religion, environment and habitat, etc.; the fourth would be 'regional phenomenology', which meant that the drawing up of the vocabulary for a religio-phenomenological model must presuppose a general historical, ecological, and sociological analysis within a given, relatively homogeneous cultural area. In addition to these, what other methods could be used to make phenomenology of religion more empirical?

The study of religion, argued J. van Baal, always involved materials from a religion, which was always a system, a circle of concepts and ideas: and this was impossible unless agreement could be reached on what the terms meant which were used to describe it.

Biezais' paper had included a discussion of Ugo Bianchi's concept of 'types', and the latter asked to be able to reply to this. He agreed that his concept was ambivalent, but he borrowed Biezais' own quotation from Mensching to justify this: 'Der Begriff des Typus ist doppeldeutig: einerseits bezeichnet er ein *Gemeinsames* innerhalb verschiedener Religionsorganismen, andererseits aber auch das 'typisch' Einmalige und Eigenartige jeder Religion.' Bianchi suggested that 'type' should be understood as a 'universal concrete', in a historical-comparative sense of the term: not as an *Idealtypus*, nor in the other meanings outlined at the end of Biezais' paper. One should remember the distinction between the typology of religion and the typology of religions. Moreover, while he agreed with Sharpe that the times of a evolutionism based on a unilinear conception of religious evolution were over, this did not necessarily mean that a rapprochement was impossible between the historical and the phenomenological methods. One had to start with historical research, i. e. into religious facts as historical processes; it was this, then, which the phenomenology had to deal with — so that one was always in touch with the historical and concrete. In this way a rapprochement between history and phenomenology of religion was perhaps not only possible, but indeed the necessary and unique way forward. (The discussion on this point was taken up again in session 5, following the presentation of Bianchi's own paper: see below).

The chairman had been wrong, claimed the next speaker, Lauri Honko, in prophesying that they would spend their time attacking past methodology: that was precisely what they had not done. In any case, the methodology of Van der Leeuw, for instance, was hardly worth 'evaluating' any more. But turning to the question of the typology of religion and of religions, he described a distinction which he had found useful in his own teaching, between 'core typologies' — which try to give the essence of each religion (and this might then include the testing of the 'essence' obtained, against the views of the believers, as Bleeker had suggested) — and 'contrastive typologies', which involved the comparison of different religions with each other, even in simple ways (e. g. national versus universal, etc.). Above all, however, he was very pleased to find how interested the contributors had been in the metatheory, or second-order tradition, of their discipline. It was of far more value, methodologically speaking, to investigate the presuppositions from which they set out, than to define some operational term for a specific purpose.

Replying to the comments and questions, Biezais referred to the fact that both Colpe, and the other speakers, had been denigrating phenomenology and the phenomenological method; but what mattered was to establish what these really were. He alluded to a recent article by Rudolph in the *Nederlands Theologisch Tijdschrift* which had shown the necessity of a (rightly-understood) phenomenology, which really consisted of no more than the comparison of the various facts which history of religions could demonstrate. He considered, therefore, that phenomenology – as a comparative branch within the science of religions – continued to be justified. He had however criticized the older phenomenology very sharply himself: especially with reference to its claims as a revelation of the essence or of God ('Schau, Wesensschau, oder Gottesschau'). This presupposed a special talent, and such preconditions were unscientific. He turned then to put a question to Bianchi about what he had said about 'concrete universals' and 'historical typology', which he did not fully understand. Historical typology dealt with the classification of empirical data, and therefore belonged to empirical research. He found the term 'concrete universal', on the other hand, unjustified, and indeed self-contradictory. A 'concrete' could never be 'universal', since the empirical world consisted of manifold but unique facts. As far as Mensching was concerned, he protested that he was not a Mensching disciple, and that his paper contained a clear critique of the various kinds of typology; he had simply wished to offer his fellow-researchers a survey of what had so far been achieved with their aid. On terminology, he wished to add his voice to Van Baal's and Sharpe's. The terminological situation in history of religions was appalling: it would hardly be an exaggeration to say that one person could refer to 'doorposts' and somebody else would assume they were talking about bricks. Without agreement on terminology, discussion was impossible. Finally, he wished to emphasize an important distinction, between the widely-voiced wish to understand (which was indeed a basic human need), and the pursuit of science. What mattered was how to transpose understanding, which might be attained in a number of ways, into scientific statement: i. e. a question of epistemology. It was easy to criticize Van der Leeuw; but he had been faced with the problem of how to recognize and express the holy, and, with the limited epistemological possibilities available to him, all he had been able to do was to say, 'I perceive the essence' ('Ich schaue das Wesen'). The second step was then to arrange the perceptions — science was, indeed, merely the ordering of perceptions — since if the understanding remained un-ordered, there would be no science of religion. The difficulties, then, were twofold: the epistemological aspect, i. e. the gathering of information, and the problem of what scientific system could be built up on the basis of the information thus gathered. If, as had repeatedly been stated, the science of religion was an empirical science, then it must be pursued according to the rules imposed on empirical science by epistemology and the theory of science. Scientists of religion, after all, could not be an exclusive group with a unique epistemology, or they would never be accepted as partners in scientific discussion. On this note, the chairman declared the session adjourned.

Religio-ecological Approach

ÅKE HULTKRANTZ   *Ecology of Religion:*
Its Scope and Methodology

1. To the student of religion, in particular the historian of religion, the mere hint of a religio-ecological approach may be challenging and provocative in a negative sense. Is there not sufficient testimony that religions, more than any other segments of culture, are part of the traditional heritage of mankind and as such can only be understood against their historical background? Moreover, are not religious data too subtle to be dealt with from ecological points of view? Indeed, what has ecology as a whole to do with religion?

Criticism of this sort that has crept up now and then following the publication of my first articles in the subject[1] is understandable. A research program like ecology of religion undoubtedly sounds like a *contradictio in adiecto*. Still, properly seen it is not unrealistic. The critics omit the fact that religions, in their formal manifestations, make use of environment and adapt themselves to it. This is exactly what ecology of religion is about: the study of the environmental integration of a religion and its implications. Superficially, this aspect of religion has little importance, touching only the peripheral stones of the religious edifice. If we look closer into the issue however we soon become aware that new forms of access offer themselves to the understanding of religion. Ecology of religion is, as I see it, not the alternative to the historical or phenomenological approaches, but a way of securing new information for these approaches.

1. 'Type of Religion in the Arctic Hunting Cultures: A Religio-Ecological Approach', in H. Hvarfner, ed., *Hunting and Fishing*, Luleå, 1965, pp. 265-318; and 'An Ecological Approach to Religion', *Ethnos* 31 (1966), pp. 131-150.

At this point we may return to the critical views, presented above. The objection that religious data should only be handled in their historical framing can easily be dismissed. The historical nature of religions is a matter of course. However, this in itself does not rule out other lines of inquiry than those of history. There is as we know the psychology of religion, and the systematic comparison of religious elements that we call phenomenology of religion; and there is the anthropology of religion with its efforts to apply functional and structural points of view to religious data. Similarly we now have the ecological approach, which, as was just pointed out, may enrich our historical understanding.

There is more to the other objection, that the delicate nature of religious data precludes ecological analysis.[2] Certainly, a spiritual conception like that of an invisible Supreme Being is difficult to grasp in such terms. However, if attention is paid to the fact that not single religious ideas as such, but in their organization into patterns and structures, are the targets of ecological interpretation, the legitimacy of the ecological approach will certainly become more acceptable. Still, some critics may consider that the proponents of the ecological theory favor some materialistic assumptions of the nature and origins of religion. There are undoubtedly ecological-minded researchers who cherish such convictions. However, their interpretation is not necessary. Ecology of religion is concerned with forms of religious expression, and specific religious contents motivated by these forms, but not with the communication of ultimate meaning and value. In my understanding, at least, conclusions as to the latter are not allowed by the ecological approach.

Ecology is today a theme of paramount importance not only in contemporary science but also in the practical outlook on life, in planning for the future and in the struggle for the conservation of natural resources, a meaningful milieu for mankind and, indeed, the survival of man. It seems to be part of the ecological re-awakening that man's religions should also be fitted into this total scheme. Two approaches offer themselves here to the student of religion: one is, research on man's experience of his environment, and his ideas of Nature; the oth-

---

2. In 'Crisis and Renewal in History of Religions', *History of Religions* 5-1 (1965), p. 7, M. Eliade warns against making a humanist discipline like the history of religions conform to models borrowed from the natural sciences. However, it is all a matter of what purpose we have with our investigations.

er is, the analysis of the environmental integration of man's religions. The former approach presents us with a world view which may be religious in certain instances, but not always, and definitely not in our modern society.[3] It is a kind of investigation that is not ecological *stricto sensu*, since the concern is not with the relations between religion and environment, but with man's opinion about these relations. Much work remains to be done in this field. One problem is, for instance, to what extent human beings outside our western civilization, and inside it in the pre-Rousseau days, have paid attention to the beauty of Nature as an expression of divine order. It seems certain, anyhow, that even the most impressive phenomena of Nature fail to leave a lasting stamp on the imagination of primitive peoples if they belong to the regular pattern of events.[4] On the other hand, natural actions that disrupt the ordinary pattern, or seem to do so, fire the imagination of man, and may actually change the religious order.[5]

It is the other approach, which is more truly an ecological approach, which will concern us here. Briefly, it is moderately environmentalistic in the sense that it attributes a decisive influence to environment in the organization and development of religious forms. In this context environment means the natural surroundings, topography, biotope, climate, as well as the demography and the natural resources which may be measured quantitatively in a culture. It is too often the case in ecological debates that only the latter, economic aspect is observed. Even analysts of religion have interpreted environment in such narrow terms.[6] However, an accurate application of ecology in the study of culture and religion should imply the whole range of ecological phenomena. The religio-ecological approach investigates religion in its

3. Eliade, *The Sacred and the Profane*, New York, 1959, p. 179. There are exceptions, however. S. H. Nasr (*The Encounter of Man and Nature*, London, 1968) refers to a divine harmony via Nature, and W. R. Jacobs (*Dispossessing the American Indian*, New York, 1972) insists that we have to learn 'that it is almost impossible to separate the materialistic side of conservation from the spiritual and subjective aspects of life itself'. Cf. also W. Müller, *Geliebte Erde. Naturfrömmigkeit und Naturhass im indianischen und europäischen Nordamerika*, Bonn, 1972.
4. Cf. E. E. Evans-Pritchard, *Theories of Primitive Religion*, Oxford, 1965, p. 54.
5. Hultkrantz, 'The Indians and the Wonders of Yellowstone: A Study of the Interrelations of Religion, Nature and Culture', *Ethnos* 19 (1954), pp. 34-68.
6. See e.g. C. Meinhof, *Die Religionen der Afrikaner in Ihrem Zusammenhang mit dem Wirtschaftsleben*, Oslo, 1926.

general environmental framing and should not be evaluated as a tool for economic determinism.

The question may then be asked what gain we have from an approach so all-embracing and vaguely defined. More specifically, in what way may such a complex as the Protestant creed in Northern Europe be illuminated by the ecology of religion? The answer is of course, very slightly indeed, if at all. The religio-ecological approach is primarily a key to the study of those religions whose cultures are dependent on the natural environment, that is, the so-called primitive religions.[7] As human culture has evolved, its dependency on nature has successively diminished. Religion, being tied up with the cultural development, has, in its process of evolutionary growth, increasingly become independent of the ecological factors that once held it in their grip. If we turn to those religions that have not been affected by urbanization and industrialization they evince both directly and indirectly a remarkable impact by the environment.[8] This is why we may talk of hunting religions, agricultural religions, pastoral or herding religions, etc.[9] Since religion has a conservative tendency, religious features that were adjusted to earlier ecological patterns often remain in later religious constellations. For instance, in agrarian cultures the spirits of the field appear in animal disguise, most certainly a left-over from the hunting cultures.

Fundamental to the religio-ecological approach is the insight that nature not only restricts and impedes, but also stimulates cultural processes. The early anthropogeographers and students of human ecology

7. Primitive religions, religions of primitive peoples, tribal religions, ethnographical religions, archaic religions and nonliterate (preliterate) religions are some of the labels by which these religions are known. The Germans, and after them the Scandinavians, speak about the religions of the 'nature peoples' (*Naturvölker, naturfolk*), distinguishing them from the religions of the 'culture peoples' (cf. e. g. Th. Achelis, *Die Religionen der Naturvölker im Umriss* (Sammlung Göschen), Berlin/-Leipzig, 1919; R. Karsten, *Naturfolkens religion*, Stockholm, 1926). Although this dichotomy suffers from an old-fashioned evolutionism it communicates, in a general way, the distance between religions submitted to a strong environmental impact and religions of technologically advanced societies.

8. Actually, religions in modern cultures may also be evaluated from an ecological point of view. There are, for instance, the different patterns of urban and rural religions (D. Luth *et al.*, 'An Ecological Approach to the Study of Religious Movements', *Bulletins of the American Anthropological Association* 1-3 (1968), pp. 87 ff.

9. Even Father Schmidt makes use of these concepts. He made the mistake however of relying on historical instead of ecological criteria in delineating them.

took the positive, change-promoting power of environmental influence for granted. Their exaggerations were repudiated by one well-known scholars from their own ranks, Friedrich Ratzel, and by later researchers in anthropology and ethnology. Indeed, in insisting on the limiting but not creative importance of environment the anthropologists reacted too strongly against the ecologists. At the same time they rightly underscored the role of culture and tradition in forming culture. Daryll Forde expressed their standpoint in these words: 'Between the physical environment and human activity there is always a middle term, a collection of specific objectives and values, a body of knowledge and belief: in other words, a cultural pattern.' In evaluating the process by which environment and culture interact he pronounced that 'physical conditions have both restrictive and permissive relations to human activities'.[10]

Permissive, but not creative. A student like Julian Steward who had an extreme natural region as the *entourage* of his field research in ethnography — the Great Basin — was soon aware that something was missing in the interpretations of his colleagues. He accepted Forde's establishment of the middle term, the cultural tradition, but combined it with a positive appreciation of the creative force of the environment. That is, culture growth is no automatic response to environment, as the old 'environmentalists' thought, but 'cultural ecological adaptations constitute creative processes'.[11] Although many students have attacked the problem of cultural ecology since the 1950's, Steward's methodology remains the most fruitful approach. It will be followed to a certain extent in the present effort to delineate the methods and goals of an ecology of religion.

The ecological approach to religion is not new. It was part of the older procedures in human ecology, it was practiced in the religio-historical analyses of Near Eastern religions,[12] and it was implied in the doctrine of the older evolutionists that experiences of Nature provided

10. C. D. Forde, *Habitat, Economy and Society*, 7th ed. London/New York, 1949, p. 463.
11. J. H. Steward, *Theory of Culture Change: the Methodology of Multilinear Evolution*, Urbana, Ill., 1955, p. 34.
12. Cf. H. and H. A. Frankfort, 'The Emancipation of Thought from Myth', in H. Frankfort *et al.*, eds., *The Intellectual Adventure of Ancient Man*, pp. 363-73, Chicago, 1946. The Frankforts describe ecological situations that influence the religions, but do not systematize the theoretical framework of their approach.

man with gods and myths. We do not say today that volcanoes gave birth to gods, but we recognize that they formed, or contributed to form, the expressions for the beliefs in gods attached to such mountains. Today the ecological ideas of the past reappear refined and modified, at the same time as we have become conscious of them and their methodological importance. In this sense the religio-ecological approach is new in the study of religions.[13]

We shall now see how it may be used, and to what conclusions it may lead us.

2. First of all, new insights into a particular religion, its pattern and functioning may be gained by an ecological analysis. It is very common today that religions are interpreted via an investigation of the social system. However, the social system is in a high degree dependent on, yes, even an outgrowth of, the ecological system. For instance, a vegetational area is the natural habitat of an agricultural people, the woman, once a collector of plants, is the cultivator of the soil (the man being the hunter, a heritage from a preceding hunting culture), matrilocality and uxorilocality becomes the convenient rule, and, as Murdock and others have proved, a matrilinear social organization is built up on this foundation. This may seem to be a very simplified scheme, but it indicates how the process mechanism in social evolution has a primal driving force that, in this case, is ecology.

Now, the observation that a religion, or part of it, may be described in ecological terms does not involve any 'reductionistic' attitude. We do not touch the religious values as such — they have their anchorage in the psychic equipment of man. We find, however, that the forms of a tribal religion may be meaningfully described in their interactions with the ecological adaptation of the culture as a whole, and, as a matter of fact, that they are partly produced by this process. Steward[14] has, in his 'method of cultural ecology', tried to relate the adaptational process with historical preformative aspects and levels of socio-cultural

13. This presentation of religio-ecological approaches does not take in the modern study of the geography of religion that is primarily concerned with the changes on the landscape brought about by religious cults. See, for example, P. Deffontaines, *Géographie et religions*, Paris, 1948; G. Imbrighi, *Lineamenti di geografia religiosa*, Roma, 1961; and D. E. Sopher, *Geography of Religions*, Englewood Cliffs, 1967.

14. Steward, *op. cit.*, pp. 36-42.

integration. According to him, ecological adaptation is most discernible in subsistence and technology, whereas it is less observable in social organization and tends to fade away in religion and intellectual culture. In principle, Steward is right of course. Since his interest is to show as clearly as possible the nature of the culture-ecological process he dismisses religion from his analysis. I think it is possible to accept Steward's model in its gross features, and to apply it to religion and develop it further.[15]

Religion is in most respects a creation of man's psychic experience and cultural tradition. In particular this is the case with mythology and other epical religious traditions, although their setting may be colored by the physical environment. Also more abstract notions, like soul and beliefs, are usually part of a traditional pattern that is validated by individual psychic experiences. In some important aspects however religion is tied up with the cultural structure and thereby, in some religions, with the ecological foundations of culture. In other aspects it reflects the environment more directly. We can say that ecology acts creatively on these religions — the 'primitive' religions — by enforcing or stimulating cultural and religious adaptation through a filter of technological possibilities, value patterns and belief traditions. It is possible to arrange the levels of religio-ecological integration according to the following scale, which is purely functional and should not be mistaken for an evolutionary diagram:

a) Primary integration: environmental adaptation of basic cultural features, such as subsistence and productive arrangements, technology etc. and behavior patterns associated with these features, such as certain social and religious attitudes. Steward calls this constellation of features a 'cultural core', an appellation that may be accepted here. To the cultural core belong such religious beliefs and rituals that are, as it were, part of the subsistence activities. So-called animal ceremonialism, or rituals around the slain animal in a hunting culture, and the calendar cycle of rites around the crops in an agricultural milieu, belong to these 'subsistence rituals'. In their exact appearance they are influenced by

15. Steward claims that his approach is particularistic insofar that he seeks 'to explain the origin of particular features and patterns which characterize different areas rather than to derive general principles applicable to any cultural-environmental situation' (*op. cit.*, p. 36). Actually, his cultural ecology implies sweeping conclusions — see below.

historical factors, such as diffusion and inheritance of specific forms; in their general pattern they reflect ecological adaptational processes.

An important instance of primary integration exists in those cases where the religious value system is structured to correspond with subsistence needs. Thus, the Naskapi of Labrador have developed a complex divination system in order to be able to locate the game in times of severe cold and scarcity of food. Indeed, their whole religion can be defined as one of divination.[16]

b) Secondary integration: the indirect adaptation of religious beliefs and rituals. The latter are organized into a framework that takes its forms from the social structure, which is, in its turn, a model suggested by the economic and technological adaptation to environment. It is a well-known fact that a complicated, stratified pantheon only occurs where there is a stratified social structure that owes its existence to a rich agricultural environment, an environment that allows a surplus economy, a dense population and professional specialization. Again we are talking about patterns and structures, not about specific beliefs and specific rites that have historical accidental circumstances as their cause.

c) Morphological integration: the covering of religious features with forms taken from the physical and biological environment. Religious concepts and rites are by their very nature traditional but borrow their formal appearance from phenomena within the actual biotope. Thus, the hunter's spirits show themselves in animal disguise, the shaman dresses himself in deer attire, the offerings are performed in sacred groves, etc. The choice of forms is not arbitrary but is related to the symbolism that is inherent in them. For instance, the bird dress of a shaman tells us of the bird-like supernatural powers of the shaman or his assistant spirits. It has already been pointed out that myths often depict the natural environment in the area where they are narrated.

It should be obvious that the interaction between environment, cultural core and traditional factors gives us a most useful key to the understanding of religious forms and religious process. We realize that it is not enough to analyze an exotic religion by referring to cultural index, cultural history and social structure; environment is also a factor to be taken into account. In particular we can assess those religions

16. Hultkrantz, 'La divination en Amérique du Nord', in A. Caquot and M. Leibovici, eds., *La divination*, Vol. II, Paris, 1968, p. 75.

in ecological terms whose cultures are most exposed to the forces of environment. In technically more advanced civilizations the ecological factor is negligible, but some of the religious symbols that have been transmitted historically still reveal an origin dependent on ecological adaptation. In Christianity, for example, the good shepherd and the lamb of God are symbols taken from a pastoral environment.

The religio-ecological method applied to a single area is illustrated in the present author's paper on the religion of the aborigines of the Great Basin in North America.[17]

3. A second target for the religio-ecological approach is the phenomenological comparison between religions and religious traits. As we know, phenomenology of religion tries to identify types which have a universal or regional representation. The scientific control of the investigated materials for the establishment of such types is of course more rigid and reliable in restricted regional areas where the researcher is a specialist.[18] Such areas are usually defined as historical-geographical units, the ethnologist's 'culture' or 'culture area'. In principle, at least, such cultures represent a certain degree of environmental adaptation; the culture-area designation is however more inclusive (cf. for instance the Southwest of North America). Cultural ecology and ecology of religion provide us with a new operative concept that allows bolder comparisons, a type concept relating to whole cultures and religions.

Again we turn back to Steward and his concept of the 'cultural core'. As we remember, the cultural core is the constellation of basic features in a culture. If, now, we find similar cultural cores in other cultures, and they have 'similar functional interrelationships resulting from local ecological adaptations and similar levels of sociocultural integration', we arrive at a 'culture type'.[19] 'Level of sociocultural integration' means here the form of society involved in the ecological process, such as the family unit, or band, or village, or nation, etc.; different cultures are organized on different social levels. The cultural-type concept thus

17. Hultkrantz, 'Religion and Ecology among the Great Basin Indians', pp. 137-150 in *The Realm of Extra-Human. Ideas and Actions*, ed. by A. Bharat. The Hague-Paris, Mouton Publishers (World Anthropology series).
18. Hultkrantz, 'The Phenomenology of Religion: Aims and Methods', *Temenos* 6 (1970), pp. 68-88.
19. Steward, *op. cit.*, pp. 5-6.

transcends the culture-area concept with its continuous and limited extent. For instance, Steward finds a cultural type represented by the patrilineal band occurring among the Bushmen, Congo Pygmies, Philippine Negritos, Australian aborigines, Tasmanians, Southern California Shoshoneans and the Ona of Tierra del Fuego.[20] Steward declares that he 'seeks cross-cultural regularities and explanations' but 'presupposes no universal schemes'.[21] It is however difficult to see how regularities could be established without universal implications.

Just as we may identify a cultural type cross-culturally we may, I think, identify its religious correlate, the 'type of religion', in the same perspective. Of course, there is a major difference between the two type concepts: one refers to the cultural core as a whole, the other to the religious and magic behavior associated with the main features of the cultural core (or primary integration, as it has been called above). Furthermore, where Steward talks of levels of socio-cultural integration I should like to emphasize subsistence activities as the most important means for identifying a cross-cultural type of religion. It should be repeated here that this is no sign of a materialistic interpretation of religion; idealistic culture historians like Schmidt and Jensen have also differentiated between religions with reference to subsistence activities. And indeed, Steward's socio-cultural grouping has also an economic basis: patrilineal bands occur where animals confined within a restricted territory are hunted, while composite bands exist where migratory herds of animals are hunted, etc. Actually, it would have been more advantageous to his analysis if Steward had defined the cultural type with recourse to varieties of subsistence.

The type of religion may thus be found in widely different regions where the level of ecological adaptation and basic subsistence systems are identical. For instance, it is possible to delineate an Arctic hunting religion, appearing in the Circumpolar regions in the Old and New Worlds, a type of religion that formerly probably had a more southerly representation, when the climate was more harsh and tundra and taiga forests covered places that today have a temperate climate. This Arctic religion is characterized by the following general features:[22] hunting rituals,

20. Steward, *op. cit.*, pp. 122-42.
21. Steward, 'Some Problems Raised by Roger C. Owen's *The Patrilocal Band*', *American Anthropologist* 67-3 (1965), p. 733.
22. Hultkrantz, 'Type of Religion...', *op. cit.* in n. 1.

including the animal ceremonialism mentioned before, cult of land-marks, sky worship, shamanism and burials above the ground. In the same way we can distinguish desert nomadic religion as another type of religion,[23] and as a third type semi-desert gathering religion.[24]

The advantage with this comparative ecological approach is that features which were formerly interpreted as solely historical here reveal their attachment to the cultural adaptation to environment. It is for instance obvious that the spirits of the wild in the hunting cultures recede to territorial spirits in agrarian cultures, or that the Supreme Being of the reindeer herders on the tundra extends his influence and absorbs the functions of the lord of animals.[25] Such observations open up new insights into the functional mechanism of religious traits.

The specific historical features give to the different religions within the type of religion their characteristic profile: Lapp religion is not the same as Naskapi religion although the primary ecologically integrated traits are common to both. However, the distinction between the core features and the historical features is often very difficult to make. It is no exaggeration to say that we have here the vulnerable spot of the religio-ecological approach and, for that matter, the culture-ecological theory as proposed by Steward. The latter paid only casual attention to this vital problem. His interests in the interior dynamics of culture preoccupied him to the exclusion of other cultural aspects.

Is there perhaps even an 'ecological fallacy' here? The stricture has been made that Steward dismissed the importance of historical factors in forming culture. One critic, Morris Freilich, tested Steward's cultural ecology on the Negroes and East Indians of Trinidad and found that these groups, who differ in cultural traditions but make the same ecological adaptation, lack a common 'core of culture' related to the mode of adaptation. Thus, their kinship and authority systems are very different, the Negroes having a matrifocal-consanguineal family and a loose, equalitarian authority system, whereas the East Indians have a joint family and a hierarchical authority system. Freilich's conclusion is that Steward's model is wrong: historic factors like the cultural traditions

23. Hultkrantz, 'An Ecological Approach...', *op. cit.* in n. 1, p. 147.
24. Hultkrantz, *op. cit.* in n. 17.
25. I. Paulson, 'Wildgeistvorstellungen in Nordeurasien', *Paideuma* 8-2 (1962), pp. 79-80, 81-82.

of groups are of a decisive import.[26] However, this argument is scarcely convincing. First of all, Freilich is theoretically confused when he sets out to demonstrate the difference between the two populations in their cultural practices, 'in areas of social life not directly connected to subsistence activities'[27] — Steward would not have denied this possibility. Secondly, both populations are newcomers to Trinidad, particularly the East Indians. It is most probable that, as time goes by, their social organization will be adjusted to the simple technology and productive arrangements. After all, in primitive societies there is a reciprocity between ecological integration and social system.[28]

Another objection to the ecological approach is more important: that we have no fixed criteria by which to judge whether features should be attributed to the cultural core or to invention, diffusion or cultural heritage.[29] It is easy to see that a religious idea like the belief in divine twins belongs to historical tradition, not the cultural core. However, the exact position of such a complex as animal ceremonialism is difficult to pinpoint. It stands for all rituals and beliefs centred around the slain game, aiming at the renewal and possibly rebirth of the food animals. We have treated this complex earlier as part of the primary integration of a hunting religion; but it could be argued that it constitutes a cultural tradition, for the following reasons. Firstly, the bear cult, obviously a subcomplex under animal ceremonialism, is a connected historical phenomenon, as Hallowell was able to point out.[30] Both quantitative and qualitative criteria support this conclusion. Secondly, animal ceremonialism is missing from Australian hunting religions, or almost so. However, even if animal ceremonialism is a connected historical complex, which seems possible, its diffusion was facilitated by ecological adaptation processes of the same kind and on the same level of technological and economic integration. Since there is a residuum of animal

26. M. Freilich, 'The Natural Experiment, Ecology and Culture', *Southwestern Journal of Anthropology* 19-1 (1963), pp. 21-39; cf. also N. Fock, 'Man as a Mediating Agent between Nature and Culture', *Folk* 6-1 (1964), pp. 47-52.
27. Freilich, *op. cit.*, p. 30.
28. Cf. G. Gjessing, *Etnografiens rolle i geografistudiet*, Oslo/Bergen, 1960, pp. 16-18.
29. More on this difficult problem in Hultkrantz, *Metodvägar inom den jämförande religionsforskningen*, Stockholm, 1973, Chapter IV: 1.
30. A. I. Hallowell, 'Bear Ceremonialism in the Northern Hemisphere', *American Anthropologist* 18-1 (1926), pp. 1-175.

ceremonialism in Australia[31] the best solution of this particular problem seems to be that animal ceremonialism was part of the primary ecological integration (or cultural core), although, as time went by, it also formed a more or less coherent historical ceremonial complex. This is, of course, a hypothetical assumption.

The case of animal ceremonialism illuminates the vicissitudes the student meets when he makes a comparative religio-ecological approach.

4. A third goal for the ecology of religion is to arrange the types of religion into historical strata. The gain of this procedure would be that religious traits that can be interpreted ecologically will be referred to particular historical configurations. The historian of religion will be aware of the fact that theriomorphic spirits have their natural beginnings in hunting religions of a very early date, or that priests attending to idols and sacred bundles make their first appearance in agricultural religions of a later date. I am here referring to a relative chronological order, to the general succession of forms, not to specific cases; for in the actual cases some hunting cultures may be younger than agrarian cultures, or they may have adopted a hunting existence after having been agriculturists, as the Cheyenne Indians did in the 18th century. In other words, our perspective is here 'evolutionistic'.[32] The evolution of cultural and religious forms is interpreted on the basis of comprehensive historical investigations. Or, as a critic of cultural theories has put it, it is a question of 'a reduction of historical findings to the generalization of formula'.[33] Some would call it history, perhaps.

Anyhow, the ecologically motivated coupling of particular idea or rite complexes to particular religious types enables us to relate them to the succession of cultural stages as defined by prehistorians and ethnologists. In particular that will be possible when the cultures that are discussed are independent, that is, not organized within the wider framework of a technically and socially more complex culture.

---

31. J. G. Frazer has brought together some evidence for Australia that may be interpreted this way, cf. 'Spirits of the Corn and of the Wild', Vol. II (*The Golden Bough*, Part V: II), London, 1912, p. 258 n. 2 and p. 259 n. 1. Later works on Australian religions (by Elkin, Worms-Petri, Eliade etc.) ignore this material.

32. On the legitimacy of the new evolutionism, see Hultkrantz, *op. cit.* in n. 29, Chapter IV: 2.

33. A. L. Kroeber, *The Nature of Culture*, Chicago, 1952, p. 103.

Here we can proceed one step further. Provided that religious patterns and their cultural setting constitute a holistic unity, or nearly so (there is no such thing as a complete integrative culture with all parts functioning positively), we may establish credible hypotheses concerning prehistoric religions. I say hypotheses, for what is not revealed to us by documents cannot be empirically verified. Most hypotheses on prehistoric religions proceed from the concept of analogy: one reconstructs a possible religious situation by adducing religious facts from contemporary primitive societies. By anchoring the interpretation in a religio-ecological approach we may restrict the selection of analogies to those which conform with the cultural type of the prehistoric remains. The method presupposes that we know the cultural type, including the probable pattern of social organization, from the analysis of settlements, graves, temples, rock-drawings, etc. As we know, modern archaeology is striving to reach results in these complicated matters.

The procedure chosen by the ecologist of religion may take the following course. First, he tries to identify the cultural type, and the social organization as revealed by archaeological facts. Next, he associates the cultural core and social organization with a specific kind of type of religion, and perhaps a segment within this type of religion. The type of religion must have been defined before, as an outcome of comparative religio-ecological research on religions in contemporary primitive societies. It is therefore a necessary task for ecologists of religion to contribute to an index of religious types.[34] By relating archaeological data to an appropriate type of religion the researcher will be able to disclose the general nature of religious ideas at a certain site. Specific archaeological traits – a bear grave, a rock-drawing – may communicate direct evidence for the general religious interpretation, and corroborate the religio-ecological operation.

Ecology of religion thus introduces a new way of dealing with the difficult subject of prehistoric religions. It cannot as such illuminate single beliefs and ideas, but it equips us with credible hypotheses concerning religious structures and patterns.[35]

34. An effort to create an acceptable index of culture types has been made by J. J. Hester, 'A Comparative Typology of New World Cultures', *American Anthropologist* 64-5 (1962), pp. 1001-15.

35. Hultkrantz, 'The Religio-Ecological Method in the Research on Prehistoric Religion', *Actes du 1er symposium international sur les religions de la préhistoire*, Valca Monica, 1975.

5. The fourth and last contribution that the religio-ecological approach can achieve for us is to indicate an imminent process of religious change. If the holistic thesis holds good that phases of religious expression belong to the primary ecological integration of culture, then changes in the basic structure of the cultural core should be expected to affect the structure of religion. Here again we must return to Steward's culture-ecological theory.

It is Steward's conviction that modifications in ecological integration are the most powerful factor in bringing about the evolution of culture, or, as he also calls it, cultural process or cultural change.[36] He states: 'over the millenia cultures in different environments have changed tremendously, and these changes are basically traceable to new adaptations required by changing technology and productive arrangements.[37] This opinion seems to be justified as far as it concerns the primitive cultures, the cultures of the foragers, hunters, hoe-cultivators, nomads, etc., but has also some bearing on modern civilization. Its implication is that in the long run the organization of religious features will conform to the new state of environmental adaptation. In other words, once we know the changes in the basic features of the cultural core we realize that changes will take place in the religious structure. In some cases the direction of these changes can be anticipated.[38]

On the other hand, where changes in society are not dependent on changes in ecological integration they do not affect that part of religion that is affected by environmental conditions. Monberg[39] reports the following from Bellona Island in Polynesia: 'The sky gods were the representatives of the ecological milieu of the Bellonese. This milieu was static; no great changes took place in the natural surroundings and the supernaturals controlling these powers were not subject to changes

36. Steward makes use of the concept of 'multilinear evolution'. His theory of culture ecology is intimately bound up with the idea of cultural evolution, or culture change. The ecology of religion presented in this article is to a certain extent, but not in all aspects, coupled to evolutionary theory.

37. Steward, *op. cit.* in n. 11, p. 37.

38. I discriminate here between 'regularities' that may be observed in the empirical material and are part of the religio-ecological theories as formulated here, and 'laws' that can exactly predict future courses. We are not in a position to identify such laws.

39. T. Monberg, *The Religion of Bellona Island*, Part 1: The Concepts of Supernaturals, Copenhagen, 1966, p. 115.

either. Transactions with these forces were uniform no matter which social group one belonged to. Not so the district deities. This group of gods was connected with society and its organization. When this organization changed, the system of transactions between social groups changed too, and the supernatural forces involved in this system necessarily changed in step with it.' It is evident that the concept of religious change stands for a complicated process and that the mechanisms involved need further investigation, not least concerning the ecological factor.

6. It should have emerged from the foregoing how many new vistas will be opened by the application of a religio-ecological perspective. Such topics are illuminated as the interaction between nature and religion — more important than was recently assumed —, ecological integration or convergence as an alternative to historical diffusion in the explanation of similar religious forms in different places, the interpretation of pre-historic religions, and religious change. It is important to remember that ecology of religion never supplants other methods, but offers more solutions.

Above all, ecology of religion helps us to achieve a deeper perspective on religious dynamics. We perceive that the forms and patterns of religion often depend on exterior conditions and that much of what we usually conceive to be genuine expressions of religious content are actually fortuitous manifestations. For instance, in the belief in an afterlife the realms of the dead mirror the environment of living man; the central idea is the faith in the next existence, whereas its forms are casual. It is often nowadays considered that some elementary religious symbols convey a universal import. Without denying this possibility I should like to point out that many symbols are in reality determined by social milieu or natural environment. It is therefore important to analyze the outworks of religion before interpreting its meaning.

Ecology of religion thus diverts religion of its fortuitous forms; it shows what is the casual expression and the genuine belief. By removing the external attributes of a religion, suggested by environmental adaptation and historical process, we may arrive at the basic ideas and values of that religion. A more profound view of the intrinsic values of so-called primitive religions will, I think, provide us with a key to the understanding of those great religious traditions that are dominant today.

SVEIN BJERKE   *Ecology of Religion, Evolutionism and
Comparative Religion*

1. In several papers Hultkrantz has outlined a new approach to the study
of religion called 'ecology of religion', as well as demonstrated in particular cases that the approach is a highly productive one.[40] My own
interest in this subject has been aroused by his papers and I have not as
yet myself attempted any detailed analysis of concrete data in accordance with his procedure. In this paper I shall mainly try to relate this
approach to the wider issues of causality and evolutionary change and
to assert the significance of evolutionary theory for our discipline. First,
however, I want to give a brief presentation of what I conceive of as
being fundamentally involved in a religio-ecological approach and I can
in this respect do little more than cast the insights of Hultkrantz in my
own mould of understanding.

2. As the present subject belongs to the section 'The future of the phenomenology of religion', of this study conference, I should perhaps first
of all try to make it clear what I take 'phenomenology of religion' to
be. In the study of religion as in all studies of the socio-cultural reality
collectively constructed by man, it is of some importance to contrast
the phenomenological approach with other possible approaches. In my
opinion the term 'phenomenology', when associated with studies of
religion, should be used in the same general sense as in the other social
sciences, namely, to refer to descriptive studies from the standpoint of
subjectivity, that is, the endeavor to understand (and possibly re-experi-
ence) a socio-cultural world from the subjective view and experiences
of those who live in that world. The non-phenomenological approaches
transcend the subjectivity of those who live in a cultural world and
take as their point of departure problems which are of professional
interest to the student with the ideal aim of explaining, and not merely
describing, socio-cultural phenomena.[41] While an ecology of religion may

40. Hultkrantz, *op. cit.* above in n.1, 5, and Hultkrantz, 'Ecology of Religion: Its
scope and methodology', in this volume, pp. 221-236.
41. Leon J. Goldstein, 'The phenomenological and naturalistic approaches to
the social', *Methodos* 14 (1961), pp. 225-238.

perhaps also be phenomenologically conceived of,[42] in what follows I shall consider ecology of religion as a non-phenomenological approach of a generalizing kind, concerned with questions of causality and regularities in religious forms of expression.

Ecology of religion is an outgrowth of the American research strategy known as 'cultural ecology' and shares its main features with its mother discipline. Cultural ecology is concerned with how man's relationship with his natural environment is mediated by culture (including society and religion), with how an adaptation to an ecosystem shapes a culture as well as with the way the ecosystem is shaped by the culture. Stressing the idea of 'interaction' between nature and culture, cultural ecology eschews the extreme position of the old environmental determinism as well as the opposed position, that of environmental possibilism.[43]

In my opinion the central concern of ecology of religion is to demonstrate how a given type of adaptation to a kind of natural environment — given a certain type of technology and society — tends to produce a certain kind of religion. Ecology of religion is thus based on the conviction that the general kind of religion met with in primitive cultures (and probably also in folk cultures in general) is not accidental, but dependent on environmental-adaptational as well as on sociological factors. We can thus no longer rest content with assumptions such as that man's experience of tropical rain forests gave rise to forest deities (environmental determinism) or with assumptions such as that given a certain type of environmental adaptation, man's experience of tropical rain forests may, or may not, give rise to forest deities (environmental possibilism).

In order to be able to disclose the relationships between religion and mode of adaptation to the natural environment, we shall have to look for parallel cases. We must use a cross-cultural method and work out types of religion associated with similar environments, technologies and societies. As the regularities which we are looking for are probably the least difficult to find in the cultures of hunting peoples, we should perhaps begin with these. Before we can be able to state with any accu-

42. C. Frake, 'Cultural ecology and ethnography', *American Anthropologist* 64 (1962), pp. 53-59.
43. Marshall D. Sahlins, 'Culture and environment: The study of cultural ecology', in Robert A. Manners and David Kaplan, eds., *Theory in Anthropology. A Sourcebook*, Chicago, 1968, pp. 367 ff.

racy what kind of religion is characteristic of hunting peoples as distinct from that of horticultural and pastoral peoples, we shall have to work out a number of types of religion belonging to hunters and gatherers. In order to be able to ascertain the significance of the natural environment we shall have to work out a typology of habitats. Thus Hultkrantz has outlined the type of religion found among the hunting peoples of the Arctic[44] and we must expect that this type of religion will be different from the type of religion found among hunters inhabiting tropical rain forests like the Pygmies of the Ituri forest, and from desert hunters like the Bushmen of the Kalahari.

Hultkrantz has worked out such a type concept, which he calls 'type of religion', which is not, however, concerned with the general features of religion as a whole, but 'contains those religious patterns and features which belong to or are intimately associated with the cultural core and therefore arise out of environmental adaptations'.[45] But as religion, more than any other aspect of culture, belongs to the secondary features of culture rather than to the core,[46] considerable parts of the religious system, and probably in inverse proportion with the complexity of the technological and socio-cultural level, must be omitted in the formulation of an ecological type of religion. The value of this type concept is obviously due to the circumstance that 'the type of religion is in its essence timeless: in principle it should occur wherever ecological and technological conditions of a similar level and integration appear. Historical influences may create changing patterns by repressing or emphasizing certain features, but the general frame of reference remains the same'.[47] This ecological type concept of religion is derived from Steward's concept of 'cultural core', '... the constellation of features which are most closely related to subsistence activities and economic arrangements. The core includes such social, political, and religious patterns as are empirically determined to be closely connected with these arrangements'.[48] The 'type' of religion is thus basically the religious aspect of the cultural core. It is, however, conceded by Steward that it is difficult to decide with some precision exactly what elements to

44. Hultkrantz, 'Type of religion...', *op. cit.* in n. 1.
45. Hultkrantz, 'An ecological approach...', *op. cit.* in n. 1, p. 146.
46. *Ibid.*, p. 142.
47. *Ibid.*, pp. 147-148.
48. Steward, *op. cit.* in n. 11, p. 37.

include in the cultural core as its definition in any given case '... will depend in part upon particular research interest, upon what is considered important; and there is still a healthy if somewhat confusing disagreement regarding these matters'.[49]

While the cultural core can be explained with reference to the dialectic relationship with the environment, the cultural features not included in the core, the 'secondary features', are seen by Steward to vary independently of the core features and thus to elude ecological explanation. Hultkrantz is well aware of the difficulties inherent in the concept of cultural core and thus of his 'type of religion',[50] but he still seems to conceive of the distinction between the ecologically explainable type of religion and the historically explainable features which are not part of the 'type of religion', as crucial to his religio-ecological approach. His position is thus that a part of the religious system can be explained nomothetically, while the rest can only be explained in a historical-particularistic way.

It would seem, however, that Hultkrantz has seen that this bi-partition of a religious system with reference to modes of explanation is not perhaps a theoretically productive one. His 'second level of religio-ecological integration' (which is not part of the 'type of religion' and thus not of the cultural core) does, after all, seem to be dependent on the 'primary integration', the 'type of religion', and cultural ~ore.[51] But if this is the case, the secondary religious features cannot vary independently of the 'type of religion' and one can hardly oppose the ecologically explainable and the culture-historically explainable parts of religious systems. It seems to me the opposition is not out there in the data, but in our modes of explanation. Given the necessary material, a religion in its totality can be explained historically or idiographically as well as in a generalizing, nomothetic mode. Through his publications on the subject of ecology of religion Hultkrantz has made us more sensitive to the importance of the natural environment for the understanding and explanation of primitive religions. None of us who are particularly interested in this category of religions (and perhaps especially if our studies are based on modern field work techniques) should in the future

49. Steward, *op. cit.*, p. 93.
50. Hultkrantz, *op. cit.* in n. 40, p. 13.
51. *Ibid.*, pp. 6-8.

fail to take into serious consideration the interaction between religion and nature. Intensive studies of the religions of particular societies should not only attempt to relate the various features of the religious system with each other and with the social structure, but society and religion should both be seen as an adaptation to a particular environment by means of a particular technology. If, however, we embark on a traditional functionalist, synchronic study only to show the inter-relatedness of things in an atemporal network, or go all the way with the functionalist programme and explain religion teleologically with reference to its role in maintaining the totality of which it is a part, we shall have lost one very important ingredient of the religio-ecological perspective. As Penner[52] and Spiro[53] cogently have shown, there can be no functional explanation of religion and 'if functionalism explains anything at all, it explains society by reference to religion'.[54] To me, the particularly important theoretical promise of ecology of religion is that it provides an effective point of departure for the breaking through of the synchronic-functionalistic web of interconnected phenomena in that it seeks to disclose the efficient causes of similarities and differences in religious phenomena.

As I understand the position of Steward, he gives research priority to the interrelationship of environment and technology[55] because the techno-economic aspect of culture tends to be the independent variable, while social organization and religion in general are dependent variables. Changes in culture 'are basically traceable to new adaptations required by changing technology and productive arrangements'.[56] The research strategy which postulates that similar technologies applied to similar natural environments tend to produce similar economic and social systems and further, similar systems of religion, is what Harris has called cultural materialism, that is, the anthropological counterpart to historical materialism.[57] This position, which does not deny that changes in

52. H. Penner, 'The poverty of functionalism', *History of Religions* 11 (1971), pp. 91-97.

53. Melford M. Spiro, 'Religion: Problems of definition and explanation', in Michael Banton, ed., *Anthropological approaches to the study of religion*, London, 1966; and *Burmese supernaturalism*, Englewood Cliffs, N. J., 1967.

54. Penner, *op. cit.*, p. 94.

55. Steward, *op. cit.*, pp. 40-41.

56. *Ibid.*, p. 37.

57. M. Harris, *The rise of anthropological theory*, New York., 1968, p. 4.

social organization or religious innovations *can* bring about changes in technology and thus change the ecological adaptation, but only states that these in general tend to be dependent factors, seems to me to be a sound one. And as is the case with historical materialism in general, it can perfectly well be conceived of as independent of a position of ontological materialism. In my opinion the distinction drawn by Marx between *Basis* and *Überbau* is theoretically more fruitful than Steward's distinction between cultural core and secondary cultural features.

Thus, in my opinion, ecology of religion can be made the point of departure for the enterprise of finding the general conditions on which the similarities and differences in primitive religions can be accounted for. We can also, on the same basis, take one further step and bring in the dimension of time. On the nomothetic level this means the reintroduction of the evolutionary approach to the study of religious phenomena.

3. It is a central fact in the history of our discipline that evolutionary points of view have been sneered at and that evolutionism has been considered an utterly outmoded strategy of research for almost two generations. The turning away from evolutionary viewpoints also in large measure accounts for the loss of interest in all kinds of general theories of religion. It would seem that the downfall of the classical evolutionary points of view created a nomothetic anxiety among historians of religion, who retreated behind the safe bastions of historical particularism and relativism. Since the turn of the century we have amassed an enormous quantity of facts, but there has in general been little in the way of formulating theories which can account for this wealth of empirical detail.

One of the most striking features of American anthropology during the last thirty years is the fact that evolutionary approaches have again been accorded academic respectability in a country where the historical particularism of Franz Boas and his school had dominated the anthropological field for half a century. In this successful resuscitation of the evolutionary approach Leslie A. White[58] and Julian H. Steward[59] have been the most important figures.

But before I deal with the new evolutionism, I shall very briefly out-

58. *The evolution of culture*, New York, 1959.
59. *Op. cit.* above in n. 11.

line the aims, methods and theories of the classical evolutionists of the latter half of the 19th century. The main interest of the classical evolutionists was the tracing of the progressive evolution of society and culture from the beginnings of human existence in the Paleolithic to modern industrial civilization, that is, they made an audacious attempt at a science of universal history. While this enterprise has its roots in the 18th century when the notion of progress became an important intellectual force,[60] its success in dominating the scientific arena in the latter half of the 19th century was to a considerable extent due to the new insights provided by geology, paleontology and archaeology.[61] By using rigorous stratigraphical methods the prehistorians were able to prove that man had originated in the distant Pleistocene (and not created by God a few thousand years ago), that an evolution of human culture had taken place, and that this evolution could be conceptualized in techno-economic stages. To a great extent the 19th-century interest in contemporary primitive peoples stemmed from the fact that the (usually inadequate) data accessible on them could be used to fill in the large gaps in the knowledge of the cultures of the prehistoric peoples. This is the procedure which became known as the 'comparative method', which was based on the conviction that contemporary primitive cultures resemble in their essential features the cultures of pre-civilized man. As is well known the evolution of religion was a major concern of most of the classical evolutionists. In order to illustrate the evolution of religion they theoretically isolated a number of stages (Tylor being an exception), Lubbock no less than seven.[62]

From about the turn of the century and onwards, the evolutionists were severely criticized from a number of quarters. Not only were the abuses of the 'comparative method' repeatedly pointed out and its general legitimacy even seriously doubted,[63] but it was clearly shown that the evolutionary stages which the comparative method was supposed to demonstrate were *a priori* constructions which to a great extent were based on judgments of value.

While the devastating criticism levelled at the evolutionists was to a

---

60. J. B. Bury, *The idea of progress*, New York, 1932.
61. Robert H. Lowie, *The history of ethnological theory*, New York, 1937, p. 21.
62. J. Lubbock, *The origin of civilization and the primitive condition of man*, London, 1870, p. 119.
63. Lowie, *op. cit.*, pp. 22 ff.; Evans-Pritchard, *op. cit.*, p. 10.

considerable extent pertinent, the critics were also guilty of severely misrepresenting the evolutionary approach. Thus it was asserted that the evolutionists regarded the evolutionary stages as fixed and necessary sequences which every single culture had to pass through, that is, the classical evolutionists were held to be defenders of what came to be known as 'universal parallelism' or 'unilinear evolution'.[64] The evolutionists, however, held that culture in general had passed through a given sequence of stages and that individual cultures tended to pass through the same sequence of stages, but they were clearly aware of the fact that not all cultures had to pass through an unvarying sequence. The British sociologist Morris Ginsberg[65] pointed this out as early as 1932 and the same point was forcefully made by White in 1945,[66] but the view that the classical evolutionists were unilinear evolutionists is, I believe, still prevalent among historians of religion.

Bound up with the issue of unilinearity is that of diffusion versus independent invention. The culture historians tended to make the principle of diffusion antithetical to that of evolution, but the evolutionists knew very well that the diffusion of culture traits was of frequent occurrence: 'Civilization is a plant much oftener propagated than developed'.[67] The contrast between diffusion and independent invention has meaning only on the level of particularistic culture-historical studies, not on that of evolutionary studies. The evolutionists were interested in the general stages through which mankind had passed and in any given case it is clearly immaterial whether a culture has passed from one stage to the next through the mechanism of independent invention, or has reached the next evolutionary stage by borrowing the necessary elements from other cultures. As Ginsberg has pointed out, diffusion cannot be contrasted with evolution, but is one of the agencies of evolution.[68]

A serious objection which can be raised against the position of the classical evolutionists is that — although they intended to fill in with socio-cultural materials the evolutionary stages revealed by prehistory — they did not feel it necessary to correlate types of subsistence with

64. Lowie, *op. cit.*, p. 190.
65. Ginsberg, *On the diversity of morals*, London, 1956, pp. 182 ff.
66. L. A. White, 'Diffusion versus evolution: An anti-evolutionist fallacy', *American Anthropologist* 47 (1945), pp. 339-356.
67. E. B. Tylor, *Primitive culture*, London, 1871, p. 53.
68. Ginsberg, *op. cit.*, p. 187.

types of society and types of religion. Bachofen must be mentioned as an exception. He did functionally relate a stage of *Mutterrecht* with a type of religion dominated by the cult of a tellurian *Urmutter* and the subsequent stage of *Vaterrecht* with male gods associated with the higher cosmic regions.[69] And it should also be noted that Wilhelm Schmidt, an anti-evolutionist according to his own programme, also related his stages of socio-cultural evolution to types of religion. His position is a particularly striking example of the point just made, namely, that there is no necessary opposition between evolution and culture history.[70]

On the assumption that the type of religion is dependent on techno-environmental and social factors, a new evolutionary enterprise cannot see the evolution of religion as an independent process related only to the progressive maturing of the human intellect. Thus Bellah in his paper on 'Religious evolution' attempts in a systematic manner to relate forms of religion to forms of society (the ecological dimension is omitted).[71] Writers within the field of history of religions still tend to follow the example of the classical evolutionists. Widengren's theory of the evolution of the idea of the high god is a case in point.[72]

An evolutionary approach can be made on different levels of abstraction. Today we have on the one hand the limited and parallelistic level of Steward, who has also gone beyond the primitive level and pointed out the parallel development of the stages in the Old World and the New World civilizations[73] and on the other the universal level of White, whose concern is with the evolution of culture as a whole and not with particular cultures.[74] At the present time, I believe that the formulations of Sahlins and Service[75] and Service[76] will prove to be of considerable utility also to a theory of religious evolution. By grouping together societies of roughly the same technology and socio-

69. Lowie, *op. cit.*, pp. 40ff.
70. *Ibid.*, pp. 189ff.
71. Robert N. Bellah, 'Religious evolution', in William A. Lessa and Evon Z. Vogt, eds., *Reader in Comparative Religion*, New York, 1965.
72. Geo Widengren, *Phänomenologie der Religion*, Berlin, 1969, p. 113.
73. Steward, *op. cit.*, and 'Cultural causality and law. A trial formulation of early civilization', *American Anthropologist* 51 (1949), pp. 1-27.
74. White, *op. cit.* in n. 58 and 66.
75. M. Sahlins and E. Service, *Evolution and culture*, Ann Arbor, 1960.
76. E. Service, *Primitive social organization*, New York, 1962.

political level of integration, one can distinguish between the familistic band level (in the definition of which the contribution of Steward[77] has been decisive) characteristic of hunters and gatherers, the tribal level of horticulturists and pastoralists, which lacks any centralized political system, the chiefdom level, which is defined on the basis of a redistributive economic system, and the state level defined on the basis of the claim for monopoly in the use of force made by the political authorities. While the last level must, for our purposes, be subdivided, I believe that these general evolutionary stages, when coordinated with ecological factors, provide, at the present time, the best general framework for a theory of the evolution of religion.

Sahlins and Service conceive of evolution as basically a dual process; on the one hand we have general evolution, the stages of which I have briefly outlined, and on the other we have specific evolution. While general evolution 'is the successive emergence of new levels of all-round development',[78] specific evolution is a 'connected, historic sequence of forms',[79] that is, the evolution of particular cultures seen in the more abstract framework of general evolution.

Sahlins and Service have not worked out the implications of their evolutionary scheme for our understanding of the evolution of religion, and its usefulness from our point of view lies in its potential for correlating decisive differences between forms of religion with these evolutionary stages. If their scheme is a productive one, it should be possible to work out general and important differences between religious systems on the band level, the tribal level, the chiefdom level and the state level (or levels). This work has hardly been initiated, but if a new evolutionary theory of religion is formulated, it can hardly overlook the point that the general form of religion is dependent on ecological and sociological factors.

4. Although the attempt may reasonably be judged to be somewhat premature, I should like in this last section of my paper to outline what I believe to be the gain from the adoption of an evolutionary research

77. J. H. Steward, 'The economic and social basis of primitive bands', in R. Lowie, ed., *Essays in anthropology presented to A. L. Kroeber*, Berkeley, 1936.
78. M. D. Sahlins, 'Evolution: Specific and general', in Manners and Kaplan, *op. cit.* (reprinted from Sahlins and Service, *op. cit.*), p. 235.
79. *Ibid.*, p. 237.

strategy for our discipline as a whole. It is often said that comparative religion (or the history of religions — I regard the terms as synonyms) basically consists of two essentially different 'disciplines': history of religions (in the narrower sense) and phenomenology of religion.[80] Some students choose to define comparative religion as a historical, that is, a particularistic and diachronic discipline, and regard phenomenology of religion as the inferior member of the pair, whose *raison d'être* lies in its usefulness in supplying the historian of religion with suitable concepts and comparative illustrations. This historical-particularist definition of our discipline is becoming increasingly difficult to defend, since it virtually leaves out of any serious consideration the overwhelming majority of religious systems. From this point of view the religions of primitive peoples can only indirectly be accommodated within our discipline, namely, as providers of material for phenomenology of religion. As it is increasingly being realized that primitive religions have as much a claim to our scholarly interest as the historical religions and must therefore be studied on a par with these, a historical perspective cannot serve as an overall integrating perspective for our discipline.

I believe that a much stronger case can be made for the other member of the pair, 'phenomenology of religion', to serve as the basis of our discipline. On this basis a clearer identity could be given to all historians of religion whatever their special fields of study, and thus protect our subject from the ever-present danger of breaking up into various philo-logical disciplines and anthropology.[81] As we all know, 'phenomenology of religion' is used as a blanket term to cover rather different types of studies of a non-diachronic and non-particularistic nature. As I have said previously, I believe that the term 'phenomenology of religion' should be restricted to denote studies written from the standpoint of subjectivity. Studies of a comparative and generalizing kind probably need no separate name, in my opinion they should form the basis for our discipline, being simply studies in comparative religion. If the core of our discipline as a whole is taken to be of a generalizing kind rather than of a particularistic historical and ethnographical one, comparative religion will be a user of idiographic studies made by philologists, his-torians, and ethnographers.

---

80. R. Pummer, '*Religionswissenschaft* or religiology?', *Numen* 19 (1972), pp. 106f.
81. Hultkrantz, *op. cit.* above in n. 18, pp. 80 ff.

There is, however, at least one important objection which can be raised against such a definition of our subject, namely, that it would tend to stress the synchronic dimension at the expense of the diachronic one. The basically synchronic nature of comparative and generalizing studies should therefore be supplemented by an approach which is both generalizing *and* diachronic. The evolutionary approach belongs to this last category. The methodological field of comparative religion as a whole can thus be represented by the following figure:

	Synchronic	Diachronic
Idiographic	A	C
Nomothetic	B	D

The figure presents us with four main types of approach and theoretical framework. Each of the boxes represents a definite choice. One has to choose between a synchronic and a diachronic approach — one clearly cannot use both at one and the same time — and one must combine the approach chosen either an idiographic or a nomothetic one.

Although I would suggest that the main emphasis of our discipline should be on generalizing, nomothetic studies, this does not of course mean that we can do without idiographic or particularizing ones, or that we should legitimately concern ourselves with history (C), ethnography of religion and synchronic studies within the historical religions (A).What is often called phenomenological studies are mainly to be accommodated within box B, and box D will comprise the evolutionary approach. To me it seems that this last box must be considered to be the most fundamental one, as A, B, and C can all be contained within the overall perspective provided by D. None of the other boxes can serve as an overall perspective for our discipline as a whole.

Commentary   by Manfred Büttner

In his paper Svein Bjerke says: 'Intensive studies of the religions of particular societies should not only attempt to relate the various features of the religious system with each other and with the social structure, but society and religion should both be seen as an adaptation to a particular environment by means of a particular technology.' He goes on: 'To me, the particularly important promise of ecology of religion is that it provides an effective point of departure for the breaking through of the synchronic-functionalist web of interconnected phenomena in that it seeks to disclose the efficient causes of similarities and differences in religious phenomena.

'As I understand the position of Steward, he gives research priority to the interrelationship of environment and technology because the techno-economic aspect of culture tends to be the independent variable, while social organization and religion in general are dependent variables.' He sums up by saying: 'Hultkrantz has made us more sensitive to the importance of the natural environment... None of us ... should in the future fail to take into serious consideration the interaction between religion and nature.'

I would like to start from this point, especially with reference to the last quotation. We geographers of religion also make similar demands, and hold a similar conception, to that expressed in the sentences quoted. We have, however, arrived there by a different route. In the brief time available to me, I would like to summarize how we have arrived at our current conception, and in what respects, despite their great similarities, it differs in detail from that expounded by the previous speaker. I would be pleased if we could then achieve a fruitful exchange of views in the discussion, for it is time to transcend the disciplinary boundaries. Geographers of religion can no longer isolate themselves from, and avoid discussion with, scientists of religion ('Religionswissenschaftler'). On the contrary, exchange of views, and in fact teamwork transcending the disciplinary boundaries, is what is now called for.

THE HISTORY OF GEOGRAPHY OF RELIGION

Current research indicates that it was Kasche who first used and defined the concept of 'geography of religion'. In his book, published in 1795, he writes that the task of the geographer of religion is to investigate the influence of the geographical environment on the ideas contained in religion. This conception of the task of the geographer of religion survived until well into the 20th century.

Among theologians and scientists of religion, in fact, the idea still persists that geographers of religion see it as their task to 'explain' religion on the basis of its geographical environment, especially of climate. I may refer here to the entries under 'geography of religion' in the pertinent works in theology and science of religion (see RGG, and König's *Lexikon*).

The geographers themselves have in fact, in the context of the general retreat from determinism, performed a total change of direction, in particular through the conscious adoption of the stock of ideas found in Max Weber. It was above all the Bonn school, under the leadership of Troll, who first embarked on the investigation and display of the way in which religion shapes its environment. In 1947 Fickeler's fundamental work pointed the direction in which geography of religion should be reoriented; here he speaks in the introduction about the mutual relationship between religion and environment, but in the text itself, he only deals with one side, i. e. the shaping of the environment that originates in religion.

Despite the fact that many of Fickeler's points were rejected in immediately subsequent publications, the idea that the geographer, as geographer of religion, should deal only with the shaping of the landscape originating in religion, was upheld up until the 1960s. Since human geography, meanwhile, was now being studied with a strongly social-geographical emphasis, Fickeler's thesis that the shaping of the landscape mainly originated in the cult component was more and more challenged; nevertheless the one-sided approach was maintained. Reference was certainly made to Max Weber, and the importance of the group for landscape-shaping was acknowledged, but the fact that the group itself, and the spiritual attitude ('Geisteshaltung') it holds, are in turn shaped by the environment — which Weber himself emphasizes and expounds at length — this was ignored.

Recently, however, and in conjunction with the methodological reorientation of cultural geography as a whole, a change has taken place in geography of religion, which I would like briefly to dwell on.

Possibly the best way of representing the difference between the old, 'two-dimensional' process of cultural geography, and the modern 'three-dimensional' process of social geography, is by means of a diagram (cf. Diagram 1, below).

For example, an urban geographer of the old school, investigating the functional network between the home and the place of work, operated (in a transferred sense) two-dimensionally. He investigated relationships on a 'plane'.

The social geographer passes on from this two-dimensional approach to a three-dimensional one; to maintain the metaphor: he regards whatever takes place on the 'lower' plane merely as an indicator of what is happening on the 'upper', i.e. social, plane. Some progressive geographers would even go so far as to say that things cannot be seen merely statically, but dynamically, i.e. in terms of process. This has given rise to the slogan that the earth's surface is the process-field of social-geographical events; and thus a four-dimensional social geography has emerged.

This then is the starting point for modern geography of religion. I would like to go briefly into this, too, by commenting on our conception, and then exemplifying this by means of the practical field research carried out by our team in Bochum.

THE NEW CONCEPTION OF GEOGRAPHY OF RELIGION

I first put this conception forward at the German Geographers' Conference at the University of Erlangen-Nuremberg. The title of my paper there was 'The dialectical process of the relation between religion and environment, and its meaning for geographers of religion and social geographers' ('Der dialektische Prozess der Religion/Umwelt-Beziehung in seiner Bedeutung für den Religions- bzw. Sozialgeographen'). All I can do here, of course, is to present some of the main ideas; anybody interested further in these questions is referred to the Geographers' Conference paper.

The starting point of our conception is the model of the dialectical spiral (cf. Diagram 2). This model is intended to illustrate the following points: Firstly, impulses are generated by religion (or, to be more precise, by the bearers of religion) out into the environment — formation — but then the environment (climate, and soil, but also the socio-economic and technological environment) operates as a modifier on religion — 'feedback'. Once it has been seen that the procedure of this network of relationships is directional, it reveals itself as a dialectical process.

The choice of whether one should start from 'above', i. e. from religion, or from 'below', i. e. from the environment, will depend on the central question being asked in the investigation and description of this spiral. The geographer's special field is the environment (including socio-economics); he cannot be alone competent for either direction of procedure, but he must necessarily and correspondingly share the competence for both directions.

Let us look more closely at the individual parts of the spiral, and attempt to see them in the total context (cf. Diagram 1, below).

First of all comes the period of development, when everything is *in statu nascendi* and, to a certain extent, 'open'. The emergent religion (or form of magic) is open to the absorption of environmental influences, and the environment, especially the social environment, is open to shaping by religion. At the end of this development phase a certain balance has been established between religion and environment — a harmony (lasting, in some cases, for thousands of years) between landscape, man, and culture, which has grown up in the framework of a dialectical process of synthesization: environment and religion have mutually given shape to each other.

This balance will be maintained for as long as major changes take place neither in the religion (i. e. in the intellectual or spiritual beliefs of the bearers of the religion) nor in the environment. Such a situation can be seen operationally as a 'beginning', from which it is possible to identify the initiation of a new dialectical process.

The disturbance of this balance may originate either from 'above' (the plane of spiritual attitude) or from 'below' (that of the socio-economic environment). A conflict situation arises, which sets off a process aimed at a new balance between a reconceived religion and a correspondingly different shaping of the environment (social constitution, pattern of settlement, etc.).

Ladies and Gentlemen, I must finish; but I would like to offer a few examples from our current research programme, so that what I have said so far does not remain too excessively or exclusively theoretical.

THE PRACTICE OF FIELD RESEARCH

It is hardly possible to research into the entire spiral (as I have, for the sake of clarity, presented it) of any complete religion or religious community. We have therefore limited ourselves for the time being to researching into partial segments of the on-going dialectical process for certain limited and surveyable religious communities: in the first place, the Moravians and Waldensians. These communities are so small that it is possible to interrogate the total group, and from this we hope to derive criteria for representative cross-sample questionnaires. In Bochum we have gathered a team which consists of about 15 members, mainly geographers, but also including sociologists, theologians, scientists of religion, and mathematicians or computer specialists.

Questionnaires were then devised, with the collaboration in particular of social psychologists in Bochum and of research teams in Amsterdam and Turin, for the Moravians in Germany and the Netherlands, and the Waldensians in Italy, respectively. These were then carried out on a house-to-house basis, with the cooperation of the local pastors, mayors, teachers, etc.

What were these questionnaires concerned with? We wanted in particular to investigate the feedback process originating from the modern industrial world, or, to maintain our image, to research into the latest twist of the spiral. We wanted to establish to what extent the effect of the modern industrial world has been to bring about changes in the spiritual attitude of the Waldensians in Italy or the Moravians in Germany; how the church leadership may be reacting to this; and to what extent these changes in spiritual attitude can be physiognomically identified in the landscape.

For example: in the early 18th century, the 'religion' of the Moravians began to develop into a solid religious organization, in which a religiously-shaped spiritual attitude, structure of society, of professions, and of the economy, and the pattern of settlement, mutually supported each other (or conformed with each other). Around the middle of the century, with the foundation of Herrnhag, a balance between religion and environment began to be achieved. They wanted to be 'soldiers of Christ', in order to fulfil their part in the spreading of his gospel. The entire 'army' was therefore put under strict organization and divided into separate groups, called 'corps'. Each corps had its own accommodation, and its special economic and social function in this religious organization. The special nature of the Moravian settlements, with their unique social and economic structure (i. e. shaping of the environment), can only be understood against this background: this constitutes the visible balance between religion and environment (cf. the diagrams; and cf. also my article in *Numen*, which is subtitled 'Fundamental insights regarding the reciprocal relationships between religion and the environment based on field research among the Herrnhuter' — 'Grundsätzliche Einsichten über die wechselseitigen Beziehungen zwischen Religion und Umwelt, gewonnen anhand von Feldforschungen bei den Herrnhutern').

Now, especially since the Second World War, the outer environment, with its competitive thinking, has been penetrating into this religious world. The consequence has been a change in the structure of the professions, in the social constitution, and, ultimately, in the spiritual attitude. Physiognomically, too, the change in the religious organization (i. e. the achievement of a new balance) has been expressed in a change in the pattern of settlement. The corps houses, for instance, which only fitted in with the older social constitution, spiritual attitude, etc., are now being demolished and replaced by buildings which one could call a manifestation of the new spirit. Through our questionnaire survey, we need to study in detail how the spiritual attitude of the Moravians living in these new houses has changed and is continuing to change.

The second example: for the Waldensians, the ideal of poverty has since the beginning been virtually a dogma. In addition, it was a particularly strict commandment for them, as for all the Reformed churches, to observe feastdays. Nowadays, however, the Waldensians commute to work in nearby industrial plants; they have, however, two jobs, since they must also carry on their farming on the side, for which they mostly only have Sunday available. At first, the Waldensians had a bad conscience about going into the fields on Sundays, and would hide themselves if the pastor happened to come past; but in the course of time a complete change has taken place. The pastors nowadays interpret the command to observe feastdays in a different way from previously. This is a particularly powerful example of the effects of the modern technological environment penetrating into the contents of belief.

A similar thing has happened to the ideal of poverty. In the commuter zone, poverty is no longer seen as something positive. While the

Waldensians in the mountains continue to consider riches, or being well-off, as an obstacle to salvation, those who work in the factories have altered their spiritual attitude on this matter fundamentally. It is nevertheless striking that the Waldensians still have no links with trade. We drew up a religious-geographical map of the Waldensian 'capital', Torre Pellice, which shows that the business world is Catholic. This seems to me to be a consequence of the Waldensian spiritual attitude about earning money. To become rich, or indeed to make money at all, through business instead of through 'proper work', still appears to the Waldensians in some way 'disreputable'.

A final example: in the Abruzzi, there are nowadays communist Waldensian communities, which are subject to attack by the Catholic environment because of their anti-ecclesiastical beliefs. It is interesting to see how communist thinking has penetrated even as far as the religious pronouncements of the leaders of the community. The Bible, and the Confession of Faith, are interpreted in a communist way. Unfortunately, the brief time available to me here does not allow me to expatiate on these questions further. An article on the communist Waldensians will however be appearing shortly in a geographical periodical.

CONCLUSION: WHAT IS 'SPIRITUAL ATTITUDE'?

Ladies and Gentlemen, I hope that the similarities and differences between the approaches of ecology and of geography of religion will have become clear to you. To simplify, I could perhaps summarize them by saying that the ecologist investigates the extent of environmental influence within religion. The geographer of religion, on the other hand, is in addition concerned with the opposite question, i. e. the extent to which religion, or the spiritual attitude held by the bearers of religion, generate impulses onto the environment.

This brings us to the concept of 'spiritual attitude'. How can this concept be defined precisely enough for one to be able to work with it?

For the older religious communities, in which the whole of one's life was still ordered on the basis of the norms of faith, and where one really lived in the faith, the definition is relatively easy. Here, what I would say is that the spiritual attitude is the shaping by religion of the thought and activity of the adherents of the religious community in question. (It must however be borne in mind that this spiritual attitude is also partly shaped, even in the 'Founder' religions, by the environment, i. e. climate, professions, social structure, etc.)

But how is one to define the concept of 'spiritual attitude' when the feedback from the forces originating in the modern industrial world is so strong as to lead to secularization? I once said that the geographer of religion who investigates these things automatically becomes a geographer of ideology. (And I entirely agree with Sopher when he argues that the geographer of religion should also consider the 'quasi-religions' such as Communism.) In a post-religious society, whose spiritual attitude is no longer shaped by religion but by ideology, should one simply speak of scales of values, and equate spiritual attitude with the ethics of values?

Yet how are these things to be quantified, and processed for the computer, in such a way as to become comparable?

At the congress at Berchtesgaden, Salzburg, I asked the scientists of religion for help in this matter, and since then there has been a constantly intensifying exchange of views. We are still at the beginning, however. At the moment, we have made a pragmatic beginning, by establishing where a change in spiritual attitude has taken place on individual points (the poverty ideal, the observation of feastdays, the idea of service, competitive thinking, etc.), and by approaching these cartographically and quantitatively and placing them in relation to their environment; for we regard these changes as the consequences of a feedback originating in the modern industrial world, with the final link in the chain of this feedback then being identifiable in a change in the shaping of the environment.

This is no more than the first step, however; an attempt to cope with a changing situation by means of modern scholarly tools. Finally, therefore, I would like to repeat the appeal which Troll made many years ago, when as Rector of the University of Bonn he appealed to the scientists of religion assembled there: Please incorporate into your discussions, and your research, the questions of geography of religion as well.

Moravian Pattern of Settlement

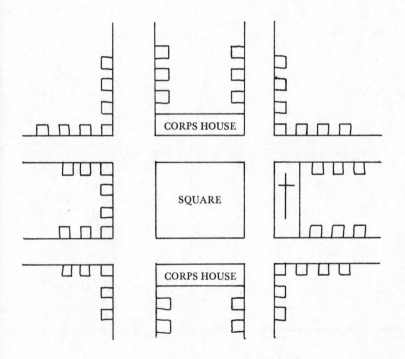

Diagram 1.
(First published in: *Münchner Studien zur Social- und Wirtschaftsgeographie*, Bd. 8.)

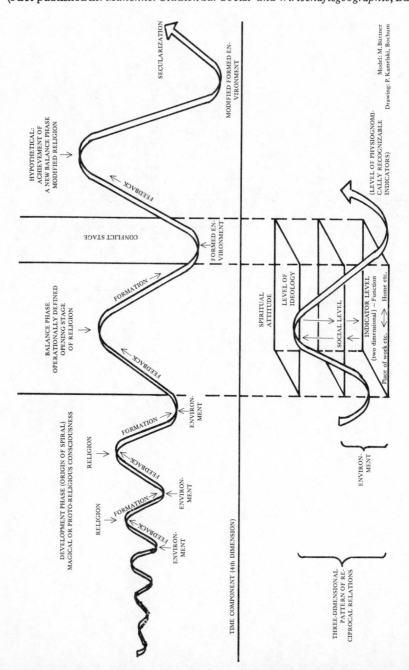

Diagram 2.
(First published in: *Münchner Studien zur Social- und Wirtschaftsgeographie*, Bd. 8.)

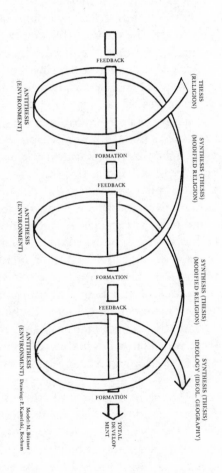

Commentary   by Asok K. Ghosh

1. New ideas always influence people who believe in the ideas or whose works have some kind of bearing on the ideas. In the same way, perhaps, Hultkrantz's ideology has influenced Bjerke, and the latter has tried to enlarge the ideas in the realm of neo-evolution. On the one hand Bjerke has been influenced by the ideas of Hultkrantz on ecology of religion, while on the other Bjerke himself concedes that he has not 'attempted any detailed analysis of the concrete data in accordance with his (Hultkrantz's) procedure'. In spite of his lack of critical understanding of the approach Bjerke has tried 'to relate this approach to the wider issues of causality and *evolutionary change* and to assert the significance of *evolutionary* theory (both italics mine) for our discipline'. Very surprisingly, Hultkrantz himself made cautions against the evolutionary approach to his ideas of ecology of religion at this stage.

In the propaedeutic part on 'phenomenology of religion', what is under consideration is a conjunctive approach, where a phenomenological approach will be part and parcel of the whole system of approach. The opinion which Bjerke has set forth on the term 'phenomenology' is more from the point of view of subjectivity. But phenomenology is essentially a method of philosophical analysis where the identification and description lie in the essence of experience with intuitive apprehension. The modern trend of phenomenology indicates the avoidance of unproductive speculation and tries to re-establish a rigorous empirical discipline. It is not very clear why Bjerke has preferred a non-phenomenological approach instead of the conjunctive approach coupled with philosophical analysis.

In dealing with the central concern of ecology of religion, emphasis has been laid on adaptation to a natural environment with a specific type of technological level of the society. Can we assume that, all the factors being equal, the forms of religion will be exactly similar? Perhaps not, as there are other factors which are also responsible for the emergence of a form of religion, though certain traits may be common in all forms of religion. The sociological factors which are dependent on ecology of religion have not properly been described. In the case of environment, the determinism comes out in the process of elimination of possibilism.

For finding out 'the relationship between religion and mode of adaptation to the natural environment', like Hultkrantz, Bjerke has also indicated parallelism through cross-cultural studies. In this connection one should not ignore time depth, and the study on parallelism must include the micro-level. Classifications of religion and habitats are more theoretically oriented, because the bases of such classification are many and the selective process for finding out the types is yet unknown. The form of religion has some amount of relationship with habitat (including the natural environment) and subsistence (which has also a bearing with ecology); besides these there are many factors which might have contributed to the form of religion.

The view point of a cultural core[82] has been necessarily assimilated in Hultkrantz's type of religion, and that too has not been rejected by Bjerke, despite his critical remarks on this issue. Before coming to any conclusive stage with the help of a theoretical assessment of the classification of types of religion — it is perhaps high time to carry out intensive work in different areas with ecology, subsistence pattern, social groups, cultural tradition — and their relation with religion. Scholars interested in this field are found in different countries, and in a Study Conference preliminary discussions might be made for bringing out an atlas on the types of religion, which would not only indicate the distribution, but also point out the ecological niche and socio-cultural forms of the areas in which the types of religion are found to exist. This basic and fundamental work would serve as a guide line for different problems, including the ecology of religion.

Of course, the totality of a religion can be viewed from various perspectives, such as historical, idiographic, and nomothetic modes, as well as generalization. But to understand religion in a meaningful way, the best approach is the integration of all the above mentioned perspectives. The theoretical model of religion can never be worked out until it is practically examined. Often the correlation has been made between ecology on the one hand, and society and religion on the other. But society is viewed from a materialistic level while the level of religion is purely ideological. As a matter of fact the interaction between ecology and society, and between ecology and religion, will have different results. Ecology certainly changes the levels of technology and subsistence

82. J. H. Steward, *op. cit.* above in n. 11.

to achieve a balance,[83] while in the case of religion, it may not be changed with the change of ecology, but some amount of moulding may be possible. This is only due to the fact that in case of the former there is direct relationship of survival while it is indirect in the sphere of religion. In order to examine the role of society in religion, one cannot ignore the fact that society is not merely social structure, but is a complex of social processes. 'The relationships, values, and goals of society are at any given moment only relatively stable; slow but cumulative changes are continually taking place. Other changes are more rapid — so rapid in fact that they cause a visible disruption of the established structure'.[84] Religion may be included here in the first category where slow change takes place with the process of development. On the other hand, technological change may be brought about either due to change in the total cultural pattern with the influence of some responsible factors, or change may take place towards betterment.

The role of religion in human society is not universal. Examples of such kinds of 'moral order' have been put forward by Redfield,[85] and this again indicates the risk of parallelism of interpretation in the ecology of religion.

The central theme of Bjerke's paper is on evolutionism, in the perspective of ecology of religion. It is more apt to say that he has made attempts to take up neo-evolutionism, rather than evolutionism. The ecological process has a 'tendency in time towards special forms of spatial and sustenance groupings of the units comprising ecological distribution. There are five major ecological processes: concentration, centralization, segregation, invasion, succession'.[86] The last one, i.e. the process of succession, cannot be considered as evolution. It may be noted that all the above mentioned processes have an opposite or negative aspect, which is not regression or negative evolution. Under the circumstances, when very little is known about the process of growth of religion, it is not justified to say that in the case of ecological bearing on religion there is no pattern of development. But until the pattern

83. R. E. Park, 'Human ecology', *The American Journal of Sociology* 42 (1936), pp. 1-15.

84. Th. F. O'Dea, *The sociology of religion*, New Jersey, 1966.

85. R. Redfield, *The primitive world and its transformations*, New York, 1953.

86. R. D. McKenzie, 'The scope of human ecology', *Publications of the American Sociological Society* 20 (1926), pp. 141-154.

has been recognized, the speculative assessment has hardly any significance. It is true that the techno-economic stages of culture have been found to follow evolution, and it may be expected that as religion is associated with the above stages — the evolution of religion is found to be expected. But it is still an open question how far religion is tied to cultural stages as a direct derivative. The situation becomes more complicated when ecology penetrates into the domain of society and religion. Social phenomena have patterns of their own, and the total conditions of life govern their shift.[87] In several instances it has been found that similar contrasting categories, such as ecological order and social order, reveal themselves to be largely arbitrary and erroneous.[88] Again, if religion is considered as a form of human behavior, its correlation with ecology is hardly significant.[89]

In the conceptual model of evolution of religion, attempts have been made to use the 'comparative method' where data from primitive people have been 'used to fill in the large gaps in the knowledge of cultures of the prehistoric peoples'. This method not only supplies inadequate facts but also the limitations in such a methodology are numerous. It is true that in the mechanism of evolution, independent invention has a significant role which emerges from need. But the borrowing mechanism cannot be properly identified as a part of evolution. This is evidenced by the fact that in culturology there are different schools, and among them the evolutionary and diffusionist schools are important. There is no compromise between the two schools when a specific case on evolution is concerned. It cannot be denied that in culture both the processes of universalism and regionalism are conspicuous, but the former is the expression of need while the latter is attributed to adjustment, in various ways.

To fit in the evolution on a religio-ecological model, Bjerke has adapted the formulations of Sahlins and Service[90] and Service[91] in

87. L. Wirth, 'Human ecology', *The American Journal of Sociology* 50 (1945), pp. 483-488.

88. W. E. Gettys, 'Human ecology and social theory', *Social Force* 17 (1940), pp. 469-476.

89. W. S. Robinson, 'Ecological correlations and the behavior of individuals', *American Sociological Review* 15 (1950), pp. 351-357.

90. *Op. cit.* above in n. 75.

91. *Op. cit.* above in n. 76.

which a number of levels have been identified 'by grouping together societies of roughly the same technology and socio-political level of integration'. Bjerke is optimistic about working out the evolution of religious systems 'on the band level, the tribal level, the chiefdom level and the state level (or levels)'. The idea is high-sounding, but does the form of religion follow the same pattern as that of the techno-social level? Secondly, how far does ecology play any role both in society and religion? In fact, the great chaos in human ecology resulted from the aberrant tendency to work in areas where ecology cannot properly be applied, resulting in the failure to maintain a close working relationship between human ecology and general or bioecology.[92]

It is hoped that in due course a new evolutionary theory of religion will be formulated, but the methodology for such a formulation would be different from that of Bjerke's approach. The new methodology will obviously include certain parameters to include ecology on the micro-level, considering all the possible attributes. It is only assumed at this stage that the types (forms) of religion cannot be very specific; rather, there will be considerable amount of range of variation.

Finally, the thought-process of Bjerke's paper is highly interesting in the field of history of religion, and the importance of his ideology has been provocative with the introduction of allied fields, especially anthropology. It would be more interesting if his theoretical ideas were implemented by practical work, which alone can indicate the degree of accuracy of his methodology. It is hoped that in the near future practical work in the field will show the merit of his approach as well as his methodology. Only the work, not the idea, will point out the exact working principle of the approach.

The paper includes three main facets, and they are ecology, religion and evolution. The central theme lies in religion, while the ecology works as a factor responsible for expressing the form of religion. Simultaneously, it is to be found out how religion follows a pattern of evolution which is Bjerke's own theoretical contribution. In the present context it may be said that religion has a specific entity, which is different from other areas of culture. Unlike the material and social traits, religious traits are more psychic in nature, and in the society they follow a general

92. A. H. Hawley, 'Ecology and human ecology', *Social Force* 22 (1944), pp. 398-405.

norm. Unlike other cultural constituents, religion is more traditional and conservative, and as a matter of fact the change of religion or its evolution is not as conspicuous as other traits. It is true that with ecology, there is some relationship to society, both on its material and abstract levels. It is inevitable that the material traits will change, where there is a close relationship with subsistence and survival. On the other hand, ecology cannot always convert the society in its totality. The effect of ecological forces may react with other forms in an indirect way and in such cases there is no direct encounter with ecology.

Evolution is development through time, and in the case of religion if we believe in evolution it is also apprehended that religion is mono-genetic in origin. The propounders of evolution of religion will advocate that religion under similar ecological conditions gave rise to one kind of religion. In answer to this, one may show a lot of examples where different forms of religion are found in similar ecological conditions.

The research design of ecologically oriented problems in the field of social science, especially in religion, has still to be formulated in the proper perspective. The socio-cultural aspects involve structure, function and behavior, and ecology affects all the factors. As a result, it is difficult to measure the change in any specific character, until the other characters are controlled. A tribal group in transition may or may not change its religion, and if there is any change, can we consider it as evolution?

2. In recent years ecology has started being used in almost all fields; to be very frank it has become fashionable to use ecology as a most modern and sophisticated tool for research. Ecology has its prime importance in biology (life science), where attempts have been made to treat the organism in relation to its environment with special emphasis on subsistence — the mode of which is expressed in the form of adaptation, adjustment, symbiosis, etc. Later, works started dealing with the interrelationships between human life and environment, which resulted in the emergence of human ecology. In such circumstances, environment 'includes only the material and spatial aspects of the surrounding world. It does not include non-material cultural environment or the web of human social relations'.[93] Human ecology broadly com-

93. J. A. Quinn, *Human Ecology*, New York, 1950.

prehends the multi-aspect relations between man and environment.
Perhaps the frontiers of human ecology have become wider with the
additional attention of workers working in the marginal areas of human
ecology. In this process, anthropologists and sociologists have become
involved and have emphasized the effects of climate on society and
culture.

In this connection, it may not‚ be out of place to mention the comment of Bews[94] who describes human ecology as a synthesis which
'unifies all the human sciences and enables each one to find its proper
place in a generalized study of man... Sometimes it concentrates on the
environment itself, sometimes on man himself, sometimes on the interactions between the two, but finally it always endeavors to view the
environment-function-organism triad as one definitely whole'. Hultkrantz's paper is not on human ecology proper in the conventional
sense; rather, it is concentrated on a specific facet of human society
and culture, i. e. religion. Culture in the realm of ecology has been
necessarily studied to a considerable extent, and it has been found
that the interaction of man in exposure to environmental reaction is
significantly balanced through the process of culture change.

In the words of Hultkrantz one may ask, what has ecology as a whole
to do with religion? Hultkrantz has tried to supply necessary argument
in favor of his religio-ecological approach. Before we take the approach
itself, one wishes to examine the relationship between religion and
ecology, of course of primitive people. Religion may be considered as
part of culture in its integrated form. Unlike other areas of culture,
religion is characterized by its ideology, which follows certain norms
in a specific area and time. As a matter of fact, the interaction between
religion and ecology is comparatively less in comparison to other aspects
of culture which have direct relationship with subsistence. On the other
hand, religion has perhaps an indirect bearing on ecology through other
dimensions of culture. The critics have omitted and Hultkrantz has
pointed out 'the fact that religions, in their formal manifestations,
make use of environment and adapt themselves to it'. According to
Hultkrantz 'this is exactly what ecology of religion is about: the study
of the environmental integration of a religion and its implications'. In
reality, hardly any concrete evidence can be put forward to illustrate

94. J. W. Bews, *Human Ecology*, London, 1935.

Hultkrantz's hypothesis. The environmental situation is used or adapted for cultural adjustments, and in this process of adjustment religious ideas are integrated which help to form traditions, generally found to be continued. In the context of ecology of religion, the ecology does not merely include the natural environment but also the socio-cultural environment of the people who practice the religion. It is perhaps obvious that the natural environment influences the socio-cultural matrix of a group whose religion is formulated from the components of different aspects of culture. In other words, there is a chain-reaction from ecology to culture, and from culture to religion.

The approaches put forward by Hultkrantz are more theoretical in nature and it is true that the information on man's experience of his environment and his ideas of Nature, and the analysis of the environmental integration of man's religions, will supply important and significant results along this line. The integration of the above two approaches will lead to the goal of a religio-ecological approach, from the stage of hypothesis to practical implementation. Primitive religions where the cultures are dependent on the natural environment, are appropriate situations where the religio-ecological approach can be conveniently carried out. In comparison to religions of modern cultures, the religions of primitive cultures are less changed. The process of fundamental change, which influences religion, lies in cultural evolution — towards better security and sufficiency. Under the circumstances, the ideal studies can be made among tribes living in isolation, whose overall cultural milieu is in a relatively static condition.

In my comment, it appears that my viewpoint on ecology and its relation with culture closely agrees with the cultural-ecological model set forth by Steward,[95] and his model, in general, fits in with religio-ecological problems, the main contention of Hultkrantz.

Religion has been briefly defined by Hultkrantz as 'a creation of man's experience and cultural tradition'. But to my mind it appears that it is more a psychic explanation(s) of experiences which forms the matrix of cultural tradition. The natural experiences are in reality and they are accounted for in the socio-cultural and psychological background. The recurrences of such events are not unusual and they can be reacted to, explained, and treated in the same manner. The cumulative

95. Steward, *op. cit.* above in n. 11.

form builds the tradition and is slowly assimilated in the religious ideas of the society.

The levels of religio-ecological integration, as proposed by Hultkrantz, are arbitrary, and there is scope to modify them. His first two scales, viz. (1) primary integration, and (2) secondary integration, are based on subsistence, and at times the same levels can be viewed from the level of morphological integration, without disturbing the functional approach. Strictly speaking, there is hardly any set pattern for scaling the levels. But attempts may be made only through extensive studies among the primitive groups with both similar and different levels of economy, living in similar as well as different ecological niches.

From his paper it is quite evident that Hultkrantz is in favor of classifying the type of religion. But what would be the bases for this classification? Regions with different levels of ecological adaptation, subsistence systems, etc. cannot always be considered as the criteria of classification. The comparative ecological approach by which he brings out the types of religion of arctic, desert nomadic and semi-desert gathering are not all the types. There is a broad spectrum indeed, and it is still an open question how far the above approach is a meaningful one for the classification of religion types.

Hultkrantz's third goal for the ecology of religion is to arrange the types of religion into historical strata. In this context the main problem lies in the typology of religion, which is still to be ascertained. For the convenience of discussion let us suppose that the typology of religion works well; but what would be the nature of arrangement of religion into historical strata? Hultkrantz's arrangement is not the arrangement or ordering of religion *senso stricto*, rather it is the placement of religion in relation to the development of subsistence economy. The so-called development pattern of economy is arranged as gathering, collecting, hunting, fishing, fowling and food producing in the form of agriculture or horticulture. But the above process is not always uniform, and more strikingly it has not much relationship with time; rather, there is always a spatial disconformity. The term *relative chronology* (italics mine) as used by Hultkrantz is a misnomer from the technical terminological point of view. Unconsciously if he uses the term in its appropriate meaning, the relative chronology of religion has very little chronographic connection with subsistence economy. Unlike other forms of culture, religion rarely follows a unilateral pattern of development. As early man used to live in different ecological situations, the (core) religions must have been different — and Hultkrantz has a similar hypothesis, though he slightly deviates from his own approach in the context of chronology of religion.

Again, if a group with a type of religion, living in a specific ecological condition, goes through a process of change in its economic activity in the course of time, will there be a change in religion type (provided the other factors are unchanged and equal)? According to Hultkrantz's idea the type of religion should not be changed. And if it be so, how one can pre-suppose about the arrangement of religion historically?

The recommendation made by Hultkrantz on the procedure of following the course of religion may be questioned. Identification of cultural types and the social organization from archaeological facts has still to be achieved, despite the attempts at reconstruction of complicated matters through archaeology. Prehistoric religion is still mostly in the domain of speculation. The comparison of prehistoric religion with the religion of contemporary primitive society is undoubtedly an important research consideration, but one should not forget the limitations involved in such comparative studies with spatio-temporal differentiation.

The fourth contribution, as apprehended by Hultkrantz, of the religio-ecological approach, is to indicate the process of religious change. This approach is, perhaps, more tangible than the others, and the limitations of such an approach cannot be ruled out. Change in religion is very conspicuous and the responsible factors are varied, among which ecology and subsistence, of course, play important roles. The change of religion is a slow process, because the core of religion lies in the sentimental and psychological level where fear, respect, contentment, etc. act simultaneously. With new regimens of ecology and subsistence the earlier traditional religion cannot be replaced by a completely new religion. On the other hand, some of the older traits which have no relevance in the new setup are obliterated while other new traits are associated, and a different religion is formed.

My own ideology on religion and ecology has already been expressed and I would like to bring some interesting examples from the tribal groups of India. The examples are really too many, and in this context only a few selected ones will be enumerated which will clearly bring out the religion of different tribes living in varied ecological settings.

The selected tribes, the Andamanese, the Todas, the Birhors and the Saoras, have specific economies of their own and in this aspect each is different from the others, as is also the general ecology in which they are living. The Andamanese live in the Andaman Islands, and their subsistence entirely depends upon the natural products of the forest and the sea through hunting and fishing. In connection with their isolation Radcliffe-Brown wrote: '... it is possible that they have been entirely isolated in their island home, and have not been affected by contact with other races, but have been free to develop their own culture in adaptation to their own environment'.[96] The manifestation of their religion is expressed in relation to their ecology; they believe in the spirits of the forest and the sea. The spirits are the supernatural beings and the Andamanese believe in their existence.

The Todas, living in the Nilgiri Hills of south India, have a pastoral economy. Their religion is mainly based on the care of the cow.[97]

The Birhors[98] live in the hills and jungles that fringe the Chotanagpur plateau, with a considerable concentration in the district of Ranchi. The economy is mainly collecting, gathering, hunting and substantiated by rope making. The main deities of the Birhors are certain hill-spirits, beast (tiger, wolf, orangoutang, monkey, baboon etc.) gods. Certain trees are believed to be the abode of spirits, but there is no tree worship as cult.

The Saoras[99] of the eastern ghat region are agriculturists. Different animals, such as red ants, kites, the snake, the monkey, and vegetables, such as the gourd, are considered as gods. Besides these, there are other gods such as village deities, disease deities, etc. All the gods have some kind of bearing on their livelihood.

It may be mentioned that all the above mentioned tribes, with different (types of) religions, living in varied ecological conditions, and with dissimilar subsistence patterns have the common deities of earth, sun and moon.

The other example which I would like to put forward here is from a regional study. The region of the Chotanagpur plateau in eastern India is inhabited by a large number of tribes. In other words all these tribes live in a specific ecological region. Of course, the economy is not always

96. A. R. Radcliffe-Brown, *The Andaman Islanders*, Cambridge, 1922.
97. W. E. Marshall, *A Phrenologist amongst the Todas*, London, 1873.
98. S. C. Roy, *The Birhors*, Ranchi, 1925.
99. V. Elwin, *The Religion of an Indian Tribe*, Bombay, 1955.

uniform among them. But a number of them have the same economy. In spite of the similarities of ecology and subsistence the religions are different. Again, different groups with varied economies have similar religions.

Finally, I congratulate Professor Hultkrantz for his approach on ecology of religion. Albeit it is still mostly at the theoretical stage, sufficient work along this line using his methodology, with relative modification where necessary, and the results of investigations, will help to formulate a model. In this context it may be said that India will provide an urgent area of research for collecting information on religion among the primitive (tribal) groups.

Commentary   by G. C. Oosthuizen

Ecology of religion has received the attention of some earlier anthropologists. It has become clearer that a certain kind of environment does not only inspire a certain type of culture but also a specific type of religion. Such types of religion are associated with the cultural core.

The suggestion that certain 'types of religion' are timeless needs closer attention. Historical circumstances may emphasize certain aspects but the type remains. The 'type of religion' is basically the religious aspect of the culture core. 'Secondary' features thus cannot be explained from the ecological angle. Part of a religion can be explained nomothetically while the rest can be explained in a historical-pluralistic way.

Ecology of religion indicates the efficient causes of similarities and differences in religious phenomena. Culture changes are due to changes in technology and productive arrangements and it will be shown that similar technologies produce similar systems of religion. Forms of religious expression are 'chiselled out' on the human plane, although it may be held that its final inspiration does not come from this plane. Religion encounters its surroundings; it aims at providing a certain life style. The explanatory apparatus of the African and Hindu world-view cannot map out a western-oriented world-view, and this fact has led to substantial, if not radical, changes in the South African religious context. Religion is the source of general, yet very distinctive dispositions or conceptions of the world, the self and the relations between them.

When culture changes take place it is not so much the farming techniques, the wedding customs, dances, the houses, the religious rites that change as the ideas of these matters. Culturally man enters a new world, but he enters it as an agriculturist, hunter or technologist, which affects the very core of his cultural expression. This transcendental directedness, the awareness of the living infinity of human possibilities, is influenced by the ecology which influences man's continuous entry into the 'divine' zone.

There remains thus a continuous dialectical tension between culture and religion, because the former has deep religious roots; and although western culture tries to avoid the transcendental, it needs its backing. It has within its very core a religious aspect. While in India the cosmic totality was expressed in the form of the lotus-trunk-branches, and the primordial roots of Indian civilization remain largely intact, these have been shaken in a civilization which has outwardly broken with the religious pattern.

As all culture is shaped by an ecosystem, it may first be necessary to state specifically what ecology embraces in its basic discipline. To speak merely about ecology of religion is unsatisfactory. Seven fields of ecology can be distinguished, namely: systems, production, sociological and physiological ecology and aut-, gen-, and paleoecology. Objects exist at different levels, such as the cell, the organ, the organism, the ecosystem, the ecosphere and the universe. These biological terms should be taken note of, and applied to the human sphere in an analysis of the ecology of religion.

Rowe[100] has indicated that the study of an object, whether at the environmental or structural-functional level, should encompass six primary or three derivative viewpoints. With regard to the first, these are morphology (form in space), anatomy (analytical form), physiology (relation to inner phenomena), ecology (relation to outer phenomena), and chorology (systematic relation to other phenomena in time). The derivative viewpoints are composition (quantified list of classified parts), classification (systematic relation to other phenomena by kind) and history (deductive tracing of past evolution).

100. J. S. Rowe, 'The level-of-integration concept and ecology', *Ecology* 42, pp. 420-427.

The ecosystem has *inter alia* been described as 'the system composed of physical-chemical-biological processes active within a space-time unity of any magnitude, i. e., the biotic (including man) community plus its abiotic environment'.[101] By the structure and function of ecosystem is meant the composition of the biological community including aspects such as species, numbers, life history and spatial distribution of abiotic materials. All these aspects should be applied to the human sphere and be taken into consideration in any thorough study of the ecology of religion. It is important to concentrate on a study of function rather than a study of structure.

Environmental ecology or systems ecology, i. e. the study of interactions between the different components of the system and the way it affects the dynamic equilibrium of the system, has been grossly neglected in the study of religion. Here also, as in the biological field, community environmental relationships are holocoenotic.[102] The controlling agents in the ecosystem are the means used for production and their organization. Applied to the modern urban environment the controlling agents are to be found in the industrial-technological environment.

The living part of the ecosystem adapts to modern conditions. Changes in the ecosystem may be cyclical or directional and may be caused autogenically (by interacting dependent components) or allogenically (by fluctuations of the controlling agents).[103] The changes in the ecosystem of the early Bushman were cyclical; but once the Hottentots entered the sphere of this ecosystem, the sidereal bodies to which he had mostly given magical attention, became means used to adapt to basic religious ideas of the Hottentot, and the Moon took on aspects of a High God. Applied to religion this change has been allogenically and directional. The Bushman influenced African magical terms, but this had no directional effect on the religious approach of the African. When the Hindu entered the South African westernized environment, the changes were immediately directional. While changes in the African traditional religion were cyclical, those in African religious separatism, i. e. a religious movement consisting of three thousand groups with

101. Cf. R. L. Lindeman, 'The Trophic-dynamic aspect of ecology', *Ecology* 23, pp. 399-418.

102. Cf. E. P. Odum, *Ecology*, New York, 1963.

103. G. M. Dyne, *Ecosystems, Systems Ecology and Systems Ecologists*, Oak Ridge, Nat. Lab. U. S. Atomic Energy Comm., 1966.

more than three million adherents, have been allogenically inspired, which led to a new type of religion as the later Bushman, especially the northern Bushman, changed to a new type of religion. Changes in Hinduism in South Africa, in the reform movements such as the Arya Samaj, Ramakrishna Movement and Divine Life Society, have been autogenic, but Sanathana Hinduism has experienced allogenic changes, and various aspects in it have either faded away or become stale due to the environment.

Ecology takes cognizance of the laws of thermodynamics. The first of these laws holds that energy may be transformed but is never created or destroyed. The second is that energy transformation can only occur if there is degradation from a concentrated form into a dispersed form. The second of these laws is significant for the study of religious change. The flow of western secular energy, which is based on the discovery of the laws of nature, brings chaos into various forms of religious expression, but does not destroy the religious energy. It has in its very core transcendental elements, an infinite pointing beyond itself. Religions which have not been deeply associated with the fruits of Christianity are radically changed as a result of contact with the products of Christianity, such as science, technology, democracy, socialism, nationalism and capitalism.

The number of people of a different religious orientation in a Western setting has a bearing on the speed at which change takes place. The type of religion is however the most important factor. African traditional religion is not in a position to resist the technological-industrial outlook, and is changing radically, from a cyclical to a linear type of religion. Western cultural energy or influence — to use the law of thermodynamics — cannot be dissociated from certain religious prerequisites such as monotheism or monodeism over against polytheism, or the futuristic line over against the cyclical approach. These aspects are reversed in the Hindu and African traditional world views. For such a study the understanding of community processes are necessary in order to understand more clearly which processes make for chaos and why.

When the distribution and combination of people in a certain area are analyzed, e. g. how they exist, and what the influences on them are, one can assess the speed of change. The influence of different kinds of environment is the task of physiological ecology, and applied to the South African situation it indicates that those who are bearers of the

Western culture and nurtured within the Western civilization will exert certain specific influences. An environmental phenomenon, to be classed as such, must be 'operationally significant to an organism, be directly effective at some time during the life of the organism, be effective as to sequence as ordered by the ontogeny of the organism'.[104]

The operational environment of the Bushman was associated with seasons, the moon, the stars; that of the Zulu with his cattle herd and his natural surroundings. As a pastoral people they were more stable, and the ancestor structure had been built up so that they settled where the ancestors were buried and 'lived'. The traditional African and Hindu has been profoundly influenced by technological society. Here the environmental factor is composed of many separate phenomena, such as education, the economy, social customs and so on.

In sociological ecology it is important to analyze the combination of various population groups, how they subsist and are related to their environment, and to assess closely the changes that take place within their community. The African in the city, removed from the rural setting and his family, undergoes certain changes, and even a transformation of personality can take place. These issues and the divisive and agglomerative factors have a definite bearing on religious expression.

In ecology of religion, autecology, i. e. the integration of the effect of a factor taken over the whole history of an organism, whether as an individual or a community, must be studied. This is a behavioral study. What effect has Western influence on the behavior of rural Whites, Africans and Indians in the South African context? Why is it that Islam has more power of resistance against such influences? Is it because it has very definite elements in its veins of the Judeo-Christian influences which influenced Western civilization? Is it not basically the same type of religion?

In studying ecology it is necessary to determine why and how the environment selects characteristics which enable species to adapt to changed circumstances in the course of evolution.[105] Such a genecological study is important for religion. Why are certain personalities selected as prophets or as charismatic pastors in the vast separatist

104. Cf. J. O. Grunow, 'The developing fields of plant ecology', *Proc. Grassld. Soc. Sth. Afr.*, 1968, pp. 33 and 37.
105. *Ibid.*, p. 38.

phenomenon in Africa and among the Hindu converts to Pentecostalism? Why are there distinct ecotypes? What is true of plants, namely that each species has to reach a compromise between fitness for its present environment and flexibility, is true of human beings also. This brings one to paleoecology, i. e. a study of the influences of the past and how this has influenced people with regard to their present environment: such a study will also help us to understand present dynamics in the religious sphere. The way in which the ecosystem in the past influenced the religious expression of people, could give some indications with regard to present developments.[106]

In a situation of rapid change certain control tactics are used. Syncretism tries to put brakes on revolutionary changes; basically, however, this kind of revolutionary change has taken place in the African independent movement, which aims at giving a certain life style in a new cultural context with its rejection of the cyclical religious view. While the common-sense perspective is in a sense naive and the scientific perspective is objective and critical, the religious perspective concentrates on involvement and encounter. A historical perspective thus cannot serve as an adequate explanation of religion. Phenomenology of religion should take its rightful place for various reasons.

A brief survey of certain types of religious expression in Southern Africa may clarify specific religious developments.

THE BUSHMEN

The Bushmen are in close relationship with nature, the animal world and sidereal bodies. The Moon (first quarter) is hollow because it is carrying people who are dead; the stars know the time when a Bushman dies; lightning converts people into stars.[107] Among these nomad people there was nothing 'to warrant the assumption of any regular worship of the dead'.[108] They had no strongly centralized clan relationships.

The religious cult of the Cape Bushman was largely concentrated on sidereal bodies, especially the Moon, to which all kinds of human qual-

106. Cf. J. Heslop-Harrison, 'Forty years of Genecology', *Adv. Ecol. Res.* 2, pp. 159-247.
107. I. Schapera, *The Khoisian peoples of South Africa*, London, 1963 ed., p. 161.
108. *Ibid.*, p. 172.

ities were ascribed. The /Xam Bushman of the northern Cape identified their deity with a certain antelope, and believed that /Kaggen created the eland first among animals, followed by the hartebeest.[109] Northern Bushmen in contact with the Hottentot associated //Guau with a definitely personified being.[110] A change to a more animistic type of religion took place among the Naron of the North before the Southern Cape Bushmen. !Khub was for some the sky; for others he dwelt in the sky. The Moon was still worshipped among the Naron when Bleek did his research, but they were shy to admit it. They gave the Moon a masculine and the sun a feminine ending. Dornan found no sun and moon worship among the Kalahari Bushmen but only considerable reverence for it.[111]

The Cape Bushmen, with their concentration on sidereal bodies, revealed the oldest form of Bushman religion. One detects a change that took place in the type of religion, namely from a naturalistic orientation, with its emphasis on magical rather than religious aspects, to an animistic orientation in which religious dependence plays a role, but not yet in the sense of the African emphasis on this cult. No really satisfactory account is however available of the religion of any single Bushman tribe or of the Hottentots.

THE AFRICAN (BANTU)

It is impossible to enter here on the extensive ecological influences on the religion of the Southern Bantu with their cattle cult and where among the Zulu and Mpondo certain types of snakes are personifications of ancestors and so on.

Attention will briefly be given to the vast separatist movement.[112] Much of the impact of this movement of African ecclesiastical independence is due to the clash between two radically different cultures: the

109. Cf. P. Vinnicombe, 'Myth, motive and selection in Southern African rock art', *Africa* 13 (1970), pp. 192-204.
110. D. F. Bleek, *The Naron: The Bushman tribe of the Central Kalahari*, Cambridge Univ. Press, 1928.
111. S. S. Dornan, *Pygmies and Bushmen of the Kalahari*, London, 1925, p. 52.
112. Cf. B. G. M. Sundkler, *Bantu Prophets in South Africa*, OUP, 1948; G. C. Oosthuizen, *The Theology of a South African Messiah*, London, 1968.

one cyclical, the other 'eschatological' with an on-going futuristic line.

The time concept has changed; a new type of religion has developed in the African context, which is basically Christian and at the same time revivalistic and revitalistic. The one-way flow of the dynamic energy of the Western secularization process has brought chaos to the African religious (and thus also cultural) sphere, and a syncretized Christianity with enormous dynamic energy is the outcome. Western civilization brought chaos and paved the way for this dynamic flow. 'A dynamic society must have a dynamic meaningful religion' is the motto of the average urbanized African. Old symbols are revitalized in the new futuristic context while others become obsolete; new symbols are drawn into the new context but with a magical emphasis. The Cross, for example, may have a magical connotation, water may be 'holy' but it is magical holiness and is used for healing, baptism becomes a purification rite often repeated on the same person; the old offices of Chief and diviner have paved the way for prophets and charismatic figures. The prophets are an indication of a new linear type of religion with an eschatological emphasis. The prophet becomes the source and symbol of change which is directional. He stands both in diachronic and synchronic relationship to his environment and to supernatural forces.

The prophet however could also be Moses or could become a Messianic figure. Complete symbolic displacement can take place so that a mountain becomes Sinai, a hill the New Jerusalem and the prophet the Messiah to whom people pray and in whose name they are baptized. Such a religion must restore the Zulu nation to its former glory. The linear eschatological element of modern society is partly responsible for this change. Various stages[113] are to be discerned when two cultures meet: (1) the first stage is a steady period, but there is severe stress; (2) conflict arises and as individual stress increases the pressure becomes abnormal and old stress reduction techniques are not in a position to solve the problems; (3) conflict arises and the contact culture receives the blame for destroying a meaningful way of life; (4) various revitalization movements come into existence in the fourth stage, in which reformulations take place in the light of or in reaction to the new situation. The prophet becomes the personification of the process as a

113. Cf. A. F. C. Wallace, 'Revitalization Movements', *American Anthropologist* 58 (1965), p. 265.

result of visions or dreams. Ancestors come to the forefront to save the situation and the prophet becomes mediator to the supernatural world around him. Destiny dreams give the prophet insight into the future. Genecology is here important in order to analyze the factors in the environment which led to the destiny dreams which directs the prophet. Here a synthesis is born, so that many prophets have come forward as saviors in the cultural meeting context of South Africa. The emphasis with some on a Black Messiah is not merely a reaction against a so-called white Christ, but he is 'born' out of the desire to obtain through him powerful contact with a world they fear they will lose as a result of the absorbing power of the new situation. The myth of the Black Christ is an effort to remain in intimate contact with the traditional supernatural forces in order to find direction in a situation which spells chaos. Many of the converts themselves undergo a revitalizing personality transformation. The abnormal pressures when a traditional cyclical culture meets a technological industrial culture makes a society sick; and an emphasis on physical and spiritual healing finds satisfaction in the new separatist movements. Such a traditional society thrown into a situation of radical social change cannot retain the old traditional religion in spite of revitalizing elements within it but accepts the religion which is part of the new situation.

This movement has grown from a few groups in the last century to 230 in 1937; 800 in 1948 with 800,000 adherents; 2000 in 1960 with 2 million adherents, and 3000 in 1970 with 3 million adherents. By now the majority has changed in this direction as far as basic religious concepts are concerned. Education, through the mission schools, has introduced Africans gradually into the new cultural world-view, but the illiterate and semi-literate have been thrown very suddenly into the linear or futuristic world-view through technological industrial forces. Nevertheless a new type of religion has developed in the life of the African due not so much to missionary efforts but as a result of contact with a new civilization.

INDIANS IN SOUTH AFRICA

According to the 1970 Census there were 642,000 Indians in South Africa of whom 71% were Hindus, 19% Muslims, 8% Christians and the rest Buddhists, Parsees and Jains. They speak Tamil (majority), Hindustani, Gujarati, Telugu and Urdu, but English is becoming the main language.

There is a correlation between individualism and innovative potential. This is evident in the Hindu community in South Africa, especially in Greater Durban, where more than half of South Africa's Indian population live. Coming to South Africa from 1860 as indentured laborers, and later as traders, the Indians very early experienced disruptions in their way of life distinct from the usual immigrant problems. Their caste system was affected; few women came so that the lack of 'the bearers of Hindu religion' affected its faithful continuation. The position later improved for the Hindu. In 1927 however the Cape Town Agreement was signed with the Indian Government, according to which those Indians who accepted a western way of life would not be repatriated to India.

The woman plays the major role in Hindu ritual and ceremony as it is mainly a domestic religion. Various interesting surveys on female attitudes of Indian South Africans, especially in Hindu society, have been made.[114] Indians are compelled to integrate into a completely westernized context. Group solidarity is fostered by religion at home, but forms of behavior are adopted which are considered to be prestigious. The western way of life became the model in order to overcome immigrant social status. New approaches were developed to the fundamentals of existence.

Family goals used to be in the past more important than individual goals, which now have started to predominate. Cultural differences have set in motion a whole series of adjustments. Western customs and values were advantageous; new public behavior patterns developed. Family life changed. Not one entire joint family (*kutum*) was transferred physically from India.[115] The nuclear family became more typical.

---

114. H. J. W. Rocher, *A study of the theory and practice of the Hindu religious tradition among a selected group of Tamil speaking Hindus in South Africa. A sociological approach*, M. A. thesis, Univ. of Pretoria, 1965; U. Pillay, *A comparative study of the values, attitudes and folklore across three generations of Hindu, Tamil-speaking females in Durban*, M. A. Psychology thesis, Univ. of Durban-Westville, 1972; F. Meer, 'Suicide in Durban', *Humanitas* 1 (1), p. 13.

115. Cf. S. Jithoo, *Structure and development cycle of the Hindu Joint family in Durban*, M. A. thesis, Univ. of Natal, Durban, 1970.

Family religious practices were less faithfully observed, even frowned upon by younger people. Western education brought profound changes. Land scarcity round the home led to the practical extinction of the shrine in the backyard. Western urban impersonality, rationality and diversity and tolerance of differences and a lack of concern for the behavior of others encouraged change and disregard for tradition. Factory work and commercial employment with its emphasis on production, efficiency, fixed goals and independence, led to a different world-view. Mysticism, elaborate ritual, certain rites and ceremonies seemed to be inadequate in a matter-of-fact world. Parental authority has gone for many. New household technology — electric stoves, vacuum cleaners, washing machines — changed the outlook of many a Hindu woman and brought her into the mainstream of the westernization process. Family values have changed since the family is no longer a significant productive unit: women work and the home is less a place of communal activity and daughters, through participation, no longer learn from mothers and sons from fathers. Social mobility means individualism and self-reliance and frees younger people from family and neighborhood pressures. The Indians have moved from a foreign-born ethnic people with immigrant status to a South Africanized second and third generation community and are on the way to a westernized community of which the younger generation is already westernized. There is an abnormally high suicide rate among young Indian women in South Africa, mainly due to the frustrations and barriers of old customs which still try to maintain their hold on them.

In the Pillay survey it is clear that the girls are on the whole ignorant of the various religious rituals. In spite of the ban on beef and pork, they enjoy it. They reject the priority given to religious ceremonies. Where they do observe it they demand that it be short and intelligible. Their attitude to disease is rational rather than religious. They reject going to the temple for the thanksgiving ceremony after recovery from illness.

A reconciliation is taking place between personal and environmental demands. In such a situation 'learning dilemmas' develop and desired goals cannot be reached through formerly effective means. A critical position develops and the time when the doctrines of reincarnation

116. Pillay, *op. cit.*

and Karma led them to accept their lot is over. Defense mechanisms change and one finds a continuous restructuring of conflicts and rationalization.

The grandmothers in the Pillay survey are still at home in the Indian culture; the mothers are marginal, and the daughters, the third generation, identify themselves fully with most values that predominate in a western society. Although religion is one aspect through which resistance has been built up, it is faced with a dilemma. The productive, protective, educational, recreational and religious functions, which were formerly the main responsibility of the family, have largely been transferred to other institutions and these are western.

The following answers (cf. table p. 283) to questions put to Tamil grandmothers, mothers (daughters of grandmothers) and their school-going daughters reveal some of the changes among Tamils.

Although younger people have in general a much more open approach to traditional matters, a marked change can be detected, especially in religious matters. On the one hand, the girls are critical of certain issues in their own religion; few reveal any difficulty in associating with Christians. In a survey[117] which concentrated on Tamil women students at the University of Natal, the University of Durban-Westville, and Springfield Teachers' Training College, student attitudes to student religious aspects were compared with those of their mothers. There was no marked difference between the attitudes of Christian mothers and daughters to the religion they profess. A clear difference between Hindu mothers and daughters was obvious.

1. 17.33% of the mothers and 28% of their student daughters never read any Hindu Scriptures. Only 42.66% of the students (most occasionally) read traditional sacred scriptures and 42% of the mothers.

2. 12% of the former Hindu mothers and 20% of the daughters were not affiliated with Hinduism.

3. 13.33% of the mothers and 17.33% of the daughters do not accept any of the basic concepts of Hinduism while 6.67% of the mothers and 13.37% of the students were uncertain. (Uncertainty is a sign of initial stages of rejection).

4. 8% of the mothers and 22.67% of the students reject the Hindu deities.

117. Rocher, *op. cit.*

	Grandmothers	Mothers	Daughters
	%	%	%
Reincarnation rejected	7.6	27	57
Karma rejected	7	16	26
Parents should choose life partners for children	67	10	7
Girls should be virgins at marriage	100	84	74
Marrying sister's daughter accepted	57	30	26
Authority of husband accepted	80	47	10
Reject birth control	33	7	0
Divorce accepted	13	44	80
Use of Tamil necessary	93	43	23
Males should live in nuclear family after marriage	57	100	100
First child, if girl, sign of blessing, and good fortune	93	47 (33 uncertain)	40 (53 uncertain)
Unquestioned obedience of children accepted	80	33	7
Social interaction between sexes accepted	1	67	100
Adoption of western dancing	1	37	97
Other caste members accepted as neighbors	100	100	100
Accept other caste member as roommate	67	90	100
Caste endogamy rejected	20	40	100
Object to Hindu-Tamil/Christian-Tamil marriage	90	31	3
Object to Hindu-Tamil/Muslim-Tamil marriage	93	97	33

5. 17.33% of the mothers and 46.67% of the students did not consult the Tamil almanac.

6. That menstruation meant ritual impurity was rejected by 24% of the mothers and 64% of the students.

6. 37.33% of the mothers and 61.33% of the students did not take vows during times of illness. Only 28% of the students did take vows.

7. 30.67% of the mothers and 34.67% of the students did not have faith in the healing powers of deities.

9. Certain rituals are outrightly disapproved of by 4% of the mothers and 25.33% of the students.

10. Moksha, dharma, karma, samsara, reincarnation — all of these concepts are accepted by 21.33% of the mothers and only 10.67% of the students. Only a few of the samsaras are still observed.

A rapid and definite decline of Hindu thought and practice is taking place. The religious disposition of Hindu fathers and sons is much more affected by modern secularized society. 82.6% of the above students were from urban areas, 16% from rural and small-town areas. While only 2.66% of the fathers had five years or less schooling, this was the case with not less that 38% of the mothers. None of the mothers had higher education. The home language of 62.67% of the mothers was Tamil; 47% of the fathers, but 25.33% of the students, spoke Tamil and the rest only English.

When the religious concepts of those who reject Hinduism are analyzed, God is spoken of in general terms and some reject any idea of a future supernatural destiny for man.

PENTECOSTALISM IN THE INDIAN COMMUNITY IN GREATER DURBAN

This type of Christianity, with its concentration on a few Christian truths, is making more impact on the Hindu community than anywhere else on the globe where Hindus are found. While the Indian population growth was 2.97% from 1951 to 1960, the growth of the Roman Catholic Church among Indians in South Africa was 2,15% (the only census on religion available as yet is that of 1951-1960); Anglican Church 2.52%, Methodist Church 2.86%, Baptists 5.27%, the Apostolic Faith Mission 6.27%, and the Full Gospel 6.54%. Some of the Pentecostal churches which started during the last decade had grown annually by about 20%, others 14% or 12%, but never less than 8%. Pentecostalism, it is estimated, has grown by at least 115% among Indians during the last decade.

Pentecostalism, with its direct goals, gives direction in chaos. The structure of the ecosystem brings forth leaders who give guidance in the new situation. The one-way flow of energy, and the circulation of materials, are the two great principles of the general ecology, and the one-way flow of technological-industrial energy and the circulation of

western cultural influences affects Hindu culture at its very core. A
new type of religious approach is developing, so that one has to study
the change from a nomothetic angle.

To speak merely of ecology of religion is not satisfactory. One should
take note of its various sub-sections, by means of which the complex
phenomenon of religious change and the development from one type
of religion to another could be more clearly indicated. Whether this
is a process of evolutionary or revolutionary change from one type
of the other cannot be categorically stated. Closer attention should be
given to phenomenology of religion and in such a study the different
interpretations of symbols and religious expressions will be more clearly
analyzed. One cannot merely synchronize: the symbol of the Cross can
be a magical entity or a mere sign; it all depends from which *Lebensmitte*
it is being explained. General nomothetic studies as well as particular
historical ethnographic and philological studies are important for this
field of study. Equally important are those forces which influence the
life and work of man over the years and this must lead to finer distinctions in the study of the discipline, as indicated in the initial section of
this paper. Furthermore, thorough field work and research is indispensable for the study of any discipline. The academic is fortunate when the
leaders of a university understands this and create such opportunities.
Continuous changes in religious expression are taking place, and to lecture on material that is twenty years old and more as if nothing had
happened in the meantime in the situation is to lecture in a vacuum.

Commentary   by Edmund Perry

Ecology of religion, which adapts the method and tools of cultural ecology to the analysis of certain manifestations of religion, does not satisfy
the demands of an exact science proper to religion itself. The prolifera-
tion from other sciences or approaches to the study of religions has
needlessly impeded the development of a science specific to religion as
such. In 1954, when the International Association for the History of
Religions published the first number of its periodical *Numen*, Raffaele
Pettazzoni addressed this problem in an introductory essay as if he were

addressing the crucial issue of the 1973 Study Conference on 'Methodology of the Science of Religion'. Pettazzoni wrote: 'There are today several different ways of attacking the study of religions. One of them consists in analyzing individual religious facts from a purely external point of view. The philologist striving for the most correct interpretation of a text dealing with religious matters, the archaeologist aiming at a reconstruction of the plan of an ancient sanctuary or at explaining the subject of a mythological or other scene, the ethnologist giving a detailed report of certain ritual practices of an uncivilized tribe, the sociologist endeavoring to form an idea of the organization and structure of a religious community and of its relations with the world of the profane, the psychologist analyzing the religious experience of this or that person, — all these various scholars study religious facts without quitting the bounds of their special sciences. They therefore study religious data in the very spirit of each of these sciences, as if they had to deal in the first place with philological, archaeological, ethnological or other facts, setting aside their specific and essential nature, which is religious' (quoted from the excerpt published in R. Pettazzoni, *Essays on the History of Religions*, Leiden, 1954, p. 215). Today he would include, 'the ecologist of religion trying to find out how environment stimulates religious facts, forms, and functions'.

Acknowledging the importance of these researches and the increase of knowledge of religion achieved by the application of these sciences to the study of religions, Pettazzoni nevertheless concludes, 'it is clear that they (the sciences mentioned) cannot wholly satisfy the demands of the scientific spirit. The peculiar nature, the very character, of religious facts as such give them the right to form the subject of a special science. That science is the science of religion in the proper sense of the words'.

Ecology of religion deals with religion as a cultural rather than a religious phenomenon. 'Ecology of religion is an outgrowth of the American research strategy known as *cultural ecology* and shares its main features with its mother discipline' (Bjerke, cf. above p. 238). Hultkrantz, in his earliest methodological essay, 'An Ecological Approach to Religion'[118] cautions against the expectation that ecology of religion can disclose anything other than the influence of environment on religion insofar

118. *Op. cit.* above in n. 1.

as religion constitutes an aspect of culture. Religion as such eludes the ecologist of religion. Note the scientific precision and the epistemic humility manifested by Hultkrantz in the following passage: 'More than any other cultural aspect religion belongs to what Steward calls the "secondary features" of culture, i. e., it is to a large extent transmitted by tradition and is therefore to the same extent outside the cultural core. For instance, the concept of a high god cannot be revealed by the study of ecological adaptation; it may be colored by the adaptation process, as when a zoomorphical Supreme Being occasionally occurs in a hunting culture and a lofty sky-god appears in an nomadic pastoral culture, *but this process does not account for the presence or absence of the concept as such.* Furthermore, *no religion grows out of ecological, economic or technical circumstance.* It is only the religious *forms* that may be determined by such impulses, at least partly — we must not forget that religious forms are also molded by cultural and religious tradition. *Religion as such, the religious sentiment etc., cannot be coped with ecologically*, it springs from sources associated with the psychological make-up of man.'[119]

We need a method of inquiry, a science, which can and will cope with religion religiously, that is, with religion as religion, not with religion as an aspect of culture, or as a social or psychological phenomenon. This assessment of our methodological need neither insinuates nor intends any disparagement of the contributions made to our knowledge of religions by sciences whose proper definition and method derive from data other than the religious. The achievements of sciences which study religions must not distract us from the formulation of a science which has religion as such as its proper object. Hultkrantz disclaims any such methodological capability for his ecology of religion.

Although not normative to the science of religion itself, ecology of religion has established the indispensibility of 'environmental awareness' in the study of religious forms. We ought to deliberate, however, whether the natural environment has intruded itself into the rites, beliefs, myths, and structures of the religions or, on the contrary, whether the religions, by virtue of their peculiar character, have appropriated selectively from the environment objects, imagery, values, and social forms compatible with the objectives of the religion.

119. Hultkrantz, *op. cit.*, p. 142; italics mine.

A religion's ecology comprehends considerably more than its natural environment. Religion, whether it be desert nomadic religion or Arctic hunting religion, or the religion of Bjerke's 'general evolutionary stages' (the religion of the familistic band, of the tribal level, of the chiefdom level, or of the multi-divisioned state level) — religion without reference to its geographical location or its cultural development characteristically claims to make available to humans and the human situation a reality which exceeds and cannot be exhausted in sensible experience. This reality, the 'world' of the eternal, provides to religious people a mode of existence or consciousness which is raised above the temporal and finite. The pious person, the person who devoutly cultivates his sense of the eternal, has as a present possession a sense of sharing in the life of the eternal world. Piety in this sense does not lead so much away from the natural-historical world as it locates and re-cognizes them in the world of eternity. From this viewpoint, piety brings to everything in human experience and consciousness a religious, that is, eternal, significance.

When characterized as man's experience of the eternal, religion gives to ecology a frame of reference and a meaning inaccessible to the social scientist. Furthermore, this characterization of religion compels us to inquire very closely as to the sense in which we can speak of the 'evolution of religion'. On what possible grounds could we maintain the greater accessibility of the world of the eternal to the state-level people than to the familistic bands? Or, to put it another way, to what extent does the phenomenon of religion lend itself to analysis and explanation by the evolutionary sciences?

Raising such questions in a conference such as this should remind us that the movement for a science of religion derives from two somewhat unfriendly sources, namely theology and the humanistic sciences. As would-be scientists wishing to satisfy the demands of the scientific spirit, we ought not to despise nor seek to evade either our theological heritage or the discomforting questions posed to us by theology. A central theological concern reentered the science of religion under the name phenomenology. Dissatisfied with knowing precisely what happened, under what circumstances, and in what sequences, we demanded more than the history of religions could deliver. We wanted to know the meaning of what happened. Phenomenology provided us with both a descriptive and a normative science. Phenomenology seeks to identify and classify the different structures in the various religions but without reference to the historical or cultural location of the religious phenomena in which the structures are found. As Pettazzoni said in the article previously cited, 'the structure, and it alone, can help us to find out the meaning of religious phenomena, independently of their position in time and space and of their attachment to a given cultural environment. Thus the phenomenology of religion reaches a universality which of necessity escapes a history of religion devoted to the study of particular religions, and for that very reason liable to the inevitable splitting up of specialization. Phenomenology does not hesitate to stand forth as a science *sui generis*, essentially different from the history of religion' (p. 217). Pettazzoni refused to relinquish the history of religion from the effort to effect a science of religion and expressed perplexity over the prospect of maintaining a 'division of the science of religion into two different sciences, one historical the other phenomenological'. Two decades later, Hultkrantz[120] and Bjerke[121] still are calling upon us to protect the study of religion from the danger of breaking up into divided and divisive disciplines.

I concur with Bjerke in his proposal that 'phenomenology of religion serve as the basis of our discipline'.[122] I support this proposal because phenomenology of religion 'does not hesitate to stand forth as a science *sui generis*' and because 'the phenomenology of religion reaches a universality which of necessity escapes a history of religion devoted to the study of particular religions'.[123] To pursue this proposal will require us to reconsider what constitutes the 'reality' of religion when we remove the qualifying adjectives in such phrases as 'primitive religion', 'Christian religion', 'Buddhist religion', and the like. The question of the wholeness of religion cannot be answered from the study of the entirety of one particular historical tradition. But we must question whether the wholeness of religion can be understood only from a composite of the history of all of the religions. In sum, the proposition that phenomenology constitute the basis of our discipline constrains us to reconsider whether religion is something accidental and arbitrary in human life or

120. *Op. cit.* in n. 18, pp. 80ff.
121. Cf. above p. 247.
122. *Ibid.*
123. Pettazzoni, *op. cit.*, p. 217.

something necessary, universally valid, and firmly, inseparably anchored in the life of the human consciousness.

Since religion expresses itself within history, the phenomenology of religion will never be able to escape a constant appeal to the historical manifestations of religion. Unless we understand the phenomenology of religion to include the historical studies of the historical religions, our science will become a science of the totally abstract rather than the science of religion.

Finally, as scientists of religion we cannot escape the practical implications of both our science and the subject of our science. Without exception religion claims to offer the human spirit good and sufficient resources for a better environment. Can we be thorough-going scientists of such a phenomenon unless we demonstrate a comparable concern for the human spirit?

Commentary   by Zygmunt Poniatowski

Both Hultkrantz, the proper founder of the ecology of religion, and Bjerke have pointed to the possibility and necessity of applying the ecological approach not only to the so-called primitive religions but also to the higher ones. Bjerke particularly, in revalorizing evolutionism in the science of religions, which enables the extrapolation of the sequence of the types of religion beyond the 'semi-desert gathering religions', makes us sensitive to the contemporary 'state level' of religious evolution.

1. The specific 'scientific provenience' of Hultkrantz — as an eminent investigator of the peoples of the Arctic — naturally encourages him to underline the fruitfulness of the ecological approach to the early stages of the evolution of religion. Ancient cultures and religions moreover reflect with particular clarity the dependence of man on nature, on his environment. But what is involved is first of all that the history of religion cannot be limited to the early phase(s) of development, thus leaving the question of modern religious changes to the sociology of religion, to ethnography, and to some modern trends in theology ('with a genetive case', such as the theology of secularization, of dialogue, of controversy,

and the famous 'God-is-dead-theology'). History of religion must also be concerned with (or particularly in) the present religious situation.

Secondly, we must clarify the conception 'environment' as used in ecology and in the ecology of religion. It must be stressed that environment is not something immutable, fixed for all time. The identification environment = nature (or 'ecological' = the physical and biotic as contrasted with the 'social-cultural') was correct until recently but is incorrect in the second half of our century. For there is a process of transition under our very eyes from one epoch of human history to another, from the phase of the struggle to master nature (the phase directed *against* nature) to the phase of the struggle *for* nature: for its preservation from (and for) man. This is not the place to enumerate familiar examples of the conversion by technical progress of rivers into cesspools and the air in large conurbations into gaseous fumes. We can accept Hultkrantz's statement that 'ecology is today a theme of paramount importance ... the practical outlook of life ... in the struggle for ... the survival of man'.

In other words, we are at present less than ever confronted with man's 'natural' environment, which is ever more grievously being replaced by an 'unnatural', artificial environment. The wasteland landscape of the large mining and steel centres clearly indicates that the 'technical environment' is more and more becoming man's 'ecological', 'natural' environment.

This situation has corresponding cultural, psychological, biological and religious consequences. The first three types of consequences are too well known to need discussion here. But there has been very little consideration of the consequences for religion of man's 'alienation' from his natural environment. Omitting here the extremist and unusual forms of protest of some young people (e. g. 'LSD-religion'), let us note two very common phenomena: changes in the function of sport, and the flight by city inhabitants into the bosom of nature. There are constantly increasing references to sport as a new (para-)religion. The cult of sports-idols grows in proportion to the degree to which the town-dweller is deprived of physical effort. The weekend exodus from city to country affects religion by the decline in church attendance, which is compelling religion to work out new pastoral techniques and tactics. Then the shifting of the bulk of the day's activity to the evening and even night (nocturnalism, nocturnization), typical of city dwellers, has an essential significance for the situation of contemporary religion.

The above analysis corresponds with Hultkrantz's valid assertion that 'the religio-ecological approach investigates religion in its general environmental framing'.

2. Hence if one of the central concepts of the ecology of religion requires greater precision, the question arises whether other ecological concepts (categories) should not be submitted to a similar procedure. For both papers struck this author as attempts to create a new science, a new branch of the science of religions, namely, an ecology of religion rendered in broad generalizations. This could be called a 'mega-ecology'. This science is, secondly, constructed from within our discipline (i.e. the science of religions), or (to put it differently) adopting the cognitive horizons and categories of cultural ecology: of Steward in the case of Hultkrantz, of Sahlins in the case of Bjerke. This is understandable, owing to the affinity between the science of culture and the science of religions. But this is not the only possible strategy today when the trend is for the most complete integration of the sciences.

It is possible to tackle a broader front of research, to observe the vicissitudes of development of other 'particular ecologies', such as the ecology of medicine, delinquency or politics.[124] It is especially possible to undertake attempts at the typology and periodization of the research phenomena and techniques investigated by these branches in order to avoid — or to minimize as far as possible — the repetition of errors and blind alleys in the development of our discipline.[125] Is it not possible, for instance, to seek a parallel for the troubles ('ecological fallacy'), demonstrated by Hultkrantz, and noted by Bjerke, in the histories of other ecological disciplines?

It is on the other hand possible to proceed more modestly by making

124. See Corvin E. H. Lewinsky, ed., *Ecology of Health*, New York, 1947; the study of R. Faris and H. Dunham on 'ecology of mental disorders in urban areas', Chicago, 1939; many works on 'delinquency areas'; F. W. Riggs, *The Ecology of Public Administration*, London, 1961; H. and A. Sprout, *The Ecological Perspective on Human Affairs with Special Reference to Internal Politics*, Princeton, 1965; etc.

125. W. C. Allee writes in his *Principles of Animal Ecology* (Polish transl., Warsaw, 1958, I, pp. 29-30) that the famous philosopher R. Carnap 'discovered' ecology in 1938. In dealing with systematic science he distinguished between 'biology' (proper) and 'behavioristics' (ecology). This occurred at the University of Chicago where ecology developed from the 90's of the last century and thus preceded the world-famous works of Park and Burgess by a good decade.

an inventory of general ecological concepts and attempting to adapt them to religious phenomena. This involves categories such as competition, ecological niche, climax, ecoton, distance and barriers, cyclism and rhythms, generation renewal, etc. The approach suggested here is modest enough to operate on various levels of abstraction, not only on the level in the 'mega-scale', as is the case, for instance, with Hultkrantz's typology of habitats, but on the macro- and micro-scales (for instance, the metropolis, big city, small town, various types of villages, suburbia etc. — analogical to the problems of parish typology in the sociology of religion).

3. The very reference to the sociology of religion involves an area which should also be the concern of the ecology of religion, in relation not only to other, 'particular' ecologies but also to such sciences as sociology of religion,[126] geography of religion, etc. In the case of the last, if we limit ourselves to the conceptions of Deffontaine's book, the geography of religion is really concerned with the impact of religion on the environment. Does the ecology of religion hence have the reverse task, to investigate the influence of the environment on religion? If not, since the ecology of religion pertains to the interrelations between religion and the environment, then the question arises as to the specific fields of ecology and geography in relation to religion, especially if the latter too is expanded to an investigation of the two-sided influence. It can be assumed that there too the analysis of works on ecology and (general) geography may prove useful.[127]

Discussion   Chairman: Lauri Honko

The first speaker, Åke Hultkrantz, said that he wished to concentrate on a number of points which were important, but not fully discussed in his paper, and commented first (in reply to questions earlier in the day by Walter Capps and Eric Sharpe) on the personal and intellectual

126. See F. A. Isambert, 'L'analyse écologique', in *Conférence Internationale de Sociologie Religieuse (CISR)*, Lille, 1971, pp. 449-463.

127. As, for instance, of the work of P. L. Wagner, *The Human Use of the Earth*, New York, 1960.

presuppositions of his work. He said that nature had been part of his picture of life for so long that it would be impossible for him to preclude it from entering into even the most abstract questions he was dealing with; and that his experience in fieldwork in the Great Basin desert region in North America, and among the Arctic peoples, had brought home to him the influence of nature not only on the culture but also on the religions of these peoples. Julian Steward, on whose method Hultkrantz had built up his ecology of religion, had similarly been extremely impressed by the way in which nature manipulated the cultural expressions of the Shoshonian Indians in the Great Basin. Both Steward and Hultkrantz himself felt that it was essential to experience the impact of the environment upon the human conditions and upon the expressions of religious thought, religious feelings, and religious behavior. Secondly, Hultkrantz did not see ecology of religion as anything definitely new: it simply stressed some old things which had been forgotten. While rejecting the unlimited environmentalism of Huntingdon, for instance, he believed that the perspective on the role of nature in religion should be widened beyond one of passive influence to that of active influence in the process of adaptation. Every religion was environmentally adapted, and this was precisely the premise of his whole approach.

This did not mean, on the other hand, that religion could be reduced to something made up of environmental influences; on the contrary: there were myths and beliefs, for example, which it was impossible to catch in this way. There were also, however, aspects of religion which could be grasped easily within an ecological context. He then drew attention to the three levels of integration described in his paper: 'primary integration', i.e. the environmental adaptation of basic cultural features, such as subsistence and productive arrangements, technology, etc., and behavior patterns associated with these features, such as social and religious attitudes. 'Secondary adaptation' is the indirect adaptation of religious beliefs and rituals. These are organized into a framework that takes its forms from the social structure, which is in its turn a model suggested by the economic and technological adaptation to the environment. The third possibility is 'morphological adaptation', the covering of religious features with forms taken from the physical and biological environment. Although religious concepts are by their nature traditional, they borrow their formal appearance from forms within the immediate biotope, and this choice of forms is not arbitrary, but is related to the symbolism that is inherent in them. He stressed that he was talking about the forms of religion, which some critics might object was not its *Geist*; our approach to religion should, however, also include the different ways in which the forms of religion have been made. It had long been recognized that cultural tradition and social structure contributed to this; the new dimension was the role of the environment.

Hultkrantz then went on to discuss four ways of handling these forms. The model set out in his paper, firstly, made new insights possible into the pattern and functioning of a religion through ecological analysis, not as a reductionist approach, but as a study of its functional interweaving with the forms of nature. Secondly, an ecological framework allowed comparison between religions and between religious traits, and thus also a phenomenological approach. The third possibility was the arrangement of types of religion into historical strata (in terms of the general succession of forms, rather than in individual cases): i.e. to bring the different types of religion into relation with the different historical or archaeological strata, such as gatherers, hunters, cultivators, nomads, etc. The fourth contribution ecology could provide would be to indicate an imminent process of religious change; for if the holistic thesis holds good, i.e. that phases of religious expression belong to the primary ecological integration of culture, then changes in the basic structure of the 'cultural core' (to use Julian Steward's term) should be expected to affect the structure of religion. To sum up, environmental integration affects technology, the economy, and other things, which in their turn influence the social structure and also certain facets of religious expression, i.e. the organization of religious patterns and religious structures.

Svein Bjerke then presented his paper, pointing out that it fell into three sections, the first dealing with ecology of religion, the second with the possibility of a new evolutionary viewpoint in the study of religion, and the third representing an attempt to argue from this evolutionary point of view towards an integration of the discipline as a whole. Of these he wanted to draw especial attention to the second, which he then read.

The chairman commented that the question of the evolution of religion, although it had not been suggested as an official topic for the conference, was one which was the centre of considerable interest both in the west and particularly in the socialist countries. He then invited the commentators to speak. Manfred Büttner regretted that it was not possible for him to show the maps which he had brought with him as illustrative material for his presentation of geography of religion, and therefore confined his remarks to those in his written paper. He was followed by G. C. Oosthuizen, who spoke of the specific religious interaction taking place in South Africa. In his own city of Durban, for instance, there lived 320,000 Indians, 320,000 Africans, and 250,000 whites. He wanted to emphasize the point that it was not possible to 'map out' the western-oriented world-view in terms of the explanatory apparatus of the African or Hindu world-view, which had emerged in a different context.

Turning to the papers, Oosthuizen stressed the need for differentiation and qualification when speaking about ecology of religion. He referred to the division mentioned in his commentary into seven different fields of ecology, and went on to present the main body of his written paper.

Two of the remaining commentators, Asok Ghosh and Zygmunt Poniatowski, were absent, and Edmund Perry did not wish to add anything to his written paper, which he read. The discussion was then thrown open.

The first comment from the floor was by J. van Baal, who conceded the importance of ecology in understanding religious phenomena, but sharply disagreed with Hultkrantz's paper, and particularly with his emphasis in ecology on the 'means of existence'. This was essentially the same as Murdock's position, protested van Baal, and amounted in effect to historical materialism. Moreover Hultkrantz had in his paper a very dubious passage, in which he had argued that matrilinear social organization in an agricultural culture could be derived from matrilocality and uxorilocality, whereas a very good case could be made for deriving it from virilocal marriage. There was also a misleading use of the term uxorilocate, which had been used to mean very different things in different societies, as could be illustrated with material from Australia and New Guinea.

Australian and New Guinea data also cast serious doubt on the validity of ecology of religion. In Australia the form of social organization was strikingly similar from south to north, i. e. in a temperate zone, in a tropical desert, and in a savanna area. Was it true that ecology had affected religion more than vice versa? He also cited the cultural continuity between the peoples of the Central Mountains and the Lowlands in New Guinea, which would be difficult to explain in view of ecology.

He questioned to what extent ecology even determined the means of existence; for man had, at least in part, the power to create his own ecology (e. g. by controlling the area and spread of forest).

Hultkrantz rejected van Baal's criticism that he had over-emphasized the importance of ecology of religion, and stressed the carefulness and qualification with which the ideas in his paper had been put forward. He thought moreover that Murdock's theories, although they had undergone modification, were still broadly accepted by anthropologists. As to van Baal's criticisms over matrilinear social organization, he had to point out that he had spoken of matrilinearity and not of matriarchy, and he did not find the criticism justified. Turning to the question of the Australian data, he pointed out that 'environment' includes far more than just climate; nor had he argued (as Van Baal's critique implicitly assumed) in terms of a direct link between environment and religion: on the contrary, he had repeatedly stressed the middle term in the relation, i. e. technology and the economic pattern. There was no direct impact by environment on religion. He had in any case not been talking about 'religion', but about the organization of patterns and structures of religion; nor about beliefs, but about the general way in which religious patterns are organized on the basis of the environmental integration of religion. Van Baal reiterated that, in Australia, it was not only the climate but the total ecology which varied very considerably, while the religion remained similar: he wanted to stress the limitations of ecology of religion. With this Hultkrantz willingly concurred. Nevertheless, he said, in the case of the Great Basin peoples the link was very striking — almost shocking; and although it was harder to pinpoint in the case of the Arctic peoples, he believed it held good there too.

Hans Klimkeit suggested that another very important means of adaptation between environment and culture (including religion) was that of symbols drawn from the natural environment. Conceivably even the concept of space and time was determined by the *Lebensraum* within which a people lives; this had been shown, for example, by Helmut Brunner in *Zum Raumbegriff der Ägypter*. In phenomenology there tended to be only a general concept of sacred space; it might be necessary to look more closely at the concept of space developed or inherited in the thinking of different peoples in different environments.

The precision with which Hultkrantz had defined his topic, not as the religiosity of the individual, nor as religion itself, but as the environmental conditioning of patterns of religion, was acknowledged and emphasized again by R. J. Zwi Werblowsky. He expressed surprise, accordingly, at Perry's commentary, which had dealt with the eternity of the eternal and with individual forms of piety and devotion. While these were certainly not outside the interests of a student of religion, they were completely outside the legitimate concerns in the investigation of environment, since what was important in the latter context — to put it in radical sociological terms — was not the religiosity of individuals within a social system, but the religious qualities of the social system itself. The former might be the concern of a psychologist of religion; but on the latter level, Hultkrantz's concern with the patterning of the system in interaction with environmental factors was highly pertinent.

The last contribution came from Annemarie de Waal Malefijt, who returned to the discussion between Van Baal and Hultkrantz about Murdock's work. She reported that in a special lecture, given in England the previous year, what Murdock had done was to renounce and denounce everything which he had said himself that anthropology had done on evolution, and to say that the only thing that was still any good was the basic nitty-gritty fieldwork. On this rather disconcerting note, the chairman declared the session concluded.

Religio-anthropological Approach

UGO BIANCHI   *The History of Religions and
the 'Religio-Anthropological Approach'*

1. The question of a 'religio-anthropological approach' raises problems
of (a) definition, (b) method, and (c) epistemology. Obviously, these
three questions are connected, and up to a point are the same question.
First of all it is a question of knowing what kind of method one wishes
to reach a definition of religion with — and what kind of definition; and
whether the definition, purely verbal, conventional and 'operative', or
real and 'ostensive', should abide by the methodological requirements
of history of religions; or whether this definition, conceived for research
that involves the study of religious data, but that fundamentally refers
to other subject-matter (as is the case with sociology and psychology)
may refrain from being anything more than a mere 'functional' definition, valid only case by case.

In the first of these two eventualities, it must be recalled that in
positive-inductive research, phenomenology, morphology and typology
of religion must result from and be continuously nurtured by historical
study and from the correct application of the historical-comparative
method that is the very method of history of religions.

But when we reach the other question, the one concerning the identity and 'place' of the 'anthropological approach' to religion(s), then
the question becomes interdisciplinary: what matters is to decide within what limits, and how, two apparently distinct approaches may be
brought to cooperate, one being historical, religious-historical indeed,
and the other 'anthropological'. The time of a postulatory 'anthropological' evolutionism is over,[1] whilst an intrinsic relation between history

1. Å. Hultkrantz, 'The Aims of Anthropology', *Current Anthropology* 9, 4 (1968),

of religions and a historically oriented 'religious ethnology' still remains; of course, the latter may not pretend to supply the former with general categories, although it does, within certain limits, remain specific for certain cultures and for certain problems of 'prehistory'. Moreover, with the advent of cultural anthropology and social anthropology, the anthropological approach appears to have become thoroughly estranged from the historical problem. True, the activity of the social anthropologist is of primary interest when he tries to locate the living context where the beliefs and religious praxis of a society or cultural ambient are living and behaving. But even thus, we will see, the 'anthropological approach' to religions, as they 'function' in the societies considered, cannot by itself fulfill all the requirements of a religious-historical approach.

Even Pettazzoni observed that the proper subject of 'sociology of religion' and 'psychology of religion', is not religion but, respectively, society and the psyche. For Pettazzoni, the religious 'quality' of facts that have to be studied in historical research, should be properly perceived in phenomenology of religion, which should be considered an aspect of the integral science of religion, to which it contributes a certain sensitivity to the religious fact as such, which, according to the same scholar, a merely historical survey could not supply.[2]

Elsewhere[3] we have tried to show that the problem of the identification of a religious 'quality' (even if articulated and not univocal) in the facts considered by our disciplines, falls properly within the scope of the historian of religions. In this way, it correctly excludes the programmatic reduction of the 'religious' to the social or the psychological; nor, on the other hand, should it presuppose pre-established categories as sometimes used by some phenomenologists of religion.

----

p. 295 writes that 'the dilemma of anthropology today is that evolutionism no longer plays any leading role'. He proposes (*ibid.*, p. 296) to solve the problem by means of the following distinction: 'It is not the *discipline* anthropology that we need, but the anthropological *goal*'; as a matter of fact with an interdisciplinary scope that could be proposed for teamwork.

2. 'The Supreme Being: Phenomenological Structure and Historical Development', in Eliade and Kitagawa, eds., *History of Religions*, Chicago, 1959, pp. 59-66.

3. Cf. the writer's Introduction to G. Castellani, ed., *Storia delle religioni*, Torino, 6th edition, Vol. I, pp. 1 ff. (an English translation of this Introduction is in the press, under the title *History of Religions*, Leiden); and our considerations in U. Bianchi, C. J. Bleeker, A. Bausani, eds., *Problems and Methods of the History of Religions*, Leiden, 1970 (Supplements to *Numen*, Vol. XIX), pp. 15 ff.

2. Some social and cultural anthropologists have their own way of facing the problem of a definition of religion: a definition that is sought for, in order to delimit the subject to be considered. These anthropologists will first ask what is intended by 'religion', if one is to inquire about it in the societies under study. This is what M. E. Spiro argues, when he demands starting with an 'ostensive' definition of religion, i. e., a definition clarifying the object of religion.[4]

Already here a difference in approach appears between history of religions and these anthropologists. History of religions has no need to presuppose an 'ostensive' (and conventional) definition of what religion and the religious may be, since its scope is precisely to reach, through the use of a comparative-historical method, a characterization of the forms of religion and the religious (and probably of an 'analogical', and not a 'univocal', concept of religion: see *infra*). In other words, sociology, social anthropology, or cultural anthropology (and psychology), not having as their primary object religion or religions, may feel (at their risk) the urgency of a preliminary definition of religion that might prove adequate to the societies they are studying. History of religions, by its very nature, cannot afford to exclude from consideration all those phenomena in the world, which, although partly anomalous, cannot, without risk, be prejudicially deprived of their possible 'religious' implications.

This becomes clear when one takes into consideration the comparative method that is used in history of religions on the one hand, and on the other the comparative method used in social anthropology. The former is dealt with at the end of the present paper.

As for social anthropology, we all know that it was born as a reaction to 'armchair-anthropology', and to the comparatism used by 19th century anthropology, propped up by naturalism, positivism and evolutionism. Modern social anthropology presents itself as a 'professional' discipline, implying an adequate permanence of the scholar in the society that he intends to study, using 'participant observation' that permits a good level of familiarity with the ambient, allowing him to get a good appreciation of all the aspects of the local culture as it is being lived and as it effectively 'works' within the frame of its total context. But here

4. In M. Banton, ed., *Anthropological Approaches to the Study of Religion*, London, 1966, pp. 90 ff.

one wonders what the role of comparison may be in such a situation; for the social anthropologist does not, today, renounce the method of comparison and the elaboration of general theories on the basis both of his work 'in the field' and of books and materials concerning other cultures.

3. Let us take, for instance, the inquiry of V. Turner into the symbolism of colors among the Ndembu.[5] This inquiry, suggestive as it is and at times illuminating, may recall the studies by Griaule and his school on the Dogon of Mali. But whereas the French scholars hardly go beyond the Dogon material in their argument, Turner does not hesitate to base, however hypothetically, upon the examination of the Ndembu feats and some cursory and disparate comparisons, an entire theory of culture that is intended to replace Durkheim's sociological hypothesis.

After having observed that, in Ndembu ritual, 'not only the dualism of sexes but indeed every form of dualism was contained in a wider, tripartite mode of classification', and after having stressed that this tripartite classification expresses itself through white, red and black (which — he writes — are the only primary colors in the local idiom), he affirms that 'there is no fixed correlation between the colors and the sexes. Color symbolism is not consistently sex-linked, although red and white may be situationally specified to represent the opposition of the sexes... White and red are certainly opposed in some situations, but the fact that each can stand for the same object ... suggests that more than a pair of opposites has to be taken into account': which is something that takes place, says Turner, through the symbolism of a third color, which is black.

Now, taking into account the cases that concern the symbolism of red, we find a good many elements that really allow for extremely useful comparison, e. g. with the Dogon material. The 'vitalistic' ambivalence (related to the theme of 'killing' and to the impurity connected with the vital processes: e. g. menstrual blood[6] and childbirth blood) of the elements connected with red seems clear; and this, together with certain aspects of the varied dialectic of the two colors, red and black with white, recalls the ambivalence and the ambiguity of that central figure

5. *The Forest of Symbols*, Ithaca N. Y., 1967, pp. 59-92.
6. Which, under another aspect, is also classified as 'black'.

of the Dogon ideology personified by the Pale Fox. This, in fact, is a figure connected with the essential aspects of life, which would be incomplete but for him, though he himself is typically incomplete and therefore unhappy and impure.[7]

So, Turner has unquestionably made a first-class contribution to the religious-historical problematic, in this case to the historical phenomenology of dualistic thought, with his triadic system that enriches the dualistic pattern. Turner's result illuminates a vision of the world articulated and certainly not reducible to easy outlines of symmetrical oppositions such as right and left, masculine and feminine, etc. These latter schemes appear to be, through their very nature, frigidly dyadic, static and anything but dynamic, and therefore unable to express life's movement and experience over and above its conceptualization in an ideology. And Turner's analysis has this further advantage: he can use a documentation that allows him to reduce the size of conjecture. The figure of the 'three streams', expressively characterized through the reference to the three colors, seems to express well the idea of a fundamental structure for the interpretation of the real, i.e. of the 'knowledge', or of 'gnosis' transmitted in the initiation rites that he has studied.

The rigidly inductive, analytical, documentary procedure that characterizes Turner's argument in the expository part, suddenly changes, however, when the author, after having evoked the symbolism of the three colors in other cultural ambits, lets himself get carried away in generalizations, or in generical affirmations. Turner may well be right in affirming that 'at the initiation of juniors into the rights and duties and values of the seniors, all three colors receive equal emphasis', but he adds a very conjectural and rather generical affirmation: 'In my view this is because they epitomize the main kinds of universal human organic experience. In many societies these colors have explicit reference to certain fluids, secretions or waste products of the human body'. Unfortunately, this hypothesis, though referring to 'many societies',

---

7. As for the dualistic aspects of Dogon ideology as described by M. Griaule and G. Dieterlen, *Le renard pâle*, I, 1, Paris, 1965 (see also G. Calame-Griaule, *Ethnologie et langage*, Paris, 1968 and M. Palau Marti, *Les Dogon*, Paris, 1957); see U. Bianchi, 'Pour l'histoire du dualisme: un Coyote africain, le Renard Pâle', in *Liber Amicorum* (Studies Bleeker), Leiden, 1969 (Suppl. to *Numen*, Vol. XVII), pp. 27-43, and Seth, 'Osiris et l'ethnographie', in *Revue de l'histoire des religions* 179/2 (1971), pp. 113-135.

proves to be based on a rather short-sided argumentation: 'Red is universally a symbol of blood, white is frequently a symbol of breast milk and semen (and sometimes of pus), while, as we have seen, the Chhāndogya Upanishad relates the black color with feces and urine (though other cultures connect urine with semen and both with whiteness)'.

Here the level of evidence seems to be quite different and irreductible to a single model as far as the connection of the three colors to elements of organic nature is concerned; from a 'universal' connection (that is obvious) between red and blood, he passes to a 'frequently', that concerns the white of milk and semen and also pus, and finally to the rather isolated case of black and feces in a Upanishadic text (as among the Ndembu). Nor is it enough to say generically: 'each of the colors in all societies is multivocal..., but nevertheless the human physiological component is seldom absent wherever reliable native exegesis is available', and that 'initiation rites often draw their symbolism from the situation of parturition and first lactation, where, in nature, blood, water, feces, and milk are present', where the inference that ties the notions of initiatic symbolism of generation and lactation with the notion of all the different substances of organic origin seems logically arbitrary.[8]

8. This brings up another point that Turner has discussed, in M. Gluckman, ed., *Essays on the Ritual of Social Relations*, Manchester, 1962, and which concerns leprosy among the Ndembu. He talks about the *mudyi* tree, the 'milktree', which he defines this way because of the white latex that implies a whole series of connections with woman's milk and the very principle of matrilinearity, and obviously also with itself, seen also as a pure and nutrient essence. Now, says Turner, the *mudyi* is used as a medicine to cure leprosy: in this case, the bark of a *mudyi* tree that grows in a *mukanda*, 'a place of death' (*ifwilu*) that has been abandoned. The whiteness of the latex, says Turner, is compared with the whiteness of the spots and rays that leprosy produces. Moreover, leprosy is considered to be the punishment for the violation of ritual interdictions of *mukanda* (the initiatic rite of young people. In this case the *mudyi* seems to be used as a homeopathic medicine). Turner himself gives a 'religious-historical' explanation of the whiteness (ontological) in leprosy according to the Ndembu. He says that it is not through simple analogical contamination that an equivalence is established between the whiteness of milk, the whiteness of ritual purity and the whiteness of leprosy. It is, he adds, well known that the sacred, the numinous, is also dangerous, not only benevolent. The very fact of coming into contact with it at times and modalities and places not specified by the sacerdotal authorities or by ritual customs is equivalent to provoking a disaster. Now it is somewhat surprising to find such a sudden and indiscriminate reference to such a general concept as the 'sacred'. Turner could have quoted the *mana*, a now obsolescent concept, and its connection with *tabu*, or the dialectic pure-impure in some religious contexts.

Notwithstanding a sentence that invokes extreme caution, Turner feels entitled to affirm that 'among the earliest symbols produced by man are the three colors representing products of the human body whose emission, spilling or production is associated with a heightening of emotion. In other words culture, the superorganic, has an intimate connection with the organic in its early stages, with the awareness of powerful physical experiences. These heightened bodily experiences are felt to be informed with a power in excess of that normally possessed by the individual; its source may be located in the cosmos or in society; analogues of physical experience may then be found wherever the same colors occur in nature; or else experience of social relations in heightened emotional circumstances may be classified under a color rubric.' Turner recognizes that 'few societies specifically connect black with processes and products of catabolism and decay'; he searches elsewhere for a primary reference for this color too: 'It is possible that black, which, as we have seen, often means "death", a "fainting fit", "sleep", or "darkness", primarily represents falling into unconsciousness, the experience of a "black-out" ', but he seems here to enlarge his reference to include those very specific phenomena of a physiological nature and one wonders whether he is right when using in this same context the connection death—black color.[9]

On these considerations, Turner also builds a general theory: 'Not only do the three colors stand for basic human experiences of the body (associated with the gratification of libido, hunger, aggressive and excretory drives, and with fear, anxiety, and submissiveness), they also provide a kind of primordial classification of reality. This view is in contrast to Durkheim's notion that the social relations of mankind are not based on the logic relations of things but have served as the prototypes of the latter... Against this I would postulate that the human organism and its crucial experiences are the *fons et origo* of all classifications. Human biology demands certain intense experiences of relationship'.

Of course, a correspondence between microcosmos (man) and macrocosmos is present in many religious experiences, of systematical thought as well as of an interpretation of the world, and history of religions has considered this at length (vision of Markandeya in the Mahabharata;

---

9. Death, Turner points out, is conceived by the Ndembu as an intermediate level of 'maturation', towards a new form of existence.

late-Vedic theory of the castes emerging from the various parts of the Purusha's body; Iranian speculation studied by Goetze and others;[10] interpretative hypotheses of Scandinavian scholars (Rönnow) concerning the idea of the macrocosmos and its alleged connection with human sacrifice; Platonic Timaeus etc.).

But Turner's hypothesis seems to be an extreme and hasty generalization. We cannot therefore accept Turner's general conclusion that 'since the experiences the three colors represent are common to all mankind, we do not have to invoke diffusion to explain their wide distribution'. What is at stake here is not the diffusion of the three colors or the universality of those physical experiences, but the way Turner interprets their alleged connection.

In social anthropology itself, the reflections on an analogous theme by Mary Douglas,[11] may be quoted. She writes: 'The body is a complex structure. The functions of its different parts and their relation afford a source of symbols for other complex structures. We cannot possibly interpret rituals concerning excreta, breast milk, saliva and the rest unless we are prepared to see in the body a symbol of society, and to see the powers and dangers credited to social structure reproduced in small on the human body'; and, on page 121: 'All margins are dangerous... Any structure of ideas is vulnerable at its margins. We should expect the orifices of the body to symbolize its specially vulnerable points... The mistake is to treat bodily margins in isolation from all other margins. There is no reason to assume any primacy for the individual's attitude to his own bodily and emotional experience, any more than for his cultural and social experience. This is the clue which explains the unevenness with which different aspects of the body are treated in the rituals of the world. In some, menstrual pollution is feared as a lethal danger; in others not at all. In some, excreta is dangerous, in others it is only a joke.'

A consideration of the 'marginal' as 'risky', or even as a possibility of potential crisis, could be fruitful in the gnostic (or Valentinian) conception of a divine *pleroma* that extends and develops in concentric circles, or pairs of aeons, the last of which, Sophia, Wisdom, fatally falls

10. *Zeitschr. f. Indologie und Iranistik* I, pp. 60-98; see also U. Bianchi, *Zamàn i Ohrmazd. Lo zoroastrismo nelle sue origini e nella sua essenza*, Torino, 1958, pp. 190 ff.

11. *Purity and Danger*, London, 1966, p. 115.

through a fault somewhat bound to the very mechanics of the process itself (she wants to know the First Principle closely, or wants to generate without the *aeon* that is her counterpart). This theme is well framed — as was the case with Turner's triadic outline — in the problem of religious dualism, of which the study of gnostic thought is part. Naturally, all this has to be located within research that is not based upon previous generalizing hypotheses that attempt to use one and the same outline to interpret different things — as Douglas agrees, although some kind of failing in this line has been attributed to her.[12]

In general, one can recall, when considering anthropological generalization, the cautious considerations of Evans-Pritchard;[13] referring to the attempt to establish 'laws or universals, in the sense of propositions to which there are no exceptions, by comparative analysis', he recalls Nieboer's criticism of 'the capricious practice of some writers of thinking up some plausible explanation of some social phenomenon and then searching round for illustrations which seem to support it and neglecting the rest of the material relating to the topic under consideration'. And Evans-Pritchard gives pertinent examples, criticizing Radcliffe-Brown's assertion that 'where man depends largely on hunting and collecting for the means of subsistence animals and plants are made objects of "ritual attitude", this being a particular instance of a general law: that any object or event which has important effects on the material or spiritual well-being of a society tends to become an object of the "ritual attitude" '. Now, says Evans-Pritchard (p. 16): 'This is simply just not the case, unless we are to understand by "ritual attitude" attention of any sort, thereby depriving the expression of any precise meaning'. E. g., 'there are many societies with ancestor cultus without a trace of a lineage system, and the most perfect example of a lineage system is perhaps that of the Bedouin Arabs, who are Muslims' (p. 15). True, it is clear that in the case of Bedouins one has to take into consideration that Islam is not a religion of the 'ethnological' type, but historically and cross-culturally a very specific religious manifestation, which — even more than the ethnological religions — may not be reduced to merely bi-dimensional proportions. But Evans-Pritchard's example remains

12. See Ardener's review of her book, *Man*, 1967, p. 139, pointed out to me by Dr. Matthey.
13. *The Comparative Method in Social Anthropology*, Holhouse Memorial Trust Lecture no. 33, Univ. of London, 1963, p. 14.

valid when talking about the limits to which the pretended sociological universal laws would aim to extend.

4. The fundamental problem of a 'religio-anthropological' approach, and of the relation between history of religions and anthropology, lies in the problem of comparison.

The social anthropologists themselves are not indifferent to certain questions implicit in the methodology of their science. Radcliffe-Brown and Malinowski have nowadays, in some respects, been left far behind. Today, the problem of the relations between history and social anthropology is put as follows by a social anthropologist, Beattie: 'Historians are chiefly interested in the past, whether remote or recent; their business is to find out what happened, and why it happened. On the whole, they are more interested in particular sequences of past events and their conditions, than they are in the general patterns, principles and 'laws' which these events may exhibit...' As for social anthropologists, they are 'centrally (though not exclusively) interested in understanding the present condition of the culture or community which they are studying. Their interest is as a rule explicitly general and comparative, as well as specific to the situation they are studying. Thus, for example, an anthropologist who is investigating a particular kinship system is interested not only in that particular kinship system but also in advancing his understanding of the working of all kinship systems, or at least of all kinship systems of that particular type...'[14] 'Although in a very general sense it is true that historians are concerned with what is individual and unique, social anthropologists, like sociologists, with what is general and typical, this dichotomy is altogether too simple.'[15]

Another and more definite answer to Malinowski's objections against a historical study of cultures comes from an Italian ethnologist, quite an expert in social anthropology, Vinigi L. Grottanelli: 'A questo discorso io rispondo che non esistono due modi di studiare le società e le loro culture, perché il comportamento sociale non appartiene e non può appartenere a due 'regni' al tempo stesso; o, per dirla in altri termini, perché il solo modo in cui la cultura si manifesta è ciò che noi chiamiamo

14. *Other Cultures. Aims, Methods and Achievements in Social Anthropology*, New York, 1964 (repr. 1966), p. 22.
15. *Op. cit.*, p. 25.

storia...'[16] 'Malgrado queste divergenze, l'etnologia quale l'intendiamo in Italia (e in genere nell'Europa continentale dell'occidente) e la più giovane *social anthropology* si occupano dei medesimi argomenti e non possono rinnegare il loro specifico compito comune, che è lo studio delle società senza scrittura. Da questa unità di scopi, dalla coincidenza delle ricerche sul terreno, ... emerge l'inopportunità, anzi l'irragionevolezza, dell'ammettere l'esistenza di due scienze distinte che studiano la medesima cosa.'[17]

This is not the position of Beattie, a social anthropologist who distinguishes between ethnology and social anthropology: '...Ethnology is the science which classifies peoples in terms of their racial and cultural characteristics, and attempts to explain these by reference to their history or to their prehistory... Ethnology is really the direct heir to Victorian anthropology; like it, it is a kind of history, though it differs from history in that ethnologists ordinarily lack written records upon which to base their theories. Also, ethnologists have mostly been interested in separate items of culture, whether in the actual objects used or made by people (material culture) or in such topics as myth and folklore. They have inevitably been less concerned with social institutions and values, whose history is usually a good deal more difficult to trace... But on the whole present-day social anthropology and ethnology are best regarded as distinct disciplines'.[18]

Now, it is symptomatic that Grottanelli, already quoted, has on the other hand been able to see in the aims of social anthropology the continuation of Victorian evolutionistic ethnology. For Grottanelli the claim that social anthropology might have the aim to 'scoprire leggi o tendenze generali verificabili nel caso particolare', to 'stabilire generalizzazioni che abbiano validità indipendentemente dal periodo e dal luogo', etc., recalls analogous formulations, e. g. Frazer's, aiming at 'scoprire le leggi generali che hanno regolato la storia nel passato e che, se la natura è realmente uniforme, possiamo aspettarci la regolino anche nel futuro'.

About the relations between social anthropology and historical research, E. E. Evans-Pritchard's position is quite different from that of

16. *L'etnologia e le 'leggi' della condotta umana*, Roma, 1964, p. 18.
17. *Op. cit.*, p. 24.
18. *Op. cit.*, pp. 19f.

many social anthropologists, from Malinowski to M. Fortes: 'In spite — he writes — of their claim that social anthropology aims at being a natural history of human societies, that is of all human societies, functionalist anthropologists, at any rate in England, in their general distaste for historical method, almost completely ignored historical writings. They have thereby denied themselves access in their comparative studies to the valuable material provided by historical societies structurally comparable to many of the contemporaneous barbarous societies, which they regard as being within their province.'[19] Furthermore, the historical character of the social anthropological studies should be assured, observes the same author, by the fact that today the social anthropologists also aim at the study of communities that, though minor in entity and simple in structure, form part of large historical societies (communities in India or in Ireland, Bedouin tribes, etc.). Finally, he justly asks himself whether social anthropology is not some kind of historical science, when it renders its object sociologically intelligible, discovering 'the structural patterns of a society', which are then compared to others 'to construct a typology of forms and to determine their essential features and the reasons for their variations'.

With these considerations Evans-Pritchard touches on the essential items that, all things considered, should reconcile social anthropology with historical research and ethnology. He gets close to a concept of the 'historical typology' of cultures (see *infra*) which might be adequate to historical 'comparison'.

And twelve years later — notwithstanding objections and criticism — the same author[20] insisted on his opinions, saying: 'In practice, social anthropologists today generalize little more than historians do. They do not deduce facts from laws or explain them as instances of laws, and if they see the general in the particular, so does the historian'. Evans-Pritchard clarifies: 'I am not speaking of those historians who are content to write narrative histories, *histoire-historisante*, battle-history, a history of great

19. 'Social Anthropology: Past and Present' (Marett Lecture 1950) published in *Man*, 1950, and republished as the first chapter of *Essays in Social Anthropology*, London, 1962, pp. 22 ff. Cf. also, as for the example of the Bedouins, of the same Author, in the same *Essays*, p. 24. He notes a certain tendency in a few contemporary social anthropologists to study perfectly 'historical' societies such as those of the Ancient East.

20. 'Anthropology and History', in *Essays* cit., pp. 48 f.

events, mostly political... I am speaking of the *historiens-sociologues*, those who are primarily interested in social institutions, in mass movements and great cultural changes, and who seek regularities, tendencies, types, and typical sequences; and always within a restricted historical and cultural context... Such historians speak as gaily as we of organisms, patterns, complexes, networks of relations, intelligible wholes, *Zusammenhang, ensembles*, principles of coherence, *un tout* etc. History is not a succession of events, it is the links between them... *Civitas*, feudality, class, capitalism, revolution, are all general abstractions, implying an ideal type...' (this concept of 'ideal type' is however not exactly one that can satisfy historical-comparative research). And again Evans-Pritchard: 'Both sociological historians and social anthropologists are fully aware that any event has the characters of uniqueness and of generality, and that in an interpretation of it both have to be given consideration. If the specificity of a fact is lost, the generalization about it becomes so general as to be valueless (this is what has happened to several of our categories, for example, 'tabu', 'totemism'...). On the other hand, events lose much, even all, of their meaning if they are not seen as having some degree of regularity and constancy, as belonging to a certain type of event, all instances of which have many features in common'. To be sincere, we find that the problem of comparison is not exhausted, nor properly formulated, as a matter of reconciling uniqueness and generality on a 'bi-dimensional' plane. What is needed too is the dimension of 'profundity', the historical dimension (see *infra*). In the light of these remarks by Evans-Pritchard, the hostility that he demonstrates to the problems of 'origins', which are as essential as those of 'development' to historical problematic, leads to some perplexity.[21]

We have seen how 'comparison' is treated by a social anthropologist such as E. E. Evans-Pritchard, even in the face of one of the essential presuppositions of social anthropology, i. e. 'research in the field'. Thus, he writes: 'It is sometimes forgotten that the social anthropologist relies on direct observation only in his role of ethnographer' (i. e. in his fieldwork) 'and that when he starts to make comparative studies he has to rely on documents, just as the historian does'.[22] This is a very useful

21. This is probably in reaction to the 'hantise des origines' of the evolutionists and their conception of unilinear evolution from alleged 'simple' beginnings.
22. *Essays*, cit., pp. 50 and 55.

caveat to possible temptations for the social anthropologist as a scientist in the field who wants to be, at the same time, a comparatist and a 'generalizer'. In fact, the comparative moment in anthropological and ethnological research may not be abandoned, according to the cultors of social and cultural anthropology.[23] O. Lewis[24] says that these sciences are characterized by a simultaneous interest in a holistic and intensive study of minor entities and in the comparative analysis of these societies and cultures in the world as a whole. Traditionally, the former has been based on analysis in the field and comparative research, and the latter on library research.

Now, what really matters is to define in what sense comparison must be founded on the methodology of (or at least on checking against) history. In fact, the cultural context from which the data may not be abstracted[25] is definitely a historical context and not only a functional one, and it is to this historical context that the concept of 'cultural dynamics' must refer. In other words, 'comparative' means also 'historical-comparative'. Though perhaps rather optimistic, a statement of I. M. Lewis is interesting: '... The number of essentially and explicitly historical anthropological studies is considerably larger than is often supposed...' It is not a matter of a 'fringe activity, but an integral part of the mainstream of British social anthropology', so that 'appearances based on the strictures of Radcliffe-Brown, or on the counter-arguments of Evans-Pritchard, are therefore somewhat deceptive...'.[26] And Lewis recalls approvingly the (historical) exigency of Evans-Pritchard and E. H. Carr's expression: 'the more sociological history becomes, and the more historical sociology becomes, the better for both'. Naturally, it must be added, as long as the specificity of historical method is really respected by 'sociological' history.

Finally, another social scientist, D. Forde,[27] says that 'anthropological

23. Cf. Fred Eggan, 'Comparative Method in Anthropology', in M. E. Spiro, ed., *Context and Meaning in Cultural Anthropology* (in Honor of A. L. Hallowel), New York/London, 1965, p. 358.

24. 'Comparisons in Cultural Anthropology', in *Yearbook of Anthropology*, New York, 1955, p. 277, quoted by Eggan, *op. cit.*, pp. 358 ff.

25. M. J. Herskovits, 'A Genealogy of Ethnological Theory', in Spiro, ed., *Context and Meaning*, cit., p. 411.

26. *History and Social Anthropology*, London, repr. 1970, p. xiv.

27. *African Worlds. Studies in the Cosmological Ideas and Social Values of African Peoples*, Oxford, 1954, repr. 1960, p. vii.

studies of many cultures have shown that even in small and comparatively isolated societies, where differences of wealth, rank, and power
are small, there need be no complete integration of belief and doctrine,
still less the domination of conduct in all spheres by a single system of
beliefs or basic ideas'; which means that, even if we have to pay primary
consideration to the existence of 'customary patterns and established
social duties and privileges', it must also be recognized that 'the unique
mobility and capacity for communication of the human species have
nearly everywhere prevented any population from remaining long isolated and static, culturally or socially, in an unchanging environment'.
   Which leads us back to the historical-comparative method.

5. Faced with these requirements of the historical-comparative method,
the criteria of American cultural anthropologists such as C. Kluckhohn
seem to us to be quite insufficient, when they are not averse to 'regard
cross-cultural likeness as being sub-cultural — as the limits and conditions of culture'.[28] This author refers to a formulation by Kroeber:
'Such more or less recurrent near-regularities of form or process as have
to date been formulated by culture are actually mainly sub-cultural in
nature. They are limits set to culture by physical or organic factors. The
so-called 'cultural constants' of family, religion, war, communication,
and the like, appear to be biopsychological frames variably filled with
cultural content, so far as they are more than categories reflecting the
compartments of our own occidental logico-verbal culture'. This would
be to solve the question by destroying it (a typical case of 'explaining
away'). In fact, the 'socio-situational data' to which even Kluckhohn
refers as to a source of 'invariant points of reference' for a valid cross-
cultural comparison are not 'subcultural' or naturalistic data, but data
of full historical relevance. More reasonable, and more in conformity
with the historical-comparative requirements, seem to be the following
observations by Kluckhohn: 'As for the larger groups of phenomena like
religion that make up "the universal pattern" — or even subdivisions of
these such as "crisis rites" or "fasting" — these are recurrent indeed, but
they are not uniform. Anyone can make a definition that will separate
magic from religion; but no one has yet found a definition that all other

28. 'Universal Categories in Culture', in Sol Tax, ed., *Anthropology Today*, Chicago, 1962, pp. 313-318.

students accept: the phenomenal contents of the concepts of religion and magic simply intergrade too much. This is true even though almost everyone would agree in differentiating large masses of specific phenomena as respectively religious and magical.' But even these considerations by Kluckhohn seem to be insufficient. They are not closely enough related to a historical-comparative sensitivity; this seems to be clear when he continues: 'In short, concepts like religion and magic have an undoubted, heuristic utility in given situations... After all, they are in origin common-sense concepts, like "boy", "youth", "man", "old man".' True, the point of departure should be located in the common meaning that the terms have in the historical-cultural background of the scientist (see *infra*): and in this sense the term 'religion' would be a heuristic or a 'common-sense' one. Scientific, historical-comparative and religious-comparative research will however proceed further, and it is only then that 'reciprocal degradation between magic and religion, in certain cases', and that frequent possibility of polarizing documents and dates respectively in one type and in the other, of which Kluckhohn speaks, acquire a sense that goes beyond the purely conventional or heuristic, beyond what is purely common sense, purely 'definitional' and more or less accepted by the majority. This seems to be perfectly within the terms of what Boas writes, as quoted by Kluckhohn: 'The analysis of the phenomena is our prime object. Generalizations will be more significant the closer we adhere to definite forms': which perhaps corresponds to what was said before (but cf. also *infra*) about the necessary constant adherence by historical-comparative enquiry and its results to the reality of concretes, over and above any reference to 'ideal types'.

We conclude this section by a reference to Lévi-Strauss's famous assertion,[29] that 'in ethnology, as much as in linguistics, ... it is not comparison that founds generalization, but the opposite'; an assertion which we are not able to share. Anyway one should not forget another passage from Lévi-Strauss: 'On pourrait, en effet, nous contester le droit de choisir nos mythes à droite et à gauche, d'éclairer un mythe du Chaco par une variante guyanaise, un mythe gé par son analogue colombien. Mais, si respectueuse qu'elle soit de l'histoire et empressée à profiter de toutes ses leçons, l'analyse structurale refuse de se faire enfermer

29. *Anthropologie structurale*, Paris, 1958, p. 28.

dans les périmètres déjà circonscrits par l'investigation historique. Au contraire, en démontrant que des mythes de provenances très diverses forment objectivement un groupe, elle pose un problème à l'histoire, et l'invite à se mettre à la recherche d'une solution. Nous avons construit un groupe, et nous espérons avoir fourni la preuve que c'était un groupe. Il incombe aux ethnographes, aux historiens et aux archéologues, de dire comment et pourquoi.'[30]

6. Let us now briefly dwell on some problems of definition and categorization, and then pass on to the exposition, unfortunately rather short, of the three methodological principles that we consider proper to history of religions (and to historically orientated ethnology), and which in our opinion render the contribution of these sciences indispensable for the anthropologist.

The very concept of 'religion' itself poses fundamental problems, as to its comprehension and extension. There is the danger of a concept of religion characterized by excessive or uncontrolled extension. On the other hand, not too much 'comprehensiveness' should be demanded for a concept applicable to such a disparate world as that of 'religion' truly is. Now, this tension between comprehension and extension of the concept, though it may confirm a well-known law of logic, at the same time risks making the phenomenological concept of religion itself explode.

It has already often been noticed that not much hope is offered for a solution of the problem by means of a 'lowest common denominator' of religion as a general concept, i. e. the minimum common contents of any religious system (in belief and practice).[31] Now a method should be established that might lead to a concept of 'religion' conceivable and applicable in positive research. With some reason it has been written that 'while a definition cannot take the place of inquiry, in the absence of definitions there can be no inquiry' (Spiro).[32] More simply: it is necessary to have an idea of the phenomenon to be studied, if only to direct oneself towards the things to be taken into consideration, and to eliminate, at least provisionally, the others. But it would be illusory

30. *Le cru et le cuit*, Paris, 1964, p. 16.
31. See the works cited under note 3.
32. In Banton, ed., *op. cit.*, p. 90, cf. p. 89.

to eliminate the problem in limiting the positive inquiry to particular historical-cultural milieus; nor can an apparent contradiction be denied in the words of Evans-Pritchard: 'One must not ask "what is religion?", but what are the main features of, let us say, the religion of one Melanesian people', whereas he further passes to 'generalizations about a Melanesian religion *in toto*';[33] for what is at stake is still to identify *the* religion of a particular Melanesian group, as distinct from other aspects of its culture.[34]

As already said, one can hardly solve the problem by reverting to definitions of religion that have merely conventional or at any rate previously established value, be it 'functional' or 'operative' definitions (as in two recent books by Baird[35] and Pye[36]) or be it 'ostensive' or 'substantive'. To be more explicit: it is of no use to rely on a 'functional' definition of religion as 'ultimate concern' (as Baird puts it, using Tillich's expression), if we are not at the same time prepared to define the categorical quality of what is 'ultimate' (otherwise one could say, with Spiro, that baseball too might be an ultimate concern for somebody; which would confuse the discussion in an unacceptable way). Nor could we escape the difficulty by reverting to substitutive expressions that might have more capacity to adapt to the generality of religions, as with the 'operative' definition that Pye proposes: 'the data for the study of religion are certain sets of actions and concepts together with the social groups and psychological states associated with them; these are located among the generality of sociological and psychological data, but their specific identity lies in their reference to what the persons concerned take to be fundamentally important aspects of their experience'. It seems to me that any specific qualification of 'religious' remains exterior to this definition, and may be applied to different series of human activities, unless the key-word 'fundamentally' (as here seems to be the case) proposes the same problem as already presented by 'ultimate'.

(Analogous comments also apply to other expressions often used by social anthropologists to somehow define the 'religious': 'non-rational', 'irrational', 'some mystic power', or, at times, 'metaphysical').

33. *Theories of Primitive Religion*, Oxford, 1965.
34. As observed by Spiro, in Banton, ed., *op. cit.*, p. 90.
35. *Category Formation and the History of Religions*, The Hague/Paris, 1972, pp. 1-27.
36. *Comparative Religion*, Newton Abbot, 1972, p. 12.

In our opinion, the adequate method which we are searching for, could only be the historical-comparative method, that establishes and compares historical-cultural milieus and complexes as well, when available, as historical processes in constant contact with the concrete data of religion and religions. Only a comparison of this kind is able to perceive those real 'continuities' (which does not exclude oppositions or radical innovations) which provide the basis for a general concept, but of inductive origin, of religion.

In other words: the problem of a definition of religion through inductive research (on which a historical phenomenology of religion could be based) is not a matter of a selection of facts or aspects operated *a priori*, but rather a matter of penetration. This penetration is realized through the progressive and articulated extension of the historical knowledge of the enquirer, in relation to the different milieus that he is methodically considering.[37] This will cause the knowledge of facts and contexts to spread in step with an increasingly adequate and valid articulation of the concept of inductive origin. Only this dialectic between contact with the object and progress in the conceptual determination of it makes it possible to surmount the impasse (which is, logically, otherwise insurmountable) of a definition that is at the same time the presupposition and the aim of research, and of the impossibility of a concept that the tension between comprehension and extension may cause to explode.[38]

In our opinion, only this procedure promises to let us surmount the above-mentioned difficulties, as it engenders enquiry and is continuously engendered by it.

7. Once these principles that constitute the foundation of solid comparative research have been fixed, it will be useful to see them illustrated by a few examples. Let us take the example of the Buddhism of the

37. V. Lanternari, 'Nuovi Argomenti' 49-50, 1961, p. 15, suggested a partially corresponding procedure, but only on a functional plane: to call religious those cultural manifestations which show, for the representatives of the culture under consideration, a psychological function (for the individual) and a cultural one (for the society) corresponding to that which is proper to religion for the subject (the researcher) and its society. This procedure, inasmuch it is merely functional, excludes from consideration the object of religion and a properly historical-culturally articulated concept.

38. Cf. *supra*, note 3.

'Small Vehicle', with apologies for quoting a limit case, since, contrary to what is sometimes affirmed (and sometimes quite correctly), in our case limit cases could cause some confusion for two opposite reasons: for leading one to forget that they are very particular cases, or else by giving the impression, quite falsely, that the question of the 'definition' (in the etymological sense) of 'religion' starts being complicated only when we get to the extremely peripheral zone.

The indissolubility of the historical-cultural and historical-religious ties between the historical fact of an 'extra-brahmanic' religious, soteriological experience of the Upanishadic type on the one hand, and the Buddhist illumination as it emerges from the Pali canon on the other hand, is an example of how the study of the concrete historical processes (genesis and development) and of the historical contiguities is the only viable way to orientate towards the continuities and the innovations. It is in this context that one must ask whether Pali Buddhism (and any Buddhism that relates to this) 'is' a 'religion'.[39]

Second example: 'magic' (unfortunately another limit case, but in a wider perspective). It is obvious that at certain levels of 'intention', the practice of magic and the religious practice may have something in common, both in cases where reference to the historical and cultural context imposes strict differentiation of the two practices from the point of view of rigorously religious-historical phenomenology (which is the case in some instances of modern European folklore), and in cases where a strict differentiation might seem difficult and subject to further verification (*bulla* at the neck of a Roman child, two thousand years ago; Assyrian or Egyptian ritual objects, some prehistorical symbols, the

---

39. As we mentioned in *Storia delle religioni* (quoted in n. 3), pp. 7-9 and 166f., and *Problems and Methods* (quoted in n. 3), pp. 15-26, partic. pp. 19-20, at the same time as we refuse any reductive interpretation, we also certainly do not intend to assign the 'Small Vehicle' to religion by authority, nor do we intend to assign it to religion only in behalf of some elements that are found in it and correspond to the definition which Spiro (in Banton, ed., *op. cit.*, pp. 91, 94, 96, 98) gives of religion (faith in superhuman beings, beneficient or maleficient: a definition which has much to be said for it and which is more appropriate than Tylor's faith in spiritual beings); nor do we base our argument on a pre-conceived concept of an *a priori* affirmed universality of religion (which is a conclusion, not a presupposition of positive-inductive research). All we wish to say is that, in a good historical-phenomenological method, one could not ignore and untie the historical and phenomenological knots between Buddhist reflection on *karma, samsara, nirvana* and the preceding mystical, religious experience of the Upanishads on those same themes.

fertility rites, the hierogamy of sacred kings, the Greek mystery cults, etc.). This is a series of questions that could only be treated in an adequate way by the historical-comparative method, which is indeed the method of history of religions, and which concerns not some isolated practices or concepts to render them a matter for arbitrary phenomenology, but rather concerns historical contexts. At the same time, the historical-comparative method will allow us to transcend that initial and insufficient level of enquiry (its functional level) which we would reach by limiting our consideration to the mere immediate and reflected finalities of the practices of a mother, worried about her child's health, whether in our days or in antiquity.[40]

8. And this is where we would like to let our argument culminate, as we stress the three qualifications which seem essential in defining a historical-comparative approach that is common to history and to historically-oriented ethnology.

(a) The first concept, of a 'historical typology': we take here the example of polytheistic religions. As a matter of fact, 'polytheism', in history of religions, does not correspond to an abstract typology; it is not an 'ideal type', but a 'series' of concrete affinities (though varied and certainly not interchangeable), as they result from the scientific attention brought to the phenomena of *Hochkultur* processes of the archaic phase to which polytheisms appear historically connected.[41] This cultural-historical connection between 'polytheism' and most of the *Hochkulturen* of the archaic phase, though not expressing an evolutionary determinism, is valid provided that the *Hochkulturen* under consideration have a common origin as a phenomenon of historical diffusion, or even of a stimulus diffusion, of a Mesopotamian origin (as some scientists of the historical-cultural school would admit: cf. Heine-Geldern); and it is valid even if their rise depends upon a parallel development and has an independent genesis. It is obvious that, if one were content to define polytheism as merely a 'cult of more deities', then one could not talk about historical typology, but rather of abstract

---

40. As far as 'magic' is concerned, in its more specific manifestations, it has certainly to be considered as categorically foreign to, and even opposed, to religion; nevertheless, and even up to a certain level of theoretical abstraction, the instances mentioned in the text raise problems of more articulate categorization.

41. A. Brelich, 'Der Polytheismus', *Numen* VII, pp. 133ff.

typology; without any clear idea of the types of divinity that emerge out of a concrete consideration of the polytheistic pantheons that have really existed or still exist.

(b) The second concept, 'analogy'. In our opinion many of the most diffused categories ('structures') of religion (e.g. 'sacrifice', 'priesthood', etc.), and even religion itself, once it is considered on a more vast comparative basis, extended to all the cultures and to all the ages accessible to positive research, can best be regarded — at least at the start — as great 'analogia': i.e. there will be no further urgency to choose between an univocal or — on the other hand — a merely equivocal meaning of the terms and the concepts of 'religion', 'sacrifice', etc., and of the corresponding realities. In other words, it will not be obvious that religions and religious forms are always species of one and the same genus. They will further have to be valued at the same time for what they might show to have deeply akin or deeply disparate, taken singly or gathered in types (of a historical typology) or families, in a constant pertinence of historical-typological evaluation by the scholar;[42] and this pertinence would no longer obtain should he work with 'ideal types' or with abstract categories or 'generalizations' of this type. The exigency of this becomes the more obvious when one confronts it with the significant formulation (though still insufficiently articulated from the historical-comparative point of view) given by Evans-Pritchard, *The Comparative Method, op. cit.*, p. 9: 'Are, for example, "monogamy" among the Veddahs of Ceylon and "monogamy" in Western Europe units of the same kind, or is "monotheism" in Islam equivalent to "monotheism" among the Pygmies?' (which does not exclude the possibility of tracing some historical-cultural and phenomenological links between those phenomena).

---

42. In a report concerning the book *Problems and Methods* quoted at n. 3, J.-P. De Menasce is kindly willing to accept the proposed use of the concept of analogy: 'Il s'agit (...) d'assouplir l'instrument conceptuel dont on se sert dans l'interprétation et le classement des faits, et de le faire en connaissance de cause; car rien n'est plus stérile qu'une classification trop peu analysée ... et on n'a pas perdu son temps quand on s'est appliqué, pressé par la fidélité au réel, à en investiguer et à en fixer les articulations. Le bouddhisme du sud est-il ou non une religion, tel rite de fertilité est-il ou non 'magique', tel mythe de création est-il ou non anthropomorphique? La réponse *per sic et non* fait-elle vraiment droit à la complexité du réel, ou suffit-il de brandir le mot magique d'"'ambiguité" pour situer chaque élément à la place qui lui revient?...' (*Revue de l'histoire des religions*, oct. 1972).

It is obvious that in a comparison of this kind, it will not be the single facts, or single elements of belief and practice that will alone be considered, but rather integrated wholes, structures and historical processes in which these single elements are real.

(c) And finally the third concept, the 'concrete universal' (not in the Hegelian sense) or the 'historical universal'. It considers the problem of 'universals' as they may result not from abstract and merely phenomenological or anthropological generalization, but rather from an ethnological and historical-religious survey made on a historical-comparative basis, i. e. on the basis of the above-described concept of analogy and historical typology as well as of that dialectic and synthesis between knowledge already scientifically acquired, and reflected on, and new information acquired through a historical-philological survey constantly encompassing new objects. A 'concrete or historical universal' that maintains a continuous reference to the real and to detail, and which, on this basis, can at any moment be understood and verified; and which might get also from this continuous understanding of the real and the particular a knowledge which is aware of its own limits of conceptual validity. Not universals that are pure forms without content, or abstract phenomenology.

The main problem, then, will be to explore that vast 'continuity' that might make it possible to speak of religion as an extensive and articulate 'concrete or historical universal', i. e. as a family of phenomena that, though various and often irreductibly different, nonetheless do show, if not always a continuity or real connection in a historical succession proved by facts, at least some affinities of character and of function (but not of function only); affinities that should not be less profound than the differences themselves. Of course these affinities too will have to result from the pertinent application of the historical-philological method.

MELFORD E. SPIRO   *Symbolism and Functionalism in the*
Anthropological Study of Religion

INTRODUCTION

For the historian and sociologist of science, the history of social science provides many fascinating problems for inquiry, not the least of which is the propensity of its practitioners to reject old approaches as false whenever a new approach acquires saliency. Even Marxist and Hegelian social scientists for whom antitheses must necessarily eventuate in some kind of synthesis, nevertheless view the different approaches to socio-cultural inquiry as constituting binary opposites, one of which (their own) is believed (with all the fervor of a Manichean) to represent the forces of light, the other the forces of darkness. A relevant case for this conference is the rejection of functionalism by the practitioners of the new symbolist approach to religious anthropology, much as the functionalists had rejected the evolutionary approach of the generation before them. The current symbolic approach, it might be added, is part of the contemporary *Zeitgeist*; everywhere, in politics and kinship, as well as in religion and myth, functionalism is out, symbolism is in, motivation is out, cognition is in, social processes are out, mental processes are in.

Roughly speaking, we can distinguish at least three different anthropological approaches to the study of cultural symbols and symbol systems: (a) phenomenological analysis of the philosophical meanings of the symbols, (b) structural analysis of the logical relationships among the symbols and (c) formal semantic analysis of their classificatory schemata. Although these three approaches are obviously quite different from each other, they have in common an exclusive attention to symbols and symbol systems as such, and an avoidance of attention to the relationship between cultural symbols and social experience. The latter is viewed (at best) as theoretically uninteresting, and (at worst) as an intellectual sin against the Cartesian theory of the mind held by many of them.

The previous generation of functionalists were equally dogmatic in the opposite direction. For many of them, at least, the cognitive meaning of cultural symbol systems was more-or-less ignored in favor of their relationship either to the psychobiological needs of the social actors or to the functional requirements of their social system. With some few exceptions, the cognitive meaning of the symbols, as such, was of little interest.

Despite the polemical opposition between symbolic and functionalist approaches, there is no intrinsic opposition between them. On the contrary, I would say (to paraphrase Kant) that functionalism without symbolism is blind, and symbolism without functionalism is lame. For, surely, the social functions of symbol systems largely depend on their cognitive meaning, and the meanings which symbol systems have for social actors derive from and are related to their social context. This, at least, is the thesis I wish to explore in this paper, not, however, by a logical analysis of the postulates and theorems of these respective theoretical approaches, but by a concrete comparison of a sub-set of the set of symbol systems of traditional Judaism and Theravāda Buddhism, namely, their soteriological symbols. My choice of these two religions stems primarily from the fact that I happen to have conducted research in two communities — an Israeli *kibbutz* and a Burmese village — whose cultures are informed by these two religious traditions. Theravāda Buddhism comprises the most important idea system (religious or secular) in Burma; and although the *kibbutz* (a collective agricultural settlement) which I studied is atheist, its founders — those who created its institutions and established its ethos — were reared in, and internalized most of the basic concepts and values of, orthodox Judaism.

What I hope to do, then, is to compare some basic, or core, symbols of these religions with respect to their philosophical meaning — I shall forego a structural and logical analysis of the symbols — and I shall then attempt to relate them to the cultural orientations and motivational dispositions found in Yeigyi, a village in Upper Burma, and Kiryat Yedidim, a *kibbutz* in central Israel.

THE SOTERIOLOGICAL SYMBOLISM OF JUDAISM AND BUDDHISM

Introduction

Although, at first blush, no two religions appear to be as disparate as traditional Judaism[43] and Theravāda Buddhism,[44] when they are looked

43. By 'traditional Judaism' I refer to pre-World War I Eastern European, orthodox Judaism, the faith in which the founders of Kiryat Yedidim were raised.
44. *Theravāda* Buddhism, the form of Buddhism found in South and Southeast Asia, is as different from *Mahāyāna* Buddhism, found in Northern and Eastern Asia

at more closely their basic concepts bear a remarkable resemblance to each other. Both religions are characterized by two sets of conceptual trinities — a trinity of faith and a trinity of soteriologically valued action — which, structurally viewed, are almost identical. If this proposition seems outrageous, consider, for example, the following data. In both religions there are three ultimately sacred symbols which are taken, in some important sense, to be the essential instruments of salvation, and which constitute the irreducible objects of devotion. This trinity — the trinity of faith, as I shall term it — consists of a sacred being (Jahweh— Buddha),[45] a sacred Law (Torah—Dhamma), revealed by the sacred being, and a sacred community (Israel—Saṅgha), which, prescriptively, lives in accordance with the Law. In the case of Buddhism, the Buddha, His Law, and His Order of Monks (Saṅgha) are the 'Three Gems' in whom, daily, the Buddhist 'take(s) Refuge'. In Judaism, although there can be no god but God, 'God, Torah, and Israel', as the tradition has it, 'are one'.

In any salvation religion, certain types of action are prescribed as necessary, if not sufficient, for the achievement of its soteriological goal. Again, Judaism and Buddhism seem to share a common trinity of soteriologically oriented action, *viz.*, charity (*ṣedaḳah—dāna*), morality (*miṣwah—sīla*), and a form of intellectual activity—study or meditation (*talmud torah—bhāvanā*). For both, too, the latter type of action is the most important: for Buddhism, charity and morality are merely stages *en route* to *bhāvanā*; for Judaism, the study of Scripture is (as the Mishnah puts it) 'equal to all the other commandments combined'.

This structural similarity between these Judaic and Buddhist symbols seems to pose a serious challenge to that part of functionalist theory which maintains that there is some kind of 'fit' between religious ideology, on the one hand, and society or personality, on the other. Whether from a Weberian point of view, in which ideology influences behavior, or from Freudian, Manheimian, or Marxist points of view, in which ideology is a reflection, respectively, of unconscious conflict, social structure, or economic relations, it would not have been expected that

---

as, say, Roman Catholicism differs from Calvinist Protestantism. In the rest of this paper I shall use 'Buddhism' to refer to its *Theravādist* form exclusively.

45. In this, and in all subsequent contrasted pairs of concepts, the first is Judaic, the second Buddhist.

these structurally similar symbols would be found in communities that are so markedly different in social structure, motivational disposition, and cultural ethos. Whereas the *kibbutz* is achievement-, work-, and group-oriented, village Burma is characterized, on each of these variables, by its polar opposite: work is not an intrinsic value, achievement (including change) is not an important goal, and individual concerns take precedence over group values.

Upon closer inspection, however, this challenge to the functionalist thesis becomes somewhat less formidable. When the Buddhist and Judaic symbols are compared in terms of their cultural and psychological meanings, their structural similarities are seen to be more apparent than real, for such a comparison reveals that whereas there is almost no point at which the Buddhist symbols articulate with the secular social order (either to give it value, on the one hand, or to provide a fulcrum by which it can be changed, on the other), the homologous Judaic symbols make contact with the social order at almost every point. For purposes of brevity I shall examine this thesis only with respect to those symbols which comprise the trinity of faith of these two religions.

Jahweh—Buddha

As traditionally depicted, Jahweh represents activity; He is a world-creating being. The Buddha, by contrast, represents passivity; He is a contemplative, world-negating being. Compare, for example, Michelangelo's wrathful Moses — for Judaism, Moses and Jahweh are, on many attributes, almost interchangeable — with the blissful calm of the traditional Buddha image.

Jahweh is not only a world creator, He is a world transformer. He is a Redeemer, who intercedes in the world to change it. The Buddha, on the other hand, teaches the Way to redemption, but He himself does not redeem. His Way, moreover, emphasizes the renunciation of the world, not its transformation.

Concretely, Jahweh redeemed Israel from Egypt, and, after a long struggle with a harsh desert environment and with their own 'stubbornness', He brought them to the land of 'milk and honey' which, however, was acquired only through conquest. The Exodus, Sinai, and the Conquest of the Land comprise, jointly, the symbols of the nuclear historical experience of Judaism. This set of symbols implies (a) that suffering can be overcome in this world, for (b) the world is potentially good, but that (c) to overcome suffering and to make the world good requires struggle.

The Buddha is almost the mirror image of Jahweh. As the Prince Gautama, he had tasted from birth the 'milk and honey' of the royal court, only to reject it to become, in pursuit of Enlightenment, a wandering mendicant. It is the Buddha's renunciation of the world, and His ultimate attainment of Enlightenment which comprise the symbols of the nuclear historical experience of Buddhism. Milk and honey, this symbol set implies, (a) are an obstacle to be overcome, not a goal to be desired, for (b) though suffering can only be overcome by struggle, the struggle is not with impedimenta of the external world, but with one's own impulses (specifically, a 'clinging' (*tanhā*) to the world), and (c) the aim of this struggle is not to change the world, for since (as we shall see) suffering is an irreducible attribute of all sentient existence, such an aim is but yet another snare on the way to liberation. The aim, rather, is to transcend the seductions of the world by achieving a state of detachment. It is no accident, surely, that monastic asceticism, which has never found a place in normative Judaism — the Essenes were viewed as heretics — is the key institution of Buddhism.

These differences between the Buddha and Jahweh, it should be noted, are dramatically symbolized in their respective festivals. The important holy days of Judaism commemorate those events which comprise Israel's nuclear historical experience — the redemption from slavery, the revelation of the Commandments, and deliverance into the Promised Land. The important Buddhist holydays commemorate the Buddha's nuclear experiences — His renunciation of the world and His deliverance from the realm of desire and attachment. If, then, sacred beings are not merely objects of devotion, but if they are also models for emulation, then, the Buddha is a model for the denigration of (and retreat from) the world, while Jahweh is a model for valuing the world and for attempting to change it.

Torah-Dhamma

The Buddhist Teaching, or Law (Dhamma), stresses two themes: suffering and release from suffering. Since, according to Buddhism, suffering (*dukkha*) is one of the three essential attributes of sentient existence — the other two are impermanence and non-self — any attempt to change the world which is based on the assumption that suffering can thereby be eliminated is irrational. Not only can such attempts not succeed, but they have the opposite effect; they not only increase suffering by increasing attachment (*tanhā*) to the world (the ultimate cause of suffering), but such attachment, in turn, precludes the attainment of nirvana, the only goal whose attainment signals the extinction of suffering.

Although the Judaic Law (Torah) is not blind to the existence of suffering, it views the latter not as an inevitable attribute of existence — after creating the world, God surveyed His handiwork, and pronounced it as 'very good' — but as retribution for sin. By refraining from sin, i. e., by living in accordance with the Law, suffering can be avoided. Hence, according to the Prophets, if suffering is to be overcome, it is necessary to change the world in compliance with the Law. Since, then, life is basically (or, at least, potentially) good, to try to make of the world a place in which its goods can be experienced, is rational, not (as in Buddhism) irrational.

But this contrast between Torah and Dhamma can be drawn even more sharply. The laws of the Torah were given, as Jahweh told Israel, 'so that ye may live by them'. The Dhamma, on the contrary, was given so that (literally) one may die by them. Life, according to Buddhism, comprises an endless round of rebirths (all, from the lowest hell to the highest heaven, characterized by suffering), and the Law is the means by which the wheel of life can be brought to an end (through the achievement of nirvana).

In short, while the Dhamma stresses the rejection and transcendance of the world as a means to extinction of suffering, the Torah stresses the acceptance of the 'yoke of the Law' — which, in effect, means the changing of the world — as the means to that end.

This difference between these two religions is exemplified in the difference between the Jewish and Buddhist male initiation ceremonies. (Neither has a female initiation.) In Burma, the initiation (*shimbyu*) is a reenactment and commemoration of the Buddha's transformation from world-embracing prince to world-rejecting mendicant. In Judaism, the initiation (*bar misva*) signals the acceptance of the yoke of the Law, an ontogenetic recapitulation of a phylogenetic experience.

Israel—Saṅgha

The true Buddhist is the monk. The monastic community (Saṅgha) is an elite, consisting of those few who possess the necessary spiritual qualifications (*pāramitā*) to practice the Dhamma in its entirety, including the 227 regulations that comprise the monastic Rule (Vinaya). Distinguished from this elite is the great mass of laymen who are spiritually qualified to follow only the Five Precepts (to refrain from lying, killing, stealing, drunkenness, and sexual immorality). The layman can only hope that the piety exhibited in his present birth will enable him to acquire sufficient merit so that, in a future birth, he too will have the qualifications for admission to the monastic order.

For Judaism, all of Israel is the elite, all are the Chosen People. Hence, all must observe the 613 commandments of the Torah. None can be exempt from their hereditary elitist status — and hence from this responsibility — for all equally received the Commandments on Sinai. 'You only have I known of all the families of the earth', Jahweh warns, and, therefore, 'I will visit upon you all your iniquities'. Indeed, it is not far-fetched to argue that Israel is to the rest of mankind what the Saṅgha is to the Buddhist laity, for while all of Israel must observe the 613 commandments, the Gentiles need observe the seven Noachite laws only. (These include obedience to authority, reverence for the Divine Name, and abstinence from idolatry, incest, murder, robbery, and eating the flesh of a living animal.) This same theme is implicit in the prophetic notion of Israel as the Suffering Servant.

The comparison of the respective sacred communities of Buddhism and Judaism yields yet another important difference. In Buddhism neither laymen nor Saṅgha, whether separately or jointly, comprise a church, a corporate group. Even within the monastic order each monk (or, at any event, each monastery) is a law unto himself (or itself). This organizational feature of the Saṅgha parallels the ideological structure of Buddhism: each individual must seek his own salvation. As the Master stressed in a famous Sutta, monks must 'wander alone like the rhinoceros', or, as He put it in yet another metaphor, they must 'live as islands unto [themselves]'.

For Judaism, on the other hand, the sense of corporate identity and corporate responsibility is keen. Because of a mythical kin tie — all Israel are 'descendants of Abraham, Isaac, and Jacob' — and because of a corporate contract — they all entered into the covenant with God — 'All Israel', according to the Mishnah, 'is responsible one for the other'. Hence, in the liturgical confession of sins, it is not 'my' sins, but 'our' sins that are confessed; and it is not for 'my' sins, but for 'our' sins that punishment is due. This sense of corporate responsibility, moreover, perdures through historical time, the sins of the ancestors being visited upon their descendants even unto three generations.

The Soteriological Goal

Although there is no reason to expect a univocal relationship between means and ends — many different roads, as they say, can lead to Rome — it is, nevertheless, not surprising that the dramatic differences between the belief systems of Buddhism and Judaism should be associated with radically different notions of redemption. Although both religions postulate similar conditions of proximate salvation — rebirth into some heaven-like existence — they postulate radically different conditions of ultimate salvation.

For Buddhism ultimate salvation consists in nirvana which, whatever else it might connote — and scholars and laymen alike differ concerning its meaning — signals the end of the wheel of rebirth. Since all forms of existence entail suffering, salvation means deliverance from all thirty-one realms of existence. In addition to the existential meaning of Buddhist salvation, attention must also be directed to its exclusively individualistic meaning. Nirvana is individualistic in two senses: the individual is both the object of salvation — the individual alone can be saved — and the instrument of salvation — the individual must save himself.

For Judaism, ultimate salvation consists in the attainment of the Kingdom of God, which is achieved, with the Messianic Coming, at the End of Days. Unlike the Buddhist case, however, salvation does not entail transcendence of the physical and social worlds as we know them, but, rather, in their transformation. In the words of the Prophet, the lion lies down with the lamb, the crooked is made straight, the people are comforted. It will be noted, moreover, that unlike the individualistic character of Buddhist salvation, that of Judaism is corporate. It is the group, Israel, that is saved, and it is the group, by its collective acceptance of the yoke of the Law, that is the instrument of salvation.

For Buddhism, then, salvation, (a) is individualistic, and (b) it consists in the transcendence of the world such that the normal and recognizable ethical, social, and political — not to mention physical and biological — categories are rendered non-existent. For Judaism, salvation (a) is collective, and (b) it consists in the transformation, rather than the transcendence, of the socio-political world within the known spatio-temporal world (however much the latter might be modified).

SACRED SYMBOLS AND SOCIAL BEHAVIOR

Thus far, I have attempted to show that there are differences between Buddhist and Judaic soteriologies, that each of these soteriologies is associated with a set of three sacred symbols (a sacred being, a sacred law, and a sacred community) which, though structurally isomorphic, are semantically dissimilar. Although I have only touched the tip of the symbolic iceberg, I shall forego the temptation to explore the other dimensions of these sacred symbols, and, instead, ask yet another question of them. Do these symbols essentially reflect the nature of the human mind? (Which, if such were the case, would suggest that the mind, unlike the claims of some linguistically oriented structuralists, operates not only according to binary oppositions, but also triadic complementaries.) And, if this question were to be answered in the affirmative, are such symbols created, as Lévi-Strauss once suggested about totemic symbols, because they are good to think, in splendid isolation from any social context? Although such hypotheses are very much in vogue today, no student, however, of either the Burmese or the Jews could entertain these hypotheses for long. Even ignoring the symbolic sets we have been examining — which, if space permitted, could be shown to be related to certain common dimensions of Jewish and Buddhist social life — the semantic differences in the individual symbols would alone infirm these hypotheses. These differences can be shown to be systematically related to differences in ethos and behavior found in village Burma and the Israeli *kibbutz*. To be sure, the explanations for these relationships are moot. Thus, some theorists would argue that the relationships are causal, although they would disagree about the direction of causality (one group contending that the ideas are prior, the other that the societal forms are prior). Since I wish to avoid such controversies

— my own view, which is different from both, may be found in my two books on Burmese religion — I am content to observe that such relationships do in fact exist, and that these religious concepts serve to express (and perhaps to sustain) the basic components of the ethos of each culture.

Thus, the Buddhist symbol set, which denigrates the sociocultural world, which emphasizes the renunciation of the politico-economic world, and which aims at the transcendence of the spatio-temporal world is found in a society (Burma) which places little value on social and economic change, on achievement values, or on corporate responsibility; in a society whose cynosure is the world-renouncing monk, and whose ideal is the *arhant*, the individual who, oblivious to the suffering of others, seeks and attains salvation for himself.

The Judaic model which values the sociocultural world, and which emphasizes the transformation of the politico-economic world, is found in a society (the *kibbutz*) which places great value on social and economic revolution, on achievement, and on group responsibility; in a society whose cynosure and ideal alike is the *halutz*, whose personal goals are subordinate to, and who sacrifices his needs for, the transformation of society.

Needless to say, I am not concerned here with evaluating the relative merits of these different religious orientations and their social concommitants, nor, *qua* anthropologist, am I qualified to do so. I am even less concerned with evaluating the different character types that are associated with these different orientations, especially since both are the products of social and individual histories over which social actors have little if any responsibility. I would like instead to make two additional observations concerning the relationship between religious symbols and social behavior. The first is stimulated by a contrast between Buddhism and Judaism, the second by their similarity.

RELIGIOUS SYMBOLS AND SOCIAL BEHAVIOR

I have already observed that the conceptions of ultimate salvation found in Judaism and Buddhism are found side by side with entirely different conceptions of proximate salvation. In both cases, moreover — and this is more important — the latter conceptions have usually been the more strongly cathected by the religious actors. If, as has often been the case, this latter fact is ignored, we are led not only to a distorted conception of the salient beliefs of the religious actors, but to a misleading interpretation of the relationship between religious symbols and social action.

For Buddhism, proximate salvation consists in rebirth in any of the many material paradises — the abodes of the *devas* — and, as all anthropological fieldwork in contemporary Buddhist societies has revealed, it is this form of salvation that the majority of their members most strongly desire. For although the aspiration for nirvana is reiterated by the average Buddhist in ritual formulae, the latter goal is for him more a cultural cliché than a personal motive; his *summum bonum* consists not in the extinction of desire, but in its satisfaction. And if rebirth in a heavenly abode is viewed as beyond his reach, he is happy to settle for rebirth as a wealthy and high status citizen of this planet, preferably of his present society. The Buddhist's preference for proximate salvation does not, however, require any changes in the semantics of the soteriological symbols discussed above. Moreover, the soteriological mechanism remains the same. Whether salvation is viewed in ultimate or proximate terms, it is achieved as the consequence of the impersonal law of karma, whose working is exclusively affected by individual action, and by the merit and demerit which such action produces.

For Judaism, too, it is a heavenly existence which constitutes proximate salvation, and although the End of Days occupies a central place in Jewish liturgy, the post-Exilic belief in an afterlife has been at least equally important in the soteriological concerns of post-Exilic and Diaspora Jewry. As in the case of Buddhism, this emphasis on proximate salvation requires little change in the semantics of the soteriological symbols of Judaism. It does, however, signal a change in the object of salvation from a corporate to an individualistic orientation. It is individual, not group, action which determines one's fate in the afterlife, and it is the individual, not the group, that is rewarded (or punished). The mechanism of salvation, however, is the same in both, salvation being achieved not by means of a karma-like mechanism, but by means of divine intercession. Whether from justice or mercy, God is influenced by human action to establish His Kingdom on earth (ultimate salvation), or to send the individual to His heavenly abode (proximate salvation).

In this connection, there are two psychologically interesting and historically significant aspects of the soteriology of the Eastern European founders of the kibbutz. The first aspect, already alluded to, is the restoration of corporate redemption to its pre-Exilic place of centrality. This reversal, it should be noted, occurred not only in the kibbutz movement, but it occurred much earlier in the non-socialist Zionist movement of Eastern and Central Europe, as well as in the theology of Western European Reform Judaism. Whereas the kibbutz founders, however, placed equal stress on both the parochial (Jewish) and universal (international socialist) dimensions of the Messianic Days, General Zionism stressed its parochial dimension, and Reform Judaism its universal dimension. With respect to the theoretical concern of this paper, *viz.*, the relationship between religious symbols and social action, this example illustrates the elementary principle that man manipulates his cultural symbols to serve his own needs. Man is as much the master, as the servant, of his cultural symbols.

Judaism and Buddhism, surely, are not the only religions in which alternative and even conflicting symbol systems exist side-by-side, and their differential appeal in different historical epochs, or to different social groups within the same historical epoch, remains a little-explored area of inquiry in religious research. Since these alternative symbol systems are equally normative, it seems not unlikely that their differential appeal might be explained by their differential cathexis by the social actors, in short, by their personality differences. But since in any society (especially if it constitutes a relatively endogamous breeding population), personality differences (either among its sub-groups or its historical epochs) are a function of differences in social conditions and their attendant cognitive and affective consequences, these personality differences are, in turn, related to sociological differences. Since it would take us too far afield, however, to examine the possible sociological conditions that contributed to the renewed emphasis on corporate soteriology in nineteenth and early twentieth century Judaism, I shall only observe that it is another illustration of the thesis that religious symbols, no less than any others, do not spring Athena-like from the human mind; rather, they emerge from concrete social experiences which act upon the mind and influence its activity.

A second important aspect of the soteriology of the founders of the kibbutz is the elimination of divine intercession for the achievement of the soteriological goal. Kibbutz ideology, as I have already mentioned, is based on a thoroughly naturalistic metaphysics. As in the case of Buddhism, the soteriological aspirations of the kibbutz — if I may use a religious concept to characterize a secular belief system — are achieved by human action alone; its consequences, however, are not deemed to be governed by the law of karma, but by the laws of sociology and history. Although space, again, does not permit an examination of the conditions that might possibly produce such thoroughgoing naturalism, this aspect of kibbutz soteriology — the absence of divine intercession — leads to the final section of this paper.

CHERCHER LA FEMME

Buddhism and Judaism not only share a common trinity of formal soteriological symbols — a sacred person, a sacred law, and a sacred group — but these symbols share a common attribute — none of them is feminine. To be sure, it can be argued — and empirical support can be adduced for such an argument — that feminist elements have been bootlegged into both Buddhism and Judaism in the unconscious meanings of some of their other symbols. Nevertheless, at the level of their formal and conscious meanings, their symbols, including those that have been examined in this paper, are primarily (Judaism) if not exclusively (Buddhism) masculine. I say 'primarily' in the case of Judaism because Israel may be viewed as a combined male and female symbol since its empirical referent, the people of Israel, includes both males and females. Even this statement, however, must be qualified by the observation that the female component in the symbol, Israel, is only physically, but not ritually or jurally, relevant. God's covenant with Israel, which is the jural basis for its status as a sacred people, is renewed in, and symbolized by, the circumcision ritual, which is performed for males alone. That, nevertheless, physical membership in the group is determined by the mother — by Talmudic law, the child of a Jewish father and a non-Jewish mother is not a Jew — is one of those paradoxes which might be variously resolved by structuralist, psychoanalytic, and other theories which delight in paradox. Ritually, too, Israel is essentially a masculine symbol in that, traditionally, Jewish congregational worship requires a quorum of ten adult males. Although females, like minors, may participate in the worship, they may not be counted in the quorum.

Buddhism is even more exclusively masculine in its symbolism than Judaism. Not only is the historical Buddha, Gautama, a male, but all previous Buddhas have also been, and all future Buddhas will also be, males. Buddhahood can be attained only in a masculine form. The Saṅgha, too, is an exclusively male institution. In Judaism the physical Israel, at least, includes both sexes, even though jurally and ritually females are peripheral members. This is not the case even with respect to the physical Saṅgha. To be sure, in early Buddhism, females were permitted to become monks — over the objection, it should be noted, of the Buddha — but after a few short years they were, and they have continued to be, excluded from the order. A woman's aspiration to the monkhood must be deferred until her future rebirth as a male.

To summarize, then, Judaism and Buddhism alike are characterized by a pervasive and systematic exclusion of females and feminine symbols from soteriological, devotional, and liturgical significance. On this dimension Buddhism and Judaism may not only be classified together, but (among the great religions) they are members of a class which includes Islam, Confucianism and Protestantism, and which excludes Hinduism and Catholicism. Like Buddhism and Judaism, the latter two religions are also characterized by a soteriological trinity, but, unlike the former, they include an important feminine component. Now, of course, just as Lévi-Strauss and the structuralists can always find binary oppositions, so too I can be charged with always finding trinities. In each of these cases, however, the trinity was not discovered by fancy intellectual methods; rather trinities are enunciated by the social actors themselves, and the problem consists in deciding which, among alternative trinities, is most germane to the present discussion. Thus, for example, both Hinduism and Catholicism exhibit one type of trinity which is isomorphic with that of Judaism and Buddhism: a sacred being (Brahma and God), a sacred law (Dharma and the teachings of the Church), and a sacred group (Varna and the Church). Unanalyzed, these trinities are as exclusively masculine as their Judaic and Buddhist counterparts. But the Hindu 'Brahma' and the Catholic 'God', it will be recalled, are generic terms, best glossed as 'divinity' or 'godhead', each of which, depending on the interpretation, comprises three component deities or aspects of the godhead.

These divine trinities are, of course, well known. The Hindu trinity consists of Vishnu, Shiva, and one of the forms taken by the feminine principle — Sakte — variously conceived as Parvati, Kali, or Durga. The Catholic trinity consists of God, Christ, and the Virgin Mary. In Catholic theology, to be sure, the Trinity refers to the triune God — Father, Son, and Holy Spirit. To the anthropologist, however, who follows the lead of the religious actor and his devotional concerns, the third member is not the Holy Spirit, but the Holy Virgin.

Now the difference between the presence or absence of a feminine symbol within the set of sacred symbols of a religion is not, I need emphasize, a trivial difference; and it certainly involves much more than a cognitive preference or lack of preference for binary oppositions (the opposition, in this case, of male and female). For, although I have thus far used the abstract concept, 'feminine', in referring to the Virgin and Parvati, neither, as is well known, represents a generically conceived, abstract, female principle. Rather, both represent a specific type of female, and that type is not wife, or sister, or daughter, or aunt, but Mother. Both are expressly referred to as Mother. The difference, then, between the absence of a sacred female symbol in Judaism and Buddhism (as well as in Islam, Protestantism and Confucianism), on the one hand, and its presence in Catholicism and Hinduism, on the other, is the difference between the presence or absence of a Mother Goddess. And this difference, in turn, is related, on the one hand, to the general importance of familial symbols within the sacred symbol system, and to the role of women in the secular domain, on the other.

Of the four religions we are considering here, Buddhism has most systematically expunged all familial symbols from its sacred symbol system. It not only excludes all mother symbols, but it also excludes all father symbols. The Buddha is a male, but he is never designated as father. Judaism, too, excludes all mother symbols — though the prophets had to fight a long battle before the various Astartes were expunged from the religious life of the ancient Hebrews — but the Jewish God is an expressly conceived father symbol, as is the God of Islam and Protestantism. Hinduism, on the other hand, includes both father and mother symbols. With respect to the latter it might also be observed that the mother symbol is not restricted to the Goddess, for we can hardly ignore the symbolism of Mother India or of the sacred cow. It should also be added that in the form of baby Krishna, Hinduism, like Catholicism, includes the sacred child symbol — and why is the child a son rather than a daughter? — although father, mother, and son are not integrated to form one sacred family. Family symbolism, of course, is most pervasive in Catholicism. Not only does the earthly family find its isomorphic representation in the Divine Family of Father, Mother, and Son, but the priest is 'father', the nun is 'sister', and the Church (as well as the nun) is a 'bride' (the Bride of Christ), and so on.

Now to pursue all the ramifications of the conceptual, not to mention the soteriological, differences in the sacred symbols of these religions would require a monograph. Here, I am interested only in the presence or absence of the Mother symbol. Since all human beings have mothers, why is this symbol such a salient feature in some religions, absent in others, and almost phobically avoided in still others? It is in their different answers to this type of question that contemporary symbolic approaches differ from functionalist approaches to the study of religion. The various symbolic approaches would attempt to answer this question by reference to the semantics, or syntax, or grammar of the symbol systems themselves, while the various functionalist approaches would look outside of the symbol systems for an explanation. A functionalist cannot ignore the obvious correlations, for example, between the following array of variables in India and China, respectively. The worship of mother goddesses in India is associated with an almost obsessive concern with the mother, the sacredness of the cow, the dietary importance of milk and milk products, the voluptuousness of sacred female iconography, and the heavy-breasted woman. The lesser importance of mother goddesses in China, on the other hand, is associated with the relative unimportance of the mother, the lack of concern with the cow, the rejection of milk and milk products, the absence of female iconography, and the flat-chested woman. Given what we know today about population genetics and the influence of cultural factors on biological selection, the possibility of a systematic relationship among these social, cultural and biological variables is not as farfetched as it might seem.

But these correlations do not provide an explanation for the difference between the presence or absence of mother symbols in different religions. Rather, they provide a broader context or frame in which such symbols are to be viewed, and their systematic covariation with a wide array of variables suggests to a functionalist that differences in symbols and symbol systems are best explained by differences in the social systems in which they are embedded and from which, *ex hypothesi*, they arise and derive their meaning. He would point, for example, to differences in cultural attitudes to sex, in the social status of women, in the roles of women as wives and mothers, and, if he is psychoanalytically oriented, to differences in the parent-child relationship and, especially, to the variable vicissitudes of the Oedipus complex.

On the basis of my own work in Buddhist Burma, I would suggest that the presence or absence of the mother goddess is systematically related to two feminine roles, those of mother and of wife, and to the differences in a single dimension of each of these roles, *viz.*, the nurturance dimension of the mother role and the dominance dimension of the wife role. Although preliminary research (to be published separately) supports this

Table 1. *The relationship between the presence or absence of mother goddesses and certain female roles*

	mother	wife
India	+	−
Catholicism (Italy)	+	−
Ceylon	+	−
Burma	+	+
Israel	+	+
Islam (Arab)	−	−
China	−	−
Calvinism (Reformation)	−	−

Key: mother: + = high nurturance
  − = low nurturance

   wife: + = high dominance
    − = low dominance

hypothesis, for our present purposes the specific empirical findings are less important than the assumption underlying its construction, *viz.*, religious symbols — and cultural symbols in general — though created by the human mind, do not arise from a mental *tabula rasa*. Although they are elaborated by philosophical thought, and infused with theological and metaphysical meaning, these symbols are ultimately the products of individual fantasies which are produced by (and therefore vary with) different types of social experience. Like private symbols they serve to express certain aspirations and needs which arise from such experience, to resolve the conflicts that are induced by the experience, and to integrate them in a manner which renders them existentially meaningful. For religious actors, religious symbols are created not only to think by, but also — and much more important — to live by. As *cultural* symbols, religious symbols, of course, have social, as well as psychological and existential functions, but the latter (important as they are) are not the concern of this paper.

Commentary   by Horst Cain

I found the task of commenting on Professor Spiro's paper an extremely difficult one, for several reasons. Firstly, I do not feel myself particularly competent to judge the empirical material dealt with in this paper, and secondly I had relatively little time to come to grips with it properly. Please do not expect from me, therefore, that I should speak about every point in this very exacting and stimulating text, for I shall concentrate on those points on which I think I have something to say.

In this paper Prof. Spiro is particularly concerned to demonstrate the functionality of religious symbols and symbol systems, and I would like to come straight to the main point. He fixes his starting point when he says: 'From our point of view religion is a cultural system', and I would be entirely in agreement with this, if the term 'religion' referred to the system of cultic and ritual forms and activities; but not if it also at the same time incorporates the ground or basis of that religion — what Rudolf Otto calls the experience of the numinous. Precisely this, however, appears to be the case. This is entirely clear from the fact that

Prof. Spiro describes the numen, i. e. Jahweh, as a symbol, and from the following sentence: 'The social functions of a symbol system largely depend on their cognitive meaning and the meanings which symbol systems have for social actors derive from and are related to the social context'. In order to make it clear where I agree with Prof. Spiro and where I disagree, I would like to explain what I understand by a religious symbol. The process of symbolization requires three factors: (1) a subject, which — because of its experience of the numinous, that evades its immediate grasp — searches for a suitable means to make access to the numinous and communication about it possible; (2) the means itself, which is derived from the world of sensory experience immediately available to the subject, and is found adequate on the basis of its cultural value to achieve the end in question; and (3) an object, whose reality the subject knows about, and in fact has an inescapable relation to, but which in an inexplicable manner resists incorporation into sensory, experiential reality. The pattern is thus as follows: man, as the symbolizing subject; the symbol; and the numen, as the object symbolized. The religious symbol is consequently the point of contact between two levels, i.e. between that of sensory perception (from which it originates), and that of the numinous (towards which it is directed, and which it mediates). This concept of mine of the symbol corresponds to that held by a whole range of other scholars. There is a definition in W. M. Urban, for example, which I cite from Shulamith Kreitler, which corresponds approximately to mine; I refer to the kind of symbols which he calls 'insight symbols', and which are a vehicle or medium of insight. For Urban, symbols are 'Objekte der Einheiten, der Welt der unmittelbaren sinnlichen Anschauungen entnommen und auf nicht anschauliche Objekte angewandt'. My conception also agrees with that of Prof. Goldammer, who writes in his book *Formenwelt des Religiösen* as follows (p. 286): 'Man kann nahezu alle Ausdrucks- und Gestaltungsformen der Religion und sogar ihre verschiedenen heiligen Gestalten als Symbole auffassen, insofern als die "weltliche" irdische Vermittler von etwas "Überweltlichem", begrenzte und endliche Aussagen von etwas Unbegrenztem und Unendlichem sind. Damit kann man schliesslich die ganze Religion als etwas Symbolisches begreifen, da sie in gleichsam indirekter Weise das ausdrückt und formt, was direkt nicht ausgedrückt und gestaltet werden kann. ... Bei der Verwendung des Wortes "Symbol" sollte man sich aber doch wenigstens soweit beschränken, dass man darunter im allgemeinen nur optisch wahrnehmbare, im weiteren Sinne dann auch in der Sprache verwendete Bilder und Zeichen aus der Welt der Formen und Farben und aus dem Bereich des Gegenständlichen überhaupt versteht, Dinge also, die durch den Menschen irgendwie gestaltet worden sind und auch der Gestaltung fähig sind.'

Prof. Koskinen writes, in his *Linking of Symbols* (Vol. II, p. 7): 'Symbols are regarded as a group of elements of communication between human beings. Through a perception individuals have become conscious of different real and fancied things: symbols are the means used to make others turn their interest to the same things. Roughly speaking, there are three groups of things communicated by symbols: phenomena, manifestations, and views concerning both of these.' Susanne Langer also, in my opinion, gets the character of a religious symbol right when she writes: 'Rites of supplication and offering cannot forever be addressed to a nameless symbol, a mere bundle of sticks, jaw-bone, gravemound, or monolith. The Holy One has a part, howbeit a silent part, to play in the ceremony...' (p. 132, Mentor edition).

In order not to prolong the list endlessly, since the choice is in any case arbitrary, let me finish by quoting what van der Leeuw says about religious symbols in his *Phänomenologie*: 'Das Heilige muss eine Gestalt haben, es muss "statthaft" werden, räumlich, zeitlich, sicht- oder hörbar. Noch einfacher: das Heilige muss "stattfinden". ... Ein Symbol nämlich ist keineswegs ... etwas Unwesentliches, sondern vielmehr das Zusammentreffen (συμ-βάλλειν) von Möglichkeit und Gegebenheit, von Geschehen und "Stattfinden", von Profanität und Heiligkeit' (p. 510).

What I want to say with all of this is that the religious symbol serves to link two levels of reality which confront man, one of which can only become accessible, as it were, by means of symbols. The sentence already quoted from Prof. Spiro, however, according to which not only religious symbols, but also their meanings, are derived from the social context of social activity, indicates to me that for him both the symbolizing subject and the object symbolized belong to the same level of experience, i.e. the cultural. At the beginning of his paper he says that religious symbols incorporate ideas, which I understand to mean that they serve to hypostasize the products of human thought on the basis of, and as a result of, cultural experience, as the author explicitly states at the end of his discussion. In this concrete case this applies to the idea of redemption or salvation, which emerged as a reaction to the sufferings of the world both in Buddhism and in Judaism, with the aim in the former of overcoming the world, and in the latter of changing the world for the better. In each case, however, it was the dissatisfaction of man with the world that was the cause for the emergence of the idea of redemption. No further comment is required to show that for Prof. Spiro the entire process takes place on the same level, i. e. in the concrete sensory world of man. Seen in this way, the process of symbolization is not an attempt by man to objectivate the level of the numinous, experienced existentially and grasped intuitively, so as to make it conceivable and communicable, but the projection of human ideas and ideals into a superior world, which would then have the function of establishing validity for these ideas and ideals through a kind of feedback effect. Whereas Prof. Spiro can in this way thus describe Jahweh without more ado as a soteriological symbol, this would only be acceptable to me (if at all) in the sense that as a name and a person he serves to make the numinous understandable. The *tertium quid* would however be the numen, and not a human idea.

As I said, I do not feel myself called to go into detail on the empirical material; nevertheless, I was unable to find, in the descriptions of Jahweh which I was able to consult, that either pious Jews or the scholarly literature conceives of Jahweh as a symbol. On the contrary, what I have found, for example in Heiler's introduction to the collection of essays *Die Religionen der Menschheit*, are examples of how Jahweh himself was symbolized, for instance by a rock (Ps. 18:2; see Heiler, p. 16) or fire (see Heiler, p. 17). Since man is tied to his language and culture, it is only logical that he should take names and epithets from his natural and cultural environment and attribute them to the numen, and that symbols are necessarily drawn from these. But that does not mean that religious symbols are merely being used to project social reality into a superior world in order to stabilize this reality by means of the fictive authority thus gained; they stand for the numen, which is just as real as the world of sensory perception, and on which man feels himself to be dependent. Religious symbols have therefore in my view the function of objectivizing, or perhaps rather of materializing, the numen, and religion in general the function of ordering man's relationship with it in harmony with historical and social experience and conditions. Religious systems are men's varied reactions to an unchanging situation. They are the expression of a feeling of dependence on a power outside

ourselves, as Radcliffe-Brown states at the beginning of his lecture on
'Religion and Society' (p. 157). When Prof. Spiro says at the end of his
paper that religious symbols are 'the result of individual fantasy produced by certain types of social experiences which function to express
and resolve the psychological conflicts and needs which arise from these
experiences', this stands in opposition to the opinion which I have
here put forward, since I trace the origin of these symbols back not to
social experiences but to primary religious experiences, even though
these can of necessity only express themselves in a culture-bound manner. Furthermore, I cannot see the three phenomena of 'sacred being',
'sacred law', and 'sacred community' as symbols. For Prof. Spiro these
are symbols of redemption; for me they are the numen itself: Jahweh
(I shall come back to Buddha later); the Torah and the Dhamma, as
fully concrete means of redemption; and the equally concrete object
of redemption, Israel and Sangha. With reference to Dhamma, von
Glasenapp also speaks of a means of redemption, and even Prof. Spiro
describes it as such. Nor does the historical personality of Buddha seem
to me to be a very appropriate symbol of redemption. He was a man,
who attained enlightenment, and who handed on his perception to
others in the form of teachings. He may be a model, or an example,
therefore, but not a symbol. Even if he were seen, like Jahweh, as
numen, he could not be described as a symbol, since he would then
himself require symbolization in order to be comprehensible to man.
For this process, I consider that the *triratna* could serve as a symbol of
the trinity of Buddha, Dhamma, and Sangha; that is to say, the three
precious stones are symbols, but not vice versa. It must be questioned
at this point whether all the trinities which Prof. Spiro expounds in
Judaism and Buddhism really are homologous in all their constituents,
as he postulates. To put it in concrete terms: is Buddha the pendant to
Jahweh? I doubt it. Frick, for example, put Buddha as homologous to
Jesus and Mohammed, and if we apply this here, then Buddha would
be the pendant of Moses, not of Jahweh. Von Glasenapp also compares
Buddha with Zarathustra, Mahavira, Jesus, Mohammed, and others. I am
not able to decide here whether this homology holds good, but the
resemblance between the functions of Buddha and Moses is very striking.
Both of them transmit the Law, but do not originate it. Without going
further into this matter here, I would like to question whether the
homologies between Buddha and Brahma, Jahweh and Brahma, and in

fact all the homologies in the paper are not somewhat problematical.

I must also allude to the lack of congruence between the symbols of the 'nuclear historical experiences'. Exodus, Sinai, and the conquest of the Land of Milk and Honey are historical experiences for Israel, i.e. for the holy community; whereas in Buddhism, milk and honey, rejection of the world and illumination, are historical experiences of the holy being, not of the Sangha. In his comparison of the holy communities of Israel and the Sangha, Prof. Spiro says that Israel is to the rest of the world as the Sangha is to the Buddhist laity. It must be pointed out that this parallel also contains a problem, in that the relation between the Sangha and the laity exists within Buddhism, and is acknowledged by both sides, whereas the relation between Israel and the rest of the world reaches beyond the frontiers of Judaism, and is certainly not seen by the rest of the world in the same way.

Prof. Spiro's characterization of the different conceptions of redemption, and of the ideology underlying them, is, in my opinion, very accurate: oriented towards individualism, and overcoming the world, in Buddhism, and towards corporatism, and improvement of the world, in Judaism. However, it does not seem to me to be correct, with respect to the individual and the group as the respective objects of redemption, to speak at the same time of instruments of redemption, as the author does. It seems to me to be more justified to speak in this context of the coincidence of the subject and the object, while I would describe the instrument of redemption as the Law.

Apart from the use of the concept of religious symbols, which is in my opinion not valid, the presentation of the conditions in Buddhism and Judaism seems to me to be entirely valid, so far as I can judge. With respect to the relation between social activity and religious symbols, however, the standpoint which I hold leads one to different findings. Man is certainly the master of his symbols, for he creates them himself. But is he their servant? I do not think so, for I do not believe that the phenomena which Prof. Spiro expounds as the 'trinity of faith' is a symbol, as I have explained. The cultural traces inherent in them reflect the value scales of the respective social groups, and are the expression of devotion in the face of the numen. The Law governs men's relations with the numen and with each other, from which they cannot free themselves. There is nothing surprising about the fact that the epithets and symbols for the numen change, since they originate in the cultural value system, which is in its turn subject to constant change. But this does not mean that man can fundamentally change the numinous reality or his relation of dependence on it.

What I have so far said about religious symbols also applies to the question of the evaluation of woman and the mother. The hypothesis which Prof. Spiro expounds on the basis of empirical data seems to me to be extremely interesting, and worthy of attention, though I do not have the necessary expert knowledge to be able to go into it in detail. What I would finally like to add is that once again here the varied evaluation of woman and the mother in different cultures has led either to their being felt to be an adequate symbol for the numinous, and used for this, or to their being rejected as unsuitable for this; but not vice versa. The reasons for the variations in evaluation are no doubt very complex, and cannot be discussed here.

Commentary   by Hans H. Penner

I believe it is an empirical fact that Professor Spiro is the leading American anthropologist in the study of religion. His articles and books are required reading for most students interested in religion regardless of whether they are professional anthropologists or not. His publications from the very beginning have sustained a rigorous intellectual interest in both theoretical and observational detail regarding religion. The paper he has written for our discussion continues to reflect this interest. It also attempts to provide a mediation between a contemporary conflict in the study of religion; the opposition between functionalist and symbolist approaches to culture and religion.

My comments will be divided into three parts. The first will examine Spiro's trinities and will attempt to show the arbitrariness of this approach. The second part will show that certain distortions of symbols take place because of arbitrariness. The third part will focus on the theory imbedded in Spiro's analysis of wives, mothers and goddesses.

The trinities which Spiro presents are far from outrageous. They can be found in most texts which describe world religions. In fact, they have led many comparativists to the conclusion that most world religions are variations on the same metaphysical principle. This approach and its *Zeitgeist* also seems to be out of fashion along with functionalism. The trinities, or, basic symbols, in other traditions are obvious. Beginning with Spiro's triads of faith and using his basic categories, or, ideal types we can construct the following list:

Religion	Sacred Being	Sacred Teaching (law)	Sacred Community
Judaism	Jahweh	Torah	Israel
Buddhism	Buddha	Dhamma	Sangha
Christianity	God	Bible	Ecclesia
Islam	Allah	Koran	Umma
Hinduism	Brahman	Veda	Ashrama/Varna
Zoroastrianism	Ahura Mazdah	Avesta	Mazdayasni

If we add a fourth category, the founder, to our list we discover that basic symbol systems are neither binary nor trinitarian, but quartets; add Moses, Gautama, Christ, Mohammed, Rishi/Guru, Zarathustra, as a fourth column. These quartets could in turn be reduced to a binary structure and a fifth category (e. g. either ultimate or proximate salvation) could lead to a meditation of the contraries. And I suppose that a committed symbolist might try to convince Spiro that his trinity is really a binary structure; sacred being and sacred community mediated by sacred law, or founder and law.

Of course, all of this is quite arbitrary. This is not to say that either Spiro or symbolists create their structures or types out of nothing. They all appeal to concrete, empirical data as the basic referent. The arbitrariness is to be found in the choice or 'fit' of each of the symbols. This can be seen very clearly, for example, when we compare the basic symbols Israel/Sangha or, Jahweh/Buddha. Here the similarities are more apparent than real and the analysis which would disclose the discrepancies would certainly not need to examine the social or psychological context in which they are imbedded.

The same arbitrariness can be shown with regard to types of action which are necessary in order to achieve a soteriological goal. For example, *karuna* (compassion), *sila* (morality) and *dhyana* (meditation) might be more accurate for the Buddhist triad for soteriologically oriented action. Of course, the Four Holy Truths stand out as the most obvious prescription for action and the path for practice is eightfold.

The Buddhist tradition also gives us a different set of symbols to work with regarding the Buddhist layman's soteriological goal. The goal, of course, is *sarga* (heaven), not *samadhi* (enlightenment), and the trinity of action could be described as, *dana* (donation), *sila* (virtue) and *sarga* (heaven). This trinity can be found in the Tripitaka and is confirmed in Spiro's work in Buddhist Burma.

It should now become clear that our choice of basic symbols can become as simple or complex as we wish them to be. We may want to follow Weberian typologies, Jungian archetypes, or Eliadian patterns. All are very useful, heuristically, for moving on to what we want to say about religion. However, if someone told me that he was studying two religions which involved a founder and a soteriology I would expect that each religion would have something to say about (1) the founder, (2) the goal and (3) how to get there. I suspect, however, that symbolists are after something that is not quite so self-evident.

The symbolic approach seems to be in need of a theory which will prevent it from remaining arbitrary, or, explaining in more complex terms what is already obvious. Perhaps contemporary developments in theoretical linguistics will help point out the directions we might wish to explore. For example, verb phrases, or, noun phrases do not have the syntactic ambiguity of Israel/Sangha, or Jahweh/Buddha.

Lacking a well formed theory the symbolic approach can often lead to distortions. Space does not allow for a complete analysis of Spiro's interpretation of the symbols. However, I wish to make a few brief comments on his interpretation of the Buddhist 'trinity of faith'. Spiro's analysis seems to follow the typology of 'world affirming/world negating' religions, or 'this-wordly asceticism/other-wordly asceticism'. If I am not mistaken, these two types become the basis for his interpretations of the two sets of trinities, that is to say, they are not inherent in the symbol systems.

This conference is on methodology and I do not want to re-direct our session into a discussion on the Buddhist tradition. I do wish to point out very briefly that it has become part of our ordinary language to describe Buddhism as 'world-negating', and 'world-transcending'. Spiro sums up this point of view by stating, 'that there is no point at which the Buddhist symbols articulate with the *secular* social order' (italics mine). It is taking a long time to overcome this point of view, in spite of complete translations of the Tripitaka, excellent scholarship, and field work (and here I would include Spiro's recent work *Buddhism and Society*).

I submit that the above interpretation is a distortion of the tradition. It can be falsified by an examination of the Theravada Canon; especially those sutras which contain Buddha's teaching to the laity. The teaching on property, wealth, trade, human relationships and the family make for a startling discovery concerning Buddhism and Society. These sutras together with the actual practice of Buddhism in Southeast Asia help us refute the view that Buddhist thought and symbol is concerned with renunciation, asceticism, other-worldliness and the irrelevance of social problems. In brief, according to Buddhism, if suffering is to be overcome, it is necessary to change the world in compliance with *Dhamma*; 'life is basically (or, at least potentially) good, to try to make of the world a place in which its goods can be experienced is rational'. If we need a concrete, actual example for this proposition I would submit the names of U Thant and U Nu — Burmese by birth and practicing Buddhists.

Time does not allow me to make further comments on the semantics of the trinity of faith in Judaism. If I had the opportunity I would probably enter into the discussion with the following reflection: Are 'traditional Judaism', the israeli *kibbutz*, and 'the protestant ethic' equivalent both structurally and semantically?

I will now turn to a few comments on what I belief is the main issue in the paper before us. In order to do this I must pass the fascinating hypothesis concerning mother goddesses and female roles in different societies. Prof. Spiro directs us toward the main issue by stating that, 'For our present purposes, the results of the empirical test are less important than the theory underlying the attempt, *viz.*, that religious symbols, though created by the human mind, do not arise from a mental *tabula rasa*. Rather, they are the result of individual fantasy, produced by certain types of social experiences — although they are later elaborated by philosophical and theological thought — which function to express and resolve the psychological conflicts and needs which arise from these experiences'.

The theory is obviously functional and its thesis can also be found in his brief answers to the controversy regarding the 'direction of causality' which Spiro raises earlier.

The question which arises is, how do we explain both the differences and the persistence of religious symbols (or any other symbol structure)? The question is causal, and functional theory has always been offered as a causal answer or explanation to the question.

In two of the three places where this theoretical issue is raised, we find that the alternative or opposition symbolist position is a mental *tabula rasa*. ('Symbols do not spring Athena-like from the human mind', 'religious symbols ... do not arise from a mental *tabula rasa*'.) Before entering the functional theory itself, it may be appropriate to request information on who these symbolists are? What symbolist approach begins with the notion that symbols arise from a mental *tabula rasa*, or, spring 'Athena-like' from the mind?

If I understand Spiro's theory, symbol systems 'arise from', are 'produced' (i.e. caused) by certain types of social experiences. The symbols function to both express and resolve conflicts and needs which arise from these experiences. Furthermore, they (the symbols) derive their meaning (semantics) from this causal relation. Thus, the meaning of a symbol system is its function in a society. At present I am not concerned with the psychological or sociological use of the theory. I am interested solely in the logic of the theory, for, in either case, the conclusion (the explanation) must follow from the theoretical premise.

In order to explicate the theory I shall simplify the premises. Once again, let us repeat the description of the theory: 'Symbol systems [structure] are the result of individual fantasy, produced by certain types of social experiences ... which function to express and resolve the psychological conflicts and needs which arise from these experiences.' We can re-write this statement and produce the following premises:

1) Let X = a social system, or a type of social experience.
2) Let Y = a functional requirement which is a necessary condition for X. This functional requirement could be described as a trinity of necessary conditions: (a) adaptation, (b) adjustment and (c) promotion of solidarity.
3) Let Z = the religious symbol system (the trinity of faith, or, any other symbol system) which is a sufficient condition for the satisfaction of Y.
4) Satisfaction of Y is the function of Z, both in terms of expressing and resolving the needs and conflicts which arise in X, which must be satisfied in order to maintain X.

I shall now re-write the premises into a formal (logical/causal) argument. Before doing so I wish to stress that 'functional theory' has always claimed logical validity. That is to say, the proponents of the theory claim it can explain (causally) the persistence and also the differences of cultural variables (e. g. religious symbols), by reference to the social system. In brief, the explanation of Z (religious symbols) must be taken as a satisfaction of Y, which in turn is a necessary condition for the maintenance of any X (a social system); religious symbol systems arise out of, are produced from, social experience.

The formal argument, as a logical explanation, appears to be as follows:

1. A social system X (or, a type of social experience) functions adequately only if a necessary condition Y is satisfied.
2. If Z is present in X, then as an effect Y is satisfied. (Since Z has the function of satisfying Y).
3. Therefore, Z (the religious symbol system or, any other symbolic unit) persists in X, and explains the differences between X and X_1.

It seems clear from Spiro's paper that religious symbol systems can only be sufficient conditions for satisfying the functional requirements which are necessary for the maintenance of a social system. If this were not the case we would not have different religious symbol systems, which is precisely what functional theories attempts to explain. However, the argument 'If Z then Y, Y, therefore Z', is clearly fallacious. All we can possibly conclude is that Z, its 'functional equivalent', or, some class of which Z is a member, functions to express and resolve needs and conflicts.

I wish to point out that this argument does not involve the dispute concerning teleological causes, or, the theoretical complexities of the meaning of 'need', 'aggression/conflict' or, a social system 'functioning adequately'. It has focused upon the logical, or, formal implications of the theory.

I must conclude, therefore, that the dispute between symbolists and functionalists is not just a manifestation of a *Zeitgeist*. The symbolist approach may indeed be arbitrary, methodologically. But from a theoretical standpoint, functional theories are either false, or, trivial.

Rodney Needham summed up the theoretical and methodological issues very succinctly when he wrote, 'Einstein once remarked that "the eternally incomprehensible fact about the universe is that it is

comprehensible". The solitary comprehensible fact about human experience is that it is incomprehensible' (*Belief, Language and Experience*,
p. 246).

Commentary   by Robert F. Spencer

The role of a commentator on given papers is in some measure that
of a devil's advocate. Yet the few remarks I wish to make are in fact
motivated by a vague sense of disquiet at the present condition of studies
of religion, whether anthropological or other. Let me first emphasize
that in no sense do I intend a negative reflection on Professor Spiro's
thought-provoking yet cautious summary and comparison. I use the
term 'cautious' advisedly, since I read into Prof. Spiro's remarks primarily an inclination toward the functionalist position rather than toward
a wholly committed stand on the bandwagon of symbolics, or symboli-
cism (if there is such a word). His statements remind me, in fact, of one
his earlier papers on the Micronesian atoll of Ifaluk and his formulation
of a teleological functionalism (cf. *American Anthropologist* 54 (1952),
pp. 497-503). In the paper he has presented here, I believe that he has
made, especially with his handling of comparative discontinuities in the
female role, a most significant contribution. My query, however, asks:
is it here and in statements of this kind where the future of religious
studies in anthropology may be said to lie?
    One must agree that with the essentially contemporary penchant to
locate the symbolic, there has been a growing indifference to the traditions of functionalism in anthropology. The field has had its fads, and
the current preoccupation appears to lie in symbolism and structuralism.
The two, to a degree, are linked, and yet seem to begin to take divergent
paths. And of course, just as with the earlier functionalist concerns, both
are being subjected to a scrutiny which bears hard on their primary
philosophical postulates. This has been the case each time the social
sciences evolve new or variant methodologies, and anthropology is no
exception. What are the questions and what are the answers?
    It may be supposed that for the anthropologist, at least, there is the
primary question of what it is that makes human beings human. Lévi-

Strauss and his followers find the answer in the 'pensée sauvage', in the resolution of binary oppositions. Although the Freudians have phrased their problem somewhat differently, they seem to arrive at essentially parallel conclusions. But clearly, if one is to be an anthropological 'scientist', there can be no cavilling at the kinds of generalizations about the human experience derived from a time-honored comparative method. Comparative hypotheses to test, such as that put forth by Prof. Spiro both on the element of the soteriological in Judaism and Buddhism and on the wife-mother role vis-à-vis female deities, are wholly in keeping with the comparative traditions of anthropology, whether past or present. Applied to the study of religion, how far do any of these approaches get?

Digressing on the point, and raising some rather simplistic queries, societies, recalling the Durkheimian formulation, distinguish between the sacred and the profane. Following Mary Douglas, there are thus the realms of the fitting as against the unfitting, the appropriate as against the inappropriate (cf. *Purity and Danger*, 1966). How the practical issue of resolving the place of various categories of phenomena is settled in different socio-cultural systems then becomes a problem. I do not question that man seeks some kind of order in his life, that this quest for order may reflect a series of unconscious processes, but I balk at the idea that different symbols in different cultures may be attempts to do the same thing and to answer the same questions. I am not sure exactly what I learn, for example, when I am told that the marriage between a man and his mother's brother's daughter is a reflection of a basic need or drive, a rationale whereby order is brought about in chaos. Thus I do not doubt that this is so in some instances, but I remain unconvinced that such a response is universal.

Thus the matter of human universals is still to be settled. Whether this is a reflection of a 'savage mind', a psychic, or psycho-biological unity of mankind, makes little difference. The present concerns of the ethologists, with their scrutiny of comparative animal behavior and its ostensible lessons for the human situation, begin to throw the concept of human cultural beginnings back into safe biological realms. Clearly, there can be no quarrel with this; every scientific and humanistic discipline has to come to grips with the what-is-man question. I feel merely that when religious phenomena are put into this kind of balance, something rather vital is lost in the weighing.

Social institutions other than religion can be subjected to a fairly rigorous yardstick of discussion. The economic, political, or social structures
lend themselves readily to comparison. Their bases can be easily propounded and generalizations made. Men, after all, have to eat, and there
are two sexes from which the procreative and the social proceed. Men
live in societies. But in the realm of religion there is a somewhat different
dimension. To be sure, religion as a social institution, a series of regulated
behavioral patterns of ritual and ceremony, can dovetail nicely with
other aspects to form a functioning, integrated social system. This is a
traditional functional approach. The symbolic avenue goes further, I believe, in recognizing that religion is the area where the human imagination
is given fullest rein, where man emerges as creator. But if symbolism
and its handmaiden, structuralism, are going to be employed to elicit
some universal categories reflective of a kind of human nature, I believe
that something vital is lost. In other words, as Prof. Spiro suggests, both
approaches are necessary; I should prefer to retain the view of the idiosyncratic in culture rather than to settle on those aspects which reflect
commonality.

Thus I am more struck by the uniqueness of human achievement in
various cultures than by an attempt to find underlying structures and
similarities cross-culturally. It is perhaps for this reason that I incline
to be impatient with many of the studies of religion which have been
made either in a contemporary context or in the background of the
development of anthropological thought. To me, terms like shaman,
totemism, mana, or whatever are meaningless since each must be seen in
a peculiar context. This is true in functionalist terms and I also believe
it to be true in symbolic terms. Thus I should prefer above all to take
a relativistic point of view.

I realize that to many present such a view may seem defeatist, perhaps
pessimistic, even highly old-fashioned. Yet it is a reflection of the kind
of training which I received and with which, *mea culpa*, I am most at
home. Perhaps too my view is colored by the fact of dealing with students in these and recent days when a search for universalities in the
human experience is so current and where there is no little impatience
with the need to look at societies per se, in their own terms and on the
basis of their own postulates.

It has been said that it is impossible to examine religion and religions
wholly objectively. At a certain level, this is unquestionably true. A

modern stress on phenomenological aspects would seem to wish to make true believers of us all. The other side of that coin is the scientific study of religion in hard-nosed terms. This is the argument that nothing in the area of religion can de facto be true. But it must be said that as part of the human experience of religion there are certain kinds of associations applicable to a given system which reflect the reality of that system which in turn posit its uniqueness. I should like to stop here before making broad pan-human generalizations and assumptions.

Because religion stems out of the imaginative and creative, I should like to see its studies given freer airing. Critical humanistic (in the sense of humanistic disciplines) examination holds promise in my view, if one can recognize and elicit the ways in which a mood is struck, an ethic formulated. Clearly, there is nothing new in this. Yet it is the feeling tone engendered by systems of religious thought which remains so striking. When, for example, Prof. Reichel-Dolmatoff, in his discussion of the Desana Tukano of Colombia, delineates the universe of these people as founded in a 'yellow principle' (*Amazonian Cosmos*, 1971), one becomes aware of an approach to reality. From such an existential proposition, the world of behavioral interaction may proceed as well as sets of associated and buttressing symbols. The crucial issue, however, seems to lie in the perceptions of reality; it is this distinctive and idiosyncratic aspect in different cultures that one ought to keep in mind. Ethnoscience, so-called, ethnosemantics, as well as however many other divergent sub-fields which have developed, may point in this direction. Perhaps when the nature of cultural realities is more pointedly understood, it will be possible to enter into a new phase of functional and symbolic comparisons in greater depth.

Commentary   by Annemarie de Waal Malefijt

I consider it a great privilege to have the opportunity to comment on Professor Spiro's elegant paper. My remarks will not be directed to his substantive analysis, because my own acquaintance with Judaism and Theravāda Buddhism is limited and indirect. Instead, I will attempt to discuss some of the wider theoretical implications of his approach as they bear upon the current status of anthropology and of the anthropology of religion.

At the outset, Spiro criticizes 'the propensity of our discipline to reject old approaches as false whenever a new approach acquires saliency'. It is certainly true that anthropologists have displayed a tendency to contradict and to debunk each other's theories. Boas made unkind remarks about 19th century evolutionists, Radcliffe-Brown called historical approaches 'conjectural', Kroeber took strong issue with those who felt that man himself played a role in the historical process, and most everyone pounced on Lévy-Bruhl. More recently, Marvin Harris condemned ideographic historical particularism,[46] while the movements that label themselves as the 'new' ethnology, the 'new' archeology or the 'new' physical anthropology imply by their common adjective that past theories should be discarded. Spiro himself notes that concerns with functionalism, motivation, and social processes are *passé*, while inquiries relating to symbolism, cognition, and mental processes are *bon ton*. It should be noted, however, that the inclination to brand approaches other than one's own as misleading forces of darkness is not peculiar to anthropologists. Bacon's 'Great Instauration', Vico's 'New Science', and Voltaire's slogan 'écrasez l'infâme' are but a few of the many examples that come readily to mind. Detailed examination of the 'new' theories presented by the various detractors reveals, however, that the substantive contents of their own writings are usually firmly rooted in the discoveries of their denigrated predecessors. The taunts are thus perhaps best understood as indicators of hubris or as cries for attention. In reality, anthropology evolved not by repudiating older principles and ideas, but by raising problems that were inherent in earlier formulations and seeking alternate solutions. Most theories advanced by social scientists and by humanists are neither false nor true, but themselves embedded in the social and historical matrix of space and time. While most anthropologists would probably agree with this formulation, few have made conscious efforts to interrelate and integrate older and newer insights. It is one of the merits of Spiro's paper that it demonstrates most convincingly that functionalism and symbolism are complementary approaches rather than antithetical ones.

Among those contemporary anthropologists who take partisan posi-

46. M. Harris, *The Nature of Cultural Things*, New York, 1964.

tions on the separation between functionalism and symbolism, Claude Lévi-Strauss and Marvin Harris figure prominently. Although Lévi-Strauss wrote in an early essay[47] that the meaning of myth and its symbols was to provide a logical model capable of overcoming social contradictions or problems, later on he denied even this vague reference to function. Totemic symbols are 'good to think'[48] but seem to have no necessary relationship to social reality; mythology 'has no obvious practical function';[49] and the mind itself 'is as alien to mental images as is the stomach to the foods which pass through it'.[50] By his insistence upon the unconscious origin and nature of symbols he not only divorces them from social reality but of necessity renders them non-functional, because the solution of unconscious problems by means of unconscious symbols serves no known purpose.

Marvin Harris, to the contrary, sets no store by the theoretical importance of symbolism. In *The Nature of Cultural Things* he attempts to analyze culture by the observation of non-verbal body motions alone, and even speech is reduced to 'visible mouth motions which produce audible effects'.[51] While Harris certainly does not deny the existence of symbols, he feels that taking account of verbal behavior — and thus of symbol-creating human beings — leads to 'astonishing paradoxes'.[52]

While the views of Lévi-Strauss and Harris on the relevance of symbolism are diametrically opposed, their basic premises bear a remarkable resemblance to one another, because both neglect or negate human beings and the creative autonomy of the human mind. At one point Lévi-Strauss recommends 'disregarding the thinking subject completely';[53] while Harris' 'actonic' approach finds comfort in the notion that language is a poor guide to inner psychological states and that people generally do not behave in the way they say they do.

These remarks do not invalidate the efforts of Lévi-Strauss or Harris,

---

47. 'The Structural Study of Myth', in Thomas A. Sebeok, ed., *Myth, A Symposium*, Bloomington, 1958.

48. Lévi-Strauss, *Totemism*, transl. by Rodney Needham, Boston, 1962, p. 89.

49. Lévi-Strauss, *The Raw and the Cooked*, transl. by John and Doreen Weightman, New York, 1969, p. 10.

50. Lévi-Strauss, *Structural Anthropology*, transl. by Claire Jacobson and Brooke Grundfest, New York, 1963, p. 203.

51. M. Harris, *The Nature of Cultural Things*, cit., p. 43.

52. *Ibid.*, p. 166.

53. Lévi-Strauss, *The Raw and the Cooked*, cit., p. 12.

and are not so intended. Both scholars deal with genuine problems, but would increase their scope by admitting the relevance of each other's positions. One problem underlying both approaches relates to the perennial search for a method to arrive at valid and universal cross-cultural analysis. If meaningful universal parameters can not be delimited, and if all religious systems and their social settings are uniquely defined, cross-cultural comparisons will be nothing else but an endless cataloguing of dissimilar entities, and a universal science of man or of religion becomes an impossibility. It is for this reason that Harris brackets language and the symbol-creating capacity of man and that Lévi-Strauss insists on the unconscious nature of symbols. In this manner a great deal of uniqueness and ambiguity can be avoided, but at a great cost. Spiro's paper indicates how such diminutions are not necessary, and that those female monsters, the Scylla of relativism and the Charybdis of soulless universalism, can be deluded or kept at a distance, with the assistance of Mother Goddesses. Since indeed 'all human beings have mothers', all religious systems have to take a stand, so to speak, towards the sex and nurturance of their sacred beings. The presence or absence of mother goddesses can thus be considered as a more or less universal item of human thought, and its varying values in human cultures and sub-cultures can be investigated. Spiro's tentative hypothesis, deriving from such examination, relates the presence or absence of Divine Mothers to the degree of nurturance of human mothers and to the degree of dominance of wives in specific social settings. This is a tantalizing proposition, and I certainly hope that Prof. Spiro will find occasion to discuss its theoretical rationale. My own fieldwork among Javanese immigrants in Surinam[54] seems to furnish an exception to his hypothesis. These Javanese have no mother goddesses in their folk-islamic religious system, yet mothers have high nurturance and wives low dominance. But certainly, one exception does not invalidate the hypothesis, and in Spiro's context as well as in that of my comments theories are more important than empirical data. Spiro has presented an important conceptual instrument for the assessment of certain universal human phenomena, and indicated that they are comparable precisely because they are embedded in social reality and thus also function in that reality. Nevertheless, it seems to me that not all symbolism and not all religious and social be-

54. *The Javanese of Surinam: Segment of a Plural Society*, Assen, 1963.

havior can be subjected to such universal treatment. It is the very nature of human beings and their cultures to have both universal and unique properties. The question then remains what to do with the particulars, with the many unique and seemingly bizarre religious rituals and practices that do not find their counterparts elsewhere, and that anthropologists of the past have so assiduously collected. My own tentative answer is that every bit of knowledge about human behavior, however trivial, adds to our understanding of the human potential. This does not lead to a scientific theory, but enhances our experience of the world we live in, so that we may come to recognize it not as a private experience, but as intersubjective. This in turn implies that the common-sense views we hold of the social world, of religious behavior, and of the nature of our fellow-men are continuously open to correction. If this is the case, the particular may have more existential significance than the universal.

Discussion   Chairman: Reinhard Pummer

Opening the session, the chairman, Reinhard Pummer, said that in view of the recent controversy between anthropologists and historians of religion, e. g. in a recent issue of the journal *Religion*, he anticipated an interesting discussion.

The first speaker was Ugo Bianchi, who wished to draw special attention to a number of points in his long paper, and to clarify some terminological questions which had arisen in the discussion about typology. The first point from his paper concerned a definition of religion which would be appropriate for historians of religions (in contradistinction to social and cultural anthropologists): whereas the latter needed a pragmatic definition in order to be able to proceed to studying societies and cultures as wholes, the historian of religions was aiming precisely at a characterization of the various forms of religion, and must therefore avoid the use of any prejudicially exclusive definition of what 'religion' means, but proceed by means of open-ended historical comparison. In his paper he had gone on to give examples, firstly of how religious comparison should not be carried out (Turner's study of color symbolism among the Ndembu, where very good detailed fieldwork was used in a methodologically invalid manner as the basis for generalizations about culture and society), and then of the real awareness by some anthropologists, such as Evans-Pritchard, of the necessity not to separate their discipline from historical research. This led on in his paper to the question of the crucial tension between the universal and the particular, which is the main issue in the controversy between phenomenology and history, and which in his opinion pointed towards the concept of 'historical typology of religion'. He then read several paragraphs from part 6 of his paper about the implications of choosing a suitable method for history of religions. His final point from the paper concerned the categorization of primitive Buddhism, which again raised the question of the definition of 'religion'; and he wished to stress the importance of appropriately using the words 'religion' and 'religious' in quotation marks when embarking on historical comparative research.

Bianchi then turned to the term 'concrete universal', which had caused some confusion in the discussion that morning about typology. Religious institutions occurred all over the world, as well as familial, tribal, and statual institutions, but he questioned whether they should always be regarded without qualification as belonging to the same typology or historical category. He denied the possibility of a programmatic or pre-established answer to the question, and, for this reason, argued that it was better to speak (at least originally and methodologically) of possible universals, whose validity could only be guaranteed by continuous reference to concrete, historical verification, i. e. as 'concrete (or historical) universals' (not in the Hegelian sense). It was wrong for the historian of religion, in relying on concepts such as family, tribe, state, priesthood, sacrifice, etc., to turn to *Idealtypen*, evolution, 'essence', or unqualified typology or phenomenology; he must turn to historical comparisons qualified by means of cultural history. (This did not necessarily imply cultural diffusion, or parallel evolution.) The question must be put philologically and historically, and in terms of contexts, milieux, and processes. Nor does this imply any idea of a reductive interpretation of 'religion', 'religious', or 'religions'. He pointed out that in practice the types or 'concrete universals' might be widespread rather than genuinely universal, but that they should nevertheless be studied by means of similar procedures. He closed by taking the example of polytheism, which does not simply lead to an abstract conception of more deities in one unqualified pantheon, but is deeply interconnected with the cultural historical typology of the archaic high cultures from Mesopotamia to Japan and Mexico.

He was followed by the second speaker, Melford Spiro, who opened by apologizing for his paper, which he felt tried to deal with three or four topics but failed to deal with any of them properly. He wished first to gloss his use of the word 'functionalism', which had bedevilled the social sciences since the 1920s, and was also highly ambiguous. He was not using it in the sense (in which it had occurred in some of the conference discussions) of asking what the 'functions', i. e. purposes or ends, of religion were for a social system, cultural system, personality system, etc.; where religion was the independent variable. Rather, he was using it in a mathematical sense: X, as a function of Y, therefore varies with changes in Y; e. g., in his paper, religion varies with the ethos of a society. In other words, the commitment to certain kinds of religious belief is a function of (or dependent on) a cultural ethos, i. e. on the cultural organization of the modulation of dispositions and values found in a particular social situation. This would apply not only to religious beliefs but also to political or esthetic beliefs, and so on. In his paper, therefore, he had been exploring how the 'religious' beliefs in two societies — Judaic influence as found in an atheist Israeli kibbutz, and Theravāda Buddhism as found in a Burmese village — varied with the differences in ethos. The two societies were interesting as representing, in Weber's terms, an inner-worldly and an other-worldly asceticism respectively.

He had started out from the idea that Theravāda Buddhism (as practiced by laymen in Burma) centred round the essentially soteriological belief in 'taking refuge in', i. e. finding redemption through, a trinity of sacred symbols: a sacred being (the Buddha), sacred teachings (the Dhamma), and a sacred group (the Sangha). He regarded redemption as the core of at least the higher religions. In Judaism, this triple structure of symbols was parallelled, by Jahweh, the Torah, and Israel respectively; and in view of the extreme contrast of ethos between the Judaic and Buddhist societies in question, this had constituted a challenge to the (mathematical) functionalist concept he was using. Despite the symbols' rather simplistic structural affinity, it was clear that their semantic meanings were very different. Both the soteriological goals and objects differed; what he had tried to do was to show the relationships between the differences. The other parallel between Burmese Buddhism and

Judaism was in their concepts of two kinds of salvation, proximal and ultimate: a heavenly afterlife, and the End of Days, in Judaism, and a better reincarnation, and nirvana, in Buddhism. But whereas in Burmese Buddhism the aspiration to nirvana is not at all deeply held, in the atheist Israeli kibbutz it is the belief in ultimate salvation which, in a secular form, has returned.

The final point in his paper related to the presence or absence of a female object in the soteriological trinity of objects. Both Theravada Buddhism and Judaism lack (at least on the conscious cultural level) a female or feminine principle. By contrast, Hinduism and Catholicism have, specifically, a Mother Goddess — not simply female, but maternal. This raised the question why familial roles should be expressed at the sacred level in some religions, but not in others; or to be more precise, why the symbolism of some religions included both mother- and father-figures, of others father-figures only, and of others again neither.

The chairman then invited the commentators to speak. All of the prepared comments dealt exclusively with Spiro's paper, since Bianchi's had not been available in advance. Horst Cain was the first to present his commentary, which constituted an extended critique of Spiro's use of the term and concept of symbols.

He was followed by Hans Penner, who said that he found Spiro's paper arbitrary (particularly the part about pairs and triads — why not quartets or quintets?), but that the theoretical implications were interesting. He considered that functionalism had achieved far more precision in its method than phenomenology had, but that its results were, theoretically speaking, trivial.

The third commentator was Robert Spencer, who defined his position as that of a 'traditional, old-fashioned anthropologist'. He expressed disquiet at the state of the discussion, e. g. the (insoluble) question of history versus non-history, a diachronic versus a synchronic approach. What appeared to be implicit in both Spiro's and Bianchi's papers, however, was an attempt to elicit principles which would in some way illuminate the human condition: an attempt about which he was extremely dubious. He referred to the work currently being carried out on animal behavior, which was reducing the distance that had formerly separated the human being from the animals. One assumption apparently underlying the discussions at the conference was that man was a 'religious animal', which he questioned. He preferred to understand man's various behavioral phenomena, religious and otherwise, and thus all religious systems, as essentially idiosyncratic and relative. He saw religion in humanistic terms, as an art form, and did not think it possible to reduce art to a science. The various products of religion were therefore artistic products, reflecting a particular mood, or (as Spiro had put it) ethos. It was the prevalence of a certain mood or ethos in differing religious systems which could conduce an understanding of religion in specific cultures; the generalizations could only come later.

The last commentator to speak was Annemarie de Waal Malefijt. She did not wish to go at length into the detailed points of Spiro's paper, since the theoretical implications were more important than the factual material. The paper's greatest strength, she suggested, was that it showed it was possible to take man into account and yet to come to meaningful kinds of analysis, through Spiro's refusal to treat the functionalist and symbolist approaches as incompatible. In her written commentary she had explored how Lévi-Strauss and Marvin Harris, representing the extreme versions of these two approaches, left man out of account. This had also been true of many of the conference contributions: they gave the impression of dealing with some purely abstract problem. The world 'man' (let alone 'woman' or for that matter 'student') had hardly occurred. She submitted that her learned audience were very much like Harris or Lévi-Strauss, in leaving man out of the picture, and she left it to them whether they considered this a compliment or not (laughter).

Replying to the commentators, Melford Spiro spoke first about Robert Spencer's critique. He agreed that the subject of religion should always be approached humanistically, since it was part of man's uniquely human characteristic, i.e. culture. On the other hand, he saw a problem in treating religion purely within the confines of the humanistic methodology: while it was certainly important to interpret and understand — i.e. to make propositions about — human behavior, including beliefs, it was also important to measure the validity of these propositions, and this was only possible by means of science. Consequently, it was necessary to rise above the particular, in order to make one's statements comparative. No statement about any given religion (or culture) was true, however esthetically or emotionally satisfying it might be, unless it could be compared with material from other religions and cultures. Spiro went on to say that he accepted much of Penner's critique of functionalism — but, briefly, that was not the kind of functionalism adopted in his paper, so that the critique appeared to be misdirected.

Speaking from the floor, Lauri Honko raised the question of the term 'ethos', which he thought Spiro and Spencer had been using in rather different ways. Did it refer to something the community experiences collectively, or was it something idiosyncratic? Responding first, Robert Spencer defined 'ethos' as a prevailing mood, characteristic of a given group, and probably not susceptible to scientific mensuration. The yardstick necessary would be more akin to that appropriate to artistic appreciation, e. g. the gut reaction that enables us to say with confidence that *Hamlet* is not a comedy. Melford Spiro subscribed to this in part; but he argued that it is possible to identify 'culturally organized motivations' in different communities, and said that commonality does not arise idiosyncratically, but through learned experience within certain kinds of social units, e. g. families. Replying to a question by C. J. Bleeker about the choice of the word 'ethos', Spiro said that it was often better to go on using an old word, even if it was not the most precise possible, rather than constantly calling in new ones.

Michael Pye returned to Horst Cain's commentary, and in particular to the concept of the 'numen' and the 'numinous'. He suggested that this brought out some of the points of friction between the phenomenological and anthropological approaches to the study of religion, and that it could be useful to sort out some of the real differences in approach that existed. Replying, Melford Spiro said that for the field-anthropologist, the concept of 'numen' as it was currently used was of no use; and that if it were to be operationally defined in such a way that it could be used by the fieldworker, it could then no longer be used in the same way as now.

Zwi Werblowski pointed out that there are two ways of generalizing about religious culture. One can study the scriptures, as a teacher of Judaism or Buddhism does; the scriptures, however, are always written by intellectuals, and the religious symbolism they contain should be treated with caution accordingly. Alternatively, one can study the people: what they are doing, what they are believing, and what makes them tick. The Buddhism of the Sutras, for example, is not at all the same as the Buddhism that makes a Buddhist in a Burmese or Thai village tick. To repeat a familiar truth, there were three types of Buddhism: that of the theologians, intellectuals, and academics; political Buddhism, which related to Burmese dynasties, and was of sociological and political science interest, though no longer in existence; and the living Buddhism of, for instance, the Burmese village. In the usual sense of the word, Buddhism was world-negating; yet one of the exciting things about studying Theravāda Buddhism was to see the non-world-negating character of Buddhist social and village life in action, with people drinking and dancing and getting as many children as possible, while paying lip-service to the ideal of the Sangha. This was possible, in part, because the Sangha was a mediating symbol which allowed a person to keep his distance from the world while getting involved in it, to be world-affirming while professing to be world-denying. This represented a symbolic double function.

This did not invalidate the idea of religious symbolism being born out of the contact with the numinous, even if (as a German scholar had written some 30 years earlier) students of religion tended to suffer, not from neurosis, but from numinosis. Once such a symbol had been born, however, if it was then transmitted, then this was clearly not as a religious symbol, i. e. mediating the experience of the numinous, but because it institutionalized a desirable ethos concerning the relationship to whatever is considered to be numinous, and was thus a stabilizing factor in society. It then became the legitimate prey of pure anthropological analysis, and the question would then not concern the nature of the numinous, but the nature of a numinous reference transmitted by a society and integrated in manifold ways into social, economic, and other forms of life. Werblowski did not necessarily wish to defend the substantive parts in Spiro's paper; he would have had a lot to say, in particular, about comparison, as also about what Spencer had called 'triviality' (since one man's triviality was another man's importance). What he valued in Spiro's paper was that it had shown what the anthropological approach was about, and that it should have been sufficient to convince everyone that this approach was useful, legitimate, and necessary.

Carsten Colpe said that he wanted to stress a point arising from Bianchi's paper. He felt that Bianchi had misunderstood what he (Bianchi) had set out to show. He had wanted to point out that typology and phenomenology did not need to be a-historical, and that what was needed was a historical phenomenology. Colpe suggested that what was needed was also a historical psychology and a historical sociology of religion. His second point concerned the concept of the 'type', as Max

Weber had defined it and as Bianchi had tried to develop it. The true 'ideal type' was neither a complete abstraction, nor an addition of conclusions; it was a heuristic concept, not something to be found as a concrete thing in a historical setting.

Another point from Bianchi's paper was then taken up by Helmer Ringgren. If he had understood correctly, Bianchi had criticized anthropology for ignoring history; but there were some anthropologists who admitted that they were not able to explain the present situation without recourse to history. Bianchi's criticism would therefore not be against anthropology as such; would those anthropologists who make use of history therefore be OK? (laughter).

Replying to these points, Ugo Bianchi spoke in French, to avoid the danger of making himself misunderstood. He confirmed that his criticism only applied to certain social anthropologists — clearly not to Evans-Pritchard, for example, who completely accepted the necessity of studying anthropological facts by means of the historical method. Taking up the point made by Ringgren against the alleged 'incompatibility' between research in history of religions and in anthropology, he agreed that this did not represent a real conflict, but rather an epistemological situation. He wished to reiterate his earlier statement, that while a conventional definition of religion might be permissible for social anthropologists, it was not so for historians of religions. The social anthropologists needed a working definition, e.g. by reference to belief in superhuman beings, in order to be able to study a society. The historian of religions, on the other hand, *must* start from the historical-comparative method, and, again in contrast to the social anthropologist, would possibly *never* arrive at an exhaustive 'ostensive' definition of religion; he must constantly be on route towards an ever more adequate definition, which could be applied to situations which were considerably, but not totally, different from each other. This was the purpose of the concept which he had been trying to establish in his paper, i.e. that of analogy. For the historian of religions, the concept of 'religion' is neither equivocal (otherwise it would have to be expunged) nor univocal (since the point of the enquiry is precisely to establish how far those manifestations of belief or practice which we customarily call 'religious' are in fact homologous); instead, the historian of religion's concept of religion must be analogous. Even if it is conceded that an ultimate definition of religion, even a univocal definition, could be achieved, the historian of religions may never set out from a univocal definition. This does not mean a conflict between the social anthropologist and the historian of religions, but a difference of approach to religion, as Spiro had also said.

Following up Bianchi's earlier remarks during the presentation of his paper, Ulf Drobin questioned once again the terms 'historical typology' and 'concrete universal'. The latter was a development of the concept of types; but (apart from Van der Leeuw, Heiler, and maybe Wach) 'type' was a generic concept, which was always an abstraction on a certain level, depending how many unique units it was intended to include. 'Concrete universals' therefore seemed to him to constitute a paradox. Secondly, Drobin pointed out that 'historical' can be understood in two ways: as referring to a point in time (e. g. as in anthropological case studies), or to a process in time (and some new anthropological studies did in fact investigate process). Thirdly, he took up Bianchi's discussion of typology and phenomenology. It appeared that Bianchi, like Lankow-ski, saw 'type' as a religion and 'phenomenon' as a separate unit within a religion; but Drobin did not think that typology and phenomenology could in fact be clearly distinguished, and thought that the proposed new discipline, 'historical typology', like the 'concrete universal', was an impossibility.

The closing remarks came from Bianchi. He denied that the 'concrete universal' was a logical impossibility, and stressed the distinction between the concept of religion, and religion as such. The latter consisted of all those institutions and beliefs, from all over the world, which one was to call 'religious'. This was the real thing, the historical, real, practical complex, which one could then analyze with the aid of historical methods, and draw distinctions within and find typologies of, but which constituted the concrete universal of religion.

PART THREE

Religion as Expressive Culture

Theories Concerning the Ritual Process

LAURI HONKO   *Theories Concerning the Ritual Process:*
                An Orientation

There are only three years between the principal works in the science of religion by Arnold van Gennep (1909)[1] and Émile Durkheim (1912).[2] Neither of them mentions the other; Van Gennep is slightly more generous, mentioning Hubert and Mauss,[3] Durkheim's colleagues, but for Durkheim Van Gennep does not seem to exist at all. Whether their mutual silence was deliberate remains a relatively trivial problem in the history of scholarship. Perhaps they could afford such extravagance during that Golden Age of the science of religion, when among other things research on ritual was making fast progress; and in the background of this boom period stands W. Robertson Smith,[4] the patron saint of the rite theorists.

Both Durkheim and Van Gennep presented a number of categories of rites and discussed the dynamics of the ritual process. The influence of Durkheim was more immediate, wider, and deeper; Van Gennep's theory remained latent, and then experienced a peculiarly lively renaissance during the 1960s.[5] Durkheim has been reborn several times in discussions

1. Arnold van Gennep, *Les rites de passage*, Paris, 1909; reprinted, with an author's Addendum, Paris-La Haye, Mouton, 1969; here English transl., London, 1960.
2. Émile Durkheim, *Les formes élémentaires de la vie religieuse*, Paris, 1912; here English transl., *The Elementary Forms of the Religious Life*, New York, Collier, 1961.
3. Henri Hubert and Marcel Mauss, 'Essai sur la nature et la fonction sociale du sacrifice', 1897-1898; here English transl., *Sacrifice: its Nature and Function*, London, 1964.
4. W. Robertson Smith, *Lectures on the Religion of the Semites*, 1889.
5. Cf. the foreword of the English translation of 1960 by Solon T. Kimball, in

concerning the reciprocal character and the functions of myth and rite. The concepts of 'imitative rite' and 'commemorative rite' which he uses include an embryonic conception of the general function of rites, which Bronislaw Malinowski,[6] Mircea Eliade,[7] and A. E. Jensen,[8] among others, have developed further. From a taxonomical point of view, however, his rite categories are not of much value; the least successful is the 'piacular rite', which Durkheim first discusses at considerable length, and then states that it is 'completely lacking' in Australia as the actual rite of expiation for sin or ritual error.[9] His line of thought has been misled by a badly chosen term. A more serious weakness lies in the fact that 'painful emotions' are seen as the element that unites the piacular rites, such as funerals, the prevention of drought, the curing of illnesses, etc., and that '... the explanation of the joyous rites is capable of being applied to the sad rites...', since both are 'made up out of collective ceremonies which produce a state of effervescence among those who take part in them'.[10]

Durkheim was a powerful, monolithic thinker. Even his blunders tend to acquire importance. His rite categories, however, have only been applied where they were born, i.e. in research on Australian totemism.[11] Van Gennep's situation, however, is different. One can hardly talk about unreserved admiration, or numerous disciples, in relation to him. It is characteristic that when Max Gluckman presents Van Gennep's merits to his readers, he (1) confesses that 'I find *Les rites de passage* boring now', whereas Durkheim is for him a 'modern mind';[12] (2) considers that Junod — who praises Van Gennep and does not mention Durkheim —

---

which maybe the most important among those few who have applied Van Gennep's ideas has been left unmentioned: Henri A. Junod, *The Life of a South African Tribe*, 2nd ed., revised and enlarged, 2 vols., London, 1927; cf. Max Gluckman, ed., *Essays on the Ritual of Social Relations*, Manchester, 1962, pp. 8-9.

6. Bronislaw Malinowski, *Argonauts of the Western Pacific*, London, 1922.

7. Mircea Eliade, *Le mythe de l'éternel retour: archétypes et répétition*, Paris, 1949.

8. A. E. Jensen, *Mythos und Kult bei Naturvölkern*, Wiesbaden, 1951.

9. Durkheim, *op. cit.*, p. 452.

10. *Ibid.*, p. 445.

11. See R. L. Sharp, 'Notes on Northeast Australian Totemism', in *Studies in the Anthropology of Oceania and Asia*, Cambridge, Mass., 1943; cf. Cl. Lévi-Strauss, *The Savage Mind*, transl. from the French, Chicago, 1966, pp. 236-237.

12. Gluckman, *op. cit.*, pp. 7, 11.

'had absorbed much of Durkheim';[13] and (3) claims incidentally, referring to the theory of rites of passage, that 'precisely the same mechanism
of ordering ritual had been analysed by Hubert and Mauss in their essay
on the nature and function of sacrifice, published in 1899'.[14] This last
argument, at least, can be disputed immediately (does Gluckman mean
that 'entry—victim—exit' = 'separation—transition—incorporation'?).

There is in fact quite a lot of evidence that the further development
of Van Gennep's theory has been valuable, and that parts of it have been
successfully transferred to various fields of research. *Essays on the Ritual
of Social Relations* by Daryll Forde, Meyer Fortes, Max Gluckman and
Victor W. Turner is one such piece of evidence. None of these writers
slavishly follows Van Gennep, which would in any case be impossible,
because social scientific thinking and terminology have of course made
enormous progress since 1909. Each of these social anthropologists
has his own original frame of reference, so that the stimulus given by
Van Gennep, and by other writers, is emphasized in different ways in
their analyses. Turner, for instance, moves in his later works firmly in
a direction of his own, and develops the concepts of 'liminality', 'structure', and 'communitas' into completely new tools for solving problems
such as Van Gennep did not dream of.

Van Gennep's influence has not been restricted only to the history of
religion and the phenomenology of religion, nor to social and cultural
anthropology. It has also reached into sociology. It is a case of interaction, in which social anthropology initially was the donor. In 1936, for
example, Linton defined the concepts of 'status' and 'role'. These were
needed to make Van Gennep's theory more accurate. Functional analysis
was also created within social anthropology. Subsequently, valuable
feedback has come from Robert K. Merton,[15] among others, a sociologist
who is known even by many social anthropologists: Merton's functional
analysis has relevance for empirical research on the ritual process, and
the same applies to his analyses of group, role and status. Another sociologist to be mentioned in this context is George C. Homans.[16] His

13. *Ibid.*, p. 7.
14. *Ibid.*, p. 14.
15. Robert K. Merton, *Social Theory and Social Structure*, 1949, rev. and enlarged
ed. 1968; here mentioned: Glencoe, 1957.
16. George C. Homans, 'Anxiety and Ritual: the Theories of Malinowski and
Radcliffe-Brown', *American Anthropologist* 43 (1941).

analysis of the differing opinions of Malinowski and Radcliffe-Brown on the motivation and function of ritual is still today a delicious piece of reading. There has also quite recently been some feedback from sociology in relation to Van Gennep: I refer to the work *Status Passage. A Formal Theory* by Barney G. Glaser and Anselm L. Strauss.[17] In their first sentence the authors acknowledge Van Gennep's remarkable social scientific insight, and they begin to develop further a battery of terms which is intended to facilitate the analysis of as many kinds of status passage as possible.

Even if Durkheim was venerated and Van Gennep tolerated, it must nevertheless be said that both of them are, from a scholarly point of view, very much alive. This statement, however, is not the real subject of the present paper. My aim is (1) to say something about the classification of rituals; (2) to ask what 'the study of the ritual process' is all about, and (3) to give a few examples of process analyses carried out within different rite categories.

One thing which I would like to point out immediately is that the classification of rituals represents a practical taxonomy, which is intended to make the grouping of the material easier, whereas the processual model of a rite is a tool which is intended to cast light on a particular problem and to try to find a solution to it. Thus the distinction between a 'category' and a 'model' is essential.

THE CLASSIFICATION OF RITUALS

The term 'ritual' has been used in a wide set of contexts in various disciplines. It depends on the assumptions, often meta-theoretical, of each discipline what meanings this term conveys. A sociologist is inclined to see a ritual in any 'symbolic behavior that is repeated at appropriate times, expressing in a stylized, overt form some value or concern of a group (or individual)';[18] or he sees in 'ritualism' one of the five ways of adaptation available for an individual, i.e. the rejection of some particular culturally defined goals, coupled with the cure of the consequent frus-

17. Barney G. Glaser and Anselm L. Strauss, *Status Passage. A Formal Theory*, Chicago, 1971.
18. G. A. Theodorson and A. G. Theodorson, *A Modern Dictionary of Sociology*, London, 1969, p. 351.

tration by clinging to the institutionalized routines and norms supposed to lead to those goals.[19] In psychiatry, the semantic span of the term 'ritual' extends considerably further, in the direction of idiosyncrasy.

In social anthropology and in comparative religion the crucial problem is whether to count all ceremonies and customs as rituals or not. In sociology the distinction between ceremony and ritual has been seen in the fact that 'ceremony is necessarily social, involving more than one person, whereas a ritual may be collective or individual'.[20] For the purposes of comparative religion this is not adequate. Max Gluckman therefore distinguishes, 'within the general field of "ceremonial", "ritual" from the "ceremonious", by taking "ritual" to be actions which are often similar to ceremonious actions, but which contain in addition "mystical notions"... Ritual ... is associated with notions that its performance in some mysterious way, by a process out of sensory control, affects the well-being of the participants: it is believed to protect them or in other ways achieve their well-being. The Zulu see clearly that obeisance and other actions of respect to the chief enhance his prestige: but they also believe that when he danced before his abased subjects in the first-fruit rites the prosperity and success of the nation were guaranteed'.[21] Thus in studies of religion it is most economical to restrict the use of the term 'ritual' to situations in which the density of traditional symbolic behavior is high and correlates in some way with dependence on the 'trans-human' or 'sacred'. A ritual is thus traditional, prescribed communication with the sacred. But because in most cases it is enmeshed in complicated sets of social relations, and because the 'charge' of the sacred is often linked to the importance of those relations, it is wrong from an analytical point of view to exclude the ceremonious or even the non-ceremonious elements of behavior simply because they can be classified as 'profane'. The real object of study is the relevant total behavior.

When I started preparing this paper, I automatically assumed that I would be able to take as a starting point in the classification of rites the following three-fold division, which I have been using in my teaching for almost ten years: (1) rites of passage, (2) calendrical rites, and (3) crisis rites.

19. Merton, *op. cit.*, p. 203.
20. Theodorson and Theodorson, *op. cit.*, p. 351.
21. Gluckman, *op. cit.*, pp. 30-31.

1. *Rites of passage*

I take the definition from the English summary of an article of mine, published in 1964. 'Rites of passage are traditional rituals organized by society, whereby the individual is moved from one status to another. They often include rites of separation, whereby the individual is separated and estranged from his erstwhile status. His previous role is 'de-actualized', and his old ego is put to death. They also include rites of transition, which prepare for a transition to a new status. These make the individual aware of the change in his life that is taking place, they describe new duties and rights to be expected, transmit information and test the competence of the individual concerned. At this stage the individual must adopt a role that is temporary and transmitting by nature. To rites of passage also belong rites of incorporation whereby the individual takes up a new social status and adopts a new role. Characteristic of these are, for example, symbolically performed first acts in the role, whereby the individual shows his willingness to adapt himself to his new position and demonstrates his ability in carrying out the tasks demanded by it'.[22]

Here standard rite-situations can be seen as parts of the chronological status-sequence in the life of the individual, but, as I pointed out, 'there is not just one change of status involved, but a complicated constellation of several statuses and roles. Rites of passage contain a dramatic interplay of roles and in them, all social relations subject to change are made public and legitimate'.[23] This statement has direct bearing on the process analysis of ritual.

The ritual dramas of birth, initiation, marriage and death are those which have been most fully investigated, but there are quite a number of other forms of rites of passage, both trans-cultural and culturally bound, which can be placed alongside them. Becoming a member of a children's playgroup or a member of a group of young men or women, pregnancy and fatherhood, transfer from one social class or profession to another, specialization for a job of high responsibility, all of these have also been ritualized, along with many other changes of status. I find

---

22. L. Honko, 'Siirtymäriitit' (Summary: On the Rites of Passage), *Sananjalka* 6 (Turku, 1964), p. 141.
23. *Ibid.*, p. 142.

especially helpful a three-fold division within initiation rites: (a) age-group initiation, which is passed through in principle by all members of society when they reach adulthood and become fully qualified for society; (b) esoteric initiation, which is experienced only by those who are accepted as members in a secret society, cult or mystery group, profession, etc.; and (c) vocational initiation, which always concerns only one particular individual and means to him that he has achieved exceptionally high status, for example political or religious status (the initiation of a shaman, the ordination of a priest, or the inauguration of a king or chief). Although the same kinds of elements exist in different types of initiation, it can be seen that they receive somewhat different emphasis. Thus age-group initiation is focused on ability tests, esoteric initiation on induction into the secrets of the group, and vocational initiation on the exercise of the power connected with the new status and on status symbols.[24]

Rites of passage can be regarded as primarily individual-oriented, because the change that takes place in the situation of an individual provides its initial impulse. Secondly, they are non-recurrent, because an individual experiences them only once in his life. Thirdly, they are anticipated, because it is possible to be prepared for their actualization in advance. These three criteria can also be applied to the classification of the remaining two main categories, i.e. calendrical and crisis rites.

2. *Calendrical rites*

These are cyclical rites, organized by the community, and placed at the turning points of the socio-economic seasons, often at their beginning or end. They are 'calendrical' even in cultures with no form of writing, in the sense that they follow a 'natural calendar' based on observations of nature, an 'economic calendar' based on economies which are linked together, and a 'calendar of feasts' which regulates social interaction. The New Year ritual and the period of chaos linked with it is a classic example, when the reversal of roles, the division of luck in different fields of activity (weather, cattle-breeding, marriage, health, etc.) within

24. Honko, *op. cit.*, pp. 128-129; cf. M. Eliade, *Birth and Rebirth*, transl. from the French, New York, 1958, pp. 1-3.

the rules of 'limited good' and by means of omen-taking, the regulation of social contact, masked processions, and the use and distribution of abundance, in fact overthrow the old cosmos and create a new one. Calendrical rites create the rhythm of social life; they mark out explicitly the collective and established values of the community, by demonstrating what the currently foremost aims are, what systems of norms are in operation, what possibilities exist, and what rules govern competition.

Just as the 24-hour day is the basic unit in man's physiological cycle, so as the basic calendrical unit it can act in exactly the same way in, for example, family cults; but it is the longer periods which have wider significance for the community. As Edmund R. Leach says: '... among the various functions which the holding of festivals may fulfil, one very important function is the ordering of time. The interval between two successive festivals of the same type is a 'period', usually a named period, e.g., 'week', 'year'. Without the festivals, such periods would not exist, and all order would go out of social life. We talk of measuring time, as if time were a concrete thing waiting to be measured; but in fact we create time by creating intervals in social life. Until we have done this there is no time to be measured'.[25]

The calendar is undoubtedly an important store of widely shared social traditions; one only needs to think of, say, the calendar of saints in the Catholic Church, or the sayings attached to important days in the popular calendar, to be able to understand what possibilities the calendrical system offers for the simultaneous and regular actualization of tradition. No wonder that Durkheim, who saw in the collective the main source of religious behavior and sentiment, restricted the manifestation of the sacred and the cult almost exclusively to festival days.[26] One of his successors, Mischa Titiev, sees in calendrical rites an anchor of the collective identity: '... since they are always social or communal in character, calendrical rites invariably tend to disappear when a society loses its distinctiveness or radically alters its old ways of life. Thus, when the Hopi Indians of Oraibi began to show greater interest in White than in native culture, the pueblo's calendrical observances were among the first cultural items to suffer disintegration'.[27]

25. Edmund R. Leach, *Rethinking Anthropology*, New York, 1961, pp. 134-135.
26. Durkheim, *op. cit.*, p. 347.
27. Mischa Titiev, 'A Fresh Approach to the Problem of Magic and Religion', *Southwestern Journal of Anthropology* 16 (1960), p. 294.

Calendrical rites are thus group-oriented; it is hard to imagine that any primarily individual interest could direct the pulse or rhythm of social time that beats throughout the calendrical system. These rites are recurrent, they link man with his social allegiances and socio-economic environment in a repetitive but also creative way (the New Year is really 'new', the beginning of the hunting period opens up new opportunities, etc.). The fact that these rites are anticipated is evident; they form the 'entrances' and 'exits' for periodic social and economic activities, and without the marking of those moments by ritual, the entrance into a period can easily create anxiety and other dysfunctional consequences.

3. *Crisis rites*

These are occasional rituals in unexpected situations of crisis. They are organized by an individual or a community, in situations that upset the normal world order and threaten the life of the individual or the community, or the achievement of their immediate aims. The rites organized to channel the anxiety and uncertainty caused by these crises vary greatly, from limited but rapid actions or reactive rites, to wider, collective rituals in which the whole group involved in the crisis takes part. The drama of curing an illness,[28] the prevention of fire spreading in a densely-built group village,[29] the rain-making rites organized in order to prevent the continuation of drought and a dearth of crops, the repair of a trap or a tool after a spell put on it by witchcraft, and prevention rites against theft, envy, and malice, are only the beginning of a long list of crisis rites, which takes its shape on the basis of major catastrophes and minor accidents in life. The aim of the rites is to indicate the cause of the accident, to reveal the guilty person, and to ease the problematical nature of an unexpected incident by means of explanations and counter-action. This happens in the language of myth by finding a precedent for a strange

---

28. Honko, *Krankheitsprojektile. Untersuchung über eine urtümliche Krankheits-erklärung*, (FF Communications 178), Helsinki, 1959, pp. 202-209; cf. Honko, 'Varhaiskantaiset taudinselitykset ja parantamisnäytelmä', *Tietolipas* 17 (Forssa, 1960) and 'On the Effectivity of Folk-Medicine', *Arv, Journal of Scandinavian Folklore* 18-19 (Uppsala, 1963).

29. Honko, *Geisterglaube in Ingermanland I* (FF Communications 185), Helsinki, 1962, pp. 210ff.

new phenomenon from the sacred primordial times in the history of creation: for example, an illness is cured by recalling a myth which tells about the first occurrence of the illness and its cure. The event of the myth is brought into the present, the cure is re-enacted here and now, and the illness is reassigned to its own place in the world order, just as in primordial times; the disorder is eliminated.[30]

Crisis rites are individual- and/or group-oriented; here their range is so wide that some kind of subdivision might be helpful. These rites can be said to be non-recurrent, since the catastrophes, accidents and misfortunes which are their objects are in principle experienced as unique events. For example a relapse in a chronic disease can cause a new act of healing, but it is now concerned with a different disease, a different case of falling ill. If the act of healing is declared unsuccessful — which very rarely happens — for example because of an error in the ritual, this is a new situation, a different crisis which requires a different ritual. Crisis rites are furthermore unanticipated: they surprise the individual or the community, and their timing cannot be influenced in any way. Maybe it is precisely because of this that some omen experiences are retrospectively attached to them; i.e. supra-normal, unaccountable experiences accumulate in the memory, from which they then re-emerge in association with catastrophes and acquire a post hoc interpretation.[31] If we would like to test this definition with some rather awkward marginal case, like rites of house-moving, we could say that these are group-(family-)oriented, non-recurrent, and are attached to a unique incident, the primary cause of which was unanticipated.

I have been using the trichotomy of rites outlined above for quite a long time now. When I included it in this paper I did not imagine that it would have much novelty value. But when I was searching through the literature in order to find an earlier user of this trichotomy, to my surprise I could not find one. If any member of this conference can help me, I would be grateful. But what I did find, to my irritation, was the inflation of the concept of crisis. Rites of passage are called 'life-crises' by most authors; Chapple and Coon make a distinction between 'indi-

30. L. Honko, *Maailmanjärjestyksen palauttamisen aate parannusriiteissä* (Summary: The Idea of the Restoration of the Cosmic System in Healing Rites), Verba docent, Helsinki, 1959.

31. Honko, *Geisterglaube...*, op. cit. in n. 29, p. 91 and 'Memorates and the Study of Folk Beliefs', *Journal of the Folklore Institute* I: 1-2 (Bloomington, 1964).

vidual crises', which are followed by rites of passage, and 'group crises', which are followed by rites of intensification.[32] What I have called crisis rites, above, are classified by them as rites of passage, and this is a habit which recurs in other authors. It strikes me that Chapple and Coon prefer to characterize as 'recurrent'[33] both what I have above called rites of passage and crisis rites. Their additional characteristic of 'non-periodic' does not help on this point. Their categorization is essentially a dichotomy, as is that of Mischa Titiev, who lumps together crisis rites and rites of passage as opposed to calendrical rites.[34] If we look into two standard handbooks on the anthropological study of religion, the situation is very much the same: Edward Norbeck has 'crisis rites' and 'cyclic group rites',[35] and Annemarie de Waal Malefijt sees 'the most constructive division ... between periodic and nonperiodic rituals'.[36] Rites of passage or status change go under the label of 'crisis rites' in both.

The key question for me is whether we can stop talking about 'life-crises' and save the term 'crisis', which has almost been worn out, for a narrower and more sensible use. If we can do so, it makes it possible for us to adopt the same kind of language usage as the modern sociologists who are interested in status passage; in other words, processes of status change would become a shared field of study. The above-mentioned essays by Forde, Fortes, Gluckman and Turner take a step in that direction, and Glaser and Strauss also seem to have cooperation with anthropologists in mind.[37]

The trichotomy of rites of passage, calendrical rites, and crisis rites is here being thought of as a 'cultural universal', and therefore the possible future development should not be tied too closely to one or two cultures. The sub-categories of initiation (cf. above) are also an example of cultural universals. These three types of initiation, presented by Mircea Eliade,[38] do not seem however to have interested Frank W. Young,[39]

32. E. D. Chapple and C. S. Coon, *Principles of Anthropology* (1st ed.: New York, 1942), 1947, pp. 398-401, 484-528.
33. *Ibid.*, p. 462.
34. Titiev, *op. cit.*, p. 298. See also my article in *Temenos* 11 (1976), pp. 61-77.
35. Edward Norbeck, *Religion in Primitive Society*, New York, 1961, pp. 138-168.
36. Annemarie de Waal Malefijt, *Religion and Culture*. An Introduction to Anthropology of Religion, New York, 1968, p. 189.
37. Glaser and Strauss, *op. cit.*, pp. 1-4.
38. Eliade, *Birth...*, *op. cit.* in n. 24, pp. 1-3.
39. Frank W. Young, *Initiation Ceremonies, A Cross-cultural Study of Status*

although it would not be at all impossible to try to test the generalizations of the phenomenology of religion on cross-cultural material. Nevertheless Young's work opens up interesting views of role-learning and status dramatization in connection with age-group initiation.

The classification of rites presented in this paper does not, of course, restrict a scholar who prefers to use more culture-bound categories. For example, Victor Turner is probably right when he groups the hunting cults, women's fertility cults and procreative cults of the Ndembu under the general label of 'rites of affliction' as opposed to 'life-crisis rituals' (e.g. initiation or funerals). He does this because 'the Ndembu have come to associate misfortune in hunting, women's reproductive disorders, and various forms of illness with the action of the spirits of the dead'.[40] This designation of these rites may be perfectly adequate in the case of the Ndembu, but its applicability in comparative studies is so limited that it will never approach the level of a 'cultural universal'.

If someone objects to this classification of rites on the grounds that Van Gennep's model for the rite of passage seems in fact to apply to more than one category of rite (status passage), I can only refer to what I said earlier about the difference between 'category' and 'model'. It is true that models have been elaborated on the basis of Van Gennep's ideas to elucidate, say, the structure of some calendrical feast (cf. below). It is also true that Van Gennep's model is neither the only nor a sufficient analytical device in the study of rites of passage.

PROCESS ANALYSIS AND RITUAL

During the last few years cultural anthropology has practised many forms of self-criticism. Victor Turner, referring to a collection of studies about witchcraft and sorcery in East Africa edited by J. Middleton and E. H. Winter,[41] says in one of his articles first published in 1964[42] and

---

Dramatization, Indianapolis, New York, Kansas City, 1965.

40. Victor W. Turner, *The Forest of Symbols. Aspects of Ndembu Ritual*, Ithaka, N. Y., 1967, p. 9.

41. John Middleton and E. H. Winter, eds., *Witchcraft and Sorcery in East Africa*, London, 1963.

42. V. W. Turner, 'Betwixt and Between, the Liminal Period in Rites de Passage', *The Proceedings of the American Ethnological Society*, 1964.

reprinted in *The Forest of Symbols*[43] something about methodology which I would like to quote in full: 'The fault — if fault it is — does not lie with the highly competent contributors but with the declining adequacy of the theoretical frames employed. These are the structural frame of reference and "cultural analysis" with which the editors (p. 9) hope to "develop explanatory formulations which can subsume the facts from more than one society". However, "the facts" have changed within the last decade and theory must change with them. Anthropologists are still vitally concerned to exhibit "structures" of social relations, ideas, and values, but they now tend to see these in relation to processes of which they are both the products and regulators. Process-theory involves a "becoming" as well as a "being" vocabulary, admits of plurality, disparity, conflicts of groups, roles, ideals, and ideas, and, since it is concerned with human beings, considers such variables as "goal", "motivation", "intention", "rationality", and "meaning". Furthermore, it lays stress on human biology, on the individual life cycle, and on public health and pathology. It takes into theoretic account ecological and economic processes both repetitive and changing. It has to estimate the effects on local subsystems of large-scale political processes in wider systems. These developments have taken place as a result of the increased use of the extended case method which studies the vicissitudes of given social systems over time in a series of case studies, each of which deals with a major crisis in the selected system or in its parts. Data provided by this method enable us to apprehend not only the structural principles of that system but also processes of various kinds, including those of structural change. Such case material must, of course, be analyzed in constant and close association with social "structure", both in its institutionalized and statistically normative senses. The new "facts" do not oust but complete the old'.[44]

With the aid of this somewhat rhapsodical credo, and the subsequent clarification, since 1964, of the trends, it is possible to tell which direction religious anthropological studies are going in. As a starting point for my investigation I shall take Robert K. Merton's presentation of functional analysis, and I shall presuppose that for example the concise but illuminating chapter 'A paradigm for functional analysis in

43. *Op. cit.* in n. 40.
44. *Ibid.*, pp. 112-113.

sociology'[45] is familiar to you. By means of a comparison with Merton's position in 1949 one can establish the following shifts in, among other things, methodological focus. (1) The frustrating over-emphasis of the balance model in functional analysis has been compensated for by theories which pay close attention to conflict and changes in the structure of the community. (2) Interest is switching from latent to manifest functions, and consequently the verbalized opinions and explicit attitudes of the people under study are gaining in importance. Melford Spiro, in an important article, has especially emphasized this aspect, and among other things has introduced a new pair of concepts of 'real' and 'apparent functions', which makes it possible for the opinions and motivations expressed by the bearers of a tradition to be taken into consideration in functional analysis more systematically than before.[46] (3) Instead of the construction of a static structural model, there has been an increasing shift towards process analysis, to schemes of events of a flow-chart type, in which among other things the role of feedback is strongly emphasized (for example, a religious 'need' gives the initial impetus for a particular religious institution, the results of whose activity not only 'satisfy' the need, but also strengthen it, maybe even by creating new clusters of needs); in this context one could refer, for instance, to J. Milton Yinger's field theory.[47] (4) Without turning historical or anti-phenomenological, it has become the tendency to move away from completely 'timeless' research settings; this trend has, however, been slowed down to some extent by the optimism raised by structuralism and quasi-historical evolution theories. (5) In association with the foregoing, what Turner calls 'extended case study' and some others 'depth study'[48] has acquired new significance. This is not a case of the revival of detailed description, but of the application of all those principles which emphasize the use, context, and meaning of tradition, which Malinowski already lectured about, but the negligence of which is still one of the most common defects in field work. (6) Ecological studies

45. Merton, *op. cit.*, pp. 104-108.

46. Melford E. Spiro, 'Religion: Problems of Definition and Explanation', *Anthropological Approaches to the Study of Religion* (A.S.A. Monographs 3), ed. by M. Banton, London, 1966, p. 109.

47. J. Milton Yinger, *The Scientific Study of Religion*, London, 1970, pp. 88-98.

48. Juha Pentikäinen, 'Perinne- ja uskontoantropologisen syvätutkimuksen menetelmästä' (Summary: On the method of tradition- and religio-anthropological depth research), *Sananjalka* 12 (Turku, 1970), pp. 72-119.

of tradition and religion are becoming popular; there are several forms, from a more deterministic type such as that which applies Roy A. Rappaport's model of self-regulating systems[49] to a more relativistic type which is based on socialization theories and selection models. (7) It is becoming more and more crucial to link 'culture', 'tradition', 'religion', etc., to the socio-economic and political problems of definable physical communities. Thus the attempt has been made to derive the 'burning questions' from empirical material (observation and interviews) and not from the classical ways of formulating a theory. (8) On the one hand there is a growing tendency towards detailed reporting of clearly-documented case-analyses at a relatively low level of abstraction, in which the freshness of the raw material is transmitted to the reader; on the other hand there is a tendency to create more abstract schemes of explanation, for example on the basis of the structure of linguistic categories, of symbolic systems, of values and attitudes, of social roles and groups, of behavior, or of thinking.

How can these trends of development be traced in the study of ritual? A better balance, firstly, between observation and interviews and other documentary techniques, and secondly, between the theoretical concepts operationalized for each investigation and the new data-impulses from the raw material, will provide more detailed and penetrating analyses of the ritual process as a holistic manifestation of an operating system of different individual, social, and cultural variables. Durkheim's fragmentary analyses of the ritual process have already been bettered; Radcliffe-Brown's corresponding analyses are characterized by coherence, but his material is in many places inadequate; Malinowski again has the material but lacks coherence — when he changes his frame of reference he even contradicts himself; and the analyses of Van Gennep, Hubert, and Mauss remain superficial as they rush into global generalizations. The dominance of the western life-style and of Christian frames of reference is only now beginning to break down, when the mills of cultural anthropology have been grinding for decades and the pre-literate tribal communities are becoming independent states. The latter is now happening to such an extent that investigators should have better chances of two-way communication, and of internalizing the foreign cultural

49. Roy A. Rappaport, *Pigs for the Ancestors*. Ritual in the Ecology of a New Guinea People, New Haven and London, 1967, pp. 1-7.

systems. Many a cultural anthropological 'laboratory' will be closed; the tactics and attitudes will change. The research itself will, more clearly than in the past, be understood as a situation where two or more cultures interact.

THREE EXAMPLES

Much depends on which step of the ladder of abstraction we are on at the time. Even our knowledge that research consists of climbing up the ladder from raw material towards general theories — up, down, and up again — makes it easier to adopt a position on the transformation of scientific knowledge. The rules of this transformation have been made explicit in the best pieces of research.

I would like to finish my presentation by handling briefly three examples of research from the field of ritual behavior.

1. *Liminal roles in the rite of passage*

Victor Turner is among those who have given exemplary analyses of ritual processes. The case-analysis of the *mukanda* circumcision rite of the Ndembu,[50] or the analysis of *isoma*, a procreative rite aimed at restoring the fertility of a woman,[51] give both the inside view of the Ndembu and the theoretical implications which the Ndembu are not able — or have no need — to verbalize. In spite of the very complicated systems of expression and the interconnections of symbols, in these investigations Turner keeps relatively close to the low level of abstraction of raw subject material. In some of his other writings he tries from the start to create theoretical frames of reference at a higher level of abstraction. One of these frames of reference is 'liminality'.[52] In 1964, Turner finished one of his articles 'with an invitation to investigators of ritual to focus their attention on the phenomena and processes of mid-transition. It is these, I hold, that paradoxically expose the building blocks of

50. Turner, *The Forest of Symbols...*, *op. cit.* in n. 40, pp. 151-279.
51. Turner, *The Ritual Process. Structure and Anti-Structure*, London, 1969, pp. 10-43.
52. *Ibid.*, pp. 94-130.

culture just when we pass out of and before we re-enter the structural realm'.[53] As a good scholar he himself was the first to follow his own invitation,[54] and has quite recently further developed the idea of the 'pilgrimage as that form of institutionalized or "symbolic" "antistructure" (or perhaps "metastructure") which succeeds the major initiation rites of puberty in tribal societies as the dominant historical form'.[55] What strikes me in this development, which I cannot fully sketch here, is the fact that what began as a characterization of transitional roles has fairly quickly turned into the characterization of the community. The community has sometimes, maybe wrongly, been regarded purely as a human aggregate, but Turner sees in it greater stability and social significance. In sociology there is in fact a concept which may not quite fully cover all the semantic 'charge' of Turner's concept of 'communitas', but corresponds with it fairly closely, i. e. *cohort* (all those initiated at the same time form a cohort; the same term can be applied to those taking part in a pilgrimage).

The point I want to make is that Turner's invitation to study the processes of mid-transition will probably also be taken up by others, so important is the 'liminal *persona*', which is a term Turner once coined but which he now tends to replace by 'liminal society' (or, better, by 'anti-society' or 'communitas'), a kind of safety valve or alternative way of life for people who are tightly bound to the structures of a hierarchical society and 'cannot be themselves'. It so happens that in 1963 and 1964 a couple of minor studies were published in which — although I did not yet know anything about Turner's invitation — I investigated among other things the liminal roles of an Ingrian bride and a deceased person in Karelia.[56] Because of the limited scope of this paper I cannot reiterate the results here, but if I test my results against the criteria of liminality set out by Turner on page 106 in his book *The Ritual Process*, I can state that at the most half of the 26 criteria listed by Turner can be applied to the role of a bride and/or deceased person (inter alia 'transition',

53. Turner, 'Betwixt and Between, ...', *op. cit.* in n. 42, repr. in *The Forest of Symbols...*, p. 110.

54. especially in *The Ritual Process...*, *op. cit.* in n. 51.

55. Turner, 'The Center Out There: Pilgrim's Goal', *History of Religions* 12/3 (Chicago, 1973), p. 204.

56. Honko, 'Itkuvirsirunous', *Suomen kirjallisuus* I (Keuruu, 1963), (in English in *Studia Fennica* 17, 1974, pp. 9-61) and the article mentioned supra in n. 22.

'totality', 'nakedness or uniform clothing', 'humility', 'unselfishness', 'total obedience', 'sacredness', 'sacred instruction', 'suspension of kinship rights and obligations', 'continuous reference to mystical powers', 'foolishness', 'acceptance of pain and suffering'). Unfortunately I shall have to guess to a certain extent, because Turner does not comment on the criteria of liminality very systematically. If one looks at Glaser and Strauss's twelve 'properties of status passage',[57] one gets the impression that it might be worth trying to cross them with Turner's criteria. Although I regard Turner's idea of 'communitas' as interesting, I am of the opinion that, quantitatively speaking, a clear majority of status passages can be analyzed only by starting from the individual and from his transitional role. The social relations to other individuals and groups, as well as to supranormal beings, actualized in the rite, then have to be related to the role itself. The role-sets, status-sets and status-sequence of an individual are also in formation, precisely in the transitional phase. Turner says that by 'structure' or 'social structure' he does not mean the Lévi-Straussian 'structure of "unconscious categories" located at a deeper level than the empirical, but rather what Robert Merton has termed "the patterned arrangements of role-sets, status-sets and status-sequences" consciously recognized and regularly operative in a given society and closely bound up with legal and political norms and sanctions'.[58] This is nice to hear. But I do not believe that it would be particularly fruitful to try to explain liminal rites and communities as 'anti-structural' or as being outside the concepts of role-set, status-set, etc. At this point I do not think that 'communitas' is going to revolutionize either sociology or comparative religion.

2. *Reversal of roles in calendrical rites*

The 12-day period of the Babylonian *akitu* feast, when 'the slaves were masters', and the Roman *Saturnalia*, when 'the slaves were free', are very well-known examples of periods of chaos when the world is turned upside down, the social order no longer obtains, and roles are reversed. This disorder normally comes to an abrupt end: afterwards, the social

57. Glaser and Strauss, *op. cit.*, pp. 4-5.
58. Turner, 'The Center...', *op. cit.* in n. 55, p. 216.

order is stricter than ever. In various parts of Europe, including Finland, a custom of organizing masked processions has been preserved, in which boys dress up as girls and girls as boys, walk in a group from house to house, and are usually received with hospitality. People try to recognize the masked persons behind their humorous clothes. In different tradition-areas the procession takes place on different days, but the connection with the rituals at the turn of the year seems obvious. Turner has dealt with this kind of rites, which exist in many places in the world and in various contexts. He calls them 'rituals of status reversal', and he has plenty of interesting things to say about them.[59] I do not intend to go here into things which can easily be read about in his splendid book.

Instead, I shall talk about a young Danish scholar who in the near future will be publishing his book *Helligtrekongersløb på Agersø. Socialt, statistikt og strukturelt.*[60] In it, Carsten Bregenhøj, the author, investigates the custom of masked processions and its structure in a Danish island community. Without going into detail, I shall present, with the permission of the author, a scheme which has been developed on the basis of the scheme published by Leach in his article 'Time and False Noses':[61]

Alternative life / Eternity / Feast, role reversal and masked people

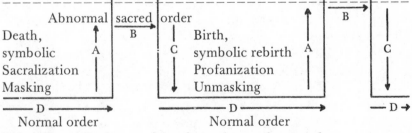

Life / Time / Profane social order and everyday people

Bregenhøj suggests that the analytical model of the rite of passage can be transferred to calendrical customs. The symbolic death, the masking, transfers the person from norm-bound everyday life into a 'sacred'

59. Cf. *The Ritual Process...*, *op. cit.* in n. 51, pp. 166-180.
60. Dansk Folkemindesamling. Skrifter 3, København, 1974.
61. In *Rethinking Anthropology, op. cit.* in n. 25.

festival, which represents 'alternative life' and 'eternity'. Role reversal is the external sign of this transfer (mask, disguised voice, etc.); the disengagement from everyday life makes it possible for the person not to need to perform the roles which he or she normally has: he becomes 'another person' (or 'real self'!), which however dies when the everyday self is reborn. The experience is, however, not negative; the act of disengagement as another person brings about catharsis, and the person who returns to everyday life is a 'new' person; the ritual can function as a catalyst for the growth of one's self-awareness.[62]

3. *The order of role-taking in crisis rites*

The practical difficulties in process analysis can be illustrated by the fact that there are, for example, about 500 books and articles about the behavior of a Siberian shaman in a healing situation, but amongst them there are only about 30 descriptions which are detailed enough to be accepted as primary material for process analysis. This was pointed out by Mrs Anna-Leena Kuusi, who is one of my students, and who is preparing her doctoral thesis on the structure of the shamanistic seance and the shamans' techniques of role-taking in Siberia. I recommended this topic because the general phenomenology of shamanism has been presented in studies again and again, but no one has taken the interest to analyze the rites in totality, at least not as far as Siberian material is concerned.

I had already become interested in shamanistic healing techniques a long time ago, but in 1969 I realized that to apply role theory to the analysis of the shamanistic healing process might reveal some structural features which would otherwise remain buried under heaps of motifs. I was also interested in the following hypothesis, which incidentally is still waiting to be verified: that in every seance, the shaman repeats central features from his own initiation vision, i.e. from the trance experience during which he finally gets to know the topography of the beyond and finds — first led by the teacher-shaman, and later by himself — the ways along which after his installation as a shaman he will often have to go in order to satisfy the expectations which the community puts on him.

62. Bregenhøj, *op. cit.*, pp. 98-100.

I have published an article about the role-taking of the shaman, and in it I analyzed one of Waldemar Jochelson's descriptions of the behavior of a Yukaghir shaman in a healing situation.[63] I have subsequently explicated the structural analysis in a different context.[64]

The structure of the seance is as follows: (1) the preparation of the audience; (2) the preparation of the shaman; (3) the invocation of the auxiliary spirits; (4) the addressing of the causer of the illness; (5) the 'inhalation' of the auxiliary spirits and possession by them; (6) change of roles and first dialogue: the shaman becomes the chief auxiliary spirit, and the shaman's assistant becomes the shaman; (7) the attack on the causer of the illness; (8) change of roles and second dialogue: the shaman becomes the demon of the illness, and the assistant and relatives = the audience; (9) the de-actualization of the demon of the illness; (10) the return to the role of shaman; (11) the de-actualization of the auxiliary spirits; and (12) the de-actualization of the role of shaman.

The following observations can be made: the general structure can be described in terms of a musical crescendo (1–7) and diminuendo (8–12). The attack on the causer of the illness (7) is the climax. The action is slow at the beginning, and introvert, but it gradually accelerates and becomes dramatic and expressive. The main part of the ecstasy technique of the shaman consists of role-taking: in the first part he actualizes his own role, then that of the minor auxiliary spirits, and then the causer of the illness, after which the first change of roles takes place (the possession by the auxiliary spirits). This is followed by the actualization of the chief auxiliary spirit and the second change of roles, in which the role of the shaman is transferred to his assistant. This is then followed by a struggle with the causer of the illness, the demon, which leads to victory and exhaustion. The de-actualization of the supranormal roles and ritual roles then begins, in exactly reverse order. The shaman acts as the demon of the illness, the audience addresses him and the chief auxiliary spirit, after which both supranormal beings are de-actualized. The shaman meanwhile returns to his own role, safeguards himself with prayers and looks after the patient. After this the minor auxiliary spirits are de-actualized — those supranormal beings who arrived first leave last. Finally the role of the shaman is discarded (the healer takes his ritual

63. Honko, 'Role-taking of the Shaman', *Temenos* 4 (Turku, 1969), pp. 41-47.
64. Honko, *Uskontotieteen näkökulmia*, Porvoo, 1972, pp. 195-198.

garments off and pretends to take his eyes out, telling them to stand guard, one from above, the other from below). Finally, a bird's shriek, like that of a diver, from the mouth of the shaman, and the last supranormal being is gone; the shaman rinses his mouth with water. The seance is at an end.

The hypothesis to which this process analysis gives rise is as follows: the order of actualization of the different ritual roles in the shamanistic seance, human as well as suprahuman roles, is constant in a particular culture and follows the rule: de-actualization of roles = actualization of roles in reverse order. It is my hope that Mrs Anna-Leena Kuusi or someone else will some day prove, disprove, or modify this assumption.

JAMES L. PEACOCK   *Notes on a Theory of the Social Evolution of Ritual*

Analyzing the 'elementary forms of religious life' among the Australian aborigines, Émile Durkheim dissected the religion of civilized society, as in his parallel between aboriginal totemism and Christian communion.[65] Informed by Durkheim's perspective, social anthropologists characteristically take a similar tack: accentuate the similarities rather than the differences between the primitive and the civilized. Of both theoretical and satirical value, the technique has yielded useful results as in Claude Lévi-Strauss' sardonic comparisons of Australian aborigines and French bureaucrats,[66] Brazilian jungle telegraphs and American homosexuals,[67] and it has even been adopted by the zoologist, reaching a limit of plausibility in Desmond Morris' graphic comparison of the European's sports car and the baboon's penis.[68]

In spite of the similarity between the 'primitive' and the 'advanced', it is obvious that things change as well as remain the same and that variation occurs among societies that exist simultaneously. Based on Durk-

65. Émile Durkheim, *The Elementary Forms of the Religious Life*, transl. Joseph Ward Swain, New York, 1965.

66. Claude Lévi-Strauss, *The Savage Mind*, Chicago, 1966.

67. Id., *Tristes Tropiques*, New York, 1964.

68. Desmond Morris, *The Human Zoo*, New York, 1969.

heim's central premise, that ritual has a social basis, one would expect that change and variation in ritual form and meaning correlate with change and variation in social structure. A simple way to schematicize this relationship is by formulating a theory of the social evolution of ritual. Serving as both history and typology, such a theory has the dual purpose of sketching both major phases of development and major variations among patterns still existing. In either instance, the object is to formulate relationships between ritual and its social context.

In attempting a rough and preliminary formulation of this type, I shall utilize the categories set forth by Robert Bellah in his theory of 'Religious Evolution',[69] though my analysis differs in substance from Bellah's. The orienting hypothesis is a suggestive one proposed by Max Gluckman[70] that the kind of ritual which Durkheim investigated among the aborigines is to be found only in those societies which possess what Gluckman terms 'multiplex social relationships'. Elaborating Gluckman's argument, I shall explore the association between successive transformations of these relationships and the form and meaning of ritual.

PRIMITIVE RITUAL AND SOCIETY

Gluckman distinguishes a type of ritual which he terms the 'ritual of social relations'. Such a ritual is stylized, it orders the particular social relationships that bind together its participants in daily life, and it is believed by these participants to bring order in the social, natural, and supernatural realms through mystical and supra-sensory processes. An example would be Durkheim's 'positive rite' which not only brings social solidarity to its aboriginal participants but is also believed to bestow fertility on the witchetty grub.

A condition that Gluckman sees as essential to the emergence and florescence of the ritual of social relations is the existence of 'multiplex' social relationships among the participants. By 'multiplex' is meant that the bonds linking one participant to another are many; fellow tribesmen

69. Robert Bellah, 'Religious Evolution', *American Sociological Review* 29 (1969), pp. 358-374. Bellah's scheme is elaborated in James Peacock and Thomas Kirsch, *The Human Direction*, New York, 1973 (rev. ed.).

70. Max Gluckman, 'Les Rites de Passage', in Max Gluckman, ed., *Essays on the Ritual of Social Relations*, Manchester, 1962.

or peasants share claims to land, are neighbors, kinsmen, fellow members of a localized political unit, educate their children together, and so forth. Because multiplex relationships are so diffuse, impinging on so many aspects of existence, disorder in such relationships has diffuse effects. Disorder disturbs the natural and supernatural orders, bringing plague, famine, and the wrath of the spirits while the ritual ordering of such relations has similarly diffuse positive effects.

Although Gluckman's theory has not been tested, it is sufficiently concrete to lend itself to checking. A negative confirmation is a Javanese funeral that failed, analyzed by Clifford Geertz.[71] While Geertz' explanation goes beyond the scope of Gluckman's theory, an essential condition of the funeral's failure is the reduction, in an urban setting, of multiplex bonds which are strong in the peasant communities where the funerals work properly. Another negative confirmation is modern drama, which fits none of the features of Gluckman's ritual of social relations. Modern drama in its typical forms is comparatively naturalistic instead of stylized; it is relatively powerless to order its actors' daily relations since they do not play their daily roles in the drama; finally, though the drama may be supposed to have psychological impact, as in Brecht's notion that drama moves an audience toward decision, only the fanatic believes that the drama directly affects the cosmic, natural, and wider social spheres through mystical and magical channels. Such dramas occur in settings and communities whose relationships are not multiplex: audience and actor are united only by the purchase of a ticket, and their daily lives are composed of similarly thin threads of relationship. Modern drama thus confirms Gluckman's theory by exhibiting an associated reduction of both the ritual form and the social relationships that Gluckman postulates as co-existing in primitive society.

Turning to the positive, where both the social conditions and the ritual are present, an exemplary case is provided by Victor Turner's study of healing among the Ndembu of Rhodesia.[72] Turner's analysis

71. Clifford Geertz, 'Ritual and Social Change: A Javanese Example', *American Anthropologist* 59 (1957), pp. 32-59.

72. Victor Turner, 'A Ndembu Doctor in Practice', in *Forest of Symbols: Aspects of Ndembu Ritual*, Ithaca, New York, 1967; *The Drums of Affliction: A Study of Religious Processes Among the Ndembu of Zambia*, London, 1968. These works and others by Turner not only analyze a case in remarkable detail but also have suggested theoretical points that underly this paper.

shows that a remarkably powerful psychotherapy can be brought about by ritual ordering of social relationships which are 'multiplex'. Gluckman asserts that both this type of ritual and these types of relationships are found in kinship-based communities in Homeric Greece, early Rome, Judea, China, Anglo-Saxon and Viking lands, and pagan Europe in general, as well as in contemporary tribal and perhaps peasant groups. The ethnological literature is of course rife with examples of Gluckman's ritual in such groups. I would prefer to distinguish, however, between the tribal or peasant communities where kinship or shared territory are the major modes of organization, and kingships, where relations between ruler and subject furnish the major axes of organization. These structures I shall discuss under a separate category though they exist in the ancient classic societies mentioned by Gluckman.

In the primitive, kinship-based societies, rites are interpreted in terms of symbolic schemes, such as totemism, which are intimately wedded to the social order. In totemism, for example, each clan is associated with a particular totem, and, as Lévi-Strauss has emphasized,[73] the totemic system as a whole is parallel in structure to the social organization. The parallel is not merely a logical one that yields intellectual meaning through classifying the social in terms of the natural, but (here Lévy-Bruhl[74] would seem to add a needed element to Lévi-Strauss) the natives felt such intimacy between the social and the totemic order, that at times they speak as if they *are* the totems. Because of this intimate association between the natural/supernatural and social orders it is relatively easy for a social rupture to disturb the natural/supernatural harmony. At least this would follow from the logic of the analysis so far.

As Max Weber[75] has pointed out, when the 'primitive' comes to differentiate his reflective (e.g., totemic) order from his active (e.g., ritual) order, he sets in motion the decline of the ritual. The reason is that by differentiating the reflective from the active, one feels a need to explain the active, and explanation comes only by systematizing or rationalizing the reflective. But the more the reflective schema is rationalized, the more it differs from the hodge podge of practice. Accordingly there

73. Claude Lévi-Strauss, *Totemism*, transl. Rodney Needham, Boston, 1963.
74. Lucien Lévy-Bruhl, *How Natives Think*, transl. Lilian A. Claire, New York, 1966. For detailed discussion see a forthcoming volume on Metaphor by Christopher Crocker and David Sapir, eds.
75. Max Weber, *Sociology of Religion*, transl. Ephraim Fischer, Boston, 1964.

develops, inevitably, an urge to reform the rituals in order to render them more consistent with the scheme. Thinking of Weber's other usage of the term 'rationalization' (*zweckrational*, the tendency to bring about a more efficient or 'rational' relationship between means and ends), one might expect that another trend in the evolution away from ritual is toward emphasizing its causal efficacy, its power as a means to achieve an end, rather than as a form providing meaning in terms of its traditional order. Once ritual is regarded as a technique, the push is strong toward stream-lining to the point that it ceases to be ritual.

ARCHAIC RITUAL AND SOCIETY

Archaic society is found wherever kingship, royalty, and aristocracy are the major units of social order, as in the classic societies mentioned by Gluckman, and in Hinduized Southeast Asia, Mesopotamia, ancient Egypt, perhaps middle America and the African kingdoms as well. In such a society social relations are multiplex but also hierarchical, rather than egalitarian as in primitive society. Master-servant, lord-serf, ruler-subject relationships are the social axes. Such relations, frequently perceived in the analogy of father-child, are multiplex in that each party depends on the other for a wide range of services — total livelihood in the case of the underlying, economic, political, military, and emotional support in the case of the superior. Owing to the diffuseness of the relationship, disturbance of it would ramify deeply and widely into the lives of its parties and their community. Accordingly, elaborate codes of etiquette, including distinctive styles of language, gesture, and honorific titles, are developed in order to maintain harmony.[76]

In archaic society, the cosmic or sacred has to a degree been removed from local or kinship groups and awarded either to gods who, though inhabiting the earth, are outside the social order, or to the king and the nobility, who are at the top of the order. In Hinduized Southeast Asia and ancient Egypt, for example, the king is a god, and in ancient China and Mesopotamia he is a priest who has special access to the divine. In either case, some of the divine charisma flows down to princes, nobles,

---

76. See Clifford Geertz, *Religion of Java*, New York, 1960, Part III, for an example of such elaboration of language, manner, and title in Java.

and lords, who are perceived as occupying a cosmic-social category totally separate from the unwashed masses. The commoner finds it difficult
if not impossible to emotionally identify with these exalted figures in
the way the primitive could identify with his totem.

Two major types of ritual that are prominent in archaic society are
the rite of sacrifice and the rite of kingship. Through sacrifice a priest
endeavors to bridge the gap that has developed between man and god. As
Lévi-Strauss[77] has observed, sacrifice differs from totemism in numerous
aspects. One difference is that sacrifice is more open to manipulation;
one can choose one's sacrificial object (but not one's totem), one performs operations with it to achieve an end (whereas the totem is a symbolic order that confers meaning), and one cannot tell for certain the
operation's outcome (whereas the totem system is a timeless structure,
raising no question of outcomes). As Bellah notes, sacrifice brings con-
tingency and anxiety as well as freedom in the relationship between
the secular and the sacred.

The ritual of kingship can be seen as bridging the gap between superior
and inferior while affirming the essential strength of the socio-cosmic
order that underlies their hierarchical relationship. Such rituals permit
mockery of the superior by the inferior, reversal of roles, or the transcendence of the inferior by the superior as when the former asserts his
wit against the latter's power. In societies where the king is in relatively
close touch with his subjects, as among the Swazi of Africa,[78] the king in
person may be ritually abused by his subjects in person. In the more complex and bureaucratized societies, such as those of Hinduized Southeast
Asia, the ritual is a drama in which actors represent the king, the princes,
and the aristocracy while the role of the people is taken by stylized
clowns, who cleverly transcend, mock, and reduce the status of the
rulers while dancers and mythic symbols affirm the basis of their order.
Whether the Swazi or Southeast Asian type, such ritual-dramas are, in
their traditional form, believed to renew through mystical channels the
cosmic-social order. Hence they qualify as rituals of social relations.

Such ritual-dramas have a distinctive form, compared to modern
drama. Because jokes, dance, costume, the shape of puppet-figures,
and other symbolic elements count more than plot-line, unwavering

77. Lévi-Strauss, *The Savage Mind.*
78. Hilda Kuper, *An African Aristocracy: Rank Among the Swazi*, London, 1965.

concentration on the narrative is not important. Accordingly the performance can last for hours, normally all night, with the audience recessing to eat, sleep, socialize, and excrete. The participants have been taught from birth not to identify with their superiors but to imitate their manners, hence the performance delves little into the psychology of the princely heroes, but instead concentrates on their manners and mien, as imitated by the clowns, mockingly, or by dancers, admiringly.[79]

In archaic society the notion of statuses separated by manners is extended to the sphere of sexuality: males and females are segregated from each other, related by codes of chivalry. This situation may explain the presence of transvestism in archaic drama. In the first place, if women are to be secluded, they are not permitted on stage: men therefore take female parts. In the second place, if women are idealized to the point of fantasy, a fantasy female — a masquerading male — may well carry a peculiar appeal. Finally, in archaic societies where the male/female opposition is enlarged into a cosmic division, the quasi-cosmic unity of the two in transvestism provides a certain charge and meaning. In the Indonesian societies, in particular, transvestism has assumed a sacral quality as it unites male and female, upperworld and underworld, right and left, and other cosmic oppositions. Clown and transvestite differ in that the clown mocks the alien status (nobility) while the transvestite joins the opposition, assuming the role of the female.[80]

HISTORIC SOCIETY AND RITUAL

Oriented around medieval Islam, Christianity, and Buddhism, historic societies retain the hierarchical relationship between inferior and superior, but the relationship's 'multiplexity' is diminished because the superior loses his sacral quality. The sacred is now located outside the social

79. The description here applies to a degree to most classical Southeast Asian drama, but especially to the *wajang kulit* and *wajang wong* of Java. See James R. Brandon, *Theater in Southeast Asia*, Cambridge, Mass., 1967.

80. These points concerning transvestite and clown in Indonesia are elaborated in James L. Peacock, 'Symbolic Reversal and Social History: the Transvestite and Clown of Java', mimeographed paper, presented at 1972 meetings of American Anthropological Association, symposium on symbolic reversal. The richest source of information on these two figures is Th. Pigeaud, *Javaanse Volksvertoningen: Bijdrage tot de Beschrijving van Land en Volk*, Batavia, 1938.

sphere, in an otherworld-afterworld — a heaven or a Nirvana — which is more sharply differentiated from the mundane realm than was any category in archaic society. Owing to the enormous importance of attaining a good afterlife, there emerge specialists in salvation such as monks, saints, and ascetics who live apart from the political order, taking from it sacral functions formerly performed by the archaic priest-or-god-king.

Historic rituals are oriented toward the otherworld, as in prayer services in church or mosque directed at God or Allah. These rituals fail to conform to Gluckman's definition of the 'ritual of social relationships' in that they are oriented around the otherworldly sphere rather than the network of relationships among members of the congregation (who may be strangers to one another). Yet the prayers do fit Gluckman's definition in that they are believed to affect the natural, supernatural, and social orders through suprasensory channels. Gluckman's theory could be extended by arguing that the historic rituals *are* ritually ordering the relationships that compose such expansive religious communities as the Christian Church or the Muslim Ummah.

The third feature of Gluckman's definition, stylization, is highly developed in these rituals. They employ special, sacred languages such as Latin, Arabic, and Pali which are incomprehensible to the laity, signifying the separation between these otherworldly rites and the worldly life. Esoteric languages, ornamental ceremonialism, and exotic mysticism affirm the special sanctity of the differentiated religious bureaucracy, the Church, the Sangha, or the Muslim semi-priesthood.

MODERNIZATION AND RITUAL

In the modernizing process, exemplified by Protestant, Muslim, and Buddhist reformation movements, by nativistic movements (e.g., the Vailala madness of Melanesia),[81] and nationalist or Communist revolutions, great stress is on the purge of traditional rituals. The most obvious reason for the purge is that the rituals have bolstered the established order, which must now be destroyed. A more subtle reason is that modernization conceives of a symbolic order (a utopia, an afterlife, a

81. Peter Worsley, *The Trumpet Shall Sound: A Study of Cargo Cults in Melanesia*, New York, 1967.

Nirvana) toward which men must struggle in this world through some kind of rationalizing rather than ritual activity. Ritual, by definition, is oriented toward celebrating the eternal, the social and cosmic structure that was, is, and ever shall be. The rationalizing of worldly activity so that it more efficiently thrusts toward some future end requires the constant modification of action, a requirement that opposes the rigidity which ritual must maintain, or appear to maintain, in order to celebrate the unchanging.

While modernizing movements reduce the ritual of conventional religion, they tend to encourage the growth of secular performances (after initial puritanical phases when all sensuous form is condemned). These are of myriad types, but two prominent ones are those that accompany collectivist modernization and those that accompany individualist modernization.

The collectivist type of performance is exemplified by films and dramas of Nazi Germany, Communist Russia and China, and the new nations of Africa and Asia. In at least some of the dramas common to such societies, the plot depicts the individual as relentlessly but enthusiastically and heroically swept along by forces of history toward a collective goal (Sigfried Kracauer[82] sees such plots in Nazi Germany as foreshadowed by horror films portraying individuals as moved by dark spiritual destinies). The plots are moralistic and didactic in order to teach the revolutionary ideals. Heroes are charismatic and superior to onlookers but lack the supernatural power of archaic princes. Enemy scapegoats are prominent as targets for the collective thrust. The archaic hierarchy is replaced by an egalitarian companionship among youths or comrades-at-arms, as in the German *Brüderschaft* or *Hitlerjugend*. With the loss of hierarchy and the mystique of the historic otherworld, there occurs a loss of popularity of such exotic figures as the clown, dwarf, and transvestite, as well as the priest, mystic, and ascetic. With the declining importance of such cosmic symbols, which furnish periodic interludes in hierarchical existence, the plot tightens, sequence becomes important, and narratives drive toward a climax as the forces of history, in Lukács' terms, 'collide'.[83]

82. Sigfried Kracauer, *From Caligari to Hitler: A Psychological History of the German Film*, Princeton, 1966.
83. Georg Lukács, *The Historical Novel*, trans. Hannah and Stanley Mitchell,

Modernizing performances of the individualist type are illustrated by American films of Hollywood's Golden Age. Depicting success mixed with romance, such films depict doing for the sake of doing rather than glorifying loyalty as an abstract, collective ideal. Plots are fast-moving, with hustle and pep. Heterosexual love instead of homosexual comradeship is romanticized. Comradeship may aid the collectivist struggle, but it can disrupt the climb to personal success. The ambitious man is held back by the gang on the streetcorner, in the barracks, or in the Bank Wiring Room.[84] The social climber is better advised to fall in love, marry, and form a mobile nuclear family unit that climbs with him. Modernizing, individualistic films tend to be short, partly in order to depict as clearly and compactly as possible the connection between initial ambition and final success, partly in order to not take too much time from the job, and partly in order to make money in the box office. Youths are not part of the political system in the society, with the result that where they are incorporated into the films (as in the American teenage romance), the themes resonate with hedonistic leisure youth culture, and the art is silly and trivial.

Particularly in the new nations or the developing regions, dramas combine aspects of both the collectivist and individualist types and retain archaic and historic elements as well. An example is the *ludruk* drama of Indonesia, analyzed elsewhere as a 'rite of modernization'.[85] The ludruk, a drama both performed and watched by working class people in East Java, has undergone an evolution from a highly stylized play containing only the clown and the transvestite to a naturalistic drama including among its plots a romance/success package where a heroine (played by a male) climbs in status through marriage to a upper-class hero. The plots have evolved from a type where this marriage failed to come about to a type where it successfully occurs. Such bourgeois plots are complemented by revolutionary plots of the collectivist type,

Boston, 1963; and 'Zur Soziologie des Modernen Drama', *Archiv für Sozialwissenschaft und Sozialpolitik* XXXVIII (1914), pp. 303-45, 662-706.

84. The groups mentioned have all been the subject of classic sociological studies: William F. Whyte on the lower class 'streetcorner gang', Edward Shils on the cohesiveness of the Germany military group, and Roethlisberger and Dickson on the manner in which workers in a bank-wiring room stifle the ambition of a rate-buster.

85. James L. Peacock, *Rites of Modernization: Symbolic and Social Aspects of Indonesian Proletarian Drama*, Chicago, 1968.

and the ludruk continues to feature clowns and transvestites, though these 'archaic' figures lose importance as the modernizing plots gain: there are instances of direct conflict between actors with vested interest in the two aspects of the dramas.

MODERN SOCIETY AND RITUAL

With modernity, the multiplexity of social relationships continues to decrease due to economic specialization, technological development, and associated social trends. Such tendencies correlate with a continuing decline of conventional ritual, whether of the archaic or historic type. Yet as alienation and disillusionment spread, countertrends emerge throughout the industrialized world.

Sociologically, the most important countertrend is the movement toward communes, the return to the soil, the establishment of quasi- villages. Long successful among such religious and ideological groups as the Hutterites and Zionists, the new movement is popular primarily among the young, whose communes lack the self-sufficiency and sta- bility of the older ones.

Associated with the communal movement has been a desire for redis- covery of meaningful ritual, a craving celebrated by a popular American magazine in its feature essay entitled 'Ritual: The Revolt Against the Fixed Smile'.[86] The essay insightfully identifies the lack of authentic ritual as a major problem of modern life. But it naively supposes that powerful ritual, as in primitive society, is made possible through orgiastic spontaneity which is lost through the 'fixed smile' of overly-rigid mod- ern rites that have become routine and empty. More correct in light of anthropological studies is the view that modern ritual is empty because the traditions which it expresses are too unstable to render the ritual rigidities meaningful. Rigid rules of primitive ritual are meaningful be- cause of the stability of the cosmic and social structures which they embody. Lacking deeply rooted structures which provide meaning and stability, the yoga, drug trips, transcendental meditation, rock festivals, Hari Krishna dances, country music and fundamentalist Christian reviv- als of the youth would not seem to be authentic ritual. Even historic

86. *Time*, October 12, 1970, p. 42.

rituals derive from a rigidly held belief in the other world, a structure of faith which has disappeared for many with the emergence of the demythologized assumption that no worlds exist 'out there', and that there are as many worlds as the individual can imagine, but all exist within himself. Such a worldview removes the drastic gap between other- and this-world, and relieves the individual of the puritan compulsion to cleanse the world of ritual in order to remove idolatrous love of wordly sensuous form, but it also deprives him of a symbolic structure that has been a source of stability and creativity.

CONCLUDING NOTE

Any formulation of the type presented here must be regarded as preliminary and temporary. The purpose is simply to place in some kind of framework particular studies, issues, and relationships that have been important in the history of religions. Significant phenomena have been omitted from discussion (for example, Greek drama and Judaic legalism, to mention only two seminal ritual forms which do not seem to fit the scheme neatly). Hopefully the conference will provide criticism, correction, and enrichment.

Commentary   by G. J. F. Bouritius

1. Both papers here presented attempt to give a deeper background to the study of rituals and ritual process, which are some of the most substantial forms of religious experience. The means to attain that purpose are different: the Honko paper offers a more extended logical classification of rituals, continuing to embroider the Van Gennep theme, after a critical survey of some well-known classical classifications of rituals. It puts the question how a better-elaborated functional analysis in the study of ritual could be traced, indicating this by means of three examples from recent literature. The Peacock paper outlines a theory of the social evolution of ritual, based on the correlation of ritual and its social basis (Durkheim): a draft meant to be of both typological and

historical character, which should also be of great interest for our out-look on the development of rituals in the future. Though the papers are rather different in design and in method, within the limited space avail-able to me I shall try to put forward some notes and offer some obser-vations concerning both papers.

2. The two papers emphasize the social background of the groups whose rituals are studied. Special attention to the social moment is explicitly claimed since ritual cannot be adequately comprehended without its social surroundings. This is an important step forward in the study of the phenomenology of religion. Too often, one-sided attention has been directed to religious phenomena as independent topics. In the last forty years only a few social anthropologists have had insight into the strong cohesion between ritual and the facts of social life. The quotation by Honko of V. Turner points clearly to the social structure and, in connec-tion with this, to processes of structural change in the societies whose rituals are being scrutinized.

3. Here, however, a problem also arises, and some points of criticism will have to be touched on, especially concerning the methods used. In the theory of ritual evolution in the Peacock paper there are a number of connections between religious ritual and social organization which seem rather inaccurate, or have been incorrectly generalized. In a very 'rough and preliminary formulation' it should not be acceptable to generalize and to join primitive kinship-based societies with totemism, a rather curi-ous system, certainly not at all typical of 'primitive society' as Durkheim supposed. It is only to be found among some tribal hunters and in such a manner, varying in forms and contents, that it is really problematic whether it can be conceived as an univocal phenomenon. Most tribal peoples are agriculturists and do not know totemism. Totemism may lend itself to some philosophical speculations, but in tribal society it is a rather obscure reality. R. Bellah's typology of primitive, archaic and historic society which Peacock utilizes is highly arbitrary: in the history of culture, there are no clear boundaries. In cultural anthropology more generally accepted levels of organization are bands, tribes, chiefdoms, primitive states and modern folk societies.[87] Ascertaining this fact is

---

87. E. R. Service, *Profiles in Ethnology*, New York, 1963.

important since 'kingship' and 'hierarchy' exist in many tribal societies as well as in societies of the civilization type. And in those societies (Ancient Egypt, Hinduized South-Asia) is the king really a god? Or a priest? What is a god or a priest? Have we clear notions of them, or is it exactly the task of our science to develop more accurate methods to be able in the future to use outstanding concepts for sound comparative study? And why should sacrifice be prominent in archaic society? I am sure we can speak with more scientific exactness about sacrifice, a central ritual in many tribal groups, after thorough investigation through fieldwork, than we can ever know about sacrifice in many ancient religions! Some such speculations are of a strongly marginal character, as is shown in the effort to compare wholly different categories like sacrifice and totemism. Such an observation by Lévi-Strauss seems more like a fascinating but gratuitous puzzle than a serious attempt at insight. Bellah himself informs us that his description of a primitive stage of religion is a theoretical abstraction and is heavily indebted to Lévy-Bruhl (1935) and Stanner (*Australian religion*, 1959).[88] It may be useful to set up a model as a means to study a complex problem, e. g. evolution, but when the stages introduced here are only 'ideal types derived from a theoretical formulation of the most generally observable historical regularities' and 'the scheme itself not intended as an adequate description of historical reality', and 'particular lines of religious development cannot simply be forced into the terms of the scheme',[89] one asks oneself whether this kind of sociological approach to the complex phenomena of religious rituals can contribute anything to our deeper knowledge of the relations between religion and society. To illustrate my problem: the *ludruk* drama of Indonesia (or of Java?)(cf. p. 399), analyzed as a 'rite of modernization' combining aspects of both the collectivist and individualist types, serves as an example of the evolution of (religious) drama 'in the new nations or the developing regions', which is very interesting. However, is this example really representative of the evolution of drama in the new nations? I should like to have some information about the old religious Islamic theater in the Husan-Husain festival of Sumatra (and Persia), too, before I could verify such generalizations: it is highly possible that such

---

88. R. Bellah, 'Religious Evolution', *loc. cit.*, cited in R. Robertson, *Sociology of Religion*, Harmondsworth, 1969, p. 269.
89. R. Bellah, *Ibid.*, pp. 266, 267.

a development is absent there, not on account of a lower degree of modernization in Sumatra, but because orthodox Islamic religion reacts upon processes of modernization in a different manner from Hindu-Javanese religion. This is important for the phenomenologist of religion; the sociologist's scheme seems then to be of less use. Another point: Peacock writes (p. 400): 'with modernity the multiplexity of social relationships continues to decrease ... correlat[ing] with a continuing decline of conventional ritual'. A first general impression seems to affirm that hypothesis. But well documented religious developments in India disclose to us another picture, which does not fit into the scheme. Ancient Hinduism, a typical country religion of the Indian agricultural village, has been new-born in the very heart of the modern industrial and urbanizing life of the Indian metropolis: immigrants from the country working in the cities in all kinds of professions assemble at fixed times to hold a religious service of which the core consists in singing songs for Krishna in the ancient classic and orthodox Hindu tradition, adapted to the new urban conditions. One of the outgrowths of these rituals: members have broken through the caste barriers and exert themselves to develop friendly attitudes to all their fellow citizens in daily life.[90] Urbanizing conditions did not destroy ancient rituals, on the contrary, they have led to a regeneration of these rituals, creating a totally new life-style for their modern adherents. I do not reject models for handling problems of our science, but I should like to plead in favor of a starting-point based more on single, well-elaborated case-studies. However fascinating the Bellah-Peacock model may be, it seems to me of little usefulness for a deeper insight into the real dynamics of religion, by generalizing about a lot of religious phenomena only from the sociological point of view.

4. The classification of rituals in the Honko paper offers us a well-fitted scheme representing a practical taxonomy, in which rites of passage, calendrical rites and crisis rites are inserted, each group characterized on the basis of trends like individual- or group-oriented, recurrent/non-recurrent, and anticipated/unanticipated. The proposal is to have these groupings of rituals as 'cultural universals', a very desirable tool for growing religious research. I would like to make some remarks on this

90. M. Singer, 'The Radha-Krishna Bhajans of Madras City', *Hist. of Religions* 2 (1963), pp. 183-226.

classification, as there is some connection with the problem mentioned above. The division of the first two groups raises no problem. A problem originates in the third group: crisis rites. Many authors use the expression for different rituals and the author points to an inflation of the concept of crisis. He pleads for saving the term crisis for a narrower and more sensible use. That is easily understood, from other than taxonomical points of view, too. Where does this confusion about the concept arise from? I suppose, on account of a rather limited starting point for the drawing up of a classification of rituals, namely only the social one: 'which are the social circumstances of the concerning ritual'; and this question put from a rather western ethnocentric point of view. In this way, 'crisis' can be conceived in a different manner; it concerns the psychic commotions of people, conceived as individuals or as members of community. The real question is: what are the deeper contents of 'crisis' in religious experience that find expression in religious rituals? Or: what is the religious implication of the concept of 'crisis'? A first analysis seems to lead to the view that a division merely of the type made by Van Gennep is unsatisfactory. My question is: don't we want a broader background to classify all religious rituals, not as loose categories on the basis of rather superficial social phenomena, but as real religious phenomena from a religious background? Religion has a wider dimension than social features alone. Or, to cite M. E. Spiro: 'we seriously err in mistaking an explanation of society for an explanation of religion which, in effect, means confusing the sociological functions of religion with the bases for its performance'.[91] The paper states (p. 380) that V. Turner is not able to classify some Ndembu-rituals within the Honko/Van Gennep scheme and he is right to group them under the general label of 'rites of affliction'. Honko, however, doubts its applicability in comparative studies: 'this designation will never approach the level of a 'cultural universal'.' Nevertheless, the fact is that hunting cults and also women's fertility cults are common rituals in many groups of the comparable type of culture. Where should they be classified? Nor is Turner's solution satisfactory, since he seems to work on the same limited base of social features alone. In his outstanding field work among the Ndembu he has given us what is up to now the richest material about

91. M. E. Spiro, 'Religion: Problems of definition and explanation', in *Anthropological Approaches to the Study of Religion*, A. S. A. Monographs 3, p. 122.

African initiation and divination cults. His interpretation of certain aspects of circumcision and curing rites within the framework of neighborhood relations and within the basic normative aspects of conflicts between kin, sex and age groups is impressive. But we have no broad account of Ndembu cosmology[92] and its relation to any of the detailed elaborated symbolic subsystems of ritual life. However, these symbols also have a religious meaning, as all religious symbolic systems have. He discusses the rituals of life crises, but there is little information about burials and funerals, or about birth and marriage rites: they could contribute to our knowledge of the typical religious aspects of their ritual, and also to our appreciation of the full implications of the already well-documented initiation rituals.

More attention, perhaps, should be given to another relation, within which social relations also exist, in order to build up a classification able to include other common rituals. This could be indicated as a macro-micro-cosmic order relationship. Most societies see the creation or origin of their community as an immediate outcome of a process of abolishing the macrocosmic primordial chaos by the establishment of a (supra-human) macrocosmic order, within which the society concerned has its place as a human microcosmic replica. Life is the continuation of that order by maintaining this relationship, which is perceived as being of a substantial and normative character. Nevertheless, there is always still the latent tension between hidden chaos and (divine) order. In this way, order is conceived of as *potential disorder* and all rituals in life are directed to the continuation and realization of this everlasting order of macrocosmic and microcosmic relationship. The order is everlasting; the forms, however, in which this order has to be realized, are always in motion, adapted to time, place, social and historical environment. All rituals can be understood as ordering a continuum. All rituals can be understood as fighting the hidden chaos manifest in all evil in life. All rituals, then, could be subdivided into three groupings accordingly: (1) *ordering*, (2) *re-ordering* and (3) *new-ordering* the macro-micro-relationship. The first group could include: (a) rites of passage: an ordering of the community which puts its members in their just place (rites de passage are rituals of the *whole* society, not only of the individual members); (b) all simple daily rituals wanted for daily life (simple hunting

92. In Turner, *Forest of Symbols...*, one page out of 322!

rituals; rituals to increase the fertility of man, animal and earth; many family rituals). The second group could comprise: (a) calendrical (I prefer: seasonal) rituals: re-ordering the human society and its concrete environment of place and time on the everlasting model of the original macro-cosmic order (solemn rituals of fertility; of harvest; New Year etc.) accompanying the renewal powers of nature; (b) rituals fighting the latent chaos in daily life: healing rituals; anti-sorcery rituals; rituals of some anti-witchcraft movements; some of Turner's rituals of affliction. (These could be named 'anti-disturbance' rituals: they re-order the macro-micro-relationship, disturbed by evil agents.) In the third group, of new-ordering rituals, should be placed all the rituals of new religious movements; syncretistic rituals (umbanda etc.), 'transitional' cults, or Turner's rituals of 'liminality'. These rituals new-order the macro-micro-cosmic relationship in totally new circumstances unbounded to kinship, time or place. The advantages of this classification would be: (1) a more open criterion, that also takes account of the typical religious aspect of ritual; (2) a less ethnocentric view of ritual, which always is a function of the community; (3) the possibility to arrange many less prominent but nonetheless very substantial daily religious rites within a scheme; (4) the possibility to arrange rituals of newly arising religions or religious movements in a general classification.

5. Special attention is required for the last grouping of rituals in connection with rituals of new religious movements. V. Turner drew attention to the concept of 'liminality'. 'The liminal stage, when the subject is in spatial separation from the familiar and habitual, constitutes a cultural domain that is extremely rich in cosmological meaning, conveyed largely by nonverbal symbols. Liminality represents a negation of many of the features of preliminal social structures and an affirmation of another order of things, stressing generic rather than particularistic relationships.'[93] Here ritual has a particular role in elucidating the actual development of religious experience, in new-ordering the macro-micro-cosmic relationship: which of the ancient religious values are to be maintained, which new values are to be accepted; an important matter not only for the study of new religions in the Third World but also for the new developments within high-culture religions. Many 'new religions' are elsewhere

93. V. Turner, 'The Center...', *op. cit.* in n. 55, p. 213.

called – in a crude, summary term – 'crisis-cults'.[94] How far the tension structure/anti-structure within these rituals can exist, as Turner thinks is open to doubt;[95] it offers, perhaps, new materials for historians who wish to look for a continuity of ritual symbolism in periods of rapid change,[96] but has not been elaborated by Turner himself, possibly on the ground of his lack of a cosmological view.[97]

6. More attention for the metasocial dimension of religious ritual can lead to a more critical hermeneutics of the many forms of ritual, and to the creation of new working concepts as general tools, more in agreement with the results of recent field work. These concepts should be able to reproduce rather more of religious reality than the rather superficial – and therefore inaccurate – indications we use today. One interesting point in this respect is their treatment in encyclopaedias of our science. It is worth noticing here that, for example, the very important concept of *divination* as a religious phenomenon is not to be found in the new *Dictionary of Comprehensive Religion*, edited by Prof. Brandon (1970), and that the concept of *sacrifice* there is described in a lot of mere accidental forms without any substantial description of its phenomenological character, to name only two examples. More methodical comparative research should try to conceive the totality of a religious ritual and to avoid as far as possible any ethnocentric approach. The question of the total context is substantial: the same phenomenon in another region in another context is clearly something different. Harwood takes to task those outstanding fieldworkers Evans-Pritchard and Middleton for their 'ethnocentric conceptions' in the somewhat inadequate context of their description of 'witchcraft'.[98]

My plea is for a methodological approach to all forms of ritual, with sufficient subtlety to interpret them, in the total context of the living community, in order to shape working concepts and working models

94. Weston la Barre, 'Materials for a History of Studies of Crisis Cults: A Bibliographic Essay', *Current Anthropology* 12 (1971), pp. 3-44.

95. R. G. Willis, *Africa* 41 (1971), p. 71.

96. *The Historical Study of African Religions*, ed. by T. O. Ranger and J. N. Kimambo, London, 1972, pp. 142-143.

97. R. Horton, 'African Conversion', *Africa* 41 (1971), pp. 93, 94.

98. A. Harwood, *Witchcraft, Sorcery and Social Categories Among the Safwa*, London, 1970, pp. 69-75.

which will be precise tools to gain insight in the always fascinating question as to what religious ritual, and religion is. In this sense I fully support the two proposals made by Prof. Honko on p. 383.

Commentary   by Jacques H. Kamstra

The remarks I have to make in this paper concern on the one hand the ritual process, as the point of departure for my thoughts, and on the other hand they touch the depth structure of religion as one of the basic elements on which the ritual process also is dependent.

Ritual Process and Human Situation

In reading the papers of Prof. Peacock and Prof. Honko I got the impression that particularly the theories of Durkheim and Van Gennep constitute for them the doorstep which opens the way to further thoughts about ritual process. In fact the theory of Van Gennep reveals somehow some basic anthropology, namely that man has to live from stage to stage and can only know more about himself by, precisely, passing through many succeeding stages of life. So human history is the history of man, who only partially and successively finds out the truth about himself. He will never be totally human at any one time, and he will always need many stages and situations in order to express all of himself and his history. The history of Christendom therefore is also the history of man encountering different situations, to which he had to react in different ways, over and over again, by reformulating dogmas and by creating new rites. The intelligibility of a ritual therefore depends on that of the situation in which it originated. As soon as the situation changes, ritual becomes ununderstandable. To my mind, this conclusion makes to some extent a general theory about ritual rather questionable. I hope to show why.

Ritual process and sociology

The authors of the papers particularly stressed the importance of sociological analysis for the understanding of ritual process. I am also convinced of the fact that phenomenology of religion until now very often
failed to take the results of sociology of religion seriously into account.
Many sociological aspects in our discipline have not been sufficiently
stressed. In my opinion this should be done in interdisciplinary cooperation together with sociologists. On the other side sociology is not
yet and will not be the only discipline to which all religious facts have
to be reduced. In rethinking Van Gennep, in confronting his theories
with those of Durkheim, sociology might help us to find appropriate
schemes in which the ritual process can be better classified, as for example Honko has shown. It might also help us to find new structures
in which it can be better understood, as there are the different stages
in polarity between the sacred and the profane in Honko's and Leach's
articles.[99] It might also enrich us with new concepts and the structures
behind them. V. W. Turner, for example, has supplied us with the term
of liminality, which illustrates how some rituals can be used in inferior
groups to restore the balance of power.[100] All of these new additions,
categories, schemes and structures, however, clarify only one aspect of
the ritual process, namely its horizontal dimension. There are still some
other dimensions left, on which — to my mind — the whole study of this
phenomenon depends. These dimensions are not to be sought in the
horizontal plane, the conscious or the subconscious of man or his savage
of domesticated mind (Lévi-Strauss)[101] but vertically: the dimension
of the sacred and the philosophy which includes that dimension. In
other words ritual cannot be studied and analyzed in isolation from the
philosophy which supports it. It has to be studied in correlation with the
ideological system of which it forms an integral part. In proposing this,
I am putting forward an idea on which I have been pondering for several years and which came to me during my stay in Japan (1954-1960).
This idea corresponds somehow with the adage: East is East and West is
West. This idea came up together with the question whether we are not

99. Cf. *supra* pp. 387ff. and the article by Edmund R. Leach mentioned *supra*
p. 387.
100. Victor W. Turner, *The Ritual Process...*, *op. cit.* in n. 51, pp. 94ff.
101. Claude Lévi-Strauss, *The Savage Mind*, Chicago, 1966.

engaged in a too western way with the phenomenon of ritual by con-
ceptualizing, classifying and structuralizing it instead of approaching it
in the eastern way by catching it, as a Zen-monk does in his satori, or by
living with it as most of the New Guinea tribesmen do. Before I start to
work out my idea I would like to draw attention to some propositions
which are needed for clarification.

Towards a more specific understanding of ritual process and ritual

1. *The propositions.* As I stated before: man lives in different situations,
and man is made by these situations. Religious facts therefore will have
to be understood within the totality of these situations, that is to say:
within the whole of the cultural and sociological environment in which
they exist. This statement implies:

a) It is impossible to isolate religious facts from their cultural, sociological and philosophical setting. I do therefore not accept the eclectic
methods of Frazer and Lévi-Strauss,[102] who try to prove their theses
simply by using all kinds of material pell-mell from all over the world
and in isolation from their own cultures and religions. It is impossible
to speak of a shamanistic ritual, for instance, if I do not have clearly in
mind in what kind of culture it functions: in Siberia or in Japan...

b) When I talk about religious elements in ritual, for instance, I always
have to keep in mind the other religious elements which together with
it constitute religion. The reason why I have to do so is simply that all
the religious elements together in some specific religion have a special
color or flavor which they derive from each other. Just by their totality,
religious elements are constituted as what they are: religious. As soon
as this totality is broken, magic comes in. Religious elements do not
deserve magical treatment. In Holland, for instance, the changes in ideas
about God and the churches can also be read from changes in ritual. So
it is impossible to speak about ritual and ritual process if I do not keep
in mind its relations with the ideas of God, world, man and society,
which are somehow fused together in the ritual.

c) Because the above-mentioned ideas about God, the world, man and
society are different all over the world, there are no two rituals from

102. Particularly in *The Savage Mind.*

two different cultures which are the same. This I would like to illustrate further. With his idea of 'Das Heilige', R. Otto thought that he had established a central idea which could be applied to the idea of the sacred in all religions all over the world. Many handbooks of comparative religion accordingly took over his description of the sacred. So it seems that all the qualifications of the sacred as depicted by R. Otto are to be found in all religions. The way in which these qualifications are met in each religion however is completely different from that of other religions. That applies particularly to Buddhism and Hinduism. In these religions Otto's beautiful system is simply useless. The same also applies to what Van der Leeuw calls 'Das Heilige als Macht'.[103] Baetke says about these generalizations: 'Ihre Verallgemeinerungen gründen sich nicht auf die kritische Lektüre der vorhandenen Zeugnisse, sondern auf die jeweiligen philosophischen Anschauungen oder Theorien über die Religionsentwicklungen, zu denen Gelehrte wie Van der Leeuw sich gerade bekennen.'[104]

d) This applies also to other generalizations, for instance the idea of the sacred and the profane or the idea of hierophany. There are undoubtedly some cultures where these distinctions can be made; there are other cultures however where this distinction (invented and inspired upon the typical structure of Christendom) is absent; for it is based on the question whether any distinction can be adequately made within the triplet: man, world and divinity. Where that does not apply, words such as profane and sacred should not be used at all. When we continue to use these terms in cultures which do not legitimate their use, we are infiltrating our own cultural and religious background and philosophy into these cultures. Our descriptions of these cultures are then only caricatures of them — no matter how well drawn they might be.

With all these considerations in mind I would propose to deal with ritual only as far as it exists in a specific situation and a specific philosophy.

2. *The multipolarity of religion.* By analyzing totemism and marriage systems Lévi-Strauss found out a specific structure of the human mind: savage and domesticated, free and suppressed, objective and engaged.

---

103. G. van der Leeuw, *Phänomenologie der Religion*, Tübingen, 1956, pp. 3 ff.
104. W. Baetke, *Das Heilige im Germanischen*, Leipzig, 1942, pp. 6 ff.

He thus established two poles, between which mankind moves. In my opinion world-religions also have something to tell about their own structures, including the structure of man. They also are able to reveal many poles, comparable with the magnetic poles; for man in his religious attitudes shows that he is living under their power of attraction or repulsion. It depends on the kind of religion whether these poles become visible or not. There are many religious poles between which mankind moves up and down. In everybody these poles are present, be they 'savage or domesticated'. These poles are the fundamental colors to which the whole worldwide spectrum of religions can be reduced. The poles are somehow in opposition to each other. In fact they include the human condition and reveal the ambivalency of religious man. These poles determine how religious man is going to act and what his ritual is going to be.

By comparing the Christian, Jewish and Moslem religions with Buddhism and Hinduism, two important poles can be found, which constitute perhaps 80 percent of world religions. From Van der Leeuw[105] I have borrowed the names and some specific elements of these poles: the poles of 'Father' and 'Mother' religions. The following scheme demonstrates how the different elements of all these religions are influenced by the central idea of the poles, i.e. separation or unity respectively within the triplet: man, divinity and the world:

FATHER RELIGIONS

fundamental: separation

God: Father in heaven; at distance:
  in time: eschatologically: in the past or in the future;
  in space: in heaven; he lives at a distance from this world, created by himself;
  metaphysically: transcendent.
Man: is independent and free and bound to God by a treaty; man can live in a profane world, the sacred being 'far away'; he lives with the profane and the sacred which are properly distinguished.

MOTHER RELIGIONS

fundamental: unity

God: Mother = earth, is present now:
  in time: can be reached now simply by introversion;
  in space: is the earth and the innermost principle of man: the Buddha-nature, atman = brahman;
  metaphysically: immanent only.
Man: man and God are but one: they permeate each other; no freedom; the profane is sacred, the sacred is profane simply by not being at a distance, but by mutual permeation. So man's body is a mandala of divinity.

105. G. van der Leeuw, *op. cit.*, p. 746.

World: is the space of man, allotted to him. Man has to secularize the world: that is his specific task; history and evolution are linear not cyclical.

Ritual: is a human approach to God; it does not make God present, but only refers to him: it is therefore the celebration of the gap and the distance: words and gestures are human only and analogous.

World: is the immense human body of God. Anything — be it a table or a frog — participates in the divinity, can be revealed in deep mystical introversion.

Ritual: is the solemn human and divine celebration of identity; man experiences the union with his innermost principle: words (mantras) and gestures (mudras) are divine and have cosmic power.

This brief survey requests some more details. In the near future I hope to find the time for a more detailed argumentation of my idea. I wonder who is going to give me the details of the other poles, which together with the two I have depicted will help us to understand better the religious nature of man.

Commentary   by Anthony Jackson

Despite the common acknowledgements to Durkheim and Van Gennep (as mediated by Gluckman) these two papers on the ritual process adopt quite different perspectives in their joint concern with typologies. Dr Peacock moves on the macro-level to survey the development of ritual while Dr Honko stays at the micro-level to examine specific types of ritual. Both papers fail, in different ways, to deal adequately with *process* since they are constrained by their a priori categories to giving a rather static picture of rituals that remain unconnected with each other and the society that performs them. Perhaps this is the fault of the methodology in trying to move from types to process by some act of intuition for it is unclear, in these papers, how this transition is to be accomplished. If we are to be able to talk about ritual process then it is necessary to know what we mean by ritual and process but this is precisely what both papers avoid discussing in any detail. It is quite unsatisfactory to simply assume that there is consensus on these two key terms and leave it at that. This criticism is a general one that applies to many discussions in the field of ritual studies. I am not suggesting that there is *a* solution to the problem of how best to discuss ritual process because this rests upon one's prior definitions. What I would plead for is greater explicitness since it would help to avoid the pitfalls that these two papers do not succeed in escaping. The two essays under consideration are of different weight and I shall deal with the lighter of the pair first.

Dr Peacock attempts to set up a typological sequence in which to discuss the evolution of ritual. He adopts a Durkheimian perspective in assuming a relation between ritual and social structure that is mediated by the nature of the social relationships involved. This schema is unsatisfactory for a number of reasons, besides reducing ritual to a mere epiphenomenon. However, Dr Peacock has a light touch as is reflected in the concluding sentence of the first paragraph and I do not think he means us to regard his essay too seriously – it is all good fun à la McLuhan. I feel that Dr Peacock has released for us a few of his favorite butterflies from his cabinet of Lepidoptera that it would be too cruel to break on the heavy wheel of criticism. Nevertheless, he asks for comment and I will be brief.

Dr Peacock sets up a number of categories of rituals and societies, then he tries to show how transformations in the social relationships induce changes in the rituals. The trouble is that these types are too simplistic and no necessary relations are shown to hold either within or between the rituals and societies, for the cement which binds this essay together is ad hoc argumentation. Reduced to its simplest terms, the schema is as follows: primitive rites are totemistic, archaic rites are kingship oriented, historic rites are otherworldly, modernizing rites are radical and secular, modern rites are empty. Dramatic presentation is the common thread upon which Dr Peacock pegs out these types of ritual but the line snaps once we ask what does he mean by ritual. He never defines his terms and the reason for this, I suggest, is because he smuggles in drama as ritual (via the discussion of kingship rituals on p. 395). From this point on we are in McLuhan country where anything goes – the medium of ritual is massaged into films or drug-induced freak-outs. While all this is entertaining, we need not entertain this as theory. I do not wish to criticize this paper too heavily since there are too many non-sequiturs to be followed up. I will only deal with a few of the possible points for discussion.

The discussion drawn between kinship and kingship societies tells us little about the form, content and meaning of rituals in such societies because this is not a true dichotomy along any axis. One cannot characterize most primitive societies as totemistic (even by implication) and 'kingship' societies as hierarchical for all societies have hierarchies in one form or another while many 'kingship' societies have totemistic beliefs. Etiquette is not simply the prerogative of archaic societies and neither are kingship rituals *the* characteristic feature of such societies. Historical societies are not exclusively otherworldly nor do superior statuses just lose their sacral quality, as the Divine Right of kings shows. Modernizing societies are not treated from a ritual viewpoint at all but from a dramatic angle. Finally there is no indication of any historical process which would lead from one type of society (and ritual) to another. It would be possible to refute each ad hoc argument with another but this serves no useful purpose. Dr Peacock fails to provide any justification for his statements on ritual and gives us no clue to the processes involved. Yet this failure raises several important questions because Dr Peacock's provocative paper forces us to realize the difficulties involved in accounting for ritual processes at the macro-level.

Dr Honko's paper is lucid, well-documented and informative even though he too has problems in coming to grips with the ritual process at the micro-level. He constructively clears away some of the dead wood in typology-making and makes the valuable distinction between category and model. This last point spotlights the weakness of Dr Peacock's paper inasmuch as he confuses these two concepts in assuming that his butterflies reveal an evolutionary trend when they are simply pinned side by side.

The first part of Dr Honko's paper is concerned with ritual and the second part with process. Unfortunately these concepts are not spelled out so clearly. A distinction is attempted between ritual and ceremony whereby ritual is defined (page 373) as 'traditional, prescribed communication with the sacred'. However, this begs the question: What is the sacred? It cannot be replied that it is that with which ritual communicates, of course. Yet how do we escape a circular argument? On this point and also on the question of process we need more clarification.

Dr Honko lays down a threefold division of ritual based on their external characteristics to form a pragmatic typology: rites of passage, calendrical rites and crisis rites. He then differentiates between them on three grounds: orientation, recurrence and anticipation.

Type	Orientation	Recurrent	Anticipated
Rites of passage	Individual	−	+
Calendrical rites	Group	+	+
Crisis rites	Individual/Group	−	−

This schema may be simplified thus:

Type of rite	Recurrent	Anticipated
Individual oriented	−	+/−
Group oriented	+/−	+/−

This simplified version of Dr Honko's trichotomy raises the problem of its apparent asymmetry as a table: why does it become skewed? The answer lies in the taking a differential attitude towards time. While it is true that from an individual's viewpoint he might not repeat the same status passage ritual because it is unique to his personal development, yet it is anticipated by him and the group as a ritual event in time, which is to make a distinction between a performance of a ritual and its possession. The uniqueness of the occasion does not make the ritual itself unique, it is only this performance in the life of the individual which is unique, for the ritual is in the possession of the group. However, if we are to argue that rites of passage are anticipated then it equally follows that crisis rites are also anticipated − the very existence of the rites prove it. Moreover, crisis rites are recurrent. These distinctions in the schema depend on a finely differentiated concept of time.

Rites of passage depend upon the life-cycle of individuals, calendrical rites are tied to the yearly cycle while crisis rites apparently occur irregularly but all ritual performances must take place in time. What is at issue is the nature of this time. If certain rites actually mark out social time − as is the case of rites of passage and calendrical rites − then it follows that the distinguishing feature of crisis rites (according to Dr Honko's thesis) is that they are not time markers either in the life of the individual or the society. Nevertheless, crisis rites are recurrent and are anticipated, for the rituals are ready to hand for just such emergencies. What is at dispute is the actual performance and the time of its occurrence. Here we must distinguish the uniqueness of every ritual performance and the placing of it within a temporal framework. While a rite of passage may be unique to the individual it is not unique to the society, indeed it may take place at fixed calendrical intervals. Similarly, crisis rites may also be performed annually, whether this is culturally or naturally determined is another matter. There is, in fact, a merging of these three categories and this may account for the lack of interest in them as 'cultural universals' in favor of the usual dichotomy of rites as seen from the viewpoint of society. If all rites occur in 'sacred time' then the apparent irregularity of crisis rites may not be seen as very significant.

Essentially, Dr Honko's trichotomy is a functional one:

(1) Rites of passage: help individual status passage;
(2) Calendrical rites: help establish the rhythm of social life;
(3) Crisis rites: help overcome threatening occasions in individual and social life.

This view could be elaborated by considering each type of rite both from the individual and social viewpoint. In this way one might be able to marry both the sorts of time involved. This double perspective is necessary, I think, if we are to be able to relate the macro- and micro-level in a processual framework.

The most interesting part of Dr Honko's paper is where he uses role concepts to explain processes within his trichotomy of rituals. He exemplifies his ideas in an illuminating manner for all three cases by concentrating upon the individuals within the rites: the transient role-taker in rites of passage, the role-reverser in calendrical rites, and the actualizing/de-actualizing roles of the shaman in crisis rites. The significant factor in all three cases is that Dr Honko chooses to analyze only role change. This may be illustrated thus:

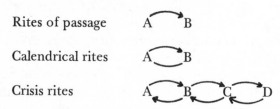

Rites of passage   A ⟶ B

Calendrical rites   A ⇄ B

Crisis rites   A ⇄ B ⇄ C ⇄ D

Now at this level of analysis a symmetry is achieved which does justify the trichotomy as long as it remains in terms of the individual actors. Should we ask how this relates to the society or to the other participants in the ritual or to the rituals as a whole, then a different sort of analysis must be called for. Thus while these examples do support Dr Honko's trichotomy of rituals they are too specific to substantiate the 'cultural universals' that are being sought. It happens that role-reversal and shamanism do not constitute paradigm cases for calendrical and crisis rites.

To my mind ritual processes must be analyzed on at least five levels:

(1) In terms of individual roles (as Honko);
(2) In terms of the social relationships between the actors (as Gluckman);
(3) Structurally in terms of the ritual itself (as Turner);
(4) In terms of the relationship between the rites (as Turner);
(5) In terms of the relationship between rites and society (as Durkheim).

The analysis of ritual process is multilateral and should take account of many factors but this does not mean that we can necessarily elicit correspondences between the different levels of analysis for this will depend upon our parameters. It is not enough to define rites in terms of their functions — as seen externally — because the importance of a rite to its performers depends on its meaning to their lives. We need to categorize rites somewhat differently perhaps from those to which we have become accustomed. Rites, like symbols, are polyvalent and may have to be doubly categorized. Thus if we wish to understand shamanistic rites across cultural boundaries then, in this case, it might be best to follow Dr Honko's lead and look at them as individual performances irrespective of the nature and purpose of the rites themselves. In other words, we could categorize rites according to the roles of the officiants and participants in the structure of the rite rather than in terms of its function.

The important aspect that Dr Honko's paper implicitly refers to is the relationship between time and ritual. If myths are machines for the abolition of time and rituals are machines for the creation of time we have a pretty paradox on our hands as to the exact relationship between myths and ritual. We might resolve this of course by employing the concepts of sacred and secular time but this is not my task. What we are primarily concerned with is ritual process and this in itself involves the concept of some sort of time. Is it clear what this type of time is? I would suggest that if one examined the ritual process from the five levels suggested then it would be found that there was an intricate criss-crossing of different forms of time. Indeed, we might even find a patterning that interrelates these different levels.

I am grateful to both contributors to this section for allowing me the opportunity of commenting on their papers which I hope they will take in good part. They have both focussed on different aspects of the problem of ritual processes which are necessary for a complete discussion. My criticisms are hopefully directed at the weaknesses of their presentation such that they will improve these tentative beginnings towards a theory which will embrace both the macro- and micro-level.

Discussion   Chairman: Melford E. Spiro

The chairman, Melford E. Spiro, introduced the discussion on ritual process, within the broader topic of 'religion as expressive culture'. He commented that the two main papers, by Honko and Peacock, beautifully complemented each other, since one looked at the problem synchronically and the other diachronically, the one inter-systematically and the other intra-systematically, the one microscopically and the other macroscopically.

Lauri Honko then presented his paper. He drew particular attention, first, to two problems: (1) the classification of rituals; and (2) the question of what ritual process actually is, and whether it is anything more than a fashionable word. Next, he drew attention to the three examples in his paper, in which he had tried to show how process analysis could be carried out, each of which was intended to illustrate one of the suggested categories of rites.

Honko went on to emphasize the distinction between 'category' and 'model'. He characterized categories as rather a simple device for grouping all sorts of material together, in either a more or a less detailed way. In a general taxonomy such as the one he wished to present here, each of the three categories would be able to include quite a large amount of material, while there might also be some which fitted into more than one category; this classification would in itself however have contributed little to the explanation of the rituals in question. A model on the other hand primarily exists in order to explain or elucidate a problem, and is thus not a taxonomical concept at all. Moreover it is transferable: in Honko's paper, for example, Van Gennep's distinction of rites of passage into rites of separation, transition, and incorporation, had been used as an explicatory model for calendrical rites, although the latter are not rites of transfer from one status to another.

Honko continued by picking out a number of points from his paper for special mention: the wide range of meaning of the word 'ritual' in different disciplines, and the difficulty — indeed in a holistic approach the practical irrelevance — of distinguishing between sacred rituals and profane ceremony. He added that what he had in mind with the word 'sacred' was the presence in the ritual of a transhuman, superhuman, or supernatural element — the name was not important — which made it of interest in the context of studies of religion.

Turning to the tripartite division of rites suggested in his paper, Honko commented especially on the concept of 'crisis rites'. One weakness, though perhaps an inescapable one at this stage, was that they were described as 'individual- and/or group-oriented': ideally, in discriminatory analysis there should never be any 'and/or's. More important, however, was the need to break away from the inflation of the concept of 'crisis', which characterized most of the standard literature on this topic. Moreover, in its implicit reliance on equilibrium models from sociology and social anthropology and on functionalism, the concept of 'crisis' was increasingly out of date, in view of the shift towards processual models. Nevertheless, a complete processual paradigm was not yet possible, and he had therefore started out from the familiar functional analysis in order to show process analysis as something different, though similar in its flexibility, and he hoped that this passage would have some prognostic value for future developments. He finished his presentation by saying that although he had criticized Victor Turner's work, he hoped that this might be due to misunderstanding; and by reiterating that the three examples in his paper were intended to particularize problems in the framework of the ritual process.

The second paper was then presented, by James Peacock, who opened

with an analogy borrowed from Lévi-Strauss: the rules in non-represen-
tational painting were those which a painter would follow in painting a
painting if he should happen to paint one; similarly, the methodology of
religion represented the rules which a scholar of religion would follow
if he should happen to analyze a religion. He had produced his own
paper, however, more like the painting itself, or rather a sketch: the rules
and underlying assumptions had not been explained, and he would like
to make up for that omission now. His basic methodology was evolutionary. The main weakness in the orthodox evolutionary methodology
to date (e.g. in Julian Steward and Leslie White) lay in the inadequate
correlation of religious phenomena with the various stages of development; it was capable of dealing with tribal culture, for instance, but
not with modern phenomena such as the Reformation or the Death of
God. Peacock had therefore taken a more sophisticated scheme put
forward by Robert Bellah in the *Sociological Review* under the title
'Religious Evolution', and had tried to speculate, in Bellah's terms, about
the correlations between change or variation in ritual, or rather in the
broader concept of 'symbolic performance', and in the social structure.

For convenience, Peacock then briefly summarized the five types
which Bellah had put forward. (1) The primitive level of religious evolution is characterized by rituals of social relationships: here ritual is
stylized, it orders everyday social relationships, and is believed by the
participants to affect their social, natural, and supernatural surroundings
through mystical and supersensory processes. According to Gluckman,
the participants' relations will be 'multiplex', e.g. they are brother,
neighbors, fellow farmers, etc.; disturbance of any of these relations will
have repercussions on the rest, and ritual restores order to them. (2) In
archaic society, however, these multiplex relationships begin to become
vertical, e.g. between the (sometimes divine) king and his subjects. Disturbance of these relations is still seen as having serious repercussions,
which ritual overcomes by re-ordering the relations. (3) Bellah's third
stage, the historic, centres round the so-called 'great religions': relations
become less multiplex; the sacred begins to die out (e.g. the divine right
of kings, instead of divine kings) and to be removed to an other-worldly
sphere. In this phase, ritual ceases to re-order relations, and becomes
other-world-directed. (4) The early modern, or modernizing, period is
typified by the purging of ritual altogether, as in the Christian, Muslim,
and Buddhist reformations. One main reason for this is that ritual re-

presents repetition, and therefore constancy, whereas a modernizing phase is characterized by change. Ritual is then replaced by drama. (5) Finally comes the modern stage, as discussed in the paper itself.

The evolutionary method, suggested Peacock, tried to do at least three things: (1) as typology, simply to define ideal types (like Weber), on the basis of distinctive characteristics; (2) in some cases it appears that this typology coincides with history, for instance in Java; and (3) on a large and rather crude scale, a combination of typology and history could be used to provide a scheme of world history from c. 5000 B. C. to the present day, in which a process akin to natural selection operates: i.e. at any given time, the type which is spreading is that which is most adaptive. He offered this final point in reply to Anthony Jackson's criticism that the evolutionary method did nothing but pin butterflies side by side, without saying anything about trends in history.

The only one of the three commentators present was G. J. F. Bouritius, who presented his commentary without additional remarks (cf. supra).

Following a short break in the discussion, Honko then replied to some of the commentators' points. He conceded to Bouritius that there was some weakness in his handling of the relationship between myth and ritual, but said that he had not wished to adopt a holistic approach to these. Some of Bouritius' points he agreed with, e.g. the idea of order being conceived of as potential disorder, but others he was at a loss to understand, e.g. what was meant by 'society as a human microcosmic replica', nor could he accept the advantages of Bouritius' alternative typology of ritual. Turning to Jacques Kamstra's commentary, Honko said that the point of view was so totally different from his own that there was little he could usefully say; nor — to put it humorously — had he the travel grants necessary to be able to achieve religious understanding through Zen satori. Honko was more impressed by Anthony Jackson's commentary, which, though sharply critical, was operating on approximately the same level as Honko himself. He found Jackson's suggested reformulation of the rituals' typology stimulating, and useful, but also distorting; and he emphatically rejected Jackson's suggestion that the mere existence of ritual meant that crises were anticipated — for example, an aeroplane crash, or a fire. He agreed with Jackson, however, that crisis rites could only function as time markers in retrospect.

Peacock then replied to the commentators. Some of Bouritius' criticisms he confessed to actually accepting: for example, the difficulty of the distinction between totemism and sacrifice; but he insisted that kingship and hierarchy, as he had defined them, did not exist in primitive society. Peacock went on to acknowledge the significance of the Indian revival of ritual following urbanization, but suggested that the breakdown of caste barriers among the Hindu actually accorded with the evolutionary scheme. All in all, Peacock was not persuaded that he should abandon sociological evolutionary typology in favor merely of well-elaborated case studies. Most of the individual points made in Jackson's commentary, Peacock felt, could be argued separately (e.g. the divine right of kings is not the same as divine kings), but Jackson's main point had been the absence of any indication of a historical process leading from one stage in the evolutionist scheme to another, whereas Peacock had been trying to deal with typology, not process. He quoted an African proverb: 'to say that a man has a mother is not to deny that he has a father'; it should be perfectly possible to talk about the sequence or process of moving from one stage to the next, but that was not what he had set out to do.

In Kamstra's commentary, he had argued that since any given ritual can only be understood in its context, it is therefore impossible to generalize either about rituals or about contexts. Peacock disagreed: he could not see why one should not be able to generalize about the correlations that emerged, and he felt that this point was important, since it linked up with a recurrent idea at the conference that typology and phenomenology were incompatible. Yet since facts can only be perceived by means of a frame of reference, which in turn required generalization, he could not see how phenomenology could be perceived without some implicit typology.

The chairman then invited comments from the floor, and Åke Hultkrantz began by criticizing the Bellah scheme, especially the primitive and archaic stages, as too simplistic: he thought that Peacock could have produced a better scheme himself. Hultkrantz endorsed the general approach in Honko's paper. Ritual involved two levels, i.e. the supernatural reference and the natural social ordering of the facts; historians of religion and social anthropologists had each over-stressed one of these levels at the expense of the other, and it was important to aim for a combination, which Honko had done. It might be better, however, instead of calendrical rites (which mainly referred to agriculture), to take 'cosmological rites', so as to include ideology; and he also disliked the ambiguity of the word 'crisis' in the term 'crisis rites'.

Michael Pye referred to Kamstra's quotation that East is East and West is West, which pointed to the question of the relation between sociological and phenomenological ways of studying religion, especially, in the latter case, participant observation. He gave two examples of participant observation of ritual which would either be difficult to place in Honko's or Peacock's schemes, or where this would fail to disclose the real meanings of the religious traditions for the participants: meditation practices in Zen Buddhism, and the Christian communion service or mass. What was important, however — *pace* Peacock — was not confrontation between the two approaches, but a more realistic engagement between them, i.e. a better machine for the valid categorization of different types of ritual in social terms, but also a real appreciation of the quite overwhelming meanings which rituals have for the participants themselves, who are important, even for the social anthropologist.

This point was supported in a brief comment by Melford Spiro, who argued that it is only through participant observation that is genuinely both participant and observation (e.g. the fact that Pye had actually taken part in and observed meditation in a Zen Buddhist monastery) that insight can be obtained into the meaning of phenomenology of religion.

J. van Baal supported Honko's valuable distinction between rites of passage and crisis rites. Rites of passage, in fact, were often not intended to solve but to provoke a crisis in the individual's life. He went on to comment on Turner's concept of 'communitas'. Turner had started out from a concept of structure borrowed from Radcliffe-Brown, and had identified in communitas an 'anti-structure'; yet this seemed in fact to be exactly what Lévi-Strauss meant by 'structure'. Van Baal also incidentally considered that many speakers at the conference had been unjust to Lévi-Strauss's interpretation of totemism in the context of man's relations with nature, however unsatisfactory the implied contrast between nature and culture might be.

At this point Th. P. van Baaren intervened to put a question to the ritual specialists present. He suggested that a law could be formulated with reference to crisis rituals: that 'the amount of ritual effort increases with the distance to be bridged, e.g. between persons, statuses, or divisions of time, or (more literally) between subjects and the king or between two subjects of equal status. It continues to increase until the distance to be bridged becomes so large that ritual is no longer considered able to bridge it at all, as happens in some forms of mysticism, and it then has to be supplemented by additional rituals, until they die of their own superabundance'. The chairman suggested that discussion of this question should be postponed for the time being, and it was not dealt with again until Peacock's closing remarks, when he offered a rephrased version of the law.

M. Heerma van Voss commented that Kamstra's idea of religion as moving between sets of poles, e.g. father/mother, was only of extremely limited applicability to the ancient religions of the Middle East.

In response to a query from Carsten Colpe about the classification of initiation rites, Honko confirmed that he saw them as rites de passage. Jan Bergman then suggested that there could be some rituals which might belong to two of Honko's categories, particularly as the result of the conscious combining of individual-oriented rites of passage and group-oriented calendrical rituals (e.g. the preference in the ancient Church for collective baptism of the *candidati* at Easter). Honko agreed; he thought that it might in some marginal cases be necessary to adopt a dual classification, e.g. in semi-anticipated catastrophes. This point was followed up by Ninian Smart, who suggested that the term 'overlap' would be more accurate than 'marginal'. He also spoke about an important overlap in method, between history of religion and social anthropology, i.e. the method of participant observation, which he considered to be extraordinarily important. Nevertheless, social anthropology and history of religion were concerned with different things. At times religion might have social, political, or psychological implications; but phenomenology of religion is mainly concerned with its religious system of meanings.

Walter Capps wished to emphasize the importance in both Honko's and Peacock's papers of the attempt to make use of developmental or process terminology, in order to get beyond the typical search for 'underlying essences' or 'core elements'. He also thought that Bellah's scheme was more impressive for its esthetic suggestiveness than as a potential literal reading of the course of human history. In Hans Penner's opinion, the evolutionist scheme was in any case quite compatible with functionalism. He thought that the categories which Honko had proposed were a useful heuristic device; but what intrigued him most was the functionalist position which seemed to underlie Honko's paper, i.e. a theory of maintenance, adjustment, adaptation, and process, which Penner said had dominated history of religions for a long time and which he felt should now be approached rather more critically. He then put the question to Peacock whether the 'Bellah-Peacock typology' could, in fact, be related to the historical process.

In Peacock's reply, which brought the session to a close, he tried to be telegraphically concise in dealing with several different speakers' points. He agreed with Hultkrantz, that the distinction between primitive and archaic society was problematical; and with Pye, that Zen Buddhism was difficult to fit into the scheme. Referring back to Van Baaren's proposition about a law defining the amount of ritual, he suggested a re-phrasal: 'The amount of ritual increases as the density of social relationships increases, to a point when the density is so slight that something replaces it' — such as the mysticism mentioned. Finally, Peacock turned to Penner's last question. By forcing the issue, he said, each type in the 'Bellah-Peacock scheme' could be seen as doing two things: (1) classifying concurrently existing societies and religions; and (2) labelling certain epochs where the type was 'born' and began to spread. He closed his remarks with a quotation from Thomas Kuhn, to the effect that scientific revolution comes about not by the destruction of old theories but by the creation of new ones.

The Language of Religion

JAMES BARR   *The Language of Religion*

I. We may begin by taking 'language' in the sense of 'natural languages', and these may be defined ostensively: thus French is a language, Sanskrit is a language, Arabic is a language. There are many such natural languages: it is characteristic of them that they are plural; they are highly diverse in structure and between them there is a high degree of mutual unintelligibility. 'Natural' language in this sense, as distinct from 'special' or 'artificial' languages (logic, mathematics, meta-languages, computer languages), is the starting point and the basic material for linguistics.

With 'religion' we may begin in the same way: we start not from the general concept of religion, but from the fact of human religions, seen descriptively. Human religions are also characteristically plural.

Historically some religions have had a particular association with some natural language, or perhaps with two or three. Islam has a very marked association with Arabic; Judaism with Hebrew; Hinduism with Sanskrit. At a formative stage the religion has expressed itself in one particular natural language; texts in that language have been preserved and have become canonical for later stages of the religion. Where this is so, the religion will meet with the fact of change and difference within natural languages. We may separate out two cases: (a) diachronic change within one language; (b) transfer between one language and another.

(a) *Diachronic change within one language.* Even within one speech community the language changes diachronically. Older texts and traditions can thus become linguistically archaic; this may lead to problems of understanding and appropriation. On the other hand the archaic diction may be regarded as a positive value within certain religious value systems. But if it is held that diachronic change in the language calls for the restatement of religious traditions, then two basic approaches may be distinguished:

1. The texts or traditions may be restated in a diachronically later ('contemporary') stage of the language, and the previous form of text or tradition may then be allowed to disappear.
2. The older form of text or tradition may be retained, but with the addition of a 'rewrite', a new version or a commentary expressed in the later stage of the language.

In many religions both forms of restatement may well have played a part. Linguistically, it is the second approach which causes an archaic form of language to be preserved within the religious structure. Where the first approach has been taken, the older stage has to be reached by historical reconstruction. Restatement of this kind is seldom motivated purely by linguistic change: it will incorporate also the effects of social, cultural and religious change.

(b) *Transfer between one language and another.* It is quite common for one religion to spread over more than one speech community. The difference between natural languages may then occasion the need for translation. In this case several different situations may obtain:

1. The basic religious texts or traditions may be retained in their original language, in spite of the difficulty in understanding that this entails (e.g. non-translation of the Qur'an among non-Arab Moslems).
2. The language of the basic religious tradition may impose itself, as the main language for religious matters, upon the co-religionists of other languages, even though for other purposes they use their own vernacular (e.g. examples in Islam and in Judaism). This produces a situation where there are two languages in the culture, with a religiously-based difference in function.
3. The basic texts or traditions may be translated into the various natural languages used by, or relevant for, the religious community.

The question of translatability may be felt as a problem within the religion, and various answers to it may relate to the values implicit within the religion itself.[1] The language of the original source may be regarded as a 'holy language' — possibly the language of the gods themselves, or the original and most 'authentic' of human languages; it is then thought of as a language having some kind of direct contact with mythological or theological reality, or a language at least in which the truths of the religion can be expressed directly and incomparably well. (However, for such conceptions to be attached to the language of a religious tradition, it is not entirely necessary that it should be the *original* language: it may be one which, though known not to be original, is otherwise dominant — e.g. Latin in traditional Roman Catholicism. Also, a language may be idealized even when it is not actually used, e.g. Egyptian is thus idealized as the true religious language in some Hermetic texts, themselves written in Greek and probably without real contact with Egyptian.[2]

The acceptance of translatability may indicate an expansive, universalistic aspect in the religion: the religion claims that it can make itself recognizably understood in a variety of languages and cultures. Conversely, the acceptance of confinement to one language may indicate the reverse, an unwillingness to move away from the original cultural and linguistic setting of the religion, a conviction that it cannot mean much to those who do not share that setting. Such an attitude may be a rather defensive one. But refusal to translate may also be an assertive and rather imperialistic phenomenon in an expansive and universalist religion (Islam; Latin in mediaeval Europe).

The purely linguistic task of translating from one language into another may be affected by the fact that the text or tradition in question is regarded as a holy one. What is linguistically viable and attainable may be distorted through the will to amplify, to introduce into the translated text interpretations which have come to be ascribed to the original, to elevate in style, to accommodate to later beliefs and religious attitudes; or, the converse of the amplificatory style, an attempt may be made to provide in the receptor language the closest possible approximation to the forms and patterns of the holy original — this 'mimetic' style of translation goes closely together with literalistic

---

1. On this see S. P. Brock, as cited in the bibliography p. 440 f., and Claire Préaux, 'De la Grèce classique à l'Égypte hellénistique: Traduire ou ne pas traduire?', *Chronique d'Égypte* 42 (1967), pp. 369-383.
2. *Corpus Hermeticum* xvi, 1 and 2 (ed. Festugière, ii. 231).

attitudes towards the original (among biblical translators notably Aquila, 2nd century A.D.).

Translation problems arise also in another way: not through the need of the religion itself to express itself in languages other than those in which it has hitherto been expressed, but through the need of the external observer to understand and describe the religion. Though he must, as far as is in his power, appropriate to himself the language of the religious community by learning it, his task is hardly complete unless he has expressed his understanding of the religion within his own language and culture. This will normally include the presentation and explanation of some of the indigenous linguistic terms which seem to the observer to be of great importance, whether (a) because of their key place in relation to the religious structure itself or (b) because there seem to be no corresponding terms in the language of the observer. This problem, in any case, belongs not to the dynamics of the religion itself but to the dynamics of the study of religion.

Thus far we have spoken as if a religion expressed itself originally in one language and later expanded into another. But the converse should also be noted: it is not uncommon for one language to be the vehicle for more than one religion (e.g. Arabic is vehicle for Christianity as well as for Islam; Sanskrit for both Hinduism and Buddhism).

In general, then, we recognize that very varie˙' relations may exist between particular natural languages and particular religions. Moreover, these relations may change through time because of linguistic diachronic change, because of changes in the religious situation, and because of more general social and cultural changes. But there is no reason for the scholar to suppose that any particular natural language is more a 'language of religion' than any other.

II. We turn therefore to the possibility that within a natural language a register or sector may be identified, which constitutes the 'language of religion' within that language. In any culture, or in many cultures, the religion (religions?) and the natural language overlap but do not coincide in scope; they are not absolutely coterminous, not a 'perfect fit'. It may thus be possible to distinguish sectors of the language which are more explicitly concerned with the religion and others which are less so. The distinction may be difficult to make, and sometimes it is said that the religion 'penetrates everything in the culture'; but it is doubtful whether this can be taken quite exclusively, and in any case the problem of identifying a linguistic sector which is the 'language of religion' would not appear to be greater than that of identifying a 'religion' itself as a concept other than that of the total culture. In fact, when we speak of 'the language of religion', we commonly mean such a sector or register within a natural language or languages. In seeking to define this, we may consider the following points:

(a) Some ancient languages are known more or less only from a corpus which itself is basically a religious text. This in turn may mean that, through the accidents of preservation, those sectors of the language which are less concerned with religion are less well known to us. That such 'less religious' sectors exist, however, should not be forgotten when we try to assess the relation between language and religion.

(b) Against this must be set the important fact, which causes many complications for our argument, that the texts taken as basic for religion do not necessarily have only religion as their subject-matter. On the contrary, they may contain a good deal of history, of geography, of cosmology, of simple classifications of animal and physical nature, of dietary rules, of folk customs, of legal systems, and so on. Thus, in general, within texts and traditions regarded as religious, only a certain proportion may have religion as its direct and explicit subject-matter. In such cases, the relation of religious texts and traditions to religion itself is an oblique one rather than a direct one. Nevertheless this observation, though it counterbalances the one made in the last paragraph, does not remove its basic force. The ultimate question, namely how one defines what is 'religious', can hardly be dealt with within the limits of this paper, and will be left aside.

(c) Thus in most situations one can perhaps say that a certain sector of the language can be roughly identified as especially concerned with religion. The elements which constitute this sector may lie on different linguistic levels. Commonly, people think first of certain lexical items ('god', 'demon', 'worship', 'pray'), but this may be only one of the phenomena in question. We may add: certain groupings of lexical items which form a small system, mapping out an area in a fairly exclusive way ('holy' as opposed to 'non-holy'; 'good' as opposed to 'evil'); groups of designations for social classes ('priests' and 'laity'), for cultic actions (names of kinds of sacrifice, etc.).[3] But more important than lexical items may be groups of collocations, in which individual items in themselves may be non-religious but the collocation is religious (e.g. 'love' might be non-religious but 'love of God' is religious, 'living' might be non-religious but 'living for ever' is religious). Moving to the more complicated structures (literary rather than strictly linguistic), certain literary types may be religious (poems of a certain structure may be 'hymns'). On the stylistic level, some styles are religious: certain adherences to archaic linguistic types, certain effects of solemnity, certain kinds of rhetoric. On yet another level, we may note certain phonetic characteristics; and these lead on to music on one side and on the other side to non-linguistic signs such as gestures, and these in turn to clothing, physical appearance, etc., which may also be a sign-system within religion and in this sense a sort of 'language'.

(d) Thus it is important not to identify the language of religion excessively on the side of terminology. Terminology in itself may be very significant, e.g. when it is the technical terminology used within a particular religion to map out concepts and actions which are characteristic of it and have systemic force within it (e.g. 'baptism' in Christianity, *jihad* in Islam). But the fact that terminology can be easily quoted (by contrast, say, with stylistic character, which is harder to describe), and that the common man's understanding of language is grossly biased in favor of word-centredness, can easily tempt us to over-emphasis on terminology. Terms in themselves are commonly equivocal in relation to religious structures, and where two religions are expressed in the same natural language they commonly share a large area of lexical material. Thus that which is characteristic of one religion as against another has to be sought on other levels than the lexical, and especially in (a) the semantic structure of sentences, and (b) the stylistic structure of the literary complexes. It is their employment within the semantic structure of the sentences that gives to the individual lexical terms their semantic content specific to a religion, and not vice versa; and where religions are in conflict within the arena of one speech community, it is their

3. Simple illustrations for Hebrew in Barr, *Vetus Test. Suppl.* xxii, pp. 15 f.

sentence-expressions which state their distinctiveness. Many questions of meaning and truth can therefore usefully be explored at sentence level. On the other hand, much religious tradition is in the form of complicated narrative or poetic expression, and here the most important tests appear to lie (a) inwardly, in the structure of the myths, legends, etc., (b) on the side of expression, in the style of the total literary complexes.

(e) In identifying a 'language of religion', which is not a natural language like Arabic or Sanskrit but a distinguishable sector or register, we have moved away from the discussion of natural languages with which we began. We now observe that there may be similarities in 'the language of religion' between one natural language and another, or even within a large number of natural languages. Though these languages, seen as total systems and stocks, are widely disparate from each other, their religious sectors appear to present similarities and points of contact; and the degree of these similarities appears to depend not on similarities of the natural languages but on the similarity or difference of the religion(s). Thus we may suspect that the 'language of religion' in Finnish Lutheranism is very similar in structure to the 'language of religion' in Swedish Lutheranism, although the two natural languages are of quite different structure and type. Conversely, an English Buddhist and an English conservative evangelical Christian may have difficulty in finding a common 'language of religion', though the natural language of both is identical. But even so *some* common elements for the 'language of religion' seem to be guaranteed — 'analytically' in the Kantian sense — by the fact that we have accepted 'religion' as a basic category to start with. This similarity in the 'language of religion', cutting across natural languages, may in turn provide some basis for the translatability of religious texts and traditions from one language to another: even a religion in conflict with another, and seeking therefore to enter its 'territory' by the translation of its own material, accepts the fact that elements of the natural languages, already used by another religion, are usable once again by itself. Secondly, this similarity in the 'language of religion', if valid, forms the basis for much of the discussion in the philosophy of religion, which appears to operate on the premise that religious statements have the same degree of validity (or otherwise) whether they are expressed in one natural language or another.

(f) Within many types of religion it may be useful to distinguish several levels within the religious language: the second level is a reflection upon (and also a criticism of, a correction of, or a more general formulation of) that which was said on the first level. The first level does not need to be defined otherwise: it is enough to say that, whatever serves as basis for second-level reflection, counts for this purpose as first-level. It is probable that more than two such levels, perhaps four or five, would have to be disengaged. Within one sacred text, such as the Bible, several such levels might be distinguished; and the use of the text within the religions in question would add yet more such levels. The way in which the various levels are patterned in relation to one another is a characteristic of the structure of each religion. Thus Christianity might have one pattern, including biblical text, liturgical language and dogmatic language, while Judaism has a different pattern, including biblical text, liturgical language and halachic language. Moreover, the higher-level language is not only superimposed upon the basic text (in this case, the Bible) but already exists within it. In some religions, where higher-level usage becomes more constant, deliberate and disciplined, it may be found useful to call it 'theology': theology might then be taken as a metalanguage reflecting upon the first-level language of religion. Theological language, while commenting upon the language of religion, may itself commonly share features with the language of disciplines such as philosophy. Theological reflection can often be seen also as the effect of conflicts and tensions within the structure of religion, these conflicts and tensions forcing a higher level of reflection and abstraction.

In general, then, we conclude that it is fruitful to consider the 'language of religion' as a register or sector identifiable within natural languages but cutting across the differences between them, displaying characteristics specific to particular religions but also at the same time providing a recognizable common arena for their differences.

III. At this point we should say something about the 'language and culture' problem. Languages are cultural and social phenomena and we understand them in that context. Religions also are deeply rooted in culture and society. It has sometimes been thought that a language (and here we return to the sense of a natural language, like Arabic or Sanskrit) carries within it or implies a particular world-view: its linguistic items

and classes represent concepts, through which the world is organized
and represented in a particular way. In an extreme form this would lead
to a 'linguistic determinism', in which there would be no possibility of
thinking other than in the manner dictated by the language used. If this
were so, since religions might also be considered as part of the world-
view, they would also be linguistically determined. But conversely, if one
believes in a correlation of language and culture (or thought) and applies
it in the opposite sense, one may suppose that religion (like culture
generally) shapes language (i.e. natural language) and that religious
change is reflected in observable changes of language.

This 'world-view' approach to language, however, cannot be sustained.[4] To say this is not to deny that *pieces* of evidence may be found
which seem to suggest such an approach; these pieces of evidence show
that there is *some* reciprocal interaction between language and world-
view. But such pieces of evidence have often been blown up far beyond
their true value, for such individual facts cannot be universalized into
a satisfactory general picture of language. To arrive at such a general
picture, one has to consider not only those facts which seem to support
a 'world-view' approach to language but also all other facts of the language, including those which argue against it and those which do not
point in either direction. There is thus a connection between language
and world-view (or, language and culture, language and thought), but
this connection is logically and psychologically haphazard.

Language is an entity which has many different levels, and these are
not necessarily, and not in fact, uniformly related to thought or to

4. See recently, for instance, the essay by the anthropologist and linguist B. Siertsema, 'Morphemic Make-up and World View (Does the Morphemic Make-up of a
Language reflect the world view of its speakers? New material to answer an old
question)', in *Studies in general and oriental linguistics*, presented to Shiro Hattori,
ed. by R. Jakobson and Sh. Kawamotu, Tokyo, 1970, pp. 525-34. For earlier material see H. Hoijer, ed., *Language in Culture*, Chicago, 1954 (also Memoir no. 79 of
the American Anthropological Association), and material cited by Barr, 'Semantics',
passim.

One of the basic arguments against the 'world-view' approach is well put by
Siertsema, citing Hattori (in his article 'The Analysis of Meaning', *For Roman Jakobson*, 1956, p. 209): 'The semene of a word is not the concept of a class of things,
events, etc. in question, but it concerns only some of the features common to the
things, events, etc. in question... The linguistic social habit trains every speaker of
the language to pay attention only to some of these features.' (See reference to this
by Siertsema, Hattori volume, p. 527.)

culture. One important distinction is that between language as a system and stock, out of which utterances can be composed, and language as a body of spoken or written complexes, i.e. *used* language. A religious text is language in the second sense: thus Hinduism is essentially related not to the Sanskrit language as a system, but to a body of texts created through selection from the resources of that system, or to a body of thoughts expressed through these resources. The content of the texts is a selection from an infinite number of possibilities made available by the language; it is to this choice, and not to the language in itself, that the religion is related. Thus languages, which have been used as the vehicles of one religion, can by a different use of their resources be used as the vehicles of another. There is a large element of redundancy in language: this is an aspect of natural languages as distinct from artificial languages. Redundancy seems wasteful but is also the factor which allows for the possibility of growth, change and originality. If there was no redundancy, and if the language thus fitted without waste and without difficulty into the thought patterns and world-view of a period and culture, the result would be to fossilize these.

As has been mentioned, one language may serve for the expression of more than one religion. Some major religious traditions have arisen in conditions of acute conflict: Hebrew was the vehicle at the same time of Baalism and of Yahwism, and 7th-century Arabic was the vehicle of pre-Islamic polytheism as well as of the message of Muhammad. This important fact is often concealed by the surviving texts, which speak only for the religious current that in the result becomes canonical. It may be conceivable that cultures of a quite homogeneous character exist, in which the common language is accompanied by a uniform way of thinking, extending throughout the culture; but even this does not show that the uniform way of thinking is directly and intrinsically tied to the common language.

Moreover, since languages are inherited from the social situation of the past, there is likely to be a time-lag, such that, in so far as language is influenced by thought and culture, it will reflect elements of the cultural situation of a past time, rather than fitting exactly with the situation of contemporary culture or thinking. Thus in major languages like Hebrew and Arabic significant elements, used in the expression of Yahwistic and Islamic religion, are probably inherited from times when the religious situation was quite different.

IV. Finally, we shall consider the topic 'the language of religion' from a more philosophical aspect. Philosophers of religion do not look at the subject in the same way as linguists do, and there is some question whether 'language' in their terminology is the same thing as 'language' when studied by linguists.[5] Certainly some philosophical studies of religious language appear to ignore the differences of natural languages and are hard to relate to facts cognizable by linguists.[6] Sometimes it seems that 'language' is used in a metaphorical sense, as 'language' being something like a 'system of thought'. When this is so, 'translation' is also metaphorical (by comparison with translation between natural languages, e.g. between Hebrew and Greek): rather, it means transfer from one system of thought to another, e.g. transfer from a mythological system to a scientific one.

However, it seems better not to conclude that the philosophical approach is talking about a different subject altogether; rather, we should suppose that it looks at the same subject in a different way and with a different purpose. Though it must make contact with natural languages, it may select from the latter (as the linguist may not do) those elements which seem to be philosophically profitable. It does not have to give an account of all the elements in natural language. Its purpose is not to describe natural language but, by using it, to uncover logical structures that underlie it. In doing this it is not, it seems, obliged to consider whether the use of a different natural language (e.g. Sanskrit rather than English) might have led to different results; but it is obliged at least to observe that this question has not been asked, if it in fact has not been asked.

The philosophical question, then, is: what sort of assertions about the universe are made or implied by the language of religion (understood, probably, in the sense of the sector of a language which is particularly concerned with religion)? What sort of meaning do its assertions have? In what ways, if any, can they be shown to be true or false? In

5. For some examples of this problem, see B. Siertsema, 'A-linguistic views on language in European philosophy', in *To honor Roman Jakobson*, The Hague and Paris, Mouton, 1967, vol. 3, pp. 1818-1826.

6. This is particularly true of G. Ebeling, *Einführung in theologische Sprachlehre*, with its almost complete lack of linguistic examples to accompany the argument; and this can be said of the use of the term 'language' throughout most of the 'New Hermeneutic' movement, connected also with Fuchs, in America with J. M. Robinson, and ultimately with M. Heidegger.

what sort of reality are they grounded? What implications do they have?

The answering of such questions lies, however, beyond the bounds of what is possible within this paper. For a conference on the methodology of the science of religion, however, it would seem profitable to emphasize one question: do the answers to the questions, which are posed from this philosophical angle, have to be religion-specific? Can they hope to find answers which will apply to all 'religion'? Or must they expect that the relationships between the various kinds of meaning, the logical structures of the various types of religious assertions, are likely to vary between one religion and another? My own preference is for the latter position, which is only a restatement of the recognition that one religion is fundamentally and structurally different from another; thus, actual religions are not just mildly variant forms of the one great 'religion'. It may be objected that there must be universals in religion which enable us to use the category 'religion' in the first place. The fact that universals may be discerned, which enable us to class differing religions together under 'religion', does not in itself mean, however, that these universals are the structurally dominant or dynamically creative elements within the individual religions. This might lead us to an analogy with what has been stated above about natural languages. A natural language is a common system through which, by different selection from its resources, widely differing positions may be expressed — e.g., two quite different religions. Though standing on quite another level, the 'language of religion' is also a resource through which radically different religions may express themselves. It should accordingly be considered possible that the 'meanings' of the language of religion in the philosophical sense — its involvements and implications, its grounding in reality, its relation to society and experience, its verifiability and falsifiability — will not be parallel for all religions but may lie in substantially different areas as between one religion and another.*

* Bibliography: There are many books on 'the language of religion' but most of them work entirely from the philosophical standpoint and pay little or no attention to problems in the natural languages as seen by the linguist; they are mostly also written from within a Christian context and do not give much thought to the variety of religions. Representative instances are:

Clarke, B. L., *Language and Natural Theology*, The Hague, 1966;
Ebeling, G., *Einführung in die theologische Sprachlehre*, Tübingen, 1971;
Evans, D. D., *The Logic of Self-involvement*, London, 1963;
Ferré, F., *Language, Logic and God*, London, 1962;

JACQUES WAARDENBURG   *The Language of Religion, and the Study of Religions as Sign Systems*[7]

Manifold problems beset the study of 'the language of religion', which is the name of the section within which this paper has been placed. Besides a number of scholarly research problems, there is a sort of peculiar involvement on the side of the scholar working in this field. For the scholar himself lives within one or more languages, without which he cannot think and express himself; and if he is interested in the study of religion as something that gives meaning to people, he will observe that such a study inevitably leads to language problems. It is in language that

---

Macquarrie, J., *God-talk*, New York, 1967;

Ramsey, I. T., *Religious Language*, New York, 1957.

From the side of general linguistics I have not found much that faces the general problems of the study of religion. One work, by a competent general linguist, and written from within a Roman Catholic context, is:

Crystal, D., *Linguistics, Language and Religion*, New York, 1965.

For the background to the writer's own approach, arising from semantic questions in the language of the Bible, the following may be cited:

Barr, J., *The Semantics of Biblical Language*, London, 1961 (transl. in French, German and Italian exist);

——, *Biblical Words for Time*, 2nd ed., London, 1969;

——, 'Common Sense and Biblical Language', *Biblica* 49 (1968), pp. 377-387;

——, 'Semantics and Biblical Theology', *Vetus Testamentum Supplements*, xxii (1972), pp. 11-19.

For semantic studies in another religious field, cf.:

Izutsu, T., *God and Man in the Koran: Semantics of the Koranic Weltanschauung*, Tokyo, 1964;

——, *Ethico-religious Concepts in the Qur'an*, Montreal, 1966.

On the translation of religious texts, see recently:

Nida, E. A., *Toward a Science of Translating*, Leiden, 1964;

——, *Theory and Practice of Translation*, Leiden, 1969;

Rabin, Ch., 'The Linguistics of Translation', in *Aspects of Translation Studies in Communication*, London, 1958;

——, 'The Translation Process and the Character of the Septuagint', *Textus* 6 (1968), p. 1-26;

Brock, S. P., 'The Phenomenon of the Septuagint', *Oudtestamentische Studien* 17 (1972), pp. 11-36.

Cf. also other works as cited in the footnotes.

7. Words like 'sign', 'sign system', 'signification', 'symbol', 'meaning', 'reference', 'use', 'language', 'to express', 'to communicate', etc., which are technical terms of linguistics and semiotics, are used here not as precisely defined terms, but as words of everyday speech, in a relatively loose, informal and free way.

meaning — religious or otherwise — can be expressed and understood in the most precise way possible.

The following lines are intended to present the main elements of a more general theory towards fruitful research on religion as a kind of language.

First, we are concerned with language as a vehicle of meaning, providing the possibility of a transmission of meanings through sets of signs. Here we deal with the semantic aspect of language: the question what it means.

Second, we are concerned with the communicative function of language, as a transmission of something from one person or group to another, establishing a kind of communication between them. Here we pay attention more particularly to the hermeneutical aspect of language: the question which meaning is, or perhaps should be, understood by the receiving party.

Third, we are concerned with language as a way of human expression, as a reverberation of something felt to be meaningful. Here we have to do with the expressive aspects of language: the question what is expressed by it.

Seen as a whole, this paper is devoted to the problem of meaning in general, that is, meaning as expressed by and in language, and to the problem of religious meaning in particular. This meaning, valid for specific persons or groups, has our attention and interest as a matter of contents much more than of form. In the major part of the paper we are dealing with word-language; only at the end will such word-language be seen within the wider context of language, signification, and communication as such.

THE LANGUAGE OF RELIGION

What may be understood by 'the language of religion'? At first, one may tend to think of things like Bible reading, sermon, prayer, myth, hymn, and so on. And we may then ask what distinguishes such 'languages of religion' from other 'languages' like detective stories, commemorative speech, human dialogue, Little Red Riding-hood, love song, and so on. To put the question more broadly: what kind of difference is there between language 'without' religion and language 'of' religion? There may be, especially in the case of religious texts, a difference of vocabulary, but this may not always be clear and it certainly is not absolutely necessary if one thinks of the use of metaphors. The difference, consequently, does not lie alone in the words as such: a number of words may be 'religious' as well as 'not religious'. The difference cannot be found either in grammatical or in formal linguistic structure as such, although in certain concrete cases there may be a difference in syntax or in the recurrence of phonemes. Even the existence of words which are felt to be primarily, if not exclusively religious — like the word 'God' for instance —, does not throw much light on the language of religion as a whole, in terms of meaning.

Without diminishing the importance of this aspect of vocabulary, we would like to approach the problem in a different way. The difference between religious and non-religious language — which does not belong in the first place to words and to sentences as patterns proper to religion — would seem to be essentially a problem of meaning: there appears to be a difference in the 'kind' of meaning between religious and non-religious language. Apart from the difference in words, religious language — broadly the language of religion — would distinguish itself by a particular or specific kind of meaning, not to be found in non-religious language. In certain cases there is a clear general framework of reference, with particular concepts which determine the semantic fields within which the other concepts and words function. In many cases, however, such a framework of reference is not expressed explicitly. Consequently we have to look for another criterion for the 'language of religion', of which not only the vocabulary but also the conceptual framework itself is a function. Since this criterion cannot be found in the words themselves — also for the simple reason that the concepts in the background are not necessarily, and in many cases necessarily not, expressed in words — we have to look at the use which is made of the words. Rather than specific words it would be a particular use of words which makes the language religious: it is the religious 'use' of a language which makes such language religious.

So religious language is anything but a thing in itself. Our hypothesis is that the religious use of language makes this language point to something basically meaningful which is signified by the words, but which does not coincide with the sum of the particular meanings of the words. In its religious use, a certain kind of reference is built into the language so that it becomes a 'double decker': it is a reference to something which is not only to be distinguished from language itself, but also from factual, empirical reality as such, with regard to which it is 'transcendent'. According to this hypothesis not only 'professionally' religious language but also ordinary 'non-religious' language may be used religiously through the introduction of such a kind of reference. This holds true not only for the speaker. On the side of the listener too, it would be precisely the sensitivity to this kind of reference — the discovery of the particular 'double decker' nature of the language itself — which makes it possible for him to perceive and understand not only the religious character of the language in question, but also the meaning conveyed by it; at least he may understand it partially. In the same way as the speaker is 'touched' by the reference for the expression of which his speech is used, in that same way the listener is 'touched' when grasping that very reference. Religious language or the language of religion, as an expression and vehicle of meaning, presupposes a sensitivity to different shades of reality.

An extreme case of the religious use of language is that whereby a wording is considered to be a vehicle not only of 'religious' meaning, but of divine meaning and even of the divine itself. There is here a particularly strong and intimate connection between the religious nature of the reference of the language and the religious use of that language itself.

An extreme case of an opposite nature is that a 'religious' vocabulary may be used in a non-religious way. That is to say, such a vocabulary has become objectified and reified, the ideas contained in it have become things in themselves, and the religious reference may be considered to have been lost. This may happen in many ways, for example when religious language has become subject to rationalization for the sake of rational mastering.

In view of the hypothesis submitted above, religious language is not as vague, contradictory, ambiguous, and confused as it sometimes is held to be. On the contrary, it is precise, effective, and to the point; but it evokes, proclaims, or points to realities of its own without which it cannot be understood. The difficulty in any study of religious language is, how to grasp its meaning or meanings in view of the intended realities.

There is no reason to suppose that certain language systems would not allow for religious references, though it may be difficult to express a particular kind of reference in a particular language. No living language confines itself to its linguistic reality; it does not confine itself either to empirical reality. That the 'transcendent' references may vary to a very great extent, and that they may correspond with different religious truths is a problem in itself. The point we want to make here is that a religious use can be made of any language. To the people concerned, such a religious use may be like the 'bringing down' or the 'breaking through' of a basic meaning which gives sense to life. The scholar may call it a 'signification' of a reference which functions as a source of meaning.

Before coming to the theory proper, it is useful to stress another aspect of religious language, or of 'the language of religion'. We observed that it is the use of language which makes it religious; it should be observed, equally, that it is people who use language 'religiously'. Any use of something, also the religious use of it, is determined by the user; consequently, if something at a certain moment is used religiously, the user at that particular occasion or moment may be considered to have been 'religious'. As soon as we define 'religious' in terms of use and meaning, we cannot but see religious language as a language of people who use this language in order to express, transmit and convey — make understood — a specific meaning of a particular kind to someone else or to certain other people. It is the person who speaks or writes this language who is at the very centre of religious language; important thereby is the concrete situation and the life situation out of which he speaks or writes that religious language.

Turning from the speaker to the listener, from the person who conveys meanings to the one who asks what he means, we come up against a hermeneutical problem. The terms of the hermeneutical problem, and consequently the direction from which its solution is looked for, largely depends upon how we conceive of 'meaning', and in this case of 'religious meaning'. We return here to our starting point of studying religion as a kind of language, and in the framework of our theory we narrow this down to the study of a religion as a 'sign system' as far as its 'objective' sense is concerned, and as 'intentions' as far as the so-called 'subject' of religion is concerned.

THE STUDY OF RELIGIONS AS SIGN SYSTEMS

Our point of departure is the concept of symbol system as this concept is used in the social sciences. Just as one speaks of the symbol system of a concrete society which is the subject of investigation, so also could we speak of a 'second grade' symbol system to indicate that system which is basic to the different symbol systems of a number of societies and by which they ultimately identify themselves. In order to distinguish the 'first grade' from the 'second grade' symbol system, it is preferable to term the latter 'sign system'. A sign system (like Islam, for instance), consequently, comprises a number of symbol systems. It suggests that people in different societies, at different times and places, deal in certain particular ways with problems of the world, of society, and of themselves. Such a sign system will contain one or more basic views with regard to reality, views which have some permanency through historical and social variations, a permanency which guarantees the continuity of the given tradition. Such basic views largely determine the orientations which exist within a given civilization or religion, as, for instance, the way in which in a given context the tension between the ideal and the real is articulated.

The concept of sign system is explicitly intended to do justice to the signifying aspect of a given culture and/or religion respectively. It is particularly appropriate in the study of world religions and world ideologies, and of their corresponding societies and cultures. It is appropriate, too, to elucidate the problem of speech, language and communication, with which we are concerned in this paper. Through its specific 'cores' of significance a signification system provides a world of discourse, a space of speech beyond the given local cultures, which makes possible to the people concerned a common discourse on the basis of what is held to be a common evidence or an implicit self-evidence, thanks to the common recognition of certain 'intended objects' as supreme truth and value. And it would seem to be through the communication of appeals or messages via the 'symbolic' cores of significance that the people can communicate with reality and with each other, and that a religion may be said to be a communication system as well as a sign system.

The basic concept, however, is that of 'meaning'. Although the problem of meaning arises in research in many ways, we are concerned here only with 'subject's meaning' as subject of investigation. Under subject's meaning is understood the explicit or implicit meaning which a given fact or set of facts has for a given group or person, or the specific meaning or relevance which is assigned by a group or person to a given fact or set of facts. Our main concern here is that of the meaning, importance and relevance of facts to people.

It would be characteristic for 'meaning' in this sense that it always occurs in particular clusters, patterns or fields which often seem to contradict each other and often are only partly explicit, and that such 'patterns' of meaning are linked to certain intentions which may be supposed to be at their origin. The perception or assignment of such meaning nearly always leads to a certain action or at least behavior on the part of the people involved. Understanding a culture or religion would be, from this point of view, essentially decoding its codes of meaning as contained in its symbol and sign systems.

As a rule of thumb, we would suggest that meanings are 'religious' to the extent that they have an absolute quality for the people concerned. This happens by means of symbols and signs which, as 'cores' of meaning, assume an absolute quality — for instance an absolute self-evidence — for the people concerned. It would seem that in those cultures or communities which we are used to calling 'religious', specific 'cores' of meaning signify or have a reference to something which cannot be 'defined', that feeds significance and meaning to the life of the community or the individual concerned, and that is felt to be 'religious'.

The difference between a religious and a non-religious sign system would not be easy to discern in practice. Both signify something which may be called transcendent with regard to common sense and daily life. Theoretically speaking, a typical religious sign system may be said to appeal to a source of meaning and significance which is at the origin of meaning itself, whereas a typical non-religious sign system would appeal to a source of meaning and significance which is not its own absolute origin. In the study of any culture, whether religious or not, it will be necessary to pay special attention to the transcendent references or significations which are characteristic for it, and to develop some kind of sensitivity to the orientations contained in them as well as to the intentions they evoke in people.

Seen from this theoretical angle, 'religion', in the way it is commonly understood, is that specific kind of sign system which, to the people involved, has or represents an absolute quality and which, consequently, contains references and significations which have some absolute connotation to these people. Religion will be linked to symbols and signs which also have themselves an absolute quality for the people; and further, the relationship between the people and their religious symbols will have absolute connotations.

It is a peculiar trait of the religious signifying process that it does not remain restricted to certain fixed symbols and signs which function as 'cores' of meaning. It has a typical radiation effect by which, in the light of one perceived meaning, a number of other facts are seen according to a new meaning pattern which determines a whole communal or personal perception of reality and actions with regard to it. According to this interpretation, religion is bound to empirical realities, but sees these realities as transparent in view of certain significations that are assumed to have an absolute origin or to be 'revealed'. This implies that the study of any religion with a view to understanding its 'meaning', basically requires, besides paying due attention to the transparent character of its references or significations, an attempt to reconstitute the signifying character of the religious data and to look at their radiation effect.

A crucial question, of course, is that of the objectivity and certainty of knowledge of such sign systems. Like facts, meanings too, in order to be known, require evidence; be it through documents, direct observation, or otherwise. Meanings in the sense of this paper can be known or understood only through the intermediary of expressions of people: whether one investigates such expressions in their factual reality or as vehicles of conveying meaning, they have to be there. Only on the basis of such expressions can certain intellectual inferences be made. If a particular scholar is of the opinion that he has a more immediate perception of what has been meant, he still has to check and verify his 'intuition' before presenting his inferences as scholarly conclusions.

This kind of research, basically, is of a hermeneutical nature and various hermeneutical theories have already tried to come to terms with the problems of such research. For any 'meaning' which was or is valid for certain people at a certain time and place with a certain religion, it is a long way from being expressed in the cultural forms of its time and situation to being perceived by a scholar working in another context at a different time, who takes upon himself the task to understand, express, and interpret that 'meaning' adequately.

A special problem is that by objectifying our subject-matter we automatically tend to neglect the possible transcendent references of significations which these materials may have or have had for the people concerned. One apparently has to ask explicitly for the 'subject's meaning' of such materials for such people if one wants to avoid considering, explicitly or implicitly, such materials as 'dead' objects in themselves apart from the people living with them. There certainly is a point in the reproach commonly made against scholars of religion with the charge that they reduce religion to a dead thing by not taking into account its signifying function and its subject's meaning. The same reproach is made against orientalists by people originating from the cultures which were and are studied, that the scholars 'kill' such cultures, if not by conscious action, then by studying them as 'objects'. It is worthwhile asking whether it is research itself that makes something a 'dead' object, or whether such a result is due to something that may accompany this research but is not necessarily identical with it. The act of studying a signified value does not necessarily mean declaring it 'false'; the 'ultimate' truth or reality of the signified reality will rather be suspended or bracketed and the scholar will concentrate on the question what this signified reality may mean or may have meant to people in given circumstances.

With regard to the study of religion as 'intentions' as far as the so-called 'subject' of religion is concerned – whereas its study as a 'sign system' rather deals with religion in its 'objective' sense – there is a clue to meaning when intentional research (*Intentionsforschung*) is applied. We may interpret a religious meaning, for instance, as a proposed solution for a specific problem or set of problems. This solution is provided by an 'intentional' view, on a more or less 'sublimated' level, with the awareness of a possible 'ultimate' sense of life and reality. In this way, we may say that religious significances and meanings have an anthropological dimension as far as intentionality is a basic characteristic of human reality. Concretely, this would imply that the analyst, in order to understand the appeal or 'message' of a religious meaning to a particular person or community, will have to reconstruct the underlying problem to which this meaning provides some kind of solution. The question to what extent such a 'religious' solution is adequate in given circumstances is of course most interesting.

A systematically working intentional research (*Intentionsforschung*) is concerned with the various designs or projects which man, as a member of a community and as an individual, has given and gives to his existence in this world and beyond, starting with the need for survival. We hold such designs to express intentions which are basically answers to existential problems with which mankind has been confronted. When analyzing such designs on their intentions, we should stress the internal logic of these designs and the reasonable nature of the scholarly effort. The scholar's sole concern here is to X-ray the real world of man in terms of its intentionalities: religion is not to be reduced, for example, to some kind of ideal reality, but it is to be interpreted in terms of human reality, very much as ideality itself is to be understood in terms of human existence.

This intentional research (*Intentionsforschung*) is a technique to grasp, at least approximately, meanings of expressions or significances of phenomena for people. And just as we can approach the phenomenon of religion now in a way different from a hundred or even fifty years ago, we do this equally with regard to meaning and significance. This may have to do in part with new ways in which something is felt to be 'religious' or 'meaningful'; in any case, not only the problem of religion but also that of meaning has been reformulated. It has to do also, indeed, with a development of our notion of rationality in the discipline. Against an older rationalistic climate there came an anti-rationalistic reaction stressing the irrational both in religion and in semantics. At present logic is claiming its dues again, and we have come to the point where we can speak of the 'logic' of myths and symbols, and of 'fields' of intelligibility so that an intelligence entering into a new field is able to arrive at a set of evidence which has its own logic in this field. In this search for logic in the religious materials themselves it is an absurd alternative of being either 'against' or 'for' religion; this question is of a different nature.

Evidently a hermeneutics of a subject's religious meaning, as sketched above, leads to an interpretation of religious data in terms of human existence. Its starting-point is that man meets reality and that he confronts problems which are given with his environment and with his own nature. Our hypothesis is that situations and problems can be digested by man in many ways, depending on his basic intentions; this 'digestion' may result in solutions which have some definite quality for those concerned, and which express themselves as 'religious' meanings of which mankind's religious past bears evidence in a long record of religious expressions. The analyst using those data which have a clear ideational content and about which sufficient evidence is available, tries to uncover their subject's meaning by questioning and interrogating the material in terms of certain basic questions, with a view to opening up the implied intentions. Religion, in this way, is studied as a self-expression of human existence in different cultures, societies and circumstances. Structure and meaning of human expressions, including the religious ones, are related to the very core of human existence: its intentionality. And if religion cannot be studied directly as existential reality, at least its expressions can be interpreted as to their subject's meaning, in the light of human intentions: in so far, of course, as the materials allow us to uncover them.

In the case of religious signification, the signified referent is beyond empirical facticity itself, functions as a source of meaning, and in principle cannot be verified empirically in an objective, that is, a scholarly way. From a scholarly perspective, the signified reality is unverifiable. It can be studied, however, through the human ideals which are attached to it. The fact itself of signification, and the relationship between sign — in this case: word sign — and signified reality, is a philosophical problem. The 'double decker' nature of religious signification gives to religious language its particular 'double decker' character. It gives to the language of religion, or religious language, its suggestive if not convincing force, at least to those who are sensitive to the transcendent references involved. Indirectly this may happen by means of ritual texts, myths, sacred histories, descriptions of states of the soul, meditative language, etc.; in a more direct way this may happen in sermons, magic formulas, prayers, hymns, prophetic language, etc. It should be stressed again that the language of religion is not confined to these particular language expressions, but also that ordinary language expressions may transmit the same 'double decker' meaning — and evoke the same 'double bottom' experience — when a religious use is made of them, so that they become instrumental to (1) religious signification in general and (2) the transmission of religious meaning in particular.

We do not intend to dwell on the problem in what ways specific religious truths are and can be verbally expressed, or on the problem of the consequences of each language for the way in which reality can be interpreted meaningfully in the light of a specific religious truth. But as far as a religious sign system as a whole is concerned, together with the meanings or 'truths' which it intends to convey, a general statement may be made. Such a religious sign system allows at least in principle for many different language expressions, for the simple reason that it must be applicable to different societies and peoples, to different social and personal situations. And the different language expressions of a religious sign system may be said to correspond with the different social and individual settings and to refer to what they consider to be the common — religious — truth. Put into one formula, the different situations are the variables of reality, to which the different language expressions correspond as variables of the given — religious — sign system.

This all may sound somewhat abstract and it cannot be otherwise. There is no opportunity here to offer as an example the analysis of one particular religious language or 'language of religion'. If we can mention nevertheless the case of the Koran, it may be called a demonstration case, not so much because it is held to be sacred scripture — there are many of the kind —, but because it is one unified whole which is due to the intermediation of one religious person, and which contains a great number of religious language expressions that convey an all encompassing religious world-view and framework of action. A first semantic analysis of Koranic vocabulary has already yielded good fruits. It would require a next step to ascertain, on the basis of this semantic analysis, the signification structure of the Koran itself; through this structure the Koran has a cornerstone place in the Islamic religious sign system as a whole. The Koran represents one religious language: as a 'language of religion' it provides precious materials for the study of Islam as a sign system, and consequently a system of communication.

SOME METHODOLOGICAL CONSEQUENCES

What would be the methodological consequences of this theory which allows one to study a religion as a sign system, with particular bearings on the study of the language of religion?

First of all, meanings can, of course, be divided and classified in many ways, but for the study of religious meanings, also when expressed through and in language, a differentiation appears to be mandatory according to different kinds of transcendent references. Such a differentiation is simply a requirement for a precise assessment of the religious use of language.

Second, a distinction can be made between different language systems — not taken here in the sense of what we call 'languages' in daily speech, connected with particular peoples and groups — as different views of reality. Such a distinction is especially useful when religious views are considered. Such views are directed ultimately to particular truths, and their corresponding languages may be considered to be the corresponding 'pointers' to such (metaphysical or religious) truths. This is important for an assessment, through the analysis of a specific language system, of the religious character of a particular view on reality.

Third, the study of a religion as a sign system, through its religious language(s) or otherwise, implies that attention should be given not only to the transcendent references proper to one particular sign system, but also to the historical and social situations to which this sign system is applied and in which it functions. The schemes of reference, not to speak of the vocabulary itself, are borrowed from the social reality — in its broadest sense — within which a particular language of the sign system is used. This is important to establish the dependence of a particular religious language on given social realities. Moreover, the fact that certain cultures cultivate language and speech, and that others are relatively poor in language expression has serious implications for the possibilities of a rich religious language in such cultures.

Fourth, it would be useful to make more proper distinctions between different 'languages of religion', not only according to criteria of form, but also according to criteria of content. Let us give some examples of possible distinctions:

1. according to that to which the language refers: spiritual realities existing in themselves, the spiritual background of the life world, or the significance of commonly experienced reality;
2. according to the very nature of the reality which is expressed by the language, or of the ideal which is reverberated by it;
3. according to whether the language puts the 'objective' things in a new light, or whether it rather leads to 'subjective' experiences which take place in this light;
4. according to whether man is addressed in his 'existential' condition in time and space by a language dealing with existential problems, or whether he is addressed rather in his 'eternal' condition between his origin and his destiny by a language dealing with spiritual problems;
5. according to active aspects which dynamize the person's will and emotion and which lead to action, or rather according to passive aspects which are connected with knowledge and feeling and which

lead to a deepening of the person himself in a more interiorized way;
6. according to whether the language functions primarily in structuring a
   person's mind by inculcating basic terms, keywords and fundamental
   phrases, or whether it rather articulates the mind by stimulating reflection, research and self-criticism.

One could even think of distinguishing all directly inspired religious
language — e.g. ecstasy, trance and non-articulated sounds — from all
other religious language; of distinguishing religious language in which
the words are experienced as addressing the person and coming from
elsewhere, from religious language in which the words are experienced as
arising from man's most inner self; of distinguishing 'revealed' language
as containing a divine quality or message from all other — non-revealed —
religious language. Other distinctions could be made too.

The most adequate distinction between different languages of religion, however, in terms of meaning content, would seem to be a distinction made in the following way. There can be devised a scale based
upon the smaller or greater difference between the 'common sense'
contained in the religious language — according to the criteria of the
religious sign system to which it belongs —, and on the other hand the
'common sense' expressed in ordinary language and speech. The greater
the distance between both forms of 'common sense', the more meaningless the religious language would seem to be in terms of common language and experience.

SOME THEORETICAL CONSEQUENCES

We would like to limit ourselves here to two more theoretical consequences of the theory of religion as a sign system, as far as language
expression is concerned.

1. *Word language*

We are concerned here with the communicative function of language.
Language is learnt from others; it is the cultural context which offers a
language to man, so that the child or grown-up person can communicate
with his 'word-givers'. In using the words himself, especially in speech

but also in writing, man makes meaning available, really or potentially, to others as well as to himself. On the other side, in being addressed, man is exposed to the words of others as a possible but not a necessary form of communication. Seen on a more fundamental level, man is enabled to communicate with reality itself in a more or a less articulated way by the very fact of his capacity to 'name' this reality, to identify it, and to identify himself with regard to it, whereby, through continuous corrections in the learning process, a kind of 'dialogue' takes place between man on the one hand, reality — world and other men — on the other hand.

Language and the use made of it is one of the major factors that constitute man's mind and its range of communication with other minds and people, and with reality as such. This happens not only in a direct way but also indirectly: because it channels the way in which man understands himself and can act accordingly in his communicative relationships. It would indeed seem to make a great difference both for man's understanding of himself and for his communicating with others and the world, whether his language knows of a religious use or not. In the first case a particular kind of transcendent reference is introduced into his understanding; in the second case the language deals with reality in order to name it, explain it, and make it instrumental for action as a thing in itself. The one does not lead as such to 'religious' communication, the other not necessarily to 'non-religious' communication. But the possibility of religious communication depends of course to a large extent on the existence, if not the availability of transcendent references or 'significations'.

The very fact that a language is religious because of the religious use which is made of it, and that such a religious language is used by people who, at the moment of using it, are religious, throws some light on the particular kind of communication which is linked to the use of religious language. One may think of the fact that such a language, to the people concerned, throws a particular light on reality; this 'light' refers back to some 'truth' about this reality, which determined in part the conceptual framework in the language. People are enabled to communicate 'religiously' one with another by means of this language, that is, in view of the common transcendent referent to which the truth in question is linked. Religious language, then, in religious communication, would serve largely as a transmission — by means of words — of a spiritual direction in which the people who communicate are moving or aspire to be moving, be it individually or be it as a community. The signification character of this language – in as far as it signifies a basic meaning of the second degree (that is, a meaning which is itself meaning-giving to other meanings) – is constitutive both for the meaning of the language and for the communication which it may bring about among people involved in a common search. In their view, probably, it is only religious language which founds communication.

It is perhaps interesting to note, parenthetically, that scholarly language too has this character of transmitting a direction in which the mind is moving. The search here, however, is of another nature. The common search leads here to a communication of the minds too, but this time of a scholarly nature; and that means subjected to norms that differ from the norms which prevail in religious communication.

2. *Non-word language*

It is now time to put word language with which we have been concerned until now within the wider context of language as such, which is for the larger part non-word language. Word language appears to be a special case of language in general; religious language in particular is basically a language of symbols with particular transcendent references – a symbolization system – in which words play a role, but often actually a rather modest one. This supports the theory of the study of religion as a sign system; signification may take place often through words in particular circumstances under particular conditions, but this is no absolute necessity.

Language taken in this broad sense is a mode of communication and may be said to function on at least three levels of communication.

The first level may be called that of basic reality. This is the fundamental communicative network or infrastructure within which man lives at a given time and place, and which contains a given mental or spiritual direction. There are many different kinds of such networks, and they are not necessarily of a harmonious nature: they show the break, encounter, and wrestling of different wills. To the extent that such a network itself is religiously qualified, it is as such somehow related to particular transcendent references which may either be considered as self-evident or consciously believed as true or truths. The use of language, verbal or non-verbal, is to be considered on this level as making dense or condensing the basic communicative network.

The second level may be called that of social reality. This is the communicative network which exists between people as persons, be it in a given society or be it across the borders of different societies. Religious language is to be considered on this level as enhancing communication between people in view of a common mental or spiritual direction. As suggested earlier, the 'transcendent' reference and its truth is constitutive of the kind of communication, prescribed and actually realized, between the people involved.

The third level may be called that of the mind. By this we mean the superimposition of articulated normative patterns of meaning on the basic reality and on the social reality, be it through non-verbal be it through verbal language. Each religion can be analyzed as a sign system on all three levels of communication.

Let me close this modest contribution to the first international conference on 'Methodology of the Science of Religion' with a plea for the recognition of the study of method and theory in the science of religion — with its different approaches — as a special branch of our field of study. Subjects like the one broached here call for further research on a fundamental level, if possible by teams of specialists working on an interdisciplinary basis. As in the natural sciences, in this field too a distinction between factual and fundamental research should be made. The fundamental relevance of the one for the other will prevent a separation between these two levels of research, both of which are basic to scholarship.*

* Bibliography:
Izutsu, T., *God and Man in the Koran: Semantics of the Koranic Weltanschauung* (Studies in the Humanities and Social Relations V), Tokyo, The Keio Institute of Cultural and Linguistic Studies, 1964.
——, *Ethico-Religious Concepts in the Qur'ân* (McGill Islamic Studies I), Montreal, McGill University Press, 1966.
Waardenburg, J., *L'Islam dans le miroir de l'Occident* (Recherches Méditerranéennes, Études III), Paris-La Haye, Mouton, 1970[3] (ch. IV).
——, 'Grundsätzliches zur Religionsphänomenologie', *Neue Zeitschrift für systematische Theologie und Religionsphilosophie* XIV/3 (1972), pp. 315-335.
——, 'Research on Meaning in Religion', in: *Religion, Culture and Methodology*.

Commentary   by Aili Nenola-Kallio

I would like to start my commentary at one of the few points where the two papers by Prof. Barr and Dr. Waardenburg coincide. They both emphasize that the terminology (i.e. lexical items) that seem to the common man the most conspicuous element in religious language must not be regarded as a primary criterion for this language. Maybe they are right, but as far as I can see, this is the only criterion that can be applied to all religious language. And moreover, all other elements of religious verbalization can change: sentence structures, literary forms, and styles; but if the terminology changes, this also means a profound change in the religion itself. Terminology is also the criterion that most clearly distinguishes religious language from other so-called social dialects or professional languages. So I would not underestimate the value

------
Papers of the Groningen working-group for the study of fundamental problems and methods of science of religion. Edited by Th. P. van Baaren and H. J.W. Drijvers (Religion and Reason 8), The Hague-Paris, Mouton, 1973, pp. 110-136.
------, 'Islam studied as a Symbol and Signification System', in: *Humaniora Islamica* II (The Hague-Paris, Mouton, 1974), pp. 267-285.
------, *Reflections on the Study of Religion, including an Essay on the Work of Gerardus van der Leeuw* (Religion and Reason 15), The Hague-Paris-New York, Mouton Publishers, 1978.

It is appropriate to stress the exploratory nature of this paper which wants to put the study of religious language within the wider context of the study of religions and ideologies as systems of signs, whereby religiosity and ideational creativity are studied in terms of human basic intentions. Just as intentions are important on the personal level (providing meaningful human subjectivity), sign systems are important on the communicative level (providing shared meanings and significances). Besides the study of intentions and sign systems as such, research on the interrelation between a given sign system in a society and given intentions of individuals and groups within that society may prove to be rewarding.

The first thing to be done is to operationalize the theory which has been outlined here so that it can lead to concrete investigations. In studies of this kind we are concerned with man's search for meaning, with or without religion; within *Religionswissenschaft* we are dealing in this way with the significance aspect of religion.

The author wants to express his sincere gratitude to Prof. W. Dupré, of the University of Nijmegen, the Netherlands, and to Prof. R. L. Nettler, of Carleton University, Ottawa, who kindly read and corrected the English style of this paper. Professor J. Pelc, of the University of Warsaw, was kind enough to read the text and to make some useful suggestions for which the author is most grateful.

of terminology in defining the notion of the language of religion.

There are, of course, other important criteria, too, according to which the language of religion can be defined — and described. Those which Prof. Barr presents in his paper in part II(c) — linguistic and literary ones —, undoubtedly apply very well to many texts of the book-religions. For Dr Waardenburg the central criterion for the language of religion is the religious use of the language; in other words, language used in religious situations, by people who are to be regarded as religious at the moment of use, is in his words religious language. Now here we have two kinds of criteria: Prof. Barr's linguistic and literary criteria and Dr Waardenburg's 'use' and 'people who use the language'. Let me try to formulate an operational definition of religious language on the basis of the two kinds of criteria mentioned above plus one of my own, i.e. the religious tradition: Religious language consists of certain linguistic and literary elements, whose choice in different religious contexts depends on religious tradition.

1. It may sound a bit trivial to say that a language consists of linguistic and literary elements. But in this case these elements are not just any elements: they are specific elements and what exactly they are depends on the natural language, the context and the religious tradition.

Since the elements are from a natural language, their recognition and systematization is not especially difficult. The same lexical and syntactical rules apply to them as to any part of a natural language. There are exceptions, but I shall return to them later. So the study of the lexical and syntactical levels of religious language can be carried out by any linguist who masters the natural language in question. And this is true even if the linguist in question does not master the semantics of religious language.

2. Linguistics provides a very good start in studying a language. But if we add to the language the attribute 'religious', the matter becomes more complicated. And it is here we must start to pay attention to the notions of context and tradition. Context here includes both the use of the language and the users of the language. Use refers to the situation of use, performance or actualization of particular religious language[8] or

8. Juha Pentikäinen, 'Perinne- ja uskontoantropologisen syvätutkimuksen mene-

a particular religious genre. Thus one aspect that must be taken into account when studying a particular piece of language assumed to be religious, is that of its situation of actualization: as a matter of fact one often cannot decide whether a piece of language is to be considered as religious before knowing its real situation of use. This applies especially to many materials collected from illiterate peoples and tribes. Let me offer an example: Victor Turner presents in his book *The Ritual Process* an example of an obscene song, that is performed in a certain ritual by the Ndembus.[9] The song is intended to delight the spirit of the female ancestor whose good will guarantees the luck of the tribe. Thus it belongs to the cult of the dead and therefore must be considered as religious. However, the only elements in the song which would reveal that it is not ordinary obscenity are the names given to the female ancestor.

Of course we could also find examples from closer at hand, in our own culture, but this one reminds us of the fact that religious language, or religiously-used language does not always have to be solemn and in high style, as we would be bound to think on the basis of our own religious tradition.

The other aspect to be considered, when speaking of the context, are the users of the language: the speakers (or the writers). They are the bearers of the religious tradition and this tradition directs their choice of vocabulary, sentence structures, literary forms etc. Of course they have their idiosyncratic speech habits, which can be heard in their speech besides the traditional elements. To take an example: The use of dialects does not belong to religious tradition. But a lay preacher may use in his sermon the dialect of his region, which is the only language he has ever learned to express himself in. The religiously traditional elements of his sermon are still the same as those of a preacher of the same church using a more 'civilized' language, e.g. a priest. I am referring to the studies of one of my colleagues here, Päivikki Suojanen, who has studied the speech habits of some lay preachers from the revivalist movement known as *Beseechers* here in South-Western Finland.[10]

---

telmästä' (Summary: On the Method of Tradition- and Religio-Anthropological Depth Research), *Sananjalka* 12 (Turku, 1970), p. 94.

9. Victor Turner, *The Ritual Process. Structure and Antistructure*, London, 1969, pp. 77-80.

10. Päivikki Suojanen, 'Spontaani saarna' (Summary: Spontaneous Sermon), *Sananjalka* 14 (Turku, 1972).

The religious speaker's possibilities of choice or improvization (within the limits of the tradition, of course) are bound to the nature of the speech situation. If the situation is relatively free, say a prayer meeting, the speakers have freer choice than for example at a funeral. This brings out clearly one of the clearest distinctions within religious language: I would call it the opposition between ritual and casual language. And here I mean ritual in the strict religio-scientific sense, not in the sense the psychologists and sociologists use the term to describe generally 'patterned behavior'. That is to say, ritual language is the verbal part of ritual expression. Casual religious language would then be any other language used religiously or referring to religious reality. Let me consider them in turn a bit more closely.

3. Ritual language. The verbalization connected with religious rituals is in most cultures very strictly limited. Not in amount, but in quality. In most cases the ritual verbalizations have fixed 'literary' forms, i.e. their texture, content and structure are or aim to be the same for one time to another: prayers, charms, incantations, myths, hymns and other songs, dialogues etc. I would like to call these ritual genres. In most cases, an expert or many experts are needed to perform these verbalizations at rituals: priest, shaman, witch doctor or other ritual specialist. Using ritual language belongs to their ritual role, it is part of their role behavior. There are cases when the use of ritual language belongs to the role behavior of other participants, too. In initiation rites all over the world the habit of using a secret language, totally different from everyday speech, is known.[11] Comparable to this habit is the way in which for example an Ingrian bride must express her emotions and expectations between the time of betrothal and the marriage ceremony in all situations belonging to the ceremonies; she does so by lamenting i.e. performing laments, whose vocabulary, content and even structure and way of performance are traditional.[12]

In the last two cases, the secret language of the initiands, and the laments of the bride, and also in laments for the dead, the ritual language

11. Cf. Arnold van Gennep, *The Rites of Passage*, London, 1960, p. 169.
12. Cf. my articles 'Itkuvirsien henkilönnimitysten typologiaa' (Summary: Typology of the Personal Names in Laments), *Sananjalka* 14 (Turku, 1972), and 'Lucky Shoes or Weeping Shoes' (Structural analysis of Ingrian shoeing laments), *Studia Fennica* 17 (Turku, 1975).

has often become so much differentiated from everyday language that it is hard or even impossible for a non-expert to interpret. Everyday things may have acquired different names. Here it takes more than just mastering the natural language to recognize the elements and explain them. In many cases, the only way to get to know the secrets of the language is, then, to go and ask the experts, the bearers of the tradition, though other contextual knowledge may also be of help.

The limited role of verbalization in rituals can, of course, be explained by the fact that it is only a part of ritual expression. There are also other elements of expression: gestures, music, material instruments, clothing etc., each of which has its message for the participants in the ritual. All of these together with the verbal expression has sometimes been called the ritual language, but in my opinion it would be better to distinguish between ritual expression and ritual language.

Ritual language being only a part, though in many cases a very significant part, of ritual expression, it should not be studied apart from its context. Of course it is possible to take a myth, a prayer, or a lament as a text, a literary form, which can be analyzed in terms of linguistic aspects or in terms of aesthetic aspects. But in this way the meaning of this text will never reveal itself. And by the meaning of this text, I refer to its meaning for the bearers of tradition, not just the literal meaning. Thus my proposition for the methodology of studying the ritual language would be, that the object of the study should be the whole ritual, which would be analyzed as emic units, entities which form the ritual expression. To study only the verbal part of the ritual expression means, in my opinion, shutting one's eyes to the emotions, thoughts and ideas which cannot be expressed in words, but which nevertheless are expressed in other ways. Of course the kind of study I propose seems difficult for us, who have grown up within a culture and religion where rituals play a rather insignificant role and where a general belief seems to be that everything, even our innermost feelings, can be expressed in words.[13]

4. Casual language. I would be tempted to define the casual language of religion by saying that any language that does not belong to ritual

13. Cf. Mary Douglas, *Natural Symbols. Explorations in Cosmology*, Plymouth, 1970, pp. 19-36.

expression is casual, and leave it at that. This would, however, be a rather too easy, and not quite satisfactory, explanation, I believe. There are cases where the boundary between ritual and casual language is a shifting one. Casual language, or parts of it, may become ritual when used within a ritual context. But normally the context of casual language is casual, i.e. it is not determined beforehand. Thus it could be a conversation between two believers, a person telling about his religious experiences, or a witness story in a Salvation Army meeting. Common features for all these speech events may include the use of specific terminology, particular sentence structures etc. that belong to the religious tradition in question, but the most important common feature is the freedom of the choice of the speaker. He may use whatever elements he thinks are best in order to tell of his thoughts and emotions.

5. To speak of ritual and casual religious language is of course to speak about first-level language of religion: it leaves out other levels, to which Prof. Barr in his paper refers, though it does not deny their existence. Anyhow, for me the problem of religious language and the methodology of its study consists more of the problem of the objects of study: real speech situations. Religion is not in the language, it is in the use of it and most of all, it is in the people who use the language.

Commentary   by Ninian Smart

First, I shall state my own general position on a number of the key issues. I shall then relate that position to the contributions of the main papers.

1. The main sense in which we can talk of the language of religion is one where it is treated functionally and as a domain: *functionally*, for it has certain uses, such as expressing worship, commandments, religious experiences, etc.; *as a domain*, for it has to do with an aspect or domain of human existence – e.g. it often has to do with gods, and typically with some entity or event which is transcendent. It thus differs from language about art, sport, physics, etc. (Obviously, though, there can be overlaps.)

2. The analysis of religious language needs to be comparative and plural, as for example is done in my *Reasons and Faiths*,[14] and in William Christian's *Meaning and Truth in Religion*.[15]

3. The language of a given religion must be analyzed with a view to its being organic and thus in certain respects necessarily particular — e.g. the concept of creation in a given faith has to be understood in the light of the concept of God, history, the content of various myths and so on. Moreover this 'horizontal organicness' is to be seen in the light of the 'vertical' connection between belief and practice — e.g. the concept God and its relation to worship.

4. From the point of view of the history of religions, the main point analysis of religious language is descriptive and not directed towards the truth or otherwise of religious beliefs (but much philosophical analysis is really directed towards the latter task). The corollary is that the reference of religious language must be bracketed (in a manner like that worked out in my *The Phenomenon of Religion*[16]).

5. Analysis should as far as possible be geared to particular problems — e.g. the examination of performatives can illuminate the 'vertical' relationship referred to above.

Comments on the papers, in relation to the five headings above:

1. This is in line with the thinking of both papers: but perhaps more stress could have been put in both the papers on the functional embedding of language in practice and experience. This arises partly because of the reluctance of the analytical tradition to follow through its own logic. From this perspective the analysis of religious language is a branch of the comparative study of religion.

2. This is in line with the two papers.

3. This is an overlap both with James Barr's remarks in III and with Jacques Waardenburg's stress on religion as a sign system. However, I draw attention to the notion of the 'vertical' connection.

4. I perceive a conflict with James Barr's remarks in II(f) re theology. I do not see that theology (as systematic) primarily functions as a metalanguage though, of course, it may incorporate metalinguistic

---

14. Ninian Smart, *Reasons and Faiths*, Routledge and Kegan Paul, 1958.
15. William Christian, *Meaning and Truth in Religion*, Princeton U. P., 1964.
16. Ninian Smart, *The Phenomenon of Religion*, Macmillan, 1973.

remarks. Of course, there may be some ambiguity in the idea of meta-language. But if it is language about primary statements, etc., then surely the systematization of the primary material (which is what a lot of theology is) is not properly metalinguistic.

5. This is consistent with both papers.

Commentary   by Hans Wissman

On isolating the concept 'religious language'

If one accepts the concept 'religious language', applies it or deals with the term, then it is necessary in this paper to reflect upon the origin of the concept.

I shall begin with the presuppositions implicated in the use of the concept 'religious language'.

1. First of all it is evident that one can qualify the word 'language' with various adjectives, and as such one can qualify it with 'religious'. The concept 'religious language' then presupposes a distinction from other languages.[17] For the sake of clarifying this distinction it is necessary to consider other possibilities. If language can be differentiated in a number of ways, then an account of these possibilities will show us so to speak *e contradictione* the presupposition implicated in the concept 'religious language'.

a) One can distinguish between religious language and any other languages (such as political or scientific languages) which are defined by their main reference to a sector of the out-of-speech reality. The point of distinction is in this case the main reference itself, since these languages make communication possible in and about these sectors to which they primarily refer.

17. Cf. on the problem of isolating and distinguishing religious language also: Hans Grass, 'Erwägungen über den religiösen Satz', *NZSystTh* 9 (1967), pp. 129-138; Tord Simonsson, 'Der religiöse Satz', *ibid.*, pp. 218-227; J. Wils, 'Aspects of Sacral Language', *Babel* 9, pp. 36-48; Manfred Kaempfert, 'Logik und Linguistik der Religion', *LingBibl* 7/8 (1971), pp. 17-27.

b) One can further distinguish between religious language and any languages (such as poetical, literary or theatrical languages) belonging to a certain sector of social and cultural reality such as poetry, theatre etc. In contrast to those in point (a), these languages mainly constitute that sector of reality for which they are specific.

c) One can make a distinction between religious language and profane or secular language, whereby this distinction is based upon metaphysical or ontological arguments.

d) Finally, one can make a distinction between religious and the logical-argumentative language, in which the distinction depends on the presupposed different systems of argumentation and the different axiomatic systems of conclusions.

Before we consider the logical steps presupposed in the oppositions listed above, we must point out that there is a certain invalidity of such a scheme: since a concept like, for example, 'poetical' language is based on a naive meta-linguistic use of language, it therefore cannot be employed as an exactly and well defined term with clear significance (intention) or with defined validity (extension). Therefore it is not possible either to map out a field in which any 'language' would have its systematically valid place. Because we are here primarily concerned with the distinction between 'religious' and 'non-religious' language, as well as with the inherent presuppositions, we shall deal with the term 'language' only as it can be defined through the above-mentioned contrasts.

In considering these oppositions, it immediately becomes obvious that the distinction between religious language and political language, for example, is quite different than the distinction between religious and poetical language. What the phenomenon 'religious language' might be can be clarified on different levels by its respective opposite.

This observation can easily be proved by another observation: there is a different meaning of 'language' in any given opposition:

a) when comparing religious and political language, the word 'language' is considered to have an instrumental meaning as a vehicle to propagate ideas on reality, without constituting these ideas themselves;

b) however, when comparing religious and literary language, the term 'language' means rather a specific modality of the *parole*, a style or a specific mode to deal with reality;

c) a similar meaning of 'language' is assumed in the comparison of religious and profane language; furthermore 'language' here means a
different structure of argumentation and reasoning as well;

d) when constrasting religious and logical-argumentative language, one
conceives 'language' not in the sense of parole but of a 'Denkform',[18]
based on a sort of system of organizing certain kinds of inner imagination of reality.

This short outline of the different contrastive presuppositions ('religious
language is not..., is unlike...') implies the following consequences:

a) when distinguishing religious language from non-religious, several
different arguments can be employed;

b) the criteria must be indicated for differentiation of religious and
non-religious language in order for it to become clear how religious
language is conceived;

c) each contrast of religious language with any other results in the altering of the meaning of 'language'.

2. These different 'languages' mentioned above have been regarded as
different sectors of one given natural language (like English, German,
Sanskrit etc.). In facing the plurality of natural languages, we must
conceive these sectors in a multidimensional way. In this interlingual
or intercultural application of the oppositions and distinctions made
above, one can presuppose that their relevancy and validity change in
the various languages and cultures.

While it would be worthwhile to discuss this interlingual change of
their relevancy and validity, I feel this would be beyond the scope of
my paper.

*On the problem of the distinction between a religious and a non-religious
sector of reality*

If, as we have shown, the varying oppositions or contrasts through which
the different sectors of a natural language are distinguished each emphasize a different meaning of language, then it is clear that the same

18. See on this concept: Hans Leisegang, *Denkformen*, Berlin, 1951².

must be valid regarding the concept 'religious'. Therefore it is necessary to use the same method in differentiating the religious from the non-religious. In addition it is obvious that varying qualities of the 'religious' must be differentiated in the same way.

The oppositions with their different criteria let us make a distinction between the religious and the languages of other sectors of reality. Therefore the implicit distinction between religion and non-religion is clear. If it is, for example, possible to make a distinction between the religious and the political — using any criteria whatsoever — then it must be possible, too, by means of the same criteria, to distinguish a sector which is regarded as 'religious' from a sector not regarded as 'religious'. Since there are obviously possibilities to distinguish between religion and other sectors of reality, there are therefore possibilities to distinguish between religion and non-religion. The opposite must also be valid: if such a distinction between religion and other sectors of reality is very difficult to make, then we shall find the same difficulties in distinguishing religion from non-religion. When one speaks in a given culture of religion, the reality signified by this word must be limitable by means of contradiction to that area of validity excluded from other sectors of reality.

One may recall the well-known difficulties in describing Hinduism as a religion, a difficulty which can be transformed into the two questions: which reality belongs to this religion at all? and: which belongs to Hinduism which we (as non-Hindus) would not signify as religion?[19]

We can state the following hypothesis as a consequence of this problem: The concept 'religion' presupposes its possible contradiction by other sectors of reality. If it is not possible to isolate the sector 'religion' in a given culture in which the distinction between religion and non-religion is difficult, then the methodologically sound consequence of the hypothesis would be to demonstrate the problematical character of this very concept 'religion'.

The concept 'religion' with this implicitly presupposed distinction from non-religion seems to be characterized by the phenomenon of a 'positive' religion: if a religion is founded in an historical event, then there is the possibility or necessity to make this distinction,

---

19. Cf. on the problem of a *religious* 'proprium' of Hinduism: Jan Gonda, *Die Religionen Indiens* (RdM 11), Stuttgart, 1960, pp. 348 ff.

a) because it is possible to distinguish between the situation before and after this foundation – the situation before the foundation is very unlike the situation afterwards, and it is possible to distinguish the founded religion from the situation before its foundation;

b) because it is possible even after the foundation to distinguish religion from non-religion: that which refers to the foundation – regardless of the reasoning – is easily to be distinguished from that which implicitly or explicitly does not refer to the foundation;

c) because these distinctions can also be made in a transcultural way: it is possible to distinguish the founded religion from another which refers either to another founder or which does not refer to the founder of this religion.

These three possibilities of distinction presuppose implicitly the possibility of distinguishing between religion and non-religion inasmuch as the distinction can also be described in the following form: religion vs. non-(or: not-this)religion. One would have to test whether the concept 'religion' refers to these possibilities (a-c) as implicated by the special case of a founded religion. This question must be affirmed at the meta-level of a science which is concerned inter alia with the problem of the religious language: if, as we have seen, the main problem of observing the phenomenon 'religious language' consists in the problem of recognizing the specifics of this language as distinguished from other languages as sectors of a given natural language, then it will be true that this searching for the specifics presupposes the distinction of religion and non-religion.

If 'religion' in the case of this special theoretical concern with religious language shows the exclusive quality of the founded religion, then we arrive at the following problem: do the presuppositions of the concept 'religion' as characterized by the founded religion (with its possibilities of distinguishing from non-religion) exclude the application of this concept to cultures which we cannot regard as founded in this exclusive way? If that should be true, I would propose the continuing utilization of the concept 'religion', aware of its confining implications, instead of disregarding the concept as unuseable. The concept, comprehended in this manner, would no longer be a generic term, but something like a model. If one applies a model for the sake of elucidating reality, it is from the outset clear that a model

–is not reality itself, but expression of an attempt at its more or less adequate representation,

—has a well defined realm of validity which the model can help to represent,

—has a well defined function in representing and describing reality for someone.[20]

If we wish to avoid distorting reality through concepts which may prove to be inadequate standards, we should try to describe reality in terms of existence and degree of distinctness of chosen characteristics.[21] Unlike the generic term, the model makes clear that the degree of distinctness of a characteristic is not absolute but is relative to a frame of reference which discloses and qualifies it.

In these terms the description and representation of reality is only possible in relation to the recognition of this degree of distinctness; mapping out this degree presupposes an implicit comparison of 'cognate' or similar phenomena which can be interpreted and described by means of this arrangement.

Some consequences for the problem of distinguishing and isolating religious language

From the model-character of the concept 'religion' it becomes evident that our purpose here cannot be to define religious language in an absolute way. Rather it is necessary to describe this reality in relative terms (i.e. *e contradictione*). By means of this relationality, that which is called 'religious' is determined relatively, i.e. in relation to its possible oppositions. This is above all necessary in the case of distinguishing and isolating religious language from non-religious. One can easily see that the oppositions mentioned above are not pure ones such as binary oppositions. They can only be as pure as the opposite concepts, for example the concept of political language.

In addition, the oppositions cannot be considered as absolutes inasmuch as different characteristics become relevant depending on various

20. Cf. the article 'Modell' in: Georg Klaus and Manfred Buhr, eds., *Philosophisches Wörterbuch*, vol. 2, Berlin, 1971[8], 729-733.

21. Cf. on this typological procedure: Carl Gustav Hempel and Paul Oppenheim, *Der Typusbegriff im Lichte der neuen Logik*. Wissenschaftstheoretische Untersuchungen zur Konstitutionsforschung und Psychologie, Leiden, 1936.

levels of analysis. For example, if we choose the word-level as level of analysis, then the occurrence of certain words should represent the variances between two or more languages. If we suppose 'God' to be a typical religious word and 'leadership' a typical political one, then we observe that 'God' occurs in political speech as well as 'leadership' in religious. Therefore the occurrence of 'God' or 'leadership' does not establish an opposition of two languages at that word-level of analysis. At best we could say that the degree of recurrence of these two words is different in the two languages, which indicates a higher or lower degree of distinctness of a characteristic such as we demanded for the application of model-concepts. The distinction between religious and political language can therefore only be grasped on a scale which has at the one extreme the religious language and at the other the political. Besides the fact that this procedure functions statistically and that one cannot distinguish between religious and other languages solely by means of the distribution of frequency of certain words, it should be emphasized, as shown in the two main papers, that there is no word with a 'naturally' religious meaning or significance. Instead, it is the usage which makes these words become religious or non-religious.[22]

To apply the word-level as the only level of analysis in a research on religious language means abandoning the possibility of learning the character of a language since the knowledge of word-usage presupposes a level of analysis which is superior to the word-level.

If one calls, according to the recent linguistics, this level of analysis 'pragmatic', one can, by means of this pragmatic component, choose 'texts-in-function' as a level of analysis.[23] This component would include everything making possible a description of the given use of a word in a certain communicative situation. By this method of analysis, as well, there is no rigid opposition between religious and, say, political language, but instead only a more or less high degree of distinctness on a scale in the sense mentioned above.

a) If this pragmatic component primarily represents the situative con-

22. Cf. the research which is restricted to the word-level (excluding pragmatical aspects of language): Manfred Kaempfert, 'Skizze einer Theorie des religiösen Wortschatzes', *Muttersprache* 81 (1971), pp. 15-22.
23. Cf. on this pragmatical aspect of a theory concerning texts-in-function: Siegfried J. Schmidt, 'Text als Forschungsobjekt der Texttheorie', *Der Deutschunterricht* 1972, 4 (= Linguistik II), pp. 7-28 (Lit.).

text making a text or a word within a text become religious, then it is still possible without contradiction that a religious word (spontaneously so defined) be used in a political speech, or vice versa.

b) A further aspect of the pragmatic component can be seen in the *'partner-taktischen Programm'*,[24] in other words the attempt to answer the questions —who says something
  —to whom
  —for what reasons.

In light of these questions, it seems very probable that 'naturally' political speeches are religiously motivated if the speaker or his listener(s) have religious motives in speaking and listening. Would that be then religious language?

c) A third aspect of the pragmatic component should be mentioned. The analysis of a concrete situation is not only dependent upon those factors present in the actual communication but also upon factors existing independent of this situation, i.e., before it, in the course of it, and afterwards. Such factors are, for example, the roles and functions which the partners in communication individually assume or accord to each other. Such factors can be determined as belonging to the specific realm of reality considered by many as religious.

It therefore seems worthwhile to give, by means of these different aspects of the pragmatic level of analysis, the following hypotheses as model-situations. With the aid of these models of pragmatic units we can make advances in operationalizing the distinction between religious and non-religious language.

1. As we have been able to see, the concept of the 'religious' and its crucial distinction from the 'non-religious' becomes helpful in describing reality because it gives well defined characteristics for which the degree of distinctness is observable. The situation regarding religious language is analogous: the criteria which allow a decision on whether a communicative situation is more or less religious also allow a decision on whether the language itself uttered in that situation is to be considered as more or less religious.

---

24. Cf. the model of production and perception of texts by: Georg F. Meier, 'Wirksamkeit der Sprache', *Zeitschrift für Phonetik, Sprachwissenschaft und Kommunikationsforschung* 22 (1969), pp. 482f.

2. In addition, if one considers certain ideas and concepts of reality to be more religious than others, one must assume that the utterances belonging to these (more likely) religious ideas and concepts are themselves more religious than other utterances not belonging to these ideas and concepts.

3. If a certain person, when speaking in a realm regarded as more religious than another and by means of his belonging to this realm, is considered more religious than another person when speaking, then his utterances must also be considered more religious. This problem belongs to the so-called religious 'performatives'.[25]

4. We must clarify the presuppositions of the term 'belonging to' as a twofold relationship dependent upon the acceptance of both parties concerned. Ideally, it is not possible to answer the question whether someone belongs to a certain realm unless one knows of the acceptance of both parties involved. On the other hand, it is also possible to think of the term 'belonging to' in a dialectical sense. We may think here of a mystic's leaving the official realm or institution of the Church and his interpreting the basis (basic texts, life history of the founder, etc.) of that institution in a new way.[26] We must extend our theoretical minimal-frame characteristics in order to decide upon the term 'belonging to' in this case. We shall concentrate on the identity of the basis of both the institution and of the interpreting mystic. I think this identity will prove an indicator for an 'objective' belonging-to relationship even though both parties of this relationship (institution and mystic) may refuse the relationship subjectively.

5. In considering the basis which may, in certain cases, constitute a belonging-to relationship, we must concentrate inter alia on the texts functioning as a basis. If one regards certain texts as a basis of a party which is considered more probably religious, then one must concede that the texts themselves have the same religious quality, insofar as the various aspects or parts of the given text actually do function as the basis. Prof. Barr gave us an important point in his paper when he states that within holy scriptures we can find, in addition to religious utterances, other things such as geography or 'classifications of animal

25. Cf. Lars Bejerholm, 'Religiöse Performative', *NZSystTh* 8 (1966), pp. 255-264.
26. Cf. Günter Lanczkowski, *Begegnung und Wandel der Religion*, Düsseldorf and Köln, 1971, pp. 64 ff.

nature' etc.; therefore we face the problem to what extent these texts actually function as a basis for an institution or realm regarded as religious. I think we can solve this problem approximately by answering the following twofold question: In which way does the (religious) institution depend on the specific text and in which way does the specific text depend on the conserving and/or producing institution? The *balance* of these two questions and the balance of their answers seems to be a sound indicator for the question whether a text is a basis of an institution or not.

In these very few observations we see a great need for further explication and supplementation. The question of isolating and distinguishing first a religious sector and then religious language has not been answered at all. The purpose of these observations has been the indication of the direction which must be taken in order to ask the appropriate questions. If the problem of isolating religious language can be solved, then it is possible to elucidate the different problems regarding its content. One can discuss, for example, the mutual influencing or interaction between language and religion,[27] or the linguistic characteristics of religious language, or further, the 'logic'[28] presupposed in this very language. In addition, one can discuss the function of language as constituting reality as well as religious reality, and, facing these problems, make a contribution worthwhile for the methodology of the theory of religion.

Discussion   Chairman: Ugo Bianchi

The first speaker, James Barr, said that all he wished to do in the time available to him was to go through some of the salient arguments in his paper, and to add one or two footnotes. It fell into four sections: the first dealing with his starting point, i.e. the natural language of hu-

27. Cf. inter alia Fritz Tschirch, 'Religion und Sprache. Bestandsaufnahme des wechselseitigen Verhältnisses', in *Solange es HEUTE heisst, Festschrift für Rudolf Herrmann*, Berlin, 1957, pp. 260-292.
    28. Cf. Joseph M. Bocheński, *The Logic of Religion*, New York, 1965; cf. also Manfred Kaempfert, *op. cit.* in n. 17.

manity (in opposition to a philosophical concept of the language of religion); the second dealing with the attempt to identify a special register within a natural language which would constitute, for that language, the language of religion; section three, which he supposed was somewhat polemic, dealt with language and culture; and finally, section four approached the question of the language of religion from a more philosophical aspect.

Starting out from an ostensive definition of both human languages and human religions (and leaving aside the question as to a final essence or identity of religions), he had explored some of the consequences of the diversity of human languages in which religion is expressed. (It was also implicit in his thinking that some religious expression was non- or sub-linguistic: gesture, etc.) He had first considered two situations involving linguistic change: diachronic change within one language, and transfer from one language to another. The latter referred to situations where a single religion was represented in more than one speech community, and he had set out the various possible ways in which this could be handled (pp. 430, 1–3); in retrospect, possibilities (1) and (2), i.e. the non-translation of canonical texts as against the retention of a special language for religious discourse, seemed very close to each other, but he still felt that the distinction was worth making: e.g. if not only the Qur'an, but also productive religious discussion, were to be carried on in Arabic within for instance a Persian or Turkish speech community. He had then discussed the various attitudes associated with different approaches to the question of translatability of religious texts.

In section II he had investigated the difficulties inherent in the attempt to define a religious register in language. It seemed to him that this could not be identified on the basis of terminology alone, but rather by groups of collocations and more complicated structures. One point fundamental to his own thinking was that terms, in themselves, were commonly equivocal in relation to religious structures. He also suggested that there would be considerable overlap between the language of two religions within the same natural language, or of the same religion spreading over two natural languages: a factor which would promote translatability of religious texts. In point II(f), he then suggested that within religious sectors of language there could be several levels operating, with the higher-degree language 'commenting' on the lower degree.

There had been a very powerful idea in the 20th century, he said, that the adoption of a particular language, as a linguistic system, necessarily carried with it a specific world-view, with consequent effects upon society and thus also on religion. This seemed to imply linguistic determinism of religion, and in section III he had given some reasons for considering this to be wrong. He did not deny that there was a connection between language and world-view, or that evidence could be found to support it: but he claimed that this connection was haphazard. Religion was not tied to a (natural) language, but to a particular use of language resources. And an obvious, yet often neglected, point was that one natural language could be used to express more than one religion.

Finally, in discussing philosophical questions about religious language (section IV), he suggested that the paramount issue was whether the answers should be universal in application, or (as he believed) religion-specific. The philosophy of religion had largely arisen within the context of a single religious community, and would need adjustment to accommodate to the plurality of religions: and while universal statements might be possible subsequently, this could, he felt, only be achieved following a preliminary, religion-specific stage.

Barr was followed by Jacques Waardenburg, who began by identifying the main question as being how language could be tackled, within the study of religions, when it was being used in a religious sense, religion being considered in its function as a source of meaning. Just as in his paper he had called religious language 'double-decker', so, he suggested, was his paper itself double-decker: it worked on two levels. He wanted to show that the problem of the language of religion could not be treated adequately except on the basis of a more general theory of religion as a system of signs, which he had tried to outline in his paper. Language can be seen in three ways: as a transmission of meaning; according to its communicative function; and as a human expression. The basic question of this kind of research, he considered, was why a particular fact had particular meaning for a particular group or person. Classical phenomenology had looked for meanings and meaningful structures according to essences; he was interested, however, first, in the meaning that was valid for concrete human beings. Secondly, he was more interested in content than in form; thirdly, in language within the context of communication: between persons and texts, persons and persons, and directly with 'reality' (nature, etc.).

The definition of religious language (both verbal and non-verbal), which was a question that had exercized many commentators, should be, he suggested, in terms of its 'religious use' by the speakers, referring to something beyond empirical reality. Communication in religious language presupposes that the speaker and the listener share some understanding of that reference. Granted this, the use of religious language is very precise in evoking, proclaiming, or 'pointing to' kinds of reality different from those to which other kinds of language refer. This led into the central part of the paper, the attempt at a general theory of religions as sign systems. Once made operational, this theory would facilitate a hermeneutical effort to explicitate the (subject's) meaning of particular things for particular people within a particular tradition and in a given socio-historical context. For this hermeneutics, two terms are crucial: subjectively, the intention(s) of the person or group; objectively, the sign system(s) (culture, religion, social code, etc.) in which they find themselves. Finally, at the end of his paper, he had discussed some methodological and theoretical consequences of this theory for the study of religions.

Introducing her commentary, Aili Nenola-Kallio described Barr's paper as a very clear-cut presentation of the relations between religions and natural languages and of the language of religion as a sector within natural languages. With Waardenburg's paper, she had the feeling that she and he were in fact talking about the same thing, but in different terms; and she described her own commentary as a pragmatic approach to an operational definition, on the basis of the criteria put forward by Barr and Waardenburg plus one of her own, i.e. the religious tradition.

The second commentator was Ninian Smart, whose prepared commentary was, as he said, the shortest on the conference (2 pages). Before expanding on it, he wanted first to explain his understanding of philosophy, since he really wanted to concentrate on the philosophical points arising at the end of Barr's paper. By 'philosophy' he did not mean metaphysics, nor what he called the 'impure' version of philosophical or linguistic analysis, which was concerned with matters of *truth*; most of the books cited by Barr, and the influential *New Essays in Philosophical Theology* edited by Flew and MacKintyre, fell into this category. What mattered now, however, was 'pure' philosophical enquiry, and their concern was with the descriptive, scientific approach to religion: i.e. the analysis of actual religious language and of the connections of different elements in a system of beliefs with each other and with the expressive or formative use of language in ritual (an example of this was Donald Evans, *The Logic of Self-Involvement*; but Evans was religion-specific, instead of comparative). What was needed then was the comparative analysis of religious language and concepts in their living environment, as both Aili Nenola-Kallio and Jacques Waardenburg had been saying. The philosophical traditions both of the European continent, and of Britain and the USA, hindered this, but he felt that the way forward was through the comparative analysis of religious concepts, in close relation to the history of religions. Thus he disagreed with Ugo Bianchi, if he had understood him correctly, about 'universals': rather, there could be analogy between the central concepts of different religious systems, which were however always embedded in the particularity of their own system, and could be compared in the same way as one compared rituals, religious art objects, etc. One way of expressing this (to barbarize Wordsworth) was to say that every religious doctrine does not come in nakedness, but 'trailing clouds of doctrine and myth and institution does it come'. He also wanted to stress the importance of checking the living context, and avoiding the distressingly frequent false generalizations about 'what the believer would say' which occurred in philosophical literature.

One point common to both the main papers was their use of the concept of multiple levels, but he took issue with James Barr's description of theology as functioning as a meta-language. 'Meta-language' was a systematically ambiguous term, and inappropriate here: most theology should be categorized simply as religious utterance (i.e. rather than as utterance about utterance). Smart preferred the admittedly not very good term 'vertical' to describe the intrinsic relation between religious concepts (doctrine, myth, etc.) and religious practice (i.e. ritual).

The papers in this session provoked an unusual amount of discussion from the other members of the conference. The first two questions came from Joseph Kitagawa, who related first how he had come across a strange change in the character of the Ainu epics, depending whether they were recited by the fireside, in which case they formed a kind of entertainment, or formally chanted. Nothing was altered except the mode of delivery, yet the character changed completely, and he asked whether any of the speakers could comment on this in the context of religious language. Secondly, could they comment on Oswald Spengler's remark that language may be transferable, but connotations and mean-

ings are not: e.g. that when the Buddhist missionaries in India and China
had tried to transplant Indian Buddhist meanings, the Chinese Buddhists
had understood them quite differently, merely in fact re-ordering their
own world of meaning.

The third comment was offered by Hans Klimkeit, who welcomed
Waardenburg's re-definition, in effect, of the phenomenological approach; the difficulty arose, however, if meaning was to be exclusively
understood in the context of intention, since this virtually made comparison impossible. On the other hand it was extremely important to
escape from the hitherto dominant conception of meaning, which had
been ontological.

Kurt Rudolph had a series of points which he wanted to raise in connection with Waardenburg's paper. Firstly, what was Waardenburg's
understanding of 'religion'? He appeared to adopt a Tillichian position,
when he talked about 'absolute significance'. Secondly, he doubted
whether the distinction between the religious and the non-religious was
one of meaning: while not defending functionalism, he argued that the
distinction was one of function within tradition, as the commentators
had said. Thirdly, he suggested that Waardenburg's concern to reach the
meaning of a religion (which approached Kristensen's position) went
beyond the task of a historian of religion. Fourthly, in response to the
question whether science made its objects 'dead', he argued that this
was fundamentally the case, and that it represented a basic scientific
problem. Fifthly, he characterized Waardenburg's understanding of
Religionswissenschaft as a basic science of intention, or a humanist science of culture: possibly this was the only form of phenomenology
of religion which was still viable, and he looked forward to following
Waardenburg's further developments. His last point concerned Waardenburg's assertion of the presence in religious language of a 'transcendent
reference', which Rudolph argued was not necessarily true of all religious
language.

The same point was immediately taken up by Hans Penner: the term
'transcendent' raised the danger of moving back into ontology.

The discussions in this session, on language of religion in a restricted
sense of the term 'language', were placed in a wider context by R. J. Zwi
Werblowsky, by relating them to the discussions in earlier sessions about
symbol theory and ritual. He suggested it would be better to set the question of 'religious language', or 'religion as language', in the framework

of communications theory — including non-verbal communication — as a system of communicating with the beyond, the transcendent, the cosmos, society, etc. Thinking of language, however, had also suggested a valuable analogy between religious studies and linguistics. Both religions, and languages, constituted positive phenomena in the social and cultural life of human groups. The study of linguistics, however, abstracted from these actual natural languages, in search of formal structures 'underlying' every language — until the point was reached where in many respectable schools of linguistics it was considered an unnecessary luxury to actually know the languages: what mattered was the linguistic concept of a meta-language. He saw the danger of the same thing happening in phenomenology of religion: i.e. the development of a conceptualized version of the underlying principles of religion, which could then in fact lose contact with the actual existing natural religions.

Thinking in terms of religious vocabulary, C. J. Bleeker described the difficulties facing investigation into ancient Egyptian religion, and suggested concrete working method for the future. It had been asserted that ancient Egyptian had had no distinct vocabulary for religion: certainly the *Wörterbuch der Ägyptischen Sprache* did not include it, in contrast to the words for things pertaining to culture, etc. What this in fact meant was that the compilers of the *Wörterbuch* had overlooked the religious by-meanings of the relevant terms. What was needed, then, was a new dictionary comprising the religious use of language in Egypt, since this was the only means, in his opinion, to get at the real feelings and thought-forms of the people. This led into his second point, which was the suggestion that the actual different terms used in different cultures for the deity or its equivalent — e.g. *deus, theos, kami,* etc. — should be scrutinized in detail, since this was a more productive method than to speculate about symbols and ideas of the deity.

Replying, Ninian Smart regretted having used the term 'transcendent' (which Penner had criticized): a better term would be 'foci of religious belief', since this could leave aside completely the question as to the truth or not of the focus of the religious beliefs under investigation. The lack of such a neutral way of referring to the focus of religious belief had been a constant problem in phenomenology of religion, since it obscured the difference between descriptive studies of religion, and crypto-theology. Similarly, Jacques Waardenburg said that in discussing the 'double-decker' nature of religious language, he had used the term 'transcendent' (in quotation marks) as a convenient form of shorthand to refer to that which the believers saw as transcendent ('transcending' daily life reality for them).

Barr's paper had ended, interposed Ugo Bianchi, with the question whether the results of investigation would apply to all religions, or would show that the relationships between various kinds of meaning, etc., varied between one religion and another. He wondered whether this alternative could be avoided by positing that religion was not univocal or equivocal, but analogical. Replying, James Barr preferred not to commit himself as to whether fundamental analogies could be constated between different religions: he saw the term 'religion' not as the definition of a class of objects, but as a bundle of features, the presence of a sufficient number of which would constitute a certain entity as a religion in the speech of a people. In response to Bianchi's further question about these features, or 'universals', he said that some of them might be nominalistic, for the convenience of scholars, but that he believed most of them to be real historical continuities between religions.

The point about the 'transcendent' was reverted to by Walter Capps. It had been widely asserted that the distinctive feature of religious language was its reference to the supra-empirical; yet it also meant something — i.e. also referred to empirical reality. He also took issue with Waardenburg's use of the term 'point to' ('the religious use of language makes this language point to something basically meaningful...'): language could express, name, refer, describe, connote, denote, etc., but he did not understand how it could 'point to'. Similarly, the word 'meaning' had been over-used to the point of meaninglessness, and he suggested that 'discernment' would be a far better term, if this was acceptable to others.

Kurt Rudolph spoke again, to challenge what Barr had said against the interrelationship between language and world-view. He recalled Landsberger's study of Babylonian culture ('Die Eigenbegrifflichkeit der babylonischen Welt', *Islamica* II (1926), pp. 355-372; rpt.: Libelli 142, Darmstadt, 1965), in which he had closely investigated the world-view and also the structure of the language, and had concluded that there was a close interrelationship which was both logical and psychologically necessary.

The chairman now invited the two main speakers to reply to the points that had been raised, and James Barr spoke first. He defended his use of the term of 'meta-language' to describe the relationship between theology and religion, against the criticism in Smart's written commentary. Not all religions developed a theology; in those which did, part at least of its function was to systematize, and to state the conditions of validity, for utterances within that religion: in this sense, it was a kind of meta-language of the religious thinking of that religion. Turning to Rudolph's last remark, he regretted that he could not recall Landsberger's study, but in fact considered that Mesopotamian culture strongly supported his own argument, in view of the very close similarity of the cultural and religious material from two languages, Sumerian and Akkadian, which were structurally completely differently from each other. He then took up the metaphor of speaking of religion as itself being a language. A natural language, however, was a sign system, with a very large number of signs, which could be used to indicate all kinds of different things; whereas a religion, on this analogy, could only say one thing — itself. He thought the analogy was therefore of limited value. Finally, he thought the major outstanding point concerned a divergence between his own paper and Waardenburg's: he was unhappy about defining religious language solely in terms of meaning, since one could not be sure that one knew adequately the meanings or intentions involved. Moreover it seemed to him to be false to separate consideration of semantic content from that of form: he believed that these could only be properly understood if equally and simultaneously related to each other.

The final speaker was Jacques Waardenburg. He accepted Aili Nenola-Kallio's reassertion of the importance of enquiring into religious terminology, and he felt that this had not been emphasized enough in his own paper. He also agreed as to the importance of the religious tradition within which people live, so that individual intentions and significations are never plucked out of the air, as it were, but drawn from the reservoir of the tradition. The same applied to ritual language, which he had neglected. Similarly, he agreed with point 4 in Smart's commentary, that the reference of religious language must be 'bracketed' for the purposes of research, i.e. the question as to the truth or falsehood of the religious assertions under investigation (but not the fact that the assertions are made) should be excluded from consideration.

Answering Kitagawa's second question, he agreed that in the strict sense meanings themselves were not transferable as such from one culture to another, only sequences of signs. On the other hand, cultures were not static, but themselves changed with their sign systems, for example through interaction with other cultures. In reply to Klimkeit's criticism that comparison would be impossible if religion were to be interpreted entirely in terms of intention, he shared the anxiety about the difficulty of comparing a series of subjective impressions. What he wanted to do was to get away from mere intuitive phenomenology and to establish a rational investigation of meaning cores and structures.

It was more difficult to reply adequately to Rudolph's question as to what he understood by the term 'religious'. Waardenburg wanted to make a clear distinction between the ontological implications of Tillich's concept of 'ultimate concern' and the heuristic character of his own concept of 'absolute significance for (someone)'. He also insisted that in the present context his problem was that of distinguishing between religious and non-religious uses. Waardenburg went on to discuss the analogy between poetry and religion which had been raised from the floor. Since there is both 'religious' and 'non-religious' poetry, the prob- is complex. Although poetry and religion touch and move deeper layers of man, the scholar has the task to investigate even the most involving emotions in a rational way. Waardenburg defended the rational nature of the study of religion. He finished his reply, and the session, by giving a description of religious language as referring on the one hand to the reality in which we live, and therefore being concrete, but envisaging the concrete on the other hand by way of basic intentions and ultimate referents. So it has a 'double decker' character.

Depth Structures of Religious Expression

J. VAN BAAL   *The Scandal of Religion*

Prior to making any statement on the methodological implications of the study of depth-structures of religious experience, I have to make clear what, to my mind, these depth-structures are. For a proper performance of this twofold task it is inevitable to devote the greater part of this paper to these depth-structures as I cannot simply refer to the formulation of my views on this point in the final two chapters of my book *Symbols for Communication* (1971). Even if I had the arrogance to expect them to be known at all to this distinguished company, I should still have to confess that this first exposition of my views is not sufficiently systematic to do duty as a basis for our present discussions.

I. Current definitions of religion tend to veil the notorious but meaningful fact that religion is based upon notions and ideas, accepted as true, concerning a reality which cannot be verified empirically in any way. As we do not know of any living being better equipped for empirical observation and experiment, there is hardly anything more surprising than man's inclination to submit his conduct to rules dictated by notions concerning a non-verifiable reality. To the scientific mind its absurdity is obvious, and yet this behavior is not abnormal. Religion is so widespread as to be almost universal. It is by definition impossible to call abnormal what is common. Besides, the religious believer is not more frequently given to other forms of deviant behavior than the unbeliever. If religion really were abnormal, it would still stand apart from all other forms of abnormal behavior which practically never are confined to one single idiosyncrasy. Religion, then, is both normal and absurd, moreover widely valued as important and respectable. Briefly: religion is a scandal.

It does not serve any useful purpose to evade the truth by using definitions which make religion seem more respectable. After all, we cannot and do not expect that comparative religion shall give us better information about God. All we hope for, is more information about man, and in that context the confrontation with an absurdity which is normal and highly valued, offers a promising clue to further studies of the depth-structures of religious behavior. The supposition seems justified that it must be based on a vast human problem, a supposition strongly supported by the multifarious emotional overtones attending religious language and behavior. This human problem cannot be one which is culturally defined. Religion being found in the widest possible diversity of cultures imaginable, its foundations must necessarily be sought for in some fundamental contradiction in the human condition generally.

The phenomenologists have opened our eyes to the fact that the human condition is defined primarily by man's being in the world. Man is in a world or — in Merleau-Ponty's phrasing — to a world. What does this mean? In the first place that man belongs to the highly differentiated category of living beings. They all have in common the remarkable phenomenon of life which begins where matter stops being subject to purely physical and chemical processes by organizing itself in persistent patterns of selected chemicals, constituting more or less autonomous wholes called organisms. Each organism has its own standard pattern and accumulates matter (including matter taken from other organisms) for the sake of organizing itself in conformity with its pattern by a process called growth. All organisms have the faculty of repeating themselves by means of a process called procreation and, with the exception of monocellular organisms, they all return to inanimate matter through a process called senilization. Finally we note that they all seem to have the faculty of mutating their own standard pattern after an unknown — but certainly very high — number of self-repetitions in a process called evolution.

Among the characteristics mentioned two are of specific interest in this context. One holds our attention because it is perfectly redundant, namely the process called senilization. Nature disposes of more effective methods such as starvation or decimation by other species, to liquidate an overspill of individuals in any one species. It is as if nature wishes to emphasize that all living matter must in the end return to the state of inanimate matter. It is such a remarkable phenomenon that we cannot help feeling reminded of the analogies between death and sleep, a feature common to higher organisms which, in spite of its apparent obviousness, has never been satisfactorily explained (cf. Buytendijk, 1965, p. 127).

The second characteristic requiring a short comment is the organism's autonomy. The organism 'does something', and in this respect the organism differs fundamentally from inanimate matter. The problem is, whether the organism does anything of its own accord or simply reacts in conformity with its hereditary pattern to inward and outward stimuli. If the latter be the case the organism remains fully subject to the laws of nature and this is what we think (rightly or wrongly) to be the rule of life of all living creatures, except man. Man's situation is different, and his presumed freedom a moot problem. Man has the gift of reason, a gift making itself known *inter alia* by his power of speech. Language implies the use of linguistic symbols which enable man to deal with a situation even in its absence. A signal is a sign bound to a situation, a symbol refers to a situation. Confronted with a problem man can imagine different solutions, that is that by stepping aside from the world he lives in, his actual world, he can summon up other worlds, different worlds, which are the products of his imagination but may, by his well-considered effort, become reality. The important point is that he summons up other possibilities, other worlds as it were, and makes a choice. To all appearances man does act on his own accord and has a free will. Does he?

First of all, the choosing between various possibilities does not in itself imply a free will. Every organism, confronted with conflicting stimuli, makes a choice, reacting positively to the one and negatively to the other. It is an inbuilt mechanism that it must react as a whole. The choice itself is – or at least can be – predictable. How is this with man whom, in his capacity of willing or choosing things, we usually call a subject or an I? What about the freedom of the I? Does it escape the laws and necessities of nature, granting the organism its autonomy, invested in the structure of the organism? After all, man has the gift of reason, and insofar as choices and decisions are consciously made by weighing the possibilities against each other on their reasonable merits, such choices and decisions should be held to be free. But does man really weigh his choices on only reasonable grounds? The problem *de libro et servo arbitrio* is, since Freud, not what it used to be before he disclosed to us the powers of the subliminal. What then about the subject?

We owe a debt to Merleau-Ponty for redirecting the philosophical discussions on the 'subject' to hard facts, the first of them being that the I cannot simply be divorced from the body. I am my body. And, indeed, when I play a game of tennis it is not the hand with the racket which drives the ball, but it is I who does it, unaware of any specific part or posture of my body. I am all intent on the game and react with my whole body. It is simply me. Yet, when I strain my ankle, I suddenly realize that I have an ankle. As soon as something goes wrong with my body, my attitude changes. The I withdraws as it were from my body, to contemplate on it as an object of thought and inspection. My body is no longer I (at least not in its totality), but has turned into a part of my world in a similar way as it makes part of the world of others who know me through my body (cf. Buytendijk, 1965, pp. 74ff.). The I is elusive.

In fact, the I is always elusive. Whenever I reflect on myself, the reflecting I is necessarily another than the I on which I reflect, an I characterized by certain qualities, preferences and deficiencies. The reflected I, the object of my thought, is as such part of my world. It is no longer my real I which is the reflecting I whose characteristics are unknown to me until I try to reflect on it. But at that very moment the I has again taken refuge and differs as a reflecting I from its object, the reflected I. The reflecting I is elusive, always escaping from observation, ever withdrawing from its world, and in this power of recession uncontrollable and really free. The other I, however, the I which is object of reflection and which, for the sake of clarity, shall from now on be termed the 'self', is the product of an I which has taken up a position in the world by assuming a certain way of being in the world, a life-project in the sense of the 'projet-de-vie' as proposed by Sartre and Merleau-Ponty, through which it (the I) has turned into a driving force in its world, whose activities are open to observation and even to prediction. As seen from this angle, we can define the self as the subject (or I) which has become part of the world.

There is little room left for freedom in this definition. And, indeed, a man's most fundamental attitudes, his basic life-project, are initially forced upon him by his education, the contingencies of his personal life-history, and those of his individual genes-pattern. Since Freud we know how difficult it is to explicitate the real motives directing our personal behavior, let alone to reform its basic traits. And yet the basic life-project is not immutable. It changes throughout our life-time, usually not as much as it should do, but quite enough to refute the idea of immutability. There is always the subject, the elusive I, escaping every effort for captivation. Heavily committed by its preceding engagements with its world which turned it into a self, the subject in its elusiveness remains free to reconsider the position of the self. The subject's possibilities and opportunities for free choice may be curtailed by the restrictions imposed by the basic self as the censor of the subconscious, the subject never loses the awareness of its freedom to reconsider its position and the preferences of the self. The nature of the subject is that it is always in confrontation with its world, always challenged by it to define its proper position. The individual, although a part of his world, must necessarily be a subject. He cannot help being it because he is it.

In conclusion we now can formulate the basic contrariety of the human condition in the following terms: as a subject man must be part of his world, as part of his world he must be a subject. The wording of the statement is ambiguous, as ambiguous as the human condition. The word 'must' indicates an inescapable necessity, a constraint by nature on the one hand, an obligation (and the foundation of moral obligation) on the other. The freedom proper to the elusive subject enables the subject to revise the modus of its being part of its world as a self, and to decide on the extent to which a man as part of his world shall realize himself as a subject, i.e. the extent to which he shall realize the freedom which is the essence of the elusive subject which he also is, which necessarily he always is. The point is that man can be a self in many ways. The fundamental life-project of the self may be based upon an image of his world, which differs profoundly from his real world; he can also choose to live so much in peace with his world as to neglect his potentialities to take a proper stand in that world where and whenever its conditions call for the individual's action. The modalities of realizing the necessity of being a subject who is part of his world, of being a part which is a subject, are as manifold as they are divergent. Their description and evaluation call for a system of ethics in which freedom and participation are conceived not as a gift, 'eine Gabe', but as a task, 'eine Aufgabe'. The devising of such a system is not of our concern here. Our present concern is the problem of religion, to which we now return.

II. To begin with, a somewhat closer inspection of the concept of the self is required. A little while before we stated that, from a certain angle, the self is the subject which has become part of its world. From another angle, however, it must be admitted that this is only half the truth because the opposition of subject and world is repeated in the structure of the self. The proper core of the self is the I, and the I remains relentlessly elusive, withdrawing from every effort to make it the object of observation or self-reflection. Always in need of self-realization in and vis-à-vis its world, it associates itself with the world in assuming a self which participates in the world. Yet the I retains its proper nature, which is to escape from the world in a movement opposing participation, and affirming its own otherness. The two movements, the one towards and the one away from the world, together define the constitution of the self. Through its body and by means of expressive action the self makes itself known to the world. Expression necessarily is the same as making a communication, an entering into a relation of some sort with the world. Simultaneously, the self tries to conceal itself, hiding out from observation by others — i.e. the world — and even by itself. It is the elusive I which in withdrawing hides out, shrouding the basic life-project, its own intimate choice of how to be in the world, from introspection by the self, a vigilant 'censor' waking over the secrets of the heart. The self cannot become integrally part of its world because it is also a subject steering away from the world. The self is divided in itself.

Consequently, being part of one's world is never a matter of simply surrendering oneself to it. This is only possible during sleep, the period during which the subject is allayed. An active subject, however, is always a conscious subject, with greater or lesser acuity aware of its self and of its world. Partaking, participating in the affairs of that world means partaking as a self which, in its core, is opaque and impenetrable, moreover forever at any moment capable of breaking away from participation. Thus being a part necessarily takes the form, not of identification or unification, but of interaction between two parties, the self and his world, wherein the latter stands for his fellow-men, for his society at large, and for his natural surroundings. The most expressive form of such interaction we call communication, communication always implying the interaction of parties who consider themselves as such. However, we shall not take the word in the narrow sense admitted to it in the theory of communication, that of the exchange of messages, but in that wider sense which includes all intercourse generally, and carries as a connotation a reference to the emotional values represented in the word communion. The crucial point is that an exchange of messages as such is incapable of persuading the self that it really is part of its world. Being a part is not primarily something which must be explicitly known, it must be implicitly lived. It requires the affirmation of feeling, the curious sensation so admirably analyzed by Merleau-Ponty in his *Phéno-ménologie de la perception* and explained as a pre-reflectory knowledge the individual has of his world. Although intellectually it can never be denied that the self is part of its world, everything depends on the way how it is part. On this point the self is often better served by its feelings than by the rationalizations of the intellect. Feelings warn the self well before the need or opportunity for rational explicitation arises, an explicitation which need not turn out to be altogether reassuring either. Man must feel emotionally secure as part of his world and it is exactly this emotional security which repeatedly fails him in his contacts with his fellow-men in his daily face-to-face relations, in those with his group or society at large, and in those with his natural surroundings.

Elsewhere I have dealt somewhat more elaborately with the deficiencies haunting each of the three modes of relationships just mentioned (1971, Ch. X). Here I may confine myself to emphasizing that these deficiencies are not primarily the effect of rationalization (though reflection tends to make matters worse) but are founded in the self-experience, conscious as well as pre-conscious, of a being who repeatedly errs in his choices of how to be part of his world, and whose world is bad enough to thwart even his best efforts really to exist as a subject who is part and as a part who is a subject. All this may lead to open conflicts between the individual and his world, a consequence in this context of smaller importance than the less dramatic but certainly more general and more lasting feelings of nostalgia for a more homely world. The actual world is resistant and exacting, making the individual feel like an outsider who is excluded from its intimacy. The individual has not the proper access to a world which behaves inimically or at best indifferently and unconcerned about his (the individual's) private cares. He feels that, to his world, he is somebody who just happens to be there but could as well be missing, because he is one out of many and hardly anyone cares what he is or does. What he hopelessly misses is a way of access which would help him restore the reassuring feeling of pertaining to his world as a part, and this is not only the matter with modern man who feels oppressed by what he calls the System, or forlorn as an anonymous in the multitude of the city, but also with primitive man who is ill-prepared to meet all the vicissitudes of a whimsical Nature. The difference between primitive and modern man can be summarized roughly (very roughly actually) as follows: the former's relations with his society are direct and authentic, whereas Nature is to him untransparent and hostile. To modern man Nature is a friendly source of recreation but modern man's relations with society are untransparent and unauthentic.[1] In both cases frustrations prevail which are vague but persistent and sometimes even obsessive. They are doomed to be vague and ill-defined because they proceed from a contradictory state of mind in which resentment against the world goes hand in hand with hankering after it.

Man expresses himself in symbols; if his mind is clear he does so in the conceptual symbols of language, if it is confused and his attendant feelings strong enough, in the contradictory symbols of dream and vision. There can be little doubt that the gods, spirits and demons occupying the religious scene, reflect man's conflicting condition, that of a part failing to be one, of an alienated wanderer in a familiar world which he loves and hates, trying to find access. All the gods and spirits are double-faced like Janus: they threaten and promise, punish and reward, they are always present and always distant, they are exacting and yet willing to help, never wholly reliable even when the reverse is claimed, whereas the worst among them can, under certain conditions, even be willing to help. The age-long efforts of theology to overcome the contradictions of the Christian faith have not been able to wipe out the conviction that God's love has a counterpart in his anger, nor have they ever found any better explanation for the fact that so many prayers remain unanswered (in spite of promises to the contrary) than making an appeal to the higher wisdom of God. And in folk-belief even the blackest of creatures, Satan, appears to be willing to give aid to those who are prepared to pay his price. In fact, the whole spectrum of man's contradictory experience with his world is reflected in his gods. One of their most intriguing traits is that — however elevated and separate they otherwise may be — the gods are always within hearing distance. The one and only phenomenon of daily life which can serve as a prototype of

---

1. I thank Mr. Platvoet (Utrecht) for suggesting the formula.

the omnipresence of the gods is the individual's universe, always present and rarely fully accessible. The gods reflect all man's projected fears and hopes concerning his world. They even reflect the permanence and immutability of the I which, unaffected by the variations of the self, is always I, always identical with itself and in this respect extemporal and immutable like the gods.

The most significant characteristic of the religious symbol is that it is socially accepted, even accepted as true. Most of our knowledge of the symbols of dream and vision derives from neuropathic and psychopathic cases, from patients who have developed their symbolic actions and idiosyncrasies as deviants in their society and at variance with its norms. Symbols of this kind do not and cannot find social recognition for the simple reason that this would imply approval of the disapproved, and the denial of the accepted rules of the society which were rejected by the patient. Religious symbols, on the other hand, are expressions of frustrations (and elations) common to all members of society who live, broadly speaking, in conformity with its rules. These symbols can and do find recognition. The reverberations of common hopes and fears in impressive dreams or visions are naturally proper objects of deliberation because they do not merely reflect the dreamer's hopes and frustrations, but in no lesser degree his need for communication and unison. The dreamer or visionary cannot keep such experiences for himself; he must communicate them to the members of his group, who will pay due attention to them, and, if they appeal to them as expressions of their own inner unrest, accept them as a myth or revelation. The dream or vision, if accepted, necessarily leads to ritual; born from the need to acquire access to partnership with the world, it holds indications for the realization of partnership by ritual acts. We have many examples of this in recent cargo-cults and prophetic movements.

In the ritual, dream or vision find their fulfilment. The ritual is common symbolic action. Its effect is not limited to the reconciliation of the faithful with the object of their veneration, i.e. their symbolized world or a certain aspect of it. The ritual is a matter of common action, persuading the participants that they are all one in their faith and thus strengthening the belief in its truth and value. It also affects the relations between the participants among themselves, not merely by creating a kind of 'solidarité mécanique' (as it also does) but in particular by requiring the collaboration of all participants in common action.

Anticipating my remarks on methodology I must point out here that the accomplished forms of communal action and participation induced by ritual are most convincingly demonstrated by the rites of sacrifice as celebrated in simple societies of agriculturalists. The sacrifice offered to the gods introduces a distribution of food which makes part of a system of food-exchange between the feast-givers and their guests in which the gods and spirits share. Part of the food is taken home by the guests where they will redistribute it among the members of the household, offering titbits to the ancestors and spirits who are inmates of the house. Very often a sacrifice is an elaborate demonstration that gods, ancestors and men are members of one great family, the gods and ancestors giving protection to the living who offer sacrifice which by distribution must serve to restore or maintain good relations among the members of the group and their guests. A rite is always a social affair.

The social significance of myth and ritual favors the further development of religious symbols into religious ideas. Being accepted as socially significant affairs, myth and ritual become objects of continuous rationalization and elaboration, resulting in religious systems which give intellectual support to the credibility of the whole. The logical constructions of the system and the integration of its various parts into a common pattern confirm the trustworthiness of the ideas, enabling the community to accept them as ultimate truth.

We conclude that religion is a normal reaction to the inner controversies ensuing from the human condition. Subject to the provision that religious symbols are accepted as true and reliable vehicles for communication with one's universe, religion is also an effective instrument for restoring the individual's spiritual balance, and for cementing social solidarity in the society concerned. When religious symbols lose their credibility — a process clearly observable in our society today — religion changes or it disappears from the scene. There is no religion without faith in its truth. We cannot dwell here on the interesting question whether religion really can be expected to disappear or to be replaced by something else. My personal views on this matter — the conviction that the ultimate mystery of our universe signifies something to us, calling upon us to answer the signifying with a signified — are not in order here. We must come at last to the theme of this conference, methodology.

III. Religious symbols represent the believer's universe. Neither these symbols nor the believer's relevant behavior can be properly understood without adequate knowledge of that universe, i.e. of the social and ecological conditions determining the believer's way of life. In their religion a people's experience of their world is integrated with their own attitudes into a coherent system of beliefs and practices. From the system the component parts derive their meaning and specific form. For this reason we cannot study religious phenomena after the manner of — for example — Van der Leeuw in his *Phänomenologie der Religion*. Divorcing the data from their systematic context, he mutilated the religious phenomena, turning them into sterile cases which, at best, could affirm the presence or absence of certain preconceived notions, but were incapable of serving any other purpose than that for which they had been selected. For the increase of knowledge and the refinement of our notions we must study the phenomena in their cultural context. I may illustrate my point by briefly discussing two cases, that of the theory of sacrifice, and that of Australian tribal rituals, the first as a correction of current concepts of sacrifice, the second as a critique of certain inconsistencies in social anthropological theory.

The most recent general theory of sacrifice worth its name is 74 years old, the 'Essai sur la nature et la fonction sociale du sacrifice', published by Hubert and Mauss in *L'Année Sociologique* II of 1899. The valuable comments on sacrifice made by Mauss 24 years later in his 'Essai sur le don' (cf. pp. 164-169 of the reprint in *Sociologie et Anthropologie par Marcel Mauss*) hold a promise for a revised theory but fail to bring it. The paucity of theoretical comment on sacrifice is a typical example of the paralyzing influence familiar terms have on critical observation. Say sacrifice, and everyone thinks that he knows what it is, a present offered to the gods or an effort to overcome the separation of the sacred from the profane. Descriptions of rites of sacrifice usually give elaborate information on the preparations and on the act of dedication, whereas the sequel, the distribution of the food, following its presentation to the deity, among the sacrificers and their retinue, is dispatched in a few words expressing the author's conviction that the culminating-point of the ritual is the dedication. But is it really? The sacrificers and their guests more often than not are of a different opinion; they assembled to partake in the meal and the distribution of food. Observers tend to interpret this seemingly irreverent attitude as a degeneration engendered by greed, because they start from the idea that a sacrifice is essentially an affair between the sacrificer and his god.

A closer inspection both of the theory and of current field-reports raises serious doubts. In the first place, the rigid separation of the sacred and the profane, so strongly emphasized by Hubert and Mauss in their theory of sacrifice, typically represents the views of a priestly caste in a literate society; with sacrifices celebrated in primitive societies the opposition of the sacred and the profane is not such a prominent characteristic. And secondly, the texts of the holy books composed by Hebrew and Hindu priests are naturally more concerned with the duties of the priest in the celebration of sacrifice; the distribution of the food is not a priestly task. A rapid inspection of the data available on sacrifices made in more or less primitive communities in Indonesia or Africa gives evidence that the distribution of the sacrificial food is a matter of great importance, so great as to allow us to interpret a sacrifice as a common meal in which gods, spirits, hosts and guests are united, a meal intended to settle old debts and to restore good relations or to cement a new alliance. A sacrifice is a typical act of communication between the sacrificer and his gods on the one hand, between him and his fellow-men on the other. It depends on the situation for whom the sacrifice is actually intended, his gods or his fellow-men. What we need are a number of comprehensive analyses to acquire a better understanding of what a sacrifice is or can be.

My second case is that of Australian so-called tribal rituals. They rarely are tribal rituals at all, and should be described as rituals commonly celebrated by intermarrying groups. The extreme value attached to ritual by Australian aborigines (they devote an uncommonly great part of their time to religious occupations) is of decisive influence on their social organization and their highly complicated marriage customs. The moiety-dualism and the opposition between successive and alternate generations characterizing the social organization and the concomitant marriage system, have such an important function in ritual that we should recognize their ritual importance as the ultimate basis for the explanation of the section- and subsection-systems which combine moiety-dualism with generational opposition. Failing to connect the ritual and social aspects of Australian cultures, social anthropologists have greatly hampered their own efforts to explain the intricacies of the social system. On the other hand, a study of ritual is impossible without a precise knowledge of the connubium-relations between the co-operating groups. It demands even more. Australian totemism, far from being the form of magic for which it was held by Frazer, is in fact an elaborate system of mystical relations between the native and his country, every landmark of any significance being mythically connected with a totemic ancestor and through that ancestor with the living members of his clan. The strong emotional value attached to the own country is validated in myth and ritual, but one cannot really study it without a fair knowledge of the ecological conditions and of the life-habits of the various animals figuring in the totemic system.

If we wish to study depth-structures a lot of spadework at surface-level must be carried out previously. We must have a thorough knowledge of the context of our religious data, and this can only be acquired by giving systematic attention to the composition of critical monographs. It is a very rewarding occupation. I made the experiment in my book 'Dema' in which all the previously published and otherwise available data on Marind-anim culture were worked up. It took me my spare time for five years during which I also had other work to do. However, I was privileged. I had written my doctoral thesis on the same subject thirty years earlier, and I was stationed for two years in Marind-anim country as the local administrator. My own fieldwork in the area was very limited in scope, but I collected a fair amount of illuminating data on social organization from the archives of the office of the administration. Yet the composition of the book only became a success because I had a collaborator in the field, the late Father Verschueren MSC, who had lived among the Marind-anim for more than thirty years, who spoke their language and enjoyed their confidence. He read the raw draft of every chapter, went out to acquire further information, and thus provided me with some 200 pages of critical comments and supplementary data. It meant a lot of work, but it opened astounding vistas on the thoroughly systematic coherence of Marind-anim religious thought. The data now can be used for studies of depth-structures. Similar work should be done among other peoples and it should be done without delay. This implies an almost discouraging amount of work, at least if we really wish to make headway. However, I never heard that there are reliable methods which permit us to skip the systematic collection and testing of data.*

* Bibliography:
Baal, J. van, *Dema*. Description and Analysis of Marind-anim Culture. The Hague,

KURT GOLDAMMER   *Is There a Method of Symbol Research Which Offers Hermeneutic Access to Depth-Dimensions of Religious Experience?*

It is possible to think and theorize about symbols as a stratified phenomenon in history and anthropology and as a functional form in religion, but it is not possible to understand them primarily or exclusively from the point of view of the problem of depth-dimensions. The historical origin of the word in Greek has little to do with this. There is nothing of depth-dimensions in the original sense of the word 'symbolon' – at the most, the veiling and unveiling of hidden things or of secrets. This does not need to be anything 'deep', however, at least not in the sense of the sub-rational, the sub-conscious or the unconscious.[2] On the other

Martinus Nijhoff, 1966.

——, *Symbols for Communication*. An introduction to the anthropological study of religion. Assen, Van Gorcum, 1971.

——, *De boodschap der drie Illusies*. Assen, Van Gorcum, 1972.

Buytendijk, F.J.J., *Prolegomena van een antropologische Fysiologie*. Utrecht, Het Spectrum, 1965.

Hubert, H., and M. Mauss, 'Essai sur la nature et la fonction sociale du sacrifice', *Année Sociologique* II (1899), pp. 29-138.

Leeuw, G. van der, *Phänomenologie der Religion*. Tübingen, Mohr, 1933.

Mauss, M., 'Essai sur le don. Forme et raison de l'échange dans les sociétés archaïques', *Année Sociologique*, nouv. série I (1923/24), pp. 30-186. (References to the reprint in *Sociologie et Anthropologie par Marcel Mauss*, Paris, PUF, 1950: pp. 143-279.)

Merleau-Ponty, M., *Phénoménologie de la Perception*. Paris, Gallimard, 1945.

Sartre, J.-P., *L'Etre et le Néant*, Paris, Gallimard, 1943.

2. What is involved is a 'mysterium'. To this extent, there is an interesting emphasis on the meaning of 'symbolon' in the Pythagorean-Neo-Platonic tradition, in the *Vita Pythagorica* of Iamblichus (XXIII, 103-105). According to this, symbols are a method of instruction (didaskalía) in the form of symbolic modes of speech, prized by almost all the Greeks because of their antiquity, and variously used by the Egyptians as well. They were supposed to guard secret things in an enigmatic form, and then reveal their correctness and truth unambiguously to the higher being of these philosophers. None of the great Pythagoreans communicated in the ordinary mode of speech, but kept silent about the divine mysteries in accordance with the command of Pythagoras; and they protected their speeches and writings, which were supposed to be kept secret, with symbols. On correct exegesis, these become visibly illuminating, and resemble in their meaning the utterances of the Pythian oracles. They fill the initiated friends of Reason with divine breath (inspiration). Iamblichus then mentions examples of types of instruction through symbols, which we would

hand, during their history, and especially since the 16th century, symbols have been understood as a conscious masking of depths, as indirect religious statement, and as a surface form. Evidence for this can be found in the use of the concept 'symbolum' in Zwingli's 'symbolistic' doctrine of the Last Supper, following a specific medieval sense of 'symbolum' and 'signum': the cultic 'symbol' is intended to restrain intrusion into the ultimate depths of religious reality, the numen praesens; to make these depths merely transparent; to provide rational access to their understanding; and as it were to ward off the advance of sub-rational events and behavior. The distance between the symbol, and the depths and realities which it represents, is increased. The depths themselves, however, are undisputed; but the 'symbols' do not represent a way into them. The symbolism and iconography of the Bodhisattvas and gods in Mahāyāna Buddhism is a highly-rationalized dogmatic-mythological system combining individual symbolic elements.[3] But it does not necessarily lay claim to any esoteric value, except insofar as it seeks to offer a statement in concrete form of central contents of the theology of Buddha and of the Buddhist doctrine of salvation. At the same time it also makes concessions to popular religious feeling, and therefore also has an exoteric side. It is difficult to say whether this should be understood as a mediator of special depth-perspectives.

ASPECTS OF THE SYMBOL AS A STATEMENT FOR DEPTH-STRUCTURES
AND FOR THEIR ANALYSIS

There are without doubt aspects of the symbol as a statement of religious depth-experiences and their analysis. Reflections on the stratified character of the symbol from the viewpoint of history of religions point of necessity at least to the 'depths' of its historical development. On

---

call aphorisms or proverbial profundity: religious rules and wise sayings with reference to the divine, and to philosophical and ritual behavior. Not only the teaching and masking technique of this method is worth attention, but also the halo of its antiquity. Despite all the emphasis on secrecy, the rational component is very prominent (cf. *Iamblichi De vita Pythagorica Liber*. Graece et Germanice. Ed. Michael von Albrecht. Stuttgart/Zürich, 1966, pp. 108ff.).

3. Cf. Willibald Kirfel, *Symbolik des Buddhismus* (Symbolik der Religionen, ed. F. Herrmann, vol. V), Stuttgart, 1959, p. 52ff.

this point one can only consult the religion and its symbols themselves. In Buddhism, the wheel and lotus symbols, and possibly also the triple *triratna* symbol, are intended to lead one into such depths, since they appeal to the knowledge of the initiated through the economical indications of their relatively simple, concrete forms; since they require completion, and challenge the ability of the informed to make associations and combinations; and since they simultaneously contain the centre of the Buddhist doctrine of salvation.[4] Possibly one could also see 'symbols' in this sense in the *tjurunga* objects of the central Australians, which are interwoven in a complex religious-social background, in individual experience, and in man's existential self-understanding. Within Christianity, the world of images in the *Areopagitica* of Pseudo-Dionysius and in other mystics contains statements which are explicitly intended to attain the depths of the religious and of the experience of God. Here the symbolic image, in this sense, is interpreted in a literary manner.

Following this tradition, Heinrich Seuse makes the female disciple in his *Vita* ask the master: 'Canst thou not cast the concealed thoughts in a pictorial likeness for me, according to thy insight, that I may understand them the better?' The answer runs: 'That images may be expelled with images, I shall speak to thee here in images, and give thee a pictorial testimony, so far as that is possible, of those unpicturable thoughts, as they are to be grasped in reality.' And he then uses the mathematical symbol of the circle whose focus is everywhere, and whose circumference nowhere, for the 'deep abyss' of the divine Trinity.[5] Nicholas de

4. The teaching of Buddha, with its acosmic, reality-denying tone, saw the world of sensory phenomena and spiritual processes, including the human ego, as doomed to decay. It would seem that this offered little opportunity for symbolic thinking, and it remains uncertain whether original Buddhism possessed real symbols. Even the earlier publication of the Buddhist canon, however, is rich in images, at least, though it is not known whether these can be subsumed under our concept of symbols as 'vehicles of meaning'. The biographical legend of the Founder contains many elements which are interpretable as various stages of the symbolic. It thus simultaneously becomes clear that in Buddhism both the depths of experience of holiness and of salvation, and those of the private ego, which combine and divide in a unique manner, are in themselves non-structured, but that they become structured by images and symbols as well as by rational reflection.

5. Schülerin: 'Könnt ihr mir nicht die verborgenen Gedanken nach eurer Einsicht in bildgebendem Gleichnis entwerfen, damit ich sie umso besser verstände?' Meister: 'Damit man die Bilder mit Bildern austreibe, so will ich dir hier in gleichnisgebender Redeweise bildlich Zeugnis geben, sofern das überhaupt möglich ist, von denselben bildlosen Gedanken, wie sie in Wahrheit aufzufassen sind.' (Heinrich Seuse, *Deutsche*

Cusa, in his comprehensive meditations on the contribution which mathematical laws and figures can make to the knowledge of the divine and the infinite, points out that those things which in themselves are unattainable for us can be tracked down by symbols, since all things have 'a secret and incomprehensible relationship to each other', and in the one universe everything is the unity itself. No (symbolic) image, however, is ever completely like its original ('exemplar'). Through its function as image, the symbol leads in a more or less approximative manner (preferably highly so) into the depths of the divine unity. Nevertheless, it is not identical with this, since it can never fully attain it.[6] A symbol as such is not a 'depth'.

In many mystics, especially in the Christian ones, we are fortunate enough to be able to study their reflections on the function of symbols, and on their relation to the divine and to the depths of their own experiences, through personal statements. It is a separate question whether this produces depth-'structures'. At any rate, we can speak here of depth-'dimensions' of individual religious experience.

Accordingly, we can analyze a 'mediating' function of religious symbols. By nature, they are a medium for religious experience and its object. There are interesting aspects of symbols from this point of view, and bearing these aspects in mind, we could attempt to describe their function.

Schriften, ed. Karl Bihlmeyer, Stuttgart, 1907, pp. 190 ff.; modern High German version quoted above from: Hermann Kunisch, *Eckhardt, Tauler, Seuse. Ein Textbuch aus der altdeutschen Mystik*, Hamburg, 1958, pp. 125 ff.)

6. 'Hoc autem quod *spiritualia, per se a nobis inattingibilia, symbolice investigentur*, radicem habet ex his, quae superius dicta sunt, quoniam omnia ad se invicem *quandam nobis tamen occultam et incomprehensibilem habent proportionem*, ut ex omnibus unum exsurgat universum, et omnia in uno maximo sint ipsum unum. Et quamvis omnis imago accedere videatur ad similitudinem exemplaris, tamen praeter maximam imaginem, quae est hoc ipsum quod exemplar in unitate naturae, non est imago adeo similis aut aequalis exemplari, quin per infinitum similior et aequalior esse possit...' (Nicolaus de Cusa, *De docta ignorantia*, Lib. I, Cap. XI; ed. Gero Wilpert, Hamburg, 1964, p. 40, italics mine). A structure of the infinite divine is, on this account, in itself unknowable or even non-existent, since it is the unity of being in the greatest and the smallest. Symbols and images, however, operate, in the sense of a transcendental process, so as to impart structure. They structure the unstructured (or merely rationally-discursively or dogmatically structured) depth-image of the divine in a new way.

1. Symbols can be understood as ciphers, which create secret signs within systematic and codified concealment and diversion, in order to reveal and to disclose, or which veil, in order to unveil. Or symbols are a kind of puzzle, whose solution is known by the initiated.[7] The enigmatic function of picture-puzzles (rebuses) builds a bridge between symbol and object, symbol and writing. The tension between giving up or solving a puzzle resembles the tension in the deciphering of a symbol, between its 'here' and 'beyond'. We know the great significance of puzzles from ethnology and folklore: both how close they often are to the religious, and their profane-sacral, poetic, and mythological aspects. It is possible to attribute a certain depth-tendency to both ciphers and puzzles. Nevertheless, they come about as the result of a rational process, even if this may make use of sub-rational facts.

2. Symbols are transparencies or television screens. Their essence is a two-sided perspective: the projection, and the object projected, from one side, and the observer watching from the other. The transparency or the television screen fulfil the function of a partition, but at the same time open the way to a secret and interesting world 'beyond' this frontier: they render things 'transparent'. The 'diaphany'[8] of a symbol is important because of what lies behind it — the unknown, which it renders visible. The symbol gives the 'trans' its structure.

3. Symbols are a pivot or joint — as Plato already said;[9] a hinge, i.e. something that allows the movement of a part that is connected to a

---

7. In the mystical spiritualism of the 15th and 16th centuries the idea of the enigmatic reappears in connection with the indirect, 'symbolic' manner of expressing the infinite and divine, concerning which speech is impossible. (Nicholas of Cusa, *Idiota de sapientia*, at the end: fol. 80v; Sebastian Franck, *Paradoxa*, 1534 (n.b. the programmatic title). For the Pythagoreans, symbols are related by definition to puzzles (cf. note 2, above).

8. This concept is employed in art history for the effect of stained glass painting, and also to describe the essence and function of supports, walls and windows in Gothic cathedral architecture, which is strongly influenced by symbolist transcendental conceptions (cf. Hans Jantzen, *Kunst der Gothik*, Hamburg, 1957). Stained glass windows in their architectonic setting, especially in Gothic, make the walls transparent, and so in fact functionally reveal part of the essence of the religious symbol.

9. *Phaedrus* 98d. Cf. Franz Vonessen, 'Der Symbolbegriff im griechischen Denken', in: *Bibliographie zur Symbolik*, 3 (Baden-Baden, 1970), p. 8.

fixed wall. The continuous alternation between the view being first shut off and then re-opened reveals the instrumental-mediating function as connector and divider. It brings about the junction and operation of two mutually related parts of a technical device that is simultaneously communicative and demarcational: a door.

4. Symbols are keys, i.e. (in comparison with the door device) a further instrument for opening or closing access to an 'other side' or a 'beyond' from the room. Its use must be a deliberate act. It can get lost or spoilt. It can be isolated, and has an independent existence. Keys may open up hidden things, secrets, or the unexpected. Susanne Langer used this expression in an appropriately programmatic manner for her symbolist 'philosophy in a new key'.[10]

5. Symbols are a bridge between two separate spheres of existence, 'the inner sphere of motivation and the outer sphere that is asked to answer', as Kahler has put it in a convincing comparison.[11]

In all of these cases the symbol demarcates the place where two parts meet, a here and a there, one 'citra' and one 'trans' or 'post', which encounter each other in the symbol. Through this encounter the symbol has the character of an enduring hermeneutic event. The static sign becomes, for those who know how to use it correctly, dynamized as an interpretative event of comprehension. In order to complete the symbol experience, and within the existence of the person confronted with the symbol, it becomes present, the comprehending 're-presentation' of a 'beyond' or something hidden (an important topos in literary evidence about the symbolic!) and its depths, but also of the withdrawn and the past. It can be a re-activation of previous events.

6. It is characteristic that in attempting a hermeneutic of the concept of symbols one tends to make descriptions or definitions by speaking 'symbolically', in the widest sense, through images and comparisons: i.e. we attempt to expound the symbol through its own methodology.

10. Susanne Langer, *Philosophy in a New Key. A study in the symbolism of reason, rite and art*, Cambridge, Mass., 1963.
11. Erich Kahler, 'The nature of the symbol', in Rollo May, ed., *Symbolism in Religion and Literature*, New York, 1960, p. 4.

In abstract terms, the symbol and its relational function are linked with, among other things, questions of representation, of analogy, of images in view of the interrelationship between their prototypes and the re-production of them, and thus of resemblance (similitudo), of participation, and finally of equivalence and identity. There can be no doubt that the symbol is supposed to represent the thing it indicates, and as-sist participation in it in concrete or more spiritual form. The stages of representational reality of the 'other', the 'trans', can range from correspondence and similarity through to the adoption of congruence or identity. The task of the symbol appears to end, however, at identity with the thing meant. The symbol can be a real re-presentation, but a distinction must be drawn between the realistic character of the symbol, and identity with the thing meant in a purely concrete understanding of the holy.[12] There seems to be approximative and maximum con-vergence between the symbol and the thing symbolized, a progressive increase in concretization. The crucial question, however, is whether identity with the 'numen praesens' still is symbolic representation. On the other hand the symbol is certainly not simply a comparison, but a more binding utterance. It is not a likeness, parable, allegory, or anything like that. This also applies to the question about the convergence in the symbol between the depths of the divine and of the human. For this reason, it is very dubious whether one can agree with Tillich in describing God as a symbol,[13] since symbols should be transcended in God — unless, that is, the concept of 'God' is relativized and advanced into the sphere of the conditional and concrete. At any rate, the symbol structures the holy.

   In contrast, in works of religious visual art there is an artistic realism,

---

   12. There are a wide range of possibilities for this identity and concreteness of the conception of the symbol, some of them contradictory. The symbolic concrete-ness may indeed be spiritually pictorial, but at the same time may be meant in a purely real sense, as is shown by the Christian cult symbolism of the Last Supper: e.g. in Schwenckfeld's teaching on the Last Supper ('This [bread, spiritual food] is my body', i.e. this bread is a special, heavenly food); or in Karlstadt's teaching (at the historical Last Supper in Jerusalem, Christ pointed to himself: 'This is my body'). Or it is purely metaphysical: the identity of the thing shown with the thing that shows it or with the thing that gives meaning (transubstantiation in Roman Catholic teaching on the Last Supper). In both cases, the character of the symbolic is put in question.
   13. Paul Tillich, 'Religionsphilosophie', *Gesammelte Werke*, Stuttgart, 1959– . Vol. I, p. 334.

concreteness, and 'identity' with the thing represented, which rules out the possibility of a symbolic character in the work of art: this is the case when the work of art aims at being the realistic reproduction of a person (i.e. a portrait) or of a historical or mythological narrative scene — that is to say, of a person or event from the concrete world, and not from the area of the transcendent or 'beyond'. In this case the religious work of art approaches the concreteness of historical painting or photographic reportage. For this reason, not all religious paintings are symbols, although they can subsequently become so through a secondary process of symbolization.

7. The analysis and determination of the concept of the religious symbol is the task of phenomenology of religion and philosophy of religion, having regard to the precise interpretation of the historical facts (including the psychological and sociological facts). This term is not intended to be used thoughtlessly or emphatically, nor as a ready-made, inflexible concept, as has happened so often. My intention is not to add another definition to the countless ones already available.[14] There have been explicit and authoritative explanations of what a symbol is since classical times, and especially since Christian theology, becoming particularly prominent in Pseudo-Dionysius, and then in mystical, theological, and devotional literature. These are most important directional aids, which cannot be replaced by arbitrary modern opinions about symbols. We should aim far rather at understanding symbols functionally and operationally within religion, in the terms of our formulation of the problem. Here once again the depth-dimensions of the religious element enter our field of vision. The application of a conceptualization that has been developed outside religion, around the word 'symbol', in the scientific analysis of general anthropological and sociological objects, should only be undertaken with critical caution.

Another question which needs critical investigation is whether our concept of symbols (which derives beyond doubt from Greek language and thought, belongs to European culture, and is the expression of a very precise stage of culture and its religious and spiritual development) can simply be transferred to other cultures, and the religious conceptions and utterances pertaining to them. This question applies particularly

14. Cf. Vonessen, *op. cit.*, p. 5.

to primitive races and to pre-historic religions. Here there could be a totally different evaluation of what we call 'symbolic'. Maybe, in this thinking, 'symbols' do not exist at all, or are an inappropriate expression.[15] This question also applies, mutatis mutandis, to Buddhism, i. e. to its concept of 'appearances' and its conception of reality. The functional and operational understanding of symbols is important for the solution of this problem. The religious symbol could be regarded (as the concept is understood in general scientific usage) as the re-projection of a differentiated self-reflection (which is in this form alien and incomprehensible to many cultures), by means of religious objects, from the viewpoint of advanced religion, into supposed depth layers and original conditions of religion. In the symbol, the dilemma of experienced, and rationally-analyzed, religion already becomes recognizable, and with this a certain distancing of religion from the depths of its experience.

We do not need here to go into the extension of the concept to describe general forms of communication such as language and mathematics, nor into the width of its current non-religious usage. To put it in general terms, the religious symbol is (in the sense used in the considerations above) something meaningful, something which structures and interprets meaning, but not something that gives meaning.[16] The symbol is a hermeneutic attempt to express and render comprehensible that which is in fact unsayable about something that gives meaning. We may leave open the question as to whether — in Tillich's sense, for instance — we ought to make a distinction between the symbol, as 'non-proper', and the 'proper' ['das Uneigentliche' and 'das Eigentliche']. At least it aims to mediate the 'proper', probably because the 'proper' is not, or is no longer, accessible. More precisely, the symbol is a vehicle of meaning ['Bedeutungsträger'], in most cases not verbal in origin, which refers to a meaning and, where possible, to the depths of this

15. There is much stimulus for reflection in this respect in the rich material which Hurault recently published about Guyana (Jean Hurault, *Africains de Guyane. La vie matérielle et l'art des noirs réfugiés de Guyane*, The Hague/Paris, 1970). The mingling of symbol, ornament, and abstract image motif, with individual, social, economic, and mythical references, provokes enquiry about the emergence, essence, function, and decay of symbolism in this culture, a symbolism which is perhaps only partly so.

16. Cf. Wilhelm Weischedel, *Der Gott der Philosophen. Grundlegung einer philosophischen Theologie im Zeitalter des Nihilismus*. 2. Band: *Abgrenzung und Grundlegung*. Darmstadt, 1972, p. 168.

meaning. The meaning does not lie in the concreteness of the symbol itself, but beyond it. Words, and verbal constructions, are not primarily symbols, but something which takes part in the process of symbolization and which is capable of symbolization.[17] It would be useful if at least within religious studies there could be agreement about restricting the concept of the symbol along these lines.

OBSERVATIONS ON PROBLEMS OF THE METHODOLOGICAL TREATMENT OF SYMBOLS, HAVING REGARD TO THE ASPECTS MENTIONED

1. In order to obviate misunderstandings, false theoreticizations, and illusions about symbols, a historical analysis of their components and origins is first necessary, once one has come to the conclusion that a particular object could constitute a symbol. In view of the difficulty of many symbols for the modern rational-reflective understanding, one needs as exact a knowledge as possible of the historical background of the thing represented, both as it has emerged and in its origins, and moreover in its particular historical context, and in its application and assimilation. The following questions must be considered:

a) What — in essential content and concretely — is the thing symbolically represented? What could it be? Is it a symbol at all? What context does it belong to? These questions must be put constantly and relentlessly.

b) When does it first appear in an area pertaining to history of religions? When was it first used in a symbolic utterance?

c) Can it have come from other cultural contexts and have been put into connection with religion only later?

d) What symbolic significance does it present?

e) What symbolic relations did it have in the period from which the presentation in question dates? What symbolic relations did it have originally?

f) Does the thing represented occur in other religious cultures or epochs? If so, are they related or different?

---

17. E.g. in its components, sounds and letters: cf. Weischedel, *op. cit.*, pp. 167f. On the concept of the vehicle of meaning, cf. Günther Bandmann, *Mittelalterliche Architektur als Bedeutungsträger*, 1951.

g) What meaning and function does it have there? What context does it stand in? Could it have been adopted from there?

h) Does its meaning change or develop historically? If so, continuously or discontinuously? What kind of change or decay in meaning has taken place?

There must be at least an attempt to answer these questions, even if it is not always fully successful. In particular — and precisely in order to avoid false depth meanings — attention should be paid to non-religious, 'secular' elements in the symbol, as well as its original or subsequent 'secular' evaluation, use, or function. Individual and social factors, economics and technology, nature and culture, and the connection with human behavior, in other words the ethological aspects, can be crucial in the emergence and meaning of a symbol. The use of symbols in general can be seen from the point of view of 'behavior'.[18] The question also arises whether animals possess a symbolism of their behavior and imagination,[19] but this can only be given limited consideration in connection with religion.

Religious symbols, including central ones, become so at a specific historical point in time. This is very clear in the cases of the central symbols of Buddhism and Christianity (wheel, lotus, cross, and fish). Of course, this point in time may be quite different for particular symbols within different cultural and religious circles. It may be repeated, especially through individual assimilation following up on original experience. The life of a symbol may come to an end, either definitively, or for a long time: this is true, for example, of the Christian fish symbol.

There is no scientific evidence that symbols exist or emerge independently of time and their surrounding external world of meaning and perception, or that they are a kind of 'Ding an sich'[20] which could enter from elsewhere into the human consciousness, i.e. history, at a particular point in time, disappear from it, and — via the individual —

18. This fact is already indicated in the title of Theodore Thass-Thienemann's psycholinguistic work, *Symbolic Behavior* (New York, 1968), though this book is otherwise of limited value for religious symbols, and lies on the frontiers of linguistic philosophy.

19. Cf. Kahler, *op. cit.*, p. 58, following on Silviano Arieti and Susanne Langer.

20. On the symbol as a 'Ding an sich', and on the primordial character of inner images, from the viewpoint of depth psychology, cf. Edward C. Whitmont, *The Symbolic Quest. Basic concepts of analytical psychology*, New York, 1969, pp. 29 ff.

reappear again. Rather, they belong inseparably together with the outer world, and cannot be regarded as *a priori* facts, nor take over the role of ideas in a kind of Platonism. They can only ever be explained *a posteriori* from an analysis of their historical context. For all of the spiritual life of men is in fact history, and is fed by history. It is epistemologically impossible to take refuge in the *'ante'* of spiritual or cosmic space: neither man as such, nor a human collective, can be *'extra'* or *'ante historiam'*.

The access to the depths of the divine or the human which is expected from symbols only becomes available to scientific investigation, therefore, through historical analysis. We can get at the structure of the symbol only through methodical, empirical procedures from the outside, not from the inside. The symbol itself is the product, not of the depth, but of an attempt to seize the depths sensorily through given historicized natural and cultural media.[21] But could there have been at least certain symbols in man's thinking or consciousness before the beginning of the process of symbolization, independently of the outer world? The basic symbolic figures of geometry, for example? Several earlier symbol theoreticians, e.g. Nicholas of Cusa, appear to think so. But this question can really only be applied to the elementary mathematical symbols, and not to other concrete vehicles of meaning. Like mathematics, the question of symbol formation does however raise the question of human perception and means of perception; a question which undoubtedly bursts out in man in the depths of his beings.[22] This question ought not to exist for a religious man's feelings towards the symbol, for he is not primarily interested in where the symbol has come from. The scientific method of research into the genesis of symbols, on the other hand, is not interested in the religious or ideological access achieved by the possessor of the symbol, for whom it is filled with life and an immediate presence.

21. The investigation of the role of human body symbolism in the classification of societies and their cosmologies in Mary Douglas, *Natural Symbols. Explorations in cosmology*, London, 1970, is very interesting from this point of view. It is not possible to enquire here whether the ethno-sociological framework shown by Douglas justifies the use found here of the concept of 'symbol' in a religious sense. Basically, however, the ethno-psychological and ethno-sociological considerations carried out here appear to confirm our conception.
22. It should not be disputed that individuals' intuition and emotion contribute to the creation of symbols, and that many absurd symbolic forms may originate in the human imagination and fantasy. Yet even monstrous symbolic forms can for example be traced back in their details to sensory impressions which have been combined, developed, and finally worked over rationally.

It is not only the historical formation of symbols which argues against their independence or transcendence of time, but also their interchangeability and even reversibility. This is particularly clear in the symbolism of colors, numbers, noises, and sounds, whose symbolic value can alter, be reversed, or even be contradictory in different religions (e.g. red as the color of sovereignty, of feasting, of joy, of life, but also of death). Numbers and colors show this most clearly of all.[23] It would seem that the change and decay of symbols, of their meanings and symbolic relations, also point to the same conclusion. This also makes it correspondingly more dubious whether they provide binding and universally valid information about the depths of man's inner life. It should also be mentioned here that the question of sound and music symbolism, and of the meaning of sounds and sound figures, is especially difficult. The variety of structures in the construction of musical forms points to a close connection between symbolism and historical-cultural formation, and to their interchangeability.

2. The depth psychology and analytical theories see things differently. One of the classical and exemplary works on the analytical concept of symbols, Silberer's fascinating book on mysticism and its symbolism, finds 'types of the truth' and 'the unchanging' in symbols, despite their changing individual meanings. '[Sie] sagen jedem seine Wahrheit',[24] i.e. they lead into the depths of individual being, which is also where they emerge. Fromm gives a precise definition of the subjectivist psychoanalytical concept of the symbol: 'Das Symbol ist etwas ausserhalb unser selbst; das, was es symbolisiert, ist etwas in uns selbst'.[25] According to this, an inner experience is expressed in the language of symbols as if it originated from sensory perception. In reality, the outer world is the symbol of our inner world, of the soul and of the spirit.[26] It veils wishes, and to that extent forms a secret code, which is deciphered through the

23. On the variations in number symbolism, cf. for example Ferdinand Herrmann, 'Die Sechs als bedeutsame Zahl. Ein Beitrag zur Zahlensymbolik', *Saeculum* XIV/2 (1963), pp. 141-169.

24. Herbert Silberer, *Probleme der Mystik und ihrer Symbolik*, Vienna, 1914 (rpt. Darmstadt, 1969), pp. 256f.

25. Erich Fromm, *Märchen, Mythen und Träume* (tr. from the English: *The Forgotten Language*), Zürich, 1947, p. 14.

26. Fromm, *op. cit.*, p. 24.

interpretation of dreams.[27] When one looks more closely, many of the objects which are particularly referred to as symbols in psychoanalysis and depth psychology and picked out as paradigms seem not to possess the quality of symbols, at any rate in the sense used in religious studies.

Silberer's book is a classic early example of this. The 'symbols' described here in many cases do not have the prerequisite mediating function, at any rate not directed towards transcendence or divine depth. Many of them are parables, allegories, or *exempla*. They could be understood as images or visual statements, but their relations to the sphere of the numinous are very remote. Or they may contribute in a rational, scientific way to the explanation of the contents of numinous experience through the depth layers of spiritual processes, and in this way they could dissolve the special qualities of the numinous. In this case they are phenomena of the consciousness or the sub-conscious. In Silberer's work, not only the concept of symbols, but also that of mystery, is transformed towards mysticism and allegorism.

Nor is the example of a dream experience of a dark, swampy hole,[28] which Rollo May expounds programmatically and with many consequences as a symbol of the vulva, convincing evidence. The whole of so-called sexual symbolism and feminine symbolism, with its countless details,[29] is a favorite child of analytical symbol theories (mainly gained from literary documents and dreams, and often hypertrophied), and its allocation within the symbolic is problematical. The powerful role of the symbolism and representation in images of the maternal as an aspect of the numinous in various religions is undisputed. Are 'mother' and 'father', in mythology and theology, symbols, however? And has the priapic and vulva 'symbolism' of pre-historic, early historical, and primitive religions anything to do with the drives, sexual dreams and fantasies of modern man? Here we have images, signs, forms of expression and communication, comparisons, literary ciphers and combinations of metaphors, and conflicts between the individual and himself or his environment, all being understood as symbols.[30] Yet are these media

27. Fromm, *op. cit.*, p. 66.
28. Rollo May, 'The Significance of Symbols', *Symbolism in Religion and Literature*, ed. Rollo May, New York, 1960, pp. 14 ff.
29. Cf. J.H. Phillips, *Psychoanalyse und Symbolik*, Bern, 1962, pp. 89 ff.
30. Cf. for instance Alfred Lorenzer, *Kritik des psychoanalytischen Symbolbegriffs*, Frankfurt a.M., 1970, and 'Symbol, Interaktion und Praxis', in: *Psychoanalyse*

which can make a process of the transcendence of the self, or the fathoming of depths of being, possible? Or do they only lead further into the individual's range of problems and his conflicts with social norms and conventions? Methodologically, at any rate, they can lead straight past the religious. The same applies to alchemical symbolism, which the analytical and depth-psychological side are eager to bring into the argument: it is mainly a set of images, likenesses and allegories, which are used for the rational and psychological interpretation of rationally-constructed physical and metaphysical-speculative events.

It is no accident that analytical interpretation, and often depth-psychological interpretation as well, frequently latches on to such complications — hybrid late developments, and the individual wilderness of the language of imagery. It must be asked whether they really reveal the essence of these statements, or allow themselves to be misled by them. These theories may have their own meaning, but they lead away from religion rather than towards it. From this point of view, Rollo May differentiates far better with his good distinction between 'central cultural symbols' or 'transcendent symbols', and 'psychological' or 'the individual's personal symbols', of which the latter have in modern times attracted steadily more attention, while the former have declined.[31] How far, however, are individual, psychological symbols still symbols in the sense used in religious studies? Are they not, as a rule, personal transformations of traditional symbolism, or distinctive inspirations without general interest? And what about the religious character of great 'cultural symbols' in May's sense?[32]

---

als Sozialwissenschaft, Frankfurt a.M., 1971. The concept of the symbol is already specially adapted, schematized, manipulated, and turned into a cliché here in such a manner that it can no longer be used for serious conceptualization outside psychoanalysis. As a result, the depth-structures he predicates are obscured.

31. May, *op. cit.*, pp. 24 ff.

32. The original Greek meaning of the word does not point towards personal intuition or the individual or collective depth experience of given structures, but at the deliberate, rationally shaped regulation, arrangement, and convention with reference to symbolic form (but not with reference to symbolic meaning). It is the conscious shaping of an intention explicit in the symbol (cf. pp. 498-499, n. 2). Ferdinand Weinhandl was however also right when he observed (*Über das aufschliessende Symbol*, Berlin, 1929, pp. 66 ff., 75 ff.) that the symbol is only opened up and rendered able to function through the subjectivity of the observer. This is where the individual has his central position in the functional system of the symbol. For psychoanalysis, the depth individually disclosed in each symbol is already structured. According to this view, the symbol is an expression of this given structure.

3. The religious symbol concerns not only the mystery of the divine and the holy, but also that of the cosmos, the individual, and groups in religion. It is developed on various levels of religious experience, its ambience and its expression. It is experienced especially on the collective and individual levels. For this reason, the situation of the individual, of the group, and of their environment, must all be taken into account in explaining it.[33] The structuralist treatment of myth points fundamentally with justification to the various levels of symbolism as a transformation of their respective 'logical' structures: geographical, sociological, economic, and cosmological.[34] The question of religious ethology was already mentioned in connection with the investigation of the emergence and intention of symbolic statements. Symbols refer to religious man's individual and group-oriented behavior in its immediate forms of expression. In combination with sociology, natural ethology can give valuable stimuli for the understanding of symbols in the behavior of religious man and of religious communities.

Once the question of 'roles' in religion has been put,[35] it is impossible to avoid extending this to include the question whether symbols are connected with 'role'-functions in religion. Themes and side-branches of symbolism in the wider sense, such as personification, types and anti-types, attributes, robe symbolism, 'speaking symbolism', and emblems, all demand that attention should be paid to the 'role' theory in our context from the point of view of findings in history of religions. What relation has the symbol to drama? Since the significance of the dramatic element in religion has been unfolded through myth and ritual research and the methodology of cult history, Aulén has pointed out the symbolic-dramatic motif in the image of God, which belongs to the self-representation of religion.[36] In concrete terms, what this provokes in history of religions is consideration and analysis of individual elements in this context with a view to their value as symbolic statements: motor behavior, gesture and mimicry in the behavior of religious men. Through

33. Cf. Hugh Daniel Duncan, *Symbolism in Society*, New York, 1968.

34. Claude Lévi-Strauss, 'La geste d'Asdiwal', *Annuaire 1958-1959 de l'Ecole Pratique des Hautes Etudes, Section des Sciences Religieuses*, Paris, 1958, pp. 3ff.

35. Hjalmar Sundén, *Die Religion und die Rollen* (tr. from the Swedish: *Religionen och rollerna*), Berlin, 1966.

36. Gustaf Aulén, *Das Drama und die Symbole* (tr. from the Swedish: *Dramat och symbolerna*), Göttingen, 1965, p. 6.

these, the religious man identifies himself with what is symbolically represented, and with the symbol. The role of dancing as an element in ritual, the image of dancing in the mystics, and God as a dancer, all belong here, just like the countless details of an advanced ritual: the ritualization of walking and other movements of the body, the meaning of masks in cults, and even the theologization of concepts such as prosopon and persona. Aulén puts it in this context programmatically: 'Gibt man die Symbole auf, um andere, scheinbar adäquate Bestimmungen an ihre Stelle zu setzen, dann verlässt man die Welt des Glaubens und vertauscht das lebendige Gottesbild ... gegen einen abstrakten Gottesbegriff'.[37] Here once again, however, one is led to exercise moderation in the historical analysis when considering these processes of identification, and to pay attention to the historical background in the emergence of the symbolic element in these forms of behavior.

4. In order to present the stock of religious symbols in a scientifically plausible manner, and to comprehend the total range of the concept in its phenomenological uniqueness, so as to understand its functional and operational task in religion, what is needed is the scientific operationalization of those historical findings which could be subsumed under the concept of the symbol. Symbolism ought to be systematically opened up in its historical context and ramifications, while being divided on the basis of individual religions or fields in history of religions. This could be achieved either through lexical arrangement or through presentation in monographs of the context. Special attention would have to be paid to pictorial representational material. Finally there are also the bibliographical requirements, in view of the already vast and steadily rising flood of literature. The first comprehensive, authoritative, and purely professional attempts in this direction are now available, in the series *Symbolik der Religionen*, edited by Ferdinand Herrmann, with its volumes of text and tables (1958-....; limited however to the living religions); in the *Lexikon der christlichen Ikonographie*, founded by Engelbert Kirschbaum (1968-....); and in the *Bibliographie zur Symbolik, Ikonographie und Mythologie* (1968-....), edited by Manfred Lurker. These show that the starting point must be the historical and phenomenological findings on the individual themes, but also that there are limits

37. Aulén, *op. cit.*, p. 6.

to the accuracy and completeness of the scientific method. The widest scope is justifiably covered by Lurker's bibliography.

Is it possible to elaborate, to extend, to surpass, or to transcend the purely theoretical or speculative-dogmatic approach scientifically and empirically, by means of philosophy, sociology, or psychology — or even, if this can be done, to replace it with something new? Conceivably the connection of symbols with the depth dimensions of the religious is one reason for the difficulty of accommodating them within a general rational-quantitative methodological system in a scientifically valid manner. On the other hand it can be seen that there is an immediate scientific need here, which can, within limits, be met. For this purpose, precise individual historical investigations of individual symbols in their historical context, and in a comparison of different religious fields, would be desirable. Much of this work has been too superficial.[38] Perhaps psychology of religion and sociology of religion could be stimulated by this to develop their positive empirical knowledge and their theories on the symbol question in similarly meticulously arranged historical and systematic presentations, instead of letting it rest with the brave gestures of brilliant individual interpretations. Above all, the luxuriantly blossoming chaos of depth-psychological and psychoanalytical opinions and investigations of the symbol question ought to give way to a cosmos which would display the entire broad spectrum of teachings and results there, in conjunction with the processed factual material, in reviewable form. It will then become clearer what contribution these branches of symbol interpretation can offer to historically and phenomenologically oriented research on the question of the depth aspects of religion. The advancement of the bibliographical work is a particularly important aspect for the illumination of the manifold variations in current work on the symbolic.

5. Finally, it must be made clear that symbols and symbol studies are only one side of the approach to 'religion' and its depths. To ignore this fact would impoverish our concept of religion. Religious experience and life is too rich to be exhausted by the field of the symbolic. History

38. Attempts at overcoming this have been made in the yearbook for symbol research, *Symbolon* (ed. Julius Schwabe, Basel, 1960-....; N.S. ed. Thomas Reimbold, Cologne, 1973-....), even though this yearbook needs to be approached critically in detail.

of religions is no more exclusively concerned with symbols than it can afford to forget or ignore them.

The urgent problem remains that of achieving agreement on a concept of the symbol which is more than just a tentative model. It is impossible to elaborate a comprehensive general theory of symbols and of methodical research on them within religion on the basis of the excessively vague and broad concept in general use today. Anyone who studies religious symbols is likely to find it necessary to make a statement of his personal understanding of them; otherwise he must operate with the unexplained or one-sided, set ideas of his audience. It would be urgent to clarify both a broader and a narrower concept of symbols, which would be adequately differentiated to do justice to the complexity of the phenomenon. An alternative question would be whether we ought to abandon the concept of the symbol altogether in religious studies, since it hinders or masks precise scientific statement. It is a striking fact that ethnology of religion to some extent makes extensive use of the word symbol, but to some extent seems to use it sparingly or to avoid it.

Basically, Joachim Wach has answered these questions through his compilation of several forms of 'expressions of religious experience': thought, action, and community. Since he was aware of the problems connected with the concept of symbols, he has divided the expression of religious experience in thought into 'endeictic' and 'discursive' methods.[39] Of course, it cannot be ruled out that the logical-discursive manner of religious expression provides just as much access to depth dimensions as the symbolic or 'endeictic' (which is particularly significant nowadays as a result of psychoanalysis and the attention paid to spiritual sub-structures). It should also be considered whether the expression of religion in action, in responsible activity, and in the community do not also provide insight into depth dimensions. These questions have already partly been touched on, since the cultic and collective forms of religion, at least, constitute their own forms of symbolism. Our reflections seem to point equally clearly to the fact that there is a marked interdependence between symbolic and logical-rational forms of experience, thought, and expression in religion. This also applies with reference to advances into the depth dimensions of religion.

The opposite alternative would be a 'pansymbolism' subsuming under

39. Joachim Wach, *Vergleichende Religionsforschung*, Stuttgart, 1962, pp. 80ff.

the concept of the 'symbol' all experiences, statements, and forms of behavior in religion against their background, and thus regarding them — depending on the point of view — as either a depth or a surface feature. This conception can be encountered not only in theological and meta-physical speculations, but also in theories of depth psychology, as well as in the rationalist-formalist understanding of religion as a socially-stabilizing surface form. The symbol is then either the 'proper' or the 'non-proper' in religion; religion is a 'symbol' either in the depth sense or the surface sense. Or the symbol is regarded in general as an instrument for the structuring of both the non-religious and the religious formation of conceptions, expressions, and concepts, as a means of inter-human communication of existential self-understanding, and thus as the universal key for all forms of human behavior, including the religious merely as one form among many. Whitehead and Langer have urged in this direction, and it has been followed by many others. Or finally, as in Tillich, the entire world, the visible creation, is understood as a symbol, which 'expresses symbolically the participation of the finite in its own infinite ground'.[40] These interpretations are of course a matter of method and concept formation.

Basically, it would be conceivable to regard the whole of religion as a symbol, and thus to strive for a new reading of and evaluation of the concept of the symbol. This kind of 'symbol religion', as I would like to call it, would then be a complex of 'non-proprieties' and indirect statements about reality. It would be understood as the opposite of the rational-scientific, quantitative description of factual data; or it would constitute another form of statement about the factual data which are the object of research in natural science. The latter conception is an old one, and not infrequent among natural scientists, but can also be encountered as a popular conception. It accords the symbolic element in religion a value which has rationalist, and especially mathematical, origins. Such illustrious minds as Nicholas of Cusa have defended this pansymbolist conception of religion, in conjunction with a pancosmic image of God. In his *De docta ignorantia*, he says that the only access to the world of the divine is through symbols, so that it would be appropriate to make use of mathematical signs on account of their indestructible

---

40. Paul Tillich, 'Existential analysis and religious symbols', in *Contemporary Problems in Religion*, ed. Harold A. Basilius, Detroit, 1956, p. 49.

certainty.[41] According to this idea, man possesses the mathematical faculty as something structural, which comes to the fore in him and leads him towards God, scientifically most convincingly, and most closely in fact, since it is exempt from the mutability of all sense objects. Universal validity, objectivity, certainty of knowledge, and permanence of the symbol, form the criteria for the theory of mathematical symbols as the universal and exclusive keys to the mysteries of religion.

In whatever way the extension of the concept of the symbol, and its application to religion, may be conceived, and however it is related to the depths of knowledge of God and of the image of man: the religions themselves believe in the existence of objective depth contexts, mediated through symbols, in their supporters. They find these depths, however, not merely in the sub-rational, the sub-conscious, or in the world of dreams, but primarily in the divine reality, which is, for them, the sole authority. One should respect this proper religious understanding. All that science can do with this claim to the 'depths of the self' and the 'depths of being' is to accept it, analyze it, and understand it — but not prove it, and certainly not construct it.

Nevertheless, there can be no doubt, despite all the criticisms, that symbol analysis is able to lead one into the depths of experience claimed by the religions, and to develop methods for this; nor that it is able to do this as well as or even better than the rational interpretation of written texts and of coherent, logical statements about God and man. What symbols disclose are not, however, pre-given structures: they are themselves structural and structure-imparting. In them, the depths of religious experience and of the image of God take on structure. And it is for this reason that it is desirable to render them hermeneutically fruitful.

41. '[dicimus] ... cum *ad divina non nisi per symbola* accedendi nobis via patet, quod tunc *mathematicalibus signis propter ipsorum incorruptibilem certitudinem* convenientius uti poterimus' (Nicolaus de Cusa, *De docta ignorantia*, Lib. I, cap. XI; *op. cit.*, p. 44; italics mine).

Commentary   by Th. P. van Baaren

It is an honor to be invited to comment on the papers of such distinguished scholars as Prof. van Baal and Prof. Goldammer; and it is also a
pleasure, because of the high quality of their contributions. I should like
to keep Prof. van Baal's paper to the last, as he treats religion in general,
and comment first upon Prof. Goldammer's contribution on symbolism
which is in any case somewhat more restricted in scope.

However, before commenting on these papers, I should like to say a
few words about the title chosen for this section: Depth-structures of
religious expression. Both scholars have interpreted this term as meaning
to delve into the fundamental and basic problems of religion. I agree
with this interpretation, but the indication given by the organisers of the
congress in using this title may also lead one to think of what is called
depth-research in anthropology.[42] I know, of course, that the latter is
an accepted term, but nevertheless I consider it a rather misleading one:
it is not so much research in depth as research producing individually
detailed information, perhaps better named density research.

The subject of symbols and symbolism has led to much confusion in
science of religion, because eminent scholars not only attribute an ontological value to symbols but are also convinced that it belongs to the task
of science of religion to study symbols in this light. To give an example,
I agree practically in full with Prof. Baird's criticism of Prof. Eliade on
this point.[43] To a high degree Prof. Goldammer's contribution is free
from this confusion, nevertheless even his way of considering symbols
leads from time to time to problems which could be avoided, because
they are not real problems residing in the material studied, but problems
arising from the way of thinking of the researcher. He does not differentiate clearly enough between a functional and an essential definition
of this phenomenon.[44] Most of these difficulties could, in my opinion,

42. J. Pentikäinen, 'Depth research', *Acta Etnogr. Acad. Scient. Hungaricae*, 21,
1972.
43. R.D. Baird, *Category formation and the history of religions*, Mouton, The
Hague, 1971, pp. 75-77.
44. Baird, *op. cit.*, pp. 1-16.

have been avoided by considering a symbol as an image, a metaphor, as I proposed in my article on religious symbols in 1964.[45]

The functional definition as proposed by me is: A symbol is an image or sign that expresses in this reality and by means derived from this reality a postulated different and higher reality. All symbols are images or signs, but not all images and signs are symbols. A symbol is, so to speak, an image or sign that has made a successful career in religion. By defining symbols in this way we avoid the problems which arise from the confusion between a symbol and that which is symbolized by it. A symbol is a form of communication, and like all other forms of communication a function of culture and not a natural phenomenon.

There is, of course, no time to enlarge upon this and to give my own views at greater length, neither is there enough time really to do justice to the rich contents of Prof. Goldammer's paper. In very many points his views and mine coincide and agree very well. In some other aspects we seem to differ. From these I should like to choose three points for a short discussion.

1. The speaker expresses his doubt whether we can speak of symbols in cultures and religions of the non-literate peoples. I am convinced that this doubt is completely unfounded. It is interesting to compare, for instance, the conception the Ndembu of Northern Rhodesia have of a symbol. They call a symbol *chinjikikilu*, a word derived from the verb *ju-jikijila*, meaning 'to mark a track' by cutting marks in trees or by bending boughs in a certain direction to indicate the way to follow in an unknown part of the country. Another word the Ndembu regularly use, when they discuss symbols, is the verb *kusolola*, to make visible. According to them a symbol is a sign that makes something visible. This view does not differ much from the one given by me. According to the Dogon of the Western Sudan the whole world consists of a system of symbols which have to be decoded by man.

The book by Jean Hurault, *Africains de Guyane*, which he cites, is not a fortunate choice. In the first place the culture of the Bush Negroes of Surinam is not an ordinary 'primitive' culture, it is a syncretistic culture founded by people who had lost most of their own cultural traditions

45. Th. P. van Baaren, 'Religious symbols, their essence and function', in *Verbum*. Essays on some aspects of the religious function of words, dedicated to dr. H. W. Obbink, Utrecht, 1964.

and who had passed through a period of close contact with European culture. In the second place, Hurault is specially interested in the art-historical aspect of the material he studies and uses the term symbol rather loosely. In the third place I do not find anything in his book which gives me the impression that the Bush Negroes of Surinam have no religious symbolism, as I use the term, although it may be, as is most symbolism as a matter of fact, often rather trite. The term symbol is no guarantee of depth and transcendental value.

I cannot understand why Prof. Goldammer says that 'our concept of symbols ... derives beyond doubt from Greek language and thought'. Once we understand a symbol as a metaphor which has been canonized, the need for a statement of this kind disappears completely for metaphors are, as far as our knowledge reaches, universal. This is one of the places where I put myself the question whether Prof. Goldammer has after all not been seduced by the lure of ontological thinking in a context in which this kind of thinking makes no sense at all. We know that mankind is apt to express in symbols things which it feels unable to express clearly, but the only test of the aptness of a symbol is its success among other persons, because there is no possibility at all to check it against the reality it claims to express.

2. Prof. Goldammer states that symbols are determined by the culture to which they belong. I agree with him completely in this matter, but when he says that this becomes apparent, because the 'symbolic value can alter, be reversed, or even contradictory in different religions', we must add that this as a rule is also the case within one and the same religion. Most symbols are multi-interpretable. It is rarely possible to indicate *the* significance of a certain symbol in general even within the same culture, we are lucky when we can do this within a specific context.

3. Prof. Goldammer asks whether father and mother are religious symbols. Of course they are, but their symbolic value is not so much that of individual symbols of sexual life, they are social symbols of great value and highly influential as such.

Prof. van Baal's contribution to this congress is worth a serious and prolonged discussion, and as this is not possible in these brief comments, I must begin by stating that I feel somewhat embarrassed by it. Not because I disagree with him, on the contrary most thoughts in this paper

I can share whole-heartedly, or at least follow easily, but by far the largest part of this paper is taken up by a disquisition in which Prof. van Baal enlarges upon his own beliefs regarding mankind, the human situation and religion. I repeat, I agree with much of what he says, but it is a confession of faith which is only partially open to scientific discussion. I could only enter into discussion with his views by stating my own prescientific and postscientific views on the same points. To do this, however, would be the task of a very different kind of congress, one treating the theological and philosophical bases of religion.

As I did with Prof. Goldammer's paper, again I should like to choose a few points for short comments.

1. Prof. van Baal regrets that 'current definitions of religion tend to veil the notorious but meaningful fact that religion is based upon notions and ideas accepted as true, concerning a reality which cannot be verified empirically in any way'. This is too sweeping a statement; this fact is at least implicitly very much present in Geertz's definition.[46] It is clearly expressed by Spiro.[47] Important in this respect is also the work of Baird.[48]

2. Prof. van Baal infers that the universality of religion must be explained by seeking its foundations 'in some fundamental contradiction in the human condition generally'. He may very well be right, but as our knowledge of religion is restricted to the last 5000 years of human existence, this again is rather a sweeping statement. We have no direct knowledge of prehistoric religion and even within the bounds of our historic knowledge many religions are only very imperfectly known. Statements of this kind belong to philosophy and theology but can never be empirically verified.

3. Again, we find a generalization which reminds us of the by now old-fashioned forms of phenomenology of religion. The way Prof. van Baal formulates the way in which primitive man and modern man react upon nature and society is not only open to grave doubt as to its correctness but it shares with most phenomenological statements the fact that it

46. C. Geertz, 'Religion as a cultural system', in M. Banton, ed., *Anthropological approaches to the study of religion*, London, 1966.
47. M. E. Spiro, 'Religion: problems of definition and explanation', in Banton, *op. cit.* in note 46.
48. Baird, *op. cit.* in note 43.

tells us far more about the author than about the subject he claims to speak about. As a matter of fact, I cannot at all agree with this statement. It is only up to a point that nature is 'a friendly source of recreation' to modern man. This can only be said of nature in so far as we have been able to tame it by our technical knowledge. Nature in the raw is to us far more frightening than to a primitive who is used to it from a child. On the other hand, our relations with society are 'untransparent and un-authentic' only because our society as a whole has become so large and complicated, but most of us live most of our life in smaller sections of it in which our relations are as 'direct and authentic' as Prof. van Baal states of the primitives, forgetting the many facts which invalidate that opinion.

4. I agree fully with Prof. van Baal that religion should be studied in its cultural context. This conviction led me more than five years ago to the formula of religion as a function of culture. There is no other way open to us to the understanding of religion than the understanding of man who created religion as part of his culture and there is no other way of understanding man than by considering him in the context of his culture, unless we are prepared to leave the field of science of religion and to enter into the disputed country of philosophy and theology.

Commentary   by Ulf Drobin

In a stimulating and provocative way the title of the last session is highly ambiguous. The word 'depth-structures' indicates something like essence (*Wesen*), the deepest apprehensible 'truth' of religions. An adherent of the Husserl philosophical school, of Sigmund Freud, Carl Gustav Jung, Claude Lévi-Strauss etc. would easily recognize 'depth-structural re-search' as *the* method for the science of religion. That the wording has no real core of univocal meaning, but nonetheless forces the scholar to con-template his methodological position within the discipline, is obvious from the interesting papers by Prof. J. van Baal and Prof. Kurt Goldam-mer. Indeed, these two papers have not much more in common than the use of the word symbol. But for Prof. van Baal, symbol, in the context in which he uses it, designates any item within the religious system by which man communicates with the universe, while for Prof. Goldammer symbol designates, as far as I can see, dogma within the theologies of the *Hochreligionen*.

As is evident from papers in the preceding sections, other key-concepts of the science of religion are also highly equivocal. There is, for instance, no consensus of opinion about such concepts as 'history', 'phenomenology', 'typology', 'anthropology' or even — in a defining sense — 'religion'.

From a more holistic point of view the different conceptual tools overlap so that it would be of little use to comment on structure without taking these other concepts into consideration. I am therefore not going to comment directly on the last two papers, but shall, instead, outline my own position, which indirectly but more coherently, I hope, will show my agreements and disagreements. Thus, I should like to make the following points.

Structure. Religion as well as culture is structured. By structure is meant here the relations between sub-units that build up into a comprehensive, bounded system. Sub-units are defined in relation to the structure (system, whole) and might, following the terminology of Kenneth Pike, be called emic units.[49] Concretely, this means that the units recurrent in different religions, e.g. myths, prayers, rituals etc., cannot be understood *ad hoc* but *in situ*.

Structure, in this general sense, is not to be understood only statically. The operation of parts within the system is included, so that the concept structure-function might have been used instead.[50] From one point of view structure implies a whole, but this is not to be interpreted too rigidly. Within one structure (metastructure, superorganism) there are substructures (configurations). Consequently, religion is a substructure within the wider concept culture.

Phenomenology—typology. A deep disbelief in phenomenology has been demonstrated and it has been urged that phenomenology and typology must be kept distinct.[51] This might be due to the long-standing

49. Cf. K. Pike, *Language in Relation to a Unified Theory of the Structure of Human Behavior*, Part I, Glendale, 1954; A. Dundes, 'From Etic to Emic Units in the Structural Study of Folktales', *Journal of American Folklore* 75, pp. 95 ff.

50. A. R. Radcliffe-Brown, *Structure and Function in Primitive Society*, London, 1952, pp. 1 ff.; R.K. Merton, *Social Theory and Social Structure*, New York, 1968.

51. See for instance papers and discussions in *Problems and Methods of the History of Religions*, ed. by U. Bianchi, C.J. Bleeker, A. Bausani, Leiden, 1972.

dominance of the Husserl phenomenology in Germany and the Netherlands. Intuitional concepts such as *epoche* or *eidology*, with their implications of theological philosophy of religion, hardly offer a basis for empirical culture-orientated studies.[52]

'Phenomenon', if consideration is paid to contextual (structural) meaning, might be defined as a recurrent unit in different religious systems (or in one). The last statement, of course, implies that the place of the phenomenon in time and space is considered — in other words its place in history. If two or more analogous phenomena, as Prof. Ugo Bianchi might put it, are compared and grouped together we have a type whose level of abstraction will depend on the number of individual entities included therein. Some of the contributors to this congress want to keep the concept phenomenology for the comparison of isolated phenomena and the concept typology for the comparison of religions as wholes. This distinction is, in my opinion, not easy to maintain because: (a) every particular phenomenon must be contextually apprehended, i.e. within the religion as such; (b) most phenomenological units are connected with other units — ritual behavior, for instance, might be coupled to myths, beliefs, observances of different kinds — so that a phenomenon generally forms a configuration or structure in itself; (c) a religion can never be studied *in toto*, in all its different aspects, it is an ideal never to be reached. The difference between the phenomenology and the typology of religions is quantitative, not qualitative. Moreover, specialized phenomenological and overall monographic research are, or should be, complementary to each other.

The definition of religion. In recent years there has been an intense debate on the problems of the definition of religion. Some important names, in this connection, are Clifford Geertz, Prof. Melford Spiro, Prof. Ugo Bianchi, Prof. J. van Baal and Robert D. Baird.[53]

52. Cf. Å. Hultkrantz, 'The Phenomenology of Religion: Aims and Methods', *Temenos* 6, pp. 68 ff.; Th. P. van Baaren, 'Systematische Religionswissenschaft', *Nederlands Theologisch Tijdschrift* 24/2, pp. 81 ff. See also K. Goldammer, 'Ein Leben für die Erforschung der Religion: Friedrich Heiler und sein Beitrag zur Aufgabenstellung und Methodik der Religionswissenschaft', in *Inter Confessiones: Beiträge zur Förderung des interkonfessionellen und interreligiösen Gesprächs*, Marburg, 1972, pp. 1 ff.
53. C. Geertz, 'Religion as a Cultural System', in *Anthropological Approaches to the Study of Religion*, ed. M. Banton (A.S.A. Monographs 3), London, 1966, pp. 1 ff.; M. E. Spiro, 'Religion: Problems of Definition and Explanation', *ibid.*, pp. 85 ff.;

526	*Depth-Structures of Religious Expression*

There may be an element of paradox in the whole process of definition. We cannot start an investigation without knowing what to investigate and which questions to put. But the initial definition may easily,
as is well-known from the history of our discipline, slant or give a bias
to the approach, so that the researcher sees nothing but those aspects
or manifestations of a complex reality which support his frame of reference; he is then trapped in the vicious circle of his own definition. This
was typical of the great evolutionists, who took their material without
system from all over the world. When the research object is limited to a
community, a tribe or a coherent religious area the danger is still present.
Today we are acquainted with some social anthropological models —
another term for definition — which turn out to be nothing but self-
fulfilling prophecies. Thomas' theorem that 'if men define situations
as real, they are real in their consequences'[54] might to a certain degree
be applicable to the society of scholars too.

Merely to delimit the research object and to intensify the study is,
however, an illusory way out of the dilemma. A monographic study cannot be carried on without preceding knowledge of phenomenology; and
a thorough monographic study, in its turn, enriches phenomenology. In
other words, there must be a feedback between tentative definitions and
research objects, as also between phenomenology and specific research.

What has been said above is intended to apply to definitions that are
tentative in the sense that their aim is real definition (description). These
are all of limited scope.

A definition of religion is usable, or even necessary, because we have
to determine the borderlines of our discipline. Within a certain span such
a definition, however, is nominal, not real. Adjustments in different
directions are matters of conventional agreement, not of empiricism. We
may include or exclude Theravada; we can define magic psychologically
and regard religion and magic as polarities, though overlapping and affiliated, or we may choose a behavioristic definition which considerably
diminishes the gap between the two concepts.

The 'essence' of religion cannot be grasped, but its human, social and

---

U. Bianchi, 'The Definition of Religion', in *op. cit.* in note 51, pp. 15 ff.; J. van Baal,
Symbols for Communication, Assen, 1971. R. D. Baird, *Category Formation and the
History of Religion*, Mouton, The Hague, 1971.
54. W. J. Thomas and D. S. Thomas, *The Child in America: Behavior Problems and
Programs*, New York, 1928, p. 572.

cultural manifestations may be tentatively formulated and investigated. From this point of view religion is multidimensional and we have to proceed with an increasing number of sets of definitions and of approaches, each of which might be called 'reductionalistic'; *das Ding an sich* will never be unveiled.

Anthropology—philology—history. Again and again it is asserted that the science of religion is ultimately the history of religion. Written documents from literate religions, it is stressed, constitute empirical evidence, and observations of non-literate religions are looked upon as more or less hypothetical generalizations. Consequently, it is often considered that as research objects the *Hochreligionen* are of far greater importance to the science of religion. One argument is that they can be studied historically— in a time continuum. The foundation of the science of religion would then be source criticism. From this point of view anthropology and phenomenology are regarded as perhaps not quite respectable auxiliary or sub-disciplines.

When making such statements philologists seem to be unaware of the obvious fact that most documents are fragmentary. They have to be interpreted; philology reaches no further than the unequivocal reading of the corpus of texts. Interpretations depend entirely on comparisons, i.e. phenomenology.[55]

Historical documents of certain religions may be studied in a time continuum, but not in a living context. Anthropological data usually have the living context, but not the historical perspective. These two branches must necessarily support each other in the inevitable process of interpretation.

Concluding remarks. In my view there is a structural relation between the different disciplines of the science of religion. Each discipline is not only of the same importance as, but depends on and conditions the others. Progress in research may follow the *Weg der konzentrischen Kreise*, to borrow a metaphor from Friedrich Heiler.[56] In the centre we find, if not *Deus absconditus*, in any case deeper knowledge.

55. The crucial problem, of course, is to determine how to make relevant comparisons. See Å. Hultkrantz' comprehensive survey *Metodvägar inom den jämförande religionsforskningen* (Methodological approaches to the comparative study of religion), Stockholm, 1973.

56. Friedrich Heiler, *Erscheinungsformen und Wesen der Religion*, Stuttgart, 1961, pp. 18ff.

Commentary   by Michael Pye

1. The papers under discussion deal with two distinct problems thrown up by the rather opaque phrase 'depth-structures of religious expression'. The writers themselves seem to have felt some difficulty as they connived at least in changing the term 'religious expression' to 'religious experience', and Prof. Goldammer tones down 'structures' to 'dimensions' which seems to be more appropriate to the problem with which he mainly dealt. There are many incidental points of interest in the papers but this comment attempts to clarify the relationship and the distinction between the two main kinds of problems which emerge.

The two problems arise divergently in accordance with whether or not one intends to apply a certain methodological criterion which has now become established as having at least some role within the systematic study of religion. If clarity could be achieved on this point it may be that future discussions could be somewhat less tortuous. This criterion, of which some use is made in both papers, is that an account of a set of data in the study of religion should be acceptable in principle to those believers or participants who are involved in the data.[57] The application of this criterion is above all that which marks off the phenomenological study of religion from studies and theories based on theological, sociological, psychological and other kinds of theories which are alien to the self-understanding of the believers and which may easily contradict that self-understanding. This is not to say that theories which do not apply this criterion do not have a justifiable rationale.[58] After all, it may be that the meaning of what is going on in a case of religion is indeed different from what the believer assumes it to be. To give an example, we may in the end prefer to conclude that adolescents get themselves converted to various kinds of religious faith or allegiance not so much because of the intrinsic truth of any one of the systems to which they

---

57. W. Brede Kristensen, 'The Meaning of Religion', *Lectures in the Phenomenology of Religion*, The Hague, 1960, p. 14; and W. Cantwell Smith, 'Comparative Religion: Whither and Why?' in M. Eliade and J.M. Kitagawa, ed., *The History of Religions*, Chicago, 1959, p. 42.

58. The importance and at the same time the limitation of the role of this criterion were briefly discussed in the present writer's book *Comparative Religion*, Newton Abbot, 1972, especially pp. 16-19.

may be converted, but because such decision or ideological adjustment is a developmental task characteristic of adolescence.[59] Such an interpretation however, whatever force it may have, does not form part of the phenomenological study of religion strictly understood, precisely because it subverts the self-understanding of the believers. In any phase of the study of religion it should be possible to be clear about whether the criterion is being applied, or whether, contrariwise, the attempt is being made to work with some other frame of reference designed to override the self-understanding of the believer whenever necessary. The decision about whether to apply the criterion or not is very important because it leads to different kinds of studies and different kinds of problems, not least in connection with the case of 'depth-structures' in religion. To some extent the two approaches are illustrated distinctively by the two papers given on this topic and it is therefore with special reference to the turning point which this criterion provides that I should like to consider each in turn.

2. Consider first the case in which the criterion is applied, when the question about 'depth-structures' may be stated briefly as follows. By what specific means is it possible to elucidate the inward depths of experience of the religious people under study? Prof. Goldammer stresses that the religions themselves find dimensions of depth not so much for example in the world of dreams but in the divine reality with which they are above all concerned. He continues: 'One should respect this proper religious self-understanding'.[60] Since he is thus clearly wishing to apply the criterion mentioned it is quite appropriate that he spends his time clarifying what use may be made of the symbols which religious people themselves use in order to elucidate the deeper dimensions of religious experience of which they themselves seem to be aware. In particular he seeks to stabilise the term 'symbol' and to itemise the questions which need to be asked in the systematic study of symbols. It is methodological work of this kind which contributes to the delineation of a broad framework in the context of which the various religious traditions can be 'phenomenologically' understood. This is surely an important

59. Cf. writers from Starbuck onwards, especially for this formulation Argyle and Loukes: references in *Comparative Religion* (*op. cit.* in note 58), p. 213.
60. Prof. Goldammer's word is *Eigenverständnis*.

activity and perhaps the main contribution of the paper, but the present comment wishes to focus attention on the relationship between that and a subordinate but persistent thread, namely his rejection of the possibility of seeking depth-structures other than those to be found in the self-understanding of the religious people themselves.

This note appears right at the outset where he stresses that symbols have in important cases been understood as rational constructs referring to the central meanings of the system concerned rather than as anything to do with the subrational, the subconscious or the unconscious, which would be something other than that explicitly conveyed by the systems in question. Buddhist symbols 'contain the centre of the Buddhist doctrine of salvation' and the symbols of Pseudo-Dionysius and other western mystics 'are explicitly intended to attain the depths of the religious and of the experience of God'. The distinction is summed up as follows: 'It is a separate question whether this produces depth-"structures". At any rate, we can speak here of depth "dimensions" of individual religious experience'. Goldammer regularly seeks to understand this 'individual religious experience' on the basis of the data offered by the religious persons, and as this is affected by their position within a particular tradition this naturally leads to a stress on historical and cultural analysis.

The main rejection of the other type of approach is directed particularly at 'depth-psychology and analytical theories' of symbolism. The general argument is that depth-psychological interpretations of symbolism refer to far too many kinds of symbols indiscriminately and lead away from the precise character of religious symbolism. It appears that the weakness of such approaches lies in their failure to define symbols precisely with respect to religion as such, i.e. as having some reference to 'transcendence' or to 'divine depth' or to 'the sphere of the numinous'. At its sharpest the criticism is that these symbols 'may contribute in a rational, scientific way to the explanation of the contents of numinous experiences through the depth layers of spiritual processes, and in this way dissolve the special qualities of the numinous'. However the depth psychology accounts are not in themselves thereby disproved! We are left with a clash of presuppositions. Goldammer, who applies the basic criterion of the phenomenological study of religion, stresses that the 'sphere of the numinous' (etc.) should not be dissolved away but recognized as being that which for religious people is important, and therefore sets up his definition of symbols as mediators of religious depth experience of the transcendent. This approach is bound to come into conflict with theories which are not elaborated in line with the principle that it is 'the believer' himself who is in principle right about what it all means. Such theories however are sure to have their own rationale, which may or may not be justifiable or consistent, but which cannot be overturned in principle by means of a circular argument advanced on the basis of presuppositions which from the beginning they do not accept. It is precisely because of the tension between such competing interpretations that there is a methodological problem about how to approach depth structures in the first place. This problem must lie further back and an important aspect of it is how to decide when it is appropriate and when it is inappropriate to apply the criterion already referred to. A satisfactorily complex methodology can surely be satisfied neither with the view that it should always be applied nor with the view that it need never be applied. Further remarks on this are best left until after some comment has been made on the other paper, which seeks to move more positively into the field of depth-structures more broadly conceived.

3. Consider then now the case in which the criterion is not applied, when the question about depth-structures turns out differently as follows. How can one set about defining or elucidating the depth-structures which lie behind or beyond the particular forms of specific religions? Prof. van Baal for his part elected to concentrate on explaining what he believes does in fact lie behind the various patterns of religious expression. We are presented with what is, in effect, a brief *Daseinsanalyse* based on Merleau-Ponty and Sartre, and the argument is that religion arises universally because of fundamental contradictions in human existence. Indeed according to his theory, although there are some differences between cultures and some differences between primitive man and modern man, religion at a fundamental level seems to have the same function and meaning everywhere. Other theories of religion which have an approximately equivalent methodological status to that of van Baal are, *mutatis mutandis*, Jung's account of religious symbolism related to archetypes of the collective unconscious, and Lévi-Strauss' theory of myth as a kind of code reflecting fundamental polarities of human existence. There may be great strength in one or more of these approaches, but they are anyway different from studies which apply, as a matter of methodological principle, the criterion previously stated. In the end such theories

claim to know better than 'the believers' what their religion is all about.[61]

As a development of this argument it may be helpful to show in more detail that Prof. van Baal does *not* seem to intend to apply the criterion mentioned, at least not in his consideration of 'depth-structures'. In the last part of his paper, it should be admitted, he does indeed adduce the 'different opinion' of sacrificers and their guests as a corrective to some descriptions of sacrifice, but this perhaps instinctive use of the criterion is not related to the main part of his paper. Three indications suggest that he does not wish to apply the criterion in a consideration of depth-structures:

a) The basic *Daseinsanalyse* which he uses as a model to explain the meaning of religion in general does not seem to be drawn from any specific religion, such as that of Marind-anim to which he refers later. It is 'the phenomenologists' (not to be confused with those who study religion phenomenologically!) who 'have opened our eyes to the fact that the human condition is defined primarily by man's being in the world'.

b) At least part of his account of the basic human problem (which is supposed to underly *all* cases of religion) is very sophisticated and surely goes far beyond the self-understanding of some participants in some religions. For example, 'The other I, however, the I which is an object of reflection and which, for the sake of clarity, shall from now on be termed the *self*, is the product of an I which has taken up a position in the world by assuming a certain way of being in the world, a life project in the sense of the "projet-de-vie" as forwarded by Sartre and Merleau-Ponty, through which it (the I) has turned into a driving force in its world...' must surely reflect a degree of heightened individual self-consciousness which to say the least is not obviously shared by all members of the human race. In another place we find primitive man treated as a colleague of the modern existentialist.

c) The *Daseinsanalyse* contains views about the way things are, which are inconsistent with the way in which some religions understand things to be. A Buddhist for example would have to go in for apolo-

61. A clear example of this in the case of a monograph dealing with the data first in all possible detail is C. Ouwehand's book *Namazu-e and Their Themes*, Leiden, 1964. The people who drew the *namazu-e* in the first place would have been surprised indeed to read the theoretical part of this book, if indeed they could have understood it at all, which is very doubtful.

getic somersaults to be able to agree with statements like: 'The gods reflect man's projected fears and hopes concerning the world. They even reflect the permanence and immutability of the I which, unaffected by the variations of the self, is always I, always identical with itself and in this respect extemporal and immutable like the gods'.

These comments are not particularly intended to show that van Baal's theory is incorrect, but rather to bring out the nature of the theory. As was stated already it may indeed be that the real meaning of religions is something different from what it is imagined to be by some or all religious persons. It may be that there are 'depth-structures' of religious expression or religious experience which lie beyond the self-understanding of religious persons. However if that self-understanding is to be contradictable while the theory is at the same time to be related in some way to particular cases of religion, as presumably it must, there are further methodological problems to be solved. These are not taken up by Van Baal in his third section, where he stresses instead the importance of studying religion in its cultural contexts in order to attain to a refined understanding of them. Nor are these problems taken up by Goldammer who as has been pointed out takes pains to steer his work into the first type of approach to 'depth-structures'. It would take a further paper to set out these problems in their own right, and it must suffice here to indicate most briefly and tentatively the kind of question which comes to mind.

4. Some of these questions may be listed as follows:

a) If the kind of theory under consideration involves some degree of tension with the self-understanding of the religious persons, what criterion or criteria could be used to control the degree of tension or the type of contradiction which would be appropriate? This question arises because of the need to avoid a completely arbitrary interpretation of particular religions.

b) Would it be possible to maintain a distinction between giving a 'deeper', 'fuller' or 'truer' account of religions than they give of themselves, and giving an account of them which implies that their own account is definitely wrong?

c) Some religions themselves offer an approach to 'depth-structures', or at least to deep dimensions of religious experience of the sort to which Goldammer referred. How could a theory not based on the

self-understanding of the religions be related to the conceptual avenues of approach found in particular cases? Would it have to be compatible, or could these approaches too be overridden or superseded?
d) At present there exist various general accounts of the depth-structures
of religion, and no doubt more will be invented. Since each of them
in some sense aims to improve on the supposedly more superficial
or limited expressions of particular religions it is not possible to draw
criteria for evaluating the theories from the religions themselves (or
at least not entirely). Where then should such criteria be sought?
Such questions cannot be avoided if one wishes to face up to the second
kind of problem about depth-structures in religion. They seem so complex that this commentator may perhaps be allowed to express a preference for spending time on the approach which restricts itself to the
first kind of question. This leads in effect to a comparative approach to
problems of hermeneutics as these arise in specific religious traditions,
and Prof. Goldammer's positive thesis, seeking analogies in the role of
symbols in various traditions and striving to stabilise the terminology
which makes comparison feasible, is just the kind of work which is important here. It is much smoother to work in accordance with the criterion that 'the believer is always right' and to remain on the tracks
which the believers have variously laid down.

On the other side however, if only because it is quite evident that
various kinds of believers do not all agree, there must be some believers
who are wrong about some things affecting their own religious systems.
For this reason there must also be a phase in the study of religion in
which the criterion referred to can no longer be simplistically applied.
We must continue to be haunted by the possibility of a more general
theory of the meaning of depth-structures in religion, such as for example that advanced by Prof. van Baal, which must be expected in some
ways to supersede or even to contradict the self-understanding of at least
some of those involved. Unfortunately no methodologically clear lines
of approach seem to have emerged in this area yet, and it remains an
urgent problem.

Commentary   by R. J. Zwi Werblowsky

I must confess that I find it exceedingly difficult to comment in a helpful manner on the two papers by Van Baal and Goldammer, because the papers — whilst full of interest and provocative of further thought — are so disparate that at first sight they seem to be lacking any common denominator. Instead of addressing myself, therefore, to specific points in these papers, I shall rather venture a few general reflections to which I have been prompted by my reading of Van Baal and Goldammer. Perhaps what I am doing is not so much making observations as trying to think aloud.

In the first place I am a bit puzzled by the 'depth-structures' in the title of our session ('Depth-Structures of Religious Expression'). What exactly does this term mean? Varying an old proverb, 'one man's depth is another man's surface'or even superficiality. Of course anyone analyzing anything believes that he lays bare 'deeper' structures, and even if he does not use the word 'deeper' he will speak of 'underlying' structures and the like. Depth psychologists (whether belonging to the Freudian or Jungian churches) as well as anthropologists of diverse functionalist and structuralist persuasions, all pretend to penetrate to deeper layers and to uncover underlying structures, sometimes distinguishing between 'apparent' and 'real' or between 'manifest' and 'latent'. Prof. Goldammer's excellent paper has been illuminating here in many respects, but especially in its insistence on historical depth.

However, not only the term deep or depth, but also the concept of structure is more than ambiguous. What explanatory purpose does it serve apart from providing one more tautological definition and re-assuring us that our fields of study exhibit certain patterns and regularities? Most people who talk about structure define it, in the dictionary way, by offering a string of synonymous terms — the surest sign that the word is really superfluous. To define structure as pattern, *Gestalt, Gefüge*, organism, coherent system or system of relations is as correct and occasionally helpful as it is essentially trivial. One does not have to be a structuralist in order to know that the whole is more than the sum of its parts. I shall not elaborate on this point, except for saying that the more recent and fashionable notion of structure as handled by Lévi-Strauss and his followers — whether one agrees with them or not — has at least the merit of being meaningful and not merely tautologous.

The aforementioned general assumption to the effect that there are deeper viz. underlying structures, as distinct from presumably less deep ones, leads me to another problem that has been touched upon more than once during our conference. I refer to levels of description and recognition on the one hand, and levels of analysis on the other. Practitioners of the phenomenological method often describe their task as the description of religious phenomena from the inside, as it were, and in such manner that the believer or practising member of a religion recognizes himself in the description. They want to seize 'the faith of the believer'. This is surely a laudable programme though I doubt, on theoretical and methodological grounds, that it is capable of realization. But even if it were, the realization would bring us to a first level only. Once this particular job is accomplished, we have to move on to another level of analysis, and here I don't mind a bit if the believer fails to recognize himself. Very often he will not only fail to recognize himself, but vigorously object and protest. His protests will not bother me in the least, for my analysis (unlike the initial phenomenological account) is not judged by the believers but only by my professional colleagues. It is they who also have to judge whether an allegedly 'reductionist' analysis is wrong, or possibly right. I always tell my students that drawing horses' hair over cats' guts is a correct description of a string-quartet, but that this description will be singularly unhelpful when trying to understand Beethoven's Quartet op. 132. On the other hand I would not want a psychological, or sociological, or anthropological analysis to be inhibited at the start, or to be rejected out of hand at the end, merely because it is deemed to be — *horribile dictu* — reductionist. To reject an interpretation, more solid arguments are required than exorcism by means of the magic formula 'reductionism'.

The anthropological (in the philosophical sense) structures underlying all forms of human, cultural and social existence, and hence also all religion, have been well described in Van Baal's paper. In fact, Van Baal summarizes the basic anthropological notions with which every student who has read Max Scheler, or A. Gehlen, or Helmuth Plessner, approaches the study of religions. What I do not understand so well is Van Baal's title 'The Scandal of Religion'. I cannot understand why religion should be a scandal. I — and I am sure also Prof. van Baal — study the history of magic, or of alchemy, or of astrology, without being particularly scandalized. Religion is a profoundly human phenomenon (whatever its transcendent focus or reference), and I suspect that it becomes a scandal only to secularized and rationalist minds plagued by a suspicion of the continued vitality, relevance and meaningfulness of religion. If I wanted to make Van Baal's reflections fruitful for the actual study of religions — apart from merely stating the anthropological structure on which all forms of human existence, including human culture, are based — then I would proceed by asking in which religions this structure merely provides the anthropologico-existential background, and in which religions it constitutes the very stuff and central concern. Most religions are based on the structure described by Van Baal (object-subject split, and the concomitant alienation — through objectivation — from nature, from society, and even from oneself), but do not deal with it directly; in the case of Buddhism (or some forms of it) it is the explicit theme. Here the characteristic solution is that when you recognize the non-reality of the subject then no objectivation is possible, and nothing remains to be objectified.

Whatever the language we use for conducting our analyses, the material analyzed presents itself in symbols — verbal utterances, actions (i.e. ritual), organizational forms (even political office-bearers such as kings may function as symbols), images, and so on. I have little to add to Prof. Goldammer's careful review of the problem, which should be read in conjunction with Prof. Colpe's paper. Let us remember that what we nowadays call the Christian creed or confession of faith was first known as the Christian *symbolon*. Many of the religious writers said to use symbols (according to one definition of the term) merely use signs, parables and allegories (according to other definitions). In my private usage e.g. Philo of Alexandria has almost no symbols; his understanding of Scripture is not symbolic but allegorical. The wings which serve as emblems of airlines are signs; the wing that goes with the eye of Horus is probably a symbol. A symbol can be 'lowered' to the rank of a sign, e.g. when a cross on a map or on a letterhead simply indicates that a site or an organization is Christian.

Having mentioned the cross, let me add a word on the relation of iconography to literature. So much of our knowledge of e.g. ancient Greek religion is derived from archeology that I have difficulty in taking seriously the accusation that historians of religion have neglected iconographic material in favor of texts. Of course the more texts we have the more we go to them, simply because texts are more articulate. After all, as Wilfred Cantwell Smith once observed, you can stare at crosses until you are blue in the face, and, I would add, even mobilize all your Jungian archetypes and cosmic trees, and yet you will never know what the cross means to Christians unless you have read the early fathers. In fact, their *theologia crucis* was fully developed long before the cross became a Christian iconographic symbol in the 4th century. An even more instructive example is provided by Buddhism, one of the 'iconographic' religions *par excellence*. There are few Buddhist monuments more impressive than the Borobudur. Yet nothing, literally nothing, makes sense without knowledge of the relevant (Tibetan-Nepalese) texts. Many galleries would still be completely unintelligible were it not for the discovery of, and correlation with the texts (e.g. those explaining the particular system of Dhyani-Buddhas) that give us the key to the intention of the builders and sculptors of the Borobudur. I should very much like some statistically-minded student of religion to investigate how much of the extant iconographic material depends for its interpretation on texts (or is conceived *ab initio* as illustrations of texts, or as representations of textual or verbal traditions), and how much is primary iconography serving as a 'source' for subsequent textual commentary and elaboration.

Most of the terms I have used so far (structure, symbol, depth) are wildly unclear and ambiguous. Frankly, I do not mind in the least. I would make bold to say that many scholars, as they pursue their studies and engage in their work, also fashion – in the process – their terminology. Eliade's archetypes are very different from those of C.G. Jung. This often idiosyncratic vocabulary may be exasperating and confusing, but to tie him down to a fixed terminology would inhibit a scholar's intellectual mobility. Liberty, also terminological liberty (which, like every liberty, is distinct from anarchy), is essential and I would regard it as disastrous if the IAHR should ever – may the gods preserve us – appoint an Académie Française-like committee to lay down an authorized technical vocabulary. No doubt Prof. Hultkrantz is right in deploring our Babylonian confusion of tongues, but it is a small price to pay for the scholar's freedom to forge his own vocabulary as he engages in his work. My own utopia is very modest. I do not insist on the miracle of all of us speaking one tongue. I shall be satisfied with a Pentecost in the IAHR, when each speaks his own tongue but we shall have no difficulty in understanding one another.

Discussion   Chairman: Kurt Rudolph

J. van Baal described the task of speaking about depth structures of religious expression as extremely difficult, and that he thought it only possible if one first dealt with the question as to what the basic human characteristic was which gave rise to religion, even if this meant transgressing beyond the boundaries of science of religion. He realized, he said, that he had tried to cram too many eggs into the basket of his paper: some of them had got crushed; others would have to be thrown out. He wanted to insist however on his definition of religion, as 'notions which implicitly or explicitly refer to an unverifiable reality'. Too many of the current definitions attempted to save the respectability, and universality, of religion, but at the cost of failing to penetrate to the real human condition in which it originated. From a scientific point of view, however, religion was not respectable, but absurd. Why did man, who is so well equipped for experimental observation, so commonly choose to submit his conduct to rules dictated by a non-verifiable reality? – so commonly, that it could not even be classified as abnormal? This absurdity suggested a deep conflict in man, a conclusion which was reinforced by the strong emotionality of religious expression and the ambiguity in religious symbols; and he suggested that this arose from the fundamental ambiguity of man's simultaneous involvement in and detachment from the universe he lived in.

He had not tried to deal in his paper with symbols, but he would like to suggest that their ambiguity, the way in which they hide more than they reveal, stemmed from the fact that they refer to unclear states of the mind. The effort to understand them could be furthered by distinguishing between relatively lucid ones (such as mathematical symbols) and highly emotional ones such as those of dream and neurosis. The main point, however, which the investigation of symbols indicated was the conflict that they expressed between man and his universe, and the main consequence for history of religion was therefore the need to investigate every religion (tribal, sect, local or national church) within the full context of the group's life. This was why he objected to the so-called 'comparative' method, which made use of facts isolated from their cultural context. What was needed was not this, but good detailed monographs on the total cultural context of particular religions. Only when these were available would comparative and typological work become of value. In his paper he had given two examples of the two-way effect of studying cultures as a consistent whole: that the understanding of Australian aborigine kinship organization would have been achieved faster if it had been combined with the study of ritual; and that students of religion would have achieved a better understanding of sacrifice if they had taken into account the focal interest in the social context in the distribution of food.

Introducing the second paper, Kurt Goldammer said he had not been attempting to deal with symbols as such, but with the relation between symbols and the possible depths of religion. This raised a series of questions: do such depths, and depth structures, exist? how do they exist? how do they relate to symbols? what methodology of symbol research does all of this indicate? Modern psychology referred to 'depths', by which it meant the sub- or unconscious; modern theology, e.g. in Tillich, also sometimes referred to 'depths', and meant the depths of existence of the divine. These two concepts could be traced back to medieval mysticism, to the ancient world and to the Bible, and were apparently often identified with each other.

Clearly there was a distinction to be made between 'depth dimensions' and 'depth structures': one could presume the former without any knowledge of the latter. He drew attention however to the way in which 'depth' itself became a kind of metaphor for the inexpressible, and suggested that 'depth' and 'structure' were in fact incompatible formulations. 'Structure' could unquestionably be found in the totality of religion, and in its forms and forms of expression, including symbols. Indeed symbols, in their communicative function of mediating the 'depth', probably needed both to possess and to impart structurality, and thus represented the sole empirical approach to the 'depths' of religion.

'Depths' of human existence could perhaps be seen in extra-rational and sub-rational events such as dreams or behavior in ritual and predominantly emotionally-conditioned situations. It seemed to be the case that symbols, in their historical extension and virtual universality within religious development, were in themselves stratified phenomena, undergoing constant development and change in the value they had within their religions. This could best be seen in certain primordial and central symbols which recurred from prehistory, through the world religions, to mysticism and modern secular philosophy and ethics. Stratified theoretical approaches, such as those in psychology, seemed however to presume that the oldest stratum was necessarily the 'deepest'; but it had not in fact been proved that older forms of symbols were not also means of a rational structuration of religion just as later, more clearly articulated strata were. The strata of symbolic meaning reflected constant change: what Whitehead called 'symbolic transference' and Susanne Langer called 'symbolic change', a gradual, almost imperceptible change parallel to the stratified change in human history. Methodologically, therefore, the most reliable scientific approach to interpretation would be in starting out from the latest, most articulate form of the symbol. The analysis of historical strata in symbols thus could be considered as a waste of time, besides being impossible due to the lack of evidence. One could summarize by defining the symbol as a functional form with a specific communicative and cognitive task. The details and importance of this would alter historically, but the functional, operative character of the symbol would be constant.

The first two commentators, Th. P. van Baaren and Ulf Drobin, read their prepared comments without any additional remarks (other than Van Baaren offering his way of speaking and gesturing as a piece of fieldwork for, he hoped, participant observation). Michael Pye explained the starting point of his commentary as having been the observation that the two speakers, Van Baal and Goldammer, were each talking about something quite different and in quite different ways: he had tried to identify these and to explicate the difference. Goldammer's fundamental question was, he thought, 'By what specific means is it possible to elucidate the inward depth of experience of the religious people under study?', whereas Van Baal's was 'How can one define or elucidate the depth structures which lie behind or beyond the particular forms of specific religions?' These approaches were not incompatible, simply different. Goldammer's set out from the self-understanding of the religions; Van Baal's potentially led to a theory which would differ from this, though Van Baal himself did not appear to wish that. Pye had therefore gone on to explore the methodological difficulties of a theory which would or could subvert the self-understanding of the individual religions, not necessarily because this was the most important thing to do, but because it was the question posed by the two papers he had been considering. He was followed by the prepared comment of R. J. Zwi Werblowsky.

The question of the possible conflict between the self-understanding by the adherents of a religion and the theory produced by a scientist of religion was taken up by Ninian Smart. He agreed that such a conflict or disparity could arise; what was worth enquiring into was why it should do so, which necessitated a further level of theory. This pointed in the direction of a new stage that was needed in the study of religion, namely the study of the effect which study of religion had on religion, e.g. the negative effects on many Christians of New Testament scholarship over the preceding 150 years, or the positive effects of comparative studies for some people in helping them to understand their own faith. While depth structures might provide a way of describing the data under study which occurred in the minds of the people under study, one should avoid adopting too cavalier an attitude towards the self-understanding of the believer.

The use of the term *symbolon*, pointed out Carsten Colpe, was in actual fact so wide that it was not possible to ask for standardized usage, merely for clarification of what the individual speaker understood by the term. This openness was then welcomed by Hans-J. Klimkeit, who pleaded for it also to be extended in the theoretical field. There had been an opposition noted between (inadequately so-termed) 'functionalist' or 'reductionist' theories of religion and those which were not. While agreeing with Werblowsky on the need for the scholar to have the freedom to see phenomena in terms of their social, economic, psychological, etc. contexts, he also argued that knowing the conditions of the becoming (*Werden*) of a religious phenomenon did not necessarily disclose the phenomenon in its entirety. Ugo Bianchi had two comments to make about points raised by two of the commentators. He agreed with Drobin's statement that there must be feedback between 'tentative definitions and research objects', and between 'phenomenology and specific research'. He suggested however that the latter pair could be renamed 'previous concrete historical research' and 'future research'; and similarly, that in Drobin's reference to definitions which are nominal, 'within a certain span', or real, the nominal/real opposition could be rephrased as 'real, i.e. obtained by study'/'real, i.e. open to further concrete historical comparative research'. All the definitions in the study of religion, including that of religion itself, must be tentative: this did not prevent them from being 'real'. Turning to Werblowsky's commentary, he suggested that while it was necessary to work with insufficient definitions of 'religion', and while one had to be methodologically content with that, functional and anthropological definitions were not necessarily adequate to deal with the whole range of the problematics of history of religions.

Before the main speakers replied to the various comments and questions that had been raised, G. C. Oosthuizen interposed with a comment on current research into contemporary religion(s). Very little was in fact known about the existential beliefs of adherents of different religions, or for that matter of different adherents of the same religion: he would like to propose an integrated inter-university programme of detailed fieldwork, using students, for example, to obtain information.

Finally, J. van Baal and Kurt Goldammer brought the last session of the conference to a close by responding to the discussion. Van Baal agreed with the criticism put by Van Baaren that his paper had been too generalizing: but this had been necessary in order to discuss the basic human conditions relating to religion, which he referred to as 'depth structures'. The theory which he had been elaborating was, in part, still under construction; in part, it had been published in *Symbols of Communication*; in part, it dated back to his earlier work. This theory had grown out of his years of field observation (mostly not as a fieldworker), which had pointed towards certain lines of research developing from Cassirer's *Philosophy of Symbolic Forms*, in combination with the theory of symbols as worked out in depth psychology by Freud and Jung and even Sartre. Turning to another point raised by Van Baaren, he denied that his claims about the universal foundations of religion being discoverable in a fundamental contradiction in the human condition constituted a sweeping statement. Naturally he had not included consideration of prehistoric religion, since nothing was really known about it. He had started from known and described religions. Nor, thirdly, could he agree with the generalization that society was to modern man what nature was to primitive man. Agreeing that a certain trend in this direction is unmistakable, he insisted that both modern and primitive man lived in, and were at home in, their own societies (though not all individuals were comfortable in them). Primitive man might also be 'at home' in nature in the sense of knowing his way around it; but there was another phenomenon — the eternal silence of nature, a silence which speaks: and he described the experience of walking through the forest once for seven days on end, until the silence bore down not only on his own mood but also on that of his bearers. Such silence is difficult company.

Replying to a point asked by Michael Pye, he agreed that the self-understanding of the believers of a religion was important: he shared Werblowsky's view, that it constituted one's first datum. The difficulty was that the self-understanding of a religion was so often illogical. Many of the hymns sung in church, for example, amazed him: they were pure nonsense, yet people were happy to sing them. Again, as a young district officer in New Guinea he had once had to deal with a murder case. In court the murderer produced a stone, 'still red with blood', which he claimed to have massaged out of his son's stomach: it had been put there, he said, by the other man (whom he had then wounded) to make his son sick. There were no stones in the country there: it was obvious that the man must have brought it from elsewhere: yet both he and everyone else was quite convinced that it had been taken from the sick boy's belly. How was one to explain beliefs such as this? How was it possible for men to believe the things they do believe in religion? And how could one then proceed with the religions' self-understanding? Finally, Van Baal replied to Drobin's commentary on the question of the definition of religion: he had wanted to be able to delimit the field of religion in some way — to say, this is religion and that isn't — on the basis of observable characteristics rather than unobservable feelings; but this was a question on which the discussion could be endless, and there was no time to continue it now.

Kurt Goldammer wished to thank the commentators and other contributors to the discussion for having examined what he had to say, and thus helping him to see it more clearly himself; he found this very important. The problems which Werblowsky had extrapolated and appended to his paper he found himself largely in agreement over. Van Baaren had complained at the absence from his paper of an essential definition of symbols: since what he had been concerned with was the question of depth structures in religious experience, he had restricted himself to a functional description. On the question of the complicated relations between words, pictures, and symbols, he referred the discussion to his article s.v. 'Symbolism and Iconography of Religions' in the new edition of the Encyclopedia Britannica. He had not denied the existence of symbols in pre-literate and early high cultures, but he doubted whether the problems arising from symbolism were reflected on in those cultures as they were in our own, and his concern had been with this reflection and with the formation of consciousness. Discussions with indologists and iranologists had indicated that these ancient cultures did not possess a concept of the symbol equivalent to our own, which related to the distancing of modern man from himself and his own self-contemplation. With reference to Michael Pye's critique, he gave his full assent to the idea of a complex methodology. He suggested that there was a new 'projection theory' in the process of emerging within the humanities: not projections by the objects of research, i.e. religious man, but by the researchers themselves into the world of religious man. The tensions which could result, between the researcher, the object of religious research, and the world of ideas, had been clearly set out by Pye and Werblowsky. Finally he wished to thank Ulf Drobin for having worked over the questions of terminology and typology again. Drobin had however misunderstood him: he did not think symbols to be identical with the dogmas of the high religions — on the contrary: dogma was a rationally formed doctrinal category of religious statement, though it could, under certain circumstances, be understood or applied in a symbolic manner.

In his closing remarks, Goldammer related what he had said about the desirability of organized and coordinated comparative research into the stock of symbols in the various religions to Juha Pentikäinen's remarks at the beginning of the conference about 'measuring religion'. He believed that the idea of measuring religion had first originated with Rudolph Otto in the 1920s. He had to confess that it had always seemed to him rather suspect and illusionary. Nevertheless, and despite the frustrations that must be expected, here lay a task to be carried out. He did not like the idea of the quantification of a qualitative phenomenon such as religion, but science had a need for quantification, and science of religion should be able to coordinate the quantified knowledge so obtained with its qualitative understanding of its object.

Index of Names

Index of Subjects*

* Compiled by Jacques Waardenburg.

Religion (*continued*)
    traditional — 279
    truth of —
      hermeneutics of truth of — 121
    type(s) of — 234, 245, 264, 268, 269, 274
      type of — and culture core 271
      five types of — in evolutionary development 422-423
      arrangement of types of — into historical strata 233
      classification of types of — 261, 268
      concept of type of — 240
      concepts of type of — and cultural type 230
      ecological type of — 239
    typology of — 143-161
      typology of the — 202
      typology of —s 202
      historical typology of —s 186
    understanding of — 479
      understanding by believers of a — 217
    universal foundations of — 543
    urban and rural —s
      different patterns of urban and rural —s 224n
    whole of — as a symbol 517
    wholeness of — 289
    See also: Primitive religion, Ecology of religion, Geography of religion, etc..
Religionstypologie 200, 216
    See also: Typology of religion
Religionswissenschaft 201, 202, 204
    — as a basic science of intention, or a humanistic science of culture 479
    — as a kind of substitute theology 214
    history of methodology of — 134
    ideological criticism of — 214
    master builders of — 178
    originality of·— 99
    subdiscipline of methodological discussion within — 133
    unique features of — within an interdisciplinary context 133
    See also: Science of religion, Study of religion, Religious studies
Religiosity
    — and non-religiosity of a given phenomenon 46
    dimensions of (belief and) religion and — 46, 47
    evaluation of — 43
    source value of oral tradition for measuring — 45
Religious
    — anthropological studies 381
    — assertions
      logical structures of various types of — assertions 440
    — belief
      foci of — belief 480
    — change 235, 236, 269, 274, 285
    — character of a particular view of reality 453

—history
  typology of — history (*religionsgeschichtliche Typik*) 143, 144, 186
—ideas
  development of religious symbols into — ideas 494
—information 35, 36
Religious language
  —and non-religious language 471, 472
  —as a language of symbols 456
  —in the framework of communication theory 479-480
  —in which the words address the person, coming from elsewhere 454
  —not to be defined solely in terms of meaning 482
  analysis of — needs to be comparative and plural 464
    levels of analysis of — 471-474
  communication in — 477
  comparative analysis of —s and concepts in their living environment 478
  concept —
    isolating the concept — 465-467
  criteria of — 458-459
  definition of — 459, 476-477
  descriptive analysis of — 464
  difficulty in studying — 444
  directly inspired — 454
  double-decker character of — 451, 483
  horizontal organicness of a — 464
  isolating — 470-474
  levels of —
    lexical and syntactical levels of — 459
    several levels within the — 436
  philosophical studies of — 439
  reference of — 444
    the reference of — must be bracketed 464, 482
  speaker and listener of — 445
  terminology (i.e. lexical terms) in — 458-459
  transcendent references of — 445
  universal and religion-specific answers to philosophical questions about — 476
  use of — 459-460
  users of the — 460
  See also: Language of religion
Religious
  —literature
    autonomous — literature 101
    study of — literature 100-104
    Sumerian — literature 26
  —man
    ambivalency of — man 413
    projections by the researchers into the world of — man 545
    religious poles determine how — man is going to act 413
  —materials
    search for logic in the — materials 450

Symbol (*continued*)
  — as the product, not of the depth (itself), but of an attempt to seize the depths sensorily 509
  — as representation 503, 504
  — as such is not a depth 501
  — as the universal key for all forms of human behavior, including the religious 517
  — expounded through its own methodology 503
  — formation 509
  — is a vehicle of meaning 500n, 506
  — is only opened up through the subjectivity of the observer 512n
  — religion 517
  — research 498-518
    methodology of — research 540
  — seen as the 'proper' or the 'non-proper' in religion 517
  — structure 349
  — structures the holy 504
  — system(s) 333, 346, 349, 445
  — theory 161, 168, 170, 171, 172, 198
  aspects of the — as a statement for depth-structures 499-507
  basic — systems 346
  concept (term) of — 213, 340, 361, 516
    stabilizing of the term — 529
  confusion between a — and that which is symbolized by it 520
  conscious shaping of an intention becomes explicit in the — 512n
  convergence in the — between the depths of the divine and of the human 504
  definition of the subjectivist psychoanalytical concept of the — 510
  father — 336
  feminine/mother —
    presence or absence of a feminine/mother — 336-338
  function of the — 502-504
  functional definition of — 520
  identity and concreteness of the conception of the — 504n
  in the — a dilemma of experienced and rationally-analyzed religion 506
  Jahweh as a — 342
  life of a — 508
  mother — 336
  non-religious, secular elements in the — 508
  questions around the — and its relational function 504
  regarding the whole of religion as a — 517
  the religious — socially accepted and accepted as true 493
  sacred child — 336-337
  'second-grade' — system or 'sign system' 446
  study of cultural symbols and — systems 322
  See also: Religious symbols, Symbols
Symbolic
  — double function 364
  — or 'endeictic' manner of religious expression in thought 516
  — sub-systems of ritual life 406

— and phenomenology 152-153, 366, 524-525
— and phenomenology incompatible 424
— for the comparison of religions as wholes 525
Typology of religion XXVII, 143-161 (esp. 146), 185, 201, 206, 268
    historical — 146, 147, 186, 359
    relationship between — and phenomenology of religion 201
Typology of the religion 202, 203
Typology of religions 202
    difference between the phenomenology and the — is quantitative and not quali-
        tative 525
Typology of religious history (*religionsgeschichtliche Typik*) 143, 144, 186
Typology
    — of societies 402
    historical — 146, 186, 219, 319, 321, 366
    historical — of cultures 310
    horizontal and vertical sense of — 209
    mediating — 186, 187
    need of — 122
    phenomenology has an implicit — 424
    sociological evolutionary — 424
    theoretically-grounded — 155
    value of — 202
Typology-making 416
Typos 215

Umwelt
    — of a text 127
Understand
    wish to — in American anthropology 84
Understanding
    — as decoding 447
    — by believers of a religion 217
    transposing — into scientific statement 219
Unilinearity 244
Universal
    the — and the particular 358, 359
    the — concrete 218
    — human phenomena embedded in social reality 357
    need of flexible — categories XXVIII
Universalities
    search for — 353
Universals 307, 478, 481
    — in religion 440
    concrete — 219, 321, 359, 366
    cultural — 379, 380, 404, 405, 418, 419
    human — 352
    problem of — 321
    religion as a concrete or historical — 321
    religious — XXVIII

Religion and Reason
Method and Theory in the Study and Interpretation of Religion

7. *Logique et Religion*
L'Atomisme logique de L. Wittgenstein et la possibilité des propositions religieuses. Including 'Logic and Religion', a shortened and
adapted English version of the text.
par Jacques Poulain (Université de Montréal, Canada)
1973, 228 pages. Clothbound
ISBN: 90-279-7284-2

8. *Religion, Culture and Methodology*
Papers of the Groningen Working-group for the Study of Fundamental Problems and Methods of Science of Religion,
ed. by Th. P. van Baaren and H. J.W. Drijvers (University of Groningen)
1973, 172 pages. Clothbound
ISBN: 90-279-7249-4

9. *Religion and Primitive Cultures*
A Study in Ethnophilosophy,
by Wilhelm Dupré (University of Nijmegen)
1975, X + 356 pages. Clothbound
ISBN: 90-279-7531-0

10. *Christologies and Cultures*
Toward a Typology of Religious Worldviews,
by George Rupp (Harvard University)
1974, XIV + 270 pages. Clothbound
ISBN: 90-279-7461-4

11. *The Biographical Process*
Studies in the History and Psychology of Religion,
ed. by Frank E. Reynolds (University of Chicago) and
Donald Capps (University of North Carolina at Charlotte)
1976, XII + 436 pages. Clothbound
ISBN: 90-279-7522-1

12. *The Study of Religion and Its Meaning*
New Explorations in Light of Karl Popper and Emile Durkheim,
by J.E. Barnhart (North Texas State University)
1977, XIV + 216 pages. Clothbound
ISBN: 90-279-7762-3

Mouton Publishers · The Hague · Paris · New York